T0385035

Opel
Omega & Senator
Service and Repair Manual

Mark Coombs and Spencer Drayton

(3157/1469-280-5AC4)

Models covered
Saloon and Estate models with four and six-cylinder petrol engines, including special/limited editions;
1.8 litre (1796 cc), 2.0 litre (1998 cc), 2.5 litre (2490 cc), 2.6 litre (2594 cc) & 3.0 litre (2969 cc, inc. 24V)

Does not cover Diesel engine or Lotus Carlton models

© Haynes Group Limited 1999

A book in the **Haynes Service and Repair Manual Series**

ISBN **978 0 85733 918 8**

British Library Cataloguing in Publication Data
A catalogue record for this book is available from the British Library.

Haynes Group Limited
Haynes North America, Inc

www.haynes.com

The manufacturer's authorised representative in the EU for product safety is:
HaynesPro BV
Stationsstraat 79 F, 3811MH Ámersfoort, The Netherlands
gpsr@haynes.co.uk

Disclaimer
There are risks associated with automotive repairs. The ability to make repairs depends on the individual's skill, experience and proper tools. Individuals should act with due care and acknowledge and assume the risk of performing automotive repairs.

The purpose of this manual is to provide comprehensive, useful and accessible automotive repair information, to help you get the best value from your vehicle. However, this manual is not a substitute for a professional certified technician or mechanic.

This repair manual is produced by a third party and is not associated with an individual vehicle manufacturer. If there is any doubt or discrepancy between this manual and the owner's manual or the factory service manual, please refer to the factory service manual or seek assistance from a professional certified technician or mechanic.

Even though we have prepared this manual with extreme care and every attempt is made to ensure that the information in this manual is correct, neither the publisher nor the author can accept responsibility for loss, damage or injury caused by any errors in, or omissions from, the information given.

Contents

LIVING WITH YOUR VAUXHALL

Introduction to the Vauxhall Carlton/Senator	Page	0•4
Safety First!	Page	0•5

Roadside Repairs

If your car won't start	Page	0•6
Jump starting	Page	0•7
Wheel changing	Page	0•8
Identifying leaks	Page	0•9
Towing	Page	0•9

Weekly Checks

Introduction	Page	0•10
Underbonnet check points	Page	0•10
Engine oil level	Page	0•11
Coolant level	Page	0•11
Brake fluid level	Page	0•12
Power steering fluid level	Page	0•12
Screen washer fluid level	Page	0•13
Wiper blades	Page	0•13
Tyre condition and pressure	Page	0•14
Bulbs and fuses	Page	0•15
Battery	Page	0•15

Lubricants, fluids and tyre pressures

	Page	0•16

MAINTENANCE

Routine Maintenance and Servicing

	Page	1•1
Maintenance schedule	Page	1•4
Maintenance procedures	Page	1•7

Contents

REPAIRS AND OVERHAUL

Engine and Associated Systems

1.8 and 2.0 litre (OHC) engines   Page   2A•1
2.5, 2.6 and 3.0 litre (CIH) engines   Page   2B•1
3.0 litre DOHC engine   Page   2C•1
Cooling, heating and air conditioning systems   Page   3•1
Fuel and exhaust systems - carburettor models   Page   4A•1
Fuel and exhaust systems - fuel injection models   Page   4B•1
Starting and charging systems   Page   5A•1
Ignition system   Page   5B•1

Transmission

Clutch   Page   6•1
Manual transmission   Page   7A•1
Automatic transmission   Page   7B•1
Final drive, driveshafts and propeller shaft   Page   8•1

Brakes and suspension

Braking system   Page   9•1
Suspension and steering   Page   10•1

Body equipment

Bodywork and fittings   Page   11•1
Body electrical systems   Page   12•1

Wiring diagrams

                                                         Page   12•17

REFERENCE

Dimensions and Weights   Page   REF•1
Conversion Factors   Page   REF•2
Buying Spare Parts   Page   REF•3
Vehicle Identification   Page   REF•3
General Repair Procedures   Page   REF•4
Jacking and Vehicle Support   Page   REF•5
Radio/cassette unit Anti-theft System - Precaution   Page   REF•5
Tools and Working Facilities   Page   REF•6
MOT Test Checks   Page   REF•8
Fault Finding   Page   REF•12
Glossary of Technical Terms   Page   REF•19

Index

                                                         Page   REF•23

The Carlton covered by this manual was introduced to the UK market in November 1986 in four door saloon and five door estate bodyshells. Initially, the range of engines offered comprised a 1.8 SOHC unit with carburettor or electronic fuel injection fuelling, and a 2.0 litre SOHC unit with electronic fuel injection. Five speed-manual and four-speed automatic transmissions were available. Later, 2.6 litre and 3.0 litre CIH straight-six cylinder engines were offered, including a DOHC 24-valve version fitted to the GSi model from 1990 onwards.

All models are equipped with both front and rear disc brakes. Anti-lock braking is fitted as standard on all high-specification models and later lower-specification models, and was offered as an optional extra on all earlier lower-specification models.

Since its introduction, the Carlton range has continually been developed. All models have a high trim level, which is extremely comprehensive in the upper model range. Central locking, electric windows, electric sunroof, cruise control, and air conditioning were all available.

The revised Senator range was also introduced in UK during 1986. In four door saloon form only, the Senator was fitted with a number of variations of the straight-six cylinder engine, in capacities of 2.5, 2.6 and 3.0 litres, and the 24 valve DOHC 3.0 litre from 1990 onwards.

Mechanically, the Senator is virtually identical to the Carlton and this is reflected in the service and repair procedures detailed in this manual. For the home mechanic, both the Carlton and Senator are relatively straightforward vehicles to maintain and repair since design features have been incorporated to reduce the actual cost of ownership to a minimum, and most of the items requiring frequent attention are easily accessible.

Vauxhall Carlton 1.8 GLi

Vauxhall Senator 3.0i

The Carlton/Senator Team

Haynes manuals are produced by dedicated and enthusiastic people working in close co-operation. The team responsible for the creation of this book included:

Authors	Mark Coombs Spencer Drayton
Sub-editor	Carole Turk
Editor & Page Make-up	Bob Jex
Workshop manager	Paul Buckland
Photo Scans	John Martin Paul Tanswell
Cover illustration & Line Art	Roger Healing

We hope the book will help you to get the maximum enjoyment from your car. By carrying out routine maintenance as described you will ensure your car's reliability and preserve its resale value.

Project vehicles

The vehicles used in the preparation of this manual, and which appear in many of the photographic sequences were: a Carlton1.8i GL Saloon, a Carlton 2.0i GL Estate, a Carlton 2.0i CD Automatic Saloon and a Senator 3.0i 24v.

Your Vauxhall Carlton/Senator Manual

The aim of this manual is to help you get the best value from your vehicle. It can do so in several ways. It can help you decide what work must be done (even should you choose to get it done by a garage), provide information on routine maintenance and servicing, and give a logical course of action and diagnosis when random faults occur. However, it is hoped that you will use the manual by tackling the work yourself. On simpler jobs, it may even be quicker than booking the car into a garage and going there twice, to leave and collect it. Perhaps most important, a lot of money can be saved by avoiding the costs a garage must charge to cover its labour and overheads.

The manual has drawings and descriptions to show the function of the various components, so that their layout can be understood. Then the tasks are described and photographed in a clear step-by-step sequence.

References to the "left" or "right" of the vehicle are in the sense of a person in the driving seat, facing forwards.

Acknowledgements

Thanks are due to Champion Spark Plug who supplied the illustrations showing spark plug conditions. Certain other illustrations are the copyright of the Vauxhall, and are used with their permission. Thanks are also due to Draper Tools Limited, who provided some of the workshop tools, and to all those people at Sparkford who helped in the production of this manual.

We take great pride in the accuracy of information given in this manual, but vehicle manufacturers make alterations and design changes during the production run of a particular vehicle of which they do not inform us. No liability can be accepted by the authors or publishers for loss, damage or injury caused by any errors in, or omissions from, the information given.

Working on your car can be dangerous. This page shows just some of the potential risks and hazards, with the aim of creating a safety-conscious attitude.

General hazards

Scalding

• Don't remove the radiator or expansion tank cap while the engine is hot.
• Engine oil, automatic transmission fluid or power steering fluid may also be dangerously hot if the engine has recently been running.

Burning

• Beware of burns from the exhaust system and from any part of the engine. Brake discs and drums can also be extremely hot immediately after use.

Crushing

• When working under or near a raised vehicle, always supplement the jack with axle stands, or use drive-on ramps. *Never venture under a car which is only supported by a jack.*
• Take care if loosening or tightening high-torque nuts when the vehicle is on stands. Initial loosening and final tightening should be done with the wheels on the ground.

Fire

• Fuel is highly flammable; fuel vapour is explosive.
• Don't let fuel spill onto a hot engine.
• Do not smoke or allow naked lights (including pilot lights) anywhere near a vehicle being worked on. Also beware of creating sparks (electrically or by use of tools).
• Fuel vapour is heavier than air, so don't work on the fuel system with the vehicle over an inspection pit.
• Another cause of fire is an electrical overload or short-circuit. Take care when repairing or modifying the vehicle wiring.
• Keep a fire extinguisher handy, of a type suitable for use on fuel and electrical fires.

Electric shock

• Ignition HT voltage can be dangerous, especially to people with heart problems or a pacemaker. Don't work on or near the ignition system with the engine running or the ignition switched on.

• Mains voltage is also dangerous. Make sure that any mains-operated equipment is correctly earthed. Mains power points should be protected by a residual current device (RCD) circuit breaker.

Fume or gas intoxication

• Exhaust fumes are poisonous; they often contain carbon monoxide, which is rapidly fatal if inhaled. Never run the engine in a confined space such as a garage with the doors shut.
• Fuel vapour is also poisonous, as are the vapours from some cleaning solvents and paint thinners.

Poisonous or irritant substances

• Avoid skin contact with battery acid and with any fuel, fluid or lubricant, especially antifreeze, brake hydraulic fluid and Diesel fuel. Don't syphon them by mouth. If such a substance is swallowed or gets into the eyes, seek medical advice.
• Prolonged contact with used engine oil can cause skin cancer. Wear gloves or use a barrier cream if necessary. Change out of oil-soaked clothes and do not keep oily rags in your pocket.
• Air conditioning refrigerant forms a poisonous gas if exposed to a naked flame (including a cigarette). It can also cause skin burns on contact.

Asbestos

• Asbestos dust can cause cancer if inhaled or swallowed. Asbestos may be found in gaskets and in brake and clutch linings. When dealing with such components it is safest to assume that they contain asbestos.

Special hazards

Hydrofluoric acid

• This extremely corrosive acid is formed when certain types of synthetic rubber, found in some O-rings, oil seals, fuel hoses etc, are exposed to temperatures above 400°C. The rubber changes into a charred or sticky substance containing the acid. *Once formed, the acid remains dangerous for years. If it gets onto the skin, it may be necessary to amputate the limb concerned.*
• When dealing with a vehicle which has suffered a fire, or with components salvaged from such a vehicle, wear protective gloves and discard them after use.

The battery

• Batteries contain sulphuric acid, which attacks clothing, eyes and skin. Take care when topping-up or carrying the battery.
• The hydrogen gas given off by the battery is highly explosive. Never cause a spark or allow a naked light nearby. Be careful when connecting and disconnecting battery chargers or jump leads.

Air bags

• Air bags can cause injury if they go off accidentally. Take care when removing the steering wheel and/or facia. Special storage instructions may apply.

Diesel injection equipment

• Diesel injection pumps supply fuel at very high pressure. Take care when working on the fuel injectors and fuel pipes.

⚠ *Warning: Never expose the hands, face or any other part of the body to injector spray; the fuel can penetrate the skin with potentially fatal results.*

Remember...

DO

• Do use eye protection when using power tools, and when working under the vehicle.

• Do wear gloves or use barrier cream to protect your hands when necessary.

• Do get someone to check periodically that all is well when working alone on the vehicle.

• Do keep loose clothing and long hair well out of the way of moving mechanical parts.

• Do remove rings, wristwatch etc, before working on the vehicle – especially the electrical system.

• Do ensure that any lifting or jacking equipment has a safe working load rating adequate for the job.

DON'T

• Don't attempt to lift a heavy component which may be beyond your capability – get assistance.

• Don't rush to finish a job, or take unverified short cuts.

• Don't use ill-fitting tools which may slip and cause injury.

• Don't leave tools or parts lying around where someone can trip over them. Mop up oil and fuel spills at once.

• Don't allow children or pets to play in or near a vehicle being worked on.

The following pages are intended to help in dealing with common roadside emergencies and breakdowns. You will find more detailed fault finding information at the back of the manual, and repair information in the main chapters.

If your car won't start and the starter motor doesn't turn

☐ If it's a model with automatic transmission, make sure the selector is in 'P' or 'N'.
☐ Open the bonnet and make sure that the battery terminals are clean and tight.
☐ Switch on the headlights and try to start the engine. If the headlights go very dim when you're trying to start, the battery is probably flat. Get out of trouble by jump starting (see next page) using a friend's car.

If your car won't start even though the starter motor turns as normal

☐ Is there fuel in the tank?
☐ Is there moisture on electrical components under the bonnet? Switch off the ignition, then wipe off any obvious dampness with a dry cloth. Spray a water-repellent aerosol product (WD-40 or equivalent) on ignition and fuel system electrical connectors like those shown in the photos. Pay special attention to the ignition coil wiring connector and HT leads.

A Check the condition and security of the battery connections.

B Check that all sensor wiring and HT connections to the distributor are secure, and spray with water-repellent if necessary.

C Check that the crankshaft sensor connection is secure - spray with water-repellent if necessary.

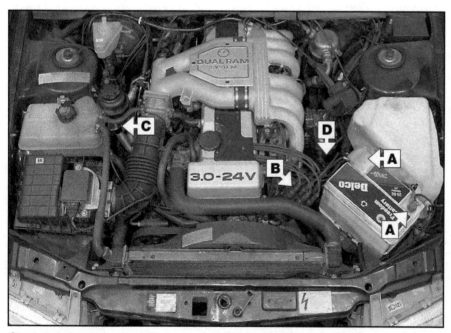

Check that electrical connections are secure (with the ignition switched off) and spray them with a water dispersant spray like WD40 if you suspect a problem due to damp

D Check that all sensor wiring and HT connections to the ignition coil are secure and spray with water-repellent if necessary.

E Check that the fuse for the fuel pump relay circuit is not blown.

Jump starting

Jump starting will get you out of trouble, but you must correct whatever made the battery go flat in the first place. There are three possibilities:

1 *The battery has been drained by repeated attempts to start, or by leaving the lights on.*

2 *The charging system is not working properly (alternator drivebelt slack or broken, alternator wiring fault or alternator itself faulty).*

3 *The battery itself is at fault (electrolyte low, or battery worn out).*

When jump-starting a car using a booster battery, observe the following precautions:

✔ Before connecting the booster battery, make sure that the ignition is switched off.

✔ Ensure that all electrical equipment (lights, heater, wipers, etc) is switched off.

✔ Take note of any special precautions printed on the battery case.

✔ Make sure that the booster battery is the same voltage as the discharged one in the vehicle.

✔ If the battery is being jump-started from the battery in another vehicle, the two vehicles MUST NOT TOUCH each other.

✔ Make sure that the transmission is in neutral (or PARK, in the case of automatic transmission).

1 Connect one end of the red jump lead to the positive (+) terminal of the flat battery

2 Connect the other end of the red lead to the positive (+) terminal of the booster battery.

3 Connect one end of the black jump lead to the negative (-) terminal of the booster battery

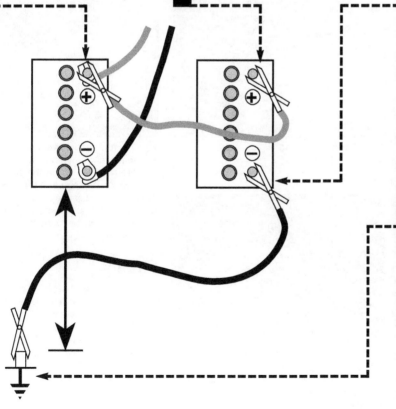

4 Connect the other end of the black jump lead to a bolt or bracket on the engine block, well away from the battery, on the vehicle to be started.

5 Make sure that the jump leads will not come into contact with the fan, drive-belts or other moving parts of the engine.

6 Start the engine using the booster battery and run it at idle speed. Switch on the lights, rear window demister and heater blower motor, then disconnect the jump leads in the reverse order of connection. Turn off the lights etc.

Wheel changing

Some of the details shown here will vary according to model. For instance, the location of the spare wheel and jack is not the same on all cars. However, the basic principles apply to all vehicles.

Warning: Do not change a wheel in a situation where you risk being hit by other traffic. On busy roads, try to stop in a lay-by or a gateway. Be wary of passing traffic while changing the wheel – it is easy to become distracted by the job in hand.

Preparation

☐ When a puncture occurs, stop as soon as it is safe to do so.
☐ Park on firm level ground, if possible, and well out of the way of other traffic.
☐ Use hazard warning lights if necessary.

☐ If you have one, use a warning triangle to alert other drivers of your presence.
☐ If a front wheel is to be changed, apply the handbrake and engage first or reverse gear (or "Park", where applicable).

☐ Chock the wheel diagonally opposite the one being removed – a couple of large stones will do for this.
☐ If the ground is soft, use a flat piece of wood to spread the load under the jack.

Changing the wheel

1 From inside the luggage compartment, fold back the trim panel, release the strap and lift out the wheel.

2 Unscrew the locking bolt and retrieve the jack and wheel brace.

3 Use a key to release the locking plate (where applicable) . . .

4 . . . then loosen each wheel bolt by half a turn.

5 Unclip the trim panel . . .

6 . . . and locate the jack head below the reinforced jacking point and on firm ground (don't jack the car at any other point on the sill), and turn the jack handle until the wheel is raised clear of the ground. For safety, put the spare wheel flat on the ground under the sill, close to the jacking point.

7 Remove the bolts and lift the wheel clear, then fit the spare wheel. Insert the wheel bolts and tighten moderately with the wheel brace.

8 Lower the car to the ground, then finally tighten the wheel bolts in a diagonal sequence. Fit the locking plate and secure the damaged wheel in the load space with the strap. Refit the trim panel.

Finally...

☐ Remove the wheel chocks.
☐ Stow the jack and tools in the correct locations in the car.
☐ Check the tyre pressure on the wheel just fitted. If it is low, or if you don't have a pressure gauge with you, drive slowly to the nearest garage and inflate the tyre to the right pressure.
☐ Have the damaged tyre or wheel repaired as soon as possible.

Identifying leaks

Puddles on the garage floor or drive, or obvious wetness under the bonnet or underneath the car, suggest a leak that needs investigating. It can sometimes be difficult to decide where the leak is coming from, especially if the engine bay is very dirty already. Leaking oil or fluid can also be blown rearwards by the passage of air under the car, giving a false impression of where the problem lies.

 Warning: Most automotive oils and fluids are poisonous. Wash them off skin, and change out of contaminated clothing, without delay.

 The smell of a fluid leaking from the car may provide a clue to what's leaking. Some fluids are distinctively coloured. It may help to clean the car carefully and to park it over some clean paper overnight as an aid to locating the source of the leak. Remember that some leaks may only occur while the engine is running.

Sump oil

Engine oil may leak from the drain plug...

Oil from filter

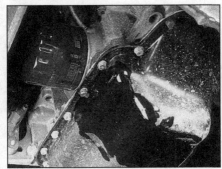

...or from the base of the oil filter.

Gearbox oil

Gearbox oil can leak from the seals at the inboard ends of the driveshafts.

Antifreeze

Leaking antifreeze often leaves a crystalline deposit like this.

Brake fluid

A leak occurring at a wheel is almost certainly brake fluid.

Power steering fluid

Power steering fluid may leak from the pipe connectors on the steering rack.

Towing

When all else fails, you may find yourself having to get a tow home – or of course you may be helping somebody else. Long-distance recovery should only be done by a garage or breakdown service. For shorter distances, DIY towing using another car is easy enough, but observe the following points:
□ Use a proper tow-rope – they are not expensive. The vehicle being towed must display an 'ON TOW' sign in its rear window.
□ Always turn the ignition key to the 'on' position when the vehicle is being towed, so that the steering lock is released, and that the direction indicator and brake lights will work.
□ Only attach the tow-rope to the towing eyes provided.
□ Before being towed, release the handbrake and select neutral on the transmission.
□ Note that greater-than-usual pedal pressure will be required to operate the brakes, since the vacuum servo unit is only operational with the engine running.
□ On models with power steering, greater-than-usual steering effort will also be required.
□ The driver of the car being towed must keep the tow-rope taut at all times to avoid snatching.
□ Make sure that both drivers know the route before setting off.
□ Only drive at moderate speeds and keep the distance towed to a minimum. Drive smoothly and allow plenty of time for slowing down at junctions.
□ On models with automatic transmission, special precautions apply. If in doubt, do not tow, or transmission damage may result.

Introduction

There are some very simple checks which need only take a few minutes to carry out, but which could save you a lot of inconvenience and expense.

These "Weekly checks" require no great skill or special tools, and the small amount of time they take to perform could prove to be very well spent, for example;

☐ Keeping an eye on tyre condition and pressures, will not only help to stop them wearing out prematurely, but could also save your life.

☐ Many breakdowns are caused by electrical problems. Battery-related faults are particularly common, and a quick check on a regular basis will often prevent the majority of these.

☐ If your car develops a brake fluid leak, the first time you might know about it is when your brakes don't work properly. Checking the level regularly will give advance warning of this kind of problem.

☐ If the oil or coolant levels run low, the cost of repairing any engine damage will be far greater than fixing the leak, for example.

Underbonnet check points

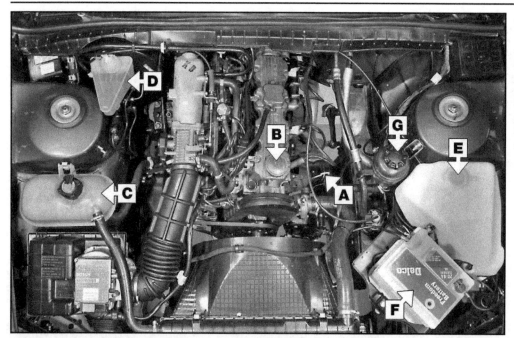

◀ 1.8 / 2.0 litre

A *Engine oil level dipstick*
B *Engine oil filler cap*
C *Coolant expansion tank*
D *Brake fluid reservoir*
E *Screen washer fluid reservoir*
F *Battery*
G *Power steering fluid reservoir*

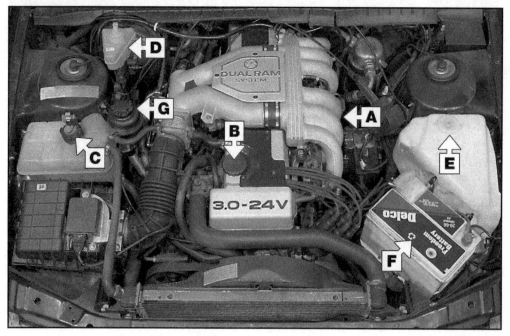

◀ 3.0 litre

A *Engine oil level dipstick*
B *Engine oil filler cap*
C *Coolant expansion tank*
D *Brake fluid reservoir*
E *Screen washer fluid reservoir*
F *Battery*
G *Power steering fluid reservoir*

Engine oil level

Before you start

✔ Make sure that your car is on level ground.
✔ Check the oil level before the car is driven, or at least 5 minutes after the engine has been switched off.

HAYNES HINT *If the oil is checked immediately after driving the vehicle, some of the oil will remain in the upper engine components, resulting in an inaccurate reading on the dipstick!*

The correct oil

Modern engines place great demands on their oil. It is very important that the correct oil for your car is used (See "Lubricants, fluids and tyre pressures").

Car Care

● If you have to add oil frequently, you should check whether you have any oil leaks. Place some clean paper under the car overnight, and check for stains in the morning. If there are no leaks, the engine may be burning oil *(see "Fault Finding").*

● Always maintain the level between the upper and lower dipstick marks (see photo 3). If the level is too low severe engine damage may occur. Oil seal failure may result if the engine is overfilled by adding too much oil.

1 The dipstick is located in its own tube at the left hand side of the engine (see *"Underbonnet Check Points"*, page 0•10 for exact location). Withdraw the dipstick.

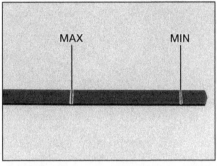
3 Hold the dipstick with the handle uppermost - if oil is allowed to run back down the blade, a false reading will be obtained. Note the oil level on the end of the dipstick, which should be between the upper ("MAX") mark and the lower ("MIN") mark.

2 Using a clean rag or paper towel, wipe all the oil from the dipstick. Insert the clean dipstick into the tube as far as it will go, then withdraw it again.

4 Oil is added through the filler cap. Twist and remove the cap, and then carefully pour in the oil. A funnel may help to reduce spillage. Add the oil slowly, checking the level on the dipstick often. Don't overfill.

Coolant level

Warning: DO NOT attempt to remove the expansion tank pressure cap when the engine is hot, as there is a very great risk of scalding. Do not leave containers of coolant about, as it is poisonous.

Car Care

● With a sealed-type cooling system, adding coolant should not be necessary on a regular basis. If frequent topping-up is required, it is likely there is a leak. Check the radiator, all hoses and joint faces for signs of staining or wetness, and rectify as necessary.

● It is important that antifreeze is used in the cooling system all year round, not just during the winter months. Don't top-up with water alone, as the antifreeze will become too diluted.

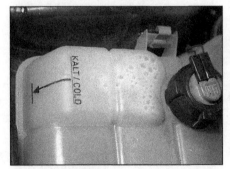
1 The coolant level varies with engine temperature. When cold, the coolant level should be up to the "KALT/COLD" mark on the side of the expansion tank (arrowed), at the right-hand end of the radiator. When hot, the level may rise slightly above the "KALT/COLD" mark.

2 The expansion tank cap must be removed to allow the coolant level to be topped up. **Wait until the engine is cold.** Turn the expansion tank cap anti-clockwise just until gas is heard to escape. Once the pressure has been released, continue turning the cap anti-clockwise until it can be lifted off.

3 Add a mixture of water and antifreeze through the expansion tank filler neck, until the coolant is up to the "KALT/COLD" level mark. Refit the cap, turning it clockwise as far as it will go until it is secure.

Brake fluid level

HAYNES HINT
• Make sure that your car is on level ground.
• The fluid level in the reservoir will drop slightly as the brake pads wear down, but the fluid level must never be allowed to drop below the "MIN" mark.

Warning:
● Brake fluid can harm your eyes and damage painted surfaces, so use extreme caution when handling and pouring it.

● Do not use fluid that has been standing open for some time, as it absorbs moisture from the air, which can cause a dangerous loss of braking effectiveness.

Safety First!
● If the reservoir requires repeated topping-up this is an indication of a fluid leak somewhere in the system, which should be investigated immediately.

● If a leak is suspected, the car should not be driven until the braking system has been checked. Never take any risks where brakes are concerned.

1 The "MAX" and "MIN" marks are indicated on the side of the reservoir - the fluid level must be kept between these two marks (make sure the car is parked on level ground when making the check).

2 If topping-up is necessary, first wipe the area around the filler cap with a clean rag before removing the cap. When adding fluid, it's a good idea to inspect the reservoir. The system should be drained and refilled if dirt is seen in the fluid (see Chapter 9).

3 Carefully add fluid, avoiding spilling it on surrounding paintwork. Use only the specified hydraulic fluid; mixing different types of fluid can cause damage to the system. After filling to the correct level, refit the cap securely. Wipe off any spilt fluid.

Power steering fluid level

Before you start:
✔ Park the vehicle on level ground.
✔ Set the steering wheel straight-ahead.
✔ The engine should be run to normal operating temperature, and then switched off.

HAYNES HINT
For the check to be accurate, the steering must not be turned once the engine has been stopped.

Safety First!
● The need for frequent topping-up indicates a leak, which should be investigated immediately.

1 The power steering reservoir cap has an integral dipstick. Before removing the cap, wipe the surrounding area clean with a rag.

2 Unscrew the cap and wipe the dipstick with a clean rag. Refit the cap, then unscrew it again and inspect the fluid level on the dipstick.

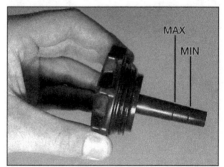

3 There are two stepped markings an the dipstick; the upper marking indicates the maximum permissible level of fluid with a warm engine, the lower marking indicates the minimum level with a cold engine.

4 If necessary, top-up to the maximum mark, using the specified type of fluid. Take great care not to allow dirt to enter the reservoir, and do not overfill the reservoir. When the level is correct, refit the cap.

Screen washer fluid level

Screenwash additives not only keep the winscreen clean during foul weather, they also prevent the washer system freezing in cold weather - which is when you are likely to need it most. Don't top up using plain water as the screenwash will become too diluted, and will freeze during cold weather. *On no account use coolant antifreeze in the washer system - this could discolour or damage paintwork.*

1 The windscreen/headlight washer fluid reservoir is located in engine compartment, in front of the left-hand suspension turret.

2 If necessary, top-up the reservoir with the recommended quantities of clean water . . .

3 . . . and screenwash additive.

Wiper blades

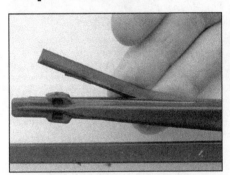

1 Check the condition of the wiper blades; if they are cracked or show any signs of deterioration, or if the glass swept area is smeared, renew them. Wiper blades should be renewed annually.

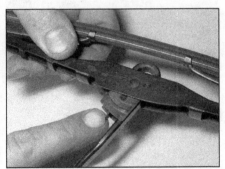

2 To remove a front wiper blade, first prise off the securing clips, and disconnect the washer tube from the arm.

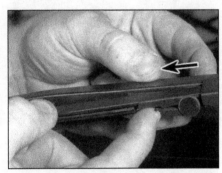

3 Pull the arm fully away from the glass until it locks. Swivel the blade through 90°, then pull up the blade securing clip, and slide the blade out of the arm's hooked end. On Estate models, to remove a tailgate wiper blade, pull the arm fully away from the glass until it locks. Swivel the blade through 90°, then press the locking tab, and slide the blade out of the arm's hooked end.

Tyre condition and pressure

It is very important that tyres are in good condition, and at the correct pressure - having a tyre failure at any speed is highly dangerous. Tyre wear is influenced by driving style - harsh braking and acceleration, or fast cornering, will all produce more rapid tyre wear. As a general rule, the front tyres wear out faster than the rears. Interchanging the tyres from front to rear ("rotating" the tyres) may result in more even wear. However, if this is completely effective, you may have the expense of replacing all four tyres at once!

Remove any nails or stones embedded in the tread before they penetrate the tyre to cause deflation. If removal of a nail does reveal that the tyre has been punctured, refit the nail so that its point of penetration is marked. Then immediately change the wheel, and have the tyre repaired by a tyre dealer.

Regularly check the tyres for damage in the form of cuts or bulges, especially in the sidewalls. Periodically remove the wheels, and clean any dirt or mud from the inside and outside surfaces. Examine the wheel rims for signs of rusting, corrosion or other damage. Light alloy wheels are easily damaged by "kerbing" whilst parking; steel wheels may also become dented or buckled. A new wheel is very often the only way to overcome severe damage.

New tyres should be balanced when they are fitted, but it may become necessary to re-balance them as they wear, or if the balance weights fitted to the wheel rim should fall off. Unbalanced tyres will wear more quickly, as will the steering and suspension components. Wheel imbalance is normally signified by vibration, particularly at a certain speed (typically around 50 mph). If this vibration is felt only through the steering, then it is likely that just the front wheels need balancing. If, however, the vibration is felt through the whole car, the rear wheels could be out of balance. Wheel balancing should be carried out by a tyre dealer or garage.

1 Tread Depth - visual check
The original tyres have tread wear safety bands (B), which will appear when the tread depth reaches approximately 1.6 mm. The band positions are indicated by a triangular mark on the tyre sidewall (A).

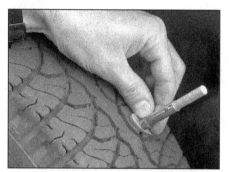

2 Tread Depth - manual check
Alternatively, tread wear can be monitored with a simple, inexpensive device known as a tread depth indicator gauge.

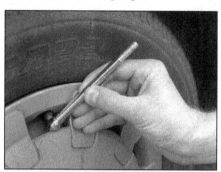

3 Tyre Pressure Check
Check the tyre pressures regularly with the tyres cold. Do not adjust the tyre pressures immediately after the vehicle has been used, or an inaccurate setting will result.

Tyre tread wear patterns

Shoulder Wear

Underinflation (wear on both sides)
Under-inflation will cause overheating of the tyre, because the tyre will flex too much, and the tread will not sit correctly on the road surface. This will cause a loss of grip and excessive wear, not to mention the danger of sudden tyre failure due to heat build-up.
Check and adjust pressures
Incorrect wheel camber (wear on one side)
Repair or renew suspension parts
Hard cornering
Reduce speed!

Centre Wear

Overinflation
Over-inflation will cause rapid wear of the centre part of the tyre tread, coupled with reduced grip, harsher ride, and the danger of shock damage occurring in the tyre casing.
Check and adjust pressures

If you sometimes have to inflate your car's tyres to the higher pressures specified for maximum load or sustained high speed, don't forget to reduce the pressures to normal afterwards.

Uneven Wear

Front tyres may wear unevenly as a result of wheel misalignment. Most tyre dealers and garages can check and adjust the wheel alignment (or "tracking") for a modest charge.
Incorrect camber or castor
Repair or renew suspension parts
Malfunctioning suspension
Repair or renew suspension parts
Unbalanced wheel
Balance tyres
Incorrect toe setting
Adjust front wheel alignment
Note: *The feathered edge of the tread which typifies toe wear is best checked by feel.*

Bulbs and fuses

✔ Check all external lights and the horn. Refer to the appropriate Sections of Chapter 12 for details if any of the circuits are found to be inoperative.

✔ Visually check all accessible wiring connectors, harnesses and retaining clips for security, and for signs of chafing or damage.

 HAYNES HINT *If you need to check your brake lights and indicators unaided, back up to a wall or garage door and operate the lights. The reflected light should show if they are working properly.*

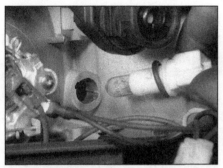

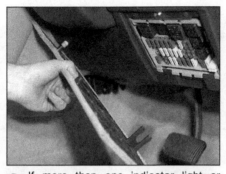

1 If a single indicator light, stop-light or headlight has failed, it is likely that a bulb has blown and will need to be replaced. Refer to Chapter 12 for details. If both stop-lights have failed, it is possible that the switch has failed (see Chapter 9).

2 If more than one indicator light or headlight has failed, it is likely that either a fuse has blown or that there is a fault in the circuit (see *"Electrical fault finding"* in Chapter 12). The fuses are mounted in a panel at the lower driver's side of the facia under a cover. Twist the clip to release the cover.

3 To replace a blown fuse, remove it, where applicable, using the plastic tool provided. Fit a new fuse of the same rating, available from car accessory shops. It is important that you find the reason the fuse blew (see *"Electrical fault finding"* in Chapter 12).

Battery

Caution: *Before carrying out any work on the vehicle battery, read the precautions given in "Safety first" at the start of this manual.*

✔ Make sure that the battery tray is in good condition, and that the clamp is tight. Corrosion on the tray, retaining clamp and the battery itself can be removed with a solution of water and baking soda. Thoroughly rinse all cleaned areas with water. Any metal parts damaged by corrosion should be covered with a zinc-based primer, then painted.

✔ Periodically (approximately every three months), check the charge condition of the battery as described in Chapter 5.

✔ If the battery is flat, and you need to jump start your vehicle, see *Roadside Repairs*.

1 The battery is located on the left-hand side of the engine compartment. The exterior of the battery should be inspected periodically for damage such as a cracked case or cover.

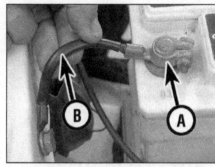

2 Check the tightness of battery clamps (A) to ensure good electrical connections. You should not be able to move them. Also check each cable (B) for cracks and frayed conductors.

Battery corrosion can be kept to a minimum by applying a layer of petroleum jelly to the clamps and terminals after they are reconnected.

3 If corrosion (white, fluffy deposits) is evident, remove the cables from the battery terminals, clean them with a small wire brush, then refit them. Automotive stores sell a tool for cleaning the battery post. . .

4 . . . and cable terminals.

Lubricants and fluids

Engine	Multigrade engine oil, viscosity SAE 10W/40 to 20W/50, to API SG or SH *(Duckhams QXR Premium Petrol Engine Oil, or Duckhams Hypergrade Petrol Engine Oil)*
Cooling system	Ethylene glycol based antifreeze *(Duckhams Antifreeze and Summer Coolant)*
Braking system	Hydraulic fluid to SAE J1703F or DOT 4 *(Duckhams Universal Brake & Clutch Fluid)*
Manual transmission:	
4 cylinder models	Gear oil, GM part no 90 297 261
6 cylinder models	Refer to vehicle handbook
Automatic transmission	Dexron II type ATF *(Duckhams ATF Autotrans III)*
Power steering	Dexron II type ATF *(Duckhams ATF Autotrans III)*

Choosing your engine oil

Engines need oil, not only to lubricate moving parts and minimise wear, but also to maximise power output and to improve fuel economy. By introducing a simplified and improved range of engine oils, Duckhams has taken away the confusion and made it easier for you to choose the right oil for your engine.

HOW ENGINE OIL WORKS

• *Beating friction*

Without oil, the moving surfaces inside your engine will rub together, heat up and melt, quickly causing the engine to seize. Engine oil creates a film which separates these moving parts, preventing wear and heat build-up.

• *Cooling hot-spots*

Temperatures inside the engine can exceed 1000° C. The engine oil circulates and acts as a coolant, transferring heat from the hot-spots to the sump.

• *Cleaning the engine internally*

Good quality engine oils clean the inside of your engine, collecting and dispersing combustion deposits and controlling them until they are trapped by the oil filter or flushed out at oil change.

OIL CARE - FOLLOW THE CODE

To handle and dispose of used engine oil safely, always:

• *Avoid skin contact with used engine oil. Repeated or prolonged contact can be harmful.*
• *Dispose of used oil and empty packs in a responsible manner in an authorised disposal site. Call 0800 663366 to find the one nearest to you. Never tip oil down drains or onto the ground.*

DUCKHAMS ENGINE OILS

For the driver who demands a premium quality oil for complete reassurance, we recommend synthetic formula **Duckhams QXR Premium Engine Oils**.

For the driver who requires a straight-forward quality engine oil, we recommend **Duckhams Hypergrade Engine Oils**.

For further information and advice, call the Duckhams UK Helpline on 0800 212988.

Tyre pressures

Saloon models	Front	Rear
Carlton:		
1.8 and 2.0 litre - 175 R 14, 185/70 R 14 tyres	2.2 bar (32 psi)	2.2 bar (32 psi)
1.8 and 2.0 litre - 195/70 R 15, 205/65 R 15 tyres	2.0 bar (29 psi)	2.0 bar (29 psi)
2.6 litre	2.2 bar (32 psi)	2.2 bar (32 psi)
3.0 litre (including early 24 valve) - 195/65 R 15, 205/65 R 15 tyres	2.5 bar (36 psi)	2.5 bar (36 psi)
3.0 litre 24 valve - 225/50 R 16 tyres	2.8 bar (41 psi)	2.7 bar (39 psi)
3.0 litre 24 valve - 235/40 R 18 tyres	2.7 bar (39 psi)	2.5 bar (36 psi)
Senator:		
All models	2.2 bar (32 psi)	2.2 bar (32 psi)
Estate models		
1.8 and 2.0 litre - 175 R 14 tyres	2.0 bar (29 psi)	2.2 bar (32 psi)
1.8 and 2.0 litre - 185/70 R 14 tyres	2.3 bar (33 psi)	2.5 bar (36 psi)
1.8 and 2.0 litre - 195/65 R 14, 205/65 R 14 tyres	2.0 bar (29 psi)	2.2 bar (32 psi)
All six-cylinder models	2.3 bar (33 psi)	2.5 bar (36 psi)

Note: *Refer to the drivers handbook for the correct tyre pressures for your particular vehicle. Pressures apply to vehicle with original-equipment tyres carrying loads of up to three persons, and may vary if loading increases or if any other make or type of tyre is fitted. Check with the tyre manufacturer or supplier for correct pressures if necessary.*

Chapter 1
Routine Maintenance and Servicing

Contents

Accelerator cable check and lubrication 10
Air cleaner element renewal 7
Air conditioning system check 29
Automatic transmission fluid change 30
Automatic transmission fluid level check .13
Auxiliary drivebelt(s) tension check and renewal 6
Auxiliary drivebelt(s) condition check 5
Brake fluid renewal 32
Brake pad lining wear check 16
Check the cooling system for leaks 4
Check the hydraulic brake lines and hoses for damage 17
Clean and check the distributor cap, rotor arm,
   HT leads and ignition coil 12
Clean the carburettor fuel inlet pipe strainer 11
Clutch pedal adjustment check - cable operated clutch 26
Coolant renewal 33
Driveshaft rubber bellows check 15

Engine oil and filter renewal 3
Examine the fuel lines 9
Final drive unit oil level check 14
Fuel filter renewal (fuel injection models only) 24
Handbrake shoe linings wear check 28
Headlamp beam alignment check 22
Idling speed and exhaust CO content check and adjustment 8
Intensive maintenance 2
Introduction 1
Level control system check 23
Lubricate hinges and locks 20
Manual transmission oil level check 27
Spark plugs renewal 25
Steering and suspension check 19
Timing belt renewal - 1.8 and 2.0 litre models 31
Underbody protection check 21
Vacuum servo unit operation check 18

Degrees of difficulty

Easy, suitable for novice with little experience	**Fairly easy,** suitable for beginner with some experience	**Fairly difficult,** suitable for competent DIY mechanic	**Difficult,** suitable for experienced DIY mechanic	**Very difficult,** suitable for expert DIY or professional

Lubricants and fluids

Refer to the end of 'Weekly Checks'

Capacities

Engine oil

Including filter:

1.8 and 2.0 litre models	4.5 litres
2.5, 2.6 and 3.0 litre models	5.5 litres

Difference between MAX and MIN dipstick marks:

1.8 and 2.0 litre models	1.0 litre
2.5, 2.6 and 3.0 litre models	1.5 litres

Cooling system

1.8 and 2.0 litre models	6.4 litres

2.5, 2.6 and 3.0 litre 12-valve models:

Manual transmission:

With air conditioning	11.3 litres
Without air conditioning	10.2 litres

Automatic transmission:

With air conditioning	11.2 litres
Without air conditioning	10.1 litres

3.0 litre 24-valve models:

Manual transmission:

With air conditioning	10.4 litres
Without air conditioning	10.0 litres

Automatic transmission:

With air conditioning	10.2 litres
Without air conditioning	9.8 litres

Manual transmission

Capacity (approximate)	1.9 litres

Automatic transmission

Capacity (approximate):

1.8 and 2.5 litre models and early (pre 1990) 2.0 litre and 3.0 litre models:

From dry	6.3 litres
Drain and refill	2.5 litres
After removing sump	3.3 litres

Later (1990 on) 2.0 litre and 3.0 litre models and all 2.6 litre models:

From dry	6.4 litres
Drain and refill	2.6 litres
After removing large sump	4.7 litres

Final drive

Saloon	0.8 litre (1.4 pints)
Estate	1.0 litre (1.8 pints)
Models with ribbed rear cover (from 08/90)	as above plus 0.1 litres

Fuel tank

Saloon models	75 litres
Estate models	70 litres

Braking system

Reservoir capacity	0.46 litres approx.

Power steering system

System capacity	0.4 litres approx.

Engine

Oil filter type:

1.8 and 2.0 litre models	Champion G102
2.5 and 2.6 litre models	Champion C108
Carlton 3.0 litre models	Champion C107 or C146
Senator 3.0 litre models	Champion C107 or C108

Cooling system

Antifreeze concentration:

Protection to -10 °C	20%
Protection to -20 °C	34%
Protection to -30 °C	44%

Fuel system

Air filter element:
1.8 litre carburettor models	Champion W103
1.8 litre and 2.0 litre fuel injection models	Champion U507
All other models	Champion U570 or U571
Fuel filter	Champion L201
Idling speed	See Chapter 4A or 4B
Exhaust idle CO content	See Chapter 4A or 4B

Ignition system

Ignition timing	See Chapter 5B

Spark plugs:
1.8 and 2.0 litre models	Champion RN9YCC
2.5, 2.6 and 3.0 litre 12-valve models	Champion RL82YCC
3.0 litre 24-valve models	Champion RC7YCC
Electrode gap*	0.8 mm

* The electrode gap is that recommended by Champion Spark Plug, for their specified plugs above. If plugs of any other type are to be fitted, consult their manufacturers for electrode gap recommendations.

Clutch

Clutch pedal stroke (cable operated clutch)	142 + 7 mm

Braking system

Friction lining material thickness (minimum)	7.0 mm (including backplate)

Tyre pressures

Refer to the end of 'Weekly Checks'

Torque wrench settings	Nm	lbf ft
Automatic transmission drain plug:		
AW03-71L and AW03-71LE transmission	20	15
AR25 and AR35 transmission	25	18
Automatic transmission fluid filter bolts:		
AW03-71L and AW03-71LE transmission	5	4
AR25 and AR35 transmission	20	15
Automatic transmission sump bolts:		
AW03-71L and AW03-71LE transmission	5	4
AR25 and AR35 transmission	12	9
Engine sump drain plug	45	33
Final drive unit filler plug	22	16
Manual transmission filler plug	30	22
Roadwheel bolts	90	66
Spark plugs:		
1.8 and 2.0 litre models	20	15
2.5, 2.6 and 3.0 litre 12-valve models	40	29
3.0 litre 24-valve models	25	18

The maintenance intervals in this manual are provided with the assumption that you will be carrying out the work yourself. These are the minimum maintenance intervals recommended by the manufacturer for vehicles driven daily. If you wish to keep your vehicle in peak condition at all times, you may wish to perform some of these procedures more often. We encourage frequent maintenance, because it enhances the efficiency, performance and resale value of your vehicle.

If the vehicle is driven in dusty areas, used to tow a trailer, or driven frequently at slow speeds (idling in traffic) or on short journeys, more frequent maintenance intervals are recommended.

When the vehicle is new, it should be serviced by a factory-authorised dealer service department, in order to preserve the factory warranty.

Every 250 miles or weekly
☐ Refer to "Weekly Checks"

Every 9000 miles (15 000 km) or 12 months - whichever comes first
☐ Change the engine oil and renew the filter (Section 3)
☐ Check the cooling system for leaks (Section 4)
☐ Check the condition of the auxiliary drivebelt(s) (Section 5)
☐ Check the tension of the auxiliary drivebelt(s) - except models with automatic tensioner (Section 6)
☐ Renew the air cleaner element (Section 7)
☐ Check and adjust the idling speed and exhaust CO content (Section 8)
☐ Examine the fuel lines (Section 9)
☐ Lubricate the throttle controls (Section 10)
☐ Clean the carburettor fuel inlet pipe strainer (Section 11)
☐ Clean and check the distributor cap, rotor arm, HT leads and ignition coil (Section 12)
☐ Check the automatic transmission fluid level (Section 13)
☐ Check the final drive unit oil level (Section 14)
☐ Check the driveshaft rubber bellows (Section 15)
☐ Check the brake pad linings for wear (Section 16)
☐ Check the hydraulic brake lines and hoses for damage (Section 17)
☐ Check vacuum servo unit operation (Section 18)
☐ Check steering and suspension balljoints (Section 19)
☐ Lubricate hinges and locks (only at 9000, 27 000, 45 000 miles etc) (Section 20)
☐ Check underbody protection (Section 21)
☐ Check the headlamp beam alignment (Section 22)
☐ Check the operation of the level control system (Section 23)

Every 18 000 miles (30 000 km) or 2 years - whichever comes first
☐ Renew the fuel filter (fuel injection models only) (Section 24)
☐ Renew the spark plugs (Section 25)
☐ Check the clutch pedal adjustment (excluding 6-cylinder engines) (Section 26)
☐ Check manual transmission oil level (Section 27)
☐ Check handbrake shoe linings for wear (Section 28)
☐ Check the air conditioning system (Section 29)

Every 36 000 miles (60 000 km) or 4 years - whichever comes first
☐ Change the automatic transmission fluid (Section 30)
☐ Renew the timing belt - 1.8 and 2.0 litre models (Section 31)

Every year, regardless of mileage
☐ Renew the brake fluid (Section 32)

Every 2 years, regardless of mileage
☐ Renew the coolant (Section 33)

Underbonnet view of a 1.8 litre OHC Carlton model

1 Brake fluid reservoir
2 Brake vacuum servo unit
3 Steering gear
4 Throttle housing
5 Auxiliary air valve (step up valve)
   for power steering
6 Distributor
7 Engine oil filler cap
8 Engine oil level dipstick
9 Additional relay box
10 Front suspension top
   mounting
11 Power steering fluid reservoir
12 Washer fluid reservoir
13 Ignition coil
14 Battery
15 Top hose
16 Power steering pump
17 Thermostat housing
18 Radiator
19 Alternator/cooling fan drivebelt
20 Alternator
21 Air cleaner cover
22 Airflow sensor
23 Coolant expansion tank
24 Brake master cylinder
25 Ignition control unit

Underbonnet view of a 3.0 litre DOHC 24-valve Senator model

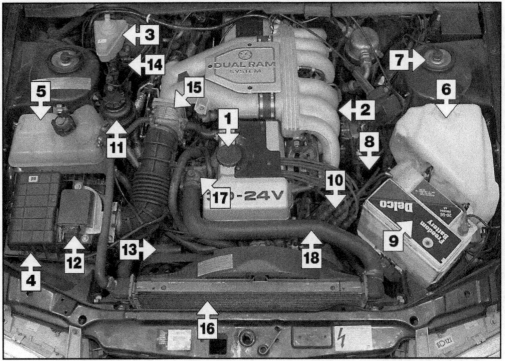

1 Engine oil filler cap
2 Engine oil dipstick
3 Master cylinder brake fluid
   reservoir
4 Air cleaner housing
5 Coolant expansion tank
6 Windscreen/tailgate washer
   fluid reservoir
7 Suspension strut upper
   mounting
8 Ignition HT coil
9 Battery
10 Distributor
11 Power steering fluid reservoir
12 Airflow meter
13 Power steering pump
14 Brake master cylinder
15 Throttle body
16 Radiator
17 Thermostat housing
18 Radiator top hose

Front underbody view of a 1.8 litre OHC Carlton model

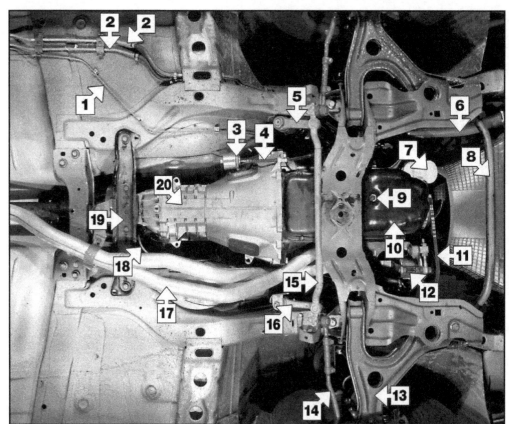

1 Rear hydraulic brake line
2 Fuel feed and return pipes
3 Clutch release arm
4 Clutch cable
5 Steering drop arm
6 Bottom hose
7 Oil filter cartridge
8 Front anti-roll bar
9 Engine oil drain plug
10 Engine oil sump
11 Power steering pump drivebelt
12 Power steering pump
13 Front lower suspension arm
14 Steering tie-rod (side)
15 Steering tie-rod (centre)
16 Steering idler
17 Exhaust front downpipe
18 Speedometer cable
19 Manual gearbox rear mounting
    crossmember
20 Manual gearbox

Front underbody view of a 3.0 litre DOHC 24-valve Senator model

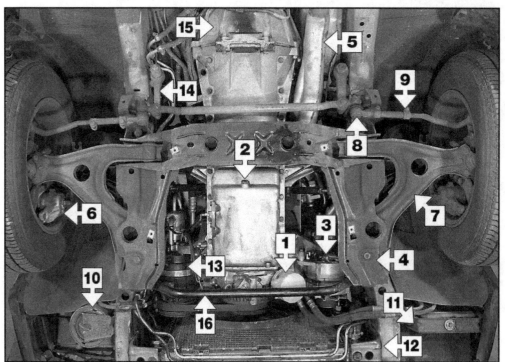

1 Engine oil filter
2 Sump drain plug
3 Alternator
4 Front suspension subframe
5 Exhaust front pipe
6 Front brake caliper
7 Front suspension lower arm
8 Track rod balljoint
9 Steering tie-rod
10 Charcoal canister
11 Engine oil cooler
12 Transmission fluid cooler
13 Air conditioning compressor
14 Steering idler
15 Automatic transmission
16 Front anti-roll bar

Rear underbody view (Senator model shown - other models similar)

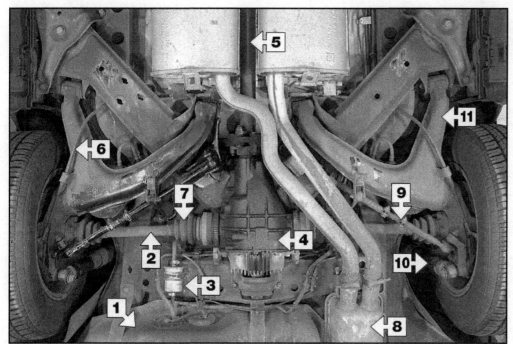

1 Fuel tank
2 Driveshaft
3 Fuel filter
4 Differential casing
5 Propeller shaft
6 Handbrake cable
7 Driveshaft rubber gaiter
8 Exhaust system tailbox
9 Rear suspension tie-rod
10 Rear damper
11 Rear suspension lower arm

Maintenance procedures

1 Introduction

General information

1 This Chapter is designed to help the home mechanic maintain his/her vehicle for safety, economy, long life and peak performance.

2 The Chapter contains a master maintenance schedule, followed by Sections dealing specifically with each task in the schedule. Visual checks, adjustments, component renewal and other helpful items are included. Refer to the accompanying illustrations of the engine compartment and the underside of the vehicle for the locations of the various components.

3 Servicing your vehicle in accordance with the mileage/time maintenance schedule and the following Sections will provide a planned maintenance programme, which should result in a long and reliable service life. This is a comprehensive plan, so maintaining some items but not others at the specified service intervals, will not produce the same results.

4 As you service your vehicle, you will discover that many of the procedures can - and should - be grouped together, because of

the particular procedure being performed, or because of the proximity of two otherwise-unrelated components to one another. For example, if the vehicle is raised for any reason, the exhaust can be inspected at the same time as the suspension and steering components.

5 The first step in this maintenance programme is to prepare yourself before the actual work begins. Read through all the Sections relevant to the work to be carried out, then make a list and gather all the parts and tools required. If a problem is encountered, seek advice from a parts specialist, or a dealer service department.

2 Intensive maintenance

1 If, from the time the vehicle is new, the routine maintenance schedule is followed closely, and frequent checks are made of fluid levels and high-wear items, as suggested throughout this manual, the engine will be kept in relatively good running condition, and the need for additional work will be minimised.

2 It is possible that there will be times when the engine is running poorly due to the lack of regular maintenance. This is even more likely

if a used vehicle, which has not received regular and frequent maintenance checks, is purchased. In such cases, additional work may need to be carried out, outside of the regular maintenance intervals.

3 If engine wear is suspected, a compression test (refer to the relevant Part of Chapter 2) will provide valuable information regarding the overall performance of the main internal components. Such a test can be used as a basis to decide on the extent of the work to be carried out. If, for example, a compression test indicates serious internal engine wear, conventional maintenance as described in this Chapter will not greatly improve the performance of the engine, and may prove a waste of time and money, unless extensive overhaul work is carried out first.

4 The following series of operations are those most often required to improve the performance of a generally poor-running engine:

Primary operations

a) Clean, inspect and test the battery (See "Weekly checks").
b) Check all the engine-related fluids (See "Weekly checks").
c) Check the condition and tension of the auxiliary drivebelt (Sections 5 and 6).
d) Renew the spark plugs (Section 25).

e) *Inspect the distributor cap and rotor arm (Section 12).*

f) *Check the condition of the air filter, and renew if necessary (Section 7).*

g) *Check the fuel filter (Section 24 or 11).*

h) *Check the condition of all hoses, and check for fluid leaks (Sections 9, 17 and 4).*

i) *Check the exhaust gas emissions (Section 8).*

5 If the above operations do not prove fully effective, carry out the following secondary operations:

Secondary operations

All items listed under "Primary operations", plus the following:

a) *Check the charging system (see relevant Part of Chapter 5).*

b) *Check the ignition system (see relevant Part of Chapter 5).*

c) *Check the fuel system (see relevant Part of Chapter 4).*

d) *Renew the distributor cap and rotor arm (see relevant Part of Chapter 5).*

e) *Renew the ignition HT leads (see relevant Part of Chapter 5)*

9000 Mile / 12 Month Service

3 Engine oil and filter renewal

1 Frequent oil and filter changes are the most important preventative maintenance procedures which can be undertaken by the DIY owner. As engine oil ages, it becomes diluted and contaminated, which leads to premature engine wear.

2 Before starting this procedure, gather together all the necessary tools and materials. Also make sure that you have plenty of clean rags and newspapers handy, to mop up any spills. Ideally, the engine oil should be warm, as it will drain more easily, and more built-up sludge will be removed with it. Take care not to touch the exhaust or any other hot parts of the engine when working under the vehicle. To avoid any possibility of scalding, and to protect yourself from possible skin irritants and other harmful contaminants in used engine oils, it is advisable to wear gloves when carrying out this work. Access to the underside of the vehicle will be greatly improved if it can be raised on a lift, driven onto ramps, or jacked up and supported on

axle stands (see "*Jacking and Vehicle Support*"). Whichever method is chosen, make sure that the vehicle remains level, or if it is at an angle, that the drain plug is at the lowest point. The drain plug is located at the rear of the sump.

3 Remove the oil filler cap from the camshaft cover (twist it through a quarter-turn anti-clockwise and withdraw it).

4 Using a spanner, or preferably a suitable socket and bar, slacken the drain plug about half a turn. Position the draining container under the drain plug, then remove the plug completely **(see Haynes Hint)**.

5 Allow some time for the oil to drain, noting that it may be necessary to reposition the container as the oil flow slows to a trickle.

6 After all the oil has drained, wipe the drain plug and the sealing washer with a clean rag. Examine the condition of the sealing washer, and renew it if it shows signs of scoring or other damage which may prevent an oil-tight seal. Clean the area around the drain plug opening, and refit the plug complete with the washer. Tighten the plug securely, preferably to the specified torque, using a torque wrench.

7 The oil filter is located at the right-hand end of the engine.

8 Move the container into position under the oil filter.

9 Use an oil filter removal tool to slacken the filter initially, then unscrew it by hand the rest of the way **(see illustration)**. Empty the oil from the old filter into the container.

10 Use a clean rag to remove all oil, dirt and sludge from the filter sealing area on the engine. Check the old filter to make sure that the rubber sealing ring has not stuck to the engine. If it has, carefully remove it.

11 Apply a light coating of clean engine oil to the sealing ring on the new filter, then screw the filter into position on the engine. Tighten the filter firmly by hand only - **do not** use any tools.

12 Remove the old oil and all tools from under the vehicle then, if applicable, lower the vehicle to the ground.

13 Fill the engine through the filler hole in the camshaft cover, using the correct grade and type of oil (refer to "Weekly Checks" for details of topping-up). Pour in half the specified quantity of oil first, then wait a few minutes for the oil to drain into the sump. Continue to add oil, a small quantity at a time, until the level is up to the lower mark on the dipstick. Adding a further 1.0 litre (1.8 and 2.0 litre) or 1.5 litre (2.5, 2.6 and 3.0 litre) will bring the level up to the upper mark on the dipstick.

14 Start the engine and run it for a few minutes, while checking for leaks around the oil filter seal and the sump drain plug. Note that there may be a delay of a few seconds before the low oil pressure warning light goes out when the engine is first started, as the oil circulates through the new oil filter and engine oil galleries before the pressure builds up.

15 Stop the engine, and wait a few minutes for the oil to settle in the sump once more. With the new oil circulated and the filter now completely full, recheck the level on the dipstick, and add more oil as necessary.

16 Dispose of the used engine oil safely, with reference to "*General repair procedures*".

HAYNES HINT

Keep the drain plug pressed into the sump while unscrewing it by hand the last couple of turns. As the plug releases, move it away sharply so the stream of oil issuing from the sump runs into the container, not up your sleeve!

3.9 Removing the oil filter cartridge (OHC engine shown)

OIL CARE
FOLLOW THE CODE

OIL BANK LINE
0800 66 33 66

Note: It is antisocial and illegal to dump oil down the drain. To find the location of your local oil recycling bank, call this number free.

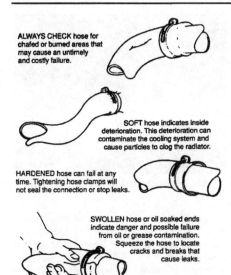

ALWAYS CHECK hose for chafed or burned areas that may cause an untimely and costly failure.

SOFT hose indicates inside deterioration. This deterioration can contaminate the cooling system and cause particles to clog the radiator.

HARDENED hose can fail at any time. Tightening hose clamps will not seal the connection or stop leaks.

SWOLLEN hose or oil soaked ends indicate danger and possible failure from oil or grease contamination. Squeeze the hose to locate cracks and breaks that cause leaks.

4.2 Possible causes of coolant hose failure

4 Check the cooling system for leaks

1 Check the security and condition of all cooling system-related pipes and hoses in the engine bay. Ensure that all cable-ties or securing clips are in place and in good condition. Clips which are broken or missing can lead to chafing of the hoses, pipes or wiring, which could cause more serious problems in the future.
2 Carefully check the radiator hoses and heater hoses along their entire length. Renew any hose which is cracked, swollen or deteriorated. Cracks will show up better if the hose is squeezed. Pay close attention to the hose clips that secure the hoses to the cooling system components. Hose clips can pinch and puncture hoses, resulting in cooling system leaks **(see illustration)**.
3 Inspect all the cooling system components (hoses, joint faces etc.) for leaks. A leak in the cooling system will usually show up as white- or rust-coloured deposits on the area adjoining the leak **(see Haynes Hint)**. Where any problems of this nature are found on system components, renew the component or gasket with reference to Chapter 3.

5 Auxiliary drivebelt(s) condition check

The belt(s) should be inspected along its/their entire length, and if found to be worn, frayed or cracked, it/they should be renewed as a precaution against breakage in service. It is advisable to carry spare drivebelt(s) of the correct type in the vehicle at all times.

HAYNES HINT

A leak in the cooling system will usually show up as white - or rust - coloured deposits on the area adjoining the leak

6 Auxiliary drivebelt(s) tension check and renewal

Tension check and adjustment

Models with manually adjusted belt(s)

1 Correct tensioning of the auxiliary drivebelt(s) will ensure a long life. Beware, however, of overtightening, as this can cause excessive wear in the alternator/power steering pump.
2 The belt(s) should be inspected along its entire length, and if found to be worn, frayed or cracked, it/they should be renewed as a precaution against breakage in service. It is advisable to carry spare drivebelt(s) of the correct type in the vehicle at all times.
3 Although special tools are available for measuring the belt tension, a good approximation can be achieved if the belt is tensioned so that there is approximately 13.0 mm of free movement under firm thumb pressure at the mid-point of the longest run between pulleys. If in doubt, err on the slack side, as an excessively-tight belt may cause damage to the alternator or other components. If necessary, adjust the belt(s) as described below.

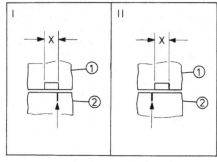

6.5 On models with a spring loaded belt tensioner, mark on tensioner arm (2) must be within mark/recess (X) on tensioner body (1) - illustration I. If mark is as shown in illustration II, the belt must be renewed

Models with a spring loaded belt tensioner

4 Working within the engine compartment, closely examine the upper edge of the spring loaded timing belt tensioner.
5 Looking down on the tensioner, check the position of the tensioner arm mark in relation to the recess/mark on the tensioner body. The mark should be positioned within the recess/mark. If the mark is outside the recess/mark, or approaching its outer limit the belt should be renewed **(see illustration)**.
6 The belt tension is automatically adjusted by the tensioner and therefore requires no adjusting.

Renewal

Alternator drivebelt - manually adjusted belt

7 To remove the belt, simply loosen the mounting nuts and bolts, and the bolt securing the adjuster bracket and slacken the belt sufficiently to slip it from the pulleys. On models with power steering it will first be necessary to remove the power steering pump drivebelt as described below.
8 Locate the belt on the pulleys and tension it as follows.
9 Lever the alternator away from the engine using a wooden lever at the mounting bracket until the correct tension is achieved (see paragraph 3), then tighten the bolt securing the adjuster bracket, and the alternator mounting nuts and bolts. On no account lever at the free end of the alternator, as serious internal damage could be caused to the alternator. **Note** *When a new belt has been fitted it will probably stretch slightly to start with and the tension should be rechecked, and if necessary adjusted, after about 5 minutes running.*

Power steering pump drivebelt - manually adjusted belt

10 Loosen the power steering pump pivot bolts.
11 Loosen the adjustment rod locknut and unscrew the adjustment nut sufficiently until the drivebelt can be released from the pulleys and removed **(see illustration)**.
12 Locate the belt on the pulleys and tension as follows.

6.11 Slackening the power steering pump adjustment nut

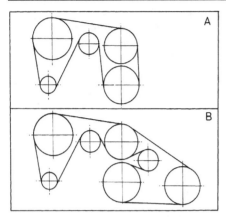

6.16 Drivebelt routing - models with a spring loaded tensioner

A Models without air conditioning
B Models with air conditioning

7.9a Air cleaner cover spring clip

7.9b Removing the air cleaner element

13 Using the adjustment nut, position the power steering pump so that the correct belt tension is achieved (see paragraph 3). Once the pump is correctly positioned, securely tighten the adjustment rod locknut and the pump pivot bolts.

Alternator/power steering pump/ air conditioning compressor drivebelt - models with a spring loaded belt tensioner

14 If necessary, to improve access remove the cooling fan as described in Chapter 3.
15 Using a suitable socket and extension bar fitted to the spring loaded tensioner arm pulley bolt, pivot the tensioner arm downwards to release the belt tension and slip the belt off the pulleys. Slowly release the tensioner arm and remove the belt from the engine, noting its correct routing.
16 Locate the new belt on all except the power steering pump pulley, making sure it is correctly routed **(see illustration)**.
17 Rotate the tensioner arm again and slip the belt onto the final pulley. Make sure the belt is correctly located on all pulleys then slowly release the tensioner arm. No further adjustment of the tension is required.

7   Air cleaner element renewal

Carburettor models

1 Disconnect the air inlet duct and warm air tube from the air cleaner.
2 Unscrew the three mounting nuts, lift the air cleaner from the carburettor, and disconnect the vacuum hose for the inlet air temperature control.
3 Remove the air cleaner gasket.
4 Remove the cover from the air cleaner, and remove the element.
5 Wipe clean the inside of the body and cover. Examine the gasket and renew it if necessary. Obtain a new element.

6 To check the operation of the inlet air temperature control, apply vacuum to the temperature switch on the bottom of the air cleaner. The flap in the inlet tube should uncover the warm air port and close the cold air port.
7 Refitting is a reversal of removal.

Fuel injection models

8 Slacken the retaining clip and disconnect the inlet duct from the air cleaner. Also disconnect the airflow sensor wiring connector.
9 Release the spring clips securing the cover to the air cleaner body and lift the cover and remove the element **(see illustrations)**.
10 Wipe clean the inside of the body and cover. Obtain a new element.
11 Refitting is a reversal of removal.

8   Idling speed and exhaust CO content check and adjustment

Refer to Chapter 4 Part A on carburettor models, and Chapter 4 Part B for fuel injection models.

9   Examine the fuel lines

1 With the vehicle raised, inspect the petrol tank and filler neck for punctures, cracks and other damage. The connection between the filler neck and tank is especially critical. Sometimes, a rubber filler neck or connecting hose will leak due to loose retaining clamps or deteriorated rubber.
2 Carefully check all rubber hoses and metal fuel lines leading away from the petrol tank. Check for loose connections, deteriorated hoses, crimped and other damage. Pay particular attention to the vent pipes and hoses, which often loop up around the filler neck and can become blocked or crimped. Follow the lines to the front of the vehicle, carefully inspecting them all the way. Renew damaged sections as necessary.
3 From within the engine compartment,

check the security of all fuel hose attachments and pipe unions, and inspect the fuel hoses and vacuum hoses for kinks, chafing and deterioration.
4 Renew any hose/pipe which shows signs of damage or deterioration.

10   Accelerator cable check and lubrication

1 Check the operation of the accelerator cable and lubricate the throttle mechanism with a light oil. If necessary, adjust the cable as described in the relevant Part of Chapter 4.

11   Clean the carburettor fuel inlet pipe strainer

⚠ *Warning: Before carrying out the following operation refer to the precautions given in Safety first! at the beginning of this Manual and follow them implicitly. Petrol is a highly dangerous and volatile liquid and the precautions necessary when handling it cannot be overstressed.*

1 Disconnect the battery negative lead.
2 Disconnect the fuel hose from the carburettor and plug the hose.
3 Withdraw the filter from the fuel inlet union (see Chapter 4A).
4 Wash it with fresh fuel to remove any debris from it. Inspect the filter for signs of clogging or splitting and renew it if necessary.
5 Refit the filter and reconnect the fuel hose.

12   Clean and check the distributor cap, rotor arm, HT leads and ignition coil

1 On 3.0 litre 24-valve models, remove the throttle housing and inlet duct assembly as described in Chapter 4B, Section 15. Undo the retaining screws and remove the spark plug cover from the centre of the cylinder head cover **(see illustrations)**.

12.1a On 3.0 litre 24-valve models, undo the retaining screws . . .

2 Ensure that the leads are numbered before removing them, if not make identification marks to avoid confusion when refitting. Pull the leads from the plugs by gripping the end fitting, not the lead, otherwise the lead connection may be fractured.

3 Check inside the end fitting for signs of corrosion, which will look like a white crusty powder. Push the end fitting back onto the spark plug ensuring that it is a tight fit on the plug. If not, remove the lead again and use pliers to carefully crimp the metal connector inside the end fitting until it fits securely on the end of the spark plug.

4 Using a clean rag, wipe the entire length of the lead to remove any built-up dirt and grease. Once the lead is clean, check for burns, cracks and other damage. Do not bend the lead excessively or pull the lead lengthways - the conductor inside might break.

5 Disconnect the other end of the lead from the distributor cap. Again, pull only on the end fitting. Check for corrosion and a tight fit in the same manner as the spark plug end. If an ohmmeter is available, check the resistance of the lead by connecting the meter between the spark plug end of the lead and the segment inside the distributor cap. Refit the lead securely on completion.

6 Check the remaining leads one at a time, in the same way.

7 If new leads are required, purchase a set for your specific car and engine.

8 Remove the distributor cap and rotor arm (see Chapter 5B). Wipe the cap clean and carefully inspect it inside and out for signs of

12.1b . . . and remove the spark plug cover to gain access to the HT leads

cracks, carbon tracks (tracking) and worn, burned or loose contacts; check that the cap's carbon brush is unworn, free to move against spring pressure and making good contact with the rotor arm. Also inspect the cap seal for signs of wear or damage and renew if necessary. Closely inspect the rotor arm. It is common practice to renew the cap and rotor arm whenever new spark plug (HT) leads are fitted. When fitting a new cap, remove the leads from the old cap one at a time and fit them to the new cap in the exact same location - do not simultaneously remove all the leads from the old cap or firing order confusion may occur. Refit the rotor arm and distributor cap.

9 On 3.0 litre 24-valve models check the spark plug cover seals for damage or deterioration and renew if necessary. Refit the cover, tightening its retaining screws securely, and refit the throttle housing and inlet duct assembly as described in Chapter 4B, Section 15.

13 Automatic transmission fluid level check

1.8 and 2.5 litre models, and early (pre-1990) 2.0 litre and 3.0 litre models - AW03-71L and AW03-71LE transmission

1 Ensure that the vehicle is on level ground. With the engine running and the brakes applied, move the selector lever through all the gear positions, finishing in "P" (Park).

2 With the engine still idling and the transmission in "P", withdraw the transmission dipstick, wipe it clean, then re-insert it and withdraw it again. Read the fluid level.

3 With the engine and transmission hot (after at least 20 km/13 miles running) the fluid level should be between the MIN and MAX marks on the side of the dipstick marked "90°C" (see illustration). The quantity of fluid required to raise the level from MIN to MAX is about 0.6 litre. With the engine and transmission cold, the fluid level should be up to the line on the side of the dipstick marked "20°C".

4 If necessary top-up the level with the specified fluid through the dipstick tube (see illustration). Take care not to allow any dust or dirt to enter the tube.

5 Refit the dipstick and switch off the engine.

Later (1990-on) 2.0 litre and 3.0 litre models, and all 2.6 litre models - AR25 and AR35 transmission

6 To check the automatic transmission fluid level, first take the vehicle on a run of approximately 12 miles/20 km to warm the transmission up to its normal operating temperature. On your return, ensure that the vehicle is parked on level ground. With the engine running and the brakes applied, move the selector lever slowly from the "P" position to the "1" position, and then return it to "P".

7 With the engine still idling and the selector lever in the "P" position, withdraw the transmission dipstick, wipe it clean, then re-insert it fully into the tube. Withdraw the dipstick and note the level of the fluid. Repeat this procedure three times, and take the average reading as the true transmission fluid level.

8 With the engine and transmission at normal operating temperature, at air temperatures above 0°C (32°F), the fluid level should be within the "HOT" portion of the dipstick (approximately 42 mm up from the base of the dipstick) (see illustration). At ambient

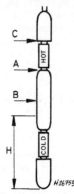

13.8 Automatic transmission dipstick level markings - AR25 and AR35 transmission

A Fill level when air temperature is above 0°C
B Fill level when air temperature is below 0°C
C Filling level after transmission overhaul (transmission completely dry)
H Fluid level from base of dipstick

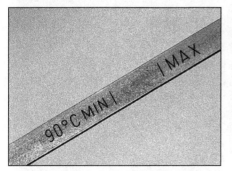

13.3 Automatic transmission fluid level dipstick markings - AW03-71L and AW03-71LE transmission

13.4 Topping up the automatic transmission

temperatures below 0°C (32°F), the fluid level should be halfway between the "HOT" portion and the "COLD" portion of the dipstick (approximately 32 mm up from the base of the dipstick).

9 If necessary, top-up the transmission fluid level with the specified fluid via the dipstick tube, and recheck the fluid level as described above. Take great care not to allow any dust or dirt to enter the tube.

10 Once the level is correct, refit the dipstick and switch off the engine.

14 Final drive unit oil level check

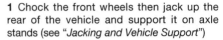

1 Jack up the front and rear of the vehicle and support it on axle stands (see "*Jacking and Vehicle Support*") so that the vehicle is level.

2 Using a hexagon key, unscrew the filler plug from the right-hand side of the final drive unit.

3 Check that the oil level is up to the bottom of the filler plug aperture using a piece of bent wire or small screwdriver as a dipstick.

4 If necessary top-up with the correct type of oil as given in the Specifications.

5 Refit and tighten the filler plug to the specified torque, and wipe clean.

6 Check the pinion final drive unit oil seal and differential bearing oil seals for leaks. If evident, renew them.

7 Lower the car to the ground.

15 Driveshaft rubber bellows check

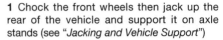

1 Chock the front wheels then jack up the rear of the vehicle and support it on axle stands (see "*Jacking and Vehicle Support*")

2 With the handbrake released turn each wheel separately and check the driveshaft rubber bellows for splits and damage **(refer to rear underbody illustration)**. Check also that the clips are secure.

3 Lower the vehicle to the ground.

16 Brake pad lining wear check

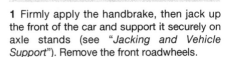

1 Firmly apply the handbrake, then jack up the front of the car and support it securely on axle stands (see "*Jacking and Vehicle Support*"). Remove the front roadwheels.

2 For a comprehensive check, the brake pads should be removed and cleaned. The operation of the caliper can then also be checked, and the condition of the brake disc itself can be fully examined on both sides. Refer to Chapter 9 for further information **(see Haynes Hint)**.

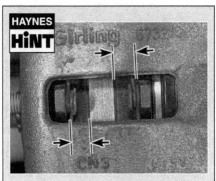

For a quick check, the thickness of the friction material on each brake pad can be measured through the aperture in the caliper body.

3 If any pad's friction material is worn to the specified thickness or less, *all four pads must be renewed as a set.*

17 Check the hydraulic brake lines and hoses for damage

1 Firmly apply the handbrake, then jack up the front of the car and support it securely on axle stands (see "*Jacking and Vehicle Support*"). Remove the front roadwheels.

2 Inspect the flexible brake hose connections to the calipers - check for evidence of damage, wear or deterioration through ageing **(see illustration)**. Brake fluid leakage should be corrected immediately, before the vehicle is brought back into service on public highway.

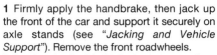

If the caliper hose union is difficult to see, use a small mirror held behind the caliper to improve visibility.

3 Repeat the inspection at the rear calipers.

4 Follow the rigid brake lines from the master cylinder through the engine bay and along the underside of the vehicle. Check carefully for signs of damage, corrosion or leakage. Renew any section that shows signs of deterioration.

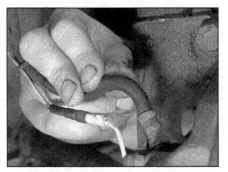

17.2 Inspecting the flexible brake hose connections to the front caliper

18 Vacuum servo unit operation check

1 To establish whether or not the servo is operating, proceed as follows.

2 With the engine stopped, apply the brake pedal several times in order to dissipate the vacuum from the servo unit.

3 Hold the brake pedal depressed, then start the engine. The pedal should move a small distance towards the floor with the additional assistance of the servo unit. If not, check the vacuum hose and non-return valve. If these prove to be satisfactory, the servo unit itself is faulty and should be renewed.

19 Steering and suspension check

Front suspension and steering check

1 Raise the front of the vehicle, and securely support it on axle stands (see "*Jacking and Vehicle Support*").

2 Inspect the balljoint dust covers and the steering rack-and-pinion gaiters for splits, chafing or damage. Any wear of these components will cause loss of lubricant, together with dirt and water entry, resulting in rapid deterioration of the balljoints or steering gear.

3 On vehicles with power steering, check the fluid hoses for chafing or deterioration, and the pipe and hose unions for fluid leaks. Also check for signs of fluid leakage under pressure from the steering gear rubber gaiters, which would indicate failed fluid seals within the steering gear.

4 Grasp the roadwheel at the 12 o'clock and 6 o'clock positions, and try to rock it **(see illustration)**. Very slight free play may be felt, but if the movement is appreciable, further investigation is necessary to determine the source. Continue rocking the wheel while an assistant depresses the footbrake. If the movement is now eliminated or significantly reduced, it is likely that the hub bearings are at fault. If the free play is still evident with the

19.4 Check for wear in the hub bearings by grasping the wheel and trying to rock it

footbrake depressed, then there is wear in the suspension joints or mountings.

5 Now grasp the wheel at the 9 o'clock and 3 o'clock positions, and try to rock it as before. Any movement felt now may again be caused by wear in the hub bearings or the steering track-rod balljoints. If the inner or outer balljoint is worn, the visual movement will be obvious.

6 Using a large screwdriver or flat bar, check for wear in the suspension mounting bushes by levering between the relevant suspension component and its attachment point. Some movement is to be expected as the mountings are made of rubber, but excessive wear should be obvious. Also check the condition of any visible rubber bushes, looking for splits, cracks or contamination of the rubber.

7 With the car standing on its wheels, have an assistant turn the steering wheel back and forth about an eighth of a turn each way. There should be very little, if any, lost movement between the steering wheel and roadwheels. If this is not the case, closely observe the joints and mountings previously described, but in addition, check the steering column universal joints for wear, and the rack-and-pinion steering gear itself.

Suspension strut/ shock absorber check

8 Check for any signs of fluid leakage around the suspension strut/shock absorber body, or from the rubber gaiter around the piston rod. Should any fluid be noticed, the suspension strut/shock absorber is defective internally, and should be renewed. **Note:** *Suspension struts/shock absorbers should always be renewed in pairs on the same axle.*

9 The efficiency of the suspension strut/shock absorber may be checked by bouncing the vehicle at each corner. Generally speaking, the body will return to its normal position and stop after being depressed. If it rises and returns on a rebound, the suspension strut/shock absorber is probably suspect. Examine also the suspension strut/shock absorber upper and lower mountings for any signs of wear.

20.2 Lubricating the bonnet lock mechanism

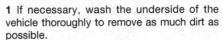

20 Lubricate hinges and locks (only at 9000, 27 000, 45 000 miles etc)

Lubricate the hinges of the bonnet, doors and tailgate with a light general-purpose oil. Similarly, lubricate all latches, locks and lock strikers. At the same time, check the security and operation of all the locks, adjusting them if necessary (see Chapter 11).

Lightly lubricate the bonnet release mechanism and cable with a suitable grease **(see illustration).**

21 Underbody protection check

1 If necessary, wash the underside of the vehicle thoroughly to remove as much dirt as possible.

2 Raise and securely support the front and rear of the vehicle, and check the underbody for damage and corrosion. Inspect the condition of the underseal. If it has been penetrated or scraped away at any point, ensure that new underseal is re-applied to the

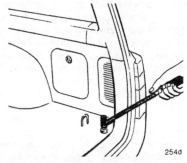

254d

23.1 Checking the pressure in the level control system (Estate model shown - others similar)

area as soon as possible, to prevent the onset of corrosion.

3 Check the security of the engine bay undertray, where applicable. Retighten/renew any fixings that may have worked loose.

22 Headlamp beam alignment check

Accurate adjustment of the headlight beam is only possible using optical beam-setting equipment, and this work should therefore be carried out by a Vauxhall dealer or service station with the necessary facilities.

Basic adjustments can be carried out in an emergency, and further details are given in Chapter 12.

23 Level control system check

Locate the level control system pressure nozzle in the load space **(see illustration).** Check that the pressure is at least 0.8 Bar (11.6 psi).

18 000 Mile / 2 Year Service

24 Fuel filter renewal (fuel injection models only)

⚠️ *Warning: Before carrying out the following operation refer to the precautions given in Safety first! at the beginning of this Manual and follow them implicitly. Petrol is a highly dangerous and volatile liquid and the precautions necessary when handling it cannot be overstressed*

1 The fuel filter is located under the rear of the vehicle, next to the fuel pump. Chock the front wheels, then jack up the rear of the vehicle,

and support securely on axle stands (see "*Jacking and Vehicle Support*").

2 Depressurise the fuel system (Chapter 4B) then disconnect the battery negative lead. Position a suitable container below the fuel filter, to catch spilt fuel.

3 Slacken the retaining clips and disconnect both hoses. To minimise fuel loss clamp the hoses either side of the filter or be prepared to plug the hose ends as they are disconnected.

4 Loosen the clamp bolt, and withdraw the filter from its clamp. Note the orientation of the fuel flow direction indicator on the filter. This will be in the form of an arrow which points in the direction of the fuel flow, or the filter will have AUS (out) stamped on its outlet side.

5 Recover the mounting rubber from the old filter, and transfer it to the new filter.

6 Fit the new filter making sure its fuel flow direction indicator is facing the right way.

7 Reconnect the hose and securely tighten their retaining clips.

8 Start the engine and check the disturbed hose connections for signs of leakage.

25 Spark plugs renewal

1 The correct functioning of the spark plugs is vital for the smooth running and efficiency of the engine. It is essential that the plugs fitted are appropriate for the engine, the suitable type being specified at the beginning of this Chapter. If the correct type of plug is used and the engine is in good condition, the spark plugs should not need attention between scheduled renewal intervals, except for adjustment of their gaps. Spark plug cleaning is rarely necessary, and should not be attempted unless specialised equipment is available, as damage can easily be caused to the firing ends.

2 To remove the plugs, first open the bonnet. On 3.0 litre 24-valve models, remove the throttle housing and inlet duct assembly as described in Chapter 4B, Section 15. Undo the retaining screws and remove the spark plug cover from the centre of the cylinder head cover.

3 If necessary, mark the HT leads 1 to 4 or 1 to 6 (as applicable), to correspond to the cylinder the lead serves (No 1 cylinder is nearest the timing belt/chain end of the engine). Pull the HT leads from the plugs by gripping the end connectors, not the leads, otherwise the lead connections may be fractured.

4 It is advisable to remove any dirt from the spark plug recesses using a clean brush, vacuum cleaner or compressed air, before removing the plugs, to prevent the dirt dropping into the cylinders.

5 Unscrew the plugs using a spark plug spanner, a suitable box spanner, or a deep socket and extension bar **(see illustration)**. Keep the socket in alignment with the spark plugs, otherwise if it is forcibly moved to either

side, the porcelain top of the spark plug may be broken off. As each plug is removed, examine it as follows.

6 Examination of the spark plugs will give a good indication of the condition of the engine. If the insulator nose of the spark plug is clean and white, with no deposits, this is indicative of a weak mixture or too hot a plug (a hot plug transfers heat away from the electrode slowly, while a cold plug transfers heat away quickly).

7 If the tip and insulator nose are covered with hard black-looking deposits, then this is indicative that the idle mixture is too rich. Should the plug be black and oily, then it is likely that the engine is fairly worn, as well as the mixture being too rich.

8 If the insulator nose is covered with light-tan to greyish-brown deposits, then the mixture is correct and it is likely that the engine is in good condition.

9 The spark plug gap is of considerable importance as, if it is too large or too small, the size of the spark and its efficiency will be seriously impaired. For the best results, the spark plug gap should be set in accordance with the Specifications at the beginning of this Chapter.

10 To set the spark plug gap, measure the gap between the electrodes with a feeler blade, and then bend open, or close, the outer plug electrode until the correct gap is achieved **(see illustrations)**. The centre electrode should never be bent, as this may crack the insulation and cause plug failure, if nothing worse.

11 Special spark plug electrode gap adjusting

tools are available from most motor accessory shops **(see illustration)**.

12 Before fitting the new spark plugs, check that the threaded connector sleeves on the top of the plug are tight, and that the plug exterior surfaces and threads are clean.

13 Screw in the spark plugs by hand where possible, then tighten them to the specified torque. Take particular care to enter the plug threads correctly, otherwise the threads in the cylinder head may be damaged **(see Tool Tip)**.

14 Reconnect the HT leads in their correct order.

15 On 3.0 litre 24-valve models inspect the spark plug cover seals for signs of damage or deterioration and renew if necessary. Refit the cover, tightening its screws securely, and refit the throttle housing and inlet duct assembly as described in Chapter 4B, Section 15.

26 Clutch pedal adjustment check - cable operated clutch

1 With the clutch pedal in the at-rest position, use a tape measure to measure the distance from the centre of the pedal pad to the base of the steering wheel rim (furthest point from the pedal). Note the measurement as (A).

2 Fully depress the clutch pedal and repeat the procedure given in paragraph 1. Note the measurement as (B).

3 Subtract measurement (A) from measurement (B) to calculate the clutch pedal stroke. This should be as shown in the Specifications at the start of this Chapter.

4 If adjustment is necessary, apply the handbrake, jack up the front of the vehicle and support it on axle stands (see "*Jacking*

25.5 Removing a spark plug (OHC engine shown)

25.10a Measuring a spark plug electrode gap using a feeler blade

25.10b Measuring a spark plug electrode gap using a wire gauge

25.11 Adjusting a spark plug electrode gap

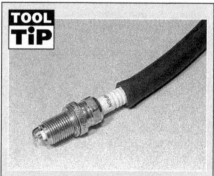

TOOL TiP

It is very often difficult to insert spark plugs into their holes without cross-threading them. To avoid this possibility, fit a short length of 5/16 inch internal diameter rubber hose over the end of the spark plug. The flexible hose acts as a universal joint to help align the plug with the plug hole. Should the plug begin to cross-thread, the hose will slip on the spark plug, preventing thread damage to the cylinder head.

26.4 Adjusting the clutch cable

and Vehicle Support"). Loosen the locknut on the clutch cable end fitting **(see illustration)** and turn the adjustment nut clockwise to increase the dimension difference, or anti-clockwise to reduce it. Tighten the locknut and recheck the dimension difference. Lower the vehicle to the ground.

5 Note that with correct adjustment the clutch pedal will be slightly higher in relation to the brake pedal. The adjustment is incorrect if both pedals are at the same height and it is likely that the clutch will not fully release.

6 As the clutch linings wear, the clutch pedal

rest position will progressively move upwards, making periodic adjustment necessary at the specified intervals.

27 Manual transmission oil level check

1 Either position the vehicle over an inspection pit, or jack up the front and rear of the vehicle and support it on axle stands (see "Jacking and Vehicle Support"). The vehicle must be level.

2 Clean the area around the filler/level plug on the right-hand side of the transmission, then slacken and remove the plug from the transmission.

3 To check the transmission oil level, it will be necessary to fabricate a suitable dipstick. This can be made out of a piece of welding rod with a right-angle bend in it. Insert the rod into the filler/level plug aperture, and check the oil level. The transmission oil level should be approximately 9 mm below the lower edge of the filler/level plug aperture.

4 If necessary, top-up using the specified type of lubricant until the transmission oil level is correct. **Note:** Do not overfill the transmission. Excess oil must be siphoned or

drained out of the transmission, otherwise the gearchange shifting action may be impaired.

5 Once the transmission oil level is correct, refit the filler/level plug and tighten it to the specified torque.

6 The frequent need for topping-up indicates a leakage, possibly through an oil seal. The cause should be investigated and rectified.

28 Handbrake shoe linings wear check

Refer to the information given in Chapter 9

29 Air conditioning system check

1 In the engine bay, check that all hoses are correctly routed and are not chaffing against other components. Check for cracking, hardening or other evidence of deterioration.

2 Where applicable, refer to Chapter 11 and remove the radiator grille. Extract any leaves or other debris that may have collected in front of the condenser.

36 000 Mile / 4 Year Service

30 Automatic transmission fluid change

1.8 and 2.5 litre models and early (pre-1990) 2.0 litre and 3.0 litre models - AW03-71L and AW03-71LE transmission

Note: Although not strictly necessary, it is also recommended that the fluid filter is cleaned at the same time the fluid is renewed. To do this remove the sump and clean the transmission filter as described in paragraphs 10 to 14, noting that the filter is retained by six bolts and that there are two magnets in the sump. Also, prior to refitting the sump, examine the

dipstick tube O-ring for signs of damage, and renew if necessary **(see illustrations)**.

1 Either position the vehicle over an

inspection pit or jack up the front of the vehicle and support it on axle stands (see "Jacking and Vehicle Support").

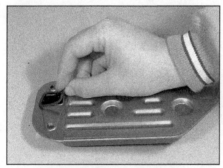

30.1a Position a new gasket on the filter housing . . .

30.1b . . . then refit the filter to the transmission . . .

30.1c . . . and tighten its retaining bolts to the specified torque

30.1d Install the cleaned magnet in the sump . . .

30.1e . . . and refit the sump using a new gasket

2 Position a container beneath the transmission sump then unscrew the drain plug and drain all the fluid.

> **Warning: If the vehicle has just been in use, the fluid is likely to be extremely hot, and care must be taken to avoid scalding.**

3 Renew the sealing washer if necessary, then refit and tighten the drain plug.
4 Lower the vehicle to the ground. Fill the transmission with the correct amount of the specified fluid through the dipstick tube.
5 Check the fluid level (see Section 13).

Later (1990-on) 2.0 litre and 3.0 litre models and all 2.6 litre models - AR25 and AR35 transmission

Note: *Although not strictly necessary, it is also recommended that the large transmission sump is removed at this interval and the transmission fluid filter cleaned. This will ensure that more of the transmission fluid is drained and renewed (only approximately half of the transmission fluid is drained when only the sump drain plug is removed), and that all debris is removed from the filter and sump.*

Fluid renewal only

6 If it is only wished to renew the transmission fluid, this can be carried out as described in paragraphs 1 to 5. On completion, fill the transmission with the specified type of fluid until the fluid level is at the correct point on the dipstick (see Section 13), then take the vehicle on a run, and check the fluid level as described earlier in this Section.

Fluid renewal and filter cleaning

7 Firmly apply the handbrake, then jack up the front of the vehicle and support it on axle stands (see "*Jacking and Vehicle Support*").
8 Position a container beneath the transmission sump, then unscrew the drain plug and allow the fluid to drain into the container.

> **Warning: If the vehicle has just been driven, the fluid will be extremely hot. Take great care to avoid being scalded.**

9 Examine the drain plug sealing washer, and renew if necessary. Once all the fluid has drained, wipe the threads clean, then refit the drain plug to the sump, tightening it to the specified torque.
10 Slacken and remove all the sump retaining bolts, then carefully lower the sump away from the transmission, being prepared for some fluid spillage. Note that the sump still contains a considerable amount of transmission fluid. Pour the fluid out of the sump and into the container, then remove the gasket and discard it.
11 Undo the three retaining bolts, then remove the filter from the underside of the transmission along with its sealing gasket. Discard the gasket; a new one should be used on refitting.
12 Clean the filter element in a bath of solvent, then examine the element for signs of clogging or damage. If the filter element is split or blocked, the filter must be renewed. Remove the magnet from inside the sump, and clean all traces of metal filings from it; the filings should be very fine - any sizeable chips of metal indicate a worn component in the transmission.
13 Ensure that the filter element is dry, then fit the new gasket onto the filter housing and offer up the filter to the transmission. Ensuring that the gasket remains correctly positioned, refit the retaining bolts and tighten them to the specified torque.
14 Ensure that the sump and transmission sealing faces are clean and dry, then position the new gasket on the sump and refit the magnet. Refit the sump to the transmission, and tighten its bolts to the specified torque.
15 Lower the vehicle to the ground, then fill the transmission with the specified type of fluid until the fluid level is at the correct point on the dipstick (see Section 13); the approximate quantity is given in the Specifications at the start of this Chapter. On completion, take the vehicle on a journey of at least 5 miles, then check the fluid level, referring to Section 13.

31 Timing belt renewal - 1.8 and 2.0 litre models

Refer to Chapter 2A.

Every Year, regardless of mileage

32 Brake fluid renewal

> **Warning: Brake hydraulic fluid can harm your eyes and damage painted surfaces, so use extreme caution when handling and pouring it. Do not use fluid that has been standing open for some time, as it absorbs moisture from the air. Excess moisture can cause a dangerous loss of braking effectiveness.**

1 The procedure is similar to that for the bleeding of the hydraulic system as described in Chapter 9, except that the brake fluid reservoir should be emptied by siphoning, using a clean poultry baster or similar before starting, and allowance should be made for the old fluid to be expelled when bleeding a section of the circuit.
2 Working as described in Chapter 9, open the first bleed screw in the sequence, and pump the brake pedal gently until nearly all the old fluid has been emptied from the master cylinder reservoir.

> **HAYNES HINT** *Old hydraulic fluid is invariably much darker in colour than the new, making it easy to distinguish them*

3 Top-up to the "MAX" level with new fluid, and continue pumping until only the new fluid remains in the reservoir, and new fluid can be seen emerging from the bleed screw. Tighten the screw, and top the reservoir level up to the "MAX" level line.
4 Work through all the remaining bleed screws in the sequence until new fluid can be

seen at all of them. Be careful to keep the master cylinder reservoir topped-up to above the "MIN" level at all times, or air may enter the system and greatly increase the length of the task.

5 When the operation is complete, check that all bleed screws are securely tightened, and that their dust caps are refitted. Wash off all traces of spilt fluid, and recheck the master cylinder reservoir fluid level.

6 Check the operation of the brakes before taking the car on the road.

Every 2 Years, regardless of mileage

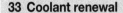 **33 Coolant renewal**

1 Refer to the information given in Chapter 3.

Chapter 2 Part A:
1.8 and 2.0 litre (OHC) engines

Contents

Compression test - description and interpretation 2
Cylinder head - overhaul 15
Cylinder head - removal and refitting with engine in car 12
Engine - complete dismantling 9
Engine - complete reassembly 16
Engine - initial start-up after major overhaul or repair 19
Engine - refitting 18
Engine - removal 6
Engine ancillaries - refitting 17
Engine ancillaries - removal 8

Engine components - examination and renovation 14
Engine dismantling - general 7
Engine mountings - renewal 11
General information 1
Major operation requiring engine removal 4
Major operations possible with engine in car 3
Method of engine removal 5
Sump - removal and refitting with engine in car 10
Timing belt - removal and refitting with engine in car 13

Degrees of difficulty

Easy, suitable for novice with little experience	Fairly easy, suitable for beginner with some experience	Fairly difficult, suitable for competent DIY mechanic 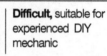	Difficult, suitable for experienced DIY mechanic 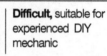	Very difficult, suitable for expert DIY or professional

Specifications

Type	. . . .	Four cylinder, in-line, single overhead camshaft

General

Bore:
- 1.8 litre models . . . . 84.8 mm
- 2.0 litre models . . . . 86.0 mm

Stroke:
- 1.8 litre models . . . . 79.5 mm
- 2.0 litre models . . . . 86.0 mm

Capacity:
- 1.8 litre models . . . . 1796 cc
- 2.0 litre models . . . . 1998 cc

Firing order . . . . 1-3-4-2 (No 1 at timing belt end of engine)

Valves

Valve clearance . . . . Automatic by hydraulic valve lifters

Valve stem-to-guide clearance:
- Inlet . . . . 0.018 to 0.052 mm
- Exhaust . . . . 0.038 to 0.072 mm

Valve stem diameter:
Inlet:
- Standard . . . . 6.998 to 7.012 mm
- 1st oversize (0.075 mm) . . . . 7.073 to 7.087 mm
- 2nd oversize (0.150 mm) . . . . 7.148 to 7.162 mm
- 3rd oversize (0.300 mm) . . . . 7.248 to 7.262 mm

Exhaust:
- Standard . . . . 6.978 to 6.992 mm
- 1st oversize (0.075 mm) . . . . 7.053 to 7.067 mm
- 2nd oversize (0.150 mm) . . . . 7.128 to 7.142 mm
- 3rd oversize (0.300 mm) . . . . 7.228 to 7.242 mm

Valve guide bore diameter:
- Standard . . . . 7.030 to 7.050 mm
- 1st oversize (0.075 mm) . . . . 7.105 to 7.125 mm
- 2nd oversize (0.150 mm) . . . . 7.180 to 7.200 mm
- 3rd oversize (0.300 mm) . . . . 7.280 to 7.300 mm

Valve guide installed height . . . . 83.50 to 83.80 mm

Cylinder head

Maximum permissible distortion of sealing face . . . . 0.025 mm
Overall height of cylinder head . . . . 95.90 to 96.10 mm

Pistons and rings

Type . . . . Alloy, recessed head
Number of piston rings . . . . 2 compression, 1 oil control
Ring end gap:
   Compression rings . . . . 0.30 to 0.50 mm
   Oil control ring . . . . 0.40 to 1.40 mm
Ring gap offset (to gap of adjacent ring) . . . . 180°
Gudgeon pin diameter . . . . 21.0 mm

Piston grades - 1.8 litre engine: . . . .

	Diameter (mm)	Marking
Production grade 1	84.76	8
Production grade 2	84.77	99
	84.78	00
	84.79	01
	84.80	02
Oversize (0.5 mm)	85.25	7 + 0.5
	85.26	8 + 0.5
	85.27	9 + 0.5
	85.28	0 + 0.5

Piston grades - 2.0 litre engine: . . . .

	Diameter (mm)	Marking
Production grade 1	85.96	8
Production grade 2	85.97	99
	85.98	00
	85.99	01
	86.00	02
Oversize (0.5 mm)	86.45	7 + 0.5
	86.46	8 + 0.5
	86.47	9 + 0.5
	86.48	0 + 0.5

Piston-to-bore clearance:
   New engine . . . . 0.02 mm
   After rebore . . . . 0.01 to 0.03 mm
Maximum permissible piston out-of-round . . . . 0.013 mm
Maximum permissible piston taper . . . . 0.013 mm

Crankshaft

Number of main bearings 5
Main bearing journal diameter:
   Standard . . . . 57.982 to 57.995 mm
   Undersizes:
      1st undersize (0.25 mm) . . . . 57.732 to 57.745 mm
      2nd undersize (0.5 mm) . . . . 57.482 to 57.495 mm
Crankpin diameter:
   Standard . . . . 48.970 to 48.988 mm
   Undersizes:
      1st undersize (0.25 mm) . . . . 48.720 to 48.738 mm
      2nd undersize (0.5 mm) . . . . 48.470 to 48.488 mm
Crankshaft endfloat . . . . 0.05 to 0.15 mm
Main bearing running clearance . . . . 0.02 to 0.04 mm
Big-end running clearance . . . . 0.01 to 0.03 mm
Big-end side-play . . . . 0.07 to 0.24 mm

Camshaft

Endfloat . . . . 0.09 to 0.21 mm
Camshaft journal diameters:
   Number 1 journal . . . . 42.455 to 42.470 mm
   Number 2 journal . . . . 42.705 to 42.720 mm
   Number 3 journal . . . . 42.955 to 42.970 mm
   Number 4 journal . . . . 43.205 to 43.220 mm
   Number 5 journal . . . . 43.455 to 43.470 mm
Maximum run-out . . . . 0.03 mm

Timing belt

Timing belt tension (using gauge KM-510-A) - early (pre 1993) models:
New belt, cold 4.5
New belt, warm 7.5
Used belt, cold 2.5
Used belt, warm 7.0

Flywheel

Ring gear maximum run-out .... 0.5 mm
Maximum machining of clutch face .... 0.3 mm

Lubrication system

Oil pump:
Gear backlash (gear to gear) .... 0.1 to 0.2 mm
Gear-to-housing clearance (endfloat) .... 0.03 to 0.10 mm
Oil pressure at idle (engine at operating temperature) .... 1.5 bar

Torque wrench settings

	Nm	lbf ft
Camshaft cover bolts	8	6
Camshaft sprocket	45	33
Crankshaft sprocket bolt:		
Stage 1	130	96
Stage 2	Angle tighten a further 40 to 50°	
Crankshaft pulley to sprocket	20	15
Flywheel/driveplate:		
Stage 1	65	48
Stage 2	Angle tighten a further 30 to 45°	
Cylinder head bolts:		
Stage 1	25	18
Stage 2	Angle tighten a further 90°	
Stage 3	Angle tighten a further 90°	
Stage 4	Angle tighten a further 90°	
Main bearing cap:		
Stage 1	50	37
Stage 2	Angle tighten a further 40 to 50°	
Big-end cap:		
Stage 1	35	26
Stage 2	Angle tighten a further 45 to 60°	
Sump	5	4
Sump drain plug	45	33
Water pump bolts	25	18

1 General information

1 On 1.8 and 2.0 litre models, the engine is of four-cylinder, in-line type with a single overhead camshaft, mounted conventionally at the front of the car. The cylinder head is of alloy and the cylinder block of cast iron.

2 The crankshaft is supported in five bearings, and the centre bearing incorporates flanges to control the endfloat.

3 The connecting rods are attached to the crankshaft by horizontally split shell bearings, and to the pistons by gudgeon pins which are an interference fit in the connecting rod small-end. The aluminium alloy pistons are fitted with three piston rings: two compression rings and a three segment oil control ring.

4 The camshaft is driven by a toothed rubber belt from the crankshaft, and operates the valves via rocker arms. The rocker arms are supported at their pivot end by hydraulic self-adjusting valve lifters (tappets), which automatically take up any clearance between the rocker arm and the valve stems. The inlet and exhaust valves are each closed by a single spring and operate in guides pressed into the cylinder head.

5 Engine lubrication is by a bi-rotor pump located in a housing attached to the front of the cylinder block. The oil pump is driven by the crankshaft, while the distributor rotor arm and, on carburettor models, the fuel pump, are driven by the camshaft. Blow-by gases in the crankcase are fed to the camshaft housing by an external tube and thereafter drawn into the inlet manifold via a hose.

2 Compression test -
description and interpretation

1 When engine performance is down, or if misfiring occurs which cannot be attributed to the ignition or fuel systems, a compression test can provide diagnostic clues as to the engine's condition. If the test is performed regularly, it can give warning of trouble before any other symptoms become apparent.

2 The engine must be fully warmed-up to normal operating temperature, the battery must be fully charged, and all the spark plugs must be removed (Chapter 1). The aid of an assistant will also be required.

3 Disable the ignition system by disconnecting the ignition HT coil lead from the distributor cap and earthing it on the cylinder block. Use a jumper lead or similar wire to make a good connection.

4 Fit a compression tester to the No 1 cylinder spark plug hole - the type of tester which screws into the plug thread is to be preferred.

5 Have the assistant hold the throttle wide open, and crank the engine on the starter motor; after one or two revolutions, the compression pressure should build up to a maximum figure, and then stabilise. Record the highest reading obtained.

6 Repeat the test on the remaining cylinders, recording the pressure in each.

7 All cylinders should produce very similar pressures; a difference of more than 2 bars between any two cylinders indicates a fault. Note that the compression should build up quickly in a healthy engine; low compression on the first stroke, followed by gradually-increasing pressure on successive strokes, indicates worn piston rings. A low compression reading on the first stroke, which does not build up during successive strokes, indicates leaking valves or a blown head gasket (a cracked head could also be the cause). Deposits on the undersides of the valve heads can also cause low compression.

8 Although Vauxhall do not specify exact compression pressures, as a guide, any cylinder pressure of below 10 bars can be considered as less than healthy. Refer to a Vauxhall dealer or other specialist if in doubt as to whether a particular pressure reading is acceptable.

9 If the pressure in any cylinder is low, carry out the following test to isolate the cause. Introduce a teaspoonful of clean oil into that cylinder through its spark plug hole, and repeat the test.

10 If the addition of oil temporarily improves the compression pressure, this indicates that bore or piston wear is responsible for the pressure loss. No improvement suggests that leaking or burnt valves, or a blown head gasket, may be to blame.

11 A low reading from two adjacent cylinders is almost certainly due to the head gasket having blown between them; the presence of coolant in the engine oil will confirm this.

12 If one cylinder is about 20 per cent lower than the others and the engine has a slightly rough idle, a worn camshaft lobe could be the cause.

13 If the compression reading is unusually high, the combustion chambers are probably coated with carbon deposits. If this is the case, the cylinder head should be removed and decarbonised.

14 On completion of the test, refit the spark plugs and reconnect the ignition system.

3 Major operations possible with engine in car

The following major operations can be carried out without removing the engine:
a) *Removal and refitting of cylinder head*
b) *Removal and refitting of sump*
c) *Removal and refitting of oil pump*
d) *Removal and refitting of timing belt*
e) *Removal and refitting of pistons and connecting rods*
f) *Removal and refitting of flywheel*
g) *Removal and refitting of engine mountings*
h) *Removal and refitting of camshaft*
i) *Renewal of the crankshaft front and rear oil seals*

4 Major operation requiring engine removal

The following major operation is only possible after removal of the engine.
a) *Removal and refitting of crankshaft and main bearings*

5 Method of engine removal

Although it is possible to remove the engine together with the manual gearbox or automatic transmission, it is recommended that the engine

be removed separately. A strong hoist will still be necessary as the engine alone is of considerable weight. The engine is removed upwards from the engine compartment.

6 Engine - removal

1 Remove the bonnet (see Chapter 11).
2 Disconnect the battery negative lead.
3 Remove the air cleaner on carburettor models, or disconnect and remove the air duct from the throttle housing and airflow sensor on fuel injection models (Chapter 4).
4 Remove the radiator (see Chapter 3).
5 Disconnect the accelerator cable, choke cable, automatic transmission kickdown cable, and cruise control cable (as applicable).
6 Unbolt the power-assisted steering pump and bracket assembly and place it on one side **(see illustrations)**. There is no need to disconnect the hoses.
7 If fitted, remove the air conditioning compressor (Chapter 11); put it on one side without disconnecting the refrigerant hoses.
8 Disconnect the heater hoses at the bulkhead **(see illustration)**.
9 Disconnect and plug the fuel feed and return hoses. Unbolt the mounting bracket from the inlet manifold.
10 Detach the HT cable from the ignition coil.
11 Note the location of the coolant hoses on the right-hand side of the engine then disconnect them **(see illustrations)**. Also disconnect the brake vacuum servo hose.

6.6a Unscrew the bolts . . .

6.6b . . . and remove the power steering pump and bracket assembly

6.8 Heater hose connections at the bulkhead

6.11a Hose connections to the front coolant housing

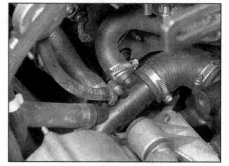

6.11b Hoses leading to water pump inlet

6.12 Engine earth strap

6.14 Wiring harness connector on the top of the fuel injection engine

6.24a Front left-hand engine mounting

6.24b Removing the engine mounting nuts

12 Unbolt the engine earth strap(s) **(see illustration)**.
13 Disconnect the top hose from the thermostat housing.
14 Note the location and routing of the engine wiring harness, and make a simple drawing of it if necessary. Disconnect and remove the harness. To ensure quick and accurate refitting, identify each wire with tape as it is removed. On fuel injection models the harness must be disconnected on the top of the engine **(see illustration)** and at the airflow sensor.
15 Apply the handbrake, then jack up the front of the car and support it on axle stands (see "Jacking and Vehicle Support").
16 Unbolt the exhaust downpipe from the exhaust manifold and remove the gasket. Where applicable unbolt the exhaust bracket at the rear of the gearbox.
17 Unbolt and remove the gearbox front cover.
18 On manual gearbox models disconnect the clutch cable from the release arm and gearbox.
19 On automatic transmission models unscrew the bolts securing the torque converter to the driveplate with reference to Chapter 6.
20 Unscrew the lower bolts securing the gearbox to the engine.
21 Lower the car to the ground.
22 Attach a hoist to the engine and just take its weight. Lifting eyes are provided at the front and rear of the engine.
23 Support the gearbox with a trolley jack.
24 Unscrew the nuts from the top of both

engine mountings, and unbolt the right-hand mounting bracket from the block **(see illustrations)**.
25 Unscrew the upper bolts securing the gearbox to the engine.
26 Pull the engine forwards to disengage it from the gearbox/automatic transmission. On automatic transmission models make sure that the torque converter is held firmly in contact with the transmission oil pump, otherwise it could fall out and fluid would be spilled.
27 When clear of the gearbox, lift the engine from the engine compartment while guiding it past the surrounding components **(see illustration)**.
28 If the engine is to be dismantled, drain the oil and refit the drain plug before lowering the engine onto the workbench.

6.27 Lifting the engine from the engine compartment

7 Engine dismantling - general

1 The engine should be dismantled in a clean area away from dust and dirt. Avoid working with the engine directly on a concrete floor, as grit presents a real source of trouble.
2 It is advisable to have suitable containers to hold small items, as this will help when reassembling the engine.
3 Thoroughly clean all components with a suitable solvent and wipe dry ready for inspection. Internal channels are best blown through with an air line.
4 Always obtain complete sets of gaskets when dismantling the engine, and fit them all.
5 When possible refit nuts, bolts and washers in their locations as this helps to protect the threads from damage and will also be helpful when the engine is being reassembled.
6 Retain unserviceable items until the new parts are obtained, so that the new part can be checked against the old part, to ensure that the correct item has been supplied.

8 Engine ancillaries - removal

Although the items listed may be removed separately with the engine installed, it is more appropriate to take these off after the engine has been removed from the car when extensive dismantling is being carried out. The items are:

a) Carburettor or fuel injection components (Chapter 4A or 4B)
b) Fuel pump on carburettor models (Chapter 4A)
c) Inlet and exhaust manifolds (Chapter 4A or 4B)
d) Clutch (Chapter 6)
e) Spark plugs, distributor cap and plate, and ignition inductive impulse sensor (Chapters 1 and 5))
f) Alternator and bracket (Chapter 5)
g) Thermo-viscous cooling fan, thermostat, and temperature gauge sender unit (Chapter 3)

9 Engine - complete dismantling

1 Using a screwdriver, prise the oil seal for the distributor plate from the rear of the camshaft housing **(see illustration)**.
2 Unscrew and remove the oil pressure switch **(see illustration)**.
3 Remove the oil dipstick.
4 Disconnect the crankcase ventilation hose from the camshaft cover **(see illustration)**.
5 On fuel injection models use an Allen key to

9.1 Prising the oil seal from the rear of the camshaft housing

9.2 Removing the oil pressure switch

9.4 Disconnecting the crankcase ventilation hose

9.5 Removing the auxiliary air valve bracket on the fuel injection engine

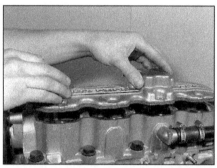

9.6a Removing the camshaft cover . . .

9.6b . . . and gasket

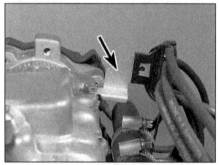

9.6c HT lead bracket (arrowed)

9.7a Remove the screws . . .

9.7b . . . and withdraw the cooling fan pulley

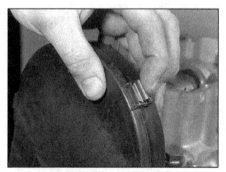

9.8a Release the clips . . .

9.8b . . . and remove the timing belt upper cover . . .

9.8c . . . and lower cover

unscrew the auxiliary air valve bracket from the camshaft housing **(see illustration)**. Recover the gasket.

6 Unbolt the camshaft cover and remove the cork gasket. Note the location of the HT lead bracket **(see illustrations)**.

7 Remove the cooling fan pulley by holding the hub stationary with a spanner while removing the pulley screws **(see illustrations)**.

8 Unclip and remove the two timing belt covers **(see illustrations)**.

9 Turn the engine with a spanner on the crankshaft pulley bolt until the mark on the camshaft sprocket is aligned with the pointer on the top of the rear timing belt cover. Also align the notch in the crankshaft pulley with the pointer on the lower part of the rear timing belt cover **(see illustrations)**.

9.9a Camshaft sprocket and cover timing marks

9.9b Crankshaft pulley notch and timing pointer

9.10 Removing the crankshaft pulley/vibration damper

9.12 Removing the timing belt

9.14 Tool for holding the flywheel stationary

9.15a Slide off the crankshaft sprocket . . .

9.15b . . . remove the Woodruff key

9.15c . . . and spacer

9.16a Unscrew the securing bolt . . .

10 Unbolt the crankshaft pulley from the timing belt sprocket **(see illustration)**.
11 Unscrew and remove the bolt securing the water pump section of the timing belt cover to the oil pump housing.
12 On early (pre 1993) models, loosen the three bolts securing the water pump to the block. Rotate the water pump body anti-clockwise and remove the timing belt from the sprockets **(see illustration)**.
13 On later (1993 on) models with a spring loaded timing belt tensioner, slacken the tensioner securing bolt slightly. Pivot the tensioner away from the belt and slip the belt off the sprockets. Remove the bolt and tensioner assembly from the engine.
14 Unscrew the crankshaft sprocket bolt while holding the flywheel/driveplate stationary using a wide blade screwdriver in the starter ring gear teeth. Alternatively make up the tool shown **(see illustration)** to hold the flywheel. Discard

the bolt, a new should be used on refitting.
15 Slide the crankshaft sprocket from the front of the crankshaft, then remove the Woodruff key and spacer **(see illustrations)**.
16 Hold the camshaft sprocket stationary using a tool as shown, then unscrew the

9.16b . . . and remove the camshaft sprocket

securing bolt. Remove the sprocket from the front of the camshaft **(see illustrations)**.
17 Unscrew and remove the three bolts and washers, and withdraw the water pump.
18 Unbolt and remove the rear timing belt cover **(see illustration)**.

9.18 Removing the rear timing belt cover

9.19 Removing the oil filter

9.20 Cooling fan hub bracket removal

9.21a Unscrew the bolts . . .

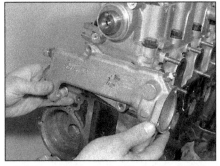

9.21b . . . and remove the front coolant and thermostat housing . . .

9.21c . . . and O-ring seal

9.22a Crankcase ventilation tube lower flange . . .

9.22b . . . and upper connecting hose

9.26 Head gasket on the block

9.27a Unscrew the bolts (arrowed) . . .

19 Unscrew the oil filter from the oil pump housing **(see illustration)**.
20 Unbolt the cooling fan hub bracket from the block **(see illustration)**.
21 Unbolt the front coolant and thermostat housing from the cylinder head, and remove the O-ring seal **(see illustrations)**.
22 Remove the crankcase ventilation tube from the camshaft housing and block by disconnecting the hose and unscrewing the flange bolts **(see illustrations)**. Recover the gasket.
23 Working in a spiral pattern from outside to inside, slacken each cylinder head bolt by a quarter turn. Following the same sequence slacken the bolts a further half turn, then remove them completely. Note that the cylinder head bolts must be renewed as a complete set whenever they are disturbed; obtain a new set of bolts for reassembly.
24 Lift off the camshaft housing and camshaft.

25 Lift the cylinder head from the block. Careful use of a wooden or hide mallet may be necessary to release the head, but do not attempt to wedge any tool between the joint faces.
26 Remove the gasket from the block **(see illustration)**.

27 Unscrew the camshaft thrustplate bolts, remove the thrustplate and withdraw the camshaft from the camshaft housing **(see illustrations)**.
28 Remove the rocker arms and thrustpads from the cylinder head. Withdraw the hydraulic valve lifters and immerse them in a

9.27b . . . remove the thrustplate . . .

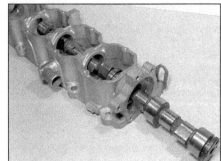

9.27c . . . and withdraw the camshaft

9.28a Removing the rocker arms . . .

9.28b . . . thrust pads . . .

9.28c . . . and hydraulic valve lifters

9.29a Unscrew the bolts . . .

9.29b . . . and lift the flywheel from the crankshaft

9.31a Unscrew the bolts . . .

9.31b . . . and remove the sump

9.32a Remove the baffle plate . . .

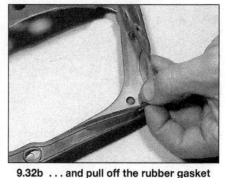

9.32b . . . and pull off the rubber gasket

container of clean engine oil to prevent the oil from draining. Keep all components identified for position to ensure correct reassembly **(see illustrations)**.
29 Hold the flywheel/driveplate stationary using the method described in paragraph 12, then unscrew the bolts and lift the unit from the crankshaft **(see illustrations)**. Discard the flywheel/driveplate bolts, new retaining bolts must be obtained for refitting.
30 Turn the engine upside-down on the workbench. Place cloth rags around it to absorb the water and oil which escapes.
31 Unscrew the sump bolts and remove the sump **(see illustrations)**.
32 Remove the baffle plate and pull the rubber gasket from its edge **(see illustrations)**.
33 Unbolt the oil pick-up tube from the block, and oil pump **(see illustration)**.
34 Unbolt the oil pump from the block and remove the gasket **(see illustrations)**.
35 Mark the big-end caps and connecting rods in relation to each other using a centre

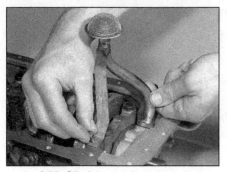

9.33 Oil pick-up tube removal

9.34a Oil pump showing mounting bolts

9.34b Removing the oil pump

9.36 Big-end cap removal

9.38 No. 1 main bearing cap

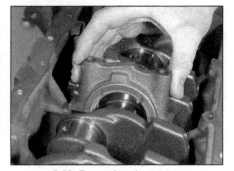

9.39 Removing the centre main bearing cap

9.40 Lifting the crankshaft out of the crankcase

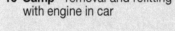

9.41 Removing No. 4 main bearing shell

punch, and numbering them from the front of the engine.

36 Lay the block on its side then unscrew the No. 1 cylinder big-end bolts and tap off the cap **(see illustration)**. Using the handle of a hammer tap the connecting rod and piston through the top of the block. Temporarily refit the cap to the connecting rod keeping the bearing shells in their original positions.

37 Repeat the procedure on the remaining pistons and connecting rods. Note that all the big-end cap bolts must be renewed whenever they are disturbed; obtain a new set of bolts for reassembly.

38 The main bearing caps should already be marked with numbers starting at the front of the engine. However if there are none, mark them with a centre punch **(see illustration)**.

39 Position the block upside-down again, then unscrew the main bearing bolts and remove the caps **(see illustration)**. Take care to keep the bearing shells with their respective caps. Note that the main bearing cap bolts must be renewed whenever they are disturbed; obtain a new set of bolts for reassembly.

40 Lift the crankshaft out of the crankcase and remove the oil seal **(see illustration)**.

41 Remove the upper halves of the main bearing shells from the crankcase and place them with their respective main bearing caps **(see illustration)**.

10 Sump - removal and refitting with engine in car

Removal

1 Apply the handbrake. Jack up the front of the car and support it on axle stands (see "*Jacking and Vehicle Support*").

2 Unscrew the drain plug and drain the engine oil into a suitable container. When completed, wipe the plug clean, refit it and tighten.

3 Unscrew the nuts from the top of both engine mountings.

4 Using a hoist or an engine support bar across the engine compartment, raise the engine approximately 25 mm.

5 On automatic transmission models unbolt both engine mounting brackets.

6 Unscrew the sump bolts, and withdraw the sump forwards over the crossmember.

7 Withdraw the baffle plate forwards while turning it to clear the oil pick-up tube.

8 Pull the rubber gasket from the edge of the baffle plate.

9 If necessary unbolt the oil level sensor from the sump and remove the gasket **(see illustrations)**.

Refitting

10 Thoroughly clean the sump and baffle plate, and clean the joint face on the crankcase.

11 Fit a new rubber gasket to the baffle plate.

12 Apply suitable sealant (Vauxhall/Opel recommend the use of GM spec 15 03 294 (Part No. 90 001 871) sealant - available from your dealer) to both sides of the gasket at the corners only.

13 Position the baffle plate on the crankcase, then fit the sump beneath it. Hold the sump temporarily with two or three bolts.

14 Apply locking fluid to the threads of the bolts then insert and tighten them progressively in diagonal sequence to the specified torque.

15 On automatic transmission models refit the engine mounting brackets and tighten the bolts.

16 Lower the engine and tighten the engine mounting nuts. Disconnect the hoist.

17 Lower the car to the ground.

18 Fill the engine with the specified quantity and grade of oil.

10.9a Oil level sensor and retaining bolts

10.9b Inner view of the oil level sensor

11.5 Locating peg on the engine mounting (arrowed)

11 Engine mountings - renewal

1 Apply the handbrake. Jack up the front of the car and support it on axle stands (see *"Jacking and Vehicle Support"*).
2 Unscrew the nuts from the top of both engine mountings.
3 Using a hoist or an engine support bar across the engine compartment, raise the engine approximately 25 mm.
4 Unscrew the lower nuts and remove the engine mountings. On automatic transmission models it will be necessary to unbolt the engine mounting brackets.
5 Fit the new mountings using a reversal of the removal procedure, but make sure that the pegs on the mountings engage with the cut-outs on the brackets **(see illustration)**.

12 Cylinder head - removal and refitting with engine in car

Note: *New cylinder head bolts will be required on refitting*

Removal

1 Disconnect the battery negative lead.
2 Remove the inlet and exhaust manifolds as described in Chapter 4.
3 Remove the spark plugs, distributor cap, and rotor arm as described in Chapters 1 and 5.
4 Unclip and remove the upper timing belt cover.
5 Remove the thermo-viscous cooling fan and drivebelt as described in Chapter 3.
6 Unbolt the camshaft cover and remove the cork gasket. Note the location of the HT lead bracket.
7 Turn the engine with a spanner on the crankshaft pulley bolt until the mark on the camshaft sprocket is aligned with the pointer on the top of the rear timing belt cover. Also align the notch in the crankshaft pulley with the pointer on the lower part of the rear timing belt cover.
8 On early (pre 1993) models, loosen the

three bolts securing the water pump to the block. Rotate the water pump body anti-clockwise and remove the timing belt from the camshaft sprocket.
9 On later (1993 on) models with a spring loaded timing belt tensioner, slacken the tensioner securing bolt slightly. Pivot the tensioner away from the belt and slip the belt off the camshaft sprocket.
10 On all models, hold the camshaft stationary with a spanner on the rear flats, then unscrew the securing bolt and remove the sprocket. Unbolt the rear timing belt cover from the cylinder head.
11 Loosen the clips and disconnect the crankcase ventilation hose from the camshaft housing.
12 Working in a spiral pattern from outside to inside, slacken each cylinder head bolt by a quarter turn. Following the same sequence slacken the bolts a further half turn, then remove them completely. Note that the cylinder head bolts must be renewed as a complete set whenever they are disturbed; obtain a new set of bolts for reassembly.
13 Lift off the camshaft housing and camshaft.
14 Lift the cylinder head from the block. Careful use of a wooden or hide mallet may be necessary to release the head, but do not attempt to wedge any tool between the joint faces.
15 Remove the gasket from the block and clean the mating faces thoroughly.

Refitting

16 Check that Nos 1 and 4 pistons are still at top dead centre with the crankshaft pulley notch and pointer aligned.
17 Check that both location dowels are inserted in the block. Locate the new head gasket on the block with the "TOP" marking uppermost and at the front.
18 Locate the cylinder head on the block so that the dowels engage in their holes. Check that the hydraulic valve lifters, thrustpads and rocker arms are correctly located.
19 Apply a uniform bead of jointing compound to the mating face on top of the cylinder head using a soft brush to ensure even coverage.

20 Check that the dowel on the front of the camshaft is uppermost, then lower the camshaft housing onto the head.
21 Insert new cylinder head bolts and tighten them in the sequence shown to the specified torque **(see illustration)**. Note that the bolts must be tightened to an initial torque then angle-tightened in stages.
22 Refit the crankcase ventilation hose and tighten the clips.
23 Insert and tighten the rear timing belt cover bolts then refit the camshaft sprocket and tighten the bolt.
24 Check that the crankshaft pulley and camshaft sprocket timing marks are correctly aligned. Reconnect the timing belt without disturbing the sprockets. Tension the belt as follows.

Early (pre 1993) models

25 Apply some tension to the belt by moving the water pump clockwise.
26 If the special tensioning gauge (KM-510-A) is available, turn the water pump clockwise to apply moderate tension to the belt then tighten the bolts. Rotate the crankshaft half a turn clockwise to tension the belt between the camshaft and crankshaft sprockets. Fit the tension gauge between the camshaft and water pump sprockets and check that the reading is as given in the Specifications **(see illustration)**. If adjustment is necessary move the water pump clockwise to increase or anti-clockwise to decrease the tension. Rotate the crankshaft through one full turn and repeat the test.
27 If the tension gauge is not available an appropriate setting may be made by checking if it is possible to twist the belt through 90° with the thumb and finger. **Note:** *If this method is used it is recommended that the belt tension should be checked by a Vauxhall/Opel dealer at the earliest possible opportunity.*
28 Once the belt is correctly tensioned, tighten the water pump bolts to the specified torque and recheck the timing mark alignment.

Later (1993 on) models with spring-loaded belt tensioner

29 Slacken the automatic tensioner securing

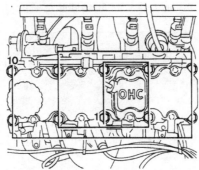

12.21 Cylinder head bolt tightening sequence, starting from 1 and working outwards in a spiral pattern

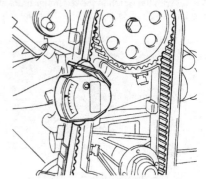

12.26 Checking the timing belt tension with a tension gauge - early (pre 1993) models

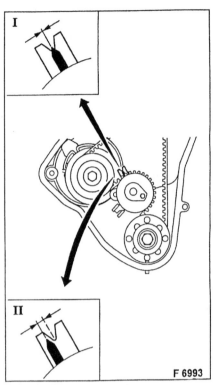

12.31 On later (1993 on) models with a spring loaded timing belt tensioner position the tensioner pointer as shown

I *New belt - align pointer with the centre of the tensioner bracket notch*
II *Used belt - position pointer about 4 mm to the left of the centre of the tensioner bracket notch*

bolt and move the tensioner arm anti-clockwise, until the tensioner pointer lies at its stop. Tighten the tensioner securing bolt to hold the tensioner in this position.
30 Turn the crankshaft through two complete turns clockwise, and check that the crankshaft pulley and camshaft sprocket timing marks are correctly aligned.
31 Slacken the automatic tensioner securing bolt and move the tensioner arm clockwise. If a new belt is being fitted, align the tensioner pointer with the notch in the tensioner bracket and if a used belt is fitted, align the pointer to

approximately 4 mm to the left of the notch **(see illustration)**. Hold the tensioner arm in the correct position and securely tighten its securing bolt. Turn the crankshaft through one complete revolution, in the normal direction of rotation, and check that the crankshaft and camshaft timing marks still align.

All models

32 Refit the camshaft cover along with a new gasket, then refit the retaining bolts and washers, and tighten them securely. Note that, to cure the problem of oil loss from beneath the cover retaining bolt heads, modified washers have been introduced; these can be purchased from your Vauxhall dealer.
33 Refit the thermo-viscous cooling fan and drivebelt with reference to Chapter 3.
34 Refit the upper timing belt cover.
35 Refit the spark plugs, distributor cap and rotor arm with reference to Chapters 1 and 5.
36 Refit the inlet and exhaust manifolds with reference to Chapter 4.
37 Reconnect the battery negative lead.
38 Start the engine and run it to normal operating temperature.

13 Timing belt - removal and refitting with engine in car

Removal

1 Disconnect the battery negative lead.
2 Remove the spark plugs (Chapter 1).
3 Remove the thermo-viscous cooling fan, drivebelt, and fan cowling. If applicable, remove the power steering pump and air conditioning compressor drivebelts.
4 Drain the cooling system (Chapter 1).
5 Unclip and remove the timing belt covers.
6 Turn the engine with a spanner on the crankshaft pulley bolt until the mark on the camshaft sprocket is aligned with the pointer on the top of the rear timing belt cover. Also align the notch in the crankshaft pulley with the pointer on the lower part of the rear timing belt cover.
7 Unbolt the crankshaft pulley from the timing belt sprocket.
8 On early (pre 1993) models, loosen the

three bolts securing the water pump to the block. Rotate the water pump body anti-clockwise and remove the timing belt from the sprockets.
9 On later (1993 on) models with a spring loaded timing belt tensioner, slacken the tensioner securing bolt slightly. Pivot the tensioner away from the belt and slip the belt off the sprockets.

Refitting

10 Locate the new timing belt temporarily on the sprockets.
11 Locate the crankshaft pulley on the crankshaft sprocket and tighten its retaining bolts.
12 Disconnect the timing belt and align the timing marks on the camshaft sprocket and crankshaft pulley with the pointers on the rear cover and reconnect the belt without disturbing the sprockets.
13 On early (pre 1993) models, tension the timing belt with reference to Section 12, paragraphs 25 to 28.
14 On later (1993 on) models with a spring-loaded belt tensioner, tension the belt as described in Section 12, paragraphs 29 to 31.
15 Refit the timing belt covers.
16 Refit and tension the drivebelt(s).
17 Refit the cooling fan and fan cowling.
18 Refit the spark plugs (Chapter 1).
19 Refill the cooling system (Chapter 1)
20 Reconnect the battery negative lead.

14 Engine components - examination and renovation

Oil pump

1 Using an impact driver, extract the cross-head screws and remove the rear cover **(see illustrations)**.
2 With a straight edge and feeler blades, check the endfloat of the two gears then check the backlash between the two gears **(see illustrations)**.
3 If any of the clearances are outside the specified tolerances, it is recommended that the oil pump is renewed, although individual parts are available.

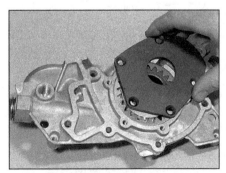

14.1a Removing the oil pump rear cover

14.1b View of the oil pump gears

14.2a Checking the outer gear endfloat . . .

14.2b . . . and inner gear

14.2c Checking the oil pump gear backlash

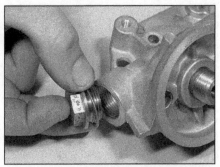

14.4a Unscrew the plug . . .

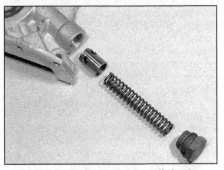

14.4b . . . and remove the relief valve spring and piston

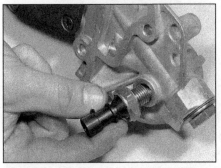

14.5 Removing the oil temperature sensor

14.6 By-pass in oil pump (arrowed)

14.7 Tightening the oil pump rear cover screws

14.9 Checking the crankshaft run-out

4 Unscrew the plug and remove the relief valve spring and piston **(see illustrations)**. Examine them for wear and damage.

5 If necessary unscrew the oil temperature sensor **(see illustration)**.

6 Check that the bypass valve ball is seating correctly **(see illustration)**. If necessary, pull out the old valve and press in a new one.

7 Thoroughly clean all components then reassemble them in reverse order, using a new plug sealing washer **(see illustration)**.

Crankshaft

8 Examine the crankpin and main journal surfaces for signs of scoring or scratches, and check the ovality and taper of the crankpins and main journals. If the bearing surface dimensions do not fall within the tolerance ranges given in the Specifications at the beginning of the Chapter, the crankpins and/or main journals will have to be reground.

9 Check the crankshaft for run-out by mounting it in the crankcase using the front and rear bearing shells only. With a dial test gauge probe on the centre main journal, rotate the crankshaft **(see illustration)**.

10 Big-end and crankpin wear is accompanied by distinct metallic knocking, particularly noticed when the engine is pulling from low revs, and some loss of oil pressure. Main bearing and main journal wear is accompanied by severe engine vibration rumble, getting progressively worse as engine revs increase, and again by loss of oil pressure.

11 If the crankshaft requires regrinding, take it to an engine reconditioning specialist, who will machine it for you and supply the correct undersize bearing shells.

12 On some engines, the crankshaft journal diameters are machined undersize in production to allow for greater manufacturing tolerances.

Big-end and main bearing shells

13 Inspect the big-end and main bearing shells for signs of general wear, scoring, pitting and scratches. The bearings should be matt grey in colour. With lead-indium bearings, should a trace of copper colour be noticed, the bearings are badly worn as the lead bearing material has worn away to expose the indium underlay. Renew the bearings if they are in this condition or if there are any signs of scoring or pitting. **You are strongly advised to renew the bearings - regardless of their condition - at time of major overhaul. Refitting used bearings is a false economy (see illustrations).**

14 The undersizes available are designed to correspond with crankshaft regrind sizes. The bearings are in fact, slightly more than the stated undersize as running clearances have been allowed for during their manufacture.

Cylinder bores

15 The cylinder bores must be examined for taper, ovality, scoring and scratches. Start by carefully examining the top of the cylinder bores. If they are at all worn a very slight ridge will be found on the thrust side. This marks the top of the piston travel. The owner will have a good indication of the bore wear prior to dismantling the engine, or removing the cylinder head. Excessive oil consumption accompanied by blue smoke from the exhaust can be caused by worn cylinder bores and piston rings.

16 Measure the bore diameter across the block and just below any ridge. This can be done with an internal micrometer or a dial

14.13a Identification numbers on the main bearing shells (except centre)

14.13b Identification numbers on the centre main bearing shells

14.13c Identification numbers on the big-end bearing shells

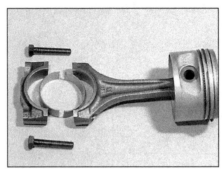

14.13d Piston, connecting rod and big-end components

gauge. Compare this with the diameter of the bottom of the bore, which is not subject to wear. If no measuring instruments are available, use a piston from which the rings have been removed and measure the gap between it and the cylinder wall with a feeler blade.

17 Refer to the Specifications. If the cylinder wear exceeds the permitted tolerances then the cylinders will need reboring.

18 If the cylinders have already been bored out to their maximum it may be possible to have liners fitted. This situation will not often be met with.

Connecting rods

19 Examine the mating faces of the big-end caps to see if they have ever been filed in a mistaken attempt to take up wear. If so, the offending rods must be renewed.

20 Check the alignment of the rods visually, and if all is not well, take the rods to your local agent for checking on a special jig.

Pistons and piston rings

21 If the pistons and/or rings are to be re-used, remove the rings from the pistons. Three strips of tin or feeler blades should be prepared and the top ring then sprung open just sufficiently to allow them to be slipped behind the ring. The ring can then be slid off the piston upwards without scoring or scratching the piston lands.

22 Repeat the process for the second and third rings.

23 Mark the rings or keep them in order so they may be refitted in their original locations.

24 Inspect the pistons to ensure that they are suitable for re-use. Check for cracks, damage to the piston ring grooves and lands, and scores or signs of picking-up the piston walls.

25 Clean the ring grooves using a piece of old piston ring ground to a suitable width and scrape the deposits out of the grooves, taking care not to remove any metal or score the piston lands. Protect your fingers - piston rings are sharp.

26 Check the rings in their respective bores. Press the ring down to the unworn lower section of the bore (use a piston to do this, and keep the ring square in the bore). Measure the ring end gap and check that it is within the tolerance allowed (see Specifications) **(see illustration)**. Also check the ring's side clearance in its groove. If these measurements exceed the specified tolerances the rings will have to be renewed, and if the ring grooves in the pistons are worn new pistons may be needed.

14.26 Checking a piston ring gap

27 Proprietary piston rings are available which are reputed to reduce oil consumption due to bore wear without the expense of a rebore. Depending on the degree of wear, the improvement produced by fitting such rings may be short-lived.

28 If new rings (or pistons and rings) are to be fitted to an existing bore the top ring must be stepped to clear the wear ridge at the top of the bore, or the bore must be de-ridged. When fitting the rings, note that the second compression ring has a tapered profile and must be installed with its "TOP" marking uppermost.

29 Check the clearance and end gap of any new rings, as described in paragraph 26. If a ring is slightly tight in its groove it may be rubbed down using an oilstone or a sheet of carborundum paper laid on a sheet of glass. If the end gap is inadequate the ring can be carefully ground until the specified clearance is achieved.

30 If new pistons are to be installed they will be selected from the grades available (see Specifications), after measuring the bores as described in paragraph 16. Normally the appropriate oversize pistons are supplied by the repairer when the block is rebored.

31 Removing and refitting pistons on the connecting rod is a job for your dealer or specialist repairer. Press equipment and a means of accurately heating the connecting rod will be required for removal and insertion of the gudgeon pin.

Camshaft

32 With the camshaft removed, examine the bearing surfaces for signs of wear. If evident, a new camshaft housing will probably be required.

33 The camshaft itself should show no marks or scoring on the journal or cam lobe surfaces. If evident, renew the camshaft.

34 The thrustplate should appear unworn and without grooves. In any event, check the camshaft endfloat, and fit a new plate where necessary.

Timing belt

35 Closely inspect the belt for cracking, fraying or tooth deformation. Where evident, renew the belt. The belt should be renewed in any case at the intervals shown in *"Routine maintenance"* at the front of this manual.

36 Whenever re-using the timing belt always note its running direction in order to prevent subsequent noisy operation.

Hydraulic valve lifters, rockers and thrustpads

37 Any sign of wear in a hydraulic valve lifter can only be rectified by renewal as the unit cannot be dismantled.

38 Inspect the rockers and thrustpads for wear or grooving, and renew if necessary.

Flywheel/driveplate

39 If the teeth on the starter ring gear are

badly worn, it is possible to renew the ring gear separately only on the flywheel.

40 Either split the ring with a cold chisel after making a cut with a hacksaw blade between two teeth, or use a soft-headed hammer (not steel) to knock the ring off, striking it evenly and alternately at equally spaced points. Take great care not to damage the flywheel during this process, and protect your eyes from flying fragments.

41 Clean and polish with emery cloth four evenly spaced areas on the outside face of the new starter ring.

42 Heat the ring evenly with a flame until the polished portions turn dark blue. Alternatively heat the ring in a bath of oil to a temperature of 200°C. (If a naked flame is used take adequate fire precautions.) Hold the ring at this temperature for five minutes and then quickly fit it to the flywheel, so the chamfered portion of the teeth faces the gearbox side of the flywheel. Wipe all oil off the ring before fitting it.

43 The ring should be tapped gently down onto its register and left to cool naturally when the contraction of the metal on cooling will ensure that it is a secure and permanent fit. Great care must be taken not to overheat the ring, indicated by its turning light metallic blue. If this happens the temper of the ring will be lost.

44 If the clutch contact surface of the flywheel is scored or on close inspection shows evidence of small hair cracks, caused by overheating, it may be possible to have the flywheel surface ground provided the overall

14.45 Spigot bearing in the rear of the crankshaft

thickness of the flywheel is not reduced too much. Consult a specialist engine repairer and if it is not possible, renew the flywheel complete.

45 If the needle bearing in the centre of the crankshaft flange is worn, fill it with grease and tap in a close-fitting rod. Hydraulic pressure will remove it. Tap the new bearing into position and apply a little grease **(see illustration)**.

Cylinder block

46 Check that all internal oil and waterways are clear of sediment or obstructions.

47 If a core plug **(see illustration)** is leaking, it may be renewed by driving a screwdriver into it and prising it out of the block. Clean the seating then use a large drift or two hammer heads to drive in the new plug. The use of sealant is not usually necessary.

14.47 Core plugs in the cylinder block

48 The crankshaft main bearing bolts and the cylinder head bolts should be renewed as a matter of course.

15 Cylinder head - overhaul

1 Clean the external surfaces of the cylinder head.

2 Remove the valves by compressing the valve spring with a suitable valve spring compressor and lifting out the collets. Release the compressor and remove the valve spring retainer and spring. Remove the inlet valve spring seat **(see illustrations)**.

3 Remove the valves, keeping them identified for location to ensure correct refitting **(see illustration)**.

15.2a Compress the valve spring and remove the collets

15.2b Removing the valve spring retainer . . .

15.2c . . . spring . . .

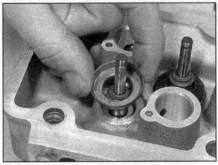

15.2d . . . inlet valve spring seat . . .

15.3 . . . and valve

15.4a Levering off the inlet valve stem oil seal

15.4b Removing the exhaust valve stem oil seal . . .

15.4c . . . and valve rotator

15.5 Piston crown

15.8 Grinding in the valves

15.10 Checking the cylinder head for distortion

4 Lever the valve stem oil seals from the valve guides, then remove the exhaust valve rotators **(see illustrations)**.

5 With the valves removed, clean the carbon from them and from the combustion chambers and ports. The piston crowns can also be cleaned at this stage but take care not to allow carbon to drop between the pistons and bores **(see illustration)**. To prevent this, clean two pistons at a time with them at the top of their bores and press a little grease between the pistons and bores. Seal off the remaining cylinders, and oil and water channels with paper. After cleaning, move the pistons down the bore and wipe out the grease which will contain the particles of carbon.

6 Examine the heads of the valves and the valve seats for pitting and burning. If the pitting on valve and seat is slight it can be removed by grinding the valves and seats together with coarse, and then fine, valve grinding paste. If the pitting is deep, the valves will have to be reground on a valve grinding machine and the seats will have to be recut with a valve seat cutter. Both these operations are a job for your local GM dealer or motor engineering specialist.

7 Check the valve guides for wear by inserting the valve in the guide and attempting to move the valve from side to side. If the specified play is exceeded the valve guides should be renewed by a GM dealer.

8 When grinding slightly-pitted valves and valve seats with carborundum paste, continue as follows. Apply a little coarse grinding paste to the valve head, and using a suction-type

15.11 Oil pressure regulating valve in the cylinder head

valve grinding tool, grind the valve into its seat with a rotary movement, lifting the valve and turning it from time to time **(see illustration)**. A light spring under the valve head will assist in this operation. When a dull matt, even surface finish appears on both the valve and the valve seat, clean off the coarse paste. Repeat the grinding operation with a fine grinding paste until a continuous ring of light grey matt finish appears on both valve and valve seat. Carefully clean off all traces of grinding paste.

9 Check the valve springs for damage and if possible compare their length with that of a new spring. Renew them if necessary.

10 Using a straight edge and feeler blade check the joint face of the cylinder head for distortion **(see illustration)**. If greater than the maximum amount given in the Specifications it may be possible to have the head machined flat. Consult a GM dealer if necessary.

15.13 Pressing the valve stem oil seals onto the guides

11 An oil pressure regulating valve in the cylinder head stabilises the oil pressure applied to the valve lifters **(see illustration)**. To renew the valve, access is gained by removing the plug in the head. The old valve must be crushed and its remains extracted, then a thread (M10) is cut in the valve seat to allow removal using a suitable bolt. A new valve and plug can then be driven into position. Care must be taken to keep foreign matter and swarf out of the oilways, and it is probably best to have the valve renewed by a GM dealer if necessary.

12 Begin reassembly by locating the exhaust valve rotators over their respective valve guides.

13 Press the valve stem oil seals onto the guides **(see illustration)**.

14 To fit the valves, lubricate the valve stem with engine oil and insert it in the valve guide. On the inlet valve, refit the spring seat.

15 Refit the spring and spring retainer, then use the valve spring compressor to compress the spring until the collets can be fitted in position in the slots in the valve stem. Release the compressor slowly, and check that the collets are seated correctly.

16 After fitting all the valves, tap the tops of the springs lightly to ensure correct seating of the collets.

16 Engine - complete reassembly

Note: *New big-end bearing cap bolts, main bearing cap bolts, flywheel/driveplate bolts, crankshaft sprocket bolt and cylinder head bolts will be required.*

1 Place the cylinder block upside-down on the bench and wipe clean the main bearing shell seats.

2 Press the main bearing shells onto the crankcase, making sure that the tags engage with the special grooves. Note that the centre shell incorporates thrust flanges.

3 Lubricate the shells with clean engine oil (**see illustration**).

4 Carefully lower the crankshaft into the crankcase. Rotate it several times and check that it is correctly seated by gently tapping the webs with a mallet (**see illustration**).

5 Check that the crankshaft endfloat is as given in the Specifications by either using a feeler blade between the flanged centre main bearing shell and the crankshaft thrust face, or by using a dial test indicator on the crankshaft rear flange (**see illustrations**).

6 Clean the backs of the lower main bearing shells and the caps, then press them into position. Lubricate the shells with clean oil (**see illustration**).

7 Coat the joint face of the rear main bearing cap with sealant (Vauxhall/Opel recommend the use of GM spec 15 04 200 (Part No. 8 983 368) sealant - available from your dealer). Fill the side grooves of the cap with RTV jointing compound (Vauxhall/Opel recommend the use of GM spec 15 04 294 (Part No. 90 001 851) sealant (**see illustrations**).

8 Fit the rear main bearing cap, then insert the new bearing cap bolts and tighten them to the specified torque setting (**see illustration**). If required, the crankshaft rear oil seal may be fitted at the same time.

9 Insert more sealant into the side grooves until it is certain that they are full (**see illustration**).

10 Refit the remaining main bearing caps, then fit the new bearing cap bolts and tighten

16.3 Lubricating the upper main bearing shells

16.4 Gently tap the crankshaft to make sure it is seated correctly

16.5a Checking the crankshaft endfloat with a feeler blade . . .

16.5b . . . and dial test indicator

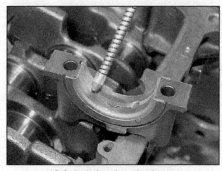
16.6 Lubricating the lower main bearing shells

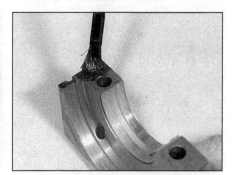
16.7a Coating the rear main bearing cap joint face with sealant

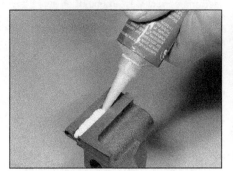
16.7b Filling the rear main bearing cap grooves with RTV jointing compound

16.8 Fitting the rear main bearing cap

16.9 Making sure the grooves are full of sealant

16.10a Torque-tightening the
main bearing cap bolts

16.10b Angle-tightening the
main bearing cap bolts

16.12a Using a piece of celluloid (arrowed)
as a guide sleeve when fitting the
crankshaft rear oil seal

16.12b Using part of a puller and the old
oil seal to fit the new oil seal

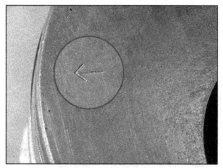

16.17a The arrow on the piston crown
must point towards the front of the engine

16.17b Inserting the piston (with piston
ring compressor) into the cylinder

16.19a Torque-tightening the
big-end bolts

16.19b Angle-tightening the big-end bolts

16.23 Oil pump gasket on the
front of the block

them to the specified torque setting. Make sure that the front cap is exactly flush with the end face of the crankcase. Note that the bolts must be tightened to an initial torque then angle-tighten **(see illustrations)**.

11 Rotate the crankshaft and check that it turns freely with no signs of binding or tight spots.

12 Lubricate the lips of the new crankshaft rear oil seal with grease. Cut a length of celluloid to act as a guide sleeve for the oil seal and locate it on the crankshaft rear flange. Locate the oil seal on the sleeve and press it into the rear main bearing cap until flush. Part of a pulley may be used effectively to press in the oil seal using two flywheel bolts and using the old oil seal to apply even pressure **(see illustrations)**. Remove the puller and celluloid.

13 Lay the block on its side and lubricate the cylinder bores and crankshaft journals liberally with oil.

14 Space the piston rings around the pistons so that their end gaps are 180° apart. In the case of the oil scraper ring, offset the gaps in the upper and lower rails by 25 to 50 mm (1 to 2 in) to right and left of the end gap of the centre section.

15 Clean the backs of the big-end bearing shells and the caps and connecting rods, then press the shells into position.

16 Turn the crankshaft so that the journal for No 1 cylinder is at bottom dead centre.

17 Fit a piston ring compressor to No 1 piston then insert it into No 1 cylinder with the arrow on the piston crown pointing towards the front of the engine **(see illustrations)**. The land extensions on the piston underside, the connecting rod and the big-end bearing cap should be towards the rear of the engine.

18 Using the handle of a hammer, tap the piston through the ring compressor while guiding the connecting rod onto the journal.

19 Fit the big-end bearing cap, ensuring it is fitted the correct way around, then insert the new big-end bearing bolts. Tighten the bolts first to the Stage 1 torque setting, and then angle-tighten them through the specified amount (see Specifications at the start of this Chapter) **(see illustrations)**.

20 Check that the crankshaft turns freely taking into consideration the resistance of the piston rings.

21 Repeat the procedure in paragraphs 16 to 20 for the remaining pistons.

22 Turn the block upside down on the bench.

23 Put a new oil pump gasket on the block, and hold it with a little grease **(see illustration)**.

24 If necessary prise out the old oil pump seal.

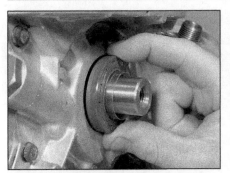

16.26a Using a piece of celluloid as a guide sleeve when fitting the crankshaft front oil seal

16.26b Using a socket to press in the crankshaft front oil seal

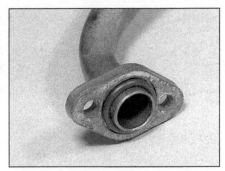

16.27 O-ring seal on the oil pick-up tube

16.29 Applying sealant to the corners of the sump gasket

16.30 Applying locking fluid to the sump bolts

16.32a Applying locking fluid to the flywheel bolts

16.32b Torque-tightening the flywheel bolts

16.32c Alternative position for the flywheel locking tool (arrowed)

16.32d Angle-tightening the flywheel bolts

25 Refit the oil pump then insert and tighten the bolts.

26 Cut a length of celluloid and wrap it around the crankshaft nose. Smear a little grease on the lips of the new oil seal and locate it on the celluloid. Press the oil seal to start it, then use a suitable socket and the crankshaft pulley bolt to press the oil seal in until flush **(see illustrations)**. Remove the celluloid and socket.

27 Fit a new O-ring seal to the oil pick-up tube then refit the tube and tighten the bolts **(see illustration)**.

28 Fit a new sump gasket to the baffle plate.

29 Apply suitable sealant (Vauxhall/Opel recommend the use of GM spec 15 03 294 (Part No. 90 001 871) sealant - available from your dealer) to both sides of the gasket at the

corners only, and locate the baffle plate on the crankcase **(see illustration)**.

30 Refit the sump. Apply locking fluid to the threads of the bolts, then insert and tighten them progressively in diagonal sequence to the specified torque **(see illustration)**.

31 Position the engine upright on the workbench using blocks of wood.

32 Locate the flywheel/driveplate on the rear of the crankshaft. Apply locking fluid to the threads of the new bolts, then insert and tighten them progressively, while holding the flywheel stationary using the method described in Section 9. Note that the bolts must be tightened to an initial torque then angle-tightened **(see illustrations)**.

33 Turn the engine so that Nos 1 and 4 pistons are at top dead centre.

34 Check that both location dowels are inserted in the block and that the joint faces on the block and cylinder head are clean **(see illustration)**.

16.34 Location dowel on the block

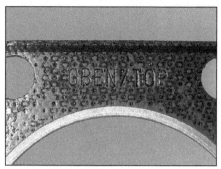

16.35 "TOP" marking on the cylinder head gasket

16.36 Rockers fitted to the valves

16.37 Cylinder head located on the block

16.38 Prising out the camshaft housing front oil seal

16.39 Lubricating the bearing surfaces in the camshaft housing

16.40 Checking the camshaft endfloat

35 Locate the new head gasket on the block with the "TOP" marking uppermost and at the front **(see illustration)**.

36 Refit the hydraulic valve lifters, thrustpads and rocker arms to the cylinder head in their original positions **(see illustration)**. If new hydraulic valve lifters are being used, initially immerse each one in a container of clean engine oil and compress by hand several times to charge them.

37 Locate the cylinder head on the block so that the dowels engage in their holes **(see illustration)**.

38 Prise the old oil seal from the front of the camshaft housing **(see illustration)**. Clean the seating and drive in the new oil seal using a block of wood. Smear the oil seal lips with grease.

39 Oil the bearing surfaces in the camshaft housing **(see illustration)**.

40 Carefully insert the camshaft into the housing. Refit the camshaft thrustplate and tighten the bolts. Using a feeler blade as shown **(see illustration)** check that the camshaft endfloat is as given in the Specifications.

41 Apply a uniform bead of jointing compound to the mating face on the cylinder head using a soft brush to ensure even coverage **(see illustrations)**.

42 Turn the camshaft so that the dowel at the front is uppermost **(see illustrations)**, then lower the camshaft housing onto the head.

43 Insert new cylinder head bolts and tighten them in the sequence shown in **illustration 12.21** to the specified torque. Note that the bolts must be tightened to an initial torque

16.41a Apply jointing compound on the cylinder head . . .

16.42a Camshaft dowel positioned uppermost

16.41b . . . and brush it to an even coverage

16.42b Camshaft housing on the cylinder head

then angle-tightened in stages **(see illustrations)**.

44 Refit the crankcase ventilation tube with a new gasket, and tighten the bolts. Refit the hose to the camshaft housing and tighten the clips **(see illustration)**.

45 Refit the front coolant and thermostat housing to the cylinder head using a new O-ring seal. Insert and tighten the bolts.

46 Refit the cooling fan hub bracket to the block. Insert and tighten the bolts.

47 Smear some oil on the sealing ring of the

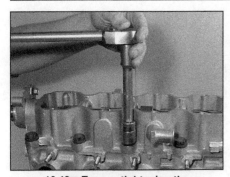

16.43a Torque-tightening the cylinder head bolts

16.43b Angle-tightening the cylinder head bolts

16.44 Crankcase ventilation tube refitted

16.52a Holding the camshaft with an open-ended spanner

16.52b Tightening the camshaft sprocket bolt

16.54 Tightening the crankshaft pulley outer bolts

new oil filter then screw it onto the oil pump housing hand tight only.

48 Refit the rear timing belt cover. Insert and tighten the bolts.

49 Apply silicon grease or equivalent to the surfaces of the water pump in contact with the block. Fit a new rubber O-ring.

50 Locate the water pump in the block with the timing cover projections correctly seated. Insert the securing bolts and washers loosely.

51 On later (1993 on) models, refit the spring loaded timing belt tensioner, making sure its lug locates in the slot in the oil pump housing, and fit its retaining bolt. Align the lug on the water pump with the mark on the block and tighten the pump bolts.

52 Locate the sprocket on the front of the camshaft and engage the peg. Insert the bolt. Hold the camshaft stationary and tighten the bolt to the specified torque. An open-ended spanner may be used on the flats provided if required **(see illustrations)**.

53 Refit the spacer, Woodruff key and sprocket to the front of the crankshaft. Fit the new sprocket retaining bolt and tighten its to the specified stage 1 torque and then through the specified stage 2 angle, holding the flywheel/driveplate stationary using the method described in Section 9.

54 Temporarily engage the timing belt with the crankshaft, camshaft, water pump sprockets and (where necessary) the tensioner and locate the crankshaft pulley damper on the crankshaft sprocket and tighten its bolts **(see illustration)**.

55 Disconnect the timing belt and align the timing marks on the camshaft sprocket and

crankshaft pulley with the pointers on the rear cover. Reconnect the belt without disturbing the sprockets and apply tension to the belt.

56 On early (pre 1993) models, tension the timing belt with reference to Section 12, paragraphs 25 to 28.

57 On later (1993 on) models with a spring-loaded belt tensioner, tension the belt as described in Section 12, paragraphs 29 to 31.

58 Insert and tighten the bolt securing the water pump section of the timing cover to the oil pump housing.

59 Refit the two timing belt covers.

60 Refit the cooling fan pulley. Insert and tighten the screws.

61 Refit the camshaft cover together with a new cork gasket. Insert and tighten the bolts.

62 On fuel injection models refit the auxiliary air valve bracket to the camshaft housing together with a new gasket. Insert and tighten the bolts.

63 Reconnect the crankcase ventilation hose to the camshaft cover.

64 Insert the engine oil dipstick.

65 Insert and tighten the oil pressure switch.

66 Using a block of wood, fit a new oil seal in the rear of the camshaft housing. Smear a little grease on the oil seal lips.

17 Engine ancillaries - refitting

Refer to Section 8 and refit the listed components, with reference to the Chapters indicated where necessary.

18 Engine - refitting

Refitting the engine is a reversal of the removal procedure given in Section 6, but in addition note the following points:

a) *Lightly grease the gearbox input shaft or torque converter spigot as applicable.*

b) *On automatic transmission models, check that the torque converter is fully engaged with the transmission oil pump with reference to Chapter 7B.*

c) *Refill the engine with the specified quantity and grade of oil*

d) *On manual gearbox models, adjust the clutch cable with reference to Chapter 6.*

e) *Adjust the tension of the power steering pump, alternator/fan, and air conditioning compressor drivebelts (see Chapter 1).*

f) *Adjust the accelerator cable, and where necessary, the automatic transmission kickdown cable and the cruise control cable as described in Chapters 4, 7B, and 12 (as applicable).*

g) *Refill the cooling system (see Chapter 1).*

19 Engine - initial start-up after major overhaul or repair

1 Make sure that the battery is fully charged and that all lubricants, coolant and fuel are replenished.

2 Double check all fittings and connections.

3 Remove the spark plugs and the negative (No 1) wiring from the ignition coil. Turn the engine over on the starter motor until the oil pressure warning light is extinguished, or until oil pressure is recorded on the gauge. This will ensure that the engine is not starved of oil during the critical few minutes running after initial start-up. The fuel system will also be primed during this operation.

4 Reconnect the ignition coil wiring and refit the spark plugs and leads. Start the engine.

5 When the engine fires and runs, keep it going at a fast tickover only (no faster) and bring it up to normal working temperature.

6 As the engine warms up there will be odd smells and some smoke from parts getting hot and burning off oil deposits. The signs to look for are leaks of water or oil, which will be obvious if serious. Check also the exhaust pipe and manifold connections as these do not always find their exact gas tight position until the warmth and vibration have acted on them, and it is almost certain that they will need tightening further. This should be done, of course, with the engine stopped.

7 When normal temperature has been reached, adjust the idle speed (see Chapter 4).

8 Stop the engine and wait a few minutes to see if any lubricant or coolant is dripping out when the engine is stationary.

9 During the initial period that the engine is running it is not unusual for the hydraulic valve lifters to be noisy, but this should gradually disappear, certainly within a few miles driving on the road.

10 Particularly if many new internal parts have been fitted, change the engine oil and oil filter after the first 1000 km (600 miles).

Chapter 2 Part B:
2.5, 2.6 and 3.0 litre (CIH) engines

Contents

Compression test - description and interpretation 2
Cylinder head - removal and refitting with engine in car 12
Cylinder head - overhaul 15
Engine - complete dismantling 9
Engine - complete reassembly 16
Engine - initial start-up after major overhaul or repair 19
Engine - refitting 18
Engine ancillaries - refitting 17
Engine ancillaries - removal 8
Engine components - examination and renovation 14
Engine dismantling - general 7

Engine mountings - renewal 11
Engine oil and filter renewal . . . . .See Chapter 1
Engine oil level check . . . . .See "Weekly checks"
Engine removal 6
General description 1
General engine checks . . . . .See Chapter 1
Hydraulic valve lifters - adjustment 13
Major operations requiring engine removal 4
Major operations possible with engine in car 3
Method of engine removal 5
Sump - removal and refitting with engine in car 10

Degrees of difficulty

Easy, suitable for novice with little experience	Fairly easy, suitable for beginner with some experience	Fairly difficult, suitable for competent DIY mechanic	Difficult, suitable for experienced DIY mechanic	Very difficult, suitable for expert DIY or professional

Specifications

General

Type	Six-cylinder, in-line, water-cooled, cam-in-head 12-valve
Engine codes:	
2.5 litre engine	25NE
2.6 litre engine	C26NE
3.0 litre engine:	
Models not equipped with a catalytic converter	30NE
Models equipped with a catalytic converter	C30NE or C30LE

Note: *The engine code forms the first digits of the engine number*

Bore:	
2.5 litre engine	87.0 mm
2.6 litre engine	88.0 mm
3.0 litre engine	95.0 mm
Stroke (all engines)	69.8 mm
Capacity:	
2.5 litre engine	2490 cc
2.6 litre engine	2594 cc
3.0 litre engine	2969 cc
Firing order	1-5-3-6-2-4 (No.1 cylinder at timing chain end)
Crankshaft rotation	Clockwise
Compression ratio	9.2:1

Cylinder block (crankcase)

Material	Cast-iron
Maximum cylinder bore out of round	0.005 mm
Maximum permissible taper	0.005 mm
Maximum rebore oversize:	
2.5 litre engine	1.0 mm
2.6 and 3.0 litre engine	0.5 mm

Crankshaft

Number of main bearings	7
Main bearing journal diameter:	
Standard	57.987 to 58.003 mm
1st undersize (0.25 mm)	57.737 to 57.753 mm
2nd undersize (0.5 mm)	57.487 to 57.503 mm
Crankpin diameter:	
Standard	51.971 to 51.990 mm
1st undersize (0.25 mm)	51.721 to 51.740 mm
2nd undersize (0.5 mm)	51.471 to 51.490 mm
Crankshaft endfloat	0.04 to 0.16 mm
Main bearing running clearance	0.02 to 0.06 mm
Big-end running clearance	0.01 to 0.06 mm
Big-end side-play	0.11 to 0.24 mm

Camshaft

Endfloat:	
Standard	0.1 to 0.2 mm
Maximum	0.25 mm
Camshaft journal diameters (number 1 at the front of the head):	
Number 1 (front) journal	48.955 to 48.970 mm
Number 2 journal	48.705 to 48.720 mm
Number 3 journal	48.580 to 48.595 mm
Number 4 journal	48.455 to 48.470 mm
Number 5 journal	48.330 to 48.345 mm
Number 6 journal	48.205 to 48.220 mm

Pistons and rings

Type	Alloy, recessed head
Number of piston rings	2 compression, 1 oil control
Ring end gap:	
Top and second compression rings:	
2.5 litre engine	0.30 to 0.50 mm
2.6 and 3.0 litre engine	0.40 to 0.65 mm
Oil control ring:	
2.5 and 3.0 litre engine	0.25 to 0.40 mm
2.6 litre engine	0.30 to 0.60 mm
Ring gap offset (to gap of adjacent ring)	180°
Gudgeon pin diameter:	
2.6 litre engine	22.0 mm
2.5 and 3.0 litre engine	23.0 mm

Piston grades - 2.5 litre engine:	Diameter (mm)	Marking
Production grade 1	86.94	6
	86.96	8
Production grade 2	86.98	00
	87.00	02
	87.02	04
Production grade 3	87.04	06
	87.06	08
Oversize (0.5 mm)	87.45	7 + 0.5
	87.46	8 + 0.5
	87.47	9 + 0.5
	87.48	0 + 0.5
Oversize (1.0 mm)	87.95	7 + 1.0
	87.96	8 + 1.0
	87.97	9 + 1.0
	87.98	0 + 1.0
Piston grades - 2.6 litre engine:	Diameter (mm)	Marking
Production grade 1	88.72	5
	88.73	6
	88.74	7
Production grade 2	88.75	04
	88.76	05
	88.77	06
	88.78	07
	88.79	08
	88.80	09

Piston grades - 2.6 litre engine (continued)	Diameter (mm)	Marking
Production grade 3	88.81	8
	88.82	99
	88.83	00
	88.84	01
	88.85	02
	88.86	03
Oversize (0.5 mm)	89.24	7 + 0.5
	89.25	8 + 0.5
	89.26	9 + 0.5
	89.27	0 + 0.5

Piston grades - 3.0 litre engine:	Diameter (mm)	Marking
Production grade 1	94.92	6
	94.93	6
Production grade 2	94.94	8
	94.96	00
	94.98	02
Production grade 3	95 00	04
	95.02	06
	95.04	08
Oversize (0.5 mm)	95.43	7 + 0.5
	95.44	8 + 0.5
	95.45	9 + 0.5
	95.46	0 + 0.5

Piston-to-bore clearance:
  2.5 and 3.0 litre engine:
    New engine .... 0.025 to 0.035 mm
    After rebore .... 0.035 to 0.045 mm
  2.6 litre engine:
    New engine .... 0.020 to 0.040 mm
    After rebore .... 0.020 to 0.050 mm
Maximum permissible piston out-of-round .... 0.005 mm
Maximum permissible piston taper .... 0.005 mm

Cylinder head

Maximum permissible distortion of sealing face:
  2.5 and 3.0 litre engine .... 0.035 to 0.045 mm
  2.6 litre engine .... 0.025 mm
Overall height of cylinder head:
  2.5 and 2.6 litre engines .... 101.45 to 101.95 mm
  3.0 litre engine:
    30NE engine .... 101.95 to 102.45 mm
    C30NE engine .... 101.45 to 101.95 mm
    C30LE engine .... 102.35 to 102.85 mm

Valves

Valve clearance .... Automatic by hydraulic valve lifters
Valve stem-to-guide clearance:
  Inlet .... 0.035 to 0.073 mm
  Exhaust .... 0.045 to 0.085 mm
Valve stem diameter:
  Inlet:
    Standard .... 8.977 to 8.990 mm
    1st oversize (0.075 mm) .... 9.052 to 9.065 mm
    2nd oversize (0.150 mm) .... 9.127 to 9.140 mm
    3rd oversize (0.300 mm) .... 9.277 to 9.290 mm
  Exhaust:
    Standard .... 8.965 to 8.980 mm
    1st oversize (0.075 mm) .... 9.040 to 9.055 mm
    2nd oversize (0.150 mm) .... 9.115 to 9.130 mm
    3rd oversize (0.300 mm) .... 9.265 to 9.280 mm
Valve guide bore diameter:
  Standard .... 9.025 to 9.050 mm
  1st oversize (0.075 mm) .... 9.100 to 9.125 mm
  2nd oversize (0.150 mm) .... 9.175 to 9.200 mm
  3rd oversize (0.300 mm) .... 9.325 to 9.350 mm

Flywheel

Maximum thickness reduction at contact surface . . . .   0.3 mm

Lubrication

Oil pump:
Tooth play (gear to gear) . . . .   0.1 to 0.2 mm
Gear-to-housing clearance (endfloat) . . . .   0.1 to 0.2 mm
Oil pressure at idle (engine at operating temperature) . . . .   1.0 bar

Torque wrench settings

	Nm	lbf ft
Big-end bearing cap bolts	45	33
Camshaft sprocket bolts	25	18
Crankshaft pulley bolt	120	90
Cylinder head bolts:		
Main bolts:		
Stage 1	60	45
Stage 2	Angle tighten a further 90 to 100°	
Wait for approximately ten minutes then:		
Stage 3	Angle tighten a further 30 to 40°	
Cylinder head to timing chain cover bolts	25	18
Engine mounting retaining nuts	40	30
Engine movement damper bolts:		
Upper bolt	40	30
Lower bolt	22	16
Flywheel/driveplate bolts:		
2.5 and 3.0 litre models	60	45
2.6 litre models:		
Stage 1	60	45
Stage 2	Angle tighten a further 30 to 45°	
Main bearing cap bolts	110	81
Oil pump cover retaining bolts	10	7
Sump drain plug	45	33
Sump retaining bolts	5	4
Timing chain cover bolts	15	11
Timing chain tensioner	50	37
Water pump bolts	15	11

1 General description

1 The engine is of six-cylinder, in-line type with a 12-valve cam-in-head (CIH) cylinder head, mounted conventionally at the front of the car. The cylinder head is of alloy and the cylinder block of cast iron.
2 The crankshaft is supported in seven bearings, and the rear bearing incorporates flanges to control the endfloat.
3 The connecting rods are attached to the crankshaft by horizontally split shell bearings, and to the pistons by gudgeon pins which are an interference fit in the pistons. The aluminium alloy pistons are fitted with three piston rings: two compression rings and a three segment oil control ring.
4 The camshaft is driven by chain from the crankshaft. The camshafts operates the valves via rocker arms and self-adjusting hydraulic tappets. The camshaft runs directly in the cylinder head. The inlet and exhaust valves are each closed by coil springs, and operate in guides pressed into the cylinder head.
5 Engine lubrication is by a gear-type pump located in the timing chain cover attached to

the front of the cylinder block. The oil pump is driven by the crankshaft; the oil pump shaft also drives the distributor rotor arm. Blow-by gases in the crankcase are fed to the camshaft housing by an external tube and thereafter drawn into the inlet manifold via a hose.

2 Compression test - description and interpretation

Refer to Part A, Section 2.

3 Major operations possible with engine in car

The following major operations can be carried out without removing the engine from the car:
a) *Removal and refitting of cylinder head.*
b) *Removal and refitting of sump.*
c) *Removal and refitting of oil pump.*
d) *Removal and refitting of pistons and connecting rods.*
e) *Removal and refitting of flywheel/driveplate.*

f) *Removal and refitting of engine mountings.*
g) *Removal and refitting of camshafts.*
h) *Renewal of the crankshaft front and rear oil seals.*

4 Major operations requiring engine removal

The following major operations are only possible after removal of the engine.
a) *Removal and refitting of crankshaft and main bearings.*
b) *Removal and refitting of the timing chain.*

5 Method of engine removal

Since it is not possible to remove the engine on its own, a strong hoist will be required to lift the engine and transmission out as an assembly. The engine/transmission is removed upwards from the engine compartment.

6 Engine removal

1 Park the vehicle on firm, level ground, chock the rear wheels then firmly apply the handbrake. Jack up the front of the vehicle and support it securely on axle stands (see "Jacking and Vehicle Support"). Remove both front roadwheels and the engine compartment undercovers.
2 Remove the bonnet (see Chapter 11).
3 Remove the battery (see Chapter 5).
4 Drain the cooling system (Chapter 1).
5 Remove the cooling fan and radiator as described in Chapter 3. Remove the upper hose, lower radiator hose and the expansion tank hose. Also disconnect hoses from the coolant pump housing. Also disconnect the hoses from the heater matrix unions on the bulkhead.
6 Working as described in Chapter 1, drain the engine oil then refit the sump drain plug and tighten it to the specified torque.
7 Slacken the union nuts and disconnect the oil cooler pipes from the engine. Unscrew the pipes from the oil cooler lines and remove them. Plug the oil cooler lines and engine ports to prevent dirt entry.
8 Remove the alternator as described in Chapter 5. Unbolt the alternator mounting bracket and remove it from the engine.
9 Working as described in Chapter 10, unbolt the power steering pump and position it clear of the engine; the fluid lines can be left connected.
10 Remove the cruise control unit as described in Chapter 12.
11 On models with air conditioning, unbolt the compressor, position it clear of the engine and unbolt the mounting bracket from the block (see Chapter 11). **Do not** disconnect the refrigerant lines from the compressor or place the lines under any strain.
12 Referring to Chapter 4B, remove the following.

a) Remove inlet duct and air cleaner housing lid assembly.
b) Mark the fuel hoses for identification and disconnect them from the manifold. On 2.6 litre models undo the retaining bolts and free the mounting bracket from the engine block.
c) Remove the exhaust front pipe and mounting brackets then remove the catalytic converter heatshield (as applicable).
d) Disconnect the necessary vacuum/breather hoses from the inlet manifold.
e) Disconnect accelerator cable from the throttle housing.
f) On 2.6 litre models mark the hoses for identification and disconnect the wiring and hoses from the dual ram system valve and purge valve.

13 Disconnect the wiring connectors from the following.

a) Thermostat housing switches and senders (Chapter 3).
b) Lambda sensor - where fitted (Chapter 4B).
c) Unbolt the earth leads from the inlet manifold and side of the cylinder block.
d) Inductive pulse sensor and distributor (Chapter 5). Also disconnect the HT lead from the coil.
e) Oil pressure switch/oil level sensor/oil temperature switch (as applicable).
f) Injectors, airflow meter and idle valve and free the wiring loom from the inlet manifold.
g) The engine wiring connectors located in the centre of the engine compartment bulkhead.

14 On manual transmission models carry out the following as described in Chapter 7A.

a) On models with a hydraulic clutch, remove heatshield and disconnect hydraulic pipe from the clutch slave cylinder. Release the pipe from its transmission clip.
b) On models with a cable clutch, disconnect the cable from the release arm (see Chapter 6).
c) Disconnect wiring connectors from the reversing light switch and speedometer drive.
d) Remove the gearchange linkage.
e) Disconnect the propeller shaft from the rear of the transmission (see Chapter 8).
f) Support the weight of the transmission with a jack then unbolt and remove the rear mounting crossmember from the transmission.

15 On automatic transmission models, carry out the following as described in Chapter 7B.

a) Disconnect the transmission breather hose and wiring connectors.
b) Disconnect the oil cooler hoses and loop them around to prevent dirt entry. Disconnect wiring connector located next to pipes.
c) Position selector lever in "N" then undo the nut and disconnect the selector lever from the transmission shaft.
d) Disconnect the propeller shaft from the rear of the transmission (see Chapter 8).
e) Support the weight of the transmission with a jack then unbolt and remove the rear mounting crossmember from the transmission.

16 On all models, unbolt the engine movement dampers from the left and right-hand side of the cylinder block and move them clear.
17 Manoeuvre the engine hoist into position, and attach it to the cylinder head lifting brackets. Raise the hoist until it is supporting the weight of the engine.
18 Unbolt the left and right-hand engine mounting brackets from the engine then make a final check that any components which would prevent the removal of the engine/

transmission from the car have been removed or disconnected. Ensure that components such as the power steering pump are secured so that they cannot be damaged on removal.
19 Tilt the front end of the engine upwards then lift the engine/transmission out of the engine compartment. As the engine is removed take great care not to damage any of the surrounding components in the engine compartment, especially those of the air conditioning system.
20 With the engine/transmission assembly removed, support the assembly on suitable blocks of wood, on a workbench (or failing that, on a clean area of the workshop floor).
21 Undo the retaining bolts, and remove the flywheel/driveplate cover plate (where fitted) from the transmission. On models with an automatic transmission recover the washer and spacer from behind the driveplate.
22 On automatic transmission models, unscrew the bolts securing the torque converter to the driveplate. To gain access to the bolts, turn the engine with a socket on the crankshaft damper bolt.
23 Slacken and remove the bolts, and remove the starter motor from the transmission.
24 Ensure that both engine and transmission are adequately supported, then slacken and remove the remaining bolts securing the transmission housing to the engine. Note the correct fitted positions of each bolt (and the relevant brackets) as they are removed, to use as a reference on refitting.
25 Carefully withdraw the transmission from the engine, ensuring that the weight of the transmission is not allowed to hang on the input shaft while it is engaged with the engine.
26 If they are loose, remove the locating dowels from the engine or transmission, and keep them in a safe place.

7 Engine dismantling - general

1 The engine should be dismantled in a clean area away from dust and dirt. Avoid working with the engine directly on a concrete floor, as grit presents a real source of trouble.
2 It is advisable to have suitable containers to hold small items, as this will help when reassembling the engine.
3 Thoroughly clean all components with a suitable solvent and wipe dry ready for inspection. Internal channels are best blown through with an air line.
4 Always obtain complete sets of gaskets when dismantling the engine, and fit them all.
5 When possible refit nuts, bolts and washers in their locations as this helps to protect the threads from damage and will also be helpful when the engine is being reassembled.
6 Retain unserviceable items until the new parts are obtained, so that the new part can be checked against the old part, to ensure that the correct item has been supplied.

8 Engine ancillaries - removal

1 Although the items listed may be removed separately with the engine installed, it is more appropriate to take these off after the engine has been removed from the car when extensive dismantling is being carried out. The items are:

a) Inlet and exhaust manifolds (Chapter 4B).
b) Clutch - manual transmission models (Chapter 6).
c) Spark plugs, distributor, and ignition inductive impulse sensor (Chapters 1 and 5).
d) Oil filter (Chapter 1).

9 Engine - complete dismantling

1 Remove the ancillary items listed in Section 8.
2 Unscrew and remove the oil pressure switch. Remove the oil dipstick.
3 Disconnect the crankcase ventilation hose from the camshaft cover.
4 Undo the bolts, noting the correct fitted locations of the HT lead/hose brackets (as applicable), then lift off the cylinder head cover and recover the seal. Undo the retaining bolts and remove the camshaft sprocket access plate and gasket from the front of the cylinder head.
5 Using a socket on the crankshaft pulley bolt, rotate the crankshaft until the pointer in the aperture on the right-hand side of the cylinder block aligns with the raised mark on the flywheel/driveplate. In this position number 1 (front) cylinder piston is at TDC. The timing dot on the camshaft sprocket should be aligned with the notch in the camshaft sprocket support plate and the recess in the camshaft should be correctly positioned to allow full access to the cylinder head bolts (see illustration 12.9a and 12.9b). If not rotate the crankshaft through another complete turn. Do not rotate the crankshaft/camshaft from this point onwards.
6 Unscrew the plastic endfloat bolt from the end of the camshaft then slacken and remove the camshaft sprocket retaining bolts using a suitable splined bit. Disengage the sprocket from the camshaft.

 HAYNES HINT *To ensure that the camshaft sprocket and timing chain remain correctly engaged secure them together with a cable-tie. Alternately, make alignment marks between the sprocket and chain.*

7 Unscrew the two small bolts securing the front of the head to the timing chain cover.

9.10 Tool for holding the flywheel/driveplate stationary

8 Working in the reverse of the sequence shown in **illustration 12.19**, progressively slacken the main cylinder head bolts by half a turn at a time, until all bolts can be unscrewed by hand and removed. Discard the bolts; new ones should be used on refitting.
9 With the aid of an assistant, lift off the cylinder head. Remove the gasket and recover the O-ring seal from the top of the timing chain cover. Also remove the head locating dowels and store them with the head.
10 Unscrew the retaining bolt and washer and slide off the crankshaft pulley assembly from the crankshaft. To prevent rotation as the bolt is slackened, hold the flywheel/driveplate stationary using a home-made tool similar to the one shown (see illustration).
11 Closely examine the flywheel/driveplate retaining bolts; find the bolt which is marked with a "P" and mark its fitted position of the flywheel/driveplate (see illustration). With the tool in position undo the retaining bolts and remove the flywheel/driveplate from the rear of the crankshaft. On models with an automatic transmission recover the washer and spacer from behind the driveplate. Discard the bolts; new ones should be used on refitting.
12 Undo the bolts and remove the water pump and gasket from the timing chain cover.
13 Unscrew the timing chain tensioner from the cover and recover its sealing washer.
14 Turn the engine upside-down on the workbench. Place cloth rags around it to absorb the water and oil which escapes.
15 Slacken and remove the retaining bolts and remove the sump and seal(s). Note the bolts are different lengths. Unbolt the inlet pipe from the base of the oil pump and remove its gasket.
16 Undo the timing chain cover retaining bolts, noting that the bolts are different lengths. Remove the cover along with both its gaskets. Remove the locating dowels.
17 Make alignment marks between the crankshaft sprocket and timing chain then unhook the timing chain and remove it along with the camshaft sprocket.
18 Remove the retaining clip(s) and withdraw the timing chain tensioner blades.
19 Undo the retaining bolt and remove the timing chain guide from the front of the block.

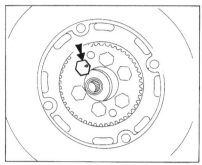
9.11 Mark the position of the bolt marked "P" (arrowed) on the flywheel/driveplate prior to removal

If necessary, also unbolt the camshaft sprocket support plate.
20 Mark the big-end caps and connecting rods in relation to each other using a centre punch, and numbering them from the front of the engine.
21 Lay the block on its side then unscrew the No. 1 cylinder big-end bolts and tap off the cap. Using the handle of a hammer tap the connecting rod and piston through the top of the block. Temporarily refit the cap to the connecting rod keeping the bearing shells in their original positions.
22 Repeat the procedure on the remaining pistons and connecting rods.
23 The main bearing caps should already be marked with numbers starting at the front of the engine. However if there are none, mark them with a centre punch.
24 Position the block upside-down again, then unscrew the main bearing bolts and remove the caps. Take care to keep the bearing shells with their respective caps.
25 Lift the crankshaft out of the crankcase and remove the oil seal. If necessary, slide off the oil pump/distributor drive gear and timing chain sprocket, noting which way around they are fitted, and remove the Woodruff key from the crankshaft slot. If the gear/sprocket are tight, a puller will be needed to draw them off.
26 Remove the upper halves of the main bearing shells from the crankcase and place them with their respective main bearing caps.

10 Sump - removal and refitting with engine in car

Removal

1 Apply the handbrake. Jack up the front of the car and support it on axle stands (see "Jacking and Vehicle Support").
2 Unscrew the drain plug and drain the engine oil into a suitable container. When completed, wipe the plug clean, refit it and tighten.
3 Unscrew the nuts from the top of both engine mountings and undo the bolts securing the engine movement dampers to the mounting brackets.

4 Using a hoist or an engine support bar across the engine compartment, raise the engine approximately 25 mm, taking care to place any undue strain any the various pipes and hoses. This will ensure that there is adequate clearance to remove the sump.
5 Where necessary, disconnect the wiring connector from the oil level sensor.
6 On models with an oil cooler, remove the oil filter (see Chapter 1) then unscrew the union nuts and disconnect the pipes from the cooler.
7 Unscrew the sump bolts, and remove it from the engine. Note the bolts are of different lengths. **Note:** *On some models it may be necessary to unbolt the anti-roll bar clamps and pivot the bar downwards slightly to enable the sump to be removed.*
8 Remove the rubber and cork gaskets from the edge of the sump/cylinder block.
9 If necessary unbolt the oil level sensor from the sump and remove the gasket.

Refitting

10 Ensure that the sump and block surfaces are clean and dry.
11 Apply a smear of suitable sealant (Vauxhall/Opel recommend the use of GM spec 15 03 294 (Part No. 90 001 851) sealant - available from your dealer) to the areas were the timing cover and rear main bearing cap abut the block.
12 Using the sealant to hold the gaskets in positions, stick the rubber gaskets to the grooves in the timing chain cover and bearing cap and the cork gaskets to the base of the cylinder block. Ensure that the joins between the gaskets are adequately coated with sealant.
13 Clean the threads of the sump retaining bolts and apply a suitable locking compound to them (Vauxhall/Opel recommend the use of GM spec 15 10 177 (Part No. 90 167 347) locking compound - available from your dealer).
14 Offer up the sump and refit its retaining bolts, making sure they are fitted in their original locations. Tighten all bolts by hand then go around and tighten them to the specified torque setting.
15 Reconnect the wiring connector to the oil level switch.
16 Lower the engine back into position and tighten the engine mounting nuts to the specified torque. Refit the movement damper bolts and tighten them to the specified torque.
17 Lower the car to the ground and fill the engine with the specified quantity and grade of oil (see Chapter 1 and "Weekly Checks").

11 Engine mountings - renewal

1 Apply the handbrake. Jack up the front of the car and support it on axle stands (see "Jacking and Vehicle Support").

2 Unscrew the nuts from the top of both engine mountings and undo the bolts securing the engine movement dampers to the mounting brackets.
3 Using a hoist or an engine support bar across the engine compartment, raise the engine approximately 25 mm, taking care not to place any undue strain on any of the various pipes and hoses.
4 Unscrew the lower nuts and remove the engine mountings. It may be necessary to unbolt the engine mounting brackets from the engine to allow this.
5 Fit the new mountings using a reversal of the removal procedure, but make sure that the pegs on the mountings engage with the cut-outs on the brackets.

12 Cylinder head - removal and refitting with engine in car

Note: *New cylinder head bolts will be required on refitting.*

Removal

1 Disconnect the battery negative lead.
2 Drain the cooling system as described in Chapter 1.
3 Remove the inlet and exhaust manifolds as described in Chapter 4B.
4 Remove the spark plugs, distributor cap and leads, and rotor arm as described in Chapters 1 and 5.
5 Remove the cooling fan (see Chapter 3).
6 Disconnect the wiring connectors from the thermostat housing sender units then slacken the retaining clips and disconnect the cooling system hoses from the thermostat housing/coolant elbow assembly.
7 Undo the bolts, noting the correct fitted locations of the HT lead/hose brackets (as applicable), then lift off the cylinder head cover and recover the seal.
8 Undo the retaining bolts and remove the camshaft sprocket access plate and gasket from the front of the cylinder head.
9 Using a socket on the crankshaft pulley bolt, rotate the crankshaft until the pointer in the aperture on the right-hand side of the cylinder block aligns with the raised mark on the flywheel/driveplate. In this position number 1 (front) cylinder piston is at TDC. The timing dot on the camshaft sprocket should be aligned with the notch in the camshaft sprocket support plate and the recess in the camshaft should be correctly positioned to allow full access to the cylinder head bolts **(see illustrations)**. If not rotate the crankshaft through another complete turn. Do not rotate the crankshaft/camshaft from this point onwards.
10 Unscrew the plastic endfloat bolt from the end of the camshaft then slacken and remove the camshaft sprocket retaining bolts using a suitable splined bit. Disengage the sprocket from the camshaft.

 To ensure that the camshaft sprocket and timing chain remain correctly engaged secure them together with a cable-tie.

11 Unscrew the two small bolts securing the front of the cylinder head to the timing chain cover.
12 Working in the reverse of the sequence shown in **illustration 12.19**, progressively slacken the main cylinder head bolts by half a turn at a time, until all bolts can be unscrewed by hand and removed. Discard the bolts; new ones should be used on refitting.
13 With the aid of an assistant, lift off the cylinder head. Remove the gasket and recover the O-ring seal from the top of the timing chain cover. Also remove the head locating dowels and store them with the head. The camshaft sprocket should be left resting on its support plate.

Refitting

14 Thoroughly clean the block and head mating surfaces. Check that Number 1 cylinder is still at top dead centre with the flywheel/driveplate mark and pointer aligned and make sure the camshaft sprocket timing mark is correctly aligned with the support plate notch.
15 Check that both location dowels are inserted in the block and apply a smear of

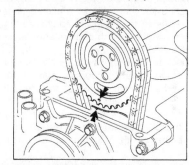

12.9a Position number 1 cylinder at TDC on its compression stroke so that the camshaft sprocket timing mark and support plate notch (arrowed) are aligned (shown with head removed for clarity) . . .

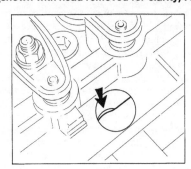

12.9b . . . and the camshaft recesses (arrowed) are correctly positioned to allow access to the cylinder head bolts

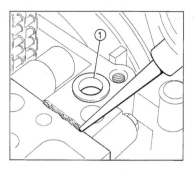

12.16 Fit the O-ring seal (1) to the timing cover recess and apply sealant to the join between the cover and cylinder block

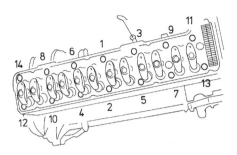

12.19 Cylinder head bolt tightening sequence

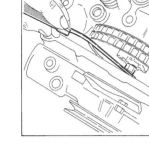

12.24 Checking camshaft endfloat

suitable sealant (Vauxhall/Opel recommend the use of GM spec 15 03 294 (Part No. 90 001 871) sealant - available from your dealer) to the areas were the timing cover and cylinder head join.

16 Fit a new O-ring to the recess in the top of the timing chain cover then fit the new cylinder head gasket making sure it is the right way up and correctly located on the dowels **(see illustration)**.

17 Make sure the camshaft recesses are correctly positioned and manoeuvre the cylinder head carefully into position.

18 Carefully enter the new cylinder head bolts into the holes (*do not drop them in*) and screw in, by hand only, until finger-tight.

19 Working progressively and in the sequence shown, tighten the main cylinder head bolts to their stage 1 torque setting, using a torque wrench and suitable socket **(see illustration)**.

20 Once all the bolts have been tightened to their stage 1 setting, working again in the specified sequence, angle-tighten the bolts through the specified stage 2 angle using a socket and extension bar. It is recommended that an angle-measuring gauge is used during this stage of the tightening, to ensure accuracy.

21 Leave the bolts to settle for approximately ten minutes then go around and angle-tighten them through the specified stage 3 angle.

22 Refit the two smaller bolts to the front of the cylinder head and tighten them to the specified torque.

23 Hook the camshaft sprocket onto the camshaft end and tighten its retaining bolts to the specified torque. Recheck that the flywheel/driveplate and camshaft sprocket timing marks are correctly positioned.

24 Screw the new plastic endfloat bolt (supplied with the gasket set) into the end of the camshaft then refit the access plate and new gasket to the front of the cylinder head. Using feeler blades, measure the clearance between endfloat bolt and cover plate; this measurement is the camshaft endfloat **(see illustration)**. Set the clearance to the specified amount by screwing the endfloat bolt in or out (as applicable) of the camshaft.

25 If the cylinder head has been overhauled, adjust the hydraulic valve lifters as described in Section 13.

26 Fit the seal to the cylinder head cover and refit the cover to the head. Refit the cover retaining bolts, making sure the HT lead/hose brackets are correctly positioned, and tighten them securely.

27 Refit the spark plugs, rotor arm and distributor cap as described in Chapters 1 and 5.

28 Reconnect the coolant hoses and wiring connectors to the thermostat housing/coolant elbow. Ensure that the retaining clips are securely tightened.

29 Refit the manifolds as described in Chapter 4B.

30 Refit the cooling fan as described in Chapter 3.

31 Refill the cooling system as described in Chapter 1.

13 Hydraulic valve lifters - adjustment

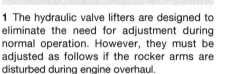

1 The hydraulic valve lifters are designed to eliminate the need for adjustment during normal operation. However, they must be adjusted as follows if the rocker arms are disturbed during engine overhaul.

Basic adjustment - engine stationary

2 On 2.6 litre engines, remove the inlet manifold dual ram air system and inlet duct components as described in Chapter 4B.

3 On all models, slacken and remove the cylinder cover retaining bolts, noting the correct fitted locations of the HT lead/hose brackets (as applicable). Lift off the cylinder head cover and recover the seal.

4 Remove the spark plugs as described in Chapter 1.

5 Using a socket on the crankshaft pulley bolt, rotate the crankshaft until the pointer in the aperture on the right-hand side of the cylinder block aligns with the raised mark on the flywheel/driveplate. In this position number 1 (front) cylinder and number 6 cylinder pistons are at TDC. Unclip the

distributor cap and check that the rotor arm is pointing to the number 1 cylinder HT lead, indicating that number 1 cylinder is at TDC on its compression stroke. If it is pointing at number 6 HT lead, rotate the crankshaft through another complete turn (360°).

6 With number 1 cylinder at TDC on its compression stroke, slacken the front rocker arm retaining nut until freeplay is evident between the rocker arm and valve lifter. From this point, slowly tighten the nut until all freeplay. Once all freeplay has been removed, tighten the rocker arm nut through one more complete turn (360°). Repeat the operation on the remaining valve of number 1 cylinder.

7 Rotate the crankshaft through a third of a turn (120°) so that number 5 cylinder is at TDC (rotor arm pointing towards number 5 cylinder HT lead). Adjust the valve lifters of number 5 cylinder as described in paragraph 6.

8 Rotate the crankshaft through a third of a turn (120°) so that number 3 cylinder is at TDC (rotor arm pointing towards number 3 cylinder HT lead). Adjust the valve lifters of number 3 cylinder as described in paragraph 6.

9 Rotate the crankshaft through a third of a turn (120°) so that number 6 cylinder is at TDC (rotor arm pointing towards number 6 cylinder HT lead). Adjust the valve lifters of number 6 cylinder as described in paragraph 6.

10 Rotate the crankshaft through a third of a turn (120°) so that number 2 cylinder is at TDC (rotor arm pointing towards number 2 cylinder HT lead). Adjust the valve lifters of number 2 cylinder as described in paragraph 6.

11 Rotate the crankshaft through a third of a turn (120°) so that number 4 cylinder is at TDC (rotor arm pointing towards number 4 cylinder HT lead). Adjust the valve lifters of number 4 cylinder as described in paragraph 6.

12 Once all hydraulic lifters have been adjusted, fit the seal to the cylinder head cover and refit the cover to the head. Refit the cover retaining bolts, making sure the HT lead/hose brackets (as applicable) are correctly positioned, and tighten them securely.

13 Refit the distributor cap making sure it is clipped securely in position.

14 On 2.6 litre engines refit the inlet manifold dual ram air system components and ducts as described in Chapter 4B. On all models except the 2.6 litre, the valves lifters can also be adjusted as described below with the engine running.

Adjustment with engine running - 2.5 and 3.0 litre engines

Note: *Since this adjustment procedure requires the engine to be running, it is not possible to carry out the operation on 2.6 litre engines with the dual ram air inlet system. On these engines, the inlet system must be removed to allow the head cover to be removed and the engine cannot be started without the inlet components in position.*

15 If it is wished, once the engine has been started and warmed up to normal operating temperature the valve lifter adjustment can be adjusted as follows.

16 Warm the engine up to normal operating temperature and stop it.

17 Remove the cylinder head cover (see paragraph 3).

HAYNES HiNT
To prevent oil being sprayed around the engine compartment when the engine is running. Make up a splash guard to fit over the top of the camshaft sprocket. Ensure that the splash guard is securely fixed to the cylinder head and in no danger of falling into the engine.

18 Start up the engine and allow it to idle at the specified speed.

19 Starting with the front valve lifter, slacken the rocker arm retaining nut until the arm beings to rattle then slowly tighten it until the rattling stops. From this point tighten the retaining nut a further quarter of a turn (90°).

20 Wait approximately 10 seconds, until the engine idles normally again, then repeat the procedure in paragraph 19 a further three times.

21 Once the front valve lifter is correctly adjusted, repeat the procedures in paragraphs 19 and 20 on the remaining eleven valve lifters.

22 Once all the valve lifters have been adjusted, stop the engine.

23 Clean up any oil splashes and refit the cylinder head cover (see paragraph 12).

14 Engine components - examination and renovation

Oil pump

1 Refer to Chapter 2C, Section 14, noting that it will be necessary to remove the inductive impulse sensor as described in Chapter 5 before the pump can be removed.

Oil pressure relief valve

Note: *This can be removed with the engine in the car.*

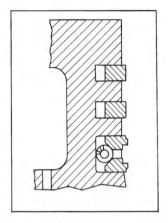

14.11 Piston ring fitting details

2 Wipe clean the area around the pressure relief valve which is situated in the oil pump cover on the base of the timing chain cover.

3 Slacken and remove the cover bolt and remove it along with the sealing washer, spring and piston (noting which way around it is fitted).

4 Inspect all components for signs of wear or damage and renew as necessary. If the piston is damaged, renew the oil pump cover assembly which is supplied complete with pressure relief valve components.

5 On refitting clean all components and lubricate then with clean engine oil. Fit the spring to the piston and slide both components into the pump cover. Refit the cover bolt and sealing washer and tighten it securely.

Crankshaft

6 Refer to Chapter 2A, Section 14.

Big-end and main bearing shells

7 Refer to Chapter 2A, Section 14.

Cylinder bores

8 Refer to Chapter 2A, Section 14.

Connecting rods

9 Examine the mating faces of the big-end caps to see if they have ever been filed in a mistaken attempt to take up wear. If so, the offending rods must be renewed.

10 Check the alignment of the rods visually, and if all is not well, take the rods to your local agent for checking on a special jig.

Pistons and piston rings

11 Refer to Chapter 2A, Section 14. When fitting the piston rings note that the compression rings are not symmetrical and must be installed the correct way up. The top compression ring has a slightly rounded upper edge and must be fitted with its "TOPKL" marking uppermost, and the second compression ring has a tapered profile and must be fitted with its "TOP" marking uppermost **(see illustration)**. **Note:** *On 2.5 litre engines, it may be found that the top*

compression ring has no markings and is symmetrical, if this is the case it can be fitted either way up.

Camshaft, rocker arms and hydraulic valve lifters

12 With the camshaft removed, examine the bearing surfaces for signs of wear. If evident, it is likely that the cylinder head camshaft bearings will require renewal; this is a task which should be entrusted to a Vauxhall/Opel dealer or suitably equipped engineering specialist.

13 The camshaft itself should show no marks or scoring on the journal or cam lobe surfaces. If evident, renew the camshaft.

14 Check the rocker arms for signs of wear or damage on their contact faces and renew as necessary.

15 If the hydraulic valve lifter mechanism is faulty, the valve lifter must also be renewed; it is not possible to overhaul the lifter.

Timing chain and tensioners

16 Examine the teeth on the camshaft and crankshaft sprockets for any sign of wear or damage such as chipped, hooked or missing teeth. If there is any sign of wear or damage on either sprocket, both sprockets and the timing chain should be renewed as a set.

17 Inspect the links of the timing chain for signs of wear or damage on the rollers. The extent of wear can be judged by checking the amount by which the chain can be bent sideways; a new chain will have very little sideways movement. If there is an excessive amount of side play in the timing chain, it must be renewed. It is a sensible precaution to renew the timing chain, if the engine has covered a high mileage or if it has been noted that the chain has sounded noisy with the engine running.

18 Examine the chain guides for signs of wear or damage to the their chain contact faces, renewing any which are badly marked.

19 The condition of the tensioner can only be judged in comparison to a new component. Renew the tensioner if there is any doubt about its condition.

Flywheel/driveplate

20 Refer to Chapter 2A, Section 14.

Cylinder block

21 Refer to Chapter 2A, Section 14.

15 Cylinder head - overhaul

Note: *To minimise wear, it is essential that the rocker arms, valve lifters, valves and associated components are refitted in their original locations. Do this by storing them in a partitioned container or in numbered bags as they are removed to prevent them being interchanged.*

1 With the cylinder head removed, unscrew the rocker arm retaining nuts and lift off the arm pivot washers. Remove the rocker arms, storing them in their original fitted locations to ensure correct refitting.

2 Withdraw the valve lifters from the cylinder head and store them with their respective rocker arms.

3 Slide the camshaft out of the front of the cylinder head.

4 Remove the valves by compressing the valve spring with a suitable valve spring compressor and lifting out the collets. Release the compressor and remove the valve spring retainer, spring and spring seat.

5 Remove the valves, storing them in their original fitted locations to ensure correct refitting.

6 Lever the valve stem oil seals from the valve guides. Lift off the valve rotators which are fitted to the exhaust valves and store them with the correct valve.

7 With the valves removed, clean the carbon from them and from the combustion chambers and ports. The piston crowns can also be cleaned at this stage but take care not to allow carbon to drop between the pistons and bores. To prevent this, clean two pistons at a time with them at the top of their bores and press a little grease between the pistons and bores. Seal off the remaining cylinders, and oil and water channels with paper. After cleaning, move the pistons down the bore and wipe out the grease which will contain the particles of carbon.

8 Examine the heads of the valves and the valve seats for pitting and burning. If the pitting on valve and seat is slight it can be removed by grinding the valves and seats together with coarse, and then fine, valve grinding paste. If the pitting is deep, the valves will have to be reground on a valve grinding machine and the seats will have to be recut with a valve seat cutter. Both these operations are a job for your local Vauxhall/Opel dealer or motor engineering specialist.

9 Check the valve guides for wear by inserting the valve in the guide and attempting to move the valve from side to side. If the specified play is exceeded the valve guides should be renewed by a Vauxhall/Opel dealer.

10 When grinding slightly-pitted valves and valve seats with carborundum paste, continue as follows. Apply a little coarse grinding paste to the valve head, and using a suction-type valve grinding tool, grind the valve into its seat with a rotary movement, lifting the valve and turning it from time to time. A light spring under the valve head will assist in this operation. When a dull matt, even surface finish appears on both the valve and the valve seat, clean off the coarse paste. Repeat the grinding operation with a fine grinding paste until a continuous ring of light grey matt finish appears on both valve and valve seat. Carefully clean off all traces of grinding paste.

11 Check the valve springs for damage and if

possible compare their length with that of a new spring. Renew them if necessary.

12 Using a straight edge and feeler blade check the joint face of the cylinder head for distortion. If greater than the maximum amount given in the Specifications it may be possible to have the head machined flat. Consult a Vauxhall/Opel dealer if necessary.

13 Begin reassembly by refitting the valve rotators to the exhaust valve guides.

14 Press the valve stem oil seals onto the guides.

15 To fit the valves, lubricate the valve stem with engine oil and insert it in the valve guide.

16 Refit the spring and spring retainer, then use the valve spring compressor to compress the spring until the collets can be fitted in position in the slots in the valve stem. Release the compressor slowly, and check that the collets are seated correctly.

17 After fitting all the valves, tap the tops of the springs lightly to ensure correct seating of the collets.

18 Lubricate the camshaft bearings and lobes with clean engine oil and slide the camshaft into the cylinder head.

19 Lubricate the valve lifter and slide them into their original locations in the cylinder head.

20 Lubricate the rocker arms and fit them onto the correct studs.

21 Lubricate the pivot washers and fit them to the rocker arms with their rounded surface downwards. Screw on the rocker arm retaining nut and adjust each valve lifter as described in Section 13, making sure each one is adjusted with the camshaft positioned at TDC. Alternatively, wait until the cylinder head is refitted to the engine and adjust the valve lifters prior to refitting the cylinder head cover.

16 Engine - complete reassembly

Note: *New flywheel/driveplate retaining bolts and new cylinder head bolts will be required.*

1 Place the cylinder block upside-down on the bench and wipe clean the main bearing shell seats.

2 Press the main bearing shells onto the crankcase, making sure that the tags engage with the special grooves. Note that the rear shell incorporates thrust flanges.

3 Lubricate the shells with clean engine oil.

4 Carefully lower the crankshaft into the crankcase. Rotate it several times and check that it is correctly seated by gently tapping the webs with a mallet.

5 Check that the crankshaft endfloat is as given in the Specifications by either using a feeler blade between the flanged main bearing shell and the crankshaft thrust face, or by using a dial test indicator on the crankshaft rear flange.

6 Clean the backs of the lower main bearing shells and the caps, then press them into position. Lubricate the shells with clean oil.

7 Apply a suitable sealant to the mating surface of the rear main bearing cap (Vauxhall/Opel recommend the use of GM spec 15 04 200 (Part No. 08 983 368) sealant - available from your dealer) **(see illustration)**.

8 Fill the grooves on each outer edge of the rear main bearing cap with a bead of sealant approximately 6 mm in diameter (Vauxhall/Opel recommend GM spec 15 03 294 (Part No. 90 001 851) sealant - available from your dealer) **(see illustration)**.

9 Refit all the main bearing caps and install the bearing cap bolts. Tighten the bolts by hand then tighten them evenly and progressively to the specified torque setting. Check that the rear main bearing cap grooves are sufficiently sealed and wipe off any excess sealant.

10 Rotate the crankshaft and check that it turns freely with no binding or tight spots.

11 Lubricate the lips of the new crankshaft rear oil seal with grease. Ease the seal over the crankshaft end, making sure its sealing lip is facing inwards, and press it into the rear main bearing cap until flush.

12 Lay the block on its side and lubricate the cylinder bores and crankshaft journals liberally with oil.

13 Space the piston rings around the pistons so that their end gaps are 180° apart. In the case of the oil scraper ring, offset the gaps in the upper and lower rails by 25 to 50 mm to right and left of the end gap of the centre section.

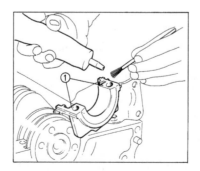

16.7 Apply suitable sealant to the mating surfaces (1) of the rear main bearing cap . . .

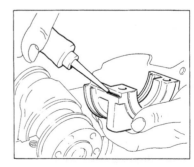

16.8 . . . and fill its outer grooves with sealant (see text)

14 Clean the backs of the big-end bearing shells and the caps and connecting rods, then press the shells into position.

15 Turn the crankshaft so that the journal for No 1 cylinder is at bottom dead centre.

16 Fit a piston ring compressor to No 1 piston then insert it into No 1 cylinder with the arrow on the piston crown pointing towards the front (timing chain end) of the engine.

17 Using the handle of a hammer, tap the piston through the ring compressor while guiding the connecting rod onto the journal.

18 Fit the big-end bearing cap, ensuring it is fitted the correct way around, then insert the big-end bearing bolts. Tighten the bolts evenly and progressively to the specified torque setting.

19 Check that the crankshaft turns freely taking into consideration the resistance of the piston rings.

20 Repeat the procedure given in paragraphs 15 to 19 for the remaining pistons.

21 Turn the block upside down on the bench.

22 Where removed, refit the Woodruff key to the crankshaft cutout. Making sure they are the correct way around, fit the timing chain sprocket and oil pump/distributor drive gear. Tap the sprocket and gear into position until they are tighten against the crankshaft shoulder.

23 Clean the threads of the timing chain guide and camshaft sprocket support plate bolts and coat them with locking compound. Refit the guide and plate and securely tighten the bolts.

24 If the threads of the new flywheel/driveplate retaining bolts are not pre-coated with locking compound, apply a coat of locking compound to them. Fit the flywheel/driveplate to the crankshaft and screw in the new retaining bolts, making sure the bolt marked "P" is fitted in the position marked on removal; on models with an automatic transmission do not forget to fit the spacer and washer between the crankshaft and driveplate. Prevent rotation using the tool shown in **illustration 9.10**, then tighten the retaining bolts to the specified torque setting. On 2.6 litre models, further tighten the bolts through the specified stage 2 angle.

25 Rotate the crankshaft so that number 1 cylinder is at TDC and align the mark on the flywheel/driveplate with pointer on the cylinder block.

26 Fit the camshaft sprocket and timing chain assembly to the engine, aligning the marks made on removal (where applicable). With the left-hand hand run of the chain taut, remove all slack from the right-hand side of the chain and check that the timing dot on the camshaft sprocket is aligned with the notch on the support plate **(see illustration)**. If necessary disengage the chain and adjust the position of the sprocket.

27 Once the marks are correctly aligned, slide the timing chain tensioner blades into position and refit the retaining clip(s).

28 Using a suitable screwdriver carefully

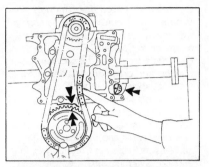

16.26 With the flywheel/driveplate mark aligned with the block pointer (arrowed), fit the timing chain and camshaft sprocket as shown, making sure the sprocket timing mark is aligned with the support plate notch (arrowed)

lever the oil seal out from the front of the timing chain cover. Fit the new seal, making sure its sealing lip is facing inwards, and press it into position until it is flush with the cover.

29 Insert the timing chain cover locating dowels to the block and fit the new gaskets.

30 Fit the timing chain cover and insert its retaining bolts, making sure they are fitted in the correct locations. Tighten the bolts to the specified torque.

31 Thoroughly clean the block and head mating surfaces and trim off the ends of the timing chain cover gasket with a sharp knife.

32 Check that Number 1 cylinder is still at top dead centre with the flywheel/driveplate mark and pointer aligned and make sure the camshaft sprocket timing mark is correctly aligned with the support plate notch. Fit the timing chain tensioner and sealing ring and screw it in a couple of turns.

33 Check that both location dowels are inserted in the block and apply a smear of suitable sealant (Vauxhall/Opel recommend the use of GM spec 15 03 294 (Part No. 90 001 871) sealant - available from your dealer) to the areas were the timing chain cover and cylinder head join.

34 Fit a new O-ring to the recess in the top of the timing chain cover then fit the new cylinder head gasket making sure it is the right way up and correctly located on the dowels.

35 Make sure the camshaft recesses are correctly positioned and manoeuvre the cylinder head carefully into position.

36 Carefully enter the new cylinder head bolts into the holes (*do not drop them in*) and screw in, by hand only, until finger-tight.

37 Working progressively and in the sequence shown in **illustration 12.19**, tighten the main cylinder head bolts to their stage 1 torque setting, using a torque wrench and suitable socket.

38 Once all the bolts have been tightened to their stage 1 setting, working again in the specified sequence, angle-tighten the bolts through the specified stage 2 angle using a socket and extension bar. It is recommended that an angle-measuring gauge is used during

this stage of the tightening, to ensure accuracy.

39 Leave the bolts to settle for approximately ten minutes then go around and angle-tighten them through the specified stage 3 angle.

40 Refit the two smaller bolts to the front of the cylinder head and tighten them to the specified torque.

41 Hook the camshaft sprocket onto the camshaft end and tighten its retaining bolts to the specified torque. Check that the flywheel/driveplate and camshaft sprocket timing marks are correctly positioned then tighten the timing chain tensioner to the specified torque setting.

42 Screw the new plastic endfloat bolt (supplied with the gasket set) into the end of the camshaft then refit the access plate and new gasket to the front of the cylinder head. Using feeler blades, measure the clearance between endfloat bolt and cover plate; this measurement is the camshaft endfloat **(see illustration 12.24)**. Set the clearance to the specified amount by screwing the endfloat bolt in or out (as applicable) of the camshaft.

43 Refit the inlet pipe to the base of the timing cover using a new gasket. Apply a suitable locking compound to the retaining bolts and tighten them securely.

44 Ensure that the sump and block surfaces are clean and dry.

45 Apply a smear of suitable sealant (Vauxhall/Opel recommend the use of GM spec 15 03 294 (Part No. 90 001 851) sealant - available from your dealer) to the areas were the timing cover and rear main bearing cap abut the block.

46 Using the sealant to hold the gaskets in positions, stick the rubber gaskets to the grooves in the timing chain cover and bearing cap and the cork gaskets to the base of the cylinder block. Ensure that the joins between the gaskets are adequately coated with sealant.

47 Clean the threads of the sump retaining bolts and apply a suitable locking compound to them. (Vauxhall/Opel recommend the use of GM spec 15 10 177 (Part No. 90 167 347) locking compound - available from your dealer).

48 Offer up the sump and refit its retaining bolts, making sure they are fitted in their original locations. Tighten all bolts by hand then go around and tighten them to the specified torque setting.

49 Refit the water pump using a new gasket and insert its retaining bolts in the correct locations. Tighten the retaining bolts to the specified torque.

50 Carefully slide the crankshaft pulley assembly into position, taking great care not to damage the oil seal lip, and align its slot with the crankshaft key. Refit the pulley retaining bolt and tighten it to the specified torque, using the flywheel/driveplate locking tool to prevent rotation.

51 Adjust the hydraulic valve lifters as described in Section 13.

52 Fit the seal to the cylinder head cover and refit the cover to the head. Refit the cover retaining bolts, making sure the HT lead/hose brackets are correctly positioned, and tighten them securely.

53 Refit the spark plugs, rotor arm and distributor cap as described in Chapters 1 and 5.

54 Refit the dipstick.

55 Refit the oil pressure switch and tighten it securely.

56 Install the ancillaries listed in Section 8.

17 Engine ancillaries - refitting

Refer to Section 8 and refit the listed components, with reference to the Chapters indicated where necessary.

18 Engine - refitting

Refitting the engine is a reversal of the removal procedure given in Section 6, but in addition note the following points:

a) *Lightly grease the gearbox input shaft or torque converter spigot as applicable (see Chapter 7A or 7B).*

b) *On automatic transmission models, check that the torque converter is fully engaged with the transmission oil pump with reference to Chapter 7B.*

c) *Refill the engine with the specified quantity and grade of oil (see Chapter 1).*

d) *On manual gearbox models, adjust the clutch cable with reference to Chapter 6.*

e) *Adjust the accelerator cable, and where necessary, the automatic transmission kickdown cable and the cruise control cable as described in Chapters 4B, 7B and 12 (as applicable).*

f) *Refill the cooling system as described in Chapter 1.*

19 Engine - initial start-up after major overhaul or repair

1 Make sure that the battery is fully charged and that all lubricants, coolant and fuel are replenished.

2 Double check all fittings and connections.

3 Disconnect the ignition HT lead from the distributor and connect it to a sound earth point using a suitable clip. Turn the engine over on the starter motor until the oil pressure warning light is extinguished, or until oil pressure is recorded on the gauge. This will ensure that the engine is not starved of oil during the critical few minutes running after initial start-up. The fuel system will also be primed during this operation.

4 Reconnect the HT lead to the distributor. Start the engine.

5 When the engine fires and runs, keep it going at a fast tickover only (no faster) and bring it up to normal working temperature.

6 As the engine warms up there will be odd smells and some smoke from parts getting hot and burning off oil deposits. The signs to look for are leaks of water or oil, which will be obvious if serious. Check also the exhaust pipe and manifold connections as these do not always find their exact gas tight position until the warmth and vibration have acted on them, and it is almost certain that they will need tightening further. This should be done, of course, with the engine stopped.

7 When normal running temperature has been reached. Stop the engine and wait a few minutes to see if any lubricant or coolant is dripping out when the engine is stationary.

8 During the initial period that the engine is running it is not unusual for the hydraulic valve lifters to be noisy, but this should gradually disappear, certainly within a few miles driving on the road.

9 If many new internal components have been fitted, it will be beneficial to change the engine oil and oil filter after the first 600 miles (1000 km).

Chapter 2 Part C:
3.0 litre (DOHC) engine

Contents

Camshafts and followers - removal and refitting with engine in car .13
Compression test - description and interpretation 2
Cylinder head - removal and refitting with engine in car 12
Cylinder head - overhaul 15
Engine - complete dismantling 9
Engine - complete reassembly 16
Engine - initial start-up after major overhaul or repair 19
Engine - refitting 18
Engine ancillaries - refitting 17
Engine ancillaries - removal 8
Engine components - examination and renovation 14
Engine dismantling - general 7
Engine mountings - renewal 11
Engine oil and filter renewal . . . . .See Chapter 1
Engine oil level check . . . . .See "Weekly checks"
Engine removal 6
General description 1
General engine checks . . . . .See Chapter 1
Major operations requiring engine removal 4
Major operations possible with engine in car 3
Method of engine removal 5
Sump - removal and refitting with engine in car 10

Degrees of difficulty

Easy, suitable for novice with little experience		Fairly easy, suitable for beginner with some experience		Fairly difficult, suitable for competent DIY mechanic		Difficult, suitable for experienced DIY mechanic		Very difficult, suitable for expert DIY or professional	

Specifications

General

Type	Six-cylinder, in-line, water-cooled, double overhead camshaft 24-valve
Engine codes	C30SE or C30SEJ

Note: *The engine code forms the first digits of the engine number*

Bore	95.0 mm
Stroke	69.8 mm
Capacity	2969 cc
Firing order	1-5-3-6-2-4 (No.1 cylinder at timing chain end)
Crankshaft rotation	Clockwise
Compression ratio	10.0:1

Cylinder block (crankcase)

Material	Cast-iron
Maximum cylinder bore out of round	0.005 mm
Maximum permissible taper	0.005 mm
Maximum rebore oversize	0.5 mm

Crankshaft

Number of main bearings	7
Main bearing journal diameter:	
Standard	57.987 to 58.003 mm
Undersizes:	
1st undersize (0.25 mm)	57.737 to 57.753 mm
2nd undersize (0.5 mm)	57.487 to 57.503 mm
Crankpin diameter:	
Standard	51.971 to 51.990 mm
Undersizes:	
1st undersize (0.25 mm)	51.721 to 51.740 mm
2nd undersize (0.5 mm)	51.471 to 51.490 mm
Crankshaft endfloat	0.04 to 0.16 mm
Main bearing running clearance	0.02 to 0.06 mm
Big-end running clearance	0.01 to 0.06 mm
Big-end side-play	0.11 to 0.24 mm

Camshaft

Endfloat	0.04 to 0.14 mm
Camshaft journal diameters	27.939 to 27.960 mm
Camshaft bearing cap diameters	28.000 to 28.020 mm

Pistons and rings

Type	Alloy, recessed head	
Number of piston rings	2 compression, 1 oil control	

Ring end gap:

Compression	0.40 to 0.65 mm	
Oil control (rail)	0.30 to 0.60 mm	
Ring gap offset (to gap of adjacent ring)	180°	
Gudgeon pin diameter	22.0 mm	
Piston gudgeon pin bore diameter	22.004 to 22.010 mm	

Piston grades:	Diameter (mm)	Marking
Production grade 1	94.92	6
	94.93	6
Production grade 2	94.94	8
	94.96	00
	94.98	02
Production grade 3	95 00	04
	95.02	06
	95.04	08
Oversize (0.5 mm)	95.43	7 + 0.5
	95.44	8 + 0.5
	95.45	9 + 0.5
	95.46	0 + 0.5

Piston-to-bore clearance:

New engine	0.025 to 0.035 mm
After rebore	0.035 to 0.045 mm
Maximum permissible piston out-of-round	0.005 mm
Maximum permissible piston taper	0.005 mm

Cylinder head

Material	Light alloy
Maximum permissible distortion of sealing face	0.025 mm
Overall height of cylinder head	129.45 to 129.75 mm

Valve seat width:

Inlet	1.1 to 1.5 mm
Exhaust	1.5 to 1.9 mm

Valves

Valve clearance	Automatic by hydraulic valve lifters (cam followers)

Valve stem-to-guide clearance:

Inlet	0.030 to 0.062 mm
Exhaust	0.039 to 0.068 mm
Valve seat angle	45°
Valve guide installed height	12.7 to 13.0 mm

Valve stem diameter:

Inlet:

Standard	6.955 to 6.970 mm
1st oversize (0.075 mm)	7.030 to 7.045 mm
2nd oversize (0.150 mm)	7.105 to 7.120 mm

Exhaust:

Standard	6.945 to 6.960 mm
1st oversize (0.075 mm)	7.020 to 7.035 mm
2nd oversize (0.150 mm)	7.095 to 7.110 mm

Valve guide bore diameter:

Standard	7.000 to 7.015 mm
1st oversize (0.075 mm)	7.075 to 7.090 mm
2nd oversize (0.150 mm)	7.150 to 7.165 mm

Flywheel

Maximum thickness reduction at contact surface	0.3 mm

Lubrication

Oil pump:

Tooth play (gear to gear)	0.1 to 0.2 mm
Gear-to-housing clearance (endfloat)	0.1 to 0.2 mm
Oil pressure at idle (engine at operating temperature)	3.0 to 3.5 bar

Torque wrench settings

	Nm	lbf ft
Big-end bearing cap bolts	45	33
Camshaft bearing cap retaining nuts:		
Stage 1	5	4
Stage 2	10	7
Camshaft sprocket bolts:		
Stage 1	90	66
Stage 2	Angle tighten a further 60°	
Stage 3	Angle tighten a further 30°	
Crankshaft pulley to vibration damper bolts	25	18
Cylinder head bolts:		
Main bolts:		
Stage 1	60	45
Stage 2	Angle tighten a further 90 to 100°	
Wait for approximately ten minutes then:		
Stage 3	Angle tighten a further 30 to 40°	
Cylinder head to timing chain cover bolts	25	18
Cylinder head cover nuts	20	15
Engine mounting retaining nuts	40	30
Engine movement damper bolts:		
Upper bolt	40	30
Lower bolt	22	16
Flywheel/driveplate retaining bolts:		
Stage 1	55	41
Stage 2	Angle tighten a further 30 to 45°	
Main bearing cap bolts	110	81
Oil pressure switch	45	33
Oil pump cover retaining bolts	10	7
Oil pump inlet pipe bolts	8	6
Primary timing chain guide retaining bolt	8	6
Primary timing chain tensioner	60	45
Secondary timing chain tensioner	20	15
Sump drain plug	45	33
Sump retaining bolts	20	15
Timing chain cover bolts	15	11
Vibration damper retaining bolt:		
Stage 1	200	148
Stage 2	Angle tighten a further 50°	
Stage 3	Angle tighten a further 15°	
Water pump bolts	15	11
Water pump pulley retaining bolts:		
Stage 1	8	6
Stage 2	Angle tighten a further 30°	
Stage 3	Angle tighten a further 15°	

1 General description

1 The engine is of six-cylinder, in-line type with a 24-valve double overhead camshaft (DOHC) cylinder head, mounted conventionally at the front of the car. The cylinder head is of alloy and the cylinder block of cast iron.
2 The crankshaft is supported in seven bearings, and the rear bearing incorporates flanges to control the endfloat.
3 The connecting rods are attached to the crankshaft by horizontally split shell bearings, and to the pistons by gudgeon pins which are secured in position with circlips. The aluminium alloy pistons are fitted with three piston rings: two compression rings and a three segment oil control ring.

4 The camshafts are driven by chain from the crankshaft; the crankshaft is linked to the exhaust camshaft by the primary chain and a secondary chain links the camshafts. The camshafts operates the valves via self-adjusting hydraulic tappets which are fitted to the cam followers. Both camshafts run in bearing caps which are bolted to the top of the cylinder head. The inlet and exhaust valves are each closed by coil springs, and operate in guides pressed into the cylinder head.
5 Engine lubrication is by a gear-type pump located in the timing chain cover attached to the front of the cylinder block. The oil pump is driven by the crankshaft; the oil pump shaft also drives the distributor rotor arm. Blow-by gases in the crankcase are fed to the camshaft housing by an external tube and thereafter drawn into the inlet manifold via a hose.

2 Compression test - description and interpretation

Refer to Part A, Section 2

3 Major operations possible with engine in car

The following major operations can be carried out without removing the engine from the car:

a) Removal and refitting of cylinder head.
b) Removal and refitting of sump.
c) Removal and refitting of oil pump.
d) Removal and refitting of pistons and connecting rods.

e) *Removal and refitting of flywheel/driveplate.*
f) *Removal and refitting of engine mountings.*
g) *Removal and refitting of camshafts.*
h) *Renewal of the crankshaft front and rear oil seals.*

4 Major operations requiring engine removal

The following major operations are only possible after removal of the engine.

a) *Removal and refitting of crankshaft and main bearings.*
b) *Removal and refitting of the primary timing chain.*

5 Method of engine removal

Since it is not possible to remove the engine on its own, a strong hoist will be required to lift the engine and transmission out as an assembly. The engine/transmission is removed upwards from the engine compartment.

6 Engine removal

1 Park the vehicle on firm, level ground chock the rear wheels then firmly apply the handbrake. Jack up the front of the vehicle and support it securely on axle stands (see *"Jacking and Vehicle Support"*). Remove both front roadwheels and the engine compartment undercovers.
2 Remove the bonnet (see Chapter 11).
3 Remove the battery as described in Chapter 5.
4 Drain the cooling system as described in Chapter 1. Slacken the nut and disconnect the coolant pipe from the right-hand, rear end of the block and allow the coolant to drain from the block.
5 Remove the cooling fan and radiator as described in Chapter 3. Remove the upper hose, lower radiator hose and the expansion tank hose. Also disconnect hoses from the coolant pump.
6 Working as described in Chapter 1, drain the engine oil then refit the sump drain plug and tighten it to the specified torque.
7 Slacken the union nuts and disconnect the oil cooler pipes from the engine. Unscrew the pipes from the oil cooler lines and remove them. Plug the oil cooler lines and engine ports to prevent dirt entry.
8 Remove the alternator as described in Chapter 5. Unbolt the alternator mounting bracket and remove it from the engine.

9 Working as described in Chapter 10, unbolt the power steering pump and move it clear of the engine; the fluid lines can be left connected.
10 Remove the cruise control unit as described in Chapter 12.
11 On models with air conditioning, unbolt the compressor, position it clear of the engine and unbolt the mounting bracket from the block (see Chapter 11). **Do not** disconnect the refrigerant lines from the compressor or place the lines under any strain.
12 Referring to Chapter 4B, remove the following.

a) *Remove inlet duct and air cleaner housing lid/airflow meter assembly.*
b) *Remove the dual ram air inlet system assembly.*
c) *Remove the exhaust front pipe and mounting brackets then remove the catalytic converter heatshields.*
d) *Disconnect the fuel hoses and necessary vacuum/breather hoses from the inlet manifold.*

13 Disconnect the wiring connectors from the following.

a) *Thermostat housing switches and senders (Chapter 3).*
b) *Knock sensors and lambda sensor (Chapter 4B).*
c) *Unbolt the earth leads from the rear of the inlet manifold and side of the cylinder block.*
d) *Inductive pulse sensor and distributor (Chapter 5). Also disconnect the HT lead from the coil.*
e) *Oil pressure switch and oil level sensor*
f) *The three wiring connectors located beneath the inlet manifold.*
g) *The engine wiring connectors located in the centre of the engine compartment bulkhead.*

14 On manual transmission models carry out the following as described in Chapter 7A.

a) *Remove heatshield and disconnect hydraulic pipe from the clutch slave cylinder. Release the pipe from its transmission clip.*
b) *Disconnect wiring connectors from the reversing light switch and speedometer drive.*
c) *Remove the gearchange linkage.*
d) *Disconnect the propeller shaft from the rear of the transmission (see Chapter 8).*
e) *Support the weight of the transmission with a jack then unbolt and remove the rear mounting crossmember from the transmission.*

15 On automatic transmission models, carry out the following as described in Chapter 7B.

a) *Disconnect the breather hose and wiring connectors located on the engine compartment bulkhead.*
b) *Disconnect the oil cooler hoses and loop them around to prevent dirt entry. Also, disconnect the wiring connector located next to pipes.*

c) *Position selector lever in "N" then undo the nut and disconnect the selector lever from the transmission shaft.*
d) *Disconnect the propeller shaft from the rear of the transmission as described in Chapter 8.*
e) *Support the weight of the transmission with a jack then unbolt and remove the rear mounting crossmember from the transmission.*

16 On all models, unbolt the engine movement dampers from the left- and right-hand side of the cylinder block and position them clear.
17 Manoeuvre the engine hoist into position, and attach it to the cylinder head lifting brackets. Raise the hoist until it is supporting the weight of the engine.
18 Unbolt the left and right-hand engine mounting brackets from the engine then make a final check that any components which would prevent the removal of the engine/transmission from the car have been removed or disconnected. Ensure that components such as the power steering pump are secured so that they cannot be damaged on removal.
19 Tilt the front end of the engine upwards then lift the engine/transmission out of the engine compartment. As the engine is removed take great care not to damage any of the surrounding components in the engine compartment, especially those of the air conditioning system.
20 With the engine/transmission assembly removed, support the assembly on suitable blocks of wood, on a workbench (or failing that, on a clean area of the workshop floor).
21 Undo the retaining bolts, and remove the flywheel/driveplate cover plate (where fitted) from the transmission. On models with an automatic transmission recover the washer and spacer from behind the driveplate. Discard the bolts, new ones should be used on refitting.
22 On automatic transmission models, unscrew the bolts securing the torque converter to the driveplate. To gain access to the bolts, turn the engine with a socket on the crankshaft damper bolt.
23 Slacken and remove the retaining bolts, and remove the starter motor from the transmission.
24 Ensure that both engine and transmission are adequately supported, then slacken and remove the remaining bolts securing the transmission housing to the engine. Note the correct fitted positions of each bolt (and the relevant brackets) as they are removed, to use as a reference on refitting.
25 Carefully withdraw the transmission from the engine, ensuring that the weight of the transmission is not allowed to hang on the input shaft while it is engaged with the engine.
26 If they are loose, remove the locating dowels from the engine or transmission, and keep them in a safe place.

7 Engine dismantling - general

1 The engine should be dismantled in a clean area away from dust and dirt. Avoid working with the engine directly on a concrete floor, as grit presents a real source of trouble.
2 It is advisable to have suitable containers to hold small items, as this will help when reassembling the engine.
3 Thoroughly clean all components with a suitable solvent and wipe dry ready for inspection. Internal channels are best blown through with an air line.
4 Always obtain complete sets of gaskets when dismantling the engine, and fit them all.
5 When possible refit nuts, bolts and washers in their locations as this helps to protect the threads from damage and will also be helpful when the engine is being reassembled.
6 Retain unserviceable items until the new parts are obtained, so that the new part can be checked against the old part, to ensure that the correct item has been supplied.

8 Engine ancillaries - removal

Although the items listed may be removed separately with the engine installed, it is more appropriate to take these off after the engine has been removed from the car when extensive dismantling is being carried out. The items are:

a) Inlet and exhaust manifolds (Chapter 4B).
b) Clutch - manual transmission models (Chapter 6).
c) Spark plugs, distributor, and ignition inductive impulse sensor (Chapters 1 and 5).
d) Oil filter (Chapter 1).

9 Engine - complete dismantling

1 Remove the ancillary items listed in Section 8.
2 Unscrew and remove the oil pressure switch.
3 Remove the oil dipstick.
4 Disconnect the crankcase ventilation hose from the camshaft cover.
5 Undo the nuts and remove the washers and seals from the cylinder head cover studs. Lift off the cover and recover the seal.
6 Unscrew the nuts and free the wiring clips from the front of the upper timing chain cover. Unscrew the retaining bolts, noting the position of wiring clip studs, and remove the cover and gasket.
7 Using a socket on the crankshaft damper bolt, rotate the crankshaft until the pointer in

the aperture on the right-hand side of the cylinder block aligns with the raised mark on the flywheel/driveplate. In this position number 1 (front) cylinder piston is at TDC. The arrows on the camshaft sprockets should be pointing **towards** each other. If not rotate the crankshaft through another complete turn. Do not rotate the crankshaft/camshafts from this point onwards.
8 Undo the bolts and remove the secondary timing chain tensioner from the top of the head.
9 Unscrew the primary timing chain tensioner from the head and recover its sealing ring.
10 Slacken and remove the inlet camshaft sprocket bolt whilst preventing the camshaft rotating by holding the rear of the camshaft with a ring spanner. Remove the sprocket and secondary timing chain. Discard the bolt, a new one should be used on refitting.
11 Unscrew the exhaust camshaft bolt whilst retaining the camshaft with a ring spanner and remove the sprocket. Discard the bolt, a new one should be used on refitting.
12 Unscrew the two small bolts securing the front of the cylinder head to the timing chain cover.
13 Working in the reverse of the sequence shown in **illustration 12.26a**, progressively slacken the fourteen main cylinder head bolts by half a turn at a time, until all bolts can be unscrewed by hand and removed. Discard the bolts, new ones should be used on refitting.
14 Lift off the cylinder head, noting how it engages with the timing chain tensioner blade. Remove the gasket and recover the head locating dowels and store them with the head.
15 Undo the bolts and remove the crankshaft pulley from the vibration damper. Retain with the damper bolt with a socket to prevent rotation as the bolts are slackened.
16 Unbolt the drivebelt pulley from the water pump. On vehicles with air conditioning, also unbolt the auxiliary drivebelt idler from the engine.
17 Unscrew the retaining bolt and remove the vibration damper assembly from the crankshaft. To prevent rotation as the bolt is slackened, hold the flywheel/driveplate stationary using a home-made tool similar to the one shown. If

necessary drive out the roll pin and separate the vibration damper and hub **(see illustrations)**. Discard the vibration damper bolt, a new one should be used on refitting.
18 With the tool in position undo the retaining bolts and remove the flywheel/driveplate from the rear of the crankshaft. On models with an automatic transmission recover the washer and spacer from behind the driveplate.
19 Undo the bolts and remove the water pump and gasket from the timing chain cover.
20 Turn the engine upside-down on the workbench. Place cloth rags around it to absorb the water and oil which escapes.
21 Slacken and remove the retaining bolts and remove the sump and seal. Note the bolts are different lengths.
22 Unbolt the inlet pipe from the base of the oil pump and remove its gasket.
23 Undo the timing chain cover retaining bolts, noting that the bolts are different lengths. Remove the cover along with both its gaskets. Remove the locating dowels
24 Remove the retaining clip and slide the timing chain tensioner off from its pivot. Remove the pivot pin if it is loose.
25 Undo the bolt and remove the timing chain guide from the front of the block. Remove the guide locating pin if it is loose.
26 Remove the timing chain.
27 Mark the big-end caps and connecting rods in relation to each other using a centre punch, and numbering them from the front of the engine.
28 Lay the block on its side then unscrew the No. 1 cylinder big-end bolts and tap off the cap. Using the handle of a hammer tap the connecting rod and piston through the top of the block. Temporarily refit the cap to the connecting rod keeping the bearing shells in their original positions.
29 Repeat the procedure on the remaining pistons and connecting rods.
30 The main bearing caps should already be marked with numbers starting at the front of the engine. However if there are none, mark them with a centre punch.
31 Position the block upside-down again, then unscrew the main bearing bolts and remove the caps. Take care to keep the bearing shells with their respective caps.

9.17a Tool for holding the flywheel/driveplate stationary

9.17b If necessary, drive out the roll pin (arrowed) and separate the vibration damper and hub

32 Lift the crankshaft out of the crankcase and remove the oil seal. If necessary, slide off the oil pump/distributor drive gear and timing chain sprocket, noting which way around they are fitted, and remove the Woodruff key from the crankshaft slot. If the gear/sprocket are tight, a puller will be needed to draw them off.
33 Remove the upper halves of the main bearing shells from the crankcase and place them with their respective main bearing caps.

10 Sump - removal and refitting with engine in car

Removal

1 Apply the handbrake. Jack up the front of the car and support it on axle stands (see *"Jacking and Vehicle Support"*).
2 Unscrew the drain plug and drain the engine oil into a suitable container. When completed, wipe the plug clean, refit it and tighten.
3 Remove the front suspension crossmember as described in Chapter 10.
4 On models with air conditioning, unbolt the compressor bracket from the sump.
5 Remove the centre tie rod as described in Chapter 10.
6 Disconnect the wiring connector from the oil level sensor.
7 Unscrew the sump bolts, and remove it from the engine. Note the bolts are of different lengths.
8 Pull the rubber gasket from the edge of the sump.
9 If necessary unbolt the oil level sensor from the sump and remove the gasket.

Refitting

10 Ensure that the sump and block surfaces are clean and dry and fit a new seal to the sump groove.
11 Apply a smear of suitable sealant (Vauxhall/Opel recommend the use of GM spec 15 03 294 (Part No. 90 001 851) sealant - available from your dealer) to the areas were the timing cover and rear main bearing cap abut the block.

12 Offer up the sump and refit its retaining bolts, making sure they are fitted in their original locations. Tighten all bolts by hand then go around and tighten them to the specified torque setting.
13 Reconnect the wiring connector to the oil level switch.
14 Refit the centre tie rod and suspension crossmember as described in Chapter 10.
15 Lower the car to the ground.
16 Fill the engine with the specified quantity and grade of oil (see Chapter 1 and "Weekly Checks").

11 Engine mountings - renewal

1 Apply the handbrake. Jack up the front of the car and support it on axle stands (see *"Jacking and Vehicle Support"*).
2 Unscrew the nuts from the top of both engine mountings and undo the bolts securing the engine movement dampers to the mounting brackets.
3 Using a hoist or an engine support bar across the engine compartment, raise the engine approximately 25 mm, taking care to place any undue strain any the various pipes and hoses.
4 Unscrew the lower nuts and remove the engine mountings. It may be necessary to unbolt the engine mounting brackets from engine to allow this.
5 Fit the new mountings using a reversal of the removal procedure, but make sure that the pegs on the mountings engage with the cut-outs on the brackets.

12 Cylinder head - removal and refitting with engine in car

Note: New cylinder bolts and camshaft sprocket retaining bolts will be required on refitting.

Removal

1 Disconnect the battery negative lead.

2 Drain the cooling system (see Chapter 1).
3 Remove the inlet and exhaust manifolds as described in Chapter 4B.
4 Remove the spark plugs, distributor cap and leads, and rotor arm as described in Chapters 1 and 5.
5 Remove the cooling fan as described in Chapter 3.
6 Disconnect the wiring connectors from the thermostat housing sender units then slacken the retaining clips and disconnect the cooling system hoses from the thermostat housing/coolant elbow assembly.
7 Free the power steering pipe from its retaining clips on the bulkhead (where necessary).
8 Disconnect the crankcase ventilation hose from the camshaft cover.
9 Undo the nuts and remove the washers and seals from the cylinder head cover studs. Lift off the cover and recover the seals **(see illustrations)**.
10 Unscrew the nuts and free the wiring clips from the front of the upper timing chain cover. Unscrew the retaining bolts, noting the position of wiring clip studs, and remove the cover and gasket **(see illustration)**.
11 Using a socket on the crankshaft damper bolt, rotate the crankshaft until the pointer in the aperture on the right-hand side of the cylinder block aligns with the raised mark on the flywheel/driveplate. In this position number 1 (front) cylinder piston is at TDC. The arrows on the camshaft sprockets should be pointing **towards** each other **(see illustrations, including 12.34)**. If not rotate the crankshaft through another complete turn until they do. Do not rotate the crankshaft/camshafts from this point onwards.
12 Undo the bolts and remove the secondary timing chain tensioner from the top of the head **(see illustrations)**.
13 Unscrew the primary timing chain tensioner from the head and recover its sealing ring **(see illustration)**.
14 Slacken and remove the inlet camshaft sprocket bolt whilst preventing the camshaft rotating by holding the rear of the camshaft with a ring spanner. Remove the sprocket and secondary timing chain. Discard the bolt, a new one should be used on refitting.

12.9a Slacken and remove the retaining nuts and washers . . .

12.9b . . . and lift off the seals from the cylinder head cover studs

12.10 Undo the nuts and free the wiring clips from the front of the timing chain upper cover

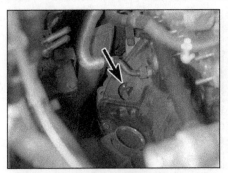

12.11a Align the flywheel/driveplate mark with the pointer on the right-hand side of the cylinder block (arrowed) . . .

12.11b . . . so that the camshaft sprocket timing arrows (arrowed) are pointing directly towards each other

12.12a Unscrew the retaining bolts . . .

12.12b . . . and remove the secondary timing chain tensioner from the head

12.13 Unscrew the primary timing chain tensioner from the right-hand side of the head

12.16 Remove the two smaller retaining bolts (arrowed) securing the cylinder head to the timing chain cover

15 Unscrew the exhaust camshaft bolt whilst retaining the camshaft with a ring spanner and remove the sprocket. Discard the bolt, a new one should be used on refitting.

16 Unscrew the two smaller (8 mm) bolts securing the front of the cylinder head to the timing chain cover **(see illustration)**.

17 Working in the reverse of the sequence shown in **illustration 12.26a**, progressively slacken the fourteen main cylinder head bolts by half a turn at a time, until all bolts can be unscrewed by hand and removed. Discard the bolts, new ones should be used on refitting.

18 Lift off the cylinder head, noting how it engages with the timing chain tensioner blade. Remove the gasket and recover the head locating dowels and store them with the head. **Note:** *On some models it may be*

necessary to lower the engine slightly to enable the head to be removed. If this is the case, remove the engine mountings (see Section 11) and lower the engine taking care not to place excess strain on the various pipes and hoses.

Refitting

19 Thoroughly clean the block and head mating surfaces.

20 Check that Number 1 cylinder is still at top dead centre with the flywheel/driveplate mark and pointer aligned.

21 Check that both location dowels are inserted in the block and apply a smear of suitable sealant (Vauxhall/Opel recommend the use of GM spec 15 03 294 (Part No. 90 001 871) sealant - available from your dealer)

to the areas were the timing cover and cylinder head join **(see illustration)**.

22 Fit the new cylinder head gasket making sure it is the right way up and correctly located on the dowels **(see illustration)**.

23 Make sure the camshafts are positioned so that the sprocket locating notches are uppermost and check that the flywheel/driveplate mark is still correctly aligned.

24 Manoeuvre the cylinder head carefully into position. Feed the timing chain up through the head and locate the head on the dowels, making sure the peg on the front of the head locates correctly with the timing chain guide cut-out **(see illustration)**.

25 Carefully enter the new cylinder head bolts into the holes (*do not drop them in*) and screw in, by hand only, until finger-tight.

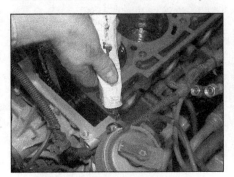

12.21 Apply suitable sealant to the areas where the timing cover joins the cylinder block . . .

12.22 . . . and fit the head gasket making sure it is correctly located on the dowels (arrowed)

12.24 Manoeuvre the cylinder head into position making sure its peg (arrowed) engages correctly with timing chain guide

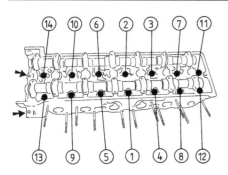

12.26a Cylinder head bolt tightening sequence (two 8 mm bolts also arrowed)

12.26b Tighten the cylinder head bolts first to the specified torque . . .

12.27 . . . and then through the specified angles

12.30 Ensure both camshafts are positioned with their sprocket cutouts (arrowed) uppermost

12.31 Engage the exhaust camshaft with the primary timing chain so that its timing arrow (arrowed) is horizontal and pointing towards the inlet camshaft

12.33 Engage the inlet camshaft and secondary timing chain with the exhaust camshaft . . .

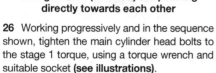

12.34 . . . making sure both sprocket timing arrows (arrowed) are pointing directly towards each other

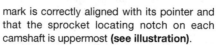

12.35a Tighten the sprocket retaining bolts to the specified torque . . .

12.35b . . . and then through the specified angle

26 Working progressively and in the sequence shown, tighten the main cylinder head bolts to the stage 1 torque, using a torque wrench and suitable socket (see illustrations).

27 Once all the bolts have been tightened to the stage 1 setting, working again in the specified sequence, angle-tighten the bolts through the specified stage 2 angle using a socket and extension bar (see illustration). It is recommended that an angle gauge is used for this stage of the tightening, to ensure accuracy.

28 Leave the bolts to settle for approximately ten minutes then go around and angle-tighten them through the specified stage 3 angle.

29 Refit the two smaller (8 mm) bolts to the front of the cylinder head and tighten them to the specified torque.

30 Make sure that the flywheel/driveplate

mark is correctly aligned with its pointer and that the sprocket locating notch on each camshaft is uppermost (see illustration).

31 Hold the timing chain taut and engage the exhaust camshaft sprocket, positioning the sprocket so that its timing arrow is horizontal and pointing towards the inlet camshaft (see illustration). When the sprocket is correctly engaged with the chain, align the sprocket with the cut-out and slide it onto the camshaft. Fit the new sprocket retaining bolt.

32 Engage the secondary timing chain with the inlet camshaft sprocket.

33 Manoeuvre the inlet sprocket and chain into position and engage it with the exhaust camshaft sprocket so the sprocket timing mark is horizontal and pointing towards the exhaust camshaft (see illustration). When the

sprocket is correctly positioned, align it with the cut-out and slide it onto the camshaft. Fit the new sprocket retaining bolt.

34 With both sprockets in position, check that the flywheel/driveplate mark is correctly aligned with its pointer and that both camshaft sprocket timing marks are horizontal and pointing directly at each other (see illustration). If not, remove the sprocket retaining bolt(s) and alter the position of the sprocket(s) as necessary.

35 Once all the timing marks are correctly positioned, retain the exhaust camshaft with a ring spanner and tighten the sprocket retaining bolt first to the specified stage 1 torque and then through the specified stage 2 angle. Use of an angle gauge is recommended to ensure accuracy (see illustrations).

12.37 Refit the primary timing chain tensioner and tighten to specified torque

12.38a Install the secondary timing chain tensioner then unscrew the grub screw . . .

12.38b . . . and prime the tensioner by pumping it full of oil

46 Refit the cooling fan as described in Chapter 3.
47 Refill the cooling system (see Chapter 1).

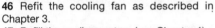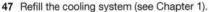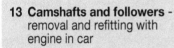

13 Camshafts and followers - removal and refitting with engine in car

Note: New camshaft sprocket retaining bolts will be required on refitting.

Removal

1 Disconnect the battery negative lead.
2 Remove the spark plugs and distributor cap and lead assembly as described in Chapters 1 and 5.
3 Remove the cooling fan as described in Chapter 3.
4 Carry out the operations described in paragraphs 8 to 15 of Section 12.
5 The camshaft bearing caps are numbered for identification purposes; the inlet camshaft caps are numbered 1 to 7, and the exhaust caps 8 to 14, the cylinder head is also numbered to prevent confusion. **Note:** Number 6 and number 9 caps have a dot next to the number to avoid confusion the number should be read with the dot at the bottom.
6 Starting with the exhaust camshaft, evenly and progressively slacken the camshaft bearing cap retaining nuts by one turn at a time to relieve the pressure of the valve springs on the bearing caps gradually and evenly. Once the valve spring pressure has been relieved, remove the nuts and washers **(see illustration)**.

12.40a Fit the spark plug hole seals to the cylinder head . . .

12.40b . . . and fit the main seal to the cylinder head cover

13.6 Unscrew the camshaft bearing cap nuts as described in text

12.41a Apply sealant to the areas where the timing cover joins the cylinder head . . .

12.41b . . . and refit the cylinder head cover

36 Retain the inlet camshaft with a ring spanner and tighten the sprocket retaining bolt first to the specified stage 1 torque and then through the specified stage 2 and stage 3 angles. Use of an angle tightening gauge is recommended to ensure accuracy.
37 Fit a new sealing ring to the primary chain tensioner and screw the tensioner into the cylinder head, tightening it to the specified torque **(see illustration)**.
38 Refit the secondary timing chain tensioner to the top of the head, making sure its oil hole screw is facing forwards. Tighten the tensioner retaining bolts to the specified torque. Unscrew the oil hole grub screw and prime the tensioner by filling it with clean engine using a suitable oil can. Once the tensioner is filled with oil, refit the grub screw and tighten it securely **(see illustrations)**.
39 Fit a new gasket and install the upper timing chain cover. Fit the cover retaining bolts, making sure the wiring clip studs are

correctly positioned, and tighten them to the specified torque. Locate the wiring clips on the studs and securely tighten their retaining nuts.
40 Fit the new spark plug hole seals to the cylinder head, making sure they are the right way up, and fit the seal to the cylinder head cover **(see illustrations)**.
41 Apply a smear of suitable sealant (see paragraph 21) to the areas where the upper timing cover abuts the head the fit the head cover **(see illustrations)**.
42 Fit the seals and washers to the head cover studs and refit the retaining nuts, tightening them to the specified torque.
43 Refit the spark plugs, rotor arm and distributor cap (see Chapters 1 and 5).
44 Reconnect the coolant hoses and wiring connectors to the thermostat housing/coolant elbow. Ensure that the retaining clips are securely tightened.
45 Refit the manifolds (see Chapter 4B).

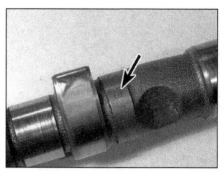

13.7 The camshafts can be identified from the letters stamped on them - inlet camshaft shown is stamped "E" (arrowed)

13.10 Removing a camshaft follower

13.15 Tighten the camshaft bearing cap retaining nuts as described in the text

7 Remove the bearing caps, noting which way around they are fitted, and lift out the exhaust camshaft. **Note:** *The camshafts are marked for identification purposes, the inlet camshaft is stamped with an "E" and the exhaust camshaft is stamped with an "A"* **(see illustration).**

8 Repeat the operations in paragraphs 6 and 7 and remove the inlet camshaft.

9 If the followers are to be removed, obtain twenty four small, clean plastic containers and number them 1 to 24 or alternatively divide a larger container into compartments.

10 Lift the first follower away from the head and store them it in its respective position in the container **(see illustration).** Remove all the remaining followers. **Note:** *Do not interchange the cam followers as the rate of wear will be increased.*

Refitting

11 Lubricate the cam follower bores with clean engine oil and slide each follower back into its original location in the head.

12 Check that Number 1 cylinder is still at top dead centre with the flywheel/driveplate mark and pointer aligned.

13 Lay the inlet camshaft (see paragraph 7) in place on the cylinder head, positioning it so its sprocket locating cut-out is uppermost.

14 Lubricate the camshaft lobes and journals with clean engine oil then refit the bearing caps, making sure they are fitted the correct way around.

15 Fit the washers and retaining nuts, tightening them by hand only. Starting from centre and working outwards, tighten the bearing cap retaining nuts evenly and progressively by half-a-turn at a time, ensuring that the camshaft is pulled squarely down onto the head. Once all the caps are in contact with the head, go around and tighten them first to the specified stage 1 torque setting and then to the specified stage 2 torque **(see illustration).** *Caution: If the retaining nuts are carelessly tightened, the bearing caps will break. The caps are not available separately (they are matched to the head to ensure that the bearing clearances are correct) and can only be purchased complete with a new cylinder head.*

16 Repeat the operations in paragraphs 13 to 15 and install the exhaust camshaft.

17 Refit the camshaft sprockets and associated components as described in paragraphs 30 to 43 of Section 12.

18 Refit the cooling fan (see Chapter 3).

14 Engine components - examination and renovation

Oil pump

Note: *This can be removed with the engine in the car.*

1 Undo the screws and remove the pump cover from the base of the timing chain cover. If the engine is upright, be prepared to catch the oil pump gears as the pump is withdrawn.

2 With a straight edge and feeler blades, check the endfloat of the two gears then check the backlash between the two gears.

3 If any of the clearances are outside the specified tolerances, both gears should be renewed. **Note:** *There are two sizes of oil pump drive gears available, standard and 0.2 mm oversize. If oversize gears are fitted, the timing chain cover will be stamped "0.2" on the left-hand side of the oil pump housing.*

4 On refitting, ensure that the gears are clean and dry and lubricate them with fresh engine oil. Apply a smear of suitable sealant (Vauxhall/Opel recommend the use of GM spec 15 03 166 (Part No. 90 094 714) sealant - available from your dealer) to the oil pump cover sealing surface; do not allow the sealant to contact the gears.

5 Refit the gears and cover and tighten the cover bolts to the specified torque.

Oil pressure relief valve

Note: *This can be removed with the engine in the car.*

6 Wipe clean the area around the pressure relief valve on the base of the timing chain cover.

7 Using circlip pliers, remove the circlip and withdraw the cover, piston (noting which way around it is fitted), spring and spring seat from the cover.

8 Inspect all components for signs of wear or damage and renew as necessary. The cover sealing ring should be renewed as a matter of course.

9 On refitting clean all components and lubricate then with clean engine oil. Fit the spring seat to the spring and slide both components into the timing cover.

10 Fit the piston, making sure it is the correct way around.

11 Fit a new seal to the cover then refit the cover and secure it in position with the circlip.

Oil cooler thermostatic valve

Note: *This can be removed with the engine in the car.*

12 Remove the engine oil filter (Chapter 1).

13 Wipe clean the area around the thermostatic valve on the base of the timing chain cover.

14 Undo the cover bolt and washer and remove the spring, noting which way around it is fitted, and valve.

15 Check components for signs of wear or damage and renew as necessary.

16 On refitting, clean the valve and spring and lubricate them with clean engine oil.

17 Insert the valve and fit the spring, noting that the spring should be fitted with its smaller diameter end facing the valve. Refit the cover bolt and sealing washer and tighten it securely.

Crankshaft

18 Refer to Chapter 2A, Section 14.

Big-end and main bearing shells

19 Refer to Chapter 2A, Section 14.

Cylinder bores

20 Refer to Chapter 2A, Section 14.

Connecting rods

21 Examine the mating faces of the big-end caps to see if they have ever been filed in a mistaken attempt to take up wear. If so, the offending rods must be renewed.

22 Check the alignment of the rods visually, and if all is not well, take the rods to your local agent for checking on a special jig.

Pistons and piston rings

23 Refer to Chapter 2A, Section 14, noting that the pistons can be removed as follows.
24 Noting the correct fitted orientation of the piston on the connecting rod then carefully hook one of the gudgeon pin circlips. Carefully tap out the pin and separate the piston and connecting rod.
25 Fit the piston to the connecting rod noting that the arrow on the piston crown should point towards the front (timing chain end) of the engine and the mark on the connecting rod shaft should face the rear (flywheel/ driveplate end) of the engine **(see illustration)**. Ensure that the piston and rod are correctly positioned then slide in the gudgeon pin. Secure the gudgeon pin in position with new circlips ensuring both clips are correctly located in the piston grooves.

Camshaft

26 With the camshaft removed, examine the bearing surfaces for signs of wear. If the camshaft bearings are worn also examine the cylinder head bearing surfaces, if they are worn the cylinder assembly must be renewed.
27 The camshaft itself should show no marks or scoring on the journal or cam lobe surfaces. If evident, renew the camshaft.

Camshaft followers

28 Examine the follower surfaces for signs of wear and renew if damaged.
29 If the hydraulic valve lifter mechanism of the follower is faulty the follower must also be renewed; it is not possible to overhaul the lifter.

Timing chains and tensioners

30 Examine the teeth on the camshaft and crankshaft sprockets for any sign of wear or damage such as chipped, hooked or missing teeth. If there is any sign of wear or damage on either sprocket, all sprockets and both timing chains should be renewed as a set.
31 Inspect the links of the timing chain for signs of wear or damage on the rollers. The extent of wear can be judged by checking the amount by which the chain can be bent sideways; a new chain will have very little sideways movement. If there is an excessive amount of side play in the timing chain, it must be renewed. It is a sensible precaution to renew the timing chain, if the engine has covered a high mileage or if it has been noted that the chain has sounded noisy with the engine running.
32 Examine the chain guides for signs of wear or damage to the their chain contact faces, renewing any which are badly marked.
33 The condition of the tensioners can only be judged in comparison to a new component. Renew the tensioner(s) if there is any doubt about their condition.

Flywheel/driveplate

34 Refer to Chapter 2A, Section 14.

Cylinder block

35 Refer to Chapter 2A, Section 14.

15 Cylinder head - overhaul

Note: *To minimise wear, it is essential that the valves and associated components are refitted in their original locations. Do this by storing them in a partitioned container or in numbered bags as they are removed to prevent them being interchanged.*
1 Remove the camshafts and followers as described in Section 13.
2 Remove the valves by compressing the valve spring with a suitable valve spring compressor and lifting out the collets. Release the compressor and remove the valve spring retainer, spring and spring seat.
3 Remove the valves, storing them in their original fitted locations to ensure correct refitting.
4 Lever the valve stem oil seals from the valve guides.
5 With the valves removed, clean the carbon from them and from the combustion chambers and ports. The piston crowns can also be cleaned at this stage but take care not to allow carbon to drop between the pistons and bores. To prevent this, clean two pistons at a time with them at the top of their bores and press a little grease between the pistons and bores. Seal off the remaining cylinders, and oil and water channels with paper. After cleaning, move the pistons down the bore and wipe out the grease which will contain the particles of carbon.
6 Examine the heads of the valves and the valve seats for pitting and burning. If the pitting on valve and seat is slight it can be removed by grinding the valves and seats together with coarse, and then fine, valve grinding paste. If the pitting is deep, the valves will have to be reground on a valve grinding machine and the seats will have to be recut with a valve seat cutter. Both these operations are a job for your local Vauxhall/Opel dealer or motor engineering specialist.
7 Check the valve guides for wear by inserting the valve in the guide and attempting to move the valve from side to side. If the specified play is exceeded the valve guides should be renewed by a Vauxhall/Opel dealer.
8 When grinding slightly-pitted valves and valve seats with carborundum paste, proceed as follows. Apply a little coarse grinding paste to the valve head, and using a suction-type valve grinding tool, grind the valve into its seat with a rotary movement, lifting the valve and turning it from time to time. A light spring under the valve head will assist in this operation. When a dull matt, even surface finish appears on both the valve and the valve seat, clean off the coarse paste. Repeat the

grinding operation with a fine grinding paste until a continuous ring of light grey matt finish appears on both valve and valve seat. Carefully clean off all traces of grinding paste.
9 Check the valve springs for damage and if possible compare their length with that of a new spring. Renew them if necessary.
10 Using a straight edge and feeler blade check the joint face of the cylinder head for distortion. If greater than the maximum amount given in the Specifications it may be possible to have the head machined flat. Consult a Vauxhall/Opel dealer if necessary.
11 Commence reassembly by refitting the spring seats and pressing the valve stem oil seals onto the guides.
12 To fit the valves, lubricate the valve stem with engine oil and insert it in the valve guide.
13 Refit the spring and spring retainer, then use the valve spring compressor to compress the spring until the collets can be fitted in position in the slots in the valve stem. Release the compressor slowly, and check that the collets are seated correctly.
14 After fitting all the valves, tap the tops of the springs lightly to ensure correct seating of the collets.
15 Refit the camshafts and followers as described in Section 13.

16 Engine - complete reassembly

Note: *New cylinder head bolts, camshaft sprocket retaining bolts, flywheel/driveplate retaining bolts and a vibration damper bolt will be required.*
1 Place the cylinder block upside-down on the bench and wipe clean the main bearing shell seats.
2 Press the main bearing shells onto the crankcase, making sure that the tags engage with the special grooves. Note that the rear shell incorporates thrust flanges.
3 Lubricate the shells with clean engine oil.
4 Carefully lower the crankshaft into the crankcase. Rotate it several times and check that it is correctly seated by gently tapping the webs with a mallet.
5 Check that the crankshaft endfloat is as given in the Specifications by either using a feeler blade between the flanged main bearing shell and the crankshaft thrust face, or by using a dial test indicator on the crankshaft rear flange.
6 Clean the backs of the lower main bearing shells and the caps, then press them into position. Lubricate the shells with clean oil.
7 Apply a suitable sealant to the areas of the cylinder block rear main bearing cap surface shown in **illustration 16.7** (Vauxhall/Opel recommend the use of GM spec 15 03 166 (Part No. 90 094 714) sealant - available from your dealer).
8 Apply a suitable sealant to the mating surface of the rear main bearing cap

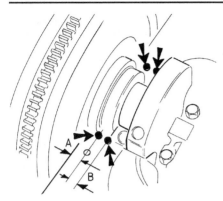

**16.7 Apply sealant to the four points
shown of the cylinder block
rear mating surface**

A = 12 ± 0.5 mm   B = 12 ± 0.5 mm

(Vauxhall/Opel recommend the use of GM spec 15 04 201 (Part No. 90 350 544) sealant - available from your dealer).

9 Refit all the main bearing caps and install the bearing cap bolts. Tighten the bolts by hand then tighten them evenly and progressively to the specified torque setting.

10 Rotate the crankshaft and check that it turns freely with no signs of binding or tight spots.

11 Lubricate the lips of the new crankshaft rear oil seal with grease. Ease the seal over the crankshaft end, making sure its sealing lip is facing inwards, and press it into the rear main bearing cap until flush.

12 Lay the block on its side and lubricate the cylinder bores and crankshaft journals liberally with oil.

13 Space the piston rings around the pistons so that their end gaps are 180° apart. In the case of the oil scraper ring, offset the gaps in the upper and lower rails by 25 to 50 mm to right and left of the end gap of the centre section.

14 Clean the backs of the big-end bearing shells and the caps and connecting rods, then press the shells into position.

15 Turn the crankshaft so that the journal for No 1 cylinder is at bottom dead centre.

16 Fit a piston ring compressor to No 1 piston then insert it into No 1 cylinder with the arrow on the piston crown pointing towards the front of the engine.

17 Using the handle of a hammer, tap the piston through the ring compressor while guiding the connecting rod onto the journal.

18 Fit the big-end bearing cap, ensuring it is fitted the correct way around, then insert the big-end bearing bolts. Tighten the bolts evenly and progressively to the specified torque setting.

19 Check that the crankshaft turns freely taking into consideration the resistance of the piston rings.

20 Repeat the procedure given in paragraphs 15 to 19 for the remaining pistons.

21 Turn the block upside down on the bench.

22 Where removed, refit the Woodruff key to the crankshaft cutout. Making sure they are the correct way around, fit the timing chain sprocket and oil pump/distributor drive gear. Tap the sprocket and gear into position until they are tighten against the crankshaft shoulder then fit the primary timing chain.

23 Ensure that the locating pin is in position and fit the timing chain guide, making sure the chain is correctly routed up through the guide. Apply a suitable locking compound to the reads of the guide retaining bolt and tighten it to the specified torque.

24 Slide the timing chain tensioner onto its pivot pin and secure it in position with the retaining clip.

25 Using a suitable screwdriver carefully lever the oil seal out from the front of the timing chain cover. Fit the new seal, making sure its sealing lip is facing inwards, and press it into position until it is flush with the cover.

26 Insert the timing chain cover locating dowels to the block and fit the new gaskets.

27 Fit the timing chain cover and insert its retaining bolts, making sure they are fitted in the correct locations. Tighten the bolts to the specified torque.

28 Refit the inlet pipe to the base of the timing cover using a new gasket. Apply a suitable locking compound to the retaining bolts and tighten them to the specified torque.

29 Ensure that the sump and block surfaces are clean and dry and fit a new seal to the sump groove.

30 Apply a smear of suitable sealant (Vauxhall/Opel recommend the use of GM spec 15 03 294 (Part No. 90 001 851) sealant - available from your dealer) to the areas were the timing cover and rear main bearing cap abut the block.

31 Offer up the sump and refit its retaining bolts, making sure they are fitted in their original locations. Tighten all bolts by hand then go around and tighten them to the specified torque setting.

32 Refit the water pump using a new gasket and insert its retaining bolts in the correct locations. Tighten the retaining bolts to the specified torque.

33 Fit the flywheel/driveplate to the crankshaft and screw in the new retaining bolts; on models with an automatic transmission do not forget to fit the spacer and washer between the crankshaft and driveplate. Prevent rotation using the tool shown in **illustration 9.17a** then tighten the retaining bolts first to the specified stage 1 torque setting and then through the specified stage 2 angle. For accuracy, it is recommended that an angle-tighten gauge is used. Leave the locking tool in position.

34 Where necessary, fit the vibration damper to the hub and secure it in position with the roll pin.

35 Carefully slide the vibration damper assembly into position, taking great care not to damage the oil seal lip, and align its slot with the crankshaft key.

36 Lubricate the threads of the new vibration damper bolt with clean engine oil and allow excess oil to drip off the bolt. Insert the bolt and tighten it to the specified stage 1 torque setting. Then angle-tighten the bolt through the specified stage 2 angle and finally through the specified stage 3 angle. To ensure accuracy, it is recommended that an angle-tightening gauge is used. Once the bolt is tighten remove the locking tool from the flywheel/driveplate.

37 Refit the auxiliary drivebelt pulley to the water pump and tighten its retaining bolts to the specified torque and then through the various angles. Where necessary refit the belt idler pulleys and securely tighten their retaining bolts.

38 Ensure that the mating surfaces are clean and refit the crankshaft pulley to the vibration damper, tightening its retaining bolts to the specified torque.

39 Thoroughly clean the block and head mating surfaces.

40 Rotate the crankshaft and position Number 1 cylinder at top dead centre, aligning the flywheel/driveplate mark with the pointer on the right-hand side of the cylinder block.

41 Check that both location dowels are inserted in the block and apply a smear of suitable sealant (Vauxhall/Opel recommend the use of GM spec 15 03 294 (Part No. 90 001 871) sealant - available from your dealer) to the areas were the timing cover and cylinder head join.

42 Fit the new cylinder head gasket making sure it is the right way up and correctly located on the dowels.

43 Make sure the camshafts are correctly positioned so that the sprocket locating notches are uppermost and check that the flywheel/driveplate mark is still correctly aligned.

44 Manoeuvre the cylinder head carefully into position. Feed the timing chain up through the head and locate the head on the dowels, making sure the peg on the front of the head locates correctly with the timing chain guide cut-out.

45 Carefully enter the new cylinder head bolts into the holes (*do not drop them in*) and screw in, by hand only, until finger-tight.

46 Working progressively and in the sequence shown in **illustration 12.26a**, tighten the main cylinder head bolts to their stage 1 torque setting, using a torque wrench and suitable socket.

47 Once all the bolts have been tightened to their stage 1 setting, working again in the specified sequence, angle-tighten the bolts through the specified stage 2 angle using a socket and extension bar. It is recommended that an angle-measuring gauge is used during this stage of the tightening, to ensure accuracy.

48 Leave the bolts to settle for approximately ten minutes then go around and angle-tighten them through the specified stage 3 angle.

49 Refit the two smaller (8 mm) bolts to the

front of the cylinder head and tighten them to the specified torque.

50 Make sure that the flywheel/driveplate mark is correctly aligned with its pointer and that the sprocket locating notch on each camshaft is uppermost.

51 Hold the timing chain taut and engage the exhaust camshaft sprocket, positioning the sprocket so that its timing arrow is horizontal and pointing towards the inlet camshaft. When the sprocket is correctly engaged with the chain, align the sprocket with the cut-out and slide it onto the camshaft. Fit the new sprocket retaining bolt.

52 Engage the secondary timing chain with the inlet camshaft sprocket.

53 Manoeuvre the inlet sprocket and chain into position and engage it with the exhaust camshaft sprocket so the sprocket timing mark is horizontal and pointing towards the exhaust camshaft. When the sprocket is correctly positioned, align it with the cut-out and slide it onto the camshaft. Fit the new sprocket retaining bolt.

54 With both sprockets in position, check that the flywheel/driveplate mark is correctly aligned with its pointer and that both camshaft sprocket timing marks are horizontal and pointing directly at each other **(see illustration 12.34)**. If not, remove the sprocket retaining bolt(s) and alter the position of the sprocket(s) as necessary.

55 Once all the timing marks are correctly positioned, retain the exhaust camshaft with a ring spanner and tighten the sprocket retaining bolt first to the specified stage 1 torque and then through the specified stage 2 and stage 3 angles. Use of an angle tightening gauge is recommended to ensure accuracy.

56 Retain the inlet camshaft with a ring spanner and tighten the sprocket retaining bolt first to the specified stage 1 torque and then through the specified stage 2 and stage 3 angles. Use of an angle tightening gauge is recommended to ensure accuracy.

57 Fit a new sealing ring to the primary chain tensioner and screw the tensioner into the cylinder head, tightening it to the specified torque.

58 Refit the secondary timing chain tensioner to the top of the head, making sure its oil hole screw is facing forwards. Tighten the tensioner retaining bolts to the specified torque. Unscrew the oil hole grub screw and prime the tensioner by filling it with clean

engine using a suitable oil can. Once the tensioner is filled with oil, refit the grub screw and tighten it securely.

59 Fit a new gasket and install the upper timing chain cover. Fit the cover retaining bolts, making sure the wiring clip studs are correctly positioned, and tighten them to the specified torque. Locate the wiring clips on the studs and securely tighten their retaining nuts.

60 Fit the new spark plug hole seals to the cylinder head, making sure they are the right way up, and fit the seal to the cylinder head cover.

61 Apply a smear of suitable sealant (see paragraph 41) to the areas where the upper timing cover abuts the head the fit the head cover.

62 Fit the seals and washers to the head cover studs and refit the retaining nuts, tightening them to the specified torque.

63 Refit the dipstick.

64 Refit the oil pressure switch and tighten it to the specified torque.

65 Install all the ancillary items listed in Section 8.

17 Engine ancillaries - refitting

Refer to Section 8 and refit the listed components, with reference to the Chapters indicated where necessary.

18 Engine - refitting

Refitting the engine is a reversal of the removal procedure given in Section 6, but in addition note the following points:

a) Lightly grease the gearbox input shaft or torque converter spigot as applicable (see Chapter 7A or 7B).

b) On automatic transmission models, check that the torque converter is fully engaged with the transmission oil pump with reference to Chapter 7B.

c) Refill the engine with the specified quantity and grade of oil (see Chapter 1).

d) On manual gearbox models, adjust the clutch cable with reference to Chapter 6.

e) Adjust the accelerator cable, and where necessary, the automatic transmission kickdown cable and the cruise control cable as described in Chapters 4B, 7B and 12 (as applicable).

f) Refill the cooling system (see Chapter 1).

19 Engine - initial start-up after major overhaul or repair

1 Make sure that the battery is fully charged and that all lubricants, coolant and fuel are replenished.

2 Double check all fittings and connections.

3 Disconnect the ignition HT lead from the distributor and connect it to a sound earth point using a suitable clip. Turn the engine over on the starter motor until the oil pressure warning light is extinguished, or until oil pressure is recorded on the gauge. This will ensure that the engine is not starved of oil during the critical few minutes running after initial start-up. The fuel system will also be primed during this operation.

4 Reconnect the HT lead to the distributor. Start the engine.

5 As soon as the engine fires and runs, keep it going at a fast tickover only (no faster) and bring it up to normal working temperature.

6 As the engine warms up there will be odd smells and some smoke from parts getting hot and burning off oil deposits. The signs to look for are leaks of water or oil, which will be obvious if serious. Check also the exhaust pipe and manifold connections as these do not always find their exact gas tight position until the warmth and vibration have acted on them, and it is almost certain that they will need tightening further. This should be done, of course, with the engine stopped.

7 When normal running temperature has been reached. Stop the engine and wait a few minutes to see if any lubricant or coolant is dripping out when the engine is stationary.

8 During the initial period that the engine is running it is not unusual for the hydraulic valve lifters to be noisy, but this should gradually disappear, certainly within a few miles driving on the road.

9 If many new internal components have been fitted, it will be beneficial to change the engine oil and oil filter after the first 600 miles (1000 km).

Notes

Chapter 3
Cooling, heating and air conditioning systems

Contents

Air conditioning system - description and precautions 15
Air conditioning system components - removal and refitting 16
Antifreeze mixture - general . . . . .See 'Weekly Checks'
Coolant pump - removal and refitting 8
Cooling fan/alternator drivebelt - renewal and adjustment 9
Cooling system - draining, flushing and refilling 2
Electric auxiliary fan - removal and refitting 4
Expansion tank - removal and refitting 10
General description 1

Heater control panel - removal and refitting 12
Heater fan motor 14
Heater matrix - removal and refitting 13
Radiator - removal and refitting 3
Temperature gauge sender unit - removal and refitting 11
Thermo-viscous cooling fan - removal and refitting 7
Thermostat - removal and refitting 5
Thermostat - testing 6

Degrees of difficulty

| Easy, suitable for novice with little experience | | Fairly easy, suitable for beginner with some experience | 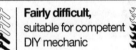 | Fairly difficult, suitable for competent DIY mechanic | | Difficult, suitable for experienced DIY mechanic | | Very difficult, suitable for expert DIY or professional | 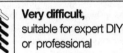 |

Specifications

System type

OHC 4-cylinder engines	Pressurised, with downflow radiator, belt-driven thermo-viscous cooling fan, centrifugal water pump driven by timing belt, bypass thermostat, expansion tank either remote or built into radiator header tank
CIH and DOHC six cylinder engines	Pressurised, with crossflow radiator, auxiliary belt driven, thermostatically controlled thermo-viscous cooling fan, electric auxiliary cooling fan, centrifugal water pump driven by auxiliary belt, bypass thermostat and remote expansion tank.

General

Pressure cap opening pressure	1.2 to 1.5 bar
System nominal boiling temperature	125°C
Electric auxiliary cooling fan thermo-switch:	
Switch on temperature	105°C
Switch off temperature	100°C

Thermostat

Opening commences	92°C
Fully open	107°C

Coolant

Type	Ethylene glycol based antifreeze, to GM spec GME L 6368, and soft water.
Capacity:	
OHC 4 cylinder engines	6.4 litres
CIH engines:	
Manual transmission:	
With air conditioning	11.3 litres
Without air conditioning	10.2 litres
Automatic transmission:	
With air conditioning	11.2 litres
Without air conditioning	10.1 litres
DOHC 6 cylinder engines:	
Manual transmission:	
With air conditioning	10.4 litres
Without air conditioning	10.0 litres
Automatic transmission:	
With air conditioning	10.2 litres
Without air conditioning	9.8 litres

Torque wrench settings

	Nm	lbf ft
Coolant pump:		
OHC engine	25	19
DOHC engine	15	11
CIH engine	15	11
Temperature gauge sender unit	10	7
Thermostat housing cover:		
OHC engine	15	11
DOHC engine	20	15
CIH engine	8	6
Cooling fan pulley (OHC engine only)	8	6
Thermo-viscous cooling fan	50	37

1 General description

The cooling system comprises a downflow radiator, belt-driven thermo-viscous cooling fan, timing belt/auxiliary belt-driven water pump (depending on engine), thermostat, and expansion tank. The expansion tank is either incorporated in the radiator header tank or of the plastic type located on the right-hand side of the engine compartment.

The system functions as follows: cold water from the water pump is forced around the cylinder block and head, then through a bypass hose back to the inlet side of the water pump. Additional circulation occurs through the car heater matrix. When the engine reaches a predetermined temperature, the thermostat starts to open and the coolant then circulates through the radiator to provide extra cooling. The thermo-viscous cooling fan is controlled by the temperature of air behind the radiator. When the predetermined temperature is reached, an internal valve opens and allows a fluid drive system to turn the fan blades. At lower temperatures the drive is reduced accordingly. The fan is therefore only operated when required, and compared with direct drive type fans, represents a considerable improvement in fuel economy, drivebelt wear and fan noise.

2 Cooling system - draining, flushing and refilling

Draining

1 Unscrew the filler cap from the expansion tank or radiator (as applicable). If the engine is hot, place a thick cloth over the cap before removing it slowly, otherwise there is a danger of scalding.
2 Place a suitable container beneath the right-hand side of the radiator.
3 Loosen the clip and disconnect the bottom hose from the radiator. Drain the coolant into the container.
4 Dispose of the old coolant, or keep it in a covered container if it is to be re-used.

Flushing

5 Flushing should not be necessary unless periodic renewal of the coolant has been neglected, or unless plain water has been used as a coolant. In either case the coolant will appear rusty and dark in colour. Flushing is then required and should be carried out as follows.
6 Drain the system as described previously.
7 Start by flushing the expansion tank where fitted. The heater may be flushed by disconnecting the hoses on the bulkhead and then inserting a garden hose.
8 Flush the radiator by inserting the garden hose into the top of the radiator and run the water until it runs clear from the bottom outlet. If, after a reasonable period the water still does not run clear, the radiator may be flushed with a proprietary cleaning agent.
9 Reverse flush the engine by removing the thermostat (Section 5) and inserting the garden hose until water flows clear from the bottom hose. Where fitted, also unscrew the cylinder block drain plug located on the front left-hand side of the engine, and allow the water to run clear.
10 In severe cases of contamination the radiator should be removed, inverted and flushed in the reverse direction to normal flow. Shake the radiator gently while doing this, to dislodge any deposits.

Refilling

11 Reconnect the hoses and tighten the clips. Where applicable, refit and tighten the cylinder block drain plug.
12 On carburettor engines, disconnect the warm air duct to provide access to the thermostat housing.
13 Disconnect the wiring and unscrew the temperature sensor from the top of the thermostat housing (see illustration).

2.13 Temperature sensor on thermostat housing - OHC engine

14 On fuel injection engines, also disconnect the coolant hose from the bottom of the throttle housing.
15 Pour the specified coolant into the radiator or expansion tank (as applicable) until it flows from the temperature sensor hole, then refit and tighten the sensor and reconnect the wiring.
16 Refit the warm air duct on carburettor engines.
17 On fuel injection engines, continue to add coolant until it runs out of the throttle housing hose, then reconnect the hose.
18 On all engines, continue to add coolant until it reaches the "cold" level mark. On the radiator this is either indicated by a level plate in the filler neck or by being 50.0 mm (2.0 in) below the top edge of the filler neck. On the remote expansion tank, a cold level mark is provided.
19 Refit the filler cap.
20 Start the engine and run it at a fast idle speed until it reaches normal operating temperature, indicated by the thermostat opening and the top hose becoming hotter when touched. Watch for any signs of overheating, and check for leaks.
21 Stop the engine and allow it to cool for two or three hours, then recheck the coolant level and if necessary top-up to the 'COLD' level. Refit the filler cap.

3 Radiator - removal and refitting

Removal

1 Where applicable, remove the engine undertray.
2 Drain the cooling system as desscribed in Section 2. Disconnect and remove the radiator top hose from the radiator and thermostat housing (see illustration).

6 cylinder DOHC engine only

3 On vehicles where the engine oil cooler is integral with the radiator, refer to the relevant Part of Chapter 2 and drain the engine oil. Unbolt the unions and disconnect the supply and return pipes from the engine oil cooler. Cover the open ports to prevent the ingress of contaminants.

3.2 Radiator top hose connection - OHC engine

3.4 Unplug the harness cabling from auxiliary cooling fan temperature switch

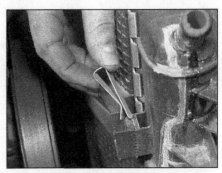

3.6a Removing a fan shroud spring clip

3.6b Removing the fan shroud

3.7 Unscrew the union nuts and detach the transmission fluid cooler pipes

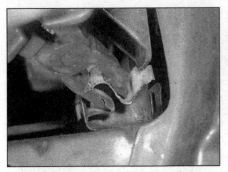

3.9 Radiator spring clip mountings

3.10 Removing the radiator - DOHC 24 valve engine shown

unions to the specified torque, then refer to the relevant Part of Chapter 2 and refill the engine with the correct grade and quantity of oil.

4 Electric auxiliary fan - removal and refitting

Removal

1 Refer to Chapter 3 and remove the radiator.
2 Unplug the fan supply cabling at the connector.
3 Remove the three screws that secure the auxiliary fan assembly to its mounting bracket.
4 Lift the auxiliary fan out of the engine bay, taking care not to damage the cooling fins of air conditioning heat exchanger radiator (where fitted).

Refitting

5 Refit the fan by following the removal procedure in reverse, noting the following points (where applicable):

a) *On completion, refill the engine with the correct quantity and concentration of coolant.*
b) *On engines fitted with an oil cooler , refill the engine with correct grade and quantity of oil, with reference to the relevant Part of Chapter 2.*
c) *On vehicles fitted with an automatic transmission fluid cooler, refer to Chapter 1 and if necessary, replenish the automatic transmission fluid.*

5 Thermostat - removal and refitting

Removal

1 Drain the cooling system as described in Section 2.
2 On carburettor engines, disconnect the warm air duct to provide access to the thermostat housing.

---

4 Unplug the harness cabling from auxiliary cooling fan temperature switch **(see illustration)**.
5 Refer to the relevant Part of Chapter 4 and remove the air inlet hose from the throttle body and air cleaner.

All engines

6 Pull out the upper clips and release the cooling fan shroud from the slots in the bottom of the radiator. The shroud may now be positioned over the cooling fan blades, however for additional working room unclip the engine wiring harness and completely remove the shroud **(see illustrations)**.
7 On automatic transmission models, place a container beneath the radiator, then unscrew the union nuts and disconnect the fluid cooler pipes from the radiator **(see illustration)**. Drain the fluid and plug the pipes to prevent entry of dust and dirt.

8 Where applicable disconnect the expansion tank hose from the right-hand side of the radiator.
9 Squeeze together and remove the spring clips retaining the rubber mountings on each side of the radiator **(see illustration)**.
10 Lift the radiator straight up from the side and bottom mountings and withdraw it from the engine compartment **(see illustration)**.
11 Check the side and bottom rubber mountings and renew them if necessary. If a new radiator is being fitted, transfer the side mountings to the new unit.

Refitting

12 Refitting is a reversal of removal. Refill the cooling system as described in Section 2 . On automatic transmission models, tighten the fluid cooler unions to the specified torque , and also top-up the transmission fluid level. Where applicable, tighten the engine oil cooler

5.3 Loosen the clip and disconnect the top hose from the thermostat housing cover

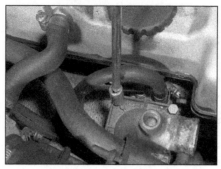

5.4a Unscrew the bolts . . .

5.4b . . .and remove the thermostat housing cover - 6 cylinder engine shown

5.4c Removing the thermostat and housing cover - OHC engine shown

5.5a On 6 -cylinder engines, prise the rubber O-ring from the housing . . .

5.5b . . . and remove the thermostat

3 Loosen the clip and disconnect the top hose from the thermostat housing cover **(see illustration)**.

4 Mark the cover in relation to the housing, then unscrew the bolts and remove the cover . On OHC engines, the thermostat is integral with the cover **(see illustrations)**.

5 On 6 -cylinder engines, prise the rubber O-ring from the housing and remove the thermostat **(see illustrations)**. On OHC engines prise the rubber O-ring from the cover.

6 On OHC engines, it is recommended that the thermostat should not be separated from the cover, as they are supplied new as one unit.

7 Clean the mating faces of the cover and housing, and obtain a new rubber O-ring.

Refitting

8 Refitting is a reversal of removal. Refill the cooling system as described in Section 2.

6 Thermostat - testing

1 A rough test of the thermostat may be made by suspending it with a piece of string in a saucepan full of water. Bring the water to the boil and check that the thermostat opens. If not, renew it.

2 If a thermometer is available, the precise opening temperature of the thermostat may be determined and compared with that given in the Specifications.

3 A thermostat which fails to close as the water cools must also be renewed.

7 Thermo-viscous cooling fan - removal and refitting

Removal

1 On carburettor engines disconnect the warm air duct and move it to one side.

2 If required, the cooling fan shroud may be moved out of the way. Pull out the upper clips, unclip the wiring harness, and lift the shroud towards the cylinder head, over the fan blades.

OHC and CIH (except 2.6 litre) engines

3 Using two open-ended spanners hold the hub stationary then unscrew the fan nut

7.3 Removing the thermo-viscous fan - OHC and CIH (except 2.6) engines

noting that it has a left-hand thread. Remove the cooling fan **(see illustration)**. **Note:** *Spanners specifically designed for the removal of viscous-coupled fans may be purchased from automobile accessory shops.*

DOHC and 2.6 litre CIH engines

4 Using an open-ended spanner, hold the hub stationary, then using a wrench and hex bit, slacken and withdraw the Allen bolt from the centre of the hub. Unscrew the fan from the water pump spindle, noting that it has a left-hand thread. **Note:** *Spanners specifically designed for the removal of viscous-coupled fans may be purchased from automobile accessory shops.*

5 The viscous-coupled clutch unit may be removed from the fan by slackening and removing the three retaining screws.

Refitting

6 Refitting is a reversal of removal.

8 Coolant pump - removal and refitting

OHC engines

Removal

1 Remove the thermo-viscous cooling fan (Section 7) and auxiliary drivebelt (Section 9).

2 Remove the radiator (Section 3).

3 Remove the screws and lift auxiliary drivebelt pulley from the cooling fan hub.

4 Unclip and remove the timing belt covers.

8.9 Removing the water pump - OHC engine shown

8.11a Twisting the timing cover section from the plate (arrowed) on the water pump - OHC engine shown

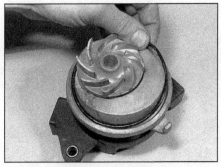

8.10 Prise the rubber O-ring from groove in the water pump - OHC engine shown

8.11b Water pump with timing cover section removed - OHC engine shown

5 Turn the engine with a spanner on the crankshaft pulley bolt until the mark on the camshaft sprocket is aligned with the pointer on the top of the rear timing belt cover. Also align the notch in the crankshaft pulley with the pointer on the lower part of the rear timing belt cover.

6 Using an Allen key loosen the three bolts securing the water pump to the block.

7 Unscrew and remove the bolt securing the water pump section of the timing cover to the oil pump housing.

8 Rotate the water pump body anti-clockwise. Release the timing belt from the water pump sprocket and tie it loosely to one side.

9 Unscrew and remove the three securing bolts and washers, and withdraw the water pump from the block **(see illustration)**.

10 Prise the rubber O-ring from the groove in the water pump **(see illustration)**.

11 If a new water pump is being fitted, transfer the timing cover section to the new pump. To do this, engage the two cut-outs and twist off the timing cover section **(see illustrations)**. Similarly fit the cover to the new water pump.

Refitting

12 Commence refitting by smearing silicon grease or equivalent to the surfaces of the water pump in contact with the block. If this precaution is not taken the water pump may seize in the block.

13 Apply the grease to the rubber O-ring and locate it in the groove.

14 Locate the water pump in the block with the timing cover projections correctly seated. Insert the securing bolts and washers loosely.

15 Engage the timing belt with the water pump sprocket. Turn the water pump clockwise to tension it. Complete the tensioning procedure with reference to Chapter 1, making sure that the timing marks are correctly aligned. Tighten the water pump securing bolts to the specified torque.

16 Insert and tighten the bolt securing the timing cover to the oil pump housing.

17 Refit the timing belt covers.

18 Refit the drivebelt pulley to the cooling fan hub and tighten the screws.

19 Refit the radiator (Section 3).

20 Refit the alternator/fan drivebelt (see Section 9) and the thermo-viscous cooling fan (see Section 7).

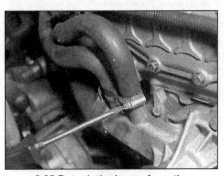

8.25 Detach the hoses from the coolant pump ports

6-cyl DOHC and 2.6 litre CIH engines

Removal

21 Remove the retaining screws and lower the engine undertray away from the underside of the vehicle.

22 Refer to Section 3 and remove the radiator and cooling fan shroud.

23 Refer to Section 7 and remove the thermo-viscous cooling fan from the coolant pump.

24 With reference to the relevant Part of Chapter 2, remove the auxiliary drivebelt.

25 Slacken the clips and detach the hoses from the coolant pump ports, noting their fitted positions **(see illustration)**.

26 On vehicles with air conditioning, the auxiliary drivebelt tensioner pulley obstructs the lower right hand coolant pump retaining bolt; to remove the tensioner pulley and hub, refer to Chapters 2, Part A or B (as applicable) and remove the alternator/power steering pump mounting bracket from the engine block.

27 With reference to Chapter 2 Part B or C as applicable, and carry out the following:

a) Slacken and withdraw the screws, then remove the drivebelt pulley from the crankshaft vibration damper.

b) Remove the vibration damper from the crankshaft flange - **Note:** The crankshaft bolt must be renewed after removal and is tightened to a very high torque setting.

28 Progressively slacken and remove the water pump retaining bolts. Note that the bolts are of different lengths; make a note of the fitted position of each bolt to ensure correct refitting **(see illustration)**

29 Lift the coolant pump away from the engine and recover the seal **(see illustrations)**.

Refitting

30 Thoroughly clean the mating surfaces of the coolant pump and cylinder block, then refit the pump by following the removal procedure in reverse, noting the following points:

a) Fit a new seal to the coolant pump.

b) Tighten the coolant pump retaining bolts progressively to the specified torque.

8.28 Removing the water pump retaining bolts

8.29a Lift the coolant pump away from the engine . . .

8.29b . . . and recover the seal

9.4 Checking the tension of the drivebelt

c) Refit and tension the auxiliary drivebelt according to the information given in Chapter 2 Part B or C as applicable.
d) On completion, refill the cooling system with the specified quantity of coolant.

CIH engines (except 2.6 litre)

Removal

31 Where applicable, remove the retaining screws and lower the engine undertray away from the underside of the vehicle.
32 With reference to Section 3 , remove the cooling fan shroud from the radiator.
33 Refer to Section 7 and remove the thermo-viscous cooling fan from the coolant pump.
34 With reference to the relevant Part of Chapter 2, carry out the following:

a) Remove the oil pump/alternator auxiliary drivebelt.
b) On vehicles with air conditioning, remove the refrigerant compressor auxiliary drivebelt.
c) Remove the auxiliary drivebelt pulley from the crankshaft. **Caution: Be prepared for an amount of oil loss from the crankshaft oil seal as the pulley is removed; place a suitable container under the shaft to catch spillage and pad the surrounding area with absorbent rags.**

35 Slacken the clips and detach the hoses from the coolant pump ports, carefully noting their fitted positions.
36 Progressively slacken and remove the water pump retaining bolts. Note that the bolts are of different lengths; make a note of the fitted position of each bolt to ensure correct refitting.
37 Lift the coolant pump away from the engine and recover the seal.

Refitting

38 Thoroughly clean the mating surfaces of the coolant pump and cylinder block, then refit the pump by following the removal procedure in reverse, noting the following points:

a) Fit a new seal to the coolant pump.
b) Insert and then tighten the coolant pump retaining bolts progressively to the

specified torque. **Caution: Ensure that the bolts are fitted in the correct positions.**
c) Refit the coolant hoses and tighten the clips securely, taking care not to overtighten them. **Caution: Ensure that the hoses are connected to the correct ports on the coolant pump, according to the notes made during removal.**
d) Refit and tension the auxiliary drivebelt(s) according to the information given in Chapter 2 Part B or C (as applicable).
e) On completion, refill the cooling system with the specified quantity of coolant.

9 Cooling fan/alternator drivebelt - renewal and adjustment

OHC engines

1 Where applicable, remove the power steering pump/oil pump drivebelt with reference to Chapter 1, Section 6.
2 It may be necessary to disconnect the warm air duct (carburettor engines) or throttle housing air duct (fuel injection engines) to improve access to the alternator.
3 Loosen the alternator pivot and adjustment link bolts, swivel the alternator towards the engine, and slip the drivebelt off the alternator, cooling fan, and crankshaft pulleys. Ease the drivebelt off over the cooling fan blades.
4 Locate the new drivebelt on the pulleys, then lever out the alternator to tension it. It will help if the adjustment link bolt is initially slightly tightened so that the alternator remains in its tensioned position. With correct adjustment the drivebelt should move approximately 13.0 mm (0.5 in) under firm finger or thumb pressure mid-way between the alternator and crankshaft pulleys **(see illustration)**.
5 Tighten the alternator pivot and adjustment link bolts.

CIH engines

6 Where applicable, remove the power steering pump/oil pump drivebelt with reference to Chapter 10 .

7 Slacken the tensioner block adjustment nuts to release the tension in the drivebelt, then carefully slide the belt off the drive pulleys and ease it off over the cooling fan blades.
8 Tighten the tensioner block locknut..

DOHC engines

9 Refer to the information given in Chapter 2 Part C.

10 Expansion tank - removal and refitting

Removal

1 Drain the cooling system as described in Section 2 .
2 Remove the filler cap.
3 Where applicable, loosen the clip and disconnect the radiator vent hose.
4 Unclip the expansion tank from the front suspension turret.
5 Loosen the clips and disconnect the coolant supply and return hoses.
6 Withdraw the expansion tank from the engine compartment.

Refitting

7 Refitting is a reversal of removal. On completion, refill the cooling system with reference to Section 2 .

11 Temperature gauge sender unit - removal and refitting

Removal

1 The temperature gauge sender unit is located on the thermostat housing. If the engine is hot, allow it to cool before attempting to remove the unit.
2 Remove the filler cap from the radiator or expansion tank to release any remaining pressure, then refit the cap - the vacuum will help to reduce the loss of coolant.
3 Disconnect the wiring from the terminal on the sender unit.

12.3 Disconnect the air distribution flap cable at the heater

12.5a Right-hand side heater control cable

12.5b Left-hand side heater control outer cable

4 Unscrew and remove the sender unit, recovering the sealing ring (where fitted). Temporarily plug the aperture with a suitable bung. **Note:** *Be prepared for an amount of coolant loss - position a container under the thermostat housing and pad the area with absorbent rags .*

Refitting

5 Refitting is a reversal of removal, using a new sealing ring. Top-up the cooling system if necessary.

12 Heater control panel - removal and refitting

Removal

Carlton

1 Disconnect the battery negative lead.
2 Prise the cover from the cigarette lighter.
3 Disconnect the air distribution flap cable at the heater **(see illustration)**.
4 Remove the two lower screws then release the top of the control panel and withdraw until the multi-plug and illumination wire can be disconnected.
5 Disconnect the control cables and remove the panel **(see illustrations)**.
6 Refitting is a reversal of removal.

Senator

7 Refer to Chapter 12 and do the following:

a) *Remove the radio/cassette/CD and amplifier unit from the facia.*
b) *Remove all the rocker switches from above the radio aperture.*

8 Refer to Chapter 11 and remove the centre console padding.
9 With the ashtray lid half-open, pull the centre console panel away from the surround slightly. At this point, unclip the bank of switch bases from the centre console panel.
10 Unplug the cabling from both temperature selector switches and the fan switch at the multiway connectors - label each connector to enable correct refitting later. **Note:** *If the control unit is to be renewed, the existing fan switch must be removed and transferred to the new unit.*

11 Prise the knobs from the fan and air distribution controls, then detach the air distribution control cables from the control panel.
12 Remove the retaining screws and lift the control panel away from the centre console panel.

Vehicles with air conditioning

13 Unplug the cabling from the electronic control unit and the compressor/air recirculation controls at the multiway connectors. **Note:** *If control unit is to be renewed, compressor/air recirculation switch unit must be transferred to new unit.*

Refitting

14 The unit can be refitted by following the removal procedure in reverse. **Note:** *If a new control unit is to be fitted, ensure that the guide pin on the fan switch control lever is correctly engaged with the corresponding guide groove of adjustment slide on the control unit.*

13 Heater matrix - removal and refitting

Removal

All models

1 Remove the pedal bracket (Chapter 9) - this gives the clearance in the floorwell to let the heater matrix be removed without damage.
2 Drain the cooling system (Section 2).

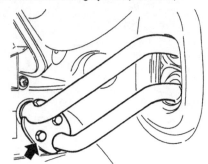

13.5 Heater matrix pipe retainer (arrowed)

Senator

3 Refer to Chapter 11 and remove the centre console.
4 Remove the retaining screws and lift off the moulded air ducting for the front and rear footwells.

All models

5 Unbolt the heater pipe retainer **(see illustration)** and disconnect the heater pipes. Be prepared for some spillage of coolant.
6 Remove the retaining screws and withdraw the matrix from the heater.

Refitting

7 Refitting is a reversal of removal but fit new O-ring seals to the two heater matrix pipes. Refill the cooling system (see Section 2).

14 Heater fan motor - removal and refitting

Removal

1 Disconnect the battery negative lead.
2 Remove the wiper arms and blades (Chapter 12).
3 Unscrew the nuts from the wiper spindle housings.
4 Pull off the weatherstrip and remove the water deflector **(see illustration)**.
5 Disconnect the wiring multi-plug, then unbolt and remove the wiper motor.
6 Disconnect the wiring plug from the fan motor.

14.4 Heater fan motor with water deflector panel removed

7 On vehicles with air-conditioning, remove the screws and lift off the air recirculation valve.

8 Remove the screws and lift off the fan shroud.

9 Remove the fan wheel covers.

10 Remove the mounting screws, then manoeuvre the motor assembly out from the vehicle. Note that the motor must be rotated in order for it to pass by the windscreen wiper bracket.

11 Disconnect the wires and remove the series resistor from the bracket.

Refitting

12 Refitting is a reversal of removal.

15 Air conditioning system - description and precautions

1 An air conditioning system is fitted as standard equipment on later high-specification models, and was available as an optional extra on some lower-specification models. In conjunction with the heater, the system enables any reasonable air temperature to be achieved inside the car, it also reduces the humidity of the incoming air, aiding demisting even when cooling is not required.

2 The refrigeration side of the air conditioning system functions in a similar way to a domestic refrigerator. A compressor, belt-driven from the crankshaft pulley, draws refrigerant in its gaseous phase from an evaporator. The compressed refrigerant passes through a condenser where it loses heat and enters its liquid phase. After dehydration, the refrigerant returns to the evaporator where it absorbs heat from the air passing over the evaporator fins. The refrigerant becomes a gas again and the cycle is repeated.

3 Various subsidiary controls and sensors protect the system against excessive temperature and pressures. Additionally, engine idle speed is increased when the system is in use to compensate for the additional load imposed by the compressor.

4 Although the refrigerant is not itself toxic, in the presence of a naked flame (or a lighted cigarette) it forms a highly toxic gas. Liquid refrigerant spilled on skin will cause frostbite.

5 Considering the above points, and the need for specialised equipment for discharging and recharging the system, any work which requires the disconnection of a refrigerant line must be left to a specialist.

6 Do not allow refrigerant lines to be exposed to temperatures in excess of 110°C (230°F), for example during welding or paint drying operations.

7 Do not operate the air conditioning system if it is known to be short of refrigerant, or damage may result.

16 Air conditioning system components - removal and refitting

Auxiliary fan

1 Refer to Section 4 .

Compressor (leaving refrigerant lines connected)

2 From the compressor, disconnect the wiring plugs for the magnetic clutch, high pressure safety switch, and auxiliary fan switch.

3 Loosen the pivot and adjustment bolts.

4 Unscrew the outer adjustment locknut to release the tension on the drivebelt then slip the drivebelt from the pulley. (On DOHC 6-cylinder engines, with a ribbed auxiliary drivebelt, refer to Chapter 2 Part C for details of releasing the tension from the drivebelt.)

5 Remove the pivot and adjustment bolts, and support the compressor to one side.

6 Refitting is a reversal of the removal procedure, tensioning the drivebelt as described in the relevant Part of Chapter 2 or in Section 9.

Chapter 4 Part A:
Fuel and exhaust systems - carburettor models

Contents

Accelerator cable - removal, refitting and adjustment 6
Accelerator pedal - removal and refitting 7
Air cleaner element renewal . . . . .See Chapter 1
Air cleaner housing - removal and refitting 2
Carburettor - adjustments 10
Carburettor - general information 9
Carburettor - overhaul 12
Carburettor - removal and refitting 11
Carburettor thermotime valve - checking .13
Exhaust manifold - removal and refitting .16

Exhaust system - removal and refitting 17
Fuel gauge sender unit - removal and refitting 4
Fuel pump - testing, removal and refitting 3
Fuel tank - removal and refitting 5
General fuel system check .See Chapter 1
General information 1
Inlet manifold - removal and refitting 15
Inlet manifold preheater element - removal, checking and refitting . .14
Unleaded petrol - general information and usage 8

Degrees of difficulty

Easy, suitable for novice with little experience	**Fairly easy,** suitable for beginner with some experience	**Fairly difficult,** suitable for competent DIY mechanic 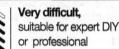	**Difficult,** suitable for experienced DIY mechanic	**Very difficult,** suitable for expert DIY or professional

Specifications

Fuel pump
Operation	Mechanical from camshaft
Pressure	0.25 to 0.36 bar

Carburettor
Type	Pierburg 2E3
Float level setting	28 to 30 mm
Accelerator pump delivery:	
Manual gearbox models	1.20 to 1.40 cm3
Automatic transmission models	0.85 to 1.05 cm3
Throttle valve gap:	
Manual gearbox models	0.95 to 1.05 mm
Automatic transmission models	1.15 to 1.25 mm
Choke valve gap:	
"Small" gap	2.0 to 2.3 mm
"Large" gap	3.0 to 3.3 mm
Fast idle cam adjustment	0.7 to 1.1 mm
Choke valve forced opening:	
Manual gearbox models	1.5 to 3.5 mm
Automatic transmission models	3.0 to 5.0 mm
Main jet:	
Primary	X107.5
Secondary	Z132.5
Idle Jet	137.5
Full load enrichment	90
Needle valve	1.5
Air correction jet:	
Primary	110
Secondary	90

Adjustment data
Idle speed:	
Manual gearbox models	850 to 900 rpm
Automatic transmission models	750 to 800 rpm
Fast idle speed	1900 to 2300 rpm
CO at idle	0.5 to 1.0%

Recommended fuel

Minimum octane rating:
Early (pre 1990) models . . . . 98 RON leaded (4-star) or unleaded (Super unleaded)*
Later (1990 on) models . . . . 95 RON leaded (4-star) or unleaded (Unleaded premium)
*If the necessary precautions are taken, 95 RON unleaded (unleaded premium) petrol can be used (see Section 8 for details)

Torque wrench settings	Nm	lbf ft
Inlet manifold	25	18
Exhaust manifold	25	18

1 General information

1 The fuel system consists of a fuel tank mounted under the rear of the car, a mechanical fuel pump and a carburettor. The fuel pump is operated by an eccentric on the camshaft and is mounted on the camshaft housing. The air cleaner contains a disposable paper filter element and incorporates a flap valve air temperature control system which allows cold air from the outside of the car and warm air from the exhaust manifold to enter the air cleaner in the correct proportions.
2 The fuel pump lifts fuel from the fuel tank via a filter and supplies it to the carburettor. Excess fuel is returned from the anti-percolation chamber to the fuel tank.

 Warning: Many of the procedures in this Chapter require the removal of fuel lines and connections which may result in some fuel spillage. Before carrying out any operation on the fuel system refer to the precautions given in Safety first! at the beginning of this Manual and follow them implicitly. Petrol is a highly dangerous and volatile liquid and the precautions necessary when handling it cannot be overstressed.

2 Air cleaner housing - removal and refitting

Removal

1 Disconnect the air inlet duct and warm air tube from the air cleaner.
2 Unscrew the three mounting nuts, lift the air cleaner from the carburettor, and disconnect the vacuum hose for the inlet air temperature control.
3 Remove the air cleaner gasket/sealing ring.

Refitting

4 Refit by reversing the removal operations, making sure that the gasket/sealing ring is in place on the carburettor.

3 Fuel pump - testing, removal and refitting

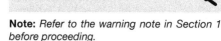

Note: *Refer to the warning note in Section 1 before proceeding.*

Testing

1 To test the fuel pump on the engine, disconnect the outlet pipe which leads to the carburettor, and hold a wad of rag over the pump outlet while an assistant spins the engine on the starter. *Keep the hands away from the electric cooling fan.* Regular spurts of fuel should be ejected as the engine turns.
2 The pump can also be tested by removing it. With the pump outlet pipe disconnected but the inlet pipe still connected, hold the wad of rag by the outlet. Operate the pump lever by hand, moving it in and out; if the pump is in a satisfactory condition the lever should move and return smoothly and a strong jet of fuel should be ejected.

Removal

3 Mark the pump inlet and outlet hoses, for identification purposes then slacken both retaining clips. Place wads of rag beneath the hose unions to catch any spilled fuel then disconnect both hoses from the pump and plug the hose ends to minimise fuel loss.
4 Unscrew and remove the pump mounting nuts and withdraw the pump from the camshaft housing. Recover the spacer/gasket **(see illustration).**

Refitting

5 Refitting is a reversal of removal, but fit a new spacer/gasket.

3.4 Removing the fuel pump (carburettor models)

4 Fuel gauge sender unit - removal and refitting

Note: *Refer to the warning note in Section 1 before proceeding.*

Removal

1 Disconnect the battery negative lead.
2 Remove the tank filler cap, and if possible syphon or pump out all of the fuel.
3 Chock the front wheels, then jack up the rear of the car and support it on axle stands (see "*Jacking and Vehicle Support*"). Disconnect the wiring from the fuel gauge sender unit.
4 Where the sender unit also incorporates the fuel feed and return hoses, identify the hoses for position then loosen the clips and disconnect them. Be prepared for loss of fuel.
5 Where a bayonet-type metal ring is fitted use two crossed screwdrivers to turn it anti-clockwise. Otherwise, unscrew the bolts. Remove the metal ring and the sender unit.
6 Remove the O-ring seal or gasket.

Refitting

7 Clean the contact faces of the sender unit and fuel tank.
8 Where applicable apply a little multi-purpose grease to the new O-ring seal and locate it in the sender unit groove.
9 Fit the sender unit to the tank with the pick-up tube facing downwards. Use a new gasket where fitted.
10 Where a bayonet-type metal ring is fitted, tighten the ring fully clockwise.
11 Where bolts are fitted, apply locking fluid to their threads then insert and tighten them in diagonal sequence.
12 Refit the hoses and wiring, and reconnect the battery negative lead. Lower the car to the ground.
13 Refill the tank and refit the filler cap.

5 Fuel tank - removal and refitting

Note: *Refer to the warning note in Section 1 before proceeding.*

Removal

1 Disconnect the battery negative lead.
2 Remove the tank filler cap, and if possible syphon or pump out all of the fuel (there is no drain plug).

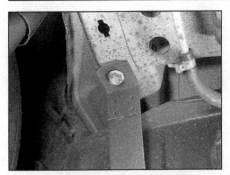

5.10 Fuel tank mounting bolt

3 Chock the front wheels, then jack up the rear of the vehicle and support it on axle stands (see "*Jacking and Vehicle Support*").
4 Disconnect the wiring from the fuel gauge sender unit and, if fitted in the fuel tank, the fuel pump.
5 Position a suitable container beneath the fuel tank to catch the spilled fuel.
6 Identify the fuel feed and return hoses for position and if available fit hose clamps to them. Loosen the clips, disconnect the hoses, and plug the open ends.
7 Where necessary, disconnect the vent pipe.
8 On models equipped with a pneumatic rear suspension levelling system, unclip the pressure line from the edge of the fuel tank.
9 Support the fuel tank using a block of wood and a trolley jack.
10 Unbolt the two retaining straps from the underbody **(see illustration)**.
11 Slowly lower the fuel tank while removing the filler neck from the rubber sleeve in the side panel.
12 Remove the rubber sleeve from the side panel.
13 Note the location of the vent lines then disconnect them.
14 Remove the fuel gauge sender unit, and where applicable the fuel pump.
15 Loosen the hose clips and remove the filler neck, vent container and hose.
16 Drain any remaining fuel from the tank.
17 If the tank is contaminated with sediment or water, swill it out with clean fuel. If the tank leaks or is damaged, it should be repaired by specialists or alternatively renewed. **Do not** under any circumstances solder or weld a fuel tank.
18 Examine the vent lines, hose and hose clips for damage and renew if necessary.

Refitting

19 Refitting is a reversal of removal, but note the following additional points:

 a) *Make sure that the vent lines and hoses are not twisted or trapped*
 b) *Refit the rubber sleeve with the "U" marking at the bottom*
 c) *Do not tighten the filler hose bottom clip until the filler neck is correctly positioned*

6 Accelerator cable - removal, refitting and adjustment

Removal

1 Remove the air cleaner (Section 2), then open the throttle by hand and unhook the inner cable from the grooved cam.
2 Slide the outer cable bush from the support bracket.
3 Working inside the car, disconnect the inner cable from the accelerator pedal.
4 Release the grommet from the bulkhead and pull the cable into the engine bay.

Refitting and adjustment

5 Refitting is a reversal of removal. Adjust the cable by selecting the appropriate position of the spring clip behind the outer cable bush, to give just a barely-perceptible amount of slack in the inner cable with the accelerator pedal released.

7 Accelerator pedal - removal and refitting

Removal

1 Disconnect the accelerator cable from the pedal with reference to Section 6.
2 Prise the spring clip from the inner end of the pivot rod, and remove the bushes, washers and return spring **(see illustration)**.
3 Remove the pedal from the bracket.

Refitting

4 Refitting is a reversal of removal, but adjust the cable as described in Section 6.

8 Unleaded petrol - general information and usage

Note: *The information given in this Chapter is correct at the time of writing and applies only to petrols currently available in the UK. If updated information is thought to be required check with a Vauxhall/Opel dealer. If travelling abroad consult one of the motoring organisations (or a*

7.2 Accelerator pedal and bracket

similar authority) for advice on the petrols available and their suitability for your vehicle.
1 The fuel recommended by Vauxhall/Opel is given in the Specifications Section of this Chapter, followed by the equivalent petrol currently on sale in the UK.
2 RON and MON are different testing standards; RON stands for Research Octane Number (also written as RM), while MON stands for Motor Octane Number (also written as MM).

Early (pre-1990) models

3 These models are designed to run on either 98 (RON) octane leaded or unleaded petrol (see Specifications). A fuel octane rating coding plug is fitted to the ignition system wiring harness. The plug which is located on the right-hand side of the engine compartment, is set during production to give optimum engine output and efficiency when run on 98 (RON) fuel. To run the vehicle on 95 (RON) unleaded fuel, the plug position can be reset to modify the timing characteristics of the ignition system. To reset the plug, release its locking clip then remove the plug and rotate it through half a turn (180°), so the "95" marking is on the same side as the clip, before reconnecting it. **Note:** *If after making the adjustment, the octane rating of the fuel used is found to be so low that excessive knocking still occurs, seek the advice of your Vauxhall dealer.*

Later (1990-on) models

4 These models are designed to run on 95 (RON) octane leaded or unleaded petrol (see Specifications).

9 Carburettor - general information

The carburettor is a Pierburg 2E3 incorporating a coolant temperature and electrically controlled automatic choke. It is of twin-barrel construction with progressively-operated throttle valves. The primary throttle valve is opened mechanically, but the secondary throttle is opened by vacuum developed in both venturis. Primary and secondary transition systems, and a part load enrichment valve, ensure efficient operation under all speed and load conditions. An idle cut-off valve stops the supply of fuel to the idle circuit when the ignition is switched off.

10 Carburettor - adjustments

Idle speed and mixture adjustment

1 A tachometer (rev counter) and an exhaust gas analyser (CO meter) are required for accurate adjustment.

10.4 Idle speed adjustment screw (1) and idle mixture adjustment screw (2) under tamperproof cap

2 Adjustment should be made with the air cleaner fitted, the accelerator cable correctly adjusted, and the engine at normal operating temperature. Ensure that the adjustment screw is not touching the fast idle cam; on models equipped with automatic transmission, position the selector lever in the "P" position.

3 Connect the tachometer and exhaust gas analyser to the engine in accordance with the manufacturers' instructions. Start the engine and allow it to idle.

4 Read the idle speed on the tachometer and compare it with the value given in the Specifications. If adjustment is necessary, turn the idle speed adjustment screw as required (see illustration).

5 Check that the CO content is as given in the Specifications. If not prise off the tamperproof cap and turn the idle mixture adjustment screw as required.

6 If necessary, repeat the procedure given in paragraph 4.

7 Switch off the engine and disconnect the tachometer and exhaust gas analyser.

Fast idle speed adjustment

8 Adjust the idle speed and mixture as described above in paragraphs 1 to 6 then stop the engine.

9 Position the fast idle adjustment screw on the second highest step of the fast idle cam. Connect a tachometer to the engine in accordance with the manufacturer's instructions. Make sure that the choke plate is fully open.

10.10 Fast idle adjustment screw under tamperproof cap (arrowed)

10 Start the engine without touching the throttle pedal and compare the engine speed with that given in the Specifications. If adjustment is necessary remove the tamperproof cap from the head of the fast idle screw by crushing it with pliers, and adjust by means of the screw (see illustration).

11 When adjustment is correct, stop the engine and disconnect the tachometer.

Carburettor throttle valve dashpot adjustment - automatic transmission models

12 Adjust the idle speed and mixture as described earlier in this Section.

13 With the throttle lever in the idle position, loosen the locknut on the dashpot and adjust the unit until the gap between the end of the plunger and the throttle lever is 0.05 mm. From this position turn the dashpot **down** 2.5 turns, then tighten the locknut (see illustration).

11 Carburettor - removal and refitting

Removal

1 Disconnect the battery negative lead.

2 Remove the air cleaner (see Section 2).

3 Drain the cooling system (Chapter 1) or alternatively fit hose clamps to the automatic choke coolant hoses.

4 Loosen the clips and disconnect the coolant hoses from the automatic choke cover.

5 Loosen the clips and disconnect the fuel supply and, if fitted, the return hose(s).

6 Disconnect the accelerator cable (Section 6).

7 Disconnect the wiring from the idle cut-off valve, the thermo time valve, and the automatic choke.

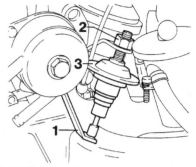

10.13 Throttle valve dashpot on automatic transmission models

1 Throttle lever   3 Dashpot
2 Adjusting nut

8 Note the location of the vacuum hoses, then disconnect them.

9 Unscrew the securing nuts then lift the carburettor off its studs. Recover the gasket.

Refitting

10 Refitting is a reversal of removal, but if necessary use a new gasket. Adjust the accelerator cable as described in Section 6. Refill the cooling system (Chapter 1) and refit the air cleaner (Section 2).

12 Carburettor - overhaul

1 With the carburettor removed from the vehicle, drain the fuel from the float chamber and vapour separator. Clean the outside of the carburettor.

2 Remove the hoses and wires from the carburettor, making identifying marks or notes to avoid confusion on reassembly (see illustration).

3 Access to the jets and float chamber is obtained by removing the top half of the

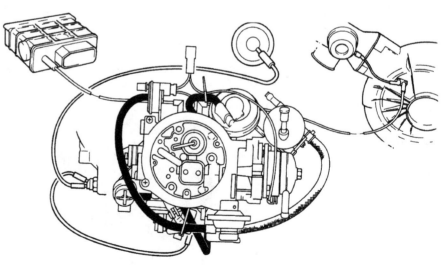

12.2 Vacuum and fuel line connections to the carburettor

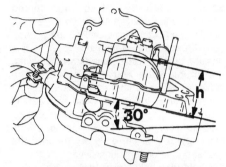

12.6 Float level checking dimension
h = 28 to 30 mm

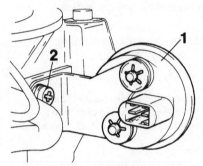

12.9 Thermo time valve (1) and mounting screw (2)

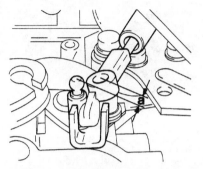

12.8 Rest position of vacuum pullrod
a = 0.5 to 2.0 mm

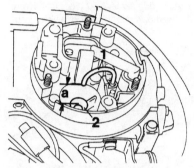

12.11 Enrichment tube adjustment

a = 24 to 26 mm   2 Venturi
1 Enrichment tube

carburettor, which is secured by five screws. Blow through the jets and drillings with compressed air, or air from a foot pump - *do not probe them with wire. If it is wished to remove the jets, unscrew them carefully with well-fitting tools.*

4 Remove the fuel strainer from the inlet pipe by hooking it out with a small screwdriver.
5 Clean any foreign matter from the float chamber. Renew the inlet needle valve if wear is evident, or if a high mileage has been covered. Renew the float if it is punctured or otherwise damaged.
6 It is not possible to adjust the float level setting as this depends on the float weight being between 5.75 and 5.95 grams. However, it is possible to check the initial setting as follows. Invert the carburettor cover and measure the distance from the joint face to the furthest edge of the float **(see illustration)**. The spring-tensioned ball in the needle valve should not be depressed during the check. The distance should be as given in the Specifications.
7 Renew the diaphragms in the part load enrichment valve and in the accelerator pump. Renew the inlet pipe fuel strainer. Obtain an overhaul kit of gaskets.
8 To remove the 2nd stage vacuum unit, prise the pullrod from the lever ball and remove the bracket screws. When refitting the unit, the rest position of the pullrod must be between 0.5 and 2.0 mm away from the lever ball as shown **(see illustration)**. This ensures that the pullrod is pre-tensioned when reconnected.

9 The thermo time valve may be removed by removing the bracket screw **(see illustration)**.
10 Reassemble the carburettor in the reverse order to dismantling using new gaskets and seals. Lubricate linkages with a little oil.
11 Check that the distance between the

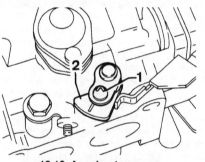

12.12 Accelerator pump adjustment bolt (1) and cam (2)

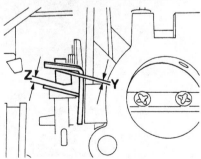

12.14 2nd stage linkage clearances
Y = 0.6 to 1.0 mm   Z = 0.2 to 0.6 mm

enrichment tube and the venturi is between 24 and 26 mm **(see illustration)**. Also check that the tube is vertically over the centre of the venturi.
12 The accelerator pump delivery may be checked as follows but the fuel level must be maintained at the correct level in the float chamber. On automatic transmission models, adjust the dashpot upwards first (Section 10). Turn the automatic choke cam clear of the fast idle adjustment screw. Position the carburettor over a suitable container, then open and close the throttle valve ten times at a rate of approximately one second per stroke, waiting approximately three seconds in between each stroke. Divide the quantity of fuel collected by ten, and compare with the amount given in the Specifications. If adjustment is necessary, slacken the bolt and reposition the cam as required, noting that rotating the cam clockwise will increase the pump delivery, and rotating it anti-clockwise will decrease the pump delivery **(see illustration)**.
13 Check that the accelerator pump jet directs the fuel towards the recess as shown, it will be necessary to remove the carburettor cover to move the jet **(see illustration)**.
14 Check that the 2nd stage linkage clearances are as shown, with the 1st stage throttle valve in its idle position **(see illustration)**. If necessary, bend the fork to correct.
15 Invert the carburettor and position the fast idle adjustment screw on the highest level of the cam. Using a twist drill check that the clearance between the primary throttle valve and the barrel is as given in the Specifications for the throttle valve gap **(see illustration)**.

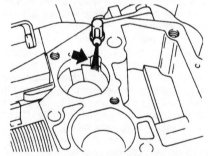

12.13 Accelerator pump jet adjustment

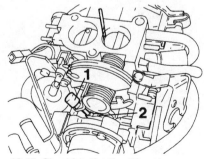

12.15 Checking the throttle valve gap
1 Fast idle screw   2 Stepped plate

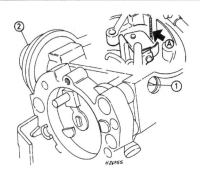

12.16 Checking the choke valve gap

1 Pulldown diaphragm rod
2 Pulldown unit adjustment screw
A Twist drill checking choke valve gap

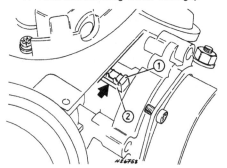

12.17b Adjust the fast idle cam setting by bending the lever, taking care not to damage the return springs - arrowed

1 Fast idle cam   2 Adjusting lever

This provides an initial setting for the fast idle speed. Adjust the fast idle adjustment screw if necessary.

16   To check the choke valve gap, first ensure that the pulldown diaphragm is not leaking, then disconnect the vacuum pipe from the diaphragm. Fully close the choke valve, and position the adjusting screw on the highest step of the fast idle cam. Using a small screwdriver, push in the pulldown diaphragm rod to the first pressure point. With the rod in this position, use a twist drill to check the "small" choke valve gap between the choke valve and bore **(see illustration)**. If necessary adjust the gap by rotating the adjustment screw on the pulldown unit. Once the "small" choke valve gap is correct, push the pulldown

12.19a Choke drive lever (1) engages with loop (2)

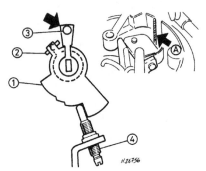

12.17a Checking fast idle cam adjustment

1 Fast idle cam   3 Choke lever
2 Adjusting lever   4 Fast idle screw
A Twist drill checking choke valve gap

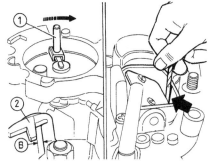

12.18 Checking the choke valve forced opening with a twist drill - arrowed

1 Choke lever   2 Adjustment segment
B Choke valve forced opening dimension

rod fully into the diaphragm, then repeat the measuring procedure and check the "large" choke valve gap. Again, if necessary adjust the gap by rotating the adjustment screw on the pulldown unit.

17   Once the choke valve gap is correctly adjusted, check the fast idle cam adjustment as follows. Open the throttle valve, press the choke lever lightly in the direction of the arrow, then close the throttle valve again; the adjustment screw should now be positioned on the second step of the cam. Using a twist drill, check the clearances between the choke valve and bore. If necessary, adjust the fast idle clearance by carefully bending the lever, taking care not to damage the return springs **(see illustrations)**.

12.19b Automatic choke cover alignment marks (arrowed)

18   Next check the choke valve forced opening as follows. Rotate the choke lever in the direction of the arrow until it abuts its stop **(see illustration)**. Retain the lever in this position using an elastic band, then fully open the throttle valve and measure the choke valve forced opening (dimension "B"). If adjustment is necessary, either carefully increase the gap using a screwdriver, or close the gap using a pair of pointed-nose pliers. Once the gap is correctly set, remove the rubber band from the choke lever.

19   Refit the choke cover to the carburettor, ensuring that the lever is correctly engaged with the cover spring loop, and align the marks provided **(see illustrations)**.

13 Carburettor thermotime valve - checking

1   Remove the air cleaner (Section 2).
2   Disconnect the wiring plug from the thermo time valve. Switch on the ignition, and use a voltmeter to check that the current supply is at least 11.5 volts.
3   Using an ohmmeter, check that the resistance across the time valve terminals is 6.0 ± 1.5 ohms at an ambient temperature of between 20 and 30°C (68 to 86°F).
4   Disconnect the vacuum hoses, then apply vacuum to the port nearest the carburettor. With the wiring still disconnected the valve should be open.
5   Reconnect the wiring and continue to apply the vacuum with the ignition switched on. From the point of reconnection, the valve should close after four to ten seconds at an ambient temperature of 20°C (68°F). Renew the valve if this is not the case (Section 12).
6   Switch off the ignition and refit the air cleaner.

14 Inlet manifold preheater element - removal, checking and refitting

Removal

1   The preheater element is located below the inlet manifold. First disconnect the wiring.
2   Remove the screws and withdraw the element from the inlet manifold. Remove the O-ring seal **(see illustration)**.

Checking

3   Using an ohmmeter check that the resistance across the element wire terminals is approximately 1.5 ohms. If not the element is probably faulty.

Refitting

4   Refitting is a reversal of removal, but use a new O-ring seal.

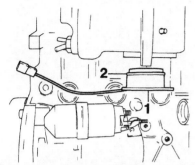

14.2 Inlet manifold preheater element (1) and O-ring seal (2)

15 Inlet manifold - removal and refitting

Removal

1 The manifold may be removed with or without the carburettor. First remove the air cleaner (Section 2).
2 Drain the cooling system (Chapter 1).
3 Disconnect all crankcase ventilation, coolant, fuel and air hoses.
4 Disconnect all electrical wires.
5 Disconnect the accelerator/kickdown cable(s) (as applicable).
6 Progressively unscrew the nuts then withdraw the inlet manifold from the studs on the cylinder head. Remove the gasket.
7 Clean the mating faces of the inlet manifold and cylinder head.

Refitting

8 Refitting is a reversal of removal but use a new gasket and tighten the mounting nuts to the specified torque.

16 Exhaust manifold - removal and refitting

Removal

1 Disconnect the HT cables from the spark plugs and ignition coil.
2 Unscrew the bolts securing the exhaust downpipe to the exhaust manifold, lower the downpipe and recover the joint.
3 Progressively unscrew the nuts, then withdraw the exhaust manifold from the studs on the cylinder head. Remove the gasket.
4 Clean the mating faces of the exhaust manifold and cylinder head.

Refitting

5 Refitting is a reversal of removal, but use a new gasket and tighten the mounting nuts to the specified torque.

17 Exhaust system - removal and refitting

Removal

1 The exhaust system is in three sections.
2 To remove the complete system, position the car over an inspection pit, or raise the car and support it on axle stands (see "Jacking and Vehicle Support").
3 Unscrew the bolts securing the exhaust downpipe to the manifold, lower the downpipe and recover the joint.
4 With the help of an assistant, unbolt the front mounting clamp and unhook the rubber mountings. The intermediate mounting rubbers are retained with metal clips. On some models the front mounting is of rubber instead of a clamp.
5 Lower the exhaust system to the ground.
6 Separate the sections by unbolting the flange and removing the clamp.

Refitting

7 Refitting is a reversal of removal, but fit a new manifold gasket. Tighten the manifold bolts with the exhaust system loose in the front clamp, then tighten the clamp.

Notes

Chapter 4 Part B:
Fuel and exhaust systems - fuel injection models

Contents

Accelerator cable - removal, refitting and adjustment 3
Accelerator pedal - removal and refitting 4
Air cleaner filter renewal . . . . .See Chapter 1
Air cleaner housing - removal and refitting .2
Catalytic converter - general information and precautions 19
Dual ram air inlet system (2.6 litre and 3.0 litre 24-valve models) -
    general information and component renewal 17
Exhaust manifold - removal and refitting 16
Exhaust system - removal and refitting 18
Fuel filter renewal . . . . .See Chapter 1
Fuel gauge sender unit - removal and refitting 9
Fuel injection system - general information .6
Fuel injection system - idle speed and mixture adjustment 11

Fuel injection system components (1.8 and 2.0 litre models) -
    removal and refitting 12
Fuel injection system components (2.5 and 2.6 litre models) -
    removal and refitting 13
Fuel injection system components (3.0 litre models) -
    removal and refitting 14
Fuel pump - testing, removal and refitting .8
Fuel system - depressurisation 7
Fuel tank - removal and refitting 10
General fuel system checks .See Chapter 1
General information 1
Inlet manifold - removal and refitting 15
Unleaded petrol - general information and usage 5

Degrees of difficulty

Easy, suitable for novice with little experience	Fairly easy, suitable for beginner with some experience	Fairly difficult, suitable for competent DIY mechanic	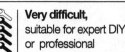 Difficult, suitable for experienced DIY mechanic	Very difficult, suitable for expert DIY or professional

Specifications

System type

1.8 litre models	L3 Jetronic
2.0 litre models:	
Pre-1990 models	Motronic ML4.1
1990-on models	Motronic M1.5
2.5 litre models	LE2 Jetronic
2.6 litre models	Motronic M1.5 with dual ram air inlet system
3.0 litre (CIH) 12-valve models:	
30NE engine	LE2 Jetronic
C30NE engine:	
Pre-1990 models	Motronic ML4.1
1990-on models	Motronic M1.5
C30LE engine	Motronic ML4.1
3.0 litre (DOHC) 24-valve models	Motronic M1.5 with dual ram air inlet system

Fuel pump

Delivery rate (approximate)	120 litres/hour
Fuel pump operating pressure (engine idling at specified speed):	
Pressure regulator vacuum hose connected:	
1.8 litre models	2.0 to 2.2 bar
2.0 litre models	
Motronic ML4.1 system	2.3 to 2.7 bar
Motronic M1.5 system	1.8 to 2.2 bar
2.5 litre models	2.3 to 2.7 bar
2.6 litre models	2.3 to 2.7 bar
3.0 litre (CIH) 12-valve models:	
30NE engine	2.3 to 2.7 bar
C30NE engine:	
Motronic ML4.1 system	2.8 to 3.2 bar
Motronic M1.5 system	2.3 to 2.7 bar
3.0 litre (DOHC) 24-valve models	2.3 to 2.7 bar

Fuel pump (continued)

Fuel pump operating pressure (engine idling at specified speed):
Pressure regulator vacuum hose disconnected and plugged:

1.8 litre models	2.3 to 2.7 bar
2.0 litre models:	
Motronic ML4.1 system	3.1 to 3.3 bar
Motronic M1.5 system	2.5 to 3.0 bar
2.5 litre models	2.8 to 3.2 bar
2.6 litre models	3.0 to 3.5 bar
3.0 litre (CIH) 12-valve models:	
30NE engine	2.8 to 3.2 bar
C30NE engine:	
Motronic ML4.1 system	3.6 to 3.9 bar
Motronic M1.5 system	3.0 to 3.5 bar
3.0 litre (DOHC) 24-valve models	3.0 to 3.5 bar

Idle speed and mixture settings

Specified idle speed:

1.8 litre models	850 to 900 rpm
2.0 litre models	720 to 880 rpm*
2.5 litre models	775 to 825 rpm*
2.6 litre models	670 to 830 rpm*
3.0 litre (CIH) 12-valve models:	
30NE engine	775 to 825 rpm*
C30NE engine	670 to 830 rpm*
C30LE engine	570 to 670 rpm*
3.0 litre (DOHC) 24-valve models	570 to 730 rpm*

Idle mixture CO level:

1.8 litre models	0.5 to 1.0%
2.0 litre models:	
Models not fitted with a catalytic converter	0.5 to 1.0%
Models with a catalytic converter	Less than 0.4%*
2.5 litre models	Less than 0.5%
2.6 litre models	Less than 0.4%*
3.0 litre (CIH) 12-valve models:	
Models not fitted with a catalytic converter	Less than 0.5%
Models with a catalytic converter	Less than 0.4%*
3.0 litre (DOHC) 24-valve models	Less than 0.4%*

*Not adjustable - controlled by the electronic control unit (ECU)

Torque wrench settings

	Nm	lbf ft
Coolant temperature sensor	15	11
Exhaust manifold:		
1.8 and 2.0 litre models	25	19
2.5 and 2.6 litre models	35	26
3.0 litre models:		
12-valve (CIH) engine	35	26
24-valve (DOHC) engine	22	16
Inlet manifold:		
1.8 and 2.0 litre models	25	19
2.5 and 2.6 litre models	35	26
3.0 litre models:		
12-valve (CIH) engine	35	26
24-valve (DOHC) engine	22	16
Lambda sensor	30	22

1 General information

The fuel system consists of a fuel tank mounted under the rear of the car, an electric fuel pump, a fuel filter, fuel feed and return lines. The fuel pump supplies fuel to the fuel rail which acts as a reservoir for the fuel injectors which inject fuel into the inlet tracts.

The fuel filter is incorporated in the feed line from the pump to the fuel rail to ensure that the fuel supplied to the injectors is clean.

Refer to Section 6 for further information on the operation of the relevant fuel injection system.

Warning: Many of the procedures in this Chapter require the removal of fuel lines and connections which may result in some fuel spillage.

Before carrying out any operation on the fuel system refer to the precautions given in Safety first! at the beginning of this Manual and follow them implicitly. Petrol is a highly dangerous and volatile liquid and the precautions necessary when handling it cannot be overstressed.

Note: *Residual pressure will remain in the fuel lines long after the vehicle was last used, when disconnecting any fuel line, depressurise the fuel system as described in Section 7.*

3.1a Accelerator cable connection to the throttle housing

3.1b Disconnecting the accelerator inner cable

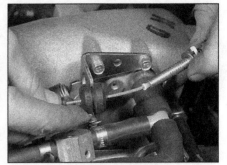

3.2 Releasing the accelerator outer cable bush

2 Air cleaner housing - removal and refitting

Removal

1 Disconnect the wiring connector from the airflow meter.
2 Slacken the retaining clip and disconnect the inlet duct from the air cleaner housing.
3 Unbolt the air cleaner housing and remove it from the engine compartment.

Refitting

4 Refitting is a reversal of removal.

3 Accelerator cable - removal, refitting and adjustment

Removal

1 Release and remove the small spring clip, and disconnect the inner cable ball end from the lever on the throttle housing (see illustrations).
2 Slide the outer cable bush from the support bracket (see illustration).
3 Working inside the car, disconnect the inner cable from the accelerator pedal.
4 Release the grommet from the bulkhead and pull the cable into the engine compartment.

Refitting and adjustment

5 Refitting is a reversal of removal. Adjust the cable by selecting the appropriate position of the spring clip behind the outer cable bush, to give just a barely-perceptible amount of slack in the inner cable with the accelerator pedal released.

4 Accelerator pedal - removal and refitting

Refer to Chapter 4A, Section 7.

5 Unleaded petrol - general information and usage

Note: *The information given in this Chapter is correct at the time of writing and applies only to petrols currently available in the UK. If updated information is thought to be required check with a Vauxhall/Opel dealer. If travelling abroad consult one of the motoring organisations (or a similar authority) for advice on the petrols available and their suitability for your vehicle.*

1 The fuel recommended by Vauxhall/Opel is given in the Specifications Section of this Chapter, followed by the equivalent petrol currently on sale in the UK.
2 RON and MON are different testing standards; RON stands for Research Octane Number (also written as RM), while MON stands for Motor Octane Number (also written as MM). Fuel requirements are as follows.

1.8 and 2.0 litre models

3 All 1.8 and 2.0 litre models are designed to run on 98 (RON) octane petrol (see Specifications).
4 On models with a catalytic converter unleaded fuel **must** be used; under no circumstances should leaded (UK "4-star") fuel be used as this will damage the catalytic converter. On models not equipped with a catalytic converter, both leaded and unleaded fuels may be used.
5 A fuel octane rating coding plug is fitted to the ignition system wiring harness (see illustration). The plug which is located on the right-hand side of the engine compartment, is set during production to give optimum engine output and efficiency when run on 98 (RON) fuel. To run the vehicle on 95 (RON) unleaded fuel, the plug position can be reset to modify the timing characteristics of the ignition system. To reset the plug, release its locking clip then remove the plug and rotate it through half a turn (180°), so the "95" marking is on the same side as the clip, before reconnecting it. Note: *If after making the adjustment, the octane rating of the fuel used is found to be so low that excessive knocking still occurs, seek the advice of your Vauxhall/Opel dealer.*

2.5 litre models

6 All 2.5 litre models are designed to run on 98 (RON) octane leaded or unleaded petrol (see Specifications). If it is wished to run the vehicle on 95 (RON) unleaded petrol, the ignition timing **must** be retarded by 3° (see Chapter 5B for details); this is necessary to avoid detonation (knocking and pinking) which could lead to possible engine damage. **Do not** use 95 (RON) unleaded petrol if the ignition timing has not been retarded. Note: *If after making the adjustment, the octane rating of the fuel used is found to be so low that excessive knocking still occurs, seek the advice of your Vauxhall/Opel dealer.*

2.6 litre models

7 All 2.6 models are fitted with a catalytic converter and are designed to run on 98 (RON) unleaded petrol **only**; under no circumstances should leaded (UK "4-star") fuel be used as this will damage the catalytic converter.
8 A fuel octane rating coding plug is fitted to the ignition system wiring harness (see paragraph 5). The plug which is located on the right-hand side of the engine compartment, is set during production to give optimum engine output and efficiency when run on 98 (RON) fuel. To run the vehicle on 95 (RON) unleaded fuel, the plug position can be reset to modify the timing characteristics of the ignition system. To reset the plug, release its locking clip then remove the plug and rotate it through half a turn (180°) so the "95" marking is on the same side as the clip, before reconnecting it. Note: *If after making the adjustment, the*

5.5 Octane rating plug (arrowed)

octane rating of the fuel used is found to be so low that excessive knocking still occurs note that it is possible to select a third (91 RON) octane rating setting using a special coding plug available from your Vauxhall/Opel dealer.

3.0 litre models

Models with 30NE engine

9 Refer to the information in paragraph 6 for the 2.5 litre engine.

Models with C30NE and C30LE engines

10 Refer to the information given in paragraphs 7 and 8 for the 2.6 litre engine.

Models with C30SE and C30SEJ (DOHC) engines

11 On these models, unleaded fuel must be used at all times; under no circumstances should leaded (UK "4-star") fuel be used as this will damage the catalytic converter. Unleaded fuel of any octane above 91 (RON) can be used, the ignition system automatically adjusts the ignition timing to suit the fuel using the information obtained from the knock sensors (see Chapter 5B). **Note:** *If 91 (RON) octane rating fuel is used, avoid placing the severe engine loads, ie. full throttle operation at low engine speeds or towing a caravan/trailer.*

---

6 Fuel injection system - general information

1.8 litre models

1 The Bosch L3 Jetronic fuel injection system is fitted to all 1.8 litre models. Refer to Chapter 5 for information on the ignition side of the system; the fuel side of the system operates as follows.
2 The fuel pump supplies fuel from the tank to the fuel rail, via a filter mounted underneath the rear of the vehicle. Fuel supply pressure is controlled by the pressure regulator in the fuel rail. When the optimum operating pressure of the fuel system is exceeded, the regulator allows excess fuel to return to the tank.
3 The electrical control system consists of the ECU, along with the following sensors:

a) *Throttle valve switch - informs the ECU of the throttle position.*
b) *Airflow sensor - informs the ECU of the amount and temperature of the air entering the inlet duct.*
c) *Coolant temperature sensor - informs the ECU of engine temperature.*
d) *Auxiliary air valve - acts as an additional air supply whilst the engine is cold to increase engine idle speed.*

4 All the above signals are analysed by the ECU, and it selects the appropriate fuelling for those values. The ECU controls the fuel injectors (varying the pulse width - the length of time the injectors are held open - to provide a richer or weaker mixture, as appropriate). The

mixture is constantly varied by the ECU, to provide the best setting for cranking, starting (with either a hot or cold engine), warm-up, idle, cruising, and acceleration.

2.0 litre models

5 All 2.0 litre models are fitted with a Bosch Motronic engine management system, this differs from the Jetronic system in that the ECU controls both the fuel injection and ignition systems. Refer to Chapter 5 for information on the ignition side of the system.
6 The fuel side of the system is very similar to that described above for the 1.8 litre models, the main change being that the auxiliary air valve is replaced with an idle speed adjuster. The idle speed adjuster is controlled by the ECU controls and keeps the idle speed constant at all times.
7 Another advantage of the Motronic system, is in its ability to store fault codes. If there is an abnormality in any of the readings obtained from the system sensors the ECU illuminates a warning light on the instrument panel and stores the relevant fault code in its memory. If the warning light comes on, the vehicle should be taken to a Vauxhall/Opel dealer at the earliest opportunity. They will be able to extract the fault code from the ECU and use it to diagnose the engine management fault.
8 Early (pre-1990) models are equipped with the Motronic ML4.1 system. From 1990 onwards, the ML4.1 system was replaced with the Motronic M1.5 system. Apart from internal changes to the ECU circuitry, the two systems are virtually identical. The only minor change was that a throttle potentiometer was fitted in place of a throttle valve switch. The advantages of the potentiometer are that it also senses the rate of opening and closing of the valve, as well as its position, and so allows greater control over the fuelling.
9 On models equipped with a catalytic converter, the system is of the "closed-loop" type; a lambda (oxygen) sensor in the exhaust system provides the fuel injection/ignition system ECU with constant feedback, enabling the ECU to adjust the mixture to provide the best possible conditions for the converter to operate. The lambda sensor tip is heated to bring the exhaust gases up to temperature on cold starts. To further reduce emission an evaporative emission control system is also fitted. The fuel tank filler cap is sealed, and a carbon canister collects the petrol vapours generated in the tank when the car is parked. The canister stores them until they can be cleared from the canister (under the control of ECU) via a solenoid valve(s). When the valve is opened, the fuel vapours pass into the inlet tract, to be burned by the engine during normal combustion.

2.5 litre models

10 All 2.5 litre models are fitted with a Bosch LE2 Jetronic fuel injection system. Refer to Chapter 5 for information on the ignition side of the system.

11 The fuel side of the system is very similar to that described above for the 1.8 litre models, the main change being that the auxiliary air valve is replaced with an idle speed adjuster. The idle speed adjuster is controlled by a separate control unit and keeps the idle speed constant at all times.

2.6 litre models

12 All 2.6 litre models are fitted with a Bosch Motronic M1.5 system (see paragraphs 5 to 9). The ECU also has control over the dual ram inlet system.

3.0 litre models

Models with 30NE engine

13 These models are fitted with a Bosch LE2 Jetronic system, which is the same as that fitted to the 2.5 litre engine (see paragraphs 10 and 11).

Models with C30NE and C30LE engines

14 These models are fitted with a Bosch Motronic engine management system, which is the same as that fitted to the 2.0 litre engine (see paragraphs 5 to 9).

Models with C30SE and C30SEJ engines

15 These models are fitted with a Bosch Motronic M1.5 system (see paragraphs 5 to 9). The ECU also has control over the dual ram inlet system. Refer to Section 16 for further details.

---

7 Fuel system - depressurisation

Note: *Refer to the warning note in Section 1 before proceeding.*

 Warning: The following procedure will merely relieve the pressure in the fuel system - remember that fuel will still be present in the system components and take precautions accordingly before disconnecting any of them.

1 The fuel system referred to in this Section is defined as the tank-mounted fuel pump, the fuel filter, the fuel injectors, the fuel rail and the pressure regulator, and the metal pipes and flexible hoses of the fuel lines between these components. All these contain fuel which will be under pressure while the engine is running, and/or while the ignition is switched on. The pressure will remain for some time after the ignition is switched off, and it must be relieved in a controlled fashion when any of these components are disturbed for servicing work.
2 Disconnect the battery negative terminal and continue as follows.

2.6 litre models and 3.0 litre 24-valve models

3 On these models a valve is incorporated in the fuel rail to more easily depressurise the

7.3 Removing the fuel depressurisation valve dust cap - 3.0 litre 24-valve models

8.7 Remote-mounted fuel pump

system. Unscrew the dust cap from the end of the fuel rail then hold a wad of rag over end of the valve and depress the valve core **(see illustration)**. Mop up any spilt fuel and securely refit the dust cap.

All other models

4 With the ignition turned off, remove the control (fuel pump) relay from its connector in the engine compartment relay box; the fuel pump relay wiring connector is black in colour.
5 Turn the engine over on the starter motor for at least 5 seconds to depressurise the fuel system.
6 Switch the ignition off and securely refit the relay to its connector.

8 Fuel pump - testing, removal and refitting

Testing

1 Depending on the model the fuel pump may be fitted inside the fuel tank, or mounted separately just in front of the fuel tank.
2 To check its delivery, disconnect the fuel feed hose at the fuel distribution rail in the engine compartment and direct it into a calibrated container of at least 5 litres capacity.
3 With the ignition turned off, remove the control (fuel pump) relay from its connector in the engine compartment relay box; the relay wiring connector is black in colour.

8.4 Bridging the fuel pump relay base terminals

8.8 Tank-mounted fuel pump (1) and fuel gauge sender unit (2)

4 Using a bridging wire, connect the terminals 30 and 87B together for a period of exactly one minute **(see illustration)**.
5 Check that 1.6 to 2.4 litres of fuel have been collected in the container. If this is not the case, the fuel filter may be blocked or the fuel pump is faulty. On completion of the test, switch the ignition off and securely refit the relay to its connector.

Removal

6 To remove the fuel pump, chock the front wheels, jack up the rear of the car and support it on axle stands (see "Jacking and Vehicle Support"). Depressurise the fuel system as described in Section 7.
7 On the remote-mounted fuel pump type, disconnect the wiring, then fit hose clamps to both hoses and disconnect them. Unscrew the clamp bolt and withdraw the fuel pump **(see illustration)**.
8 On the tank-mounted type remove the filler cap and syphon or pump out the fuel. Disconnect the wiring plug, then fit hose clamps to the feed and return hoses and disconnect them. Unscrew the bolts and remove the fuel pump. Recover the gasket **(see illustration)**.

Refitting

9 Refitting is a reversal of removal. On the tank-mounted type fit a new gasket, and apply locking fluid to the bolts before inserting and tightening them progressively.

9 Fuel gauge sender unit - removal and refitting

Refer to Chapter 4A, Section 4. Where the sender unit also incorporates the fuel feed and return hoses, depressurise the fuel system as described in Section 7 before removal.

10 Fuel tank - removal and refitting

Refer to Chapter 4A, Section 5, depressurising the fuel system as described in Section 7 before the fuel hoses are disconnected.

11 Fuel injection system - idle speed and mixture adjustment

1.8 litre models

1 Run the engine to normal operating temperature, then switch it off and connect a tachometer to it in accordance with the manufacturer's instructions.
2 Allow the engine to idle and compare the idle speed with that given in the Specifications. If adjustment is necessary locate the adjusting screw on the throttle housing and turn it as required **(see illustration)**.
3 Stop the engine and connect an exhaust gas analyser in accordance with the manufacturer's instructions.
4 With the engine idling at the specified speed, read the CO level and compare it with that specified. If adjustment is necessary turn the screw located on the side of the airflow sensor clockwise to enrich the mixture or anti-clockwise to weaken it **(see illustration)**.
5 Readjust the idle speed if necessary and disconnect the tachometer.

All other models

Models with a catalytic converter

6 On these models the both the idle speed

11.2 Adjusting the idle speed - 1.8 litre model

11.4 Idle mixture screw location (arrowed) - 1.8 litre model

and mixture CO level are automatically controlled by the ECU and are not adjustable. If the idle speed/mixture (CO level) are incorrect, a fault must be present in the injection system.

Models without a catalytic converter

7 On these models the idle speed is controlled by the ECU/idle speed regulator control unit and is not adjustable. If the idle speed is incorrect, a fault must be present in the injection system. The mixture (CO level) can be adjusted as follows.

8 Warm the engine up to normal operating temperature, and connect an exhaust gas analyser in accordance with the manufacturer's instructions. With the engine idling at the specified speed, read the CO level and compare it with that specified. If adjustment is necessary turn the screw located on the side of the airflow sensor clockwise to enrich the mixture or anti-clockwise to weaken it **(see illustration)**. Once the CO level is within the specified limits disconnect the tachometer.

---

12 Fuel injection components (1.8 and 2.0 litre models) - removal and refitting

1.8 litre models

Throttle valve switch

1 Disconnect the wiring plug from the switch **(see illustration)**.

12.6 Fuel distribution rail mounting bolt (arrowed)

11.8 Adjusting the idle mixture - 2.0 litre model

2 Remove the two mounting screws and pull the switch off the throttle valve spindle.
3 Refitting is a reversal of removal, but adjust the switch as follows.
4 With the wiring connector disconnected, connect an ohmmeter between the centre terminal (18) on the switch and each of the outer terminals in turn (2 and 3) **(see illustration)**. The resistance measured between terminals 2 and 18 should be zero, and between terminals 3 and 18 infinity. If necessary, loosen the two screws, turn the switch clockwise, then turn it slowly anti-clockwise until the microswitch is heard to click. Tighten the screws with the switch in this position and recheck the resistances. Once the switch is operating correctly, securely tighten the retaining screws and reconnect the wiring connector.

12.1 Disconnecting throttle valve switch wiring

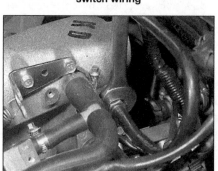

12.8 Disconnecting the brake servo vacuum pipe

Fuel injectors

5 Depressurise the fuel system (Section 7) then disconnect the battery negative lead.
6 Disconnect the wiring plugs from the injectors and unscrew the four bolts retaining the fuel distribution rail to the inlet manifold **(see illustration)**.
7 Using a screwdriver, prise out the clips holding the injectors to the distribution rail.
8 Unscrew the union nut and disconnect the brake servo vacuum pipe from the inlet manifold **(see illustration)**.
9 Remove the bracket for the fuel feed pipe.
10 Place some cloth rags around the injectors to absorb spilled fuel, then ease the distribution rail from the injectors.
11 Pull the injectors from the inlet manifold and recover all the injector seals.
12 Refitting is a reversal of removal, but if necessary renew the injector sealing rings.

Airflow sensor and electronic control unit (ECU)

13 Loosen the clip and disconnect the air duct from the airflow sensor **(see illustration)**. Disconnect the wiring multi-plug.
14 Release the spring clips and lift the airflow sensor and cover from the air cleaner body.
15 Wipe clean the sensor air valve and check it for free movement.
16 The control unit is located inside the sensor cover, which may be removed by extracting the four screws.
17 Refitting is a reversal of removal.

12.4 Checking the resistance of the throttle valve switch

12.13 Disconnecting the air duct from the airflow sensor

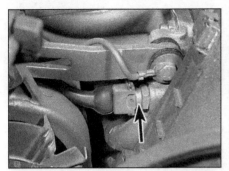

12.18 Coolant temperature sensor for the fuel injection system (arrowed)

12.25a Loosen the clips . . .

12.25b . . . and disconnect the auxiliary air valve hoses

12.26 Removing the auxiliary air valve

12.32 Fuel pressure regulator (arrowed)

12.37a Disconnecting the air inlet duct . . .

12.37b . . . and auxiliary air valve hose from the throttle valve housing

12.38a Throttle valve housing bottom coolant hose (arrowed)

12.38b Hose connections to the throttle valve housing
1 Auxiliary air valve hose
2 Crankcase ventilation hose
3 Coolant hose

Coolant temperature sensor

18 The coolant temperature sensor is located by the alternator on the side of the block **(see illustration)**.
19 Drain the cooling system (Chapter 1).
20 Disconnect the wiring plug
21 Unscrew the sensor and remove it from the engine.
22 Refitting is a reversal of removal. Refill the cooling system with reference to Chapter 1.

Auxiliary air valve

23 The auxiliary air valve is bolted to the side of the camshaft housing.
24 Disconnect the wiring plug from the valve.
25 Loosen the hose clips and disconnect the air hoses **(see illustrations)**.
26 Unbolt and remove the valve **(see illustration)**.
27 The function of the valve may be checked by looking through the hose connecting stubs. When cold the valve should be slightly

open. As the valve is heated (achieved by connecting a 12 volt supply to its terminals) the regulator disc should move round and block the hole.
28 Refitting is a reversal of removal.

Control relay

29 The control relay is located in the left-hand rear corner of the engine compartment. Unplugging the relay disables the fuel pump.
30 Lift off the cover and pull the relay from the terminal socket; its socket is black.
31 Refit in the reverse order to removal.

Fuel pressure regulator

32 The fuel pressure regulator is located between injectors 3 and 4 **(see illustration)**.
33 Place cloth rag around the regulator to absorb spilled fuel.
34 Disconnect the fuel and vacuum hoses and remove the regulator.
35 Refitting is a reversal of removal.

Throttle valve housing

36 Disconnect the battery negative lead.
37 Loosen the clips and disconnect the air inlet duct and auxiliary air valve hose **(see illustrations)**.
38 Fit hose clamps to the coolant hoses, then disconnect them from the housing **(see illustrations)**.
39 Disconnect the accelerator cable, and as appropriate the automatic transmission kick-down cable and cruise control cable.
40 Disconnect the wiring plug from the throttle valve switch.
41 Unhook the throttle return spring.
42 Detach the crankcase ventilation hose.
43 Unscrew the nuts and withdraw the throttle valve housing from the inlet manifold. Remove the gasket.

12.50 Disconnecting wiring plug
from an injector

12.52 Removing the injector clips

12.53 Disconnecting the brake servo
vacuum pipe

12.55 Removing injector from
the inlet manifold

12.56 Refitting the injector clips

12.58 Disconnecting the wiring
multi-plug from the airflow sensor

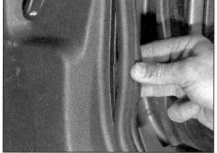

12.63 Pull back the rubber moulding and
remove the trim panel

12.64 Control unit and
upper mounting screws

44 Refitting is a reversal of removal, but fit a new gasket and adjust the cables as necessary. Top-up the coolant level.

2.0 litre models

Throttle valve switch - Motronic ML4.1 system

45 Refer to paragraphs 1 to 3, adjusting the switch as follows.
46 To adjust the switch, loosen the retaining screws and turn the switch fully clockwise. Slowly turn the switch anti-clockwise to the point where resistance is felt. Tighten the screws with the switch in this position and slowly open the throttle; if the switch is correctly positioned, it should be heard to click as the throttle opens.

Throttle valve potentiometer - Motronic M1.5 system

47 Refer to paragraphs 1 to 3, noting that no adjustment is necessary.

Fuel injectors

48 Depressurise the fuel system (Section 7) then disconnect the battery negative lead.
49 Disconnect the wiring plug from the idle speed adjuster. Disconnect the hoses and remove the adjuster.
50 Disconnect the wiring plugs from the injectors (see illustration).
51 Unscrew the four bolts retaining the fuel distribution rail to the inlet manifold.
52 Using a screwdriver, prise out the clips holding the injectors to the distribution rail (see illustration).
53 Unscrew the union nut and disconnect the brake servo vacuum pipe from the inlet manifold (see illustration).

54 Remove the bracket for the fuel feed pipe.
55 Place some cloth rags around the injectors to absorb spilled fuel, then ease the distribution rail from the injectors and pull the injectors from the inlet manifold (see illustration). Test the injectors.
56 Refitting is a reversal of removal but, if necessary, renew the injector sealing rings (see illustration).

Airflow sensor

57 Loosen the clip and disconnect the air duct from the airflow sensor.
58 Disconnect the wiring multi-plug (see illustration).
59 Release the spring clips and lift the airflow sensor and cover from the air cleaner body.
60 If necessary unbolt the sensor from the cover.
61 Wipe clean the sensor air valve and check it for free movement.
62 Refitting is a reversal of removal.

Electronic control unit (ECU)

63 Pull back the rubber moulding and remove the trim panel from the right-hand side of the driver's footwell (see illustration).
64 Remove the three mounting screws (see illustration).
65 Pull back the spring clip and disconnect the wiring multi-plug (see illustrations). Withdraw the control unit.
66 Refitting is a reversal of removal.

Coolant temperature sensor

67 Refer to paragraphs 18 to 22.

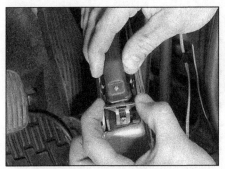

12.65a Pull back the spring clip . . .

12.65b . . . and disconnect
the wiring multi-plug

12.68 Disconnecting the wiring plug from
the idle speed adjuster

Idle speed adjuster

68 Disconnect the wiring plug from the rear of the adjuster **(see illustration)**.
69 Loosen the clips and detach the air hoses.
70 Remove the idle speed adjuster from the engine compartment.
71 Refitting is a reversal of removal.

Control relay

72 Refer to paragraphs 29 to 31.

Fuel pressure regulator

73 Refer to paragraphs 32 to 35.

Throttle valve housing

74 The procedure is basically as given in paragraphs 36 to 44, except for the disconnection of the auxiliary air valve hose.

Lambda sensor - models with a catalytic converter

Note: *The lambda sensor must be unscrewed from the exhaust system downpipe when the engine is at normal operating temperature. The sensor is delicate, and will not work if it is dropped or knocked, if its power supply is disrupted, or if any cleaning materials or solvents are used on it.*

75 Warm the engine up to normal operating temperature, then switch it off. Firmly apply the handbrake, jack up the front of the vehicle and support it on axle stands (see "*Jacking and Vehicle Support*").
76 Taking great care not to burn your hands on the hot exhaust pipe, disconnect the sensor wiring connector, and free the wiring from its retaining clips.
77 Carefully unscrew the lambda sensor, and remove it from the exhaust system along with its sealing washer.
78 If the original lambda sensor is to be refitted, remove all traces of anti-seize compound from the threads, and apply a smear of the special grease (part number 19 48 602) to the threads of the sensor; this is available from your Vauxhall dealer. In the absence of the specified grease, a smear of good-quality, high-temperature anti-seize compound can be used. Note that new lambda sensors are supplied with the grease already applied to their threads. Examine the sealing washer for signs of damage, and renew if necessary.

79 Fit the sealing washer to the end of the lambda sensor, then screw the sensor into the downpipe and tighten it to the specified torque.
80 Ensuring that the wiring is correctly routed, reconnect the wiring connector and secure the wiring with all the necessary retaining clips. Make a final check that the wiring is in no danger of contacting the exhaust system, then lower the vehicle to the ground.

Carbon canister - models with a catalytic converter

81 The carbon canister is mounted onto the engine compartment bulkhead. To remove the canister, slacken the hose clips and disconnect the hoses from the canister, noting their correct fitted positions. Slacken and remove the canister bracket mounting clamp bolt, then remove the clamp and lift the canister out of the engine compartment.
82 Refitting is a reversal of the removal procedure, ensuring that the hoses are reconnected to their original positions and the hose clamps are securely tightened.

Purge valve - models with a catalytic converter

83 Trace the outlet hose from the carbon canister (mounted on the engine compartment bulkhead) to the purge valve. Noting their correct fitted positions, slacken the retaining clips and disconnect the hoses from the valve.
84 Disconnect the valve wiring connector, then undo the retaining bolt and remove the valve from the engine compartment.
85 Refitting is a reverse of the removal procedure, ensuring that the vacuum hoses are correctly refitted and securely retained by their retaining clips.

---

13 Fuel injection components (2.5 and 2.6 litre models) - removal and refitting

2.5 litre models

Throttle valve switch

1 Refer to paragraphs 1 to 4 of Section 12.

Fuel injectors

2 Depressurise the fuel system (Section 7) and disconnect the battery negative lead.
3 Noting that the injectors are removed in pairs disconnect the wiring connectors from the relevant injectors.
4 Slacken the retaining clips and disconnect the fuel hoses from the injectors.
5 Unscrew the retaining bolt and remove the injector retaining clamp along with the pair of injectors.
6 Remove the injectors from the clamp and recover both the large and small injector seals from the manifold.
7 Refitting is the reverse of removal, using new seals.

Airflow sensor

8 Disconnect the wiring connector from the sensor then slacken the retaining clip and disconnect the inlet duct.
9 Release the retaining clips and lift off the air cleaner lid. If necessary, unscrew the retaining nuts/bolts and remove the airflow sensor and seal.
10 Refitting is the reverse of removal, ensuring that the rubber seal is correctly fitted. Also apply locking compound the retaining bolts prior to refitting.

Electronic control unit (ECU)

11 Refer to Section 12, paragraphs 63 to 66.

Coolant temperature sensor

12 Disconnect one of the small coolant hoses from the thermostat housing and drain out the coolant.
13 Disconnect the wiring connector and unscrew the sensor from the thermostat housing. Recover the sealing washer.
14 Refitting is the reverse of removal, tightening the sensor to the specified torque.

Idle speed adjuster

15 Disconnect the wiring connector from the adjuster.
16 Slacken the retaining clips and disconnect the air hoses then remove the adjuster.
17 Refitting is a reversal of removal.

Idle speed adjuster control unit

18 Peel off the rubber seal from the top of the engine compartment bulkhead and lift up the water deflector to gain access to the control unit. To further improve access remove the wiper arms and spindle nuts (Chapter 12).

19 Disconnect the wiring connectors then undo the bolts and remove the control unit.

20 Refitting is the reverse of removal.

Control relay

21 Refer to Section 12, paragraphs 29 to 31.

Fuel pressure regulator

22 Depressurise the fuel system (Section 7).

23 Disconnect the vacuum hose from the regulator.

24 Slacken the retaining clips then disconnect the fuel hoses and remove the regulator from the manifold.

25 Refitting is the reverse of removal.

2.6 litre models

Throttle valve potentiometer

26 Slacken the clips and remove the breather hose from between the throttle housing and cylinder head cover.

27 Disconnect the wiring connector then undo the retaining screws and remove the potentiometer from the side of the throttle housing.

28 Refitting is the reverse of removal, securely tightening the retaining screws.

Fuel injectors

29 Depressurise the fuel system (Section 7).

30 Remove the throttle housing and inlet duct assembly (Section 15).

31 Remove the dual ram air operating diaphragm from the manifold (Section 16)

32 Unbolt the inlet manifold support brackets from the cylinder head and remove.

33 Disconnect the vacuum hose from the pressure regulator.

34 Disconnect the wiring connectors from the thermostat housing and injectors.

35 Unbolt the cable guide strip.

36 Disconnect the fuel feed and return pipes from the fuel rail.

37 Slacken and remove the fuel rail retaining bolts.

38 Remove the bolts securing the centre and rear injector adapter to the manifold.

39 Ease the front injectors out their adapter then remove the centre and rear adapters from the injectors. Recover the injector seals.

40 Slide the fuel rail and injector assembly out of position and remove it from the engine compartment. Recover the gaskets fitted between the adapters and manifold.

41 Carefully prise off the spring clip the relevant injector and remove it from the fuel rail. Recover the seal.

42 Refitting is the reverse of removal, fitting new injector seals and adapter gaskets.

Airflow sensor

43 Refer to paragraphs 8 and 10.

Electronic control unit (ECU)

44 Refer to Section 12, paragraphs 63 to 66.

Coolant temperature sensor

45 Refer to paragraphs 12 to 14.

Idle speed adjuster

46 Undo the retaining screws and remove the cover from the top of the inlet ducts.

47 Disconnect the wiring connector and push the adjuster out from its rubber mounting.

48 From the side of the manifold, slacken the retaining clips then disconnect the air hoses and remove the adjuster.

49 Refitting is the reverse of removal making sure the adjuster is securely retained by its rubber mounting.

Control relay

50 Refer to Section 12, paragraphs 29 to 31.

Fuel pressure regulator

51 Remove the fuel rail and injector assembly as described in paragraphs 29 to 40.

52 Undo the retaining screws and remove the regulator.

53 Refitting is the reverse of removal.

Lambda sensor

54 Refer to Section 12, paragraphs 75 to 80.

Carbon canister

55 See paragraphs 81 and 82 of Section 12 noting on some models that the canister is mounted underneath the wing.

Purge valve

56 Undo the retaining screws and remove the cover from the top of the inlet ducts.

57 Disconnect the hoses, noting their correct fitted locations, undo the retaining bolt and remove the valve.

58 Refitting is the reverse of removal.

---

14 Fuel injection components (3.0 litre models) - removal and refitting

Models with non-catalyst CIH (30NE) engine

1 Refer to the information given in Section 13 for the 2.5 litre model.

Models with CIH (C30NE and C30LE) engines with a catalytic converter

Throttle valve switch - Motronic ML4.1 system

2 Disconnect the wiring plug from the switch.

3 Remove the two mounting screws and pull the switch off the throttle valve spindle.

4 Refitting is a reversal of removal, but adjust the switch as follows.

5 To adjust the switch, loosen the retaining screws and turn the switch fully clockwise. Slowly turn the switch anti-clockwise to the point where resistance is felt. Tighten the screws with the switch in this position and slowly open the throttle; if the switch is correctly positioned, it should be heard to click as the throttle opens.

Throttle valve potentiometer - Motronic M1.5 system

6 Refer to paragraphs 2 to 4, noting that no adjustment is necessary.

Fuel injectors - C30LE engine

7 Refer to paragraphs 2 to 7 of Section 13.

Fuel injectors - C30NE engine

8 Depressurise the fuel system (Section 7).

9 Disconnect the fuel feed and return hoses from the fuel rail. Slacken and remove the fuel rail retaining bolts. Ease the fuel rail and injector assembly out of position and remove it from the engine compartment. Recover the injector seals.

10 Carefully prise off the spring clip the relevant injector and remove it from the fuel rail. Recover the seal.

11 Refitting is the reverse of removal, fitting new injector seals.

Airflow sensor

12 Refer to Section 13, paragraphs 8 and 10.

Electronic control unit (ECU)

13 Refer to Section 12, paragraphs 63 to 66.

Coolant temperature sensor

14 Refer to Section 13, paragraphs 12 to 14.

Idle speed adjuster

15 Refer to Section 13, paragraphs 15 to 17.

Control relay

16 Refer to Section 12, paragraphs 29 to 31.

Fuel pressure regulator - C30LE engine

17 Refer to Section 13, paragraphs 22 to 25.

Fuel pressure regulator - C30NE engine

18 Depressurise the fuel system (Section 7).

19 Disconnect the vacuum hose from the regulator then unbolt the regulator from the fuel rail.

20 Refitting is the reverse of removal.

Lambda sensor

21 Refer to Section 12, paragraphs 75 to 80.

Carbon canister

22 Refer to Section 12, paragraphs 81 and 82, noting on some models that the canister is mounted underneath the wing.

Purge valve

23 Refer to Section 12, paragraphs 83 to 85, noting the valve is mounted onto the suspension turret.

Models with DOHC (C30SE and C30SEJ) engine

Throttle valve potentiometer

24 Refer to Section 13, paragraphs 26 to 28.

Fuel injectors

25 Remove the inlet manifold and fuel injectors as described in Section 15.

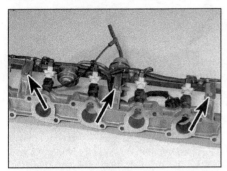

14.26 Fuel rail retaining bolts (arrowed)

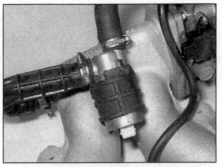

14.34 Idle speed adjuster (viewed with intake ducts removed)

14.38 Fuel pressure regulator retaining bolts (arrowed)

14.40 Diaphragm damper retaining screws (arrowed)

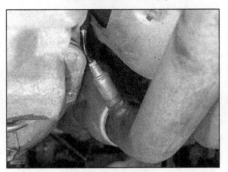

14.41 Lambda sensor is screwed into the front pipe

14.42 Removing the carbon canister

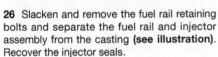

14.44 Disconnecting the purge valve hoses

26 Slacken and remove the fuel rail retaining bolts and separate the fuel rail and injector assembly from the casting **(see illustration)**. Recover the injector seals.
27 Disconnect the wiring plugs then release the clip(s) and slide the relevant injector(s) out of the fuel rail. Recover the seals.
28 Refitting is the reverse of removal using new injector seals.

Airflow sensor
29 See paragraphs 8 and 10 of Section 13.

Electronic control unit (ECU)
30 See paragraphs 63 to 66 of Section 12.

Coolant temperature sensor
31 See paragraphs 12 to 14 of Section 13.

Idle speed adjuster
Note: *To improve access, remove the throttle housing and inlet duct assembly (Section 15).*
32 Undo the retaining screws and remove the cover from the top of the inlet ducts.

33 Disconnect the wiring connector and push the adjuster out from its rubber mounting.
34 From beneath the manifold, slacken the clips then disconnect the air hoses and remove the adjuster **(see illustration)**.
35 Refitting is the reverse of removal. Ensure the adjuster is retained by its rubber mounting.

Control relay
36 See paragraphs 29 to 31 of Section 12.

Fuel pressure regulator
37 Remove the inlet manifold and fuel injectors as described in Section 15.
38 Slacken and remove the retaining bolts and remove the regulator from the fuel rail **(see illustration)**.
39 Refitting is the reverse of removal using new injector seals.

Diaphragm damper
40 Refer to paragraphs 37 to 39 **(see illustration)**.

Lambda sensor
41 See paragraphs 75 to 80 of Section 12 **(see illustration)**.

Carbon canister
42 See paragraphs 81 and 82 of Section 12 noting on some models that the canister is mounted underneath the wing **(see illustration)**.

Purge valve
43 Undo the retaining screws and remove the cover from the top of the inlet ducts.
44 Disconnect the wiring connector and hoses, noting their correct fitted locations,

undo the retaining bolt and remove the valve **(see illustration)**.
45 Refitting is the reverse of removal.

15 Inlet manifold - removal and refitting

Removal

1.8 and 2.0 litre models
1 Depressurise the fuel system (Section 7) then disconnect the battery negative terminal.
2 Disconnect the air inlet duct from the throttle housing.
3 Disconnect all crankcase ventilation, coolant, fuel and air hoses **(see illustration)**.
4 Disconnect all electrical wires.
5 Disconnect the accelerator/kickdown cable(s) (as applicable).

15.3 Disconnecting idle speed adjuster hose from inlet manifold (2.0 litre model)

15.6a Removing the inlet manifold
(1.8 litre model)

15.6b Inlet manifold gasket on the
cylinder head (1.8 litre model)

6 Progressively unscrew the nuts then withdraw the inlet manifold from the studs on the cylinder head. Remove the gasket (see illustrations).
7 Clean the mating faces of the inlet manifold and cylinder head.

2.5 litre models

Note: The inlet and exhaust manifold share the same gasket. Therefore if the inlet manifold is to be removed, the exhaust manifold should also be removed to allow the gasket to be renewed.
8 Depressurise the fuel system (Section 7) then disconnect the battery negative terminal.
9 Disconnect the exhaust front pipe from the manifold.
10 Remove the inlet duct connecting the airflow sensor to the manifold.
11 Disconnect the coolant hoses from the throttle housing. Plug the hose ends to minimise coolant loss.
12 Disconnect the crankcase ventilation hose, vacuum hose(s) from the manifold.
13 Disconnect the fuel feed and return hoses from the fuel rail.
14 Disconnect the accelerator/kickdown cable(s) (as applicable).
15 Disconnect the wiring connectors from the injectors, throttle valve switch and (where fitted) the inlet manifold temperature switch. Also disconnect the earth lead from the manifold.
16 Slacken the union nuts and free the exhaust gas recirculation valve from the manifolds.
17 Slacken and remove the inlet manifold retaining nuts/bolts and remove the inlet manifold. Recover the manifold locating pins (where fitted).
18 Remove the remaining retaining bolts and remove the exhaust manifolds and manifold gasket from the engine.

2.6 litre models

Note: The inlet and exhaust manifold share the same gasket. Therefore if the inlet manifold is to be removed, the exhaust manifold should also be removed to allow the gasket to be renewed.
19 Depressurise the fuel system (Section 7) then disconnect the battery negative terminal.
20 Disconnect the exhaust front pipe from the manifold.

21 Disconnect the accelerator/kickdown cable(s) (as applicable).
22 Slacken the clip and disconnect the inlet duct from the throttle housing.
23 Unclip the coolant pipe from the inlet manifold.
24 Undo the retaining screws and remove the cover from the inlet ducts.
25 Release the clamps securing the inlet ducts to the manifold then undo the retaining bolts. Disconnect the wiring and vacuum hoses, noting the correct location of each one, and remove the inlet duct and throttle housing assembly from the engine.
26 Undo the retaining nuts and remove the dual ram air system valve and diaphragm from the manifold.
27 Unbolt the earth cable from the manifold.
28 Unbolt the inlet manifold support brackets.
29 Disconnect the vacuum hose from the fuel pressure regulator.

15.39a On 3.0 litre 24-valve models, undo
the retaining screws . . .

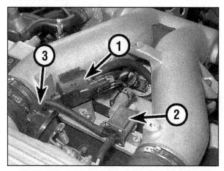

15.40 Disconnect the hoses and wiring
from the purge valve (1) and dual ram air
valve (2) and diaphragm (3)

30 Disconnect the wiring connectors from the thermostat housing and disconnect the harness wiring connector located in the front, right-hand corner of the engine compartment.
31 Noting the correct routing of the wiring, disconnect the wiring plugs from the idle speed adjuster, throttle valve potentiometer, purge valve and dual ram air valve.
32 Unscrew the fuel hoses from the fuel rail.
33 Undo the six retaining bolts and remove the inlet manifold from the engine.
34 Remove the remaining retaining bolts and remove the exhaust manifolds and manifold gasket from the engine.

3.0 litre (CIH) 12-valve models

35 Refer to paragraphs 8 to 18.

3.0 litre (DOHC) 24-valve models

36 Depressurise the fuel system (Section 7) then disconnect the battery negative lead.
37 Disconnect the wiring connector from the airflow sensor.
38 Remove the inlet duct connecting the air cleaner to the throttle housing.
39 Undo the screws and remove the top cover from the inlet ducts (see illustrations).
40 Mark the hoses for identification and disconnect the hoses from the purge valve and the dual ram air valve and diaphragm. Also disconnect the wiring connectors from the valves (see illustration).
41 Disconnect the vacuum and coolant hoses from the throttle housing. Plug the coolant hose ends to minimise coolant loss (see illustration).
42 Slacken the clips and remove the breather

15.39b . . . and remove the top cover from
the intake ducts

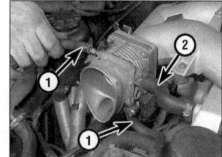

15.41 Disconnect the coolant hoses (1)
and breather hose (2) from the
throttle housing

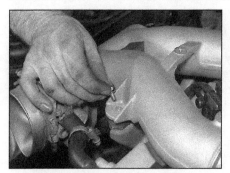

15.45a Undo the retaining bolts . . .

15.45b . . . then release the clamps and remove the intake duct and throttle housing assembly from the engine

15.46 Unbolt the earth leads from the inlet manifold

15.47 unscrew the brake servo hose union

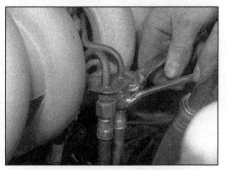

15.49 Unscrew the fuel hoses from the fuel rail

15.50 Disconnect the injector wiring connector

15.53 Unscrew the manifold nuts and release the retaining clips from the studs

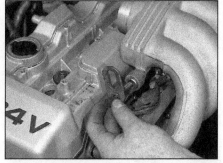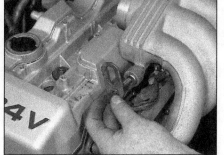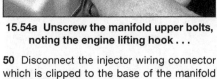

15.54a Unscrew the manifold upper bolts, noting the engine lifting hook . . .

15.54b . . . and recover the spacers

hose linking the throttle housing and cylinder head cover.

43 Disconnect the accelerator/kickdown cable(s) (as applicable).

44 Disconnect the wiring connector from the throttle potentiometer and idle speed adjuster.

45 Release the clamps securing the ducts to the inlet manifold then undo the mounting bolts and remove the inlet duct and throttle housing assembly from the engine **(see illustrations)**.

46 Unbolt the earth connections from the rear of the manifold **(see illustration)**.

47 Disconnect the brake servo hose from the manifold **(see illustration)**.

48 Disconnect the vacuum hose from the fuel pressure regulator.

49 Unscrew the fuel feed and return hoses from the fuel rail **(see illustration)**.

50 Disconnect the injector wiring connector which is clipped to the base of the manifold **(see illustration)**.

51 Remove the engine oil dipstick.

52 On models with cruise control, remove the unit as described in Chapter 12.

53 Slacken and remove the retaining nuts and free the wiring clips from the manifold lower studs, noting their correct fitted locations **(see illustration)**; new ones should be used when refitting. Discard the nuts; new ones should be used when refitting.

54 Slacken and remove the front and rear upper manifold bolts and recover the spacers which are fitted between the manifold and mounting. Note that the engine lifting bracket is also fitted to the front bolt **(see illustrations)**.

55 Manoeuvre the manifold away from the cylinder head **(see illustration)**.

56 Remove the injector casting from the

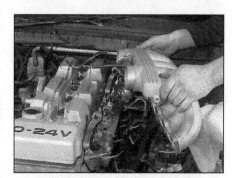

15.55 Removing the inlet manifold

head and recover the gasket spacers and sealing rings **(see illustrations)**.

Refitting

57 Refitting is a reversal of removal, using a new gasket(s) and sealing rings (as applicable)

15.56a Remove the injector casting . . .

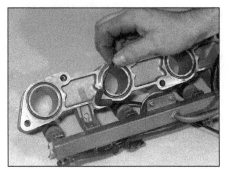

15.56b . . . and recover the sealing rings . . .

15.56c . . . and gasket spacers

and tighten the mounting nut/bolts to the specified torque. On 3.0 litre (DOHC) 24-valve models new manifold retaining nuts should be used.

16 Exhaust manifold - removal and refitting

Removal

1.8 and 2.0 litre models

1 Disconnect the HT cables from the spark plugs and ignition coil.
2 Unscrew the bolts securing the exhaust downpipe to the exhaust manifold, lower the downpipe and recover the joint **(see illustration)**.
3 Progressively unscrew the nuts, then withdraw the exhaust manifold from the studs

on the cylinder head **(see illustration)**. Remove the gasket.

2.5 and 2.6 litre models

4 Refer to Section 15.

3.0 litre (CIH) 12-valve models

5 Refer to Section 15.

3.0 litre (DOHC) 24-valve models

6 Firmly apply the handbrake then jack up the front of the vehicle and support it on axle stands (see "*Jacking and Vehicle Support*").
7 Remove the throttle housing and inlet duct assembly as described in Section 15.
8 Unscrew the bolts securing the rear of the front pipe to its mounting bracket.
9 Undo the retaining bolts and remove the heatshield from the manifold **(see illustration)**
10 Slacken and remove the manifold retaining nuts noting the correct fitted location of the engine lifting hook **(see illustration)**

11 Remove the manifolds and gaskets **(see illustrations)**.

Refitting

12 Refitting is a reversal of removal, but use a new gasket and tighten the mounting nuts to the specified torque. Note that new manifold retaining nuts should be used on 3.0 litre (DOHC) 24-valve models.

17 Dual ram air inlet system (2.6 litre and 3.0 litre 24-valve models) - general

General information

1 On 2.6 litre and 3.0 litre 24-valve models, a dual ram air inlet system is fitted to improve the low down torque of the engine. The manifold has two inlet ducts, one for the front three cylinders and another for the back three.

16.2 Exhaust downpipe and gasket

16.3 Removing the exhaust manifold

16.9 On 3.0 litre 24-valve models remove the heatshield from the manifold

16.10 Remove the manifold retaining nuts, noting the engine lifting hook

16.11a Remove the manifolds . . .

16.11b . . . and recover the gaskets

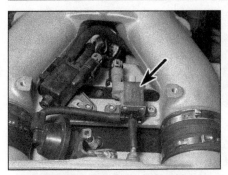

17.4 Dual ram air system solenoid valve (3.0 litre 24-valve model shown)

The inlet manifold is fitted with a butterfly valve in between the number 3 and 4 cylinder inlet duct. The valve has a vacuum diaphragm unit attached to it and is controlled by the ECU by way of a solenoid valve.

2 At engine speeds up to 4000 rpm, the butterfly valve remains closed. This effectively lengthens the inlet path and increases the low down torque output of the engine. At engine speeds of 4000 rpm and above the ECU switches the solenoid valve which in turn supplies vacuum to the diaphragm and opens up the butterfly valve. The inlet path is effectively shortened which increases the high speed torque output of the engine.

Component renewal

Solenoid valve

3 Undo the retaining screws and remove the cover from the top of the inlet ducts.

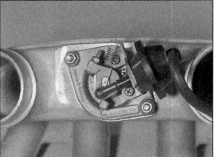

17.7 Dual ram air diaphragm unit and valve assembly

4 Disconnect the wiring connector and vacuum hoses from the solenoid valve then undo the retaining bolt and remove the valve from the engine (see illustration).
5 Refitting is the reverse of removal.

Diaphragm unit and valve assembly

6 Remove the purge valve as described in Section 14.
7 Disconnect the vacuum hose from the diaphragm the undo the retaining nuts and remove the assembly from the inlet manifold (see illustration). If necessary the valve and diaphragm can be separated and renewed individually.
8 Refitting is the reverse of removal.

18 Exhaust system - removal and refitting

Removal

1.8 and 2.0 litre models

1 On models not fitted with a catalytic converter, the exhaust system is in three sections, each with its own silencer. On models with a catalytic converter, the exhaust system consists of four sections; a shorter front pipe is fitted and the catalytic converter is fitted between the front pipe and intermediate pipe.
2 To remove the complete system, position the car over an inspection pit, or raise the car and support it on axle stands (see "Jacking and Vehicle Support"). On models with a catalytic converter, disconnect the lambda sensor wiring connector and free the wiring from its retaining clips.
3 Unscrew the bolts securing the exhaust downpipe to the manifold, lower the downpipe and recover the joint.
4 With the help of an assistant, unbolt the front mounting clamp and unhook the rubber mountings. The intermediate mounting rubbers are retained with metal clips (see illustrations). On some models the front mounting is of rubber instead of a clamp.
5 Lower the exhaust system to the ground.
6 Separate the sections by unbolting the flange and removing the clamp (see illustrations).

18.4a Exhaust front mounting clamp

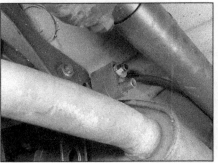

18.4b Intermediate exhaust mounting with exhaust fitted

18.4c Intermediate exhaust mounting rubber with exhaust removed

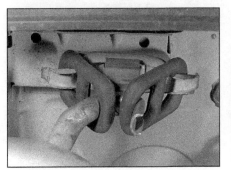

18.4d Rear exhaust mounting rubber rings

18.6a Exhaust downpipe to intermediate section flange

18.6b Intermediate to rear section clamp

2.5, 2.6 and 3.0 litre models

7 On models not fitted with a catalytic converter the exhaust system consists of four sections, the front pipe, the two intermediate pipe sections and the tailpipe. On models fitted with a catalytic converter the system is similar but the catalytic converters are fitted between the front pipe and intermediate pipes; twin catalytic converters are fitted one to each intermediate pipe.

8 Refer to paragraphs 2 to 6 for removal details.

Refitting

9 Refitting is a reversal of removal, using new gaskets (where fitted). Tighten the manifold bolts with the exhaust system loose in the front clamp, then tighten the clamp.

19 Catalytic converter - general information and precautions

1 The catalytic converter is a reliable and simple device which needs no maintenance in itself, but there are some facts of which an owner should be aware if the converter is to function properly for its full service life.

a) DO NOT use leaded petrol in a car equipped with a catalytic converter - the lead will coat the precious metals, reducing their converting efficiency and will eventually destroy the converter.

b) Always keep the ignition and fuel systems well-maintained in accordance with the manufacturer's schedule.

c) If the engine develops a misfire, do not drive the car at all (or at least as little as possible) until the fault is cured.

d) DO NOT push- or tow-start the car - this will soak the catalytic converter in unburned fuel, causing it to overheat when the engine does start.

e) DO NOT switch off the ignition at high engine speeds.

f) DO NOT use fuel or engine oil additives - these may contain substances harmful to the catalytic converter.

g) DO NOT continue to use the car if the engine burns oil to the extent of leaving a visible trail of blue smoke.

h) Remember that the catalytic converter operates at very high temperatures. DO NOT, therefore, park the car in dry undergrowth, over long grass or piles of dead leaves after a long run.

i) Remember that the catalytic converter is FRAGILE - do not strike it with tools during servicing work.

J) In some cases a sulphurous smell (like that of rotten eggs) may be noticed from the exhaust. This is common to many catalytic converter-equipped cars and once the car has covered a few thousand miles the problem should disappear.

k) The catalytic converter, used on a well-maintained and well-driven car, should last for between 50 000 and 100 000 miles - if the converter is no longer effective it must be renewed.

Chapter 5 Part A:
Starting and charging systems

Contents

Alternator - removal and refitting 7
Alternator testing and overhaul 8
Alternator drivebelt - removal, refitting and tensioning 6
Battery - removal and refitting 4
Battery - testing and charging 3
Battery check . . . . .See "Weekly Checks"
Charging system - testing 5
Electrical fault finding - general information .2
Electrical system check . . . . .See Chapter 1
General information and precautions 1
Ignition switch - removal and refitting 12
Oil level sensor - removal and refitting 14
Oil pressure warning light switch - removal and refitting 13
Starter motor - removal and refitting 10
Starter motor - testing and overhaul 11
Starting system - testing 9

Degrees of difficulty

Easy, suitable for novice with little experience	**Fairly easy,** suitable for beginner with some experience	**Fairly difficult,** suitable for competent DIY mechanic 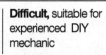	**Difficult,** suitable for experienced DIY mechanic	**Very difficult,** suitable for expert DIY or professional

Specifications

System type . . . . 12-volt, negative earth

Battery
Type . . . . Lead-acid, maintenance-free
Capacity:
   1.8 and 2.0 litre models . . . . 44 Amp-hour
   2.5, 2.6 and 3.0 litre models . . . . 44, 55 or 66 Amp-hour (depending on specification)

Alternator
Type . . . . Delco or Bosch (depending on model)

Starter motor
Type . . . . Delco or Bosch (depending on model)

Torque wrench settings	**Nm**	**lbf ft**
Alternator:		
10 mm bolts	35	26
8 mm bolts	25	18
Starter motor:		
1.8 and 2.0 litre models:		
Engine side	45	33
Transmission side	60	44
2.5, 2.6 and 3.0 litre models	70	50

---

1 General information and precautions

General information

1 The engine electrical system consists mainly of the charging and starting systems. Because of their engine-related functions, these components are covered separately from the body electrical devices such as the lights, instruments, etc (which are covered in Chapter 12). Refer to Part B for information on the ignition system.

2 The electrical system is of the 12-volt negative earth type.

3 The battery is of the low maintenance or "maintenance-free" (sealed for life) type and is charged by the alternator, which is belt-driven from the crankshaft pulley.

4 The starter motor is of the pre-engaged type incorporating an integral solenoid. On starting, the solenoid moves the drive pinion into engagement with the flywheel ring gear before the starter motor is energised. Once the engine has started, a one-way clutch prevents the motor armature being driven by the engine until the pinion disengages from the flywheel.

Precautions

5 Further details of the various systems are given in the relevant Sections of this Chapter.

While some repair procedures are given, the usual course of action is to renew the component concerned. The owner whose interest extends beyond component renewal should obtain a copy of the *"Automobile Electrical & Electronic Systems Manual"*, available from the publishers of this manual.

6 It is necessary to take extra care when working on the electrical system to avoid damage to semi-conductor devices (diodes and transistors), and to avoid the risk of personal injury. In addition to the precautions given in "Safety first!" at the beginning of this manual, observe the following when working on the system:

Always remove rings, watches, etc before working on the electrical system. Even with

the battery disconnected, capacitive discharge could occur if a component's live terminal is earthed through a metal object. This could cause a shock or a burn.

Do not reverse the battery connections. Components such as the alternator, electronic control units, or any other components having semi-conductor circuitry could be irreparably damaged.

If the engine is being started using jump leads and a slave battery, connect the batteries positive-to-positive and negative-to-negative (see "Booster battery (jump) starting"). This also applies when connecting a battery charger.

Never disconnect the battery terminals, the alternator, any electrical wiring or any test instruments when the engine is running.

Do not allow the engine to turn the alternator when the alternator is not connected.

Never "test" for alternator output by 'flashing' the output lead to earth.

Never use an ohmmeter of the type incorporating a hand-cranked generator for circuit or continuity testing.

Always ensure that the battery negative lead is disconnected when working on the electrical system.

Before using electric-arc welding equipment on the car, disconnect the battery, alternator and components such as the fuel injection/ignition electronic control unit to protect them from the risk of damage.

The radio/cassette unit fitted as standard equipment by Vauxhall/Opel is equipped with a built-in security code to deter thieves. If the power source to the unit is cut, the anti-theft system will activate. Even if the power source is immediately reconnected, the radio/cassette unit will not function until the correct security code has been entered. Therefore, if you do not know the correct security code for the radio/cassette unit do not disconnect the battery negative terminal of the battery or remove the radio/cassette unit from the car. Refer to "Radio/cassette unit anti-theft system precaution".

2 Electrical fault finding - general information

Refer to Chapter 12.

3 Battery - testing and charging

Standard and low maintenance battery - testing

1 If the vehicle covers a small annual mileage, it is worthwhile checking the specific gravity of the electrolyte every three months to determine the state of charge of the battery. Use a hydrometer to make the check and compare the results with the following table. The temperatures quoted in the table are ambient (air) temperatures. Note that the specific gravity readings assume an electrolyte temperature of 15°C (60°F); for every 10°C (50°F) below 15°C (60°F) subtract 0.007. For every 10°C (50°F) above 15°C (60°F) add 0.007.

	Above 25°C(77°F)	Below 25°C(77°F)
Fully-charged	1.210 to 1.230	1.270 to 1.290
70% charged	1.170 to 1.190	1.230 to 1.250
Discharged	1.050 to 1.070	1.110to 1.130

2 If the battery condition is suspect, first check the specific gravity of electrolyte in each cell. A variation of 0.040 or more between any cells indicates loss of electrolyte or deterioration of the internal plates.
3 If the specific gravity variation is 0.040 or more, the battery should be renewed. If the cell variation is satisfactory but the battery is discharged, it should be charged as described later in this Section.

Maintenance-free battery - testing

4 In cases where a "sealed for life" maintenance-free battery is fitted, topping-up and testing of the electrolyte in each cell is not possible. The condition of the battery can therefore only be tested using a battery condition indicator or a voltmeter.
5 Certain models my be fitted with a "Delco" type maintenance-free battery, with a built-in charge condition indicator (see illustration). The indicator is located in the top of the battery casing, and indicates the condition of the battery from its colour. If the indicator shows green, then the battery is in a good state of charge. If the indicator turns darker, eventually to black, then the battery requires charging, as described later in this Section. If the indicator shows clear/yellow, then the electrolyte level in the battery is too low to allow further use, and the battery should be renewed. Do not attempt to charge, load or jump start a battery when the indicator shows clear/yellow.

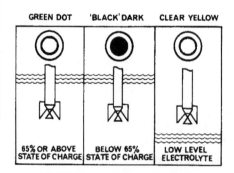

3.5 Battery "magic eye" indicator hydrometer readings

6 If testing the battery using a voltmeter, connect the voltmeter across the battery and compare the result with those given in the Specifications under "charge condition". The test is only accurate if the battery has not been subjected to any kind of charge for the previous six hours. If this is not the case, switch on the headlights for 30 seconds, then wait four to five minutes before testing the battery after switching off the headlights. All other electrical circuits must be switched off, so check that the doors and tailgate are fully shut when making the test.
7 If the voltage reading is less than 12.2 volts, then the battery is discharged, whilst a reading of 12.2 to 12.4 volts indicates a partially discharged condition.
8 If the battery is to be charged, remove it from the vehicle (Section 4) and charge it as described later in this Section.

Standard and low maintenance battery - charging

Note: The following is intended as a guide only. Always refer to the maker's recommendations (often printed on a label attached to the battery) before charging a battery.
9 Charge the battery at a rate of 3.5 to 4 amps and continue to charge the battery at this rate until no further rise in specific gravity is noted over a four hour period.
10 Alternatively, a trickle charger charging at the rate of 1.5 amps can be used overnight.
11 Specially rapid 'boost' charges which are claimed to restore the power of the battery in 1 to 2 hours are not recommended, as they can cause serious damage to the battery plates through overheating.
12 While charging the battery, note that the temperature of the electrolyte should never exceed 37.8°C (100°F).

Maintenance-free battery - charging

Note: The following is intended as a guide only. Always refer to the maker's recommendations (often printed on a label attached to the battery) before charging a battery.
13 This battery type takes considerably longer to fully recharge than the standard type, the time taken being dependent on the extent of discharge, but it can take anything up to three days.
14 A constant voltage type charger is required, to be set to 13.9 to 14.9 volts with a charge current below 25 amps. Using this method, the battery should be usable within three hours, giving a voltage reading of 12.5 volts, but this is for a partially discharged battery and, as mentioned, full charging can take much longer.
15 If the battery is to be charged from a fully discharged state (condition reading less than 12.2 volts), have it recharged by your Vauxhall dealer or local automotive electrician, as the charge rate is higher and constant supervision during charging is necessary.

4.4 Battery clamp and bolt

4 Battery - removal and refitting

Note: *If a Vauxhall/Opel radio/cassette unit is fitted, refer to "Radio/cassette unit anti-theft system - precaution" in the Reference section of this manual.*

Removal

1 The battery is located on the left-hand side of the engine compartment.
2 Slacken the clamp nut/bolt and disconnect the clamp from the battery negative (earth) terminal.
3 Remove the insulation cover (where fitted) and disconnect the positive terminal lead clamp in the same way.
4 Unscrew the bolt and remove battery retaining clamp **(see illustration)**.
5 Lift the battery out of the engine compartment. If necessary, undo the retaining bolts then release all the relevant clips securing the wiring to the tray and remove the battery tray from the engine compartment.

Refitting

6 Refitting is a reversal of removal, but smear petroleum jelly on the terminals when reconnecting the leads, and always reconnect the positive lead first, and the negative lead last.

5 Charging system - testing

Note: *Refer to the warnings given in "Safety first!" and in Section 1 of this Chapter before starting work.*
1 If the ignition warning light fails to illuminate when the ignition is switched on, first check the alternator wiring connections for security. If satisfactory, check that the warning light bulb has not blown, and that the bulbholder is secure in its location in the instrument panel. If the light still fails to illuminate, check the continuity of the warning light feed wire from the alternator to the bulbholder. If all is satisfactory, the alternator is at fault and should be renewed or taken to an auto-electrician for testing and repair.

2 If the ignition warning light illuminates when the engine is running, stop the engine and check that the drivebelt is correctly tensioned (see Chapter 1) and that the alternator connections are secure. If all is so far satisfactory, have the alternator checked by an auto-electrician for testing and repair.
3 If the alternator output is suspect even though the warning light functions correctly, the regulated voltage may be checked as follows.
4 Connect a voltmeter across the battery terminals and start the engine.
5 Increase the engine speed until the voltmeter reading remains steady; the reading should be approximately 12 to 13 volts, and no more than 14 volts.
6 Switch on as many electrical accessories (eg, the headlights, heated rear window and heater blower) as possible, and check that the alternator maintains the regulated voltage at around 13 to 14 volts.
7 If the regulated voltage is not as stated, the fault may be due to worn brushes, weak brush springs, a faulty voltage regulator, a faulty diode, a severed phase winding or worn or damaged slip rings. The alternator should be renewed or taken to an auto-electrician for testing and repair.

6 Alternator drivebelt - removal, refitting and tensioning

Refer to the procedure given for the auxiliary drivebelt(s) in Chapter 1.

7 Alternator - removal and refitting

Removal

1 Disconnect the battery negative lead. If necessary to improve access, firmly apply the handbrake then jack up the front of the vehicle and support it on axle stands (see *"Jacking and Vehicle Support"*).
2 Release the drivebelt tension as described in Chapter 1 and unhook the belt from the alternator pulley.

7.4a Loosening the alternator adjustment bolt - 1.8 litre models

3 Note the electrical connections at the rear of the alternator then disconnect them.
4 Slacken and remove the adjustment/pivot bolts and withdraw the alternator from the engine. If necessary unbolt the bracket from the block **(see illustrations)**.

Refitting

5 Refitting is a reversal of removal, tensioning the drivebelt as described in Chapter 1.

8 Alternator - testing and overhaul

If the alternator is thought to be suspect, it should be removed from the vehicle and taken to an auto-electrician for testing. Most auto-electricians will be able to supply and fit brushes at a reasonable cost. However, check on the cost of repairs before continuing as it may prove more economical to obtain a new or exchange alternator.

9 Starting system - testing

Note: *Refer to the precautions given in "Safety first!" and in Section 1 of this Chapter before starting work.*
1 If the starter motor fails to operate when the ignition key is turned to the appropriate position, the following possible causes may be to blame.

a) *The battery is faulty.*
b) *The electrical connections between the switch, solenoid, battery and starter motor are somewhere failing to pass the necessary current from the battery through the starter to earth.*
c) *The solenoid is faulty.*
d) *The starter motor is mechanically or electrically defective.*

2 To check the battery, switch on the headlights. If they dim after a few seconds, this indicates that the battery is discharged - recharge (see Section 3) or renew the battery. If the headlights glow brightly, operate the ignition switch and observe the lights. If they

7.4b Removing the alternator - 1.8 litre models

dim, then this indicates that current is reaching the starter motor, therefore the fault must lie in the starter motor. If the lights continue to glow brightly (and no clicking sound can be heard from the starter motor solenoid), this indicates that there is a fault in the circuit or solenoid - see following paragraphs. If the starter motor turns slowly when operated, but the battery is in good condition, then this indicates that either the starter motor is faulty, or there is considerable resistance somewhere in the circuit.

3 If a fault in the circuit is suspected, disconnect the battery leads (including the earth connection to the body), the starter/solenoid wiring and the engine/transmission earth strap. Thoroughly clean the connections, and reconnect the leads and wiring, then use a voltmeter or test lamp to check that full battery voltage is available at the battery positive lead connection to the solenoid, and that the earth is sound. Smear petroleum jelly around the battery terminals to prevent corrosion - corroded connections are amongst the most frequent causes of electrical system faults.

4 If the battery and all connections are in good condition, check the circuit by disconnecting the wire from the solenoid blade terminal. Connect a voltmeter or test lamp between the wire end and a good earth (such as the battery negative terminal), and check that the wire is live when the ignition switch is turned to the 'start' position. If it is, then the circuit is sound - if not the circuit wiring can be checked as described in Chapter 12.

5 The solenoid contacts can be checked by connecting a voltmeter or test lamp between the battery positive feed connection on the starter side of the solenoid, and earth. When the ignition switch is turned to the 'start' position, there should be a reading or lighted bulb, as applicable. If there is no reading or lighted bulb, the solenoid is faulty and should be renewed.

6 If the circuit and solenoid are proved sound, the fault must lie in the starter motor. In this event, it may be possible to have the starter motor overhauled by a specialist, but check on the cost of spares before proceeding, as it may prove more economical to obtain a new or exchange motor.

10 Starter motor -
removal and refitting

Removal

1 Disconnect the battery negative lead.
2 Jack up the front of the car and support it on axle stands (see "Jacking and Vehicle Support"). On 3.0 litre 24-valve models, to improve access release the cruise control unit

10.3 Electrical connections on the starter motor solenoid (1.8 litre model shown)

from its mounting bracket and disconnect the wiring connector from the rear knock sensor.
3 Note the electrical connections on the solenoid then disconnect them (see illustration).
4 Unbolt the front starter motor bracket from the cylinder block (see illustration), then unscrew the mounting bolts and remove the starter motor from below. Remove the front bracket. Note: On 3.0 litre 24-valve models, it may be necessary to disconnect the fuel lines from the manifold (See Chapter 4B) in order to gain the necessary clearance required to remove the motor.

Refitting

5 Refitting is the reverse of removal, tightening the mountings to the specified torque.

11 Starter motor -
testing and overhaul

If the starter motor is thought to be suspect, it should be removed from the vehicle and taken to an auto-electrician for testing. Most auto-electricians will be able to supply and fit brushes at a reasonable cost. However, check on the cost of repairs before proceeding as it may prove more economical to obtain a new or exchange motor.

12 Ignition switch -
removal and refitting

Refer to Chapter 12.

13 Oil pressure warning light switch/gauge sensor -
removal and refitting

Removal

1 On 1.8 and 2.0 litre models the switch/sensor is located at the front of the cylinder block, above the oil filter mounting. On 2.5,

10.4 Starter motor front mounting bracket (1.8 litre model shown)

2.6 and 3.0 litre models the switch/sensor is either screwed into the left-hand side of the timing chain cover or screwed into the left-hand side of the cylinder block (depending on model). Note that on some models access to the switch may be improved if the vehicle is jacked up and supported on axle stands (see "Jacking and Vehicle Support") so that the switch can be reached from underneath.
2 Disconnect the battery negative lead.
3 Remove the protective sleeve from the wiring plug (where applicable), then disconnect the wiring from the switch.
4 Unscrew the switch from the cylinder block, and recover the sealing washer. Be prepared for oil spillage, and if the switch is to be left removed from the engine for any length of time, plug the hole in the cylinder block.

Refitting

5 Examine the sealing washer for signs of damage or deterioration and if necessary renew.
6 Refit the switch, complete with washer, and tighten it securely. Reconnect the wiring connector.
7 Lower the vehicle to the ground then check and, if necessary, top-up the engine oil as described in Chapter 1.

14 Oil level sensor -
removal and refitting

Removal

1 Drain the engine oil into a clean container (Chapter 1) then refit the drain plug and tighten.
2 Disconnect the wiring connector from the level sensor which is situated on the side of the sump.
3 Undo the retaining bolts and remove the sensor from the sump and remove the gasket.

Refitting

4 Refitting is the reverse of removal using a new gasket. Tighten the sensor bolts securely and refill the engine with oil (Chapter 1).

Chapter 5 Part B:
Ignition system

Contents

Distributor - removal and refitting 3
General information 1
Ignition coil - removal, testing and refitting 5
Ignition system - testing 2
Ignition system check . . . . .See Chapter 1
Ignition system components - removal and refitting 6
Ignition timing - checking 4
Spark plug check and renewal . . . . .See Chapter 1

Degrees of difficulty

Easy, suitable for novice with little experience	Fairly easy, suitable for beginner with some experience	Fairly difficult, suitable for competent DIY mechanic	Difficult, suitable for experienced DIY mechanic	Very difficult, suitable for expert DIY or professional

Specifications

System type
1.8 litre models	MSTS (Microprocessor Spark Timing System)
2.0 litre models	Integrated with Bosch Motronic engine management system
2.5 litre models	MSTS (Microprocessor Spark Timing System)
2.6 litre models	Integrated with Bosch Motronic engine management system
3.0 litre models:	
Models without a catalytic converter (30NE engine)	MSTS (Microprocessor Spark Timing System)
Models with a catalytic converter (all other engines)	Integrated with Bosch Motronic engine management system

Ignition HT coil
Primary winding resistance (approximate)	0.7 to 0.8 ohm
Secondary winding resistance (approximate)	7000 ohms
Firing order:	
1.8 and 2.0 litre models	1-3-4-2 (No 1 at timing belt end of engine)
2.5, 2.6 and 3.0 litre models	1-5-3-6-2-4 (No 1 at timing chain end of engine)

Ignition timing
At specified idle speed with vacuum pipe (where fitted) disconnected and plugged):
1.8 litre models	10° ± 2° BTDC*
2.0 litre models	8° to 12° BTDC*
2.5 litre models	10° ± 2° BTDC**
2.6 litre models	8°to 12° BTDC*
3.0 litre models:	
Models without a catalytic converter (30NE engine)	10° ± 2° BTDC**
Models with a catalytic converter (all other engines)	8° to 12° BTDC*

*Ensure that the fuel octane rating plug (where fitted) is set to the "95" position (see Chapter 4)
**On 2.5 and 3.0 litre (30NE) engine models, if 95 RON petrol is to be used retard the ignition timing to 7° BTDC

Torque wrench setting
	Nm	lbf ft
Knock sensor bolt - 3.0 litre 24-valve engine	25	18

1 General information

1 To achieve optimum performance from an engine, and to meet stringent exhaust emission requirements, it is essential that the fuel/air mixture in the combustion chamber is ignited at exactly the right time relative to engine speed and load. The ignition system provides the spark necessary to ignite the mixture, and varies the instant at which ignition occurs according to the engine requirements.

2 The ignition system consists of a primary low tension (LT) circuit and a secondary high tension (HT) circuit. When the ignition is switched on, current is fed to the coil primary windings and a magnetic field is established. At the required point of ignition, the primary circuit is interrupted electronically by the sensor disc attached to the crankshaft. The magnetic field collapses and a secondary high tension voltage is induced in the secondary windings. This HT voltage is fed via the distributor rotor arm to the relevant spark plug.

After delivering the spark the primary circuit is re-energised and the cycle is repeated.

3 The ignition timing is controlled by a microprocessor within the control unit. On 1.8 litre, 2.5 litre and 3.0 litre models not fitted with a catalytic converter a separate ignition system control unit is fitted. On 2.0 litre, 2.6 litre and 3.0 litre models fitted with a catalytic converter, the control unit is integral with the Motronic engine management control unit (Chapter 4B). The control unit receives information on engine speed, load and temperature and from this determines the correct ignition timing.

2 Ignition system - testing

⚠️ *Warning: Voltages produced by an electronic ignition system are far higher than those produced by conventional ignition systems. Extreme care must be taken when working on the system with the ignition switched on. Persons with surgically-implanted cardiac pacemaker devices should keep clear of the ignition circuits, components and test equipment.*

Note: *Refer to the warning in Section 1 of Part A of this Chapter before starting. Always switch off the ignition before disconnecting or connecting any component and when using a multi-meter to check resistances.*

General

1 The components of electronic ignition systems are normally very reliable; most faults are far more likely to be due to loose or dirty connections or to "tracking" of HT voltage due to dirt, dampness or damaged insulation than to the failure of any of the system's components. **Always** check all wiring before condemning an electrical component and work methodically to eliminate all other possibilities before deciding that a particular component is faulty.

2 The old practice of checking for a spark by holding the live end of an HT lead a short distance away from the engine is not recommended; not only is there a high risk of a powerful electric shock, but the HT coil or amplifier unit will be damaged. Similarly, **never** try to "diagnose" misfires by pulling off one HT lead at a time.

Engine will not start

3 If the engine either will not turn over at all, or only turns very slowly, check the battery and starter motor. Connect a voltmeter across the battery terminals (meter positive probe to battery positive terminal), disconnect the ignition coil HT lead from the distributor cap and earth it, then note the voltage reading obtained while turning over the engine on the starter for (no more than) ten seconds. If the reading obtained is less than approximately 9.5 volts, first check the battery, starter motor and charging system as described in the relevant Sections of this Chapter.

4 If the engine turns over at normal speed but will not start, check the HT circuit by connecting a timing light (following the manufacturer's instructions) and turning the engine over on the starter motor; if the light flashes, voltage is reaching the spark plugs, so these should be checked first. If the light does not flash, check the HT leads themselves followed by the distributor cap, carbon brush and rotor arm using the information given in Chapter 1.

5 If there is a spark, check the fuel system, referring to Chapter 4 for more information.

6 If there is still no spark, check the voltage at the ignition HT coil "+" terminal; it should be the same as the battery voltage (ie, at least 11.7 volts). If the voltage at the coil is more than 1 volt less than that at the battery, check the feed back through the fusebox and ignition switch to the battery and its earth until the fault is found.

7 If the feed to the HT coil is sound, check the coil's primary and secondary winding resistance as described later in this Section; renew the coil if faulty, but be careful to check the condition of the LT connections themselves first, to ensure the fault is not due to dirty or poorly-fastened connectors.

8 If the HT coil is in good condition, the fault is probably within the control unit, the inductive impulse sensor or, on 2.5, 2.6 and 3.0 litre models, in the distributor assembly. Testing of these components should be entrusted to a Vauxhall/Opel dealer.

Engine misfires

9 An irregular misfire suggests either a loose connection or intermittent fault on the primary circuit, or an HT fault on the coil side of the rotor arm.

10 With the ignition switched off, check carefully through the system ensuring that all connections are clean and securely fastened. If the equipment is available, check the LT circuit as described above.

11 Check that the HT coil, the distributor cap and the HT leads are clean and dry. Check the leads themselves and the spark plugs (by substitution, if necessary), then check the distributor cap, carbon brush and rotor arm as described in Chapter 1.

12 Regular misfiring is probably due to a fault in the distributor cap, HT leads or spark plugs. Use a timing light (paragraph 4 above) to check that HT voltage is present at all leads.

13 If HT voltage is not present on any particular lead, the fault will be in that lead or in the distributor cap. If HT is present on all leads, the fault will be in the spark plugs; check and renew them if there is any doubt about their condition.

14 If no HT is present, check the HT coil; its secondary windings may be breaking down under load.

3 Distributor - removal and refitting

Removal

1.8 and 2.0 litre models

1 Access to the distributor is not easy since it is located on the rear of the camshaft housing near the bulkhead.

2 On carburettor engines remove the air cleaner assembly (Chapter 4A).

3 Unscrew the distributor cap retaining screws and withdraw the cap **(see illustration)**. Disconnect the HT leads from the spark plugs and ignition coil. The leads should already be marked for location, but if not, attach identification tags to them.

4 Remove the condensation seal from the rotor arm **(see illustration)**.

5 Note the position of the rotor arm, then unscrew the two Allen bolts. Remove the rotor arm from the backplate **(see illustrations)**.

3.3 Removing the distributor cap - 1.8 litre model shown (engine removed for clarity)

3.4 Condensation seal removal

3.5a Unscrew the bolts . . .

3.5b . . . and remove the rotor arm

3.6 Removing the backplate

3.8 View inside the distributor cap

3.10a Removing the distributor cap -
3.0 litre 24-valve model shown

3.10b Ensure the rotor arm is pointing
towards No 1 cylinder terminal and aligned
with the mark (arrowed) on the distributor
body (3.0 litre 24-valve shown)

disengages, and recover the sealing ring. Note that the distributor assembly is a sealed unit the only component available separately is the vacuum advance diaphragm unit (where fitted).

Refitting

1.8 and 2.0 litre models

15 Refitting is a reversal of removal, but apply a little sealing compound under the bolt heads of the backing plate before tightening them.

2.5, 2.6 and 3.0 litre models

16 Fit the insulator cover to the distributor and press on the rotor arm.
17 Check the flywheel/driveplate mark is still correctly aligned then fit a new seal to the distributor and position the rotor arm just to the side of its alignment mark; this will compensate for the clockwise movement of the arm as the drive gear engages.
18 Slide the distributor into position, aligning its drive dog with that of the oil pump as the drivegear engages. Seat the distributor fully in position and align the marks made prior to removal. Check that the rotor arm tip is correctly aligned with the mark on the distributor body. If not, lift the distributor out of position slightly and rotate the rotor arm as necessary.
19 Once the marks are correctly aligned, refit the retaining clamp and bolt and tighten securely (see illustration).
20 Reconnect the distributor wiring connector and vacuum hose (as applicable).
21 Refit the distributor cap making sure it is clipped securely in position. If necessary, check the ignition timing as described in Section 4.

6 Pull the backplate out of the oil seal (see illustration).
7 To ensure correct refitting, mark the end of the camshaft with a dab of paint in the direction the rotor arm was pointing.
8 Examine the cap and rotor arm for signs of arcing which will show up as thin black lines of carbon. Clean any build-up of carbon from the metal segments, but do not remove any metal as this will increase the gap the HT spark has to jump. Check that the carbon brush inside the cap is free to move against the spring tension (see illustration).

2.5, 2.6 and 3.0 litre models

9 Using a socket on the crankshaft pulley bolt, rotate the crankshaft until the pointer in the aperture on the right-hand side of the cylinder block aligns with the raised mark on the flywheel/driveplate.

10 Unclip the distributor cap and check that the rotor arm is pointing towards the No 1 (front) cylinder HT lead terminal; if the arm is facing number 6 cylinder terminal, rotate the crankshaft through a complete turn (360°) until the arm is correctly positioned. The rotor arm tip should be aligned with the mark on the distributor body; if no marks are visible make alignment marks to use on refitting (see illustrations).
11 Pull off the rotor arm and remove the insulator cover (see illustration).
12 Disconnect the wiring connector and (where fitted) the vacuum hose from the distributor.
13 Make alignment marks between the distributor body and engine then slacken and remove the bolt and retaining clamp.
14 Lift the distributor out of position, noting how the rotor arm rotates as the drive gear

4 Ignition timing - checking

Early (pre-1990) 1.8 litre models

1 The ignition timing can be checked as described in the following paragraphs, although no adjustment is possible since this is carried out automatically by the electronic control unit. The procedure may be used if a fault is suspected or if any of the ignition components have been renewed.
2 Run the engine to normal operating temperature, then switch off.
3 On carburettor versions disconnect the vacuum hose from the electronic control unit located in the right-hand rear corner of the engine compartment.
4 On fuel injection versions disconnect the plug from the throttle valve switch and connect together terminals 18, 3 and 2 inside the plug with bridging wires.
5 Connect a tachometer and stroboscopic timing light to the engine (No. 1 cylinder at front).

3.11 Removing the rotor arm

3.19 Align the marks made prior to
removal and tighten the clamp bolt

6 Check that the octane rating plug near the brake vacuum servo is set to the 95 octane number with the number "95" on the same side as the black plastic clip (See Chapter 4). If it is set to 98, unclip the plug and turn it round.

7 Start the engine and run it at the specified speed.

8 Point the timing light to the left-hand side of the crankshaft pulley and check that the notch in the pulley appears in line with the pointer on the rear timing cover.

9 Stop the engine. Refit the throttle valve switch plug or the control unit vacuum hose as applicable.

10 With the engine stopped disconnect the tachometer and timing light.

11 If necessary, reset the octane rating plug to the required position.

Later (1990-on) 1.8 litre models and all 2.0 and 2.6 litre models

12 On these models, the ignition timing is constantly being altered by the control unit to suit the running conditions of the engine. The ignition timing can be checked as described above but without access to the special Vauxhall/Opel test equipment the check is of little use.

2.5 litre models

13 On these models checking and adjustment of the ignition timing requires access to special Vauxhall/Opel test equipment, mainly due to the fact that there are no timing marks on the crankshaft pulley. If a temporary pointer is set up and the relevant alignment marks, one for number 1 cylinder TDC and another the correct number of degrees before TDC, are made on the pulley, the timing can be checked and adjusted as follows.

14 Warm the engine up to normal operating temperature and switch it off.

15 Connect a tachometer and stroboscopic timing light to the engine (No. 1 cylinder at front).

16 Disconnect the wiring connector from the throttle switch and connect together terminals 2, 3 and 18 of the connector using bridging wires.

17 Disconnect the vacuum hose from the distributor advance unit (where fitted) and plug its end.

18 Start the engine and run it at the specified speed. Point the timing light at the pulley and check that the timing mark made on the pulley aligns with the pointer. If adjustment is necessary, slacken the distributor clamp bolt and rotate the distributor body as required to align the marks then securely tighten the clamp bolt.

19 Stop the engine and disconnect the tachometer and timing light.

20 Reconnect the wiring connector to the throttle valve switch and (where necessary) the distributor vacuum hose.

5.2 Disconnecting the coil HT lead (arrowed)

3.0 litre models

Models without a catalytic converter (30NE engine)

21 Refer to the information given in paragraphs 13 to 20 noting that on models with the AW 03-71 LE automatic transmission, terminals 4, 5 and 6 of the throttle valve switch should be connected together (see paragraph 16). On automatic transmission models, once adjustment is complete remove any relevant fault codes from the memory by disconnecting the battery negative terminal for a short while.

Models with a catalytic converter

22 Refer to paragraph 12.

---

5 Ignition coil -
removal, testing and refitting

Removal

1 Disconnect the battery leads.

2 Disconnect the HT lead from the coil **(see illustration)**.

3 Disconnect the LT wiring connectors from the coil, noting their correct fitted positions.

4 Undo the retaining bolts and remove the coil from the car. If necessary, undo the clamp screw and remove the coil from its mounting bracket.

Testing

5 Testing of the coil consists of using a

multimeter set to its resistance function, to check the primary (LT '+' to '-' terminals) and secondary (LT '+' to HT lead terminal) windings for continuity, bearing in mind that on the four output, static type HT coil there are two sets of each windings. Compare the results obtained to those given in the Specifications at the start of this Chapter. Note the resistance of the coil windings will vary slightly according to the coil temperature, the results in the Specifications are approximate values for when the coil is at 20°C.

6 Check that there is no continuity between the HT lead terminal and the coil body/mounting bracket.

7 If the coil is thought to be faulty, have your findings confirmed by a Vauxhall dealer before renewing the coil.

Refitting

8 Refitting is a reversal of the relevant removal procedure ensuring that the wiring connectors are correctly and securely reconnected.

---

6 Ignition system components
- removal and refitting

Inductive impulse sensor

1 The inductive impulse sensor is located on the front left-hand side of the cylinder block on 1.8 and 2.0 litre models and on the front of the timing chain cover on 2.5, 2.6 and 3.0 litre models.

2 On 2.5, 2.6 and 3.0 litre 12-valve models jack up the front of the vehicle and support it on axle stands (see "Jacking and Vehicle Support") to improve access.

3 If necessary, on 3.0 litre 24-valve models, remove the auxiliary drivebelt to improve access to the sensor (Chapter 1).

4 To remove the sensor, use an Allen key to unscrew the retaining bolt, and withdraw the sensor **(see illustrations)**.

5 Disconnect the wiring plug and unclip the cable from the timing belt cover.

6 Refitting is a reversal of removal ensuring that the sensor and bracket mating surfaces are perfectly clean.

6.4a Unscrew the inductive impulse sensor Allen bolt . . .

6.4b . . . and withdraw the sensor (1.8 litre models shown)

Ignition control unit

1.8 and 2.5 litre models

7 The ignition control unit is located in the right-hand rear corner of the engine compartment. First disconnect the battery negative lead.

8 Lift the bonnet weatherstrip and plastic cover from the bulkhead on the right-hand side.

9 Disconnect the multi-plug and (where necessary) the vacuum hose from the unit.

10 Unscrew the mounting bolts and withdraw the control unit.

2.0 litre and 2.6 litre models

11 The ignition system is controlled by the Motronic ECU (see Chapter 4B).

3.0 litre models without a catalytic converter (30NE engine)

12 Refer to paragraphs 7 to 10.

3.0 litre models with a catalytic converter

13 The ignition system is controlled by the Motronic ECU (see Chapter 4B).

Oil temperature switch - 2.5 litre and 3.0 litre models without a catalytic converter

14 Jack up the front of the vehicle and support it on axle stands (see "*Jacking and Vehicle Support*").

15 Disconnect the wiring connector then unscrew the switch from the base of the timing chain cover. Plug the switch aperture to prevent oil loss and the entry of dirt. For testing purposes, there should be continuity between the switch terminals at temperatures below 65°C and an open circuit above 65°C.

16 Refitting is the reverse of removal.

Inlet air temperature switch - 2.5 litre and 3.0 litre models without a catalytic converter

17 Disconnect the wiring connector and unscrew the switch from the inlet manifold. For testing purposes, there should be continuity between the switch terminals at temperatures above17°C and an open circuit below 17°C.

18 Refitting is the reverse of removal.

Partial load sensor - 2.5 litre and 3.0 litre models without a catalytic converter

19 The partial load switch is mounted onto the right-hand suspension strut turret.

20 To remove the switch, disconnect the vacuum hose and unscrew its retaining bolts. The switch is adjustable, but adjustment requires the use of a vacuum pump.

6.22 Knock sensor - 3.0 litre 24-valve model

21 Refitting is the reverse of removal.

Knock sensors - 3.0 litre 24-valve models

22 The knock sensors are mounted onto the left-hand side of the cylinder block. There are two sensors, one for the front three cylinders and another for the rear three **(see illustration)**.

23 Disconnect the wiring connector from the relevant sensor the unscrew it retaining bolt and remove it from the cylinder block.

24 On refitting ensure that the knock sensor and block mating surfaces are clean and dry and tighten the retaining bolt to the specified torque.

Notes

Chapter 6
Clutch

Contents

Clutch - removal, inspection and refitting 8
Clutch cable - removal and refitting 2
Clutch cable - adjustment . . . . .See Chapter 1
Clutch fluid level check . . . . .See "Weekly Checks"
Clutch master cylinder (hydraulic clutch) -
    removal, overhaul and refitting 4
Clutch pedal - removal and refitting 3
Clutch release bearing and arm - removal, inspection and refitting . . .9
Clutch slave cylinder (hydraulic clutch) -
    removal, overhaul and refitting 5
General information 1
Hydraulic clutch pipe/hose - renewal 6
Hydraulic system - bleeding 7

Degrees of difficulty

Easy, suitable for novice with little experience	Fairly easy, suitable for beginner with some experience	Fairly difficult, suitable for competent DIY mechanic	Difficult, suitable for experienced DIY mechanic	Very difficult, suitable for expert DIY or professional 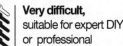

Specifications

General

Clutch type	Single dry plate, diaphragm spring pressure plate
Actuation	Cable or hydraulic (depending on model)

Friction plate

Diameter:
1.8 litre models:	
18 SV engines	200 mm
18 SEH engines	216 mm
2.0 litre models	216 mm
2.5, 2.6 and 3.0 litre models	240 mm

Total lining thickness (new):
1.8 litre models:	
18 SV engines	10.5 ± 1.0 mm
18 SEH engines	9.0 ± 1.0 mm
2.0 litre models	9.0 ± 1.0 mm
2.5, 2.6 and 3.0 litre models	9.4 ± 1.0 mm
Maximum lateral run-out (all models)	0.4 mm

Torque wrench settings

	Nm	lbf ft
Clutch cover (pressure plate) bolts:		
7 mm bolts	15	11
8 mm bolts	28	20
Master cylinder retaining bolts	20	15
Hydraulic pipe/hose union nut	16	12
Hydraulic pipe union bolt	25	18
Slave cylinder retaining nuts	25	18
Slave cylinder heatshield bolts	20	15
Slave cylinder bleed screw	9	6

1 General information

1 All models with a manual transmission have a single dry plate, diaphragm spring clutch. The clutch cover is bolted to the rear face of the flywheel.

2 The friction plate is located between the flywheel and the pressure plate and slides on splines on the gearbox input shaft. When the clutch is engaged, the diaphragm spring forces the pressure plate onto the friction plate which in turn is forced against the flywheel. Drive is then transmitted from the flywheel, through the friction plate to the gearbox input shaft. On disengaging the clutch, the pressure plate is lifted from the friction plate, and drive to the gearbox is then disconnected.

3 The clutch is operated by a foot pedal suspended under the facia. Depending on model, the clutch release mechanism is either cable operated or hydraulically operated.

4 Depressing the pedal causes the release lever to move the release bearing against the fingers of the diaphragm spring in the clutch cover. The spring is sandwiched between two rings which act as fulcrums. As the centre of the spring is moved in, the periphery moves out to lift the pressure plate and disengage the clutch. The reverse takes place when the pedal is released.

5 As the friction plate linings wear, the foot pedal will rise progressively relative to its original position. On models with a cable operated clutch it is therefore necessary to periodically adjust the clutch cable; on models with a hydraulic clutch, adjustment of the release mechanism is automatic.

2 Clutch cable - removal and refitting

Removal

1 Apply the handbrake. Jack up the front of the vehicle and support it on axle stands.

2 Using a steel rule, measure the distance from the locknut to the end of the threaded cable fitting **(see illustration)**. This will provide an initial setting when refitting the cable.

3 Unscrew and remove the locknut, and the adjustment nut noting that the inner end of the adjustment nut is ball-shaped **(see illustration)**.

4 Remove the end fitting from the release lever, and remove both the inner and outer cables from the hole in the clutch housing **(see illustration)**.

5 Working inside the vehicle, release the fasteners by rotating them anti-clockwise and remove the driver's side facia undercover. Reach up behind the facia and disengage the inner cable from the curved upper section of the clutch pedal.

6 Where necessary, unbolt the cable clip from the steering gear.

7 Withdraw the clutch cable from the bulkhead and remove it from the engine compartment **(see illustration)**.

Refitting

8 Refitting is a reversal of removal, but make sure that the cable is correctly located in the clutch pedal, bulkhead, and clutch housing. Initially adjust the cable to the setting noted in paragraph 2, but finally check the pedal adjustment as described in Chapter 1.

3 Clutch pedal - removal and refitting

Removal

Models with a cable operated clutch

1 Disconnect the clutch cable from the pedal with reference to Section 2.

2 Working inside the vehicle, disconnect the wiring from the brake stop-lamp switch, unhook the brake pedal return spring and disconnect the servo pushrod from the brake pedal.

3 Loosen the nut on the end of the pedal shaft. Unhook the clutch pedal return spring.

4 Unscrew the nuts holding the pedal bracket

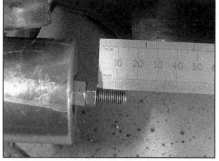

2.2 Measuring the position of the clutch cable adjustment nut and locknut

2.4 Removing the clutch cable end fitting from the release lever

to the bulkhead, and turn the bracket around the steering column to allow removal of the pedal shaft. Note that on later models, it may be necessary to remove the steering column to allow the pedal bracket to be slid off its retaining studs. The column can be removed as described in Chapter 10, Section 22, noting that it is not necessary to remove the steering wheel or the lock cylinder; the column can be removed with these items still in position.

5 Remove the pedal location clips, then unscrew the nut, remove the washer and withdraw the shaft until the clutch pedal can be removed from the bracket. Recover the pedal thrustwashers.

Models with a hydraulic clutch

6 Working inside the vehicle, release the fasteners by rotating them anti-clockwise and remove the driver's side facia undercover.

7 Reach up behind the facia and remove the retaining clip securing the return spring assembly to the pedal. Remove the retaining clip and pin securing the spring assembly to the pedal mounting bracket and manoeuvre the assembly out from under the facia, noting its correct fitted position.

8 Remove the retaining clip (where fitted) and slide out the pin securing the master cylinder pushrod to the pedal.

9 Remove the pedal as described in paragraphs 2 to 5, taking great care not to place any undue pressure on the hydraulic pipe/hose. If necessary, disconnect the pipe and hose from the master cylinder (see Section 4) to allow the pedal bracket to be turned.

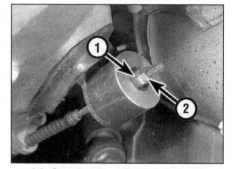

2.3 Clutch cable adjustment nut (1) and locknut (2)

2.7 Clutch cable at the bulkhead

Refitting

Models with a cable operated clutch

10 Refitting is a reversal of removal, but lubricate the shaft with grease. On completion adjust the clutch cable as described in Chapter 1.

Models with a hydraulic clutch

11 Refitting is the reverse of removal, lubricating the pedal shaft with grease. If the clutch pipe/hose were disconnected, top-up and bleed the hydraulic system as described in Section 7.

4 Clutch master cylinder (hydraulic clutch) - removal, overhaul and refitting

Note: *Before starting work, refer to the note at the beginning of Section 7 concerning the dangers of hydraulic fluid.*

Removal

1 Disconnect the battery negative terminal. On left-hand drive models, to improve access to the master cylinder hydraulic pipe/hose, remove the relay box from the suspension strut turret (see Chapter 12).

2 Remove the clutch fluid reservoir cap, and syphon the hydraulic fluid from the reservoir. **Note:** *Do not syphon the fluid by mouth, as it is poisonous; use a syringe or an old poultry baster.* Alternatively, open the bleed screw on the slave cylinder and gently pump the clutch pedal to expel the fluid through a plastic tube connected to the screw (see Section 7).

3 Peel back the rubber seal from the driver's side of the engine compartment bulkhead and lift up the water deflector to gain access to the hydraulic pipe/hose.

4 Slacken the retaining clip and disconnect the lower end of the reservoir hose from the master cylinder. Plug or tape over the hose end and master cylinder pipe, to minimise the loss of hydraulic fluid, and to prevent the entry of dirt into the system. Wash off any spilt fluid immediately with cold water

5 Carry out the operations described in paragraphs 6 to 8 of Section 3.

6 Position an absorbent rag beneath the master cylinder and have ready a suitable container to catch any spilt fluid.

7 On right-hand drive models unscrew the union nut and disconnect the hydraulic pipe from the master cylinder. Plug or tape over the pipe end and master cylinder port to minimise fluid loss and prevent dirt entry.

8 On left-hand drive models, unscrew the union bolt and recover the sealing washer from each side of the pipe union. Plug or tape over the pipe end and master cylinder port to minimise fluid loss and prevent dirt entry. Discard the sealing washers; new ones will be required on refitting.

9 Slacken and remove the retaining bolts and manoeuvre the master cylinder out from underneath the facia, taking care not to damage its feed pipe. Recover the sealing grommet from the bulkhead and renew it if it shows signs of wear or damage.

Overhaul

10 Overhaul of the master cylinder is not possible. If the cylinder is damaged of is no longer effective it must be renewed.

Refitting

11 Refitting is a reverse of the removal procedure, noting the following points.

a) *Refit the rubber grommet to the bulkhead and manoeuvre the master cylinder into position. Tighten the master cylinder retaining bolts to the specified torque setting.*

b) *On right-hand drive models connect the hydraulic pipe to the master cylinder and tighten its union nut to the specified torque setting.*

c) *On left-hand drive models position a new sealing washer on each side of the pipe union then refit the union bolt and tighten it to the specified torque setting.*

d) *On completion top-up the fluid reservoir and bleed the system as described in Section 7.*

5 Clutch slave cylinder (hydraulic clutch) - removal, overhaul and refitting

Note: *Before starting work, refer to the note at the beginning of Section 7 concerning the dangers of hydraulic fluid.*

Removal

1 Disconnect the battery negative terminal. Minimise fluid loss by removing the master cylinder reservoir cap and then tightening it down onto a piece of polythene to obtain an airtight seal.

2 Apply the handbrake, then jack up the front of the car and support it on axle stands.

3 Where necessary, to gain access to the slave cylinder, undo the retaining screws and remove the plastic undershield from beneath the engine/transmission.

4 Unscrew the retaining bolts and remove the heatshield from around the clutch slave cylinder.

5 Wipe clean the area around the slave cylinder pipe union and place absorbent rags beneath the union to catch any surplus fluid. Unscrew the union nut and carefully withdraw the pipe. Plug or tape over the pipe end and cylinder port.

6 Unscrew the retaining nuts and remove the slave cylinder from the transmission.

Overhaul

7 Overhaul of the slave cylinder is not possible. If the cylinder is damaged of is no longer effective it must be renewed.

Refitting

8 Refitting is a reverse of the removal procedure, noting the following points.

a) *Ensure that the cylinder and transmission mating surfaces are clean and dry and fit the slave cylinder. Locate the hydraulic pipe in position and screw in the union nut by a couple of turn then tighten the cylinder retaining nuts to the specified torque setting.*

b) *Tighten the hydraulic pipe union nut to the specified torque setting.*

c) *Prior to refitting the heat shield, top-up the fluid reservoir and bleed the system as described in Section 7.*

6 Hydraulic clutch pipe/hose - renewal

1 If any section of the pipe/hose is to be renewed, minimise fluid loss by first removing the clutch fluid reservoir cap, then tightening it down onto a piece of polythene to obtain an airtight seal. Alternatively, flexible hoses can be sealed, if required, using a proprietary brake hose clamp; metal pipe unions can be plugged (if care is taken not to allow dirt into the system) or capped immediately they are disconnected. Place a wad of rag under any union that is to be disconnected, to catch any spilt fluid.

2 If a flexible hose is to be disconnected, unscrew the pipe union nut before removing the spring clip which secures the hose to its mounting bracket.

3 To unscrew the union nuts, it is preferable to obtain a brake pipe spanner of the correct size; these are available from most large motor accessory shops. Failing this, a close-fitting open-ended spanner will be required, though if the nuts are tight or corroded, their flats may be rounded-off if the spanner slips. In such a case, a self-locking wrench is often the only way to unscrew a stubborn union, but it follows that the pipe and the damaged nuts must be renewed on reassembly. Always clean a union and surrounding area before disconnecting it. If disconnecting a component with more than one union, make a careful note of the connections before disturbing any of them.

4 Where a union is secured in position with a union bolt, recover the washer from each side of the union and discard them; new washers should be used on refitting.

5 If a pipe is to be renewed, it can be obtained, from Vauxhall/Opel dealers. Alternatively, most motor accessory shops can make up pipes from kits, but this requires very careful measurement of the original, to ensure that the replacement is of the correct length. The safest answer is usually to take the original to the shop as a pattern.

6 On refitting, tighten the union nuts/bolt to the specified torque. It is not necessary to exercise brute force to obtain a sound joint.

7 Ensure that the pipes and hoses are correctly routed, with no kinks, and that they are secured in the clips or brackets provided. After fitting, remove the polythene from the reservoir, and bleed the hydraulic system as described in Section 7. Wash off any spilt fluid, and check carefully for fluid leaks.

7 Hydraulic system - bleeding

Warning: Hydraulic fluid is poisonous; wash off immediately and thoroughly in the case of skin contact, and seek immediate medical advice if any fluid is swallowed or gets into the eyes. Certain types of hydraulic fluid are flammable, and may ignite when allowed into contact with hot components; when servicing any hydraulic system, it is safest to assume that the fluid is flammable, and to take precautions against the risk of fire as though it is petrol that is being handled. Hydraulic fluid is also an effective paint stripper, and will attack plastics; if any is spilt, it should be washed off immediately, using copious quantities of fresh water. Finally, it is hygroscopic (it absorbs moisture from the air) - old fluid may be contaminated and unfit for further use. When topping-up or renewing the fluid, always use the recommended type, and ensure that it comes from a freshly opened sealed container.

1 The correct operation of any hydraulic system is only possible after removing all air from the components and circuit; this is achieved by bleeding the system.

2 During the bleeding procedure, add only clean, unused hydraulic fluid of the recommended type; never re-use fluid that has already been bled from the system. Ensure that sufficient fluid is available before starting work.

3 If there is any possibility of incorrect fluid being already in the system, the hydraulic circuit must be flushed completely with clean, correct fluid, and a new master cylinder and slave cylinder should be fitted.

4 If hydraulic fluid has been lost from the system, or air has entered because of a leak, ensure that the fault is cured before continuing further.

5 Firmly apply the handbrake then jack up the front of the vehicle and support it on axle stands.

6 Where necessary, to gain access to the slave cylinder, undo the retaining screws and remove the plastic undershield from beneath the engine/transmission.

7 Unscrew the retaining bolts and remove the heatshield from around the clutch slave cylinder to gain access to the bleed screw.

8 Check that all pipes and hoses are secure, unions tight and the bleed screws closed. Clean any dirt from around the bleed screws.

9 Unscrew the clutch fluid reservoir cap, and top the master cylinder reservoir up to the "MAX" level line; refit the cap loosely, and remember to maintain the fluid level at least above the "MIN" level line throughout the procedure, or there is a risk of further air entering the system.

10 There are a number of one-man, do-it-yourself brake bleeding kits currently available from motor accessory shops. It is recommended that one of these kits is used whenever possible, as they greatly simplify the bleeding operation, and reduce the risk of expelled air and fluid being drawn back into the system. If such a kit is not available, the basic (two-man) method must be used, which is described in detail below.

11 If a kit is to be used, prepare the vehicle as described previously, and follow the kit manufacturer's instructions, as the procedure may vary slightly according to the type being used; generally, they are as outlined below in the relevant sub-section.

Bleeding - basic (two-man) method

12 Collect a clean glass jar, a suitable length of plastic or rubber tubing which is a tight fit over the bleed screw, and a ring spanner to fit the screw. The help of an assistant will also be required.

13 Remove the dust cap from the slave cylinder bleed screw. Fit the spanner and tube to the screw, place the other end of the tube in the jar, and pour in sufficient fluid to cover the end of the tube.

14 Ensure that the clutch fluid level is maintained at least above the "MIN" level line in the reservoir throughout the procedure.

15 Have the assistant fully depress the clutch pedal several times to build up pressure, then maintain it on the final downstroke.

16 While pedal pressure is maintained, unscrew the bleed screw (approximately one turn) and allow the compressed fluid and air to flow into the jar. The assistant should maintain pedal pressure and should not release it until instructed to do so. When the flow stops, tighten the bleed screw again, have the assistant release the pedal slowly, and recheck the reservoir fluid level.

17 Repeat the steps given in paragraphs 15 and 16 until the fluid emerging from the bleed screw is free from air bubbles. If the master cylinder has been drained and refilled allow approximately five seconds between cycles for the master cylinder passages to refill.

18 When no more air bubbles appear, tighten the bleed screw to the specified torque, remove the tube and spanner, and refit the dust cap. Do not overtighten the bleed screw.

Bleeding - using a one-way valve kit

19 As their name implies, these kits consist of a length of tubing with a one-way valve fitted, to prevent expelled air and fluid being drawn back into the system; some kits include a translucent container, which can be positioned so that the air bubbles can be more easily seen flowing from the end of the tube.

20 The kit is connected to the bleed screw, which is then opened. The user returns to the driver's seat, depresses the clutch pedal with a smooth, steady stroke, and slowly releases it; this is repeated until the expelled fluid is clear of air bubbles.

21 Note that these kits simplify work so much that it is easy to forget the clutch fluid reservoir level; ensure that this is maintained at least above the "MIN" level line at all times.

Bleeding - using a pressure-bleeding kit

22 These kits are usually operated by the reservoir of pressurised air contained in the spare tyre. However, note that it will probably be necessary to reduce the pressure to a lower level than normal; refer to the instructions supplied with the kit.

23 By connecting a pressurised, fluid-filled container to the clutch fluid reservoir, bleeding can be carried out simply by opening the bleed screw and allowing the fluid to flow out until no more air bubbles can be seen in the expelled fluid.

24 This method has the advantage that the large reservoir of fluid provides an additional safeguard against air being drawn into the system during bleeding.

25 Pressure-bleeding is particularly effective when bleeding "difficult" systems, or when bleeding the complete system at the time of routine fluid renewal.

All methods

26 When bleeding is complete, and correct pedal feel is restored, wash off any spilt fluid, tighten the bleed screw to the specified torque and refit the dust cap.

27 Refit the heatshield to the transmission and tighten its retaining bolts to the specified torque. Where necessary, refit the undershield and securely tighten its retaining bolts.

28 Lower the vehicle to the ground and check the hydraulic fluid level in the clutch fluid reservoir, and top-up if necessary (see "Weekly Checks" and Chapter 1).

29 Discard any hydraulic fluid that has been bled from the system; it will not be fit for re-use.

30 Check the feel of the clutch pedal. If the clutch is still not operating correctly, air must still be present in the system, and further bleeding is required. Failure to bleed satisfactorily after a reasonable repetition of the bleeding procedure may be due to worn master cylinder/slave cylinder seals.

8 Clutch - removal, inspection and refitting

Removal

1 Remove the transmission (see Chapter 7A).

2 Mark the clutch cover in relation to the flywheel (see illustration).

3 On 1.8 and 2.0 litre models, unscrew, in a diagonal progressive manner, the bolts securing the clutch cover to the flywheel. Care should be exercised to unscrew the bolts evenly otherwise there is a risk of distorting the diaphragm spring. To avoid this, GM dealers use a special tool, to depress the diaphragm spring, and the pressure plate is then held in this position with special clips while the bolts are unscrewed (see illustration). Removal of the clips and the subsequent fitting of them to the new cover requires the use of a press. However, provided that the bolts are unscrewed evenly, no distortion should occur.

4 On 2.5, 2.6 and 3.0 litre models, evenly and progressively slacken and remove the bolts securing the clutch cover to the flywheel.

8.2 Clutch cover and flywheel marked in relation to each other

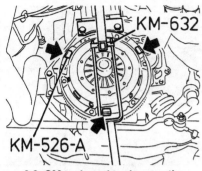

8.3 GM tool used to depress the diaphragm spring

Arrows indicate where pressure plate retaining clips are fitted

8.5 Removing the friction plate

8.12 Fitting the clutch friction disc and cover

8.14 Centralising the clutch friction disc with the special tool

8.15 Tightening the clutch cover bolts

5 On all models, lift the cover from the flywheel and remove the friction plate, noting which way round the latter is fitted **(see illustration)**.

Inspection

6 Examine the surfaces of the pressure plate and flywheel for scoring. If this is only light the parts may be re-used, but if scoring is excessive renew both the pressure plate and flywheel.

7 If the pressure plate has any blue discoloured areas, the clutch has been overheated at some time and renewal is necessary.

8 Examine the clutch cover for loose components and for distortion of the diaphragm spring.

9 Renew the friction plate if the linings are worn down to, or near the rivets. If the linings appear oil stained, the cause of the oil leak must be found and rectified. This is most likely to be a failed gearbox input shaft oil seal or crankshaft rear oil seal. Check the friction plate hub and centre splines for wear.

10 Spin the release bearing in the clutch housing and check it for roughness. If any excessive movement or roughness is evident, renew the release bearing (see Section 9).

Refitting

Note: *On 2.5 and 3.0 litre models, the flywheel assembly was modified during 1988 to prevent the clutch overheating. The modified flywheel has slots in its outer circumference to allow the heat to dissipate whereas the original flywheel had a solid outer circumference. All clutch assemblies supplied by Vauxhall/Opel are designed to be used with the modified flywheel; if the a new clutch cover is being fitted to an original flywheel it will be necessary to fit spacer plates in between the clutch cover and flywheel to ensure correct operation of the clutch. See your Vauxhall/Opel dealer for further information.*

11 Wipe clean the pressure plate and flywheel faces with a clean cloth. During the refitting procedure take care not to allow oil or grease onto the linings or friction faces.

12 Locate the friction plate on the flywheel with the raised hub facing outwards. The word

"GETRIEBESEITE" on the hub must also face outwards **(see illustration)**.

13 Fit the cover (on early 2.5 and 3.0 litre models, see the note at the start of this Section) and insert the bolts loosely. Align the previously made marks if the original cover is being refitted.

14 The friction plate must now be centralised so that when the gearbox is refitted, the input shaft will press through the friction plate splines, and enter the spigot bearing in the end of the crankshaft. Ideally a universal clutch centralising tool should be used **(see illustration)**, or if available an old gearbox input shaft. Alternatively a bar or wooden mandrel may be used, although the degree of accuracy in this instance will depend on how accurate the tool dimensions are.

15 Make sure that the centralising tool is located correctly in the friction plate and spigot bearing, then tighten the clutch cover

bolts in a diagonal progressive manner to the specified torque **(see illustration)**. Remove the centring tool.

16 Refit the transmission (see Chapter 7A).

9 Clutch release bearing and arm - removal, inspection and refitting

Removal

1 With the transmission removed in order to provide access to the clutch, attention can be given to the release bearing located in the clutch housing **(see illustration)**.

2 On models with a cable operated clutch, prise the rubber grommet from the clutch housing, and remove it from the end of the release arm. Note the arrow pointing forwards **(see illustration)**.

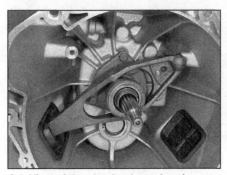

9.1 View of the clutch release bearing arm inside the clutch housing

9.2 Forward pointing arrow on the clutch housing grommet

3 Carefully pull the release arm out of the clutch housing hole until the socket and spring are disengaged from the ball pin **(see illustration)**, then slide the bearing and arm from the guide sleeve inside the clutch housing.

4 Separate the bearing from the rollers on the release arm. If necessary, remove the circlip and balance weight **(see illustrations)**.

Inspection

5 Check the release mechanism, renewing any component which is worn or damaged. Carefully check all bearing surfaces and points of contact.

6 When checking the release bearing itself, note that it is often considered worthwhile to renew it as a matter of course. Check that the contact surface rotates smoothly and easily, with no sign of noise or roughness, and that the surface itself is smooth and unworn, with no signs of cracks, pitting or scoring. If there is any doubt about its condition, the bearing must be renewed.

Refitting

7 Refitting is the reverse of removal, applying a little high melting-point grease to the contact surfaces of the ball pin, socket, guide sleeve and bearing collar contact faces. When fitted, the release arm should be held firmly in contact with the ball pin. If this is not the case, press the fork-shaped spring against the release arm to give it extra tension **(see illustration)**.

9.3 **Disengaging the clutch release arm from the ball-pin**

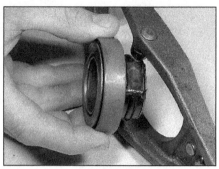

9.4a **Separating the bearing from the release arm**

9.4b **Release arm balance weight and retaining circlip**

9.7 **Fork-shaped spring on the release arm**

Chapter 7 Part A:
Manual transmission

Contents

Gearchange lever - removal and refitting 4
Gearchange lever support bracket - removal and refitting 5
Gearchange linkage - adjustment 6
General information 1
Oil seals - renewal 8

Reversing light switch - removal, testing and refitting 7
Transmission - removal and refitting 3
Transmission - draining and refilling 2
Transmission oil level check .See Chapter 1

Degrees of difficulty

Easy, suitable for novice with little experience		Fairly easy, suitable for beginner with some experience		Fairly difficult, suitable for competent DIY mechanic		Difficult, suitable for experienced DIY mechanic		Very difficult, suitable for expert DIY or professional	

Specifications

General

Type	Five forward speeds and reverse, synchromesh on all forward and reverse gears
Designation:	
3.0 litre 24-valve models	R28
All other models	R25

Lubricant

Type/specification	Gear oil, GM type 19 40 761 (Part number 90 297 261)
Capacity (approximate)	1.9 litres

Torque wrench settings

	Nm	lbf ft
Output flange	180	133
Rear crossmember bolts	45	33
Release bearing guide sleeve	22	16
Reversing lamp switch	20	15
Transmission filler/ level plug	30	22
Transmission drain plug	30	22
Transmission-to-engine bolts:		
Normal shank	75	55
Reduced diameter shank	60	44

1 General information

The manual gearbox fitted is of five-speed type with synchromesh on all gears including reverse. All gears, including the reverse idler gear, are in constant mesh with those on the laygear. Gear engagement is by locking the corresponding gear to the mainshaft with the synchro unit sliding sleeves. As the gears are engaged, the synchro-rings match the speed of the mainshaft with that of the gear being selected in order to ensure smooth engagement.

2 Transmission - draining and refilling

1 This operation is much quicker and more efficient if the car is first taken on a journey of sufficient length to warm the engine/ transmission up to operating temperature.
2 Park the car on level ground, switch off the ignition and apply the handbrake firmly. For improved access, jack up the front of the car and support it on axle stands (see "*Jacking and Vehicle Support*"). The car must be lowered to the ground and level, to ensure accuracy, when refilling and checking the oil level.
3 Wipe clean the area around the filler/level plug, which is situated on the right-hand side of the transmission. Unscrew the filler/level plug from the transmission and recover the sealing washer.

4 Position a suitable container under the drain plug and unscrew the plug.
5 Allow the oil to drain completely into the container. If the oil is hot, take precautions against scalding. Clean both the filler/level and the drain plugs, being especially careful to wipe any metallic particles off the magnetic inserts. Discard the original sealing washers; they should be renewed whenever they are disturbed.
6 When the oil has finished draining, clean the drain plug threads and those of the transmission casing, fit a new sealing washer and refit the drain plug, tightening it to the specified torque wrench setting. It the car was raised for draining, lower it to the ground.
7 Refilling the transmission is an extremely awkward operation. Above all, allow plenty of time for the oil level to settle properly before checking it. The car must be parked on flat level ground when checking the oil level.

3.6 Removing the propeller shaft from the output flange

3.7a Turn the vibration damper to align the cut-outs . . .

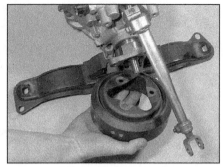

3.7b . . . and remove it

3.9 Disconnecting the wiring from the reversing lamp switch

3.10 Removing the oil drain plug

3.13 Removing the gearbox front cover plate

8 Refill the transmission with the exact amount of the specified type of oil then check the oil level as described in Chapter 1; if the correct amount was poured into the transmission and a large amount flows out on checking the level, refit the filler/level plug and take the car on a short journey so that the new oil is distributed fully around the transmission components, then check the level again on your return.

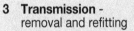

3 Transmission - removal and refitting

3.15a Gearchange linkage connection to the gear lever

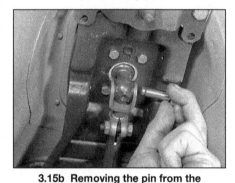

3.15b Removing the pin from the gearchange linkage

Removal

1 On carburettor models remove the air cleaner as described in Chapter 4A. On models with a catalytic converter disconnect the lambda sensor wiring connector.
2 Position the vehicle over an inspection pit, or alternatively drive the front wheels onto car ramps or jack it up and support it on axle stands (see "*Jacking and Vehicle Support*"). Apply the handbrake. Remove the engine undercover.
3 Slacken the slider joint nut on the front propeller shaft section one complete turn (Chapter 8).
4 Unbolt the exhaust system front downpipe from the intermediate section, mounting bracket, and exhaust manifold. Also unbolt the mounting bracket from the gearbox. Unbolt and remove the exhaust system heatshields.

5 Using a conventional, or Torx socket, as applicable, unscrew the bolts securing the propeller shaft front flexible disc joint to the gearbox output flange.
6 Lever the propeller shaft rearwards from the output flange and tie it to one side **(see illustration)**.
7 Where applicable, remove the vibration damper from the output flange by turning it so that the special cut-outs are aligned with the flange extremities **(see illustrations)**.
8 Disconnect the speedometer cable (where fitted) and tie it to one side.
9 Disconnect the wiring from the reversing lamp switch/speedometer sensor **(see illustration)**.
10 Position a container beneath the gearbox, then using an Allen key, unscrew the drain plug and drain the oil **(see illustration)**. Refit the drain plug on completion.
11 On models with a cable operated clutch,

disconnect the cable from the release arm (Chapter 6).
12 On models with an hydraulic clutch, disconnect the pipe from the slave cylinder and free it from the transmission (Chapter 6).
13 Unbolt the cover plate from the front of the gearbox **(see illustration)**.
14 Unscrew and remove the two lower gearbox-to-engine bolts.
15 Reach up over the propeller shaft and disconnect the gearchange linkage from the bottom of the gear lever. To do this, extract the spring clip from one end of the pivot pin and withdraw the pin **(see illustrations)**.
16 Unscrew the two bolts securing the gear lever bracket to the rear of the gearbox **(see illustration)**.
17 For additional working room, unbolt and remove the underbody crossmember located behind the gearbox.
18 Support the gearbox on a trolley jack.

3.16 Unbolting the gear lever bracket

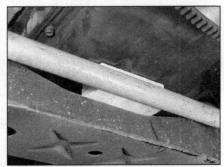

3.20 Place a piece of wood between the sump and front crossmember

3.24a Rear crossmember and exhaust mounting bracket

3.24b Gearchange linkage connection to the gearbox

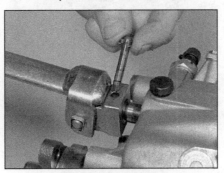

3.24c Disconnecting the gearchange linkage

3.26a Tightening the gearbox rear mounting crossmember bolts

3.26b Tightening the underbody crossmember bolts

3.26c Tightening the propeller shaft front flexible disc joint Torx bolts

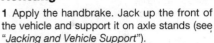

4 Gearchange lever - removal and refitting

19 Unbolt the rear mounting crossmember from the underbody.
20 Position a thin piece of wood beneath the engine sump on the front crossmember (see illustration). Alternately attach a hoist and chains to the engine.
21 Lower the gearbox until the engine sump rests on the piece of wood.
22 Unscrew and remove the remaining gearbox-to-engine bolts.
23 With the help of an assistant, lift the gearbox rearwards from the engine, then withdraw it from under the car. Take care not to allow the weight of the gearbox to bear on the input shaft while it is still engaged with the clutch friction disc.
24 If necessary, extract the spring clip, remove the pin, and disconnect the gearchange linkage from the gearchange lever shaft on the gearbox. Also unbolt and remove the crossmember and exhaust mounting bracket (see illustrations).

Refitting

25 Refitting is a reversal of removal. Check that the clutch release arm and bearing are correctly fitted, and lightly grease the input shaft splines.
26 To help engage the input shaft and clutch friction disc splines, select 4th gear and slowly turn the output flange. Note also that the friction disc must be centralised as described in Chapter 6 in order for the gearbox input shaft to enter the crankshaft spigot bearing. Check and if necessary adjust the clutch cable. Tighten all nuts and bolts to the specified torque. Before inserting the crossmember bolts, apply locking fluid to their threads. Finally fill the gearbox with the specified grade and quantity of oil, and tighten the filler plug on completion (see illustrations).

Refitting

1 Apply the handbrake. Jack up the front of the vehicle and support it on axle stands (see "Jacking and Vehicle Support").
2 Reach up over the propeller shaft and disconnect the gearchange linkage from the bottom of the gear lever. To do this, extract the spring clip from one end of the pivot pin and withdraw the pin.
3 Unscrew the four bolts securing the gear lever to the bracket (see illustrations).
4 Working inside the vehicle, prise the gaiter from the centre console surround (see illustration). Lift the gaiter so that it is inside out then untie the cord and remove the gaiter.
5 Remove the two screws and withdraw the centre console surround (see illustration).
6 Cut the strap retaining the rubber bellows on the gear lever. Release the bellows from the lower plate and gear lever (see illustration).
7 Lift out the gearchange lever assembly, and mount it in a vice.
8 Prise the two half-bushes from the bottom of the gear lever.
9 Remove the bottom foam ring and tap the gear lever out using a mallet.
10 Remove the retaining ring from the housing.
11 Using a pin punch, drive the roll pin from the shift finger tube, then tap off the shift

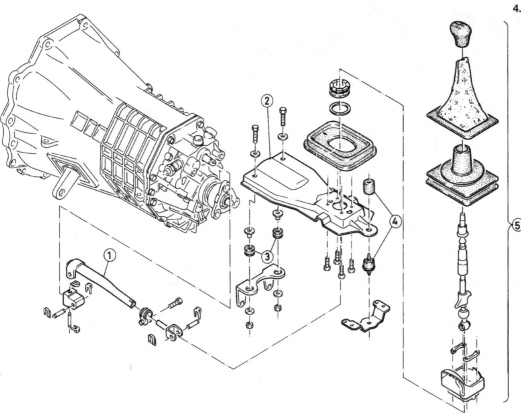

4.3a Exploded view of manual gearbox outer parts

1 Gearchange linkage
2 Gearchange lever support bracket
3 Gearchange front mounting rubbers
4 Gearchange rear mounting rubbers
5 Gear lever assembly

finger. Also remove the upper roll pin and stop sleeve.

12 If necessary remove the gear lever knob by cutting it with a hacksaw taking care not to damage the lever.

13 Remove the reverse gear block by prising off the retainer.

14 Using circlip pliers, extract the spring clip then withdraw the tube, grommet, lock washer, lower grommet and shift finger tube **(see illustration)**.

15 Remove the cable retainer and spring.

16 Clean all the components and examine them for wear and damage. Renew them as necessary and obtain a new gear lever knob.

Refitting

17 Commence reassembly by fitting the spring to the retainer.

18 Insert the retainer in the shift finger tube.

19 Push on the grommet with its open groove uppermost, then fit the spring clip and upper grommet.

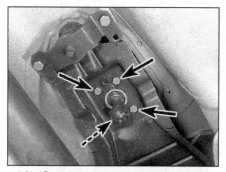

4.3b Gear lever housing bolts (arrowed)

20 Assemble the shift finger tube to the gearchange lever tube with its groove aligned with the lug. Fit the retainer.

21 Where fitted, position the O-ring on the

4.4 Removing the gear lever gaiter

4.5 Removing the centre console surround

4.6 Gearchange lever assembly (with centre console removed)

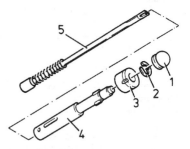

4.14 Gearchange lever components

1 Grommet
2 Lockwasher
3 Grommet
4 Shift finger tube
5 Cable retainer and spring

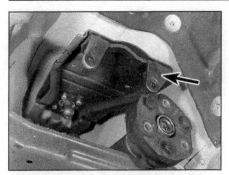

5.4 Gearchange lever support bracket

gearchange lever tube, then insert the reverse gear block.

22 Push up the cable retainer and attach to the lug.

23 Fit the stop sleeve and drive in the roll pin. The upper, long finger should point to the right.

24 Fit the shift finger and drive in the roll pin. Make sure that the stop moves freely.

25 Locate the retaining ring on the gear lever ball, then locate the assembly in the housing.

26 Press the two half bushes into the bottom of the gear lever.

27 Heat the new gear lever knob to approximately 70°C (158°F) then drive it on the gear lever in its correct position using a block of wood and a mallet.

28 Apply a little grease to the threaded plates and locate them in the shift housing.

29 Stick the foam spacer under the housing with a little grease.

30 Locate the gearchange lever assembly in the vehicle and align the bolt holes.

31 Working under the vehicle, insert and tighten the four bolts.

32 Refit the gearchange linkage pivot pin and retain with the spring clip.

33 Refit the gear lever rubber bellows using a new strap. It will help to dip the bellows in soapy water.

34 Refit the centre console surround and gaiter.

35 Lower the vehicle to the ground.

---

5 Gearchange lever support bracket - removal and refitting

Removal

1 Apply the handbrake. Jack up the front of the vehicle and support it on axle stands (see *"Jacking and Vehicle Support"*).

2 Reach up over the propeller shaft and disconnect the gearchange linkage from the gear lever by extracting a spring clip and withdrawing the pin.

3 Unscrew the four bolts securing the gear lever to the bracket.

4 Unbolt the rear mounting bracket from the underbody, and the front of the support bracket from the gearbox **(see illustration)**.

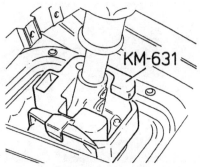

6.4 Tool KM-631 for holding the gear lever for linkage adjustment

5 Withdraw the support bracket from under the vehicle.

6 Unbolt and remove the rubber mountings. Examine them and renew them as necessary.

Refitting

7 Refitting is a reversal of removal. If the threaded plates on top of the gear lever assembly have become displaced, gain access to them with reference to Section 4.

---

6 Gearchange linkage - adjustment

Note: *Adjustment is only possible using GM tool No KM-631*

1 Apply the handbrake. Jack up the front of the vehicle and support it on axle stands (see *"Jacking and Vehicle Support"*). Position the gear lever in neutral.

2 Loosen the clamp bolt on the linkage.

3 Working inside the vehicle, prise the gaiter from the centre console surround and lift it up. Remove the two screws and withdraw the centre console surround. Release the rubber bellows and fold upwards.

4 Fit the tool No KM-631 into the housing while depressing the gear lever to the right **(see illustration)**.

5 Using a spanner on the flats provided, turn the linkage clockwise (as viewed from the driving position) up to the stop.

6 Tighten the clamp bolt.

7 Remove the tool and check for correct gear selection.

8.2 Slacken and remove the drive flange retaining nut . . .

---

8 Refit the rubber bellows, centre console surround, and gaiter.

9 Lower the vehicle to the ground.

---

7 Reversing light switch - removal, testing and refitting

Removal

1 Jack up the front of the vehicle and support it on stands (see *"Jacking and Vehicle Support"*).

2 Disconnect the wiring connector from the switch which is on the left-hand side of the top of the transmission.

3 Unscrew the switch from the transmission casing along with its sealing washer.

Testing

4 To test the switch, use a multimeter (set to the resistance function) or a battery-and-bulb test circuit to check the operation of the switch.

Refitting

5 Fit a new sealing washer to the switch, then screw it back into position in the top of the transmission housing and tighten it to the specified torque setting. Reconnect the wiring connector, and test the operation of the circuit.

---

8 Oil seals - renewal

Propeller shaft flange seal

1 Disconnect the propeller shaft from the transmission (see Chapter 8) and remove the vibration damper.

2 Bolt a suitable length of metal bar to the drive flange then slacken and remove the flange retaining nut whilst holding it stationary with the bar **(see illustration)**.

3 Remove the drive flange from the transmission **(see illustration)**.

4 Lever the seal out of position using a suitable screwdriver.

5 Examine the drive flange sealing surface for

8.3 . . . and remove the drive flange (shown with transmission removed)

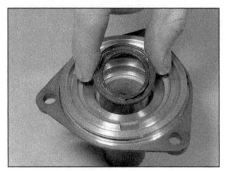

8.14 Press the new seal
into the guide sleeve

8.15a Fit a new sealing ring . . .

8.15b . . . then refit the release bearing
guide sleeve and tighten its retaining bolts
to the specified torque

signs of wear or damage and renew if necessary. Remove all traces of locking compound from the transmission shaft and retaining nut.

6 Press the new seal into position, making sure its sealing lip is facing inwards.

7 Carefully slide the drive flange into position taking care not to damage the seal.

8 Apply fresh locking compound to the retaining nut threads then refit the retaining nut and tighten it to the specified torque.

9 Reconnect the propeller shaft (Chapter 8).

Input shaft seal

10 Remove the transmission as described in Section 3.

11 Remove the clutch release arm and bearing as described in Chapter 6.

12 Undo the bolts and slide the clutch release bearing guide sleeve off the input shaft. Recover the sealing ring and discard.

13 Carefully lever the seal out from the centre of the guide sleeve.

14 Press the new seal into the sleeve so that its sealing lip is facing towards the transmission (sleeve installed) (see illustration).

15 Fit a new sealing ring to the guide sleeve and carefully slide the sleeve onto the input shaft. Refit the retaining bolts and tighten them to the specified torque setting (see illustrations).

16 Refit the clutch release bearing and arm (Chapter 6) and refit the transmission as described in Section 3.

Chapter 7 Part B:
Automatic transmission

Contents

Control unit and switches (AR25 and AR35 transmission) -
    removal and refitting 7
General information 1
Inhibitor switch - removal, refitting and adjustment 6
Kickdown cable - removal, refitting and adjustment
    (AW03-71L and AW03-71LE transmission) 3
Selector lever - removal and refitting 5
Selector lever linkage - adjustment 4
Transmission - removal and refitting 2
Transmission fluid level check ....See Chapter 1
Transmission fluid renewal ....See Chapter 1

Degrees of difficulty

Easy, suitable for novice with little experience	**Fairly easy,** suitable for beginner with some experience	**Fairly difficult,** suitable for competent DIY mechanic	**Difficult,** suitable for experienced DIY mechanic	**Very difficult,** suitable for expert DIY or professional

Specifications

Type

1.8 and 2.5 litre models and early (pre-1990) 2.0 litre and 3.0 litre models:

Manufacturer	Aisin-Warner four forward speeds and one reverse, 4th gear lock-up clutch
Designation	AW03-71L or AW03-71LE

Later (1990-on) 2.0 litre and 3.0 litre models and all 2.6 litre models:

Manufacturer	GM Powertrain computer-controlled with three operating modes, four forward speeds and reverse
Designation	AR25 or AR35

Torque wrench settings

	Nm	lbf ft
AW03-71L and AW03-71LE transmission		
Drain plug	20	15
Fluid coolant lines	35	26
Inhibitor switch	22	16
Rear crossmember	45	33
Torque converter to driveplate	30	22
Transmission to engine:		
M10 bolts	35	26
M12 bolts	55	41
AR25 and AR35 transmission		
Drain plug	25	18
Inhibitor switch bolts	12	9
Rear crossmember bolts	45	33
Selector shaft lever nut	20	15
Torque converter-to-driveplate bolts	30	22
Transmission-to-engine bolts	45	33

---

1 General information

1.8 and 2.5 litre models and early (pre-1990) 2.0 litre and 3.0 litre models - AW03-71L and AW03-71LE transmission

1 The automatic transmission of four-speed type. In 4th gear the torque converter is locked by access of an internal clutch, thereby eliminating any slip. With the selector lever in Drive (D) it is possible to select either a three or four-speed sequence by pressing the button on the lever. It is also possible to select speeds "1" and "2" separately. The transmission incorporates the normal kickdown facility to enable greater acceleration in all the gears, but in addition a kickdown switch is provided on the accelerator pedal specifically to shift from 4th to 3rd gear.

Later (1990-on) 2.0 litre and 3.0 litre models and all 2.6 litre models - AR25 and AR35 transmission

2 From 1990 model year onwards, a new electronically-controlled four speed automatic transmission was fitted. This new transmission has three driving modes; an Economy mode, a Sport mode and a Winter mode. The Economy mode, as the name suggests, is the mode for normal driving, in

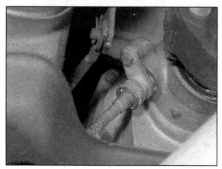

2.11 Speedometer cable connection

2.12 Selector rod connection to the transmission lever

2.13 Fluid drain plug (arrowed)

which the transmission shifts up at relatively low engine speeds to combine reasonable performance with economy. The transmission is automatically set to the Economy mode every time the ignition is switched on.

3 For increased performance, there is a Sport mode, selected using the button on the top of the selector lever. When the transmission is in Sport mode, an indicator lamp on the left-hand side of the instrument cluster is lit. In this mode, the transmission hangs on to each gear longer, shifting up at higher engine speeds to achieve maximum performance. To return to the Economy mode, simply press the selector button a second time.

4 The Winter mode is selected using the button on the centre console. When the Winter mode is selected, the LED indicator by the switch is lit. In this mode, the vehicle pulls away from rest with the transmission in third gear. This limits the torque supplied to the driving wheels, and allows the vehicle to start off safely on slippery surfaces such as snow and ice. The Winter mode can only be selected when the selector lever is in the "D" position. To return the transmission to Economy mode, simply press the mode button for a second time, or move the selector lever to position "3" or "R". Note that the transmission will automatically exit the Winter mode and return to the Economy mode if the vehicle speed exceeds 50 mph (80 kph) or if the kickdown switch is depressed for more than 2 seconds.

2 Transmission - removal and refitting

Removal

AW03-71L and AW03-71LE transmission

1 Disconnect the battery negative lead.
2 Move the selector lever to position "N".
3 Pull the fluid level dipstick from its tube.
4 Unbolt the dipstick tube from the bracket, then cut the strap and pull the filler tube from the receiver tube.
5 Unclip the cooling fan shroud from the radiator.

6 Disconnect the kickdown cable from the throttle lever, then compress the outer cable and detach it from the bracket. On carburettor models first remove the air cleaner as described in Chapter 3.
7 Disconnect the inhibitor switch plug located on the bulkhead, and cut the wiring strap from the filler tube.
8 Unbolt the exhaust system front downpipe from the intermediate section mounting bracket, and exhaust manifold. Also unbolt the mounting bracket and heat shield.
9 Slacken the slider joint nut on the front propeller shaft section one complete turn.
10 Using a conventional or Torx socket as applicable, unscrew the bolts securing the propeller shaft front flexible disc joint to the transmission output flange. Lever the propeller shaft rearwards from the output flange and tie it to one side.
11 Unscrew the knurled nut, and disconnect the speedometer cable from the transmission (see illustration).
12 Disconnect the selector rod from the transmission lever by releasing the spring clip and pivot pin (see illustration).
13 Position a container beneath the transmission sump, unscrew the drain plug and drain the fluid (see illustration). Refit and tighten the drain plug on completion.
14 Loosen the clips and disconnect the flexible rubber fluid hoses at the underbody connection. To ensure correct refitment and to prevent the entry of dust and dirt, disconnect the hoses only at diagonally

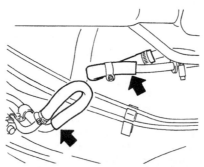

2.14 Disconnect the transmission fluid hoses at diagonally opposite ends then reconnect them as shown

opposite ends then fold them back onto the adjacent pipes (see illustration).
15 Unscrew the bolts securing the front brackets to the engine.
16 Unbolt the transmission front cover and front brackets.
17 Unscrew the bolts securing the torque converter to the driveplate. To gain access to all the bolts, turn the engine with a spanner on the crankshaft pulley bolt.
18 Lever the torque converter away from the driveplate.
19 Support the transmission on a trolley jack.
20 Unscrew the two lower bolts securing the transmission to the engine.
21 Unbolt the rear mounting crossmember from the underbody, then lower the transmission slightly.
22 Disconnect the wiring plugs for the solenoid valve and kickdown switch.
23 Unscrew the remaining bolts securing the transmission to the engine.
24 With the help of an assistant, lower the transmission and withdraw it from the engine, making sure that the torque converter remains fully engaged with the fluid pump.
25 If a new transmission is being fitted, the following parts must be transferred from the old unit:

  a) Rear mounting crossmember.
  b) Fluid lines.
  c) Inhibitor switch and wiring.
  d) Cable retainer.
  e) Selector lever.
  f) Solenoid valve.
  g) Kickdown switch.
  h) Speedometer drive gear.

AR25 and AR35 transmission

26 Firmly apply the handbrake, and place the selector lever in the "N" position. Disconnect the battery negative terminal.
27 Withdraw the dipstick from the filler tube, then undo the dipstick tube retaining bolt and washer, and remove the tube from the transmission, noting its sealing O-ring.
28 Trace the transmission inhibitor switch wiring back to its wiring connector (which is clipped to the centre of the engine compartment bulkhead). Disconnect the connector, and free the switch wiring loom from all its relevant retaining clips and ties.

29 From within the engine compartment, release the transmission breather hose from all its retaining clips and ties.

30 Chock the rear wheels, then jack up the front of the vehicle and support it on axle stands (see "*Jacking and Vehicle Support*").

31 From underneath the vehicle, release the inhibitor switch wiring and breather hose from any remaining clips.

32 Referring to Chapter 4B, on models not fitted with a catalytic converter, remove the exhaust system downpipe then unbolt the exhaust mounting bracket and heat shield. On models with a catalytic converter, remove the downpipe and converter then remove the mounting bracket and the catalytic converter heat shields.

33 Disconnect the two wiring connectors from the left-hand side of the transmission housing, and position the wiring clear of the transmission. **Note:** *When disconnecting the wiring connectors, hold the lower part of each connector firmly in position, to prevent it from being pulled out of the transmission.*

34 Release the speed sensor wiring from its retaining clip, and disconnect it at the wiring connector.

35 Slacken and remove the four retaining bolts, and remove the front crossmember from under the vehicle.

36 Carry out the operations described in paragraphs 9 to 17.

37 Place a jack with interposed block of wood beneath the transmission, and raise the jack until it is supporting the weight of the transmission.

38 Slacken and remove the nuts and bolts securing the rear crossmember to the transmission, and the four bolts securing the crossmember to the underbody, then remove the crossmember from underneath the vehicle.

39 With the jack positioned beneath the transmission taking the weight, slacken and remove the remaining bolts securing the transmission housing to the engine. Note the correct fitted positions of the bolts, to use as a reference on refitting, then make a final check that all necessary components have been disconnected.

40 With the bolts removed, move the trolley jack and transmission to the rear, to free it from its locating dowels. Once the transmission is free, lower the jack and manoeuvre the unit out from under the car, ensuring that the torque converter stays in position on the transmission shaft. If they are loose, remove the locating dowels from the transmission or engine, and keep them in a safe place.

Refitting

AW03-71L and AW03-71LE transmission

41 Refitting is a reversal of the removal procedure but note the following additional points:

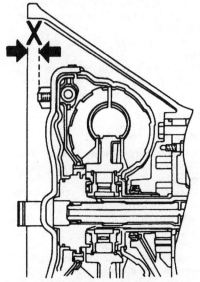

2.41 With the torque converter fully engaged, dimension "X" should be approximately 14.25 mm

a) *Before offering the transmission to the engine, check that the torque converter is fully engaged so that the dimension shown in* **illustration 2.41** *is as stated.*

b) *Apply a little grease to the torque converter centre pin.*

c) *Apply locking fluid to the threads of the rear mounting crossmember bolts before inserting and tightening them.*

d) *Tighten all nuts and bolts to the specified torque.*

e) *Adjust the kickdown cable (Section 3), and selector lever linkage (Section 4).*

f) *Fill the transmission with the specified fluid (Chapter 1).*

AR25 and AR35 transmission

42 The transmission is refitted using a reversal of the removal procedure, bearing in mind the following points.

a) *Apply a little high-melting-point grease to the splines of the transmission input shaft. Do not apply too much, however, otherwise there is a possibility of the grease contaminating the torque converter.*

3.2 Kickdown cable (A), throttle cable (B), and cruise control cable (C)

b) *Make sure the dowels are correctly positioned prior to refitting the transmission to the engine.*

c) *Tighten all nuts and bolts to the specified torque setting (where given).*

d) *Prior to installation, apply locking compound to the threads of the rear crossmember-to-underbody bolts.*

e) *Ensure that the breather hose and wiring looms are correctly routed, and secured by all the necessary retaining clamps and new cable-ties.*

f) *On completion, refill the transmission with the specified type and quantity of fluid (Chapter 1) and check the adjustment of the selector linkage (see Section 4).*

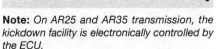

3   Kickdown cable (AW03-71L/LE transmission) - removal, refitting and adjustment

Note: *On AR25 and AR35 transmission, the kickdown facility is electronically controlled by the ECU.*

Removal

1 On carburettor models remove the air cleaner (Chapter 4A), then remove the spring clip and detent spring. Disconnect the outer cable from the segment disc and remove the safety clip if necessary.

2 On fuel injection models, disconnect the inner cable from the ball socket. Compress the plastic bracket and remove the outer cable from the bracket **(see illustration)**.

3 Cut the transmission fluid filler tube retaining strap.

4 Jack up the front of the vehicle and support it on axle stands (see "*Jacking and Vehicle Support*").

5 Position a container beneath the transmission sump then unscrew the drain plug and drain the fluid. Refit and tighten the plug on completion.

6 Unbolt and remove the transmission sump and remove the joint and filler tube.

7 Make a piece of wire to the dimensions shown **(see illustration)**. Using the wire turn the curved disc until the cable can be disconnected.

8 Release and remove the kickdown cable.

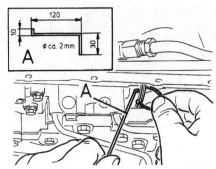

3.7 Using a piece of wire (A) to turn the curved disc

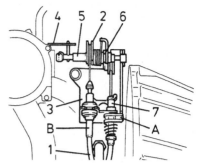

3.18 Upper kickdown cable connection on carburettor models

1 Accelerator cable	6 Lever
2 Cam	7 Kickdown cable
3 Bracket	A Spring clip
4 Throttle valve lever	B Ferrule
5 Shaft	

3.23 Upper kickdown cable connection on fuel injection models

1 Accelerator cable	5 Kickdown cable
2 Ball socket	6 Ferrule
3 Bracket	A Spring clip
4 Throttle valve lever	B Safety clip

Refitting

9 Attach the new cable to the transmission fluid filler tube with a strap.
10 Apply a little grease to the cable seal.
11 Connect the cable to the curved disc using the piece of wire. Check that the cable moves the disc easily.
12 Adjust the cable as described beneath the relevant sub-heading and reconnect the upper end of the cable.

13 Refit the transmission sump using a new joint and filler tube O-ring and tighten the sump bolts.
14 On carburettor models, refit the air cleaner.
15 Lower the vehicle to the ground.
16 Refill the transmission with the specified quantity of fluid as described in Section 2.

Adjustment

Carburettor models

17 Remove the air cleaner (Chapter 4A).
18 Release the spring clip (A) **(see illustration)**.
19 Release the accelerator cable adjustment, then pull the ferrule (B) until the throttle lever (4) rests against the throttle stop without parts (5) and (6) turning against each other. Secure the ferrule in this position.
20 Adjust the accelerator pedal so that it is free of any play in the idle position.
21 Have an assistant slowly depress the accelerator pedal until the kickdown switch is fully depressed. Refit the spring clip (A).
22 Refit the air cleaner (Chapter 4A).

Fuel injection models

23 Release the safety clip (B) **(see illustration)**.
24 Have an assistant depress the accelerator pedal until it just touches the kickdown switch **(see illustration)**.
25 Pull the ferrule until the throttle lever rests against the full throttle stop, then refit the spring clip (B).
26 With the accelerator pedal in the idle position, adjust it so that there is no free play.
27 Release the spring clip (A).
28 Have an assistant slowly depress the accelerator pedal until the kickdown switch is fully depressed. Refit the spring clip (A).

4 Selector lever linkage - adjustment

1 Position the vehicle over an inspection pit, or alternatively jack up the front end and support it on axle stands (see "Jacking and Vehicle Support").

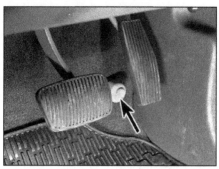

3.24 Kickdown switch (arrowed)

2 Move the selector lever to position "N".
3 Disconnect the linkage rod from the lever on the transmission by releasing the spring clip and pivot pin.
4 Check that the transmission lever is in position "N" (third notch from rear).
5 Move the linkage rod rearwards to push the selector lever against the front of the "N" position, then locate the adjustment fork on the transmission lever. Check the alignment of the holes and if necessary turn the fork until the holes are exactly aligned.
6 From this position turn the adjustment fork one complete turn clockwise onto the linkage rod.
7 Refit the spring clip and pivot pin.
8 Check that the selector lever operates correctly. Also check that the inhibitor switch functions correctly. With the selector lever in positions R, D, 2 and 1 it should not be possible to operate the starter motor. If necessary adjust the switch as described in Section 6.

5 Selector lever - removal and refitting

Removal

AW03-71L and AW03-71LE transmission

1 Using a small screwdriver prise out the gear indicator panel and remove it from the selector lever **(see illustrations)**.
2 Lift out the slot cover **(see illustration)**.

5.1a Prise out the gear indicator panel ...

5.1b ... and remove it from the selector lever

5.2 Removing the slot cover

5.3a Remove the screw . . .

5.3b . . . and release the surround panel from the centre console

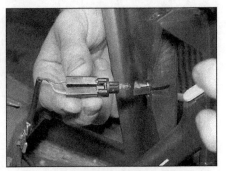

5.4 Removing the bulbholder

5.9a Right-hand view of selector lever

5.9b Left-hand view of selector lever

5.10 Separating the bulb from the bulbholder

3 Remove the front mounting screw and release the surround panel from the rear location holes (see illustrations).

4 Pull out the bulbholder and remove the surround panel (see illustration).

5 Position a block of wood on the right-hand side of the selector lever to hold it in position.

6 Jack up the front of the car and support on axle stands (see "Jacking and Vehicle Support").

7 Disconnect the linkage rod from the lever on the transmission by releasing the spring clip and pivot pin.

8 Unscrew the nut and disconnect the linkage from the selector lever shaft. Recover the corrugated washer and rubber ring. Remove the block of wood.

9 Disconnect the wiring plug, then slide the selector lever sideways from the bearing and remove it (see illustrations).

10 If necessary disconnect the wiring from the bulbholder and pull out the bulb (see illustration).

AR25 and AR35 transmission

11 Remove the centre console assembly as described in Chapter 11.

12 Firmly apply the handbrake, then jack up the front of the vehicle and support on axle stands (see "Jacking and Vehicle Support").

13 From underneath the vehicle, release the spring clip, then withdraw the pivot pin and detach the linkage rod from the base of the selector lever.

14 Return to the inside of the vehicle, and carefully drill out the five rivets securing the selector lever housing to the body. Lift the selector lever and housing out of the vehicle.

Refitting

AW03-71L and AW03-71LE transmission

15 Refitting is a reversal of removal, but adjust the linkage as described in Section 4.

AR25 and AR35 transmission

16 Remove all traces of sealing compound from the base of the selector lever housing and vehicle body.

17 Apply a bead of suitable sealing compound to the underside of the selector lever housing, then refit the housing to the vehicle.

18 Secure the selector lever housing in position using new pop-rivets.

19 From underneath the vehicle, reconnect the linkage rod to the base of the selector lever, securing the pivot pin in position with the spring clip.

20 Refit the centre console as described in Chapter 11.

21 Check the selector linkage adjustment as described in Section 4.

---

6 **Inhibitor switch** - removal, refitting and adjustment

Removal

AW03-71L and AW03-71LE transmission

1 Move the selector lever to position "N".

2 Disconnect the inhibitor switch plug located on the bulkhead. Cut the strap holding the wiring to the filler tube.

3 Jack up the front of the vehicle and support it on axle stands (see "Jacking and Vehicle Support").

4 Release the wiring from the underbody and from the clip on the transmission.

5 Disconnect the fluid cooler pipes from the transmission (see illustration). Plug the open ends to prevent entry of dust and dirt.

6 Unscrew the locknut from the front connector on the switch. Move the connector aside and plug it.

7 Unscrew the rear bolt. Bend the locktab and unscrew the nut.

8 Withdraw the inhibitor switch from the transmission.

AR25 and AR35 transmission

9 Firmly apply the handbrake, and place the selector lever in position "N".

6.5 Fluid cooler pipes

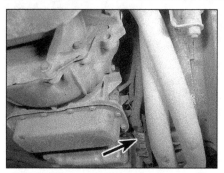

6.12 Inhibitor switch location (arrowed) -
AR25 and AR35 transmission

10 Trace the transmission inhibitor switch wiring back to its wiring connector (which is clipped to the centre of the engine compartment bulkhead). Disconnect the connector, and free the switch wiring loom from all its relevant retaining clips and ties.
11 Chock the rear wheels, then jack up the front of the vehicle and support it on axle stands (see "*Jacking and Vehicle Support*").
12 From underneath the vehicle, release the inhibitor switch wiring from any further retaining clips (see illustration).
13 Unclip the inhibitor switch cover, then slacken and remove the nut securing the selector lever to the transmission, and pull the lever off the selector shaft.
14 Undo the two retaining bolts, and slide the inhibitor switch off the selector shaft.

Refitting and adjustment

AW03-71L and AW03-71LE transmission

15 Refitting is a reversal of removal, however before tightening the rear bolt, the switch must be correctly aligned as follows. Position a steel rule or length of bar on the rear flat of the switch shaft. With the transmission in Neutral align the line on the switch with the rule then tighten the switch to the specified torque (see illustration).

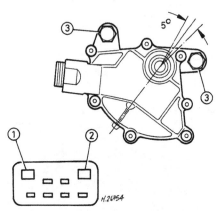

6.19 Inhibitor switch electrical adjustment
- AR25 and AR35 transmission

1 Wiring connector terminal 1
2 Wiring connector terminal 2
3 Switch retaining bolts

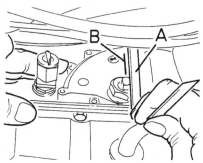

6.15 Aligning the inhibitor switch
A Straight edge   B Alignment mark

AR25 and AR35 transmission

16 Prior to refitting the switch, examine the selector shaft oil seal for signs of damage or oil leakage, and renew if necessary. To renew the oil seal, carefully lever the oil seal out of position using a small flat-bladed screwdriver. Apply a thin smear of grease to the lips of the new seal, then carefully pass the seal over the end of the shaft and press it into position in the transmission. If necessary, the seal can be tapped into place using a tubular drift which bears only on the hard outer edge of the seal.
17 Locate the inhibitor switch on the selector shaft, then install its two retaining bolts, tightening them finger-tight only at this stage. Adjust the switch as follows. Before proceeding further, temporarily refit the selector lever to the shaft, and ensure that the transmission is still in neutral ("N" position).
18 There are two ways of adjusting the switch, either mechanically or electrically. The electrical method is the far more accurate method, but requires the use of a multimeter.
19 To electrically adjust the switch, connect a multimeter, set to the resistance function, across terminals 1 and 2 of the switch wiring connector (see illustration). With the transmission in neutral, there should be continuity between the terminals. Pivot the switch slowly to determine the area of the

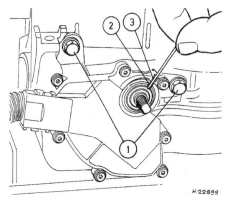

6.20 Adjusting the inhibitor switch using a
suitable piece of welding rod - AR25 and
AR35 transmission

1 Switch retaining bolts
2 Inhibitor switch grooves
3 Selector lever groove

switch where this occurs; this area forms an angle of approximately 5°. Position the switch in the centre of this area, then tighten its retaining bolts to the specified torque.
20 To adjust the switch mechanically, a welding rod of diameter 2.0 to 2.3 mm is required. With the transmission in neutral, pivot the switch until the grooves on the switch and transmission selector lever align and the rod can be cleanly inserted (see illustration). Hold the switch in this position, and tighten its retaining bolts to the specified torque. Check that the grooves are still correctly aligned, then remove the rod.
21 Once the inhibitor switch is correctly adjusted, refit the selector lever to the transmission selector shaft, and tighten its retaining nut to the specified torque.
22 Feed the switch wiring back up into the engine compartment, ensuring it is correctly routed.
23 From within the engine compartment, reconnect the inhibitor switch wiring connector, and secure the wiring in position with new cable-ties.
24 Check the selector linkage adjustment as described in Section 4, then check that the inhibitor switch operates correctly.
25 Refit the inhibitor switch cover, and lower the vehicle to the ground.

7 Control unit and switches (AR25/AR35 transmission) - removal and refitting

Electronic control unit (ECU)

1 The electronic control unit is situated under the bonnet (behind the left-hand end of the plastic water deflector).
2 To remove the unit, open up the bonnet, then peel back the sealing strip from the left-hand end of the water deflector. Carefully lift the water deflector to gain access to the control unit (see illustration).
3 Undo the retaining bolt and withdraw the control unit, disconnecting the wiring connector as it becomes accessible.
4 Refitting is a reversal of the removal procedure, ensuring that the water deflector and sealing strip are correctly seated.

7.2 Electronic control unit location -
AR25 and AR35 transmission
(water deflector lifted)

Sport mode switch

5 Using a small flat-bladed screwdriver, carefully prise out the gear indicator panel and slot cover from the surround panel, and remove them from the selector lever.

6 Undo the single retaining screw, then release the surround panel from the centre console. Pull the bulbholder out of the panel, and lift the panel off the selector lever.

7 Gently feed the Sport mode switch wiring in through the base of the selector lever, until the switch is forced out of position.

8 Using a soldering iron, carefully unsolder the two wires and remove the switch.

9 Refitting is a reverse of the removal procedure, ensuring that the wires are securely soldered onto the switch. Check the operation of the switch prior to refitting the surround panel.

Winter mode switch

10 Unclip the middle console cover, and remove it from the centre console, disconnecting the switch wiring connector(s) as they become accessible.

11 Depress the switch retaining tangs, and remove the switch from the cover.

12 Refitting is a reversal of removal.

Kickdown switch

13 The kickdown switch is situated beneath the accelerator pedal.

14 To remove the switch, disconnect the wiring, then carefully prise the switch off its retainer.

15 On refitting, ensure that the switch is correctly seated on its retainer, then reconnect the wiring connector.

Notes

Chapter 8
Final drive, driveshafts and propeller shaft

Contents

Driveshaft - removal and refitting 8
Driveshaft rubber bellows and outer constant velocity joint - renewal . .9
Final drive unit - removal and refitting 2
Final drive unit - oil level check 3
Final drive unit damping bracket - renewal .4
Final drive unit differential bearing oil seal - renewal 7
Final drive unit pinion oil seal - renewal 6
Final drive unit rear cover gasket - renewal .5
General description 1
Propeller shaft - removal and refitting 10
Propeller shaft centre bearing - renewal 11
Propeller shaft disc joints - renewal 12

Degrees of difficulty

Easy, suitable for novice with little experience	Fairly easy, suitable for beginner with some experience	Fairly difficult, suitable for competent DIY mechanic	Difficult, suitable for experienced DIY mechanic	Very difficult, suitable for expert DIY or professional

Specifications

Final drive
Type . . . . Unsprung, attached to rear suspension crossmember and underbody
Number of teeth:
   Crown wheel 37
   Pinion 10
Final drive ratio:
   All six cylinder models . . . . 3.70 : 1
   1.8 and 2.0 litre models with a catalytic converter . . . . 3.90 : 1
   1.8 and 2.0 litre non-catalyst models with manual transmission . . . . 3.70 : 1
   1.8 litre non-catalyst models with automatic transmission . . . . 3.90 : 1
   2.0 litre non-catalyst models with automatic transmission . . . . 3.70 : 1

Driveshaft
Type . . . . Maintenance-free double constant velocity joint

Propeller shaft
Type . . . . Two-piece tubular shaft with centre bearing, centre universal joint, and flexible disc joint connections to transmission and differential

Lubrication
Final drive lubricant type/specification:
   Excluding limited-slip differential . . . . Hypoid gear oil, viscosity SAE 90
   Limited-slip differential . . . . GM special lubricant 19 42 382 (9 293 688)
Final drive lubricant capacity:
   Saloon . . . . 0.8 litre (1.4 pints)
   Estate . . . . 1.0 litre (1.8 pints)
   Models with ribbed rear cover (from 08/90) . . . . as above plus 0.1 litres
Driveshaft CV joint grease type . . . . GM special grease 19 41 522 (90 007 999)

Torque wrench settings

	Nm	lbf ft
Rear damping block to underbody:		
Stage 1	30	22
Stage 2	Tighten a further 30° to 45l°	
Rear damping block to final drive unit	110	81
Final drive unit rear cover	60	44
Final drive unit to crossmember:		
Stage 1	110	81
Stage 2	Tighten a further 30° to 45°	
Driveshaft to hub:		
Stage 1	50	37
Stage 2	Tighten a further 45° to 60°	
Final drive unit filler plug	22	16
Propeller shaft slider joint nut	40	30
Propeller shaft centre bearing bracket	20	15
Propeller shaft to flexible joint (Hexagon bolt)	100	74
Propeller shaft to flexible joint (Torx bolt):		
Stage 1	50	37
Stage 2	Tighten a further 45° to 60°	
Anti-roll bar clamps	22	16
Speed sensor bracket (with ABS)	60	44
Speed sensor to bracket (with ABS)	7	5
Disc joint to propeller shaft transmission or differential:		
Hexagon bolt	100	74
Torx bolt:		
Stage 1	50	37
Stage 2	Tighten a further 45° to 60°	
Propeller shaft centre bearing to bracket	22	16
Propeller shaft centre bearing bracket to underbody	20	15
Propeller shaft slider joint nut	40	30

1 General description

1 The final drive unit is bolted directly to the rear suspension crossmember and hence is of the unsprung type. A rubber damping block attached to the rear of the final drive unit acts as a mounting for the rear suspension crossmember. Two driveshafts transmit drive from the final drive differential to the rear wheels which are attached to the fully independent rear suspension.

2 A limited-slip differential may be fitted as an option to new vehicles, or it may be service-installed at a later date, however special tools are required and the existing crownwheel must be heated to a pre-determined temperature before bolting the limited-slip differential to it. Because of this, the procedure is not included in this Chapter. General overhaul of the final drive differential is also not included.

3 A two-piece, tubular propeller shaft is fitted, incorporating a centre bearing supported in a rubber insulator. The rear section has a universal joint at its front end, and the front section has a slider joint at its rear end. The propeller shaft is attached to the transmission and differential by flexible disc joints. It is not possible to overhaul the universal joint.

2 Final drive unit - removal and refitting

Removal

1 Chock the front wheels. Jack up the rear of the vehicle and support it on axle stands (see "*Jacking and Vehicle Support*"). Remove both rear wheels.

2 Remove both driveshafts with reference to Section 8.

3 Loosen the centre slider joint nut on the propeller shaft approximately one complete turn.

4 Unhook the exhaust system mounting rubbers and lower the rear of the system approximately 300 mm (12.0 in). Support or tie the system in this position.

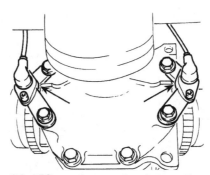

2.9 ABS speed sensor brackets on the rear of the final drive unit (arrowed)

5 Unbolt the propeller shaft centre bearing bracket from the underbody noting the location of any alignment shims.

6 Unbolt the propeller shaft rear flange from the flexible drive joint and lever the propeller shaft from the joint. Support the propeller shaft on an axle stand.

7 Support the final drive unit on a trolley jack.

8 Loosen only the bolts securing the rear damping bracket to the final drive unit.

9 On models equipped with an anti-lock braking system (ABS), unbolt the speed sensor brackets from the rear of the final drive unit (see illustration).

10 Unbolt the rear damping bracket from the underbody (see illustration).

11 Disconnect the rear brake hoses from the semi-trailing arms by pulling out the retaining clips.

12 Lower the final drive unit and rear

2.10 Rear damping bracket mounting bolts (arrowed)

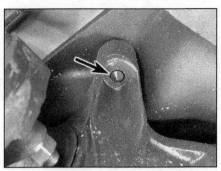

2.13 Lower view of a final drive unit front mounting bolt (arrowed)

suspension crossmember several inches, then unscrew the bolts securing the rear anti-roll bar clamps to the crossmember. Pivot the anti-roll bar upwards.

13 Unscrew the final drive front and rear mounting bolts from the top of the rear suspension crossmember **(see illustration)**.

14 Lower the final drive unit and withdraw it from under the vehicle. Unbolt and remove the rear damping bracket, and the rubber disc joint.

Refitting

15 Refitting is a reversal of removal but tighten all nuts and bolts to the specified torque. Refit the driveshafts with reference to Section 8. Check the oil level in the final drive unit as described in Section 3.

3 Final drive unit - oil level check

1 Jack up the front and rear of the vehicle and support it on axle stands (see *"Jacking and Vehicle Support"*) so that the vehicle is level.

2 Using a hexagon key, unscrew the filler plug from the right-hand side of the final drive unit.

3 Check that the oil level is up to the bottom of the filler plug aperture using a (clean) piece of bent wire or small screwdriver as a dipstick.

4 If necessary top-up with the correct type of oil as given in the Specifications.

5 Refit and tighten the filler plug to the specified torque, and wipe clean.

6 Check the pinion final drive unit oil seal and differential bearing oil seals for leaks. If evident, renew them.

7 Lower the car to the ground.

4 Final drive unit damping bracket - renewal

1 Chock the front wheels. Jack up the rear of the vehicle and support it on axle stands (see *"Jacking and Vehicle Support"*).

2 Support the final drive unit on a trolley jack.

3 Loosen the bolts securing the rear damping bracket to the final drive unit.

4 Unbolt the rear damping bracket from the underbody.

5 Lower the final drive unit and rear suspension crossmember, then unscrew the bolts and remove the damping bracket (refer to illustration 2.10).

6 Fit the new bolts using a reversal of the removal procedure, but tighten all nuts and bolts to the specified torque.

5 Final drive unit rear cover gasket - renewal

Note: *The rear cover fitted to the final drive unit from 08/90 was modified by the addition of a series of cooling ribs, cast into the outer surface of the cover - previous units had a smooth finish. Note the following deviations when working on a final drive unit fitted with a modified rear cover:*

a) *A paper gasket is no longer fitted between the cover and housing. On refitting, ensure that the cover and housing mating surfaces are clean and dry, then apply a coat of suitable sealing compound to the cover flange mating surface.*

b) *The rear cover retaining bolts must be renewed as a complete set whenever they are removed.*

c) *The lubricant capacity of the modified final drive unit is greater than that of the earlier version - refer to Specifications for details.*

1 Remove the damping bracket as described in Section 4.

2 Position a suitable container under the final drive unit, then unbolt and remove the cover. Remove the gasket and allow the oil to drain.

3 Thoroughly clean the joint faces of the cover and final drive unit.

4 Locate the new gasket on the final drive unit using a little grease to hold it in place.

5 Refit the cover, then insert and tighten the bolts progressively to the specified torque. It is recommended that new bolts are used.

6 Refit the damping bracket with reference to Section 4.

7 With the vehicle on a level surface, unscrew the filler plug from the final drive unit and pour in the specified grade of oil until it reaches the lower edge of the hole. Refit and tighten the filler plug to the specified torque.

8 Lower the vehicle to the ground.

6 Final drive unit pinion oil seal - renewal

1 Remove the final drive unit as described in Section 2.

2 Mount the unit in a vice.

3 Mark the drive flange nut in relation to the drive flange and pinion.

4 Hold the drive flange stationary by bolting a length of metal bar to it, then unscrew the nut noting the exact number of turns necessary to remove it.

5 Using a suitable puller, draw the drive flange from the pinion.

6 Lever the oil seal from the final drive casing with a screwdriver. Wipe clean the oil seal seating.

7 Smear a little oil on the sealing lip of the new oil seal, then drive it squarely into the casing until flush with the outer face. Ideally use metal tubing to fit the oil seal, but alternatively a block of wood may be used on each side of the pinion.

8 Locate the drive flange on the pinion in its original position and refit the nut to its original position as well.

9 To check that the final drive bearings are pre-loaded correctly, check that the turning torque of the drive flange is between 90 and 120 Ncm (8.0 and 10.6 lbf in). To do this, either fit a socket on the pinion nut, and use a special torque meter, or a length of string and a spring balance.

10 Refit the final drive unit with reference to Section 2.

7 Final drive unit differential bearing oil seal - renewal

1 Chock the front wheels. Jack up the rear of the vehicle and support it on axle stands (see *"Jacking and Vehicle Support"*). Remove the appropriate rear wheel.

2 Remove the appropriate driveshaft with reference to Section 8.

3 Note the fitted depth of the oil seal in the final drive casing.

4 Using a screwdriver or hooked instrument, lever out the oil seal **(see illustration)**. Wipe clean the oil seal seating.

5 Smear a little oil on the sealing lip of the new oil seal. Using suitable metal tubing drive the oil seal squarely into the casing to the previously noted position.

6 Refit the driveshaft with reference to Section 8.

7 Refit the wheel and lower the vehicle to the ground.

7.4 Differential bearing oil seal

8.9a Torque tightening the driveshaft bolts

8.9b Angle tightening the driveshaft bolts

driveshaft bolts to ensure correct alignment. Tap the cover on the joint with a mallet.

16 Extract the retaining circlip from the inner end of the driveshaft and fit a new one.

17 Refit the driveshaft with reference to Section 8.

10 Propeller shaft - removal and refitting

8 Driveshaft - removal and refitting

Removal

1 Chock the front wheels, then jack up the rear of the vehicle and support it on axle stands (see *"Jacking and Vehicle Support"*).

2 Unscrew the socket-head bolts securing the driveshaft to the rear hub while holding the rear wheel stationary. Recover the lockwashers.

3 Lever the driveshaft from the rear hub and support it above the disc brake assembly.

4 Remove the rear wheel.

5 Position a container under the final drive unit to catch any spilled oil.

6 Carefully lever the driveshaft from the final drive unit differential. On models with anti-lock braking take care not to damage the speed sensor and trigger wheel.

7 Withdraw the driveshaft from the side of the vehicle.

8 Check the circlip on the inner end of the driveshaft and if necessary renew it.

Refitting

9 Refitting is a reversal of removal, but make sure that the driveshaft is fully entered in the differential side gear with the circlip engaged in its groove. Tighten the mounting bolts in the two stages given in the Specifications **(see illustrations)**. Check and if necessary top-up the oil level in the final drive unit (see Section 3).

9 Driveshaft rubber bellows and outer constant velocity joint - renewal

1 Remove the driveshaft as described in Section 8 and mount it in a vice.

2 Using a small drift, top the metal cover from the outer joint.

3 Loosen and remove both clips from the rubber bellows.

4 Using a sharp knife slice through the rubber bellows and remove them from the driveshaft.

5 Scoop out the grease from the joint and wipe the driveshaft clean.

6 Using circlip pliers, extract the circlip from the outer end of the driveshaft.

7 Support the outer joint on a vice, then tap the driveshaft down through it.

8 Fill the inner joint with the specified type of grease using a wooden spatula.

9 Fit the new inner bellows, check that it is not twisted then fit and tighten the clips.

10 Locate the outer bellows on the driveshaft.

11 Fit the outer joint using metal tubing with the driveshaft mounted in a vice. Make sure that the joint abuts the shoulder.

12 Fit the circlip making sure that it fully enters the groove.

13 Using the wooden spatula fill the outer joint with grease.

14 Locate the outer bellows on the plate, check that it is not twisted then fit and tighten the clips.

15 Locate the cover on the joint using two

Removal

1 Chock the front wheels. Jack up the rear of the vehicle and support it on axle stands (see *"Jacking and Vehicle Support"*).

2 On models equipped with a catalytic converter, from underneath the vehicle, undo the retaining bolts and remove both the large and small catalytic converter heatshields from the vehicle underbody.

3 Apply the handbrake, then slacken the slider joint nut on the front propeller shaft section one turn **(see illustration)**.

4 Using a conventional, or Torx, socket as applicable, unscrew the bolts securing the front flexible disc joint to the transmission output flange **(see illustration)**.

5 At the rear of the propeller shaft, unscrew the bolts securing the rear disc joint to the differential flange **(see illustration)**.

6 Support the centre of the propeller shaft on an axle stand, then unbolt the centre bearing support bracket from the underbody, noting the location of any alignment shims.

7 Push the front section rearwards along the slider joint splines until clear of the transmission output flange.

8 Withdraw the propeller shaft forwards, making sure that the front section remains on the slider joint splines.

9 Unbolt the centre support bracket from the centre bearing, noting the location of any alignment shims.

10 Unbolt the front and rear disc joints from the propeller shaft. Note that on some models a vibration damper is fitted at the front of the propeller shaft.

10.3 Propeller shaft slider joint nut (arrowed)

10.4 Propeller shaft front flexible disc joint connection

10.5 Propeller shaft rear flexible disc joint connection

10.11 Tightening the slider joint nut

Refitting

11 Refitting is a reversal of removal, but tighten all nuts and bolts to the specified torque. Tighten the slider joint nut last to avoid any strain on the disc joints **(see illustration)**. If a new propeller shaft is being fitted, loosen the slider joint nut before commencing the refitting procedure.

11 Propeller shaft centre bearing - renewal

1 Remove the propeller shaft as described in Section 10.

2 Mount the rear propeller shaft section in a vice, using shaped blocks of wood to prevent damage.

3 Mark the front and rear sections in relation to each other, then pull the front section from the splines.

4 Using circlip pliers, extract the circlip from the groove in front of the centre bearing **(see illustration)**.

5 Support the centre bearing on a vice, and press or drive the rear propeller shaft section down through the bearing.

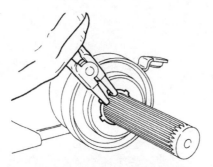

11.4 Extract the circlip from the groove in front of the centre bearing

6 Similarly press or drive the ball bearing from the centre bearing housing, and remove the dust cover.

7 Clean the removed components and the end of the propeller shaft. Lightly grease the splines.

8 Press or drive the new ball bearing into the housing, and align the dust cover.

9 Support the rear section universal joint on a vice, and press or drive the centre bearing over the splines using a metal tube on the inner track. Make sure that the bearing makes contact with its seating shoulder.

10 Mount the rear section in a vice, and fit the front dust cover and the circlip, making sure that it is correctly located in the groove.

11 Locate the dust cover over the splines, followed by the slider nut, washer and plastic sleeve.

12 Fit the front section on the rear section splines, making sure that the previously-made marks are aligned. Note that a master spline is fitted to ensure correct assembly **(see illustration)**.

13 Start the slider joint nut on its thread, but do not tighten until after the propeller shaft has been refitted.

11.12 Master spline on the slider joint (arrowed)

12 Propeller shaft disc joints - renewal

1 Chock the front wheels. Jack up the rear of the vehicle and support it on axle stands (see "*Jacking and Vehicle Support*").

2 Apply the handbrake, then loosen only the slider joint nut on the front propeller shaft section. Note that, on models equipped with a catalytic converter, it will be necessary to remove the small heatshield from the vehicle underbody to gain access to the nut.

3 Unbolt the propeller shaft flange(s) from the flexible disc joint(s).

4 Unbolt the flexible disc joint from the transmission and/or differential drive flange(s).

5 Push the appropriate propeller shaft section towards the centre bearing and remove the disc joint(s). If necessary, use a lever to prise the propeller shaft clear of the drive flange(s).

6 Fit the new flexible disc joint(s) using a reversal of the removal procedure, but tighten all nuts and bolts to the specified torque. Tighten the slider joint nut last to avoid any strain on the disc joints. Where Torx head bolts are fitted, observe the angle tightening procedure given in the Specifications.

Notes

Chapter 9
Braking system

Contents

ABS (Anti-lock Braking System) -
  general information and component removal/refitting 17
Brake disc - examination, removal and refitting 6
Brake pedal - removal and refitting 16
Front brake caliper - removal, overhaul and refitting 4
Front brake pads - inspection and renewal 2
General description 1
Handbrake cable - removal and refitting 8
Handbrake lever - removal and refitting 9
Handbrake shoes - inspection and renewal 7
Hydraulic brake lines and hoses - removal and refitting 13
Hydraulic system - bleeding 12
Master cylinder - removal, overhaul and refitting 10
Rear brake caliper - removal, overhaul and refitting 5
Rear brake pads - inspection and renewal .3
Rear brake proportioning valve - removal and refitting 11
Vacuum servo hose and non-return valve - renewal 14
Vacuum servo unit - testing, removal and refitting 15

Degrees of difficulty

Easy, suitable for novice with little experience	**Fairly easy,** suitable for beginner with some experience	**Fairly difficult,** suitable for competent DIY mechanic
Difficult, suitable for experienced DIY mechanic	**Very difficult,** suitable for expert DIY or professional	

Specifications

System type . . . . Front and rear discs, floating front caliper, fixed rear caliper, tandem master cylinder with hydraulic system split front/rear, vacuum servo unit; rear brake proportioning valve on certain models. Electronic anti-lock braking system (ABS) on some models. Cable-operated handbrake to shoes bearing on inside of rear discs.

Front brakes
Disc diameter:
  4 cylinder-engined models . . . . 258 mm
  6 cylinder-engined models to 1990 . . . . 280 mm
  6 cylinder engined models (including DOHC) from 1990-on . . . . 296 mm
Disc thickness:
  4 cylinder-engined models:
    Non-ventilated:
      New . . . . 12.7 mm
      Minimum . . . . 9.7 mm
    Ventilated:
      New . . . . 24.0 mm
      Minimum . . . . 21.0 mm
    Thickness variation (maximum) . . . . 0.007 mm
  6 cylinder-engined models to 1990:
    Ventilated:
      New . . . . 24.0 mm
      Minimum . . . . 21.0 mm
    Thickness variation (maximum) . . . . 0.007 mm
  6 cylinder-engined models from 1990-on (including DOHC):
    Ventilated:
      New . . . . 28.0 mm
      Minimum . . . . 25.0 mm
    Thickness variation (maximum) . . . . 0.007 mm
Run-out with disc fitted to vehicle (maximum) . . . . 0.1 mm
Minimum brake pad thickness (including backplate) . . . . 7.0 mm
Caliper piston diameter:
  4 cylinder-engined models . . . . 54.0 mm
  6 cylinder-engined models to 1990 . . . . 60.0 mm
  6 cylinder-engined models (including DOHC) from 1990-on . . . . 57.0 mm

Rear brakes

Discs:

Diameter, new	270 mm
Minimum thickness	7.0 mm
Thickness variation (maximum)	0.007 mm
Run-out with disc fitted to vehicle (maximum)	0.1 mm

Caliper piston diameter:

Up to 1990:

4 cylinder-engined saloons	35.0 mm
6 cylinder-engined saloons and 4 cylinder-engined estates	38.0 mm
6 cylinder-engined estates	40.0 mm

From 1991-on:

4 cylinder-engined saloons	35.0 mm
6 cylinder-engined saloons	38.0 mm
All estates	40.0 mm
Minimum brake pad thickness (including backplate)	7.0 mm
Handbrake shoes minimum thickness (lining only)	1.0 mm

General

Brake fluid type/specification	Hydraulic fluid to FMVSS 571 or 116, DOT3 or 4, or SAE J1703
Rear wheel speed sensor-to-impulse wheel clearance	0.5 to 1.5 mm

Torque wrench settings

	Nm	lbf ft
Caliper bleed screw	9	7
Brake disc detent screw	4	3
Master cylinder front mounting	20	15
Vacuum servo	20	15
Rear caliper mounting bolts	65	48
Front caliper frame to housing (GM caliper)	95	70
ABS modulator	8	6
ABS modulator front frame	10	7
Handbrake lever	20	15
Vacuum servo support	18	13
Master cylinder to vacuum servo	22	16
Brake line union nuts/bolts	11	8
Roadwheel bolts	90	60
Caliper guide bolt (ATE caliper)	30	22
Caliper guide pins (Girling caliper)	30	22
Front caliper mounting bracket-to-steering knuckle bolts (all calipers):		
Stage 1	95	70
Stage 2	Angle-tighten 30° to 45°	
Caliper brake hose union bolt	40	30

1 General description

1 The braking system is of dual hydraulic circuit type with front and rear discs. The front and rear hydraulic circuits are operated independently, so that in the event of a failure in one circuit the remaining circuit still functions. The handbrake is cable-operated to brake shoes inside the rear brake discs, the inner part of the discs being drums. The disc brakes are self- adjusting in use, however the handbrake is adjusted manually.

2 Some Saloon models and all Estate models are fitted with a rear brake proportioning valve which is deceleration-dependent. The valve prevents the rear wheels from locking due to the weight shift to the front of the vehicle during deceleration.

3 GM's anti-lock braking system (ABS) is fitted as standard equipment to some models and as optional equipment to others. It effectively regulates the hydraulic pressure to each separate brake in order to prevent one wheel locking ahead of the others. The system incorporates an electronic control unit which is supplied with signals from the wheel speed sensors. The signals are compared with each other and, if one wheel is found to be decelerating ahead of the others the hydraulic pressure to that wheel is reduced until its speed matches the other wheels. For this purpose the two front brakes are modulated separately, but the two rear brakes are modulated together. The ABS unit is fitted in the hydraulic lines leading from the master cylinder to the brakes, the vacuum servo unit and master cylinder being of similar type for both non-ABS and ABS models.

4 Should the ABS develop a fault, it is recommended that a complete test be carried out by a GM garage who will have the necessary equipment to make an accurate diagnosis.

2 Front brake pads - inspection and renewal

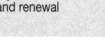

 Warning: Renew both sets of front brake pads at the same time - never renew the pads on only one wheel, as uneven braking may result. The dust created by wear of the pads may contain asbestos, which is a health hazard. Never blow it out, and don't inhale any of it. An approved filtering mask should be worn when working on the brakes. DO NOT use petroleum-based solvents to clean brake parts - use brake cleaner or methylated spirit only.

Removal

**GM caliper -
Carlton 1.8 and 2.0 litre to 1989**

1 Apply the handbrake. Jack up the front of the vehicle and support it on axle stands (see

"*Jacking and Vehicle Support*"). Remove the front wheels.

2 Turn the steering to full right-hand lock and check the wear of the linings on the right-hand brake pads. Check that the thickness of the lining including the backing plate is as shown in the Specifications using a steel rule or vernier calipers.

3 Turn the steering to full left-hand lock and check the left-hand brake pads the same way.

4 If any brake pad is worn below the minimum thickness, renew all the front pads as a set together with new anti-rattle springs.

5 Extract the spring clips from the inner ends of the brake pad pins where fitted.

6 Note how the anti-rattle spring is located, then drive out the pins using a thin punch from the inside (**see illustration**).

7 Remove the anti-rattle spring. At the same time, where applicable, disconnect the pad wear warning lamp sensor from the inner pad, and disconnect the sensor cable from the wiring harness in the engine compartment (**see illustrations**). Also release the cable from the clips and the anti-rattle spring. Note that the sensor and cable must always be renewed when fitting new brake pads as the sensor will be worn.

8 Push the brake pads apart slightly.

9 Pull the brake pads from the caliper (**see illustration**). If they are tight, use pliers or grips on the backplates. Also remove the intermediate plates where fitted.

ATE caliper - Carlton 1.8 and 2.0 litre from 1989-on

10 Firmly apply the handbrake, then jack up the front of the vehicle and support on axle stands (see "*Jacking and Vehicle Support*"). Remove both front roadwheels.

11 The thickness of the brake pads (friction material and backing plate) can be measured via the aperture in the caliper. If any pad has worn beyond the specified minimum thickness (See Specifications), all the pads must be renewed as an axle set. However, a far more thorough check can be made if the caliper is first removed, as follows.

12 Carefully lever out the large spring, and remove it from the outside of the caliper body (**see illustration**).

13 On vehicles equipped with check control, unclip the pad wear sensor from the caliper aperture, and position it clear of the caliper (**see illustration**).

14 Remove the dust caps from the caliper guide pin bolt holes, then slacken and remove the two guide pin bolts, and withdraw them from the caliper (**see illustrations**).

15 Slide the caliper off the brake disc, unclipping the outer pad from the outer edge of the caliper. Tie the caliper to the suspension strut, using a suitable piece of wire.

 Warning: Take care to avoid kinking or placing any strain on the flexible brake hose.

16 Remove the outer pad from the caliper mounting bracket.

2.6 Removing the front brake pad pins - GM caliper

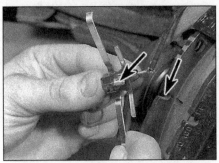
2.7b Pad wear sensor location stub and slot (arrowed)

2.7a Disconnecting the pad wear warning lamp sensor and anti-rattle spring

2.9 Removing the outer front brake pad

ATE caliper - all Senator models to 1990 and 6-cylinder Carlton models to 1990

17 Firmly apply the handbrake, then jack up the front of the vehicle and support on axle stands (see "*Jacking and Vehicle Support*"). Remove both front roadwheels.

18 The thickness of the brake pads (friction material and backing plate) can be observed via the aperture in the caliper. If any pad has worn beyond the specified minimum thickness (See Specifications), all the pads must be renewed as an axle set. However, a more thorough check can be made if the caliper is first removed, as follows.

2.12 Carefully lever out the large spring

2.13 Unclipping the pad wear sensor

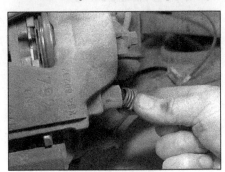
2.14a Remove the guide bolt dust covers . . .

2.14b . . . then slacken and remove the guide bolts

19 On vehicles equipped with check control, unclip the pad wear sensor from the caliper aperture, and position it away from the caliper.

20 Remove the dust caps from the caliper guide pin , then slacken and remove the two guide pin bolts, and withdraw them from the caliper.

21 Slide the caliper off the brake disc, unclipping the outer pad from the outer edge of the caliper. Tie the caliper to the suspension strut, using a suitable piece of wire.

 Warning: Take care to avoid kinking or placing any strain on the flexible brake hose.

22 Remove both brake pads from the caliper mounting bracket.

Girling caliper - all Senator models 1990-on and 6-cylinder Carlton models 1990-on

23 Firmly apply the handbrake, then jack up the front of the vehicle and support on axle stands (see "*Jacking and Vehicle Support*"). Remove both front roadwheels.

24 The thickness of the brake pads (friction material and backing plate) can be observed via the aperture in the caliper. If any pad has worn beyond the specified minimum thickness (See Specifications), all the pads must be renewed as an axle set. However, a more thorough check can be made if the caliper is first removed, as follows.

25 On vehicles equipped with check control, unclip the pad wear sensor from the caliper aperture, and position it away from the caliper.

26 Slacken and withdraw the guide pins from the caliper - use an open ended spanner to counter-hold the pin as it is slackened.

27 Grasp the caliper and lift it away from the mounting bracket. Suspend the caliper body from an appropriate point on the suspension using wire, to avoid straining the brake hose, then remove the pads.

Inspection

28 First measure the thickness of each brake pad (friction material and backing plate). If either pad is worn at any point to the specified minimum thickness (see Specifications), all four pads must be renewed. The pads should also be renewed if any are fouled with oil or grease; there is no satisfactory way of degreasing friction material, once contaminated. If any of the brake pads are worn unevenly or fouled with oil or grease, trace and rectify the cause before reassembly. On vehicles equipped with check control, if the pad wear sensor has been in contact with the brake disc, that must also be renewed.

29 If the brake pads are still serviceable, carefully clean them using a clean, fine wire brush or similar, paying particular attention to the sides and back of the metal backing. Clean out the grooves in the friction material

(where applicable), and pick out any large embedded particles of dirt or debris. Carefully clean the pad locations in the caliper body and mounting bracket. Check that the guide pins are free to slide easily in the caliper mounting bushes. Brush the dust and dirt from the caliper and piston, but do not inhale it, as it is injurious to health. Inspect the dust seal around the piston for damage, and the piston for evidence of fluid leaks, corrosion or damage. If attention to any of these components is necessary, refer to the information given in the following sub-section.

30 If new brake pads are being fitted, the caliper piston must be pushed back into the cylinder to make room for the greater depth of friction material. Either use a G-clamp or similar tool, or use suitable pieces of wood as levers. Provided that the master cylinder reservoir has not been overfilled with hydraulic fluid, there should be no spillage, but keep a careful watch on the fluid level while retracting the piston. If the fluid level rises above the maximum level mark, the surplus should be siphoned off using a syringe to avoid overflow.

Refitting

GM caliper - Carlton 1.8 and 2.0 litre to 1989

31 Press the piston fully into the caliper in order to accommodate the new brake pads. Where applicable, the edges of the cut-away recess in the piston should be positioned as shown **(see illustration)**.

2.31 The edges of the piston recess (arrowed) should be horizontal to the caliper body

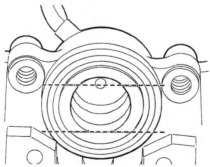

2.39 Ensure the recess on the caliper piston is horizontal to the caliper body

32 Insert the new brake pads and intermediate plates in the caliper, and check that they are free to move.

33 Locate the anti-rattle spring on the pads then insert the pins from the outside, with the springs located beneath the pins **(see illustration)**.

34 Fit the spring clips to the inner ends of the brake pad pins where applicable.

35 Where applicable, fit the new pad wear warning lamp sensor to the slot on the inner pad then feed the cable into the engine compartment and connect it to the wiring harness. Attach the cable to its clips.

36 Renew the brake pads on the remaining front wheel in a similar manner .

37 Depress the footbrake pedal several times in order to reset the brake pads to their normal position.

38 Refit the front wheels and lower the vehicle to the ground.

ATE caliper - Carlton 1.8 and 2.0 litre 1989-on

39 Prior to installing the inner pad, ensure that the recess on the caliper piston is positioned horizontally in relation to the caliper body **(see illustration)**. If necessary, rotate the piston until the recess is correctly positioned.

40 Once the piston is correctly positioned, clip the inner pad into position in the caliper piston, and install the outer pad in the caliper mounting bracket, ensuring that its friction material is facing the brake disc **(see illustration)**.

2.33 Inserting the front brake pad pins

2.40 Clip the inner pad into position in the caliper piston . . .

2.41 Slide the caliper into position over the brake disc and outer pad

2.44 Refitting the caliper spring

41 Slide the caliper into position over the brake disc and outer pad **(see illustration)**.

42 Thoroughly clean the threads of the guide pin bolts, then apply a few drops of a suitable locking compound to them. Refit the bolts in the caliper holes, then tighten them to the specified torque and refit the dust covers.

43 On vehicles equipped with check control, clip the pad wear sensor into position on the inner brake pad. If a new sensor is being installed, trace the wiring of the original sensor back to the connector, then disconnect it and remove the old sensor from the vehicle. Connect the wiring connector of the new sensor, ensuring that the wiring is correctly routed and retained by all necessary clips.

44 Refit the caliper spring, ensuring that its ends are firmly located in the holes in the caliper body **(see illustration)**.

45 Check that the caliper body slides smoothly on its guide pins, then depress the brake pedal until the pads are pressed into firm contact with the brake disc, and normal (non-assisted) pedal pressure is restored.

46 Repeat the above procedure on the remaining front brake caliper.

47 Refit the roadwheels, then lower the car to the ground and tighten the roadwheel bolts to the specified torque setting.

48 Check and top-up the hydraulic fluid level.

ATE caliper - Senator models to 1990 and 6-cylinder Carlton models to 1990

49 Prior to refitting the caliper, ensure that the recess on the caliper piston is positioned horizontally in relation to the caliper body. If necessary, rotate the piston until the recess is correctly positioned.

50 Apply a smear of high temperature grease to the caliper mounting bracket, at the points which contact the brake pad backing plates *Caution: Don't get any grease onto the pad friction material or brake disc surface.*

51 Install the brake pads in the caliper mounting bracket, ensuring that the friction material faces the brake disc.

52 Slide the caliper into position over the brake disc and brake pads, ensuring the outer pad backing plate spring hooks over the edge of the caliper. Ensure that both pad tension springs bear on the inner surface of the caliper and do not protrude through the caliper aperture.

53 Thoroughly clean the threads of the guide pin bolts, then apply a few drops of a suitable locking compound to them. Refit the bolts in the caliper holes, then tighten them to the specified torque and refit the dust covers.

54 On vehicles with check control, clip the pad wear sensor into position on the inner brake pad. If a new sensor is being installed, trace the wiring of the original sensor back to the connector, then disconnect it and remove the old sensor from the vehicle. Connect the wiring connector of the new sensor, ensuring that the wiring is correctly routed and held by all the necessary clips.

55 Check that the caliper body slides smoothly on its guide pins, then depress the brake pedal until the pads are pressed into firm contact with the brake disc, and normal (non-assisted) pedal pressure is restored.

2.60 Apply a smear of high temperature grease to the caliper mounting bracket, at the points which support the brake pad backing plates

2.61b ... then install the brake pads in the caliper mounting bracket

56 Repeat the above procedure on the remaining front brake caliper.

57 Refit the roadwheels, then lower the car to the ground and tighten the roadwheel bolts to the specified torque setting.

58 Check the hydraulic fluid level and if necessary top it up.

Girling caliper - all Senator models 1990-on and 6-cylinder Carlton models 1990-on

59 Prior to refitting the caliper, ensure that the recess on the caliper piston is positioned horizontally in relation to the caliper body. If necessary, rotate the piston until the recess is correctly positioned.

60 Apply a smear of high temperature grease to the caliper mounting bracket, at the points which support the brake pad backing plates **(see illustration)**. *Caution: Don't get any grease onto the pad friction material or brake disc surface.*

61 Apply a smear of high temperature grease to the rear surface of the brake pad backing plate, then fit the brake pads in the caliper mounting bracket. Ensure the friction material faces the brake disc **(see illustrations)**.

62 Lift the caliper into position over the brake disc and brake pads, ensuring that both pad tension springs bear on the inner surface of the caliper and do not protrude through the caliper aperture.

63 Thoroughly clean the threads of the guide pins, then apply a little thread-locking compound to them **(see illustration)**. Refit the

2.61a Apply a smear of high temperature grease to the rear surface of the brake pad backing plate . . .

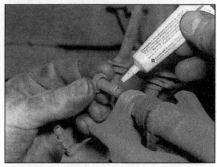

2.63 Apply a few drops of a suitable thread-locking compound to the guide pins

3.4 Removing the rear brake pad pins

3.6 Removing the inner rear brake pad

3.9 Checking the rear caliper piston recess angle with a card template
A Angle = 23°

pins in the caliper holes, then tighten them to the specified torque - counter-hold the pins with a open ended spanner as they are being tightened.

64 On vehicles equipped with check control, clip the pad wear sensor into position on the inner brake pad. If a new sensor is being installed, trace the wiring of the original sensor back to the connector, then disconnect it and remove the old sensor from the vehicle. Connect the wiring connector of the new sensor, ensuring that the wiring is correctly routed and retained by all the necessary clips.

65 Check that the caliper body slides smoothly on its guide pins, then depress the brake pedal repeatedly until the pads are pressed into firm contact with the brake disc, and normal (non-assisted) pedal pressure is restored.

66 Repeat the above procedure on the remaining front brake caliper.

67 Refit the roadwheels, then lower the car to the ground and tighten the roadwheel bolts to the specified torque setting.

68 Check the hydraulic fluid level and if necessary top it up.

---

3 Rear brake pads -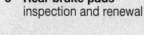
inspection and renewal

Note: Before starting work, refer to the note at the beginning of Section 2 concerning the dangers of hydraulic fluid, and asbestos dust.

1 Chock the front wheels then jack up the rear of the vehicle and support it on axle stands (see *"Jacking and Vehicle Support"*). Release the handbrake. Remove the rear wheels.

2 Inspect the brake pad linings for wear. Using a steel rule or vernier calipers, check that the thickness of the lining including the backing plate is as shown in the Specifications.

3 If any brake pad is worn below the minimum thickness, renew all the rear pads as a set together with new anti-rattle springs.

4 Note how the anti-rattle spring is located, then drive out the pins using a thin punch from the outside **(see illustration)**.

5 Remove the anti-rattle spring.

6 Push the brake pads apart slightly to give a small clearance then pull them from the caliper together with the intermediate plates **(see illustration)**. If they are tight, use pliers or grips to remove them.

7 Brush the dust and dirt from the caliper and intermediate plates, but take care not inhale it. Clean any rust from the edge of the brake disc.

8 Press both pistons fully into their cylinders using a length of wood or a hammer handle.

9 Check that the cut-away recesses on the pistons are positioned downwards at approximately 23° to the horizontal. A template made of card may be used to check the setting **(see illustration)**. If necessary, turn the pistons to their correct positions.

10 Apply a little brake grease to the top and bottom edges of the backplates on the new brake pads.

11 Insert the new brake pads and intermediate plates in the caliper and check that they are free to move.

12 Locate the anti-rattle spring on the pads, then insert the pins from the inside while depressing the spring. Tap the pins firmly into the caliper.

13 Renew the brake pads on the remaining rear wheel using the procedure given in paragraphs 4 to 12.

14 Depress the footbrake pedal several times in order to reset the brake pads to their normal position.

15 Refit the rear wheels and lower the vehicle to the ground.

4.2 Brake hose clamp in position on a typical flexible brake hose

---

4 Front brake caliper - removal, overhaul and refitting

Removal

Note: Before starting work, refer to the note at the beginning of Section 2 concerning the dangers of hydraulic fluid, and asbestos dust.

1 Apply the handbrake then jack up the front of the vehicle and support it on axle stands (see *"Jacking and Vehicle Support"*). Remove the wheel.

2 Fit a brake hose clamp to the flexible hose leading to the brake caliper **(see illustration)**. Alternatively remove the cap from the hydraulic fluid reservoir and refit it with a piece of polythene sheeting covering the opening to help minimise the loss of brake fluid when the caliper hose is disconnected.

3 Remove the brake pads as described in Section 3.

4 Clean the area around the union, then undo the brake hose union bolt, and disconnect the hose from the caliper **(see illustration)**. Plug the end of the hose and the caliper orifice, to prevent dirt entering the hydraulic system. Discard the sealing washers; they must be renewed whenever disturbed.

GM caliper - Carlton 1.8 and 2.0 litre to 1989

5 Lever the caps from the caliper mounting bolts with a screwdriver **(see illustration)**.

6 Using a hex bit, unscrew the mounting bolts

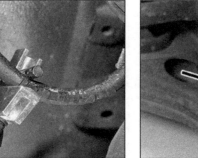

4.4 Brake hose union bolt (arrowed) - GM caliper shown

4.5 Removing the front brake caliper mounting bolt caps

and withdraw the caliper from the steering knuckle.

7 Prise the outer plastic caps from the sliding sleeves.

8 Press the sliding sleeves slightly inwards, and remove the inner caps from their grooves.

9 Remove the sliding sleeves but identify them for location.

10 Mount the caliper in a vice and unbolt the frame.

ATE caliper (all versions)

11 Refer to Section 2 and remove the brake pads from the relevant caliper. Lift the caliper from the vehicle and clean it thoroughly.

Girling caliper

12 Refer to Section 2 and remove the brake pads from the relevant caliper, then unbolt the caliper upper guide pin and lift the caliper away from the carrier bracket.

Overhaul - all calipers

13 With the caliper on the bench, wipe away all traces of dust and dirt using copious quantities of brake cleaning fluid.

 Warning: Avoid inhaling the dust, as it may contain asbestos which is injurious to health.

14 On Girling calipers, prise open the three tangs and remove the protective plate from the face of the cylinder **(see illustration)**.

15 Withdraw the piston from the caliper body, and remove the dust seal. The piston can be withdrawn by hand, or can if necessary be pushed out by applying compressed air to the

brake pipe union bolt hole. Only low pressure should be required, such as is generated by a foot pump - place a block of hardwood between the end of the piston and the caliper body to prevent damage to the piston as it exits from the cylinder.

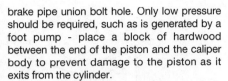 **Warning: Use eye protection during this procedure, as droplets of brake fluid may be ejected if the piston leaves the cylinder under pressure.**

16 Using a blunt plastic instrument (such as the end of a cable-tie), extract the piston hydraulic seal, taking great care not to damage the caliper bore **(see illustration)**

17 Press the guide sleeves out of the caliper body using a suitable socket.

18 Thoroughly clean all components, using only methylated spirit, isopropyl alcohol or clean hydraulic fluid as a cleaning medium. Never use mineral-based solvents such as petrol or paraffin, as they will attack the hydraulic system's rubber components. Dry the components immediately, using compressed air or a clean, lint-free cloth. Use compressed air to blow clear the fluid passages. Wear eye protection when using compressed air!

19 Check all components, and renew any that are worn or damaged. Pay particular attention to the cylinder bore and piston; these must be renewed if they are scratched, worn or corroded in any way.

 Warning: Do not use abrasives or tools to remove any material from the piston or cylinder in an attempt to effect a repair or remove corrosion - the piston and caliper body must be renewed as a complete assembly.

20 Where applicable, check the condition of the guide bolts/pins and their sleeves; both guide bolts/pins should be undamaged and (when cleaned) a reasonably-tight sliding fit in the sleeves. If there is any doubt about the condition of any component, renew it.

21 If the assembly is fit for further use, obtain new piston and dust seals, and a tube of brake cylinder paste from a Vauxhall dealer.

22 Smear a little brake cylinder paste onto

the surfaces of the caliper bore, piston and piston seal.

23 Install the piston seal in the caliper bore, using only your fingers to manipulate it into its groove - do not use tools that may damage the new seal. Fit the new dust seal over the piston, pushing it to the end that will enter the cylinder first. Offer up the dust seal and piston to the cylinder and ease the lip of the dust seal into the groove in the cylinder.

24 Carefully fit the piston to the caliper bore, using a twisting motion, ensuring that it enters the bore squarely.

25 Press the piston fully into the bore, until the outer edge of the dust seal catches in the groove at the outer edge of the piston. Where applicable, rotate the piston so that the recess in the brake pad contact surface is positioned horizontally in relation to the caliper body **(refer to illustration 2.39)**.

26 On Girling calipers, fit the protective plate in position on the cylinder face and press the three tangs into the corresponding recesses.

27 Where applicable, lubricate the caliper guide sleeves with a little soapy water, then press them into position in the caliper body.

Refitting

GM caliper

28 Refit the caliper frame and tighten the bolts to the specified torque. Locate the caliper on the steering knuckle, insert the mounting bolts and tighten them to the specified torque.

29 Fit the plastic caps over the mounting bolts.

30 Check that the caliper moves freely on the sliding sleeves.

31 Refit the brake pads (see Section 2).

ATE caliper - all versions

32 With reference to Section 2 , fit the remaining brake pad into position, then slide the caliper over the brake disc and outer pad.

33 Thoroughly clean the threads of the guide bolts, and apply a few drops of suitable thread-locking compound to them. Refit the bolts in the caliper holes, then tighten them to the specified torque and refit the dust covers.

34 On vehicles with check control, clip the pad wear sensor into position on the inner brake pad.

35 Refit the caliper spring, ensuring that its ends are firmly located in the holes in the caliper body.

Girling caliper

36 With reference to Section 2, fit the brake pads into position on the caliper carrier, then slide the caliper over the brake disc and pads.

37 Thoroughly clean the threads of the guide bolts, and apply a few drops of suitable thread-locking compound to them. Refit the bolts in the caliper holes, then tighten them to the specified torque and refit the dust covers.

38 On vehicles with check control, clip the pad wear sensor into position on the inner brake pad.

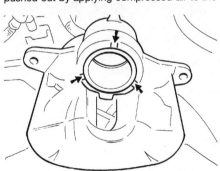

4.14 Prise open the three tangs (arrowed) and remove the protective plate from the face of the cylinder

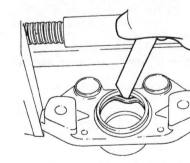

4.16 Extracting the piston hydraulic seal from the caliper bore

39 Refit the caliper spring, ensuring that its ends are firmly located in the holes in the caliper body.

All calipers

40 Position a new sealing washer on each side of the hose union, and refit the brake hose union bolt. Ensure that the brake hose union is correctly positioned against the lug on the caliper, and tighten the union bolt to the specified torque setting.

41 Remove the brake hose clamp, where fitted, and bleed the hydraulic system as described in Section 12. Note that, providing the precautions described were taken to minimise brake fluid loss, it should only be necessary to bleed the relevant caliper.

42 Refit the roadwheel, then lower the car to the ground and tighten the roadwheel bolts to the specified torque.

43 Thoroughly check the operation of the braking system before bringing the vehicle back into service on the public highway.

5 Rear brake caliper - removal, overhaul and refitting

Removal

1 Chock the front wheels then jack up the rear of the vehicle and support it on axle stands (see "*Jacking and Vehicle Support*"). Remove the wheel.

2 Fit a brake hose clamp to the flexible hose leading to the brake caliper (**refer to illustration 4.02**). Alternatively remove the cap from the hydraulic fluid reservoir and refit it with a piece of polythene sheeting covering the opening to help prevent loss of brake fluid when the caliper hose is disconnected.

3 Remove the brake pads (see Section 3).

4 Unscrew the union nut securing the rigid brake line to the caliper, and remove the brake line.

5 Unscrew the hexagon mounting bolts and withdraw the caliper from the semi-trailing arm (**see illustration**).

Overhaul

6 Clean the outer surfaces of the caliper.

7 Note that no attempt must be made to separate the two halves of the caliper.

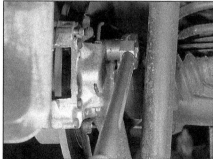

5.5 Removing the rear brake caliper mounting bolts

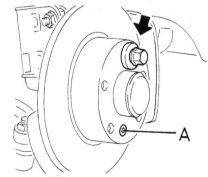

5.8 Removal of rear brake caliper dust cover ring

8 Prise the rings and dust covers from each side of the caliper and pull the covers from the piston grooves (**see illustration**).

9 Position a thin piece of wood between the pistons, then using air pressure from an air line or foot pump through the fluid inlet, carefully force the pistons from the cylinders. Remove the pistons.

10 Prise the piston seals from the cylinders, taking care not to scratch the bore surfaces.

11 Clean the pistons and cylinders with methylated spirit and allow to dry. Examine the surfaces of the pistons and cylinder bores for wear, damage and corrosion. If evident, renew the caliper complete, however if the surfaces are good obtain a repair kit which includes piston seals and dust covers. Also obtain a tube of brake cylinder paste.

12 Apply a little brake cylinder paste to the pistons, cylinder bores and piston seals.

13 Locate the piston seals in the cylinder grooves, then insert the pistons carefully until they enter the seals. It may be necessary to rotate the pistons to prevent them jamming in the seals.

14 Ease the dust covers into the piston grooves then locate them on the caliper housing. Press the retaining rings over the dust covers.

15 Press the pistons into their cylinders, then turn them so that the cut-away recesses are positioned downwards at an angle of approximately 23°. Make up a card template to check the setting (**refer to illustration 3.9**).

Refitting

16 To refit the caliper locate it on the semi-trailing arm, insert the mounting bolts and tighten them to the specified torque.

17 Locate the rigid brake line on the caliper and tighten the union nut to the specified torque.

18 Refit the brake pads (see Section 3).

19 Remove the brake hose clamp or polythene sheeting and bleed the hydraulic system as described in Section 12. Provided that there has been no loss of brake fluid, it should only be necessary to bleed the caliper which was removed, however if brake fluid has been lost bleed the complete system.

20 Refit the wheel and lower the vehicle to the ground.

6 Brake disc - inspection, removal and refitting

Inspection

1 Jack up the front or rear of the vehicle as applicable and support it on axle stands (see "*Jacking and Vehicle Support*"). Release the handbrake and chock the front wheels if checking a rear disc. Remove the appropriate wheel.

2 Check that the brake disc securing screw is tight, then refit and tighten a wheel bolt opposite the screw using a spacer washer approximately 10.0 mm (0.4 in) thick (**see illustration**).

3 Rotate the brake disc and examine it for deep scoring or grooving. Light scoring is normal, but if excessive, the disc should be removed and either renewed or machined within limits by a suitable engineering works. It is worth mentioning that some garages may be able to regrind the discs in position using a specially adapted electric grinder.

4 Using a dial gauge, or metal block and feeler blades, check that the disc run-out does not exceed the amount given in Specifications, measured 10.0 mm (0.4 in) from the outer edge of the disc. Check the run-out at several positions around the disc.

5 If the run-out is excessive, remove the disc and check that the disc-to-hub surfaces are perfectly clean. Refit the disc and check the run-out again.

Removal

6 To remove the brake disc, first remove the brake pads as described in Section 2 or 3 (as applicable).

7 To remove a front disc, remove the securing screw then withdraw the disc from the hub, tilting it as necessary to clear the brake caliper. On some models it may be necessary to unbolt the frame from the caliper.

8 To remove a rear disc, unbolt the brake caliper from the semi-trailing arm, and support it away from the disc taking care not

6.2 Tighten the disc securing screw, then refit a wheel bolt, together with a 10 mm washer (arrowed), to seat the disc

A Disc securing screw

6.8a Removing the rear brake disc securing screw

6.8b Removing the rear brake disc

screwdriver through the unthreaded hole in the disc and hub then turn the adjuster upwards until the disc/drum is locked. Back off the adjuster until the disc/drum just turns freely **(see illustration)**.
23 Refit the rear wheels.
24 Pull up the handbrake lever to the sixth notch, then working under the vehicle tighten the cable adjustment nut until both rear wheels are locked. The adjustment nut is of the self-locking type. Check the adjustment by releasing and applying the handbrake lever two or three times.
25 Lower the vehicle to the ground.

to damage the rigid brake line. Remove the securing screw and withdraw the disc from the hub **(see illustrations)**.

Refitting

9 Refitting is a reversal of removal, but make sure that the mating faces of the disc and hub are perfectly clean, and before inserting the securing screw apply a little locking fluid to its threads. Refit the brake pads with reference to Section 2 or 3 (as applicable).

7 Handbrake shoes - inspection, removal and refitting

Inspection

1 Remove the rear brake discs as described in Section 6.
2 Brush the dust and dirt from the shoes, backplate and from inside the disc drum.
3 Check the thickness of the linings on the shoes and if less than shown in the Specifications, renew the shoes on both sides as a set.
4 Also check the surface inside the drums. These should not normally be worn unless the handbrake has been binding.

Removal

5 Unhook the return spring from the lever on the backplate then unhook the handbrake cable.
6 Using a screwdriver through a hole in the hub flange, twist and remove the anti-rattle springs **(see illustration)**.
7 Mark the brake shoes for location. Also note the fitted positions of the return springs.
8 Prise the brake shoes from the adjuster and lever, and disconnect the return springs **(see illustrations)**.
9 Remove the adjuster and lever.
10 Clean the backplate, springs, adjuster and lever.
11 Apply a little brake grease to the threads of the adjuster then screw it together to its minimum length.

Refitting

12 Fit one brake shoe and secure to the backplate with the anti-rattle spring.
13 Fit the lever in position.

14 Fit the remaining brake shoe and secure with the anti-rattle spring.
15 Hook the lower return spring onto the brake shoes.
16 Fit the adjuster between the upper ends of the shoes, then hook the upper return spring to the shoes.
17 Refit the handbrake cable and return spring to the rear of the backplate.
18 Refit the rear brake disc (see Section 6) but do not refit the wheel at this stage.
19 Repeat the above procedure at the opposite wheel.
20 In order to hold the discs centrally while adjusting the shoes, fit and tighten a wheel bolt opposite the securing screws using a spacer washer roughly 10.0 mm (0.4 in) thick.
21 At the front end of the handbrake cable, loosen the cable adjustment nut to the end of the threaded handbrake lever rod.
22 Working on each rear disc in turn, insert a

7.6 Handbrake shoe anti-rattle spring (arrowed)

7.8b Handbrake shoe lower lever assembly

8 Handbrake cable - removal and refitting

Removal

1 Chock the front wheel, then jack up the rear of the vehicle and support it on axle stands (see "*Jacking and Vehicle Support*"). Remove the rear wheels and release the handbrake.
2 At the front of the handbrake cable, unscrew the adjustment nut from the threaded handbrake lever rod and slide off the compensator bar **(see illustration)**.
3 Working on each side in turn, unhook the return spring from the lever on the backplate then unhook the cable.
4 Pull the rear of the outer cable from the guide on the semi-trailing arm on both sides.
5 Bend back the intermediate clips and release the cables.

7.8a Handbrake shoe adjuster (A) and spring (B)

7.22 Method of adjusting handbrake shoes (rear brake disc removed for clarity)

8.2 Front end of handbrake inner cables, and compensator bar

6 Pull the front ends of the outer cables from the guides **(see illustration)**, and unhook the inner cables. Withdraw the cable assembly from under the vehicle.

Refitting

7 Refitting is a reversal of removal but note that the shorter, black sheathed cable is fitted on the right-hand side. Apply some molybdenum disulphide paste to the plastic guides at the front of the inner cables. Finally adjust the handbrake shoes and the cable as described in Section 7.

---

9 Handbrake lever - removal and refitting

Removal

1 Chock the front wheels then jack up the rear of the vehicle and support it on axle stands (see "*Jacking and Vehicle Support*").
2 On vehicles fitted with a catalytic converter, remove the screws and lower the metal heat shield away from the floorpan.
3 At the front of the handbrake cable unscrew the adjustment nut from the threaded handbrake lever rod, and slide off the compensator bar.
4 Prise the rubber gaiter from the underbody and remove it from the handbrake lever rod.
5 Refer to Chapter 11 and carry out the following:

a) On manual transmission models unclip the gear lever gaiter from the centre

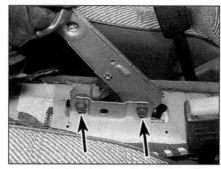

9.6a Handbrake lever mounting bolts (arrowed)

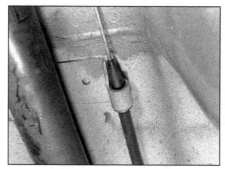

8.6 Front end of handbrake outer cable in the guide

console inside the vehicle, and pull upwards over the gear lever so that it is turned inside out. Untie the cord and remove the gaiter. Remove the screws and withdraw the gear lever surround.
b) *On automatic transmission models unclip the selector lever position panel and flexible slot cover. Remove the screw, lift the selector lever cover and disconnect the illumination lamp and switch cabling.*
c) *Remove the centre console.*

6 Unscrew the handbrake lever mountings bolts, then disconnect the wiring from the warning switch **(see illustrations)**.
7 Remove the handbrake lever from the vehicle.

Refitting

8 Refitting is a reversal of removal, but on completion adjust the handbrake cable as described in Section 7.

---

10 Master cylinder - removal, overhaul and refitting

Caution: Do not dismantle the master cylinder on models equipped with ABS.

Removal

1 Depress the footbrake pedal several times to dissipate the vacuum in the servo unit.
2 Disconnect the wiring for the brake fluid level warning lamp from the reservoir filler cap.
3 If available use a pipette or syphon to

9.6b Warning switch wiring location (arrowed)

remove the brake fluid from the reservoir. This will reduce loss of fluid later.
4 Locate a container beneath the master cylinder to catch spilled fluid.
5 Identify the brake lines for position, then unscrew the union nuts and pull the lines from the master cylinder.
6 Unbolt the front bracket.
7 Unscrew the mounting nuts and withdraw the master cylinder from the studs on the vacuum servo unit. Take care not to drop any brake fluid on the body paintwork. If accidentally spilt, wash off immediately with copious amounts of cold water.

Overhaul

8 Clean the exterior surfaces of the unit then prise out the fluid reservoir and rubber seals.
9 Depress the primary piston slightly with a screwdriver, then extract the circlip from the mouth of the master cylinder.
10 Withdraw the primary piston assembly.
11 Depress the secondary piston and unscrew the stop pin from the cylinder body.
12 Withdraw the secondary piston assembly by tapping the unit on the bench.
13 Clean all the components in methylated spirit and examine them for wear and damage. In particular check the surfaces of the pistons and cylinder bore for scoring and corrosion. If the bore is worn renew the complete master cylinder, otherwise obtain a repair kit which will include pistons and seals. If the pistons are in good condition it may be possible to obtain just the rubber seals.
14 Check that the inlet and outlet ports are clear. If applicable, fit the new seals to the pistons using the fingers only to manipulate them into position. The open ends of the seals must face the appropriate ends of the pistons.
15 Dip the secondary piston assembly in clean brake fluid and insert in the cylinder. Depress the secondary piston and tighten the stop pin in the body.
16 Dip the primary piston assembly in clean brake fluid and insert in the cylinder. Depress the piston and refit the circlip.
17 Press in the rubber seals and refit the fluid reservoir.
18 If necessary renew the O-ring seal on the master cylinder flange.

Refitting

19 Refitting is a reversal of removal but tighten the mounting nuts and union nuts to the specified torque, and finally bleed the hydraulic system as described in Section 12.

---

11 Rear brake proportioning valve - removal and refitting

Removal

1 Chock the front wheels. Jack up the rear of the vehicle and support it on axle stands (see "*Jacking and Vehicle Support*").

2 Remove the cap from the brake fluid reservoir and refit it with a piece of polythene sheeting covering the opening to help prevent loss of brake fluid when the valve is removed.
3 Unscrew the union nuts and disconnect the two brake lines from the valve. Plug the ends of the brake lines.
4 Pull out the locking plate and remove the valve from the bracket.

Refitting

5 Refitting is a reversal of removal, but bleed the rear hydraulic system as described in Section 12.

12 Hydraulic system - bleeding

⚠ *Warning: Hydraulic fluid is poisonous; thoroughly wash off spills from bare skin without delay. Seek immediate medical advice if any fluid is swallowed or gets into the eyes. Certain types of hydraulic fluid are inflammable and may ignite when brought into contact with hot components; when servicing any hydraulic system, it is safest to assume that the fluid is inflammable and to take precautions against the risk of fire as though it were petrol that was being handled. Hydraulic fluid is an effective paint stripper and will also attack many plastics. If spillage occurs onto painted bodywork or fittings, it should be washed off immediately, using copious quantities of fresh water. It is also hygroscopic i.e. it can absorb moisture from the air, which then renders it useless. Old fluid may have suffered contamination and should never be re-used. When topping-up or renewing the fluid, always use the recommended grade, and ensure that it comes from a new sealed container.*

General

1 The correct operation of any hydraulic braking system relies on the fact that the fluid used in it is incompressible, otherwise the effort exerted at the brake pedal and master cylinder will not be fully transmitted to the brake calipers or wheel cylinders. The presence of contaminants in the system will allow the fluid to compress - this results in a 'spongy' feel to the brakes and unpredictable performance, in the form of brake fade or at worst brake failure. In addition, brake fluid deteriorates with age through oxidation and water absorption. This lowers its boiling point and may cause vaporisation under hard braking, again affecting brake performance. For this reason, old or contaminated fluid must be renewed - this is achieved by bleeding the system.
2 When refilling the system, use only clean,

new hydraulic fluid of the recommended type and grade; *never* re-use fluid that has already been bled from the system. Ensure that sufficient fluid is available before starting work.
3 If there is any possibility of there being incorrect fluid in the system already , the brake components and circuits must be flushed completely with new fluid of the correct type and grade and new seals should be fitted throughout the system.
4 If hydraulic fluid has been lost from the system, or air has entered because of a leak, ensure that the fault is corrected before proceeding further.
5 Park the vehicle on level ground, switch off the engine and select first or reverse gear (manual transmission) or 'Park' (automatic transmission), then chock the wheels and release the handbrake.
6 Check that all pipes and hoses are secure, unions tight and bleed screws closed. Remove the dust caps and clean off all dirt from around the bleed screws.
7 Unscrew the master cylinder reservoir cap, and top the master cylinder reservoir up to the 'MAX' level line; refit the cap loosely, and remember to maintain the fluid level at least above the 'MIN' level line throughout the procedure, otherwise there is a risk of further air entering the system, as the level drops.
8 There are a number of one-man, do-it-yourself brake bleeding kits currently available from motor accessory shops. It is recommended that one of these kits is used whenever possible, as they greatly simplify the bleeding operation, and also reduce the risk of expelled air and fluid being drawn back into the system. If such a kit is not available, the basic (two-man) method must be used, which is described in detail below.
9 If a kit is to be used, prepare the vehicle as described previously, and follow the kit manufacturer's instructions, as the procedure may vary slightly according to the type being used. Generally, they are as outlined below in the relevant sub-section.
10 Whichever method is used, the same sequence must be followed to ensure that the removal of all air from the system.

⚠ *Warning: On Saloon models equipped with an anti-lock braking system (ABS), the front wheel brake circuits must always be bled before the rear circuit.*

Note: *On Estate models with an anti-lock braking system (ABS), only **manual** bleeding of the braking system is possible.*

Bleeding sequence

11 It is possible to partially bleed the system, i.e. just one brake line and caliper at a time. Providing fluid loss is kept to a minimum and air is not drawn into the system, it will not be necessary to bleed the other brake lines as well.
12 The entire system can be bled completely,

12.14 Brake bleeding kit connected to the caliper bleed nipple (arrowed)

if necessary; the order in which the brakes lines are dealt with is not important, as each caliper has its own connection to the master cylinder. Refer to Chapter 1 for a description of the brake fluid renewal procedure.

Bleeding - basic (two-man) method

13 Obtain a clean glass jar, a suitable length of plastic or rubber tubing which is a tight fit over the bleed screw, and a ring spanner to fit the screw. Alternatively, a proprietary brake bleeding kit can be obtained. **Note:** *The help of an assistant will also be required.*
14 Remove the dust cap from the first caliper's bleed screw. Fit the spanner over the bleed screw and push the tube onto the bleed screw nipple **(see illustration)**. Place the other end of the tube in the jar and pour in sufficient fluid to cover the end of the tube.
15 Throughout the procedure, keep an eye on the reservoir fluid level and ensure that it is maintained above the 'MIN' level line as the brakes are bled; top it up if necessary.
16 Have the assistant fully depress the brake pedal several times to build up pressure - then on the final downstroke, keep it depressed.
17 While pedal pressure is maintained, slacken the bleed screw (approximately one turn) and allow the brake fluid to flow into the jar . Pedal pressure should be maintained throughout; follow the pedal down to the end of its travel if necessary, but do not release it. When the flow stops, tighten the bleed screw again, then have your assistant release the pedal slowly. Re-check the reservoir fluid level and top it up if necessary.
18 If air is present in the brake lines, it will appear as bubbles in the expelled fluid. Repeat the steps given in the two previous paragraphs until the fluid emerging from the bleed screw is free from air bubbles. If the master cylinder has been drained and refilled and air is being bled from the first brake line in the sequence, allow approximately five seconds between cycles for the master cylinder passages to refill.
19 When no more air bubbles appear, tighten the bleed screw securely, remove the tube and spanner then refit the dust cap. *Caution: Do not overtighten the bleed screw.*
20 Repeat the procedure on the remaining brake lines to be bled, until all air is removed

from the system and the brake pedal feels firm again. **Note:** *On models fitted with ABS, at least fifteen pedal depressions are required to bleed the rear brake circuit.*

Bleeding - using a one-way valve kit

21 As their name implies, these kits consist of a length of tubing with a one-way valve fitted, to prevent expelled air and fluid being drawn back into the system; some kits include a translucent container, which can be positioned so that the air bubbles can easily be seen flowing from the end of the tube.

22 The kit is connected to the bleed screw, which is then opened. The user returns to the driver's seat, depresses the brake pedal with a smooth, steady stroke and slowly releases it; this process is repeated until the expelled fluid is free of air bubbles .

23 Note that the use of these kits can simplify the bleed operation so much, that it is easy to forget the reservoir fluid level. Ensure that it is maintained at least above the 'MIN' level line at all times, or air may be drawn into the system.

Bleeding - using a pressure-bleeding kit

24 These kits are usually powered by the reservoir of pressurised air contained in the spare tyre. However, note that it will probably be necessary to reduce the tyre pressure to a lower level than normal; refer to the instructions supplied with the kit.

25 The method involves connecting a pressurised, fluid-filled container to the master cylinder reservoir. Bleeding can then be carried out simply by opening each bleed screw in turn, and allowing the fluid to flow out under moderate pressure until no more air bubbles can be seen in the expelled fluid.

26 This method has the advantage that the large reservoir of fluid provides an additional safeguard against air being drawn into the system during bleeding.

27 Pressure-bleeding is particularly effective when bleeding 'difficult' systems, or when bleeding the complete system at the time of routine fluid renewal.

All methods

28 When bleeding is complete, and firm pedal feel is restored, wash off any spilt fluid, tighten the bleed screws securely, and refit their dust caps (where applicable).

29 Check the hydraulic fluid level in the master cylinder reservoir; top it up if necessary.

30 Dispose of any hydraulic fluid that has been bled from the system; it cannot be re-used.

31 Check the feel of the brake pedal. If it feels at all spongy, it is probable that air is still present in the system; further bleeding will therefore be required. If the bleeding procedure has been repeated several times and brake feel has still not been restored, the problem may be

caused by worn master cylinder seals - see Section 10 for a description of the master cylinder overhaul procedure.

13 Hydraulic brake lines and hoses - removal and refitting

1 Remove the cap from the brake fluid reservoir and refit it with a piece of polythene sheeting covering the opening to help prevent subsequent loss of brake fluid.

2 Jack up the vehicle and support it on axle stands (see *"Jacking and Vehicle Support"*).

Front flexible hose

3 Remove the front wheel.

4 Turn the steering on full lock. Unscrew the bolt securing the hose to the caliper and recover the copper washers.

5 Pull the locking plates from the mountings. On models with ABS disconnect the hose from the clips.

6 Unscrew the rigid brake line union, and remove the hose.

7 Refitting is a reversal of removal, but make sure that the hose is not twisted. Bleed the hydraulic system as described in Section 12 .

Rear flexible hose

8 Pull the locking plates from the mountings.

9 Unscrew the rigid brake line unions, and remove the hose.

10 Refitting is a reversal of removal, but make sure that the hose is not twisted. Bleed the hydraulic system as described in Section 12 .

Brake lines

11 Some commonly-used brake lines can be obtained from GM parts stores already formed complete with unions, however other brake lines must be prepared out of 4.75 mm (0.19 in) diameter brake pipe. Kits for making the brake lines can be obtained from motor accessory shops.

12 To remove a brake line, unscrew the unions at each end and release it from the clips.

13 Refitting is a reversal of removal. Bleed the hydraulic system, referring to Section 12.

14 Vacuum servo hose and non-return valve - renewal

1 When new, the vacuum hose is shrunk onto the non-return valve using a heat process, therefore when the valve is first renewed it is necessary to fit a conventional vacuum hose, using clips to secure it. Thereafter the hose and valve may be renewed separately.

2 Unscrew the hose union nut at the inlet manifold.

3 Pull or prise the elbow connector out of the servo.

4 Release the hose from the plastic straps.

5 Cut the hose off the non-return valve, the elbow and the inlet manifold union.

6 Cut the new hoses to length (it is sold in 5.0 metre lengths) and secure to the non-return valve, elbow and union using clips. Make sure that the arrows on the valve point towards the inlet manifold end.

7 Press the elbow into the servo rubber grommet and tighten the union nut on the inlet manifold. Fit new plastic straps.

15 Vacuum servo unit - testing, removal and refitting

Testing

1 To establish whether or not the servo is operating, proceed as follows.

2 With the engine stopped, apply the brake pedal several times in order to dissipate the vacuum from the servo unit.

3 Hold the brake pedal depressed, then start the engine. The pedal should move a small distance towards the floor with the additional assistance of the servo unit. If not, check the vacuum hose and non-return valve. If these prove to be satisfactory, the servo unit itself is faulty and should be renewed.

Removal

4 Depress the footbrake pedal several times to dissipate the vacuum in the servo unit.

5 Disconnect the wiring for the brake fluid level warning lamp from the reservoir filler cap.

6 Unbolt the master cylinder front bracket.

7 Unscrew the master cylinder mounting nuts and pull the unit from the studs on the vacuum servo unit sufficiently to allow room for removal of the servo unit. Leave the brake lines connected to the master cylinder.

8 Pull or prise out the vacuum hose elbow connector. Move the bulkhead wiring harness to one side.

9 Working inside the vehicle unhook the return spring from the brake pedal.

10 Extract the spring clip and pull out the clevis pin securing the servo pushrod to the brake pedal **(see illustration)**.

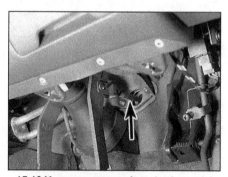

15.10 Vacuum servo unit-to-brake pedal pushrod (arrowed)

11 Unscrew the mounting nuts, then tilt the servo unit and remove it from the bulkhead into the engine compartment. Recover the gasket.

12 Loosen the locknut and unscrew the clevis fork from the pushrod. Unscrew the locknut.

13 Unscrew the nuts and remove the support bracket and gasket from the servo unit.

Refitting

14 Commence refitting by screwing the locknut and clevis fork onto the pushrod. With the pushrod in its rest position adjust the fork so that the distance between the servo mounting face and the clevis pin centre line is 211.0 + 1.0 mm (8.31 + 0.04 in). Tighten the locknut.

15 Locate the support bracket on the servo unit together with a new gasket. Fit and tighten the nuts.

16 Refit the servo unit to the bulkhead using a new gasket. Fit and tighten the mounting nuts.

17 Connect the pushrod to the brake pedal with the clevis pin and spring clip.

18 Reconnect the brake pedal return springs.

19 Press the vacuum hose elbow connector in the servo rubber grommet.

20 If necessary, renew the O-ring seal on the master cylinder flange then locate the unit on the servo studs. Fit and tighten the mounting nuts.

21 Refit and tighten the bolts for the master cylinder front bracket to the specified torque.

22 Reconnect the wiring to the brake fluid reservoir filler cap.

16 Brake pedal - removal and refitting

Removal

1 Working inside the vehicle disconnect the wiring from the brake stop-lamp switch, then unscrew the switch from the pedal bracket noting its fitted position (see illustration).

2 Unhook both the brake and clutch pedal return springs.

3 Extract the spring clip and pull out the clevis pin securing the servo pushrod to the brake pedal.

16.1 Brake stop-lamp switch

4 Disconnect the cable from the clutch pedal with reference to Chapter 6.

5 Unscrew the nut from the end of the pedal shaft, and remove the washer.

6 Unscrew the nuts holding the pedal bracket to the bulkhead and turn the bracket around the steering column to allow removal of the pedal shaft. Note that, on later models, it may be necessary to remove the steering column to allow the pedal bracket to be slid off its retaining studs. The column can be removed as described in Chapter 10, noting that it is not necessary to remove the steering wheel or the lock cylinder; the column can be removed with these items still in position.

7 Remove the pedal location clips and withdraw the shaft until the brake pedal can be removed. Recover the thrustwashers.

Refitting

8 Refitting is a reversal of removal, but lubricate the shaft with grease. Where applicable, adjust the clutch cable and check the clutch pedal adjustment as described in Chapter 6.

17 Anti-lock braking system (ABS) - information and component removal/refitting

General information

1 If the ABS develops a fault, it is recommended that the complete system is tested by a GM dealer, who will have the special equipment necessary to make a quick and accurate diagnosis of the problem. Because of the electronic nature of the system, it is not practical for the DIY mechanic to carry out the test procedure.

2 To prevent possible damage to the integrated circuits, always disconnect the multi-plug from the ABS electronic control unit before carrying out electrical welding work. It is recommended that the control unit is removed if the vehicle is being subjected to high temperatures as may be encountered, for instance, during certain paint drying processes. *Caution: Do not disconnect the control unit multi-plug with the ignition switched on. Do not use a battery booster to start the engine.*

ABS hydraulic modulator

Removal

3 Disconnect the battery negative lead.

4 Remove the cap from the brake fluid reservoir and refit it with a piece of polythene sheeting covering the opening to help prevent subsequent loss of brake fluid.

5 Unscrew the bolt from the power steering reservoir clamp and tie the reservoir to one side.

6 Remove the screw and withdraw the cover from the hydraulic modulator.

7 Remove the screws and lift away the wiring harness securing clamp.

8 Pull off the multi-plug, if necessary using a screwdriver to lever it from the terminals.

9 Identify all the brake lines on the modulator for location, then unscrew the union nuts and pull the brake lines just clear of the modulator. If possible, plug the ends of the brake lines, or at least cover them to prevent the ingress of dust and dirt. Also cover the modulator ports.

10 Unscrew the modulator mounting nuts and remove the cover.

11 Slightly tilt the modulator and pull it forward from the bracket, then unscrew the nut and disconnect the earth cable.

12 Remove the modulator from the engine compartment taking care not to spill brake fluid on the vehicle bodywork.

13 If a new modulator is being fitted, unscrew the two relays and transfer them to the new unit. No attempt must be made to dismantle the modulator.

14 Check that the modulator mounting bracket bolts are tight, and that the rubber mountings on the modulator are in good condition.

Refitting

15 Refitting is a reversal of removal but tighten all nuts and bolts to the specified torque, and finally bleed the hydraulic system as described in Section 12. Check that the ABS warning light goes out at the first application of the brake pedal after starting the engine. On completion take the vehicle to a GM dealer and have the complete system tested with the ABS test equipment.

ABS electronic control unit (models to 1989)

Removal

16 With the ignition switched off, disconnect the battery negative lead.

17 Inside the car, remove the trim panel from the left-hand side of the passenger footwell.

18 Pull the bonnet release lever then unclip the electronic control unit from its mounting.

19 Disconnect the wiring multi-plug and withdraw the unit.

Refitting

20 Refitting is a reversal of renewal. Check that the ABS warning light goes out at the first application of the brake pedal after starting the engine. On completion take the vehicle to a GM dealer and have the complete system tested with the ABS test equipment.

ABS electronic control unit (1989-on models)

Removal

21 From 1989 model year onwards, the ABS electronic control unit is situated underneath the front passenger seat. To remove the unit, first disconnect the battery negative terminal.

22 Push the passenger seat fully forwards, so that access to the unit can be gained from the rear of the seat.

23 Open up the plastic cover, then slide the control unit out of the rear of the plastic

housing. Disconnect the wiring connector, and remove the unit from the vehicle.

Refitting

24 Refitting is a reversal of removal.

ABS front wheel speed sensors

Removal

25 Disconnect the battery negative lead.
26 Jack up the front of the vehicle as applicable and support it on axle stands (see "*Jacking and Vehicle Support*").
27 Remove the front wheels.
28 Inside the engine compartment unclip the sensor wiring harness plug from the bracket, then separate the plug halves.
29 Under the wheel arch, release the sensor wiring from the hose clips.
30 Pull the wiring grommets from the hose brackets.
31 Using an Allen key, unscrew the bolt securing the sensor to the steering knuckle, then lever out the sensor with a screwdriver.
32 Prise the wiring grommet from the inner panel and remove the wheel speed sensor.

Refitting

33 Refitting is a reversal of removal but smear a little anti-friction grease on the sensor casing before inserting it. Have the complete ABS function checked by a GM dealer.

ABS rear wheel speed sensors

Removal

34 Disconnect the battery negative cable and position it away from the terminal.
35 Chock the front wheels, then jack up the rear of the vehicle as applicable and support it securely on axle stands (see "*Jacking and Vehicle Support*").
36 Remove the rear roadwheels.
37 Working beneath the vehicle unclip the sensor wiring harness plug from the bracket on the underbody, then carefully separate the plug halves using a screwdriver.
38 Using an Allen key, unscrew the bolt securing the sensor to the bracket on the differential, then pull out the sensor together with any shims located under the flange.

Refitting

39 Refitting is a reversal of removal but smear a little anti-friction grease on the sensor casing before inserting it. After tightening the bolt check that the clearance between the sensor and the impulse wheel is as specified using a feeler blade. If necessary adjust the shim thickness as required. Finally, have the complete ABS function checked by a GM dealer.

Solenoid valve and pump motor relays

Removal

40 The solenoid valve and pump motor relays are mounted on the hydraulic modulator. First disconnect the battery.
41 Unscrew the bolt from the power steering reservoir clamp; tie the reservoir to one side.
42 Remove the screw and withdraw the cover from the hydraulic modulator.
43 Pull out the appropriate relay. The small relay is for the solenoid valve, and the large one is for the return pump motor.

Refitting

44 Fit the new relay using a reversal of the removal procedure.

Surge arrester relay

Removal

45 The surge arrester relay is located on the left-hand side of the engine compartment, behind the left-hand front suspension mounting. First disconnect the battery.
46 Remove the relay cover, and pull out the relay.

Refitting

47 Fit the new relay and cover, and re-connect the battery negative lead.

Chapter 10
Suspension and steering

Contents

Front anti-roll bar - removal and refitting 6
Front anti-roll bar link - removal and refitting 7
Front hub and bearings - removal and refitting 9
Front lower suspension arm - removal and refitting 4
Front suspension crossmember - removal and refitting 10
Front suspension lower balljoint - renewal 5
Front suspension strut - overhaul 3
Front suspension strut - removal and refitting 2
General description 1
Power steering pump - removal and refitting 25
Rear anti-roll bar - removal and refitting 14
Rear axle (complete) - removal and refitting 15
Rear coil spring - removal and refitting 13

Rear hub and bearing - removal and refitting 18
Rear semi-trailing arm - removal and refitting 12
Rear shock absorber - removal and refitting 11
Rear suspension crossmember - removal and refitting 16
Rear suspension crossmember mountings - renewal 17
Steering column - removal and refitting 20
Steering gear - adjustment *in situ* 22
Steering gear - removal and refitting 21
Steering idler - removal and refitting 24
Steering knuckle - removal and refitting 8
Steering tie-rods - removal and refitting 23
Steering wheel - removal and refitting 19
Wheel alignment - checking and adjustment 26

Degrees of difficulty

Easy, suitable for novice with little experience	**Fairly easy,** suitable for beginner with some experience	**Fairly difficult,** suitable for competent DIY mechanic	**Difficult,** suitable for experienced DIY mechanic	**Very difficult,** suitable for expert DIY or professional

Specifications

Front suspension
Type .... Independent MacPherson struts, coil springs and anti-roll bar, double-acting telescopic shock absorbers

Rear suspension
Type .... Independent, semi-trailing arms and coil springs, anti-roll bar, double-acting telescopic shock absorbers, air pressure type levelling system on some models. Adjustable track control arms on later Senator and 3.0 litre Carlton models

Rear shock absorber air pressure (when fitted):
    Unladen .... 0.8 bar (11.5 psi)
    Laden .... 3.0 bar (43.5 psi)

Steering
Type .... Recirculating ball, worm shaft and nut with sector shaft and drop arm, power-assisted

Ratio:
    All models except Carlton 3000 GSi 14.5:1
    Carlton GSi 13.5:1
Lubricant type .... Dexron II type fluid
Lubricant quantity .... 1.0 litre

Front wheel alignment

Camber:
    Carlton models except 3000 GSi .... -1°55' to -0°25'
    Carlton 3000 GSi and Senator .... -2°15' to -0°45'
    Maximum deviation, left to right wheel .... 1° 0'
Toe-setting (total) .... 0° to 0°2' toe-in

Rear wheel alignment (laden*)

Camber:
    Carlton saloon (except GSi) .... -2°20' to -1°
    Senator, Carlton 3000 GSi .... -2°40' to -1°20'
    Carlton estate .... -2° 5' to -0° 45'
    Maximum deviation, left to right wheel .... 0° 45'
Toe-setting:
    Carlton saloon (except GSi) .... 0°5' toe-out to 0°45' toe-in (0.5 to 5.5 mm)
    Senator, 3000 GSi Carlton .... 0°10' to 0°30' toe-in (1.0 to 4.0 mm)
    Estate (except 3.0 litre 24v) .... 0°10' toe-out to 0°40' toe-in (1.0 to 5.0 mm)
    Estate, 3.0 litre 24v .... 0° to 0°50' toe-in (0.0 to 6.0 mm)
    Maximum deviation left to right wheel .... 0°25'
Note: *Laden indicates a vehicle containing two front seat occupants and a half-filled fuel tank.*

Wheels

Type   .... Pressed steel or alloy
Size   .... 5.5J x 14, 6J x 15, 7J x 15, depending on model

Tyres

Sizes

Carlton 4 cylinder models .... 175 R 14, 185/70 R 14
Carlton 6 cylinder models .... 195/65 R 15, 205/65 R 15
Senator .... 195/65 R 15, 205/65 R 15
* Refer to vehicle handbook or Vauxhall dealer for tyre speed ratings.

Pressures

See end of 'Weekly Checks'

Torque wrench settings

	Nm	lbf ft

Front suspension

	Nm	lbf ft
Lower suspension arm pivot bolt:*		
Front:		
Stage 1	120	89
Stage 2	Angle-tighten a further 30° to 45°	
Rear:		
Stage 1	70	52
Stage 2	Angle-tighten a further 45° to 60°	
Anti-roll bar front mounting	40	30
Strut to steering knuckle:*		
Stage 1	50	37
Stage 2	100	74
Stage 3	Angle-tighten a further 30° to 45°	
Hub nut	320	236
Strut top mounting	70	52
Anti-roll bar link	65	48
Front crossmember	170	126
Lower balljoint to knuckle	100	74
Lower balljoint to arm	35	26

Note *Values indicating angle-tightening apply to special bolts that must be renewed after removal.*

Rear suspension

	Nm	lbf ft
Crossmember	125	92
Driveshaft to rear hub:		
Stage 1	50	37
Stage 2	Angle-tighten a further 45° to 60°	
Track control arm to semi-trailing arm	60	44
Track control arm to crossmember	90	66
Semi-trailing arm pivot bolt	100	74
Anti-roll bar	22	16
Rear hub nut	300	221

Torque wrench settings (continued)	Nm	lbf ft
Rear suspension		
Shock absorber lower mounting	110	81
Shock absorber upper mounting	20	15
Steering		
Steering column	22	16
Steering wheel	25	19
Flexible coupling	22	16
Steering gear adjustment locknut	30	22
Steering gear mounting	40	30
Steering gear cover	30	22
Bearing cap locknut	150	111
Drop arm	160	118
Power steering union	42	31
Power steering pump	25	19
Tie-rod balljoint nut	60	44
Outer tie-rod clamp bolt	10	7
Idler mounting	55	41
Idler arm	45	33
Wheels		
Wheel bolts	90	66

1 General description

The front suspension is of independent MacPherson strut type incorporating coil springs and double-acting telescopic shock absorbers. An anti-roll bar is mounted forward of the suspension arms.

The rear suspension is of independent type with coil springs, double-acting telescopic shock absorbers and semi-trailing arms - 3.0 litre Carlton models and Senator models from 1990 were fitted with a revised multi-link rear suspension system, incorporating adjustable track control arms. The anti-roll bar is mounted on the crossmember. A rear suspension levelling system is fitted to some models, which enables the rear ride height to be adjusted by means of air pressure from an air line.

Power-assisted steering is fitted to all models. It is of worm and sector shaft type with a recirculating ball type nut. On fuel injection models automatic transmission, the hydraulic system includes a pressure switch. This operates an auxiliary air valve in order to increase the engine idling speed and compensate for the additional load imposed by the power steering pump.

2 Front suspension strut - removal and refitting

Removal

1 Apply the handbrake, then jack up the front of the vehicle and support it on axle stands (see "*Jacking and Vehicle Support*"). Remove the front wheel.

2 Prise off the metal caps, and unscrew the brake caliper mounting bolts using an Allen key.
3 Remove the brake caliper and support it so that the hydraulic hose is not strained.
4 Pull out the clip and disconnect the hydraulic hose from the bracket on the strut.
5 On models fitted with an anti-lock braking system (ABS), remove the wheel speed sensor and cable with reference to Chapter 9.
6 Unscrew the nut and separate the bottom of the link from the anti-roll bar. To prevent the ball-pin from turning, hold it stationary with a spanner on the two flats provided.
7 Unscrew the nut from the steering tie-rod balljoint, and use a proprietary balljoint separator to release the ball-pin from the steering knuckle.
8 Unscrew and discard the pinch-bolt, and pull down the lower suspension arm to release the balljoint from the steering knuckle.
9 Support the suspension strut then unscrew the nut from the upper mounting. Withdraw the strut from under the vehicle (**see illustrations**).

Refitting

10 Commence refitting by inserting the strut up into the upper mounting. Refit the nut and tighten it to the specified torque while holding the piston rod stationary with an Allen key.
11 Insert the balljoint in the steering knuckle, then fit a new pinch-bolt with its head facing the rear. Tighten to the specified torque.
Note: *On no account should the old pinch-bolt be used again.*
12 Reconnect the steering tie-rod balljoint and tighten the nut to the specified torque.
13 Reconnect the link to the anti-roll bar and tighten the nut to the specified torque.
14 On models with ABS refit the wheel speed sensor and cable.

15 Clip the hydraulic hose to the bracket on the strut.
16 Refit the brake caliper with reference to Chapter 9.
17 Refit the front wheel and lower the vehicle to the ground.
18 Finally have the front wheel alignment checked and if necessary adjusted. If the strut has been dismantled the camber setting will also have to be checked by a Vauxhall dealer using specialised equipment.

2.9a Front suspension strut upper mounting

2.9b View of front suspension strut under the vehicle

3 Front suspension strut - overhaul

Note: *A purpose-made spring compressor is essential for this work. Use of makeshift or unsuitable tools may result in injury.*

1 Remove the strut as described in Section 2 and mount it in a vice.
2 Fit the spring compressor and tighten it to unload the pressure on the upper seat and mounting.
3 Hold the piston rod stationary with an Allen key, then unscrew the nut and withdraw the upper seat and mounting. Separate the bearing from the mounting and recover the piston rod stop washers.
4 Remove the coil spring and upper seat, and remove the rubber boot, damping rings, and rubber buffer.
5 Unbolt the anti-roll bar link from the strut.
6 Mark the top of the steering knuckle in relation to the strut in order to retain the camber setting, then unscrew the bolts, and remove the knuckle **(see illustration)**. Note that the bolt heads face forwards.
7 It is not possible to separate the shock absorber from the strut, so if the shock absorber is faulty the strut assembly must be renewed. The shock absorber may be tested by mounting the strut upright in a vice and moving the piston rod up and down. If the movement of the rod is uneven, weak or loose, a new unit is required.
8 Clean all the components and examine them for wear and damage. If renewing the coil spring, both front springs should be renewed at the same time.
9 Commence reassembly by locating the steering knuckle on the strut. If the original strut is being refitted, insert the new bolts from the front, align the previously-made marks and tighten the new nuts to the specified torque. If a new strut is being fitted, secure the steering knuckle to the strut using the old bolts, tighten to the specified torque and have the camber angle adjusted by a Vauxhall dealer immediately on completion of the refitting operation. The new bolts can then be fitted during the camber angle adjustment.

10 Refit the anti-roll bar link and tighten the nut.
11 Mount the strut in a vice and fully extend the piston rod.
12 Locate the lower damping ring on the strut followed by the coil spring.
13 Fit the spring compressor to the coil spring.
14 Refit the rubber buffer.
15 Fit the rubber boot and upper damping ring on the coil spring upper seat.
16 Position a stop washer on the piston rod with its concave side facing downwards, then locate the upper seat on the coil spring. The 8 mm hole in the upper seat must be positioned on the opposite side of the steering knuckle **(see illustration)**.
17 Locate the bearing in the upper mounting with the yellow coloured inner race facing out, then fit the mounting onto the piston rod.
18 Position a stop washer on the piston rod with its concave side uppermost. Refit and tighten the nut.
19 Release the spring compressor and make sure that the coil spring locates correctly on the damping rings.
20 The front suspension strut may now be refitted with reference to Section 2 .

4 Front lower suspension arm - removal and refitting

Removal

1 Apply the handbrake, then jack up the front of the vehicle and support it on axle stands (see "*Jacking and Vehicle Support*"). Remove the front wheel.
2 Unscrew and remove the pinch-bolt, and pull down the lower suspension arm to release the balljoint from the steering knuckle.
3 Unscrew the nuts and separate the bottom of the links from the anti-roll bar. Support the anti-roll bar as far upwards as possible.
4 Unscrew the vertical front mounting bolt and the horizontal rear mounting bolt, discard them, and withdraw the lower suspension arm from under the vehicle. Note the horizontal bolt head faces forwards.

5 Refer to Section 5 if renewing the suspension balljoint. Examine the rubber bushes in the arm and if necessary renew them by pressing out the old ones and pressing in the new bushes. Use a long bolt, nut, metal tubing and packing washers, and dip the new bushes in soapy water before fitting them. The vertical bush should be removed upwards from the arm, and the new bush pressed downwards. The horizontal bush should be removed from front to rear, and the new bush fitted from rear to front. The narrow lead on the horizontal bush must face forward.

Refitting

6 Commence refitting by locating the arm on the underbody and inserting the new mounting bolts. **Note:** *On no account must the old bolts be used again.*
7 Hold the arm horizontally and tighten the nuts and bolts to the specified torque.
8 Insert the balljoint in the steering knuckle and fit a new pinch-bolt with its head facing the rear. **Note:** *On no account must the old pinch-bolt be used again.* Tighten to the specified torque.
9 Reconnect the links to the anti-roll bar and tighten the nuts.
10 Refit the front wheel and lower the vehicle to the ground.
11 Finally check and if necessary adjust the front wheel alignment (Section 26).

5 Front suspension lower balljoint - renewal

1 Remove the front lower suspension arm as described in Section 4.
2 The balljoint is riveted to the suspension arm when new, with subsequent balljoints bolted on. Where necessary drill out the rivets using a 12.0 mm (0.47 in) drill. One side of each rivet has a centre punch to facilitate accurate drilling in order to prevent enlarging the holes in the arm **(see illustration)**.
3 Using only the special bolts supplied, fit the new balljoint and tighten the nuts to the specified torque. The nuts must face downwards.
4 Refit the front lower suspension arm with reference to Section 4.

3.6 Front suspension strut-to-knuckle

3.16 Correct position of the front coil spring upper seat in relation to steering knuckle (arrows)

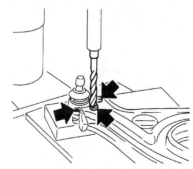

5.2 Drilling the front suspension lower balljoint rivets

6 Front anti-roll bar - removal and refitting

Removal

1 Apply the handbrake, then jack up the front of the vehicle and support it on axle stands (see "*Jacking and Vehicle Support*"). Remove the front wheels.
2 Unscrew the nuts and separate the bottoms of the links from the anti-roll bar **(see illustration)**. Prevent the link ball-pins from turning by holding them with a spanner on the two flats provided.
3 From inside the engine compartment unscrew the anti-roll bar mounting clamp bolts, and unclip the clamps **(see illustration)**.
4 Withdraw the anti-roll bar from under the vehicle.

Refitting

5 Examine the mounting rubbers for wear and deterioration and, if necessary, prise them from the bar. Dip the new rubbers in silicone oil and fit them on the bar with their slits facing forwards.
6 Insert the anti-roll bar from under the front of the vehicle, and refit the clamps. Insert the bolts loosely.
7 Reconnect the links and tighten the nuts to the specified torque.
8 Tighten the mounting clamp bolts to the specified torque.
9 Refit the front wheels and lower the vehicle to the ground.

6.2 Front anti-roll bar link connection

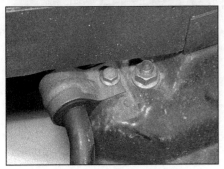
6.3 Front anti-roll bar mounting clamp and bolt

7 Front anti-roll bar link - removal and refitting

Removal

1 Apply the handbrake, then jack up the front of the vehicle and support it on axle stands (see "*Jacking and Vehicle Support*"). Remove the appropriate front wheel.
2 Note which way round the link is fitted then unscrew the nuts while holding the ball-pins with a spanner on the two flats provided **(see illustration)**.
3 Remove the link from the strut and anti-roll bar.

Refitting

4 Refitting is a reversal of removal but tighten the nuts to the specified torque.

8 Steering knuckle - removal and refitting

Removal

1 Remove the front hub as described in Section 9 .
2 Unbolt the disc shield from the steering knuckle.
3 Unscrew the nut from the steering tie-rod balljoint, and use a proprietary balljoint separator to release the ball-pin.
4 On models with an anti-lock braking system remove the wheel speed sensor and cable with reference to Chapter 9.
5 Unscrew and remove the pinch-bolt, and pull down the lower suspension arm to release the balljoint from the steering knuckle.
6 Mark the top of the steering knuckle in relation to the strut in order to retain the camber setting, then unscrew and discard the bolts and remove the knuckle. Note that the bolt heads face forwards.

Refitting

7 Refitting is a reversal of removal, but be sure to use new bolts and nuts. On no account should the old bolts be used. Tighten to the specified torque wrench settings and if necessary have the camber and wheel alignment checked by a Vauxhall dealer.

9 Front hub and bearings - removal and refitting

Note: *A torque wrench capable of measuring the high torque of the front hub nut should be obtained before commencing work. If such a torque wrench is not available, the work should be entrusted to a Vauxhall dealer.*

Removal

1 Apply the handbrake, then jack up the front of the vehicle and support it on axle stands (see "*Jacking and Vehicle Support*"). Remove the appropriate front wheel. On vehicles fitted with alloy wheels remove the disc in the centre of the wheel.

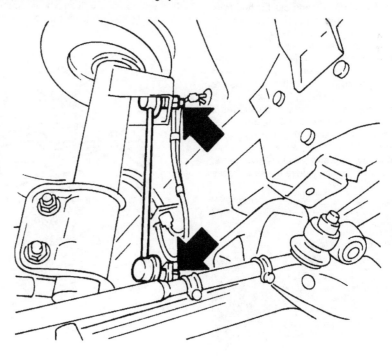
7.2 Front anti-roll bar link mounting nuts

9.9a Remove the front hub nut . . .

9.9b . . . and the front hub

9.10 Plastic sleeve for retaining the bearing inner tracks during fitting (arrowed)

2 Lever the metal cap from the hub, refit the wheel and lower the vehicle to the ground. (Leave the wheel cover off if fitted.)
3 Place blocks of wood, or similar, behind every wheel to ensure that the vehicle cannot move in either direction.
4 Using a socket, sturdy T-bar and a long extension bar for leverage, slacken the hub nut half a turn. Note that the nut is tightened to an extremely high torque setting, and a considerable effort will be required to slacken it.
5 Jack up the front of the vehicle and support it on axle stands (see "Jacking and Vehicle Support"). Remove the appropriate wheel.
6 Prise off the metal caps and unscrew the brake caliper mounting bolts using an Allen key.
7 Remove the brake caliper and support it so that the hydraulic hose is not strained.
8 Unscrew the retaining screw and remove the brake disc.
9 Remove the hub nut, and pull the hub from the stub axle. If the inner bearing track remains on the stub axle, remove it with a puller and recover the oil seal which will have been pulled out of the hub (see illustrations).
10 The bearings cannot be renewed separately to the hub, so if the bearings are worn or the oil seal leaking the complete hub must be renewed. The new hub includes a plastic sleeve which holds the bearing inner tracks together while fitting the hub (see illustration).
11 Locate the hub and plastic sleeve on the stub axle, then carefully drive the inner tracks

onto the stub axle using a suitable size socket or metal tube (see illustration). Remove the plastic sleeve.

Refitting

12 Refit the components in the reverse order to removal but note the following points:
a) Tighten all nuts and bolts to the specified torque.
b) Apply locking fluid to the threads of the brake disc retaining screw and tighten it to 4 Nm (3 lbf ft).
c) Refit the brake caliper as described in Chapter 9.

10 Front suspension crossmember - removal and refitting

Removal

1 Apply the handbrake, then jack up the front of the vehicle and support it on axle stands

(see "Jacking and Vehicle Support") positioned under the underbody channel sections.
2 Remove both front lower suspension arms as described in Section 4.
3 From inside the engine compartment, unscrew the anti-roll bar front mounting clamp bolts and unclip the clamps.
4 Unscrew the nuts securing both engine mountings to the crossmember and engine brackets. Recover the washers.
5 Support the weight of the engine using a hoist or engine support bar (see illustration). If using a hoist, remove the bonnet first (Chapter 11).
6 Support the crossmember on a trolley jack and stout length of wood.
7 Unscrew the four mounting bolts and lower the crossmember to the ground. Recover the engine mountings.

Refitting

8 Refitting is a reversal of removal, but tighten all nuts and bolts to the specified torque settings.

9.11 Driving the bearing inner tracks onto the stub axle

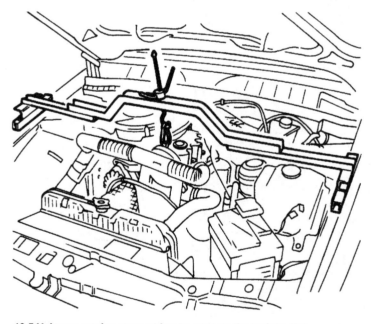

10.5 Using an engine support bar to support the weight of the engine

11.2a Rear shock absorber upper mounting - Saloon

11.2b Rear shock absorber upper mounting - estate (arrowed)

11.3 Unplugging the cabling from the top of the shock absorber - vehicles with electronic ride control

11 Rear shock absorber - removal and refitting

Removal

1 Position the vehicle over an inspection pit or on car ramps. The rear of the vehicle may be jacked up and supported by axle stands under the semi-trailing arms, but the downward slope of the arms makes it difficult to position the axle stands safely. Alternatively jack up the semi-trailing arm with a trolley jack and suitable wooden saddle.
2 On Saloon models open the boot lid and remove the rubber cap from the top of the shock absorber. On Estate models remove the screws and lift the cover over the shock absorber **(see illustrations)**.
3 Unscrew the upper mounting nuts and remove the washer and rubber buffer. Note: *On vehicles with electronic ride control, unplug the cable connector from the top of the shock absorber* **(see illustration)**.
4 On models with rear suspension levelling, release the pressure from the Schrader valve then unclip the pressure line from the shock absorber.
5 Unscrew the bottom mounting bolt and remove the shock absorber **(see illustrations)**.
6 Commence refitting by locating the shock absorber on the semi trailing arm and inserting the bottom mounting bolt loosely. Ensure that the bush engages with the recess in the lower mounting **(see illustration)**.
7 On models fitted with rear suspension

levelling, refit the pressure line and carefully inflate the shock absorber until it protrudes through the top mounting.
8 Refit the upper mounting rubber buffer and washer, and tighten the nut and locknut to the specified torque. The distance between the locknut and the top of the shock absorber stub must be 13.0 mm (0.5 in)
9 Tighten the bottom mounting bolt to the specified torque.
10 Refit the cover (Estate models) or rubber cap (Saloon models).
11 Lower the vehicle to the ground.

Refitting

12 On models fitted with rear suspension levelling, inflate the system to the specified pressure.

12 Rear semi-trailing arm - removal and refitting

Removal

1 Chock the front wheels, then jack the rear of the vehicle and support it on axle stands under the crossmember mountings.
2 Using an Allen key unscrew the socket-head bolts securing the driveshaft to the rear hub while holding the rear wheel stationary. Recover the lock washers.
3 Lever the driveshaft from the rear hub and support it to one side.
4 Disconnect the hydraulic brake hose from the bracket on the semi-trailing arm.

5 Remove the rear wheel, then unbolt and remove the brake caliper and support it to one side without straining the hydraulic brake hose.
6 Unscrew the retaining screw and remove the brake disc.
7 Unhook the return spring and disconnect the handbrake cable from the lever on the semi-trailing arm. Disconnect the cable from the bracket.
8 Using a socket through the unthreaded holes in the hub unscrew the brake anchor plate bolts and remove the locking plate.
9 Remove the rear hub with reference to Section 18 , then withdraw the brake anchor plate and brake shoes as an assembly.
10 On vehicles with multi-link suspension, remove the nut from the joint between the track control arm and the trailing arm, then using a suitable ball-joint splitter, press the joint from the trailing arm **(see illustration)**

11.5a Unscrew the bottom mounting bolt ...

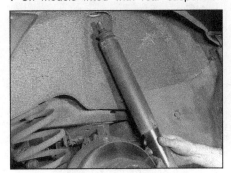

11.5b ... and remove the shock absorber

11.6 Ensure that the bush engages with the recess in the lower mounting (arrowed)

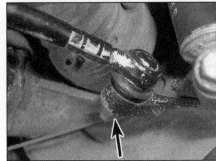

12.10 Remove the nut (arrowed), then detach the track control arm

12.19 Rear semi-trailing arm pivot bolt

12.22 Rear track control arm adjustment nut and locking collars

13.9 Rear coil spring and damping rubbers

11 If removing the left-hand semi-trailing arm disconnect the exhaust rear mounting rubbers and lower the exhaust approximately 30 cm (12 in). Support the exhaust in this position with wire or string.

12 Unbolt the rear anti-roll bar link from the semi-trailing arm and turn the link upwards. Remove the rubber mounting from the semi-trailing arm.

13 Using a trolley jack slightly raise the semi-trailing arm.

14 On models fitted with rear suspension levelling, release the air pressure from the schrader valve then unclip the pressure line from the shock absorber.

15 Unscrew the shock absorber bottom mounting bolt.

16 Lower the jack until the rear spring and damping rubbers can be removed.

17 Completely lower the jack.

18 Support the final drive unit on the trolley jack and unbolt the rear damping bracket from the underbody.

19 Slightly lower the final drive unit then unscrew and remove the pivot bolts and withdraw the semi-trailing arm from the crossmember **(see illustration)**.

20 If the pivot bushes are worn, they may be renewed. Cut the rubber shoulders from the old bushes and press out the bushes using a long bolt, nut, washers and suitable metal tube. Fit the new bushes in a similar way, but dip them in soapy water first to assist fitting.

Refitting

21 Refitting is a reversal of removal, but adjust the handbrake with reference to Chapter 9 and on models fitted with rear suspension levelling inflate the system to the specified amount. Tighten all nuts and bolts to the specified torque. Note that the semi-trailing arm pivot bolt heads must face each other.

22 On vehicles with multi-link rear suspension, it is strongly recommended that the rear wheel toe-in be checked and if necessary adjusted by a Vauxhall dealer **(see illustration)**.

13 Rear coil spring - removal and refitting

Removal

1 Chock the front wheels, then jack up the rear of the vehicle and support on axle stands positioned under the crossmember mountings. Remove the rear wheel.

2 Disconnect the hydraulic brake hose from the bracket on the semi-trailing arm by pulling out the locking plate.

3 Using a trolley jack, slightly raise the semi-trailing arm.

4 On models fitted with rear suspension levelling, release the air pressure from the schrader valve, then unclip the pressure line from the shock absorber.

5 Unscrew the shock absorber bottom mounting bolt.

6 If removing the left-hand coil spring disconnect the exhaust rear mounting rubbers and lower the exhaust approximately 30 cm (12 in). Support the exhaust in this position with wire or string.

7 On models fitted with ABS, unclip the wheel speed sensor cables from the underbody.

8 Using a further trolley jack or bottle jack support the final drive unit then unbolt the rear damping bracket from the underbody.

9 Lower the final drive unit and semi-trailing arm until the rear coil spring and damping rubbers can be removed. Note that the upper damping rubber incorporates a buffer **(see illustration)**.

Refitting

10 Refitting is a reversal of removal, but tighten all nuts and bolts to the specified torques.

14 Rear anti-roll bar - removal and refitting

Removal

1 Chock the front wheels, then jack up the rear of the vehicle and support on axle stands

(see "*Jacking and Vehicle Support*").

2 Support the final drive unit on a trolley jack. Unbolt the rear damping bracket from the underbody, then lower the final drive unit slightly.

3 Unbolt the two links from the semi-trailing arms, and remove the rubber mountings **(see illustration)**.

4 Unscrew the clamp bolts from the top of the crossmember, release the clamps, and withdraw the anti-roll bar from under the vehicle.

5 Remove the links and mounting rubbers from the anti-roll bar. If necessary the rubbers may be pressed from the links and renewed, using metal tubing, washers and long bolt and nut. Dip the new rubbers in soapy water to assist fitting them.

Refitting

6 Refitting is a reversal of removal, but tighten all nuts and bolts to the specified torques.

15 Rear axle (complete) - removal and refitting

Removal

1 Chock the front wheels, then jack up the rear of the vehicle and support it on axle stands positioned under the rear underbody channel sections. Remove both rear wheels.

2 Remove the intermediate and rear sections

14.3 Rear anti-roll bar link

15.15 Rear crossmember front mounting

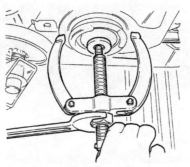

17.6 Withdrawing the crossmember mountings

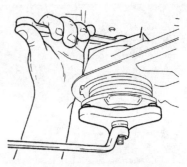

17.7 Pressing in the crossmember mountings

of the exhaust system with reference to Chapter 4.

3 Note the position of the adjustment nut on the handbrake rod, then unscrew it and slide off the compensator bar.

4 Working on one side disconnect the return spring and unhook the handbrake cable from the shoe operating lever. Disconnect the cable from the bracket on the semi-trailing arm.

5 Disconnect the hydraulic brake hose from the bracket on the semi-trailing arm by pulling out the locking plate.

6 Unbolt the rear brake caliper from the semi-trailing arm and support it away from the disc, taking care not to damage the rigid brake line.

7 Repeat the procedure described in paragraphs 4, 5, and 6 on the remaining side of the vehicle.

8 On models fitted with ABS, unbolt the wheel speed sensors from the final drive unit.

9 Loosen the slider joint nut on the propeller shaft front section one complete turn.

10 At the rear of the propeller shaft unscrew the bolts securing the rear disc joint to the differential flange. Push the propeller shaft forwards and disconnect it from the flange. Support it on an axle stand.

11 Position a length of wood beneath the semi-trailing arms and support in the middle with a trolley jack.

12 Unbolt the final drive unit rear damping bracket from the underbody and lower the unit onto the length of wood.

13 Unscrew the shock absorber bottom mounting bolts on each side.

14 Lower the trolley jack until both rear coil springs and damping rubbers can be removed. Note that the upper damping rubbers incorporate buffers.

15 Raise the trolley jack until the rear damping bracket touches the underbody, then unscrew the three bracket bolts and centre bolt from the crossmember front mountings **(see illustration)**. As a precaution, have an assistant steady the assembly to prevent it falling from the trolley jack.

16 Lower the rear axle assembly to the ground and withdraw from under the vehicle.

Refitting

17 Refitting is a reversal of removal, but tighten all nuts and bolts to the specified torques.

16 Rear suspension crossmember - removal and refitting

Removal

1 Remove the rear axle assembly as described in Section 15.

2 Unscrew the anti-roll bar clamp bolts from the top of the crossmember and release the clamps.

3 Unscrew the final drive unit mounting bolts and lower the unit from the crossmember.

4 Unscrew and remove the semi-trailing arm pivot bolts, noting that the bolt heads are facing each other on each arm. Remove the crossmember.

5 If necessary renew the mountings with reference to Section 17 .

Refitting

6 Refitting is a reversal of removal, but tighten all nuts and bolts to the specified torques. The semi-trailing arms should be positioned horizontally before tightening the pivot bolts.

17 Rear suspension crossmember mountings - renewal

1 Chock the front wheels, then jack up the rear of the vehicle and support on axle stands positioned under the rear underbody channel sections. Remove both rear wheels.

2 Disconnect the exhaust rear mounting rubbers and lower the exhaust approximately 30 cm (12 in). Support the exhaust in this position with wire or string.

3 Disconnect the hydraulic brake hoses from the brackets on the semi-trailing arms by pulling out the locking plates.

4 Support the final drive unit on a trolley jack.

5 Unscrew the three bracket bolts and one

centre bolt from the crossmember mountings on each side and remove the brackets.

6 The mountings must now be pulled from the crossmember. The Vauxhall tool for this task is shown in **(see illustration)**. The crossmember is lowered slightly and the mounting bolt inserted from the top, then the puller is assembled as shown and the nut tightened to withdraw the mounting. If a similar arrangement using a conventional puller is not possible, use metal tubing, a long bolt, and large washers or a metal plate to remove the mounting.

7 The Vauxhall tool for inserting the mountings is shown in **(see illustration)**, and here again a similar tool may be fabricated from metal plate and a long bolt.

8 Refitting is a reversal of removal.

18 Rear hub and bearing - removal and refitting

Note: *A torque wrench capable of measuring the high torque of the rear hub nut should be obtained before commencing work. If such a torque wrench is not available, it is recommended that the work is entrusted to a Vauxhall dealer.*

Removal

1 Chock the front wheels, then jack up the rear of the vehicle and support it on axle stands (see "Jacking and Vehicle Support").

2 Unscrew the socket-head bolts securing the driveshaft to the rear hub while holding the rear wheel stationary. Recover the lockwashers.

3 Lever the driveshaft from the rear hub and support it to one side.

4 Remove the rear wheel.

5 Disconnect the hydraulic brake hose from the bracket on the semi-trailing arm by pulling out the locking plate.

6 Unbolt and remove the brake caliper and support it to one side without straining the hydraulic brake hose.

7 Unscrew the retaining screw and remove the brake disc.

8 Using an Allen key through an unthreaded

18.9 Driveshaft flange and rear hub nut

19.3 Disconnecting the horn pad wiring

19.5a Unscrew the retaining nut . . .

19.5b . . . and remove the locktab

19.6 Removing the steering wheel

19.8 Spring on the top of the inner column

hole in the hub drive flange, unscrew the brake backplate mounting bolts. Note that the upper bolts are shorter and are fitted with a locking plate.

9 Insert the wheel bolts and use a long bar to hold the hub stationary, then unscrew the central nut from the inner side of the hub (see illustration).

10 Pull off the driveshaft flange using a suitable puller.

11 Press the rear hub outwards from the bearing using a suitable puller bolted to the semi-trailing arm.

12 Extract the circlip from the semi-trailing arm then press out the bearing, again using a puller bolted to the arm.

13 If the inner bearing track has remained on the hub remove it with a puller.

14 Clean all the components and examine them for wear and damage. Obtain a new bearing.

Refitting

15 Press the new bearing into the semi-trailing arm using pressure on the outer track. If necessary, a long bolt and washers may be used to do this.

16 Fit the bearing retaining circlip.

17 Support the wheel bearing inner track on the inside with a metal tube, then carefully drive in the rear hub from the outside.

18 Fit the driveshaft flange on the inside of the hub. If necessary, support the outside of the hub and drive the flange fully on from the inside.

19 Refit the hub nut and tighten to the specified torque while holding the hub

stationary. Drive in the special collar to lock the nut.

20 Refitting is a reversal of removal but note the following points:
  a) *Tighten all nuts and bolts to the specified torque wrench settings*
  b) *Adjust the handbrake with reference to Chapter 9.*

19 Steering wheel - removal and refitting

Removal

1 Disconnect the battery negative lead.

2 Set the front wheels in the straight-ahead position.

3 Prise the horn pad from the centre of the steering wheel and disconnect the two wires (see illustration).

4 With the ignition key inserted check that the steering lock is disengaged.

5 Bend back the locktab and unscrew the retaining nut. Remove the locktab (see illustrations).

6 Mark the inner column and steering wheel in relation to each other then remove the steering wheel by carefully rocking it from side to side (see illustration). Do not use a hammer or mallet to remove it.

7 If necessary, unclip the horn contact ring from the steering wheel, noting that the direction indicator return segment points to the left.

8 Check that the spring is located on the inner column (see illustration), and lightly lubricate the horn contact finger with a copper-based grease.

Refitting

9 Refitting is a reversal of removal, but tighten the nut to the specified torque and bend up the locktab to lock it.

20 Steering column - removal and refitting

Removal

1 Disconnect the battery negative lead.

2 Working inside the vehicle, mark the inner column in relation to the flexible coupling, then unscrew and remove the clamp bolt.

3 Remove the steering wheel as described in Section 19.

4 Where applicable unscrew the height adjustment lever.

5 Remove the screws and withdraw the shroud sections from the steering column (see illustrations).

6 With the ignition key inserted at position II, depress the small detent spring and pull out the lock cylinder. Also disconnect the wiring plug.

7 Depress the plastic clips and remove the direction indicator switch and the windscreen wiper switch (see illustration).

8 Disconnect the wire from the horn contact finger.

20.5a Remove the screws . . .

20.5b . . . and withdraw the lower shroud . .

20.5c . . . and upper shroud

20.7 Removing the windscreen wiper switch

20.12 Locating the switch rubber grommets in the upper shroud

9 Unscrew the lower mounting bolt.
10 The upper column mounting consists of a nut and a shear bolt. Ideally a bolt extractor should be used to remove the shear bolt by first drilling a 3.2 mm hole then using the extractor to unscrew the bolt. Alternatively, drill off the head and use grips to unscrew the remainder of the bolt later.
11 Unscrew the upper mounting nut and withdraw the steering column rearwards from the flexible coupling. The column should be handled carefully to avoid damage to the latticed safety outer column and special inner column.

Refitting

12 Refitting is a reversal of removal but tighten all nuts and bolts to the specified torque. Before tightening the shear bolt, check that the column is correctly aligned then tighten the bolt until the head shears off. Check that, with the front wheels in the straight-ahead position, the clamp bolt on the flexible coupling is horizontally at the top, and that the steering wheel spokes are centred and pointing downwards. Before tightening the clamp bolt, pull the inner column upwards until it touches the stop on the ball bearing, then hold it in this position while tightening the bolt. Make sure that the switch rubber grommets are correctly located in the upper shroud (see illustration).

21 Steering gear - removal and refitting

Removal

1 Where applicable, remove the fixings and lower the undertray away from the engine bay.
2 Working inside the vehicle by the foot pedals lift the cover, then unscrew and remove the clamp bolt from the steering column flexible coupling.
3 Position a container beneath the steering gear to catch any spilt fluid.
4 Identify the pressure and return lines for location then unscrew the union nuts and pull the lines from the steering gear. Plug the line ends and steering gear ports.
5 On Senator models with automatic transmission, remove the bracket fixings and detach the fluid cooler lines from the chassis rail.
6 Apply the handbrake then jack up the front of the vehicle and support it on axle stands (see "*Jacking and Vehicle Support*").
7 On Carlton models fitted with ABS remove the front exhaust downpipe (see Chapter 4).
8 Unscrew the nut securing the steering drop arm to the bottom of the steering gear, then use a suitable puller to pull the arm from the splines on the sector shaft **(see illustration)**.
9 Unscrew the mounting bolts and nut and withdraw the steering gear downwards from under the vehicle **(see illustration)**. Recover any shims fitted to the upper stud. Where applicable, remove the exhaust heat shield.
10 Unscrew the clamp bolt and remove the flexible coupling from the steering gear.

Refitting

11 Commence refitting by locating the flexible coupling on the worm shaft splines, so that the clamp bolt hole on the column side of the coupling is horizontally on top with the worm shaft in its central position. The shaft and housing are marked as shown **(see illustration)**. Insert and tighten the clamp bolt,

21.8 Steering gear drop arm

21.9 View of the power-assisted steering gear (engine removed for clarity)

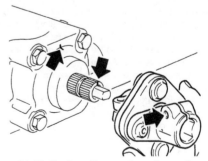

21.11 Centre alignment marks on the worm shaft and housing

but check that the rubber cap on the steering gear is not pressed against the housing.

12 With the steering wheel centralised lift the steering gear into its position and engage the flexible coupling with the inner column.

13 Insert the mounting bolts and hand-tighten.

14 Refit the removed shims and hand-tighten the upper mounting nut.

15 Tighten the flexible coupling upper clamp bolt followed by the steering gear mounting bolts and nut to the specified torque.

16 Refit the exhaust heat shield where applicable.

17 Refit the steering drop arm to the sector shaft and tighten the nut to the specified torque.

18 Refit the front exhaust downpipe on models fitted with ABS.

19 Lower the vehicle to the ground.

20 Remove the plugs, refit the pressure and return lines, and tighten the union nuts to the specified torque.

21 Refit the cover to the bulkhead.

22 Check and if necessary top-up the fluid level in the power steering fluid reservoir. Refit the cap.

23 With the engine idling, turn the steering from lock to lock several times in order to bleed trapped air from the system, then recheck and top-up the fluid level.

22 Steering gear -
adjustment *in situ*

1 The steering gear may be adjusted whilst in the vehicle. First jack up the front of the car and support it on axle stands (see "*Jacking and Vehicle Support*").

2 Unscrew the nut securing the steering drop arm to the bottom of the steering gear, then use a suitable puller to pull the arm from the splines on the sector shaft.

3 Prise the horn pad from the centre of the steering wheel.

4 Centralise the steering wheel by turning it from lock to lock then halving the number of turns. Turn the steering wheel approximately one turn anti-clockwise from centre.

5 Using a torque meter on the steering wheel nut, measure and record the turning torque. Now measure the torque while passing through the centre position. The second torque should be between 50 and 80 Ncm (4.4 and 7.1 lbf in) greater than the first, and the torque recorded should be between 110 and 150 Ncm (9.7 and 13.3 lbf in).

6 If necessary, adjust the sector shaft adjustment screw on the steering gear as required, then tighten the locknut and recheck the setting.

7 Refit the drop arm and tighten the nut to the specified torque, then lower the vehicle to the ground.

23.2 Side tie-rod outer balljoint

23 Steering tie-rods -
removal and refitting

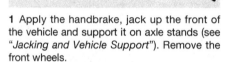

1 Apply the handbrake, jack up the front of the vehicle and support it on axle stands (see "*Jacking and Vehicle Support*"). Remove the front wheels.

2 To remove a side tie-rod unscrew the nuts and use a proprietary balljoint removal tool to press out the ball-pins **(see illustration)**. If it is required to renew just one tie-rod end, disconnect the appropriate end only.

3 Loosen the clamp bolts and unscrew the tie-rod ends, counting the exact number of turns required to remove them.

4 To remove the centre tie-rod, the side tie-rods must first be disconnected at their inner ends as described in paragraph 2.

5 Unscrew the nuts and disconnect the tie-rod from the drop arm and idler arm using the balljoint removal tool **(see illustration)**.

6 Refitting is a reversal of removal, but use new self-locking nuts and tighten all nuts and bolts to the specified torques. On completion check and if necessary adjust the front wheel toe-in setting as described in Section 26 .

24 Steering idler -
removal and refitting

1 Apply the handbrake, jack up the front of the vehicle and support on axle stands (see

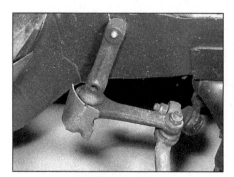

24.2 Steering idler

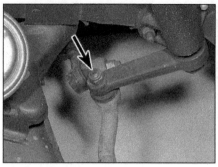

23.5 Centre tie-rod-to-drop arm nut (arrowed)

"*Jacking and Vehicle Support*"). Remove the left-hand wheel.

2 Disconnect the centre tie-rod by unscrewing the nut and using a balljoint removal tool to press out the ball-pin **(see illustration)**.

3 Unscrew the nut from the bottom of the idler bracket, and remove the heat shield followed by the idler arm. It is not possible to renew the bush separately from the arm.

4 If necessary, unbolt the idler bracket from the underbody.

5 Refitting is a reversal of removal, but use new self-locking nuts, and tighten nuts and bolts to the specified torques. When fitting the idler bracket bolts apply a little locking compound to their threads.

25 Power steering pump -
removal and refitting

All 4-cylinder models and 6-cylinder models to 1990

Removal

1 Loosen the two pivot bolts on top of the pump.

2 Loosen the tensioner nut and bolt under the pump, and the inner adjustment rod nut.

3 Unscrew the outer nut on the adjustment rod until the drivebelt can be released from the two pulleys **(see illustrations)**.

4 Position a container beneath the pump, then unscrew the union nut and disconnect

25.3a Loosening the adjustment rod outer nut

25.3b Removing the power steering pump drivebelt

25.10 Power steering fluid reservoir cap and dipstick

the pressure pipe. Loosen the clip and disconnect the supply hose. Drain the fluid into the container.

5 Support the pump and remove the three mounting bolts. Withdraw the pump from the engine compartment.

Refitting

6 Refit the pump using a reversal of the removal procedure, however leave the mounting bolts loose until completing the following tensioning procedure.

7 With the drivebelt on the two pulleys, unscrew the inner adjustment locknut then tighten the outer adjustment locknut until there is approximately 13.0 mm movement under firm thumb pressure mid-way between the pulleys. Ideally a tension gauge should be used to set the drivebelt to the correct tension, but the above method should be satisfactory. Tighten the inner locknut on completion.

8 Tighten all nuts and bolts to the specified torques.

9 Pour fresh fluid into the reservoir to the maximum level. Start the engine briefly, then

switch off and top-up the fluid level. Do this several times until the level remains constant. With the engine idling, slowly turn the steering several times from lock to lock in order to purge air from the system.

10 With the engine stopped top-up the fluid to the hot or cold level on the dipstick depending on the temperature of the engine (see *'Weekly Checks'*). Refit the cap on completion **(see illustration)**.

6-cylinder models from 1990-on and DOHC 24V

Removal

11 Refer to Chapter 4 and remove the air inlet hose.

12 With reference to Chapter 2, remove the ribbed auxiliary drivebelt.

13 Position a container beneath the pump, then unscrew the union nut and disconnect the pressure pipe. Loosen the clip and disconnect the supply hose. Drain the fluid into the container.

14 Slacken and withdraw the three pump mounting bolts - note that the third is

accessible through the aperture in the crankshaft pulley.

15 Remove the pump from the engine

Refitting

16 Refit the pump using a reversal of the removal procedure, on completion refit and tension the auxiliary drivebelt as described in Chapter 2. Refill and bleed the hydraulic system as described earlier in this Section.

26 Wheel alignment - checking and adjustment

1 Accurate wheel alignment is essential for good steering and to prevent excessive tyre wear. Before checking it, make sure that the car is only loaded to kerbside weight and that the tyre pressures are correct.

2 Camber and castor angles are best checked by a garage using specialised equipment. The castor angle is not adjustable but the camber angle is.

3 The toe-in setting may be checked as follows. Place the car on level ground with the wheels in the straight-ahead position, then roll the car backwards 4 metres (13 feet) and forwards again.

4 Using an accurate wheel alignment gauge, check that the front wheels are aligned as given in the Specifications.

5 If adjustment is necessary loosen the clamp bolts on the side tie-rods and turn the adjustment tubes by equal amounts. Both tie-rods must be equal in length.

6 After making an adjustment, centralise the balljoints and tighten the clamp bolts.

Notes

Chapter 11
Bodywork and fittings

Contents

Bonnet - removal and refitting 4
Bonnet release cable 5
Boot lid - removal and refitting 6
Bumpers - removal and refitting 26
Centre console - removal and refitting 30
Door - removal and refitting 16
Door exterior mirror - removal and refitting 21
Door lock - removal and refitting 15
Door speaker - removal and refitting 11
Door trim panel - removal and refitting 10
Electric window components 19
Exterior door handle - removal and refitting 13
Facia - removal and refitting 29
Front door lock cylinder - removal and refitting 14
Front door window - removal and refitting 18

General information and maintenance 1
Interior door handle - removal and refitting 12
Major body damage - repair 2
Minor body damage - repair 3
Radiator grille - removal and refitting 9
Rear door fixed window - removal and refitting 23
Rear door window - removal and refitting 20
Rear headrest guides - removal and refitting 24
Rear side window - removal and refitting 22
Seat belts - removal and refitting 25
Seats - removal and refitting 27
Sunroof - general 28
Tailgate - removal and refitting 7
Tailgate/bootlid trim panel - removal and refitting 8
Windscreen and tailgate rear window - removal and refitting 17

Degrees of difficulty

Easy, suitable for novice with little experience	**Fairly easy,** suitable for beginner with some experience	**Fairly difficult,** suitable for competent DIY mechanic 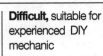
Difficult, suitable for experienced DIY mechanic	**Very difficult,** suitable for expert DIY or professional	

Specifications

Torque wrench settings	Nm	lbf ft
Bonnet hinge:		
To bonnet	20	15
To bulkhead	25	19
Seat belts	35	26
Bumpers	12	9

1 General information and maintenance

General information

The bodyshell is of all-steel welded construction, treated extensively for corrosion protection. One unusual feature is that the bulkhead assembly is glued to the bodyshell using the same glue as for bending the windscreen in position. The manufacturing process includes the use of robots and electronic measurement equipment.

Maintenance - bodywork and underframe

The general condition of a vehicle's bodywork can significantly affects its value. Maintenance is easy but needs to be regular. Neglect, particularly after minor damage, can lead quickly to further deterioration and costly repair bills. It is important also to keep watch on those parts of the vehicle not immediately visible, for instance the underside, inside all the wheel arches and the lower part of the engine compartment.

The basic maintenance routine for the bodywork is washing -preferably with a lot of water, from a hose. This will remove all the loose solids which may have stuck to the vehicle. It is important to flush these off in such a way as to prevent grit from scratching the finish. The wheel arches and underframe need washing in the same way to remove any accumulated mud which will retain moisture and tend to encourage rust. Strange as it may seem, the best time to clean the underframe and wheel arches is in wet weather when the mud is thoroughly wet and soft. In very wet weather the underframe is usually cleaned of large accumulations automatically and this is a good time for inspection.

Periodically, except on vehicles with a wax-based underbody protective coating, it is a good idea to have the whole of the underframe of the vehicle steam cleaned, engine compartment included, so that a thorough inspection can be carried out to see what minor repairs and renovations are necessary. Steam cleaning is available at many garages and is necessary for removal of the accumulation of oily grime which sometimes is allowed to become thick in certain areas. If steam cleaning facilities are not available, there are one or two excellent grease solvents available which can be brush applied. The dirt can then be simply hosed off. Note that these methods should not be used on vehicles with wax-based underbody protective coating or the coating will be removed. Such vehicles should be inspected annually, preferably just prior to winter, when the underbody should be washed down and any damage to the wax coating repaired using underseal. Ideally, a completely fresh coat should be applied. It would also be worth considering the use of such wax-based protection for injection into door panels, sills, box sections, etc, as an additional safeguard against rust damage where such protection is not provided by the vehicle manufacturer.

After washing paintwork, wipe off with a chamois leather to give an unspotted clear finish. A coat of clear protective wax polish will give added protection against chemical pollutants in the air. If the paintwork sheen has dulled or oxidised, use a cleaner/polisher combination to restore the brilliance of the shine. This requires a little effort, but such dulling is usually caused because regular washing has been neglected. Care needs to be taken with metallic paintwork, as special non-abrasive cleaner/polisher is required to avoid damage to the finish. Always check that the door and ventilator opening drain holes and pipes are completely clear so that water can be drained out. Bright work should be treated in the same way as paint work. Windscreens and windows can be kept clear of the smeary film which often appears by the use of a proprietary glass cleaner. Never use any form of wax or other body or chromium polish on glass.

Maintenance - upholstery and carpets

Mats and carpets should be brushed or vacuum cleaned regularly to keep them free of grit. If they are badly stained remove them from the vehicle for scrubbing or sponging and make quite sure they are dry before refitting. Seats and interior trim panels can be kept clean by wiping with a damp cloth and a proprietary cleaner. If they do become stained (which can be more apparent on light coloured upholstery) use a little liquid detergent and a soft nail brush to scour the grime out of the grain of the material. Do not forget to keep the headlining clean in the same way as the upholstery. When using liquid cleaners inside the vehicle do not over-wet the surfaces being cleaned. Excessive damp could get into the seams and padded interior causing stains, offensive odours or even rot. If the inside of the vehicle gets wet accidentally it is worthwhile taking some trouble to dry it out properly, particularly where carpets are involved. *Do not leave oil or electric heaters inside the vehicle for this purpose.*

2 Minor body damage - repair

Repair of minor scratches in bodywork

If the scratch is very superficial, and does not penetrate to the metal of the bodywork, repair is very simple. Lightly rub the area of the scratch with a paintwork renovator, or a very fine cutting paste to remove loose paint from the scratch and to clear the surrounding bodywork of wax polish. Rinse the area with clean water.

Apply touch-up paint to the scratch using a fine paint brush; continue to apply fine layers of paint until the surface of the paint in the scratch is level with the surrounding paintwork. Allow the new paint at least two weeks to harden then blend it into the surrounding paintwork by rubbing the scratch area with a paintwork renovator or a very fine cutting paste. Finally, apply wax polish.

Where the scratch has penetrated right through to the metal of the bodywork, causing the metal to rust, a different repair technique is required. Remove any loose rust from the bottom of the scratch with a penknife, then apply rust inhibiting paint, to prevent the formation of rust in the future. Using a rubber or nylon applicator fill the scratch with bodystopper paste. If required, this paste can be mixed with cellulose thinners to provide a very thin paste which is ideal for filling narrow scratches. Before the stopper-paste in the scratch hardens, wrap a piece of smooth cotton rag around the top of a finger. Dip the finger in cellulose thinners and then quickly sweep it across the surface of the stopper-paste in the scratch; this will ensure that the surface of the stopper-paste is slightly hollowed. The scratch can now be painted over as described earlier in this Section.

Repair of dents in bodywork

When deep denting of the vehicle's bodywork has taken place, the first task is to pull the dent out, until the affected bodywork almost attains its original shape. There is little point in trying to restore the original shape completely, as the metal in the damaged area will have stretched on impact and cannot be reshaped fully to its original contour. It is better to bring the level of the dent up to a point which is about 1/8 in (3 mm) below the level of the surrounding bodywork. In cases where the dent is very shallow anyway, it is not worth trying to pull it out at all. If the underside of the dent is accessible, it can be hammered out gently from behind, using a mallet with a wooden or plastic head. Whilst doing this, hold a suitable block of wood firmly against the outside of the panel to absorb the impact from the hammer blows and thus prevent a large area of the bodywork from being "belled-out".

Should the dent be in a section of the bodywork which has a double skin or some other factor making it inaccessible from behind, a different technique is called for. Drill several small holes through the metal inside the area - particularly in the deeper section. Then screw long self-tapping screws into the holes just sufficiently for them to gain a good purchase in the metal. Now the dent can be pulled out by pulling on the protruding heads of the screws with a pair of pliers.

The next stage of the repair is the removal of the paint from the damaged area, and from an inch or so of the surrounding "sound" bodywork. This is accomplished most easily by using a wire brush or abrasive pad on a power drill, although it can be done just as effectively by hand using sheets of abrasive paper. To complete the preparation for filling, score the surface of the bare metal with a screwdriver or the tang of a file, or alternatively, drill small holes in the affected area. This will provide a really good "key" for the filler paste.

To complete the repair see the Section on filling and re-spraying.

Repair of rust holes or gashes in bodywork

Remove all paint from the affected area and from an inch or so of the surrounding "sound" bodywork, using an abrasive pad or a wire brush on a power drill. If these are not available a few sheets of abrasive paper will do the job just as effectively. With the paint removed you will be able to gauge the severity of the corrosion and therefore decide whether to renew the whole panel (if this is possible) or to repair the affected area. New body panels are not as expensive as most people think and it is often quicker and more satisfactory to fit a new panel than to attempt to repair large areas of corrosion.

Remove all fittings from the affected area except those which will act as a guide to the original shape of the damaged bodywork (eg headlamp shells etc). Then, using tin snips or a hacksaw blade, remove all loose metal and any other metal badly affected by corrosion. Hammer the edges of the hole inwards in order to create a slight depression for the filler paste.

Wire brush the affected area to remove the powdery rust from the surface of the remaining metal. Paint the affected area with rust inhibiting paint; if the back of the rusted area is accessible treat this also.

Before filling can take place it will be necessary to block the hole in some way. This can be achieved by the use of aluminium or plastic mesh, or aluminium tape.

Aluminium or plastic mesh or glass fibre matting is probably the best material to use for a large hole. Cut a piece to the rough size and shape of the hole to be filled, then position it in the hole so that its edges are below the level of the surrounding bodywork. It can be retained in position by several blobs of filler paste around its periphery.

Aluminium tape should be used for small or very narrow holes. Pull a piece off the roll and trim it to the approximate size and shape required, then pull off the backing paper (if used) and stick the tape over the hole; it can be overlapped if the thickness of one piece is insufficient. Burnish down the edges of the tape with the handle of a screwdriver or similar, to ensure that the tape is securely attached to the metal underneath.

Bodywork repairs - filling and re-spraying

Before using this Section, see the Sections on dent, deep scratch, rust holes and gash repairs.

Many types of bodyfiller are available, but generally speaking those proprietary kits which contain a tin of filler paste and a tube of resin hardener are best for this type of repair. A wide, flexible plastic or nylon applicator will be found invaluable for imparting a smooth and well contoured finish to the surface of the filler.

Mix up a little filler on a clean piece of card or board - measure the hardener carefully (follow the maker's instructions on the pack) otherwise the filler will set too rapidly or too slowly. Alternatively a proprietary no-mix filler can be used straight from the tube without mixing, but daylight is required to cure it. Using the applicator apply the filler paste to the prepared area; draw the applicator across the surface of the filler to achieve the correct contour and to level the filler surface. As soon as a contour that approximates to the correct one is achieved, stop working the paste - if you carry on too long the paste will become sticky and begin to "pick up" on the applicator. Continue to add thin layers of filler paste at twenty-minute intervals until the level of the filler is just proud of the surrounding bodywork.

Once the filler has hardened, excess can be removed using a metal plane or file. From then on, progressively finer grades of abrasive paper should be used, starting with a 40 grade production paper and finishing with 400 grade wet-and-dry paper. Always wrap the abrasive paper around a flat rubber, cork, or wooden block - otherwise the surface of the filler will not be completely flat. During the smoothing of the filler surface the wet-and-dry paper should be periodically rinsed in water. This will ensure that a very smooth finish is imparted to the filler at the final stage.

At this stage the "dent" should be surrounded by a ring of bare metal, which in turn should be encircled by the finely "feathered" edge of the good paintwork. Rinse the repair area with clean water, until all of the dust produced by the rubbing-down operation has gone.

Spray the whole repair area with a light coat of primer, this will show up any imperfections in the surface of the filler. Repair these imperfections with fresh filler paste or bodystopper, and once more smooth the surface with abrasive paper. If bodystopper is used, it can be mixed with cellulose thinners to form a really thin paste which is ideal for filling small holes. Repeat this spray and repair procedure until you are satisfied that the surface of the filler, and the feathered edge of the paintwork are perfect. Clean the repair area with clean water and allow to dry fully.

The repair area is now ready for final spraying. Paint spraying must be carried out in a warm, dry, windless and dust free atmosphere. This condition can be created artificially if you have access to a large indoor working area, but if you are forced to work in the open, you will have to pick your day very

carefully. If you are working indoors, dousing the floor in the work area with water will help to settle the dust which would otherwise be in the atmosphere. If the repair area is confined to one body panel, mask off the surrounding panels; this will help to minimise the effects of a slight mis-match in paint colours. Bodywork fittings (eg chrome strips, door handles etc) will also need to be masked off. Use genuine masking tape and several thicknesses of newspaper for the masking operations.

Before commencing to spray, agitate the aerosol can thoroughly, then spray a test area (an old tin, or similar) until the technique is mastered. Cover the repair area with a thick coat of primer, the thickness should be built up using several thin layers of paint rather than one thick one. Using 400 grade wet-and-dry paper, rub down the surface of the primer until it is really smooth. While doing this, the work area should be thoroughly doused with water, and the wet-and-dry paper periodically rinsed in water. Allow to dry before spraying on more paint.

Spray on the top coat, again building up the thickness by using several thin layers of paint. Start spraying in the centre of the repair area and then, with a single side-to-side motion, work outwards until the whole repair area and about 2 inches of the surrounding original paintwork is covered. Remove all masking material 10 to 15 minutes after spraying on the final coat of paint.

Allow the new paint at least two weeks to harden, then, using a paintwork renovator or a very fine cutting paste blend the edges of the paint into the existing paintwork. Finally, apply wax polish.

Plastic components

With the use of more and more plastic body components by the vehicle manufacturers (eg bumpers, spoilers, and in some cases major body panels), rectification of more serious damage to such items has become a matter of either entrusting repair work to a specialist in this field, or renewing complete components. Repair of such damage by the DIY owner is not really feasible owing to the cost of the equipment and materials required for effecting such repairs. The basic technique involves making a groove along the line of the crack in the plastic using a rotary burr in a power drill. The damaged part is then welded back together by using a hot air gun to heat up and fuse a plastic filler rod into the groove. Any excess plastic is then removed and the area rubbed down to a smooth finish. It is important that a filler rod of the correct plastic is used, as body components can be made of a variety of different types (eg polycarbonate, ABS, polypropylene).

Damage of a less serious nature (abrasions, minor cracks etc) can be repaired by the DIY owner using a two-part epoxy filler repair material like which can be used directly from the tube. Once mixed in equal proportions this is used in similar fashion to the bodywork filler

used on metal panels. The filler is usually cured in twenty to thirty minutes, ready for sanding and painting.

If the owner is renewing a complete component himself, or if he has repaired it with epoxy filler, he will be left with the problem of finding a suitable paint for finishing which is compatible with the type of plastic used. At one time the use of a universal paint was not possible owing to the complex range of plastics encountered in body component applications. Standard paints, generally speaking, will not bond to plastic or rubber satisfactorily, but paints to match any plastic or rubber finish can be obtained from dealers. However, it is now possible to obtain a plastic body parts finishing kit which consists of a pre-primer treatment, a primer and coloured top coat. Full instructions are normally supplied with a kit, but basically the method of use is to first apply the pre-primer to the component concerned and allow it to dry for up to 30 minutes. Then the primer is applied and left to dry for about an hour before finally applying the special coloured top coat. The result is a correctly coloured component where the paint will flex with the plastic or rubber, a property that standard paint does not normally possess.

3 Major body damage - repair

Where serious damage has occurred or large areas need renewal due to neglect, it means that completely new sections or panels will need welding in, and this is best left to professionals. If the damage is due to impact, it will also be necessary to completely check the alignment of the bodyshell structure. Due to the principle of construction, the strength and shape of the whole car can be affected by damage to one part. In such instances the services of a GM dealer with specialist checking jigs are essential. If a body is left misaligned, it is first of all dangerous as the car will not handle properly, and secondly uneven stresses will be imposed on the steering, engine and transmission, causing abnormal wear or complete failure. Tyre wear may also be excessive.

4 Bonnet - removal and refitting

Removal

1 Support the bonnet in its open position and place some cardboard or rags beneath the corners.

2 As applicable, disconnect the wiring and tubing from the engine compartment light and washer jets and feed through the bonnet frame **(see illustration)**.

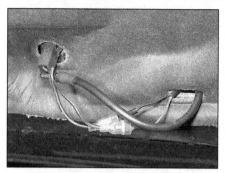

4.2 Heated windscreen washer jet wiring and tubing

4.3b . . . and remove the bonnet

3 With the help of an assistant, support the bonnet then unscrew the single central bolts on both hinges and lift the bonnet from the car **(see illustrations)**.

4 If the hinges remain undisturbed on the bonnet and body, no adjustment will be necessary when refitting the bonnet, however if the hinge sections require renewal, unbolt them.

Refitting

5 Refitting is a reversal of removal. If necessary, adjust the hinge positions so that the bonnet is central within its aperture, and aligned with the surrounding bodywork. The height of the front edge of the bonnet can be adjusted by the two screw-in rubber grommets. Check that the dimension between the striker pin nut and washer is 45.0 mm, and if necessary adjust it by loosening the nut and turning the pin **(see illustration)**.

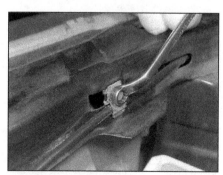

5.2 Removing the bonnet release cable clamping bolt

4.3a Unscrew the central bolts . . .

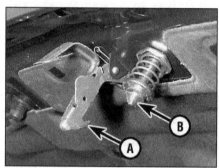

4.5 Bonnet latch components
A Safety catch   B Striker pin

5 Bonnet release cable - renewal and adjustment

Renewal

1 Open up the bonnet, and remove the radiator grille as described in Section 9.
2 Slacken and remove the release cable clamping bolt and clamp from the bonnet locking platform **(see illustration)**.
3 Detach the inner cable from the bonnet lock, then work back along the length of the cable, releasing it from any necessary retaining clips, and noting how it is routed.
4 From within the car, unclip the bonnet release lever from the right-hand footwell side trim panel, and remove the lever from the vehicle, withdrawing the cable as it is removed. Remove the rubber grommet and examine it for damage, renewing as necessary.
5 Fit the grommet to the new cable and lever assembly, then have an assistant feed the cable through the bulkhead from the inside of the vehicle, while you ensure that the cable is correctly routed around the engine compartment.
6 Once the cable is correctly routed, clip the release lever into position on the side trim panel, and press the grommet into the bulkhead aperture.
7 Connect the cable to the bonnet lock, then refit the cable clamping bolt and plate, tightening the bolt finger-tight only. Secure the cable in position with all the necessary clamps and ties.

Adjustment

8 To adjust the bonnet release cable, position the outer cable in the clamp plate so that there is no free play present at the lock end of the inner cable. Once the outer cable is correctly positioned, tighten the clamping bolt securely. Have an assistant operate the release lever, and check that the lock catch moves sufficiently to release the bonnet. Close the bonnet, and check the operation of the release lever. Adjust as necessary.
9 Re-open the bonnet, and refit the radiator grille as described in Section 9.

6 Boot lid - removal and refitting

Removal

1 Open the boot lid and mark around the bolts on the hinges with a pencil **(see illustration)**.
2 On models fitted with a rear spoiler, disconnect the pneumatic strut.
3 With the help of an assistant unscrew the hinge bolts and withdraw the boot lid.
4 The torsion springs may be removed if necessary, but it is recommended that the special GM tools KM-125 and KM-614 are used, as inappropriate tools may result in personal injury. The tools enable the torsion springs to be unhooked from their locations.
5 If necessary the lock may be removed from the bootlid: first remove the bootlid trim panel (where fitted). Remove the screws, disconnect the central locking motor link rod and latch control rod **(see illustrations)**. **Note:** *On*

6.1 Boot lid hinge

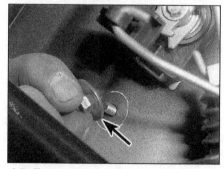

6.5a To remove the boot lid lock, unscrew the mounting nuts (one of two arrowed) . . .

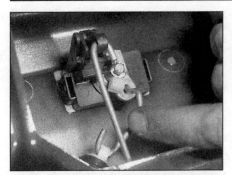

6.5b . . . disconnect the central locking motor link rod . . .

6.5c . . . and latch control rod (arrowed)

6.6 Book lid striker

Senator models, it will be necessary to remove the bootlid light cluster/number plate panel; refer to Chapter 12 for details.

Refitting

6 Refitting is a reversal of removal. Check that the boot lid is central in its aperture and aligned with the surrounding bodywork. Check the striker **(see illustration)** enters the latch centrally, and if necessary adjust its position.

7 Tailgate - removal and refitting

Removal

1 Support the tailgate in its open position.

2 Disconnect the struts by prising out the spring clips **(see illustration)**.
3 Remove the trim panel (Section 8).
4 Disconnect the wiring, and washer tubing.
5 With the help of an assistant remove the hinge clips, drive out the pins and withdraw the tailgate from the car.
6 The lock may be removed by disconnecting the control rod and removing the four retaining screws **(see illustration)**.
7 Access to the striker is gained by removing the screws and rear plastic protector. The striker may then be unbolted.

Refitting

8 Refitting is a reversal of removal, but adjust the striker so that it enters the lock centrally.

8 Tailgate/bootlid trim panel - removal and refitting

Removal

1 On Estate models, remove the speakers by extracting the screws with an Allen key and disconnecting the speaker wires **(see illustration)**.
2 Remove the fixings and withdraw the trim panel **(see illustrations)**.
3 Where necessary on Estate models, unbolt the speaker mounting frames **(see illustration)**.

Refitting

4 Refitting is a reversal of removal.

7.2 Disconnect the struts by prising out the spring clips

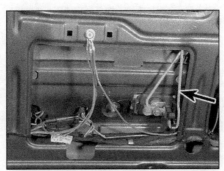

7.6 Tailgate lock control rod (arrowed) and central locking operating rod

8.1 Removing the tailgate speakers

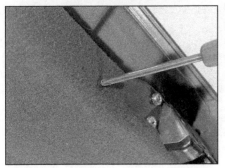

8.2a Removing the trim panel screws

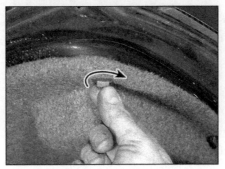

8.2b Removing the trim panel twist-lock studs

8.3 Tailgate speaker mounting frame (Estate models)

9.2a To remove the radiator grille on Carlton models, slacken and withdraw the three securing screws . . .

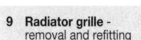

9 Radiator grille - removal and refitting

Removal
1 Open the bonnet.
2 On Carlton models, remove the three securing screws, then push the bottom of the grille inwards to release it from the cut-outs in the front bumper. Lift the grille away from the bumper **(see illustrations)**.
3 On Senator models, remove the screws and lower the radiator grille away from the bonnet aperture.

Refitting
4 Refitting is a reversal of removal.

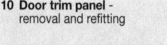

10 Door trim panel - removal and refitting

Note: *This Section describes the removal of the front door trim panel; the removal of the rear door panel is very similar.*

Removal
1 Disconnect the battery negative cable and position it away from the terminal.

Carlton
2 Where manually operated windows are fitted, fully close the window and note the position of the regulator handle.

10.7b . . . for access to the screw (arrowed)

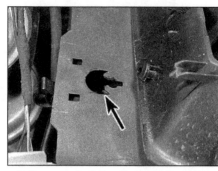

9.2b . . . and release the grille from the cut-outs (arrowed) in the front bumper

3 Slide a piece of cloth behind the handle. Move it from side to side to release the spring clip, then remove the handle **(see illustration)**.
4 Remove the plastic collar **(see illustration)**.

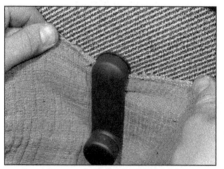

10.3 Method of releasing the window regulator handle spring clip

10.6 Removing the locking knob surround

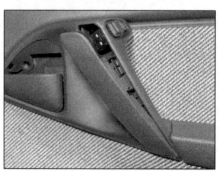

10.8a Prise out the plastic insert . . .

5 Disconnect the locking knob from the control rod. To do this it should be possible to prise out the red plastic insert, then to remove the knob from the rod. In most instances however, it will be found that this action breaks the insert, necessitating its renewal.
6 With the knob removed unscrew the screw and remove the surround **(see illustration)**.
7 Prise out the inner door handle finger plate and remove the screw **(see illustrations)**.
8 Prise the plastic insert from the grip and remove the exposed screws **(see illustrations)**.
9 Where applicable extract the exterior mirror control switch and disconnect the wires.
10 On models with electric front windows, prise out the window switch and disconnect the wiring.
11 Where applicable, remove the door pocket screws **(see illustration)**, then release the rear clip inside the pocket.

10.4 Remove the plastic collar

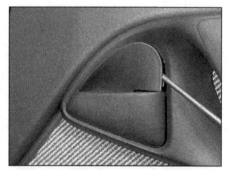

10.7a Prise out the inner door handle fingerplate . . .

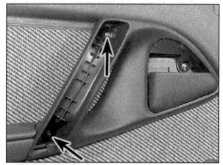

10.8b . . . and remove the screws (arrowed)

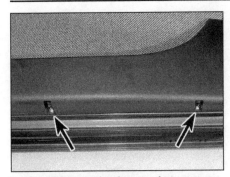

10.11 Remove the door pocket screws (arrowed)

10.12 Using a wide-bladed screwdriver or a purpose-made tool, prise off the panel

10.14a Prise the intake grille from the air flow control unit

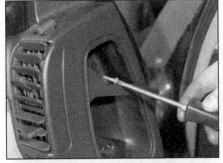

10.14b Remove the screws and lift off the air flow control unit . . .

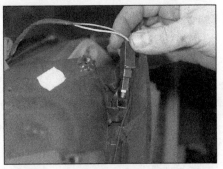

10.14c . . . unplugging the wiring for the illumination bulb at the connector

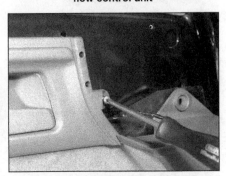

10.14d Remove the door trim panel securing screw

10.16a Unclip the door courtesy/hazard lamp unit, and unplug the wiring

10.16b Remove the trim panel securing screw behind

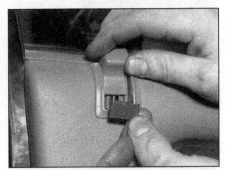

10.17 Removing the red plastic insert from the door locking knob

12 Using a wide-bladed screwdriver or a purpose-made tool (see illustration) prise the trim panel from the door. To avoid breakage of the plastic clips insert the tool as near to them as possible.
13 Remove the trim panel while slightly opening the inner door handle. As applicable, disconnect the switch wiring plugs.

Senator

14 Open the door and prise the inlet grille from the air flow control unit. Remove the screws and lift off the air flow control unit, unplugging the wiring for the illumination bulb at the connector. Remove the door trim panel securing screw that becomes exposed (see illustrations).
15 Unclip the cover from the grab handle and remove the trim securing screws behind.
16 Unclip and lift out the door courtesy/hazard lamp unit, unplugging the wiring at the

harness. Remove the trim panel securing screw behind (see illustrations).
17 Disconnect the locking knob from the control rod. To do this it should be possible to prise out the red plastic insert, then to remove the knob from the rod. In most instances however, it will be found that this action breaks the insert, necessitating its renewal (see illustration).
18 With the knob removed unscrew the screw and remove the surround.
19 Remove the three concealed screws at the lower edge of the door trim panel, then carefully pull the panel away from the door slightly.
20 Disconnect the wiring for the electric mirror at the connector, then unhook the link rod from the rear of the door latch handle.
21 Remove the trim panel from the door (see illustration).

Refitting

22 Refitting is a reversal of removal. When refitting the locking knob, pull up the control rod to its unlocked position, locate the knob on the rod so that the red insert slot is just showing, then press in the insert.

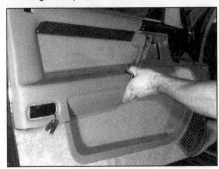

10.21 Removing trim panel from the door

11.2 Using an Allen key to unscrew the door speaker screws

11.3 Disconnecting the door speaker wires

11.4 Remove the screws and withdraw the enclosure

11 Door speaker - removal and refitting

Removal

1 Remove the door trim panel as described in Section 10.
2 Using an Allen key unscrew the mounting screws **(see illustration)**.
3 Withdraw the speaker and disconnect the wiring noting which way round the wires are connected **(see illustration)**.
4 Remove the screws and withdraw the enclosure **(see illustration)**.

Refitting

5 Refitting is a reversal of removal.

12 Interior door handle - removal and refitting

Removal

1 Remove the door trim panel as described in Section 10.
2 Push the handle forwards and release it from the aperture in the door, then twist it to release it from the control rod **(see illustrations)**.

Refitting

3 Refitting is a reversal of removal.

13 Exterior door handle - removal and refitting

Removal

1 Remove the door trim panel as described in Section 10.
2 Disconnect the control rods.
3 Slide out the retaining clip and remove the handle from the outside **(see illustration)**.

Refitting

4 Refitting is a reversal of removal.

14 Front door lock cylinder - removal and refitting

Removal

1 Remove the door trim panel (Section 10) and the exterior door handle (Section 13). Peel back the plastic membrane as far as required.
2 Remove the door handle fingerplate. Disconnect the central locking motor wires where applicable.
3 Extract the circlips and remove the lock cylinder from the fingerplate.

Refitting

4 Refitting is a reversal of removal.

12.2a Push the handle forwards and release it from the door aperture . . .

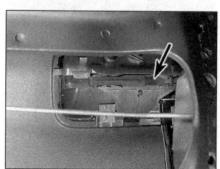

13.3 Exterior door handle retaining clip (arrowed)

15 Door lock - removal and refitting

Removal

1 Remove the door trim panel (Section 10). Peel back the plastic membrane as far as required.
2 Disconnect the control rods from the lock, and on 1988-on models, disconnect the wiring connector from the central locking servo motor.
3 Using a Torx bit, undo the screws and withdraw the lock assembly from inside the door **(see illustration)**.

Refitting

4 Refitting is a reversal of the removal procedure, noting that on 1988-on models

12.2b . . . then twist it to release it from the control rod

15.3 Front door lock mounting Torx screws (arrowed)

equipped with central locking, prior to refitting the lock assembly, the servo motor should be adjusted as described in Chapter 12. On all models, on completion check that the striker enters the lock centrally, and adjust if necessary.

16 Door - removal and refitting

Removal

1 Remove the door trim panel (Section 10). Peel back the plastic membrane as far as required.
2 Disconnect the wiring for the electric mirror, electric window, door-mounted speakers, and central locking as applicable.
3 Disconnect the check arm from the door pillar by extracting the pin.
4 Support the door on blocks of wood.
5 Remove the lower caps and use a suitable drift to drive out the hinge pins in an upwards direction. Withdraw the door from the car.

Refitting

6 Refitting is a reversal of removal. Check that the striker enters the lock centrally, and if necessary, adjust its position.
Note: *On later models, when removing the door assembly, it will not be necessary to remove the inner trim panel to gain access to the various wiring connectors. All the wiring connectors are joined to a master wiring*

connector, fitted to the front edge of the door, which can be disconnected once the door has been opened.

17 Windscreen and tailgate/rear window - removal and refitting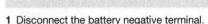

The windscreen and tailgate/rear windows are bonded to the body with special adhesive. As purpose-made tools are required to remove the old glass and to fit the new glass, this work is best entrusted to a specialist.

18 Front door window - removal and refitting

Removal

1 Remove the door trim panel (Section 10) and peel back the plastic membrane.
2 Remove the window regulator by unscrewing the bolts, drilling out the rivets, and disconnecting the arms from the bottom glass channels. On electrically operated windows, disconnect the wiring **(see illustrations)**.
3 Remove the exterior mirror (Section 21).
4 Carefully remove the weatherseal strip and moulding from the door.
5 Unbolt and remove the front guide rail **(see illustration)**.
6 Lift the window from the door.

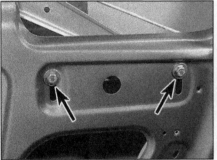

18.2a Window regulator adjustment bolts (arrowed)

18.2c Window regulator arm connection to glass channel

18.2b Electrically operated window regulator

18.5 Front door window guide rail and bolt (arrowed)

Refitting

7 Refitting is a reversal of the removal. Check that the rail and stops are correctly fitted to the front edge of the window. Adjust the position of the regulator so that the upper edge of the window is parallel to the upper door frame. Check that the window operates smoothly.

19 Electric window components - removal and refitting

1 Disconnect the battery negative terminal.

Window motor and regulator assemblies

2 Refer to Section 18 or 20 as applicable.

Centre console switches

3 Remove the centre console (Section 30).
4 Depress the retaining tabs, and remove the switch from the console.
5 Refitting is a reversal of the removal procedure.

Rear door switches

6 Carefully prise the switch out of the door trim panel, and disconnect its wiring connector.
7 Refitting is a reverse of the removal procedure.

Door lock operating switch

8 Refer to the information given for the central locking system in Chapter 12.

Electric windows (1988-on models) - reprogramming

9 On 1988-on models, whenever the battery is disconnected, or if any of the electric window components are removed, the electric window controls must be reprogrammed as follows to restore one touch operation.
10 Close all doors, then switch on the ignition.
11 Close one of the windows by pressing the relevant operating switch until the window is fully closed. With the window closed, press and hold the switch down for a further two seconds.
12 Repeat the procedure on the remaining window(s).

20 Rear door window - removal and refitting

Removal

1 Remove the door trim panel (Section 10) and peel back the plastic membrane.
2 Remove the window regulator by unscrewing the bolts, drilling out the rivets, and disconnecting the arms from the bottom glass channels. On electrically operated windows, disconnect the wiring.

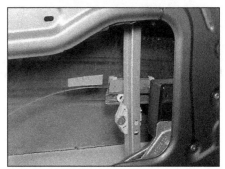

20.4 Rear door window guide rail

3 Carefully remove the weatherseal strips and moulding from the door.
4 Lower the window then unbolt and remove the centre guide rail (see illustration).
5 Lift the window from the door.

Refitting

6 Refitting is a reversal of removal. Make sure that the window stops are not pushed off the centre guide rail. On completion, check that the window operates smoothly.

21 Door exterior mirror -
removal and refitting

Removal

1 Prise out the screw cap (see illustration).
2 Remove the screw and unclip the plastic cover (see illustration).
3 Support the exterior mirror, then unscrew the three cross-head screws and remove the mirror (see illustration). Note that, on electrically-operated mirrors, it will be necessary to disconnect the wiring connector as the mirror is removed.

Refitting

4 Refitting is a reversal of removal.

Electrically-operated door exterior mirror - glass removal and refitting

Removal

5 Press the mirror glass in at its lower, inner

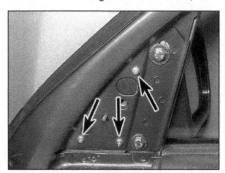

21.3 Exterior mirror retaining screws (arrowed)

corner, and carefully lever out the glass at its upper, outer corner, using a suitable flat-bladed tool, to release the glass from its retaining clips. Remove the glass from the mirror unit, disconnecting its wiring connectors as they become accessible (see illustrations).

Refitting

6 Ensure that both the mirror adjustment rods are fully retracted into the motor assembly, then offer up the glass and reconnect its wiring connectors.
7 Align the glass with its central mounting point and adjustment rods, and press it firmly in until it clicks into position.
8 Switch on the ignition, and adjust the mirror to the required position.

Electrically-operated door exterior mirror - component removal and refitting

Mirror motor

9 Remove the mirror glass as described earlier in this Section.
10 Undo the three retaining screws, then remove the motor from the mirror housing, disconnecting the wiring connector as it becomes accessible.
11 Refitting is a reverse of the removal procedure.

Mirror operating switch

12 Remove the door trim panel as described in Section 10.
13 Depress the retaining tangs, and remove the switch from the door panel.

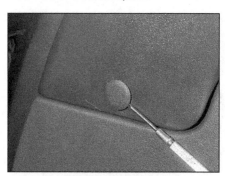

21.1 Prise out the trim panel screw cap

21.5a Lever out the mirror glass upper, outer corner, using a suitable tool

14 Refitting is a reverse of the removal procedure.

Mirror heating time relay

15 On pre-1989 models, the mirror heating time relay is situated behind the passenger footwell left-hand side panel. To remove the relay, peel back the rubber moulding, and remove the trim panel from the left-hand side of passenger footwell. Disconnect the wiring connector, and slide the relay off its retaining plate.
16 On 1989-on models, the mirror heating time relay may be combined with (or in place of) the rear screen wash/wipe time relay, which is situated in the relay holder behind the fusebox. Refer to Chapter 12 for further information.

22 Rear side window -
removal and refitting

Removal

1 Remove the trim strip from the bottom of the side window.
2 Working inside the car remove the inner trim panels and the rear seat belt guide. Where necessary, also remove the outer seat upholstery.
3 Unscrew the cap nuts and withdraw the window outwards.

Refitting

4 Refitting is a reversal of removal.

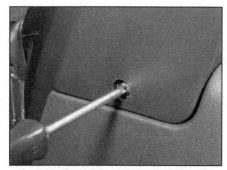

21.2 Remove the screw and unclip the plastic cover

21.5b Disconnect the wiring connectors as they become accessible

23 Rear door fixed window - removal and refitting

Removal

1 Remove the door trim panel (Section 10). Peel back the plastic membrane as necessary.
2 With the window lowered, unscrew the middle and upper screws holding the rear window guide channel. Push the channel forwards.
3 Prise out the upper and lower weatherseal strips, and withdraw the window forwards.

Refitting

4 Refitting is a reversal of removal, but apply soapy water to the window channels when inserting the window.

24 Rear headrest guides - removal and refitting

Removal

1 Depress the side plungers, and withdraw the headrest from the guides.
2 Move the seat backrest forwards. Reach up behind the guides, depress the plastic tabs, then withdraw the guides.

Refitting

3 Refitting is a reversal of removal.

25 Seat belts - removal and refitting

Removal

Front

1 Remove the B-pillar trim panel.
2 Unscrew the bolt securing the lower (rigid) belt to the B-pillar.
3 Feed the belt through the B-pillar panelling.
4 Unscrew the bolt securing the inertia reel unit and withdraw it from the B-pillar.
5 Unscrew the belt from the height adjuster.
6 To remove the seat belt stalk, first remove the seat as described in Section 27.

Rear (Saloon)

7 Remove the rear seat cushion and backrest (Section 27). Also remove the side upholstery.
8 Unscrew the bolt securing the lower (rigid) belt to the floor.
9 Unscrew the belt from the height adjuster.
10 Unscrew the bolt securing the inertia reel unit.
11 Pull the belt sideways from the rear quarter trim panel.
12 Unbolt and remove the stalk.

Rear (Estate)

13 Remove the rear seat cushion (Section 27).

14 Unscrew the bolt securing the lower (rigid) belt to the floor.
15 Unscrew the belt from the height adjuster.
16 Remove the trim panels from the under rear quarter window and wheel housing.
17 Where fitted remove the luggage cover and the panel covering the roller channel.
18 Unscrew the bolt securing the inertia reel unit and remove the belt.
19 Unbolt and remove the stalks.

Refitting

20 Refitting is a reversal of removal.

26 Bumpers - removal and refitting

Removal

Front

1 Jack up the front of the vehicle and support it on axle stands (see "Jacking and Vehicle Support").
2 Where necessary, disconnect the wiring connectors from the front foglamps and outside air temperature sensor (as applicable), and free the wiring from any relevant retaining clips and ties.
3 Extract the press stud fixings and remove the wheel arch protection panels (see illustration).
4 Unscrew and remove the bolts securing the brackets to the underbody channel sections (see illustration)

5 Release the plastic clips from the channel sections, and remove the brackets.
6 Disconnect the side sections and withdraw the bumper forwards (see illustration)

Rear

7 Remove the rear lamp clusters as described in Chapter 12.
8 Disconnect the wiring for the number plate lights.
9 Where applicable, remove the screws and lift off the inner wheel arch protection panels (see illustration).
10 Remove the spare wheel on Estate models.
11 Remove the rear protector and trim panel from the inside of the load space.
12 Working in the load space, slacken and remove the bumper bracket bolts (see illustration).

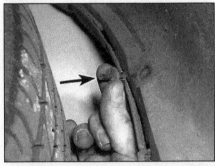

26.3 Extract the press stud fixings (arrowed) and remove the wheel arch protection panels

26.4 Unscrew and remove the bolts (arrowed) securing the brackets to the underbody channel sections

26.6 Withdraw the bumper forwards (Senator model shown)

26.9 Remove the screws and lift off the rear inner wheel arch protection panels

26.12 Working in the load space, slacken and remove the bumper bracket bolts

26.13 Unbolt the cotton rubber mountings at the leading edge of the bumper

13 Where applicable, unbolt the rubber mountings at the leading edge of the bumper adjacent to the wheel arches **(see illustration)**.
14 Slide the leading edges of the bumper off the mounting clips and lift off the bumper.

Refitting

15 Refitting is a reversal of removal.

27 Seats - removal and refitting
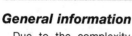

Removal

Front

1 Adjust the seat fully rearwards and unscrew the front rail mounting bolts **(see illustration)**.
2 Adjust the seat fully forwards and unscrew the rear rail mounting bolts.
3 If applicable disconnect the seat heating wiring.
4 Remove the seat from the car.

Rear

5 Release the rear seat cushion from the lower brackets by pulling the special handles. Where applicable, disconnect the seat heating wiring.
6 Unbolt the backrest brackets and remove the backrest(s).

Refitting

7 Refitting is a reversal of removal.

28 Sun roof - general

General information

Due to the complexity of the tilt/slide sunroof mechanism, considerable expertise is required to repair, renew or adjust the sunroof components successfully. Removal of the sunroof first requires that the headlining be removed, an operation which is difficult to carry out successfully. Therefore it is recommended that problems related to the sunroof are referred to a GM dealer.

27.1 Front seat mounting bolt removal

29 Facia - removal and refitting

Removal

1 Remove the centre console (Section 30).
2 Unbolt and remove the glove compartment from the passenger side of the facia panel. Also disconnect the illumination light wiring.
3 As applicable unbolt the ashtray, or remove the cassette storage case.
4 Remove the radio and, where necessary, the CD player or graphic equaliser, as described in Chapter 12.
5 Remove the heater control panel and on Senator models, the rotary temperature selector knobs (Chapter 3).
6 Remove the facia panel switches (see Chapter 12).
7 Carefully lever the centre fresh air vents

29.7a Removing a centre fresh air vent

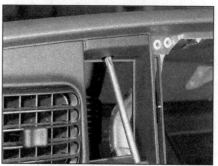

29.13a Remove the screws securing the centre surround panel . . .

from the facia using a hooked plastic instrument and disconnect the control rod(s) **(see illustrations)**. On Senator models, the centre fresh air vents are removed with the trip computer module - refer to Chapter 12.
8 Remove the steering wheel and steering column shroud panels (Chapter 10).
9 Remove the steering column combination switches (Chapter 12).
10 Disconnect the ignition switch wiring connector.
11 Remove the instrument panel (see Chapter 12).
12 Remove the clock/trip computer module (as applicable) with reference Chapter 12.
13 Remove the screws securing the centre surround panel, and disconnect the plug block **(see illustrations)**. Disconnect the wiring from the cigarette lighter and illumination bulb, and withdraw the surround panel.
14 Remove the heater matrix (Chapter 3).
15 Unclip the side panels, remove the screws and lift off the side fresh air vents.
16 Remove the fusebox (Chapter 12).
17 Pull the weatherstrips from the A-pillars and remove the covering from the front loudspeakers. Remove the loudspeakers.
18 Disconnect all the air distribution ducts, making a careful note of their routing to aid correct refitting.
19 Using a cranked screwdriver remove the front screws and lift off the facia panel cover, by first raising its centre.
20 Note the location of the wiring harness then starting from the left disconnect it, labelling each connector to aid correct refitting later and withdraw it into the driver's footwell.

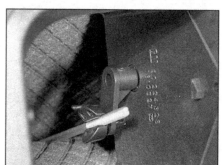

29.7b Centre fresh air vent control rod

29.13b . . . and disconnect the plug block - Carlton model shown

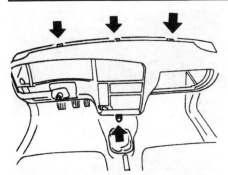

29.21a Facia panel front mounting bolts (arrowed) - LHD shown, RHD similar

21 Unscrew the facia panel mounting bolts. There are two at each side, three at the top front, and one at the bottom (see illustrations).
22 With the help of an assistant remove the facia panel from the car.

Refitting

23 Refitting is a reversal of removal.

30 Centre console - removal and refitting

Removal

Carlton

1 Disconnect the battery negative lead.
2 On models with a centre console rear armrest, open up the storage compartment lid, then carefully prise the cassette storage

30.3 Prise out the plastic cover from the base of the rear console compartment

30.7c Centre console side retaining screws (arrowed)

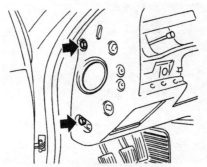

29.21b Facia panel side mounting bolts - LHD shown, RHD similar

box out of the console, or remove the retaining screw and lift the oddments box out of the console (as applicable).
3 On earlier models without a console armrest, using a screwdriver, carefully prise out the plastic cover from the base of the rear console compartment (see illustration).
4 On manual gearbox models, prise out the gear lever gaiter frame, then extract the two retaining screws and remove the gear lever surround panel.
5 On automatic transmission models, using a small flat-bladed screwdriver, carefully prise out the gear indicator panel and slot cover from the surround panel, and remove them from the selector lever. Undo the single retaining screw, then release the surround panel from the centre console. Pull the bulbholder out of the panel, and lift the panel off the selector lever.
6 Prise the middle cover out and remove it from

30.7a Centre console rear retaining screws (arrowed)

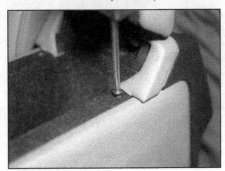

30.10a Remove the retaining screw . . .

29.21c Facia panel lower mounting bolt (arrowed)

the console (if necessary), disconnecting the switch connector(s) as they become accessible.
7 Prise out the trim caps, then slacken and remove the six console retaining screws (two at the front, two at the rear and one either side) (see illustrations).
8 Release the handbrake lever gaiter from the centre console, then lift the console over the gear/selector lever and handbrake lever whilst feeding the handbrake lever gaiter through the console aperture. Where necessary, disconnect the electric window switch wiring connectors, and remove the console from the vehicle.

Senator

9 Disconnect the battery negative cable and position it away from the terminal.
10 Open up the centre console storage compartment lid, then remove the retaining screw and lift the oddments compartment/cassette storage box out of the console (see illustrations).

30.7b Centre console front retaining screws (arrowed)

30.10b . . . and lift the oddments/cassette storage box out of the centre console

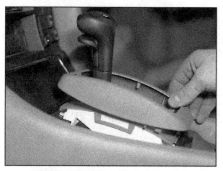

30.11a Models with automatic transmission: Unclip the selector lever indicator panel from the console . . .

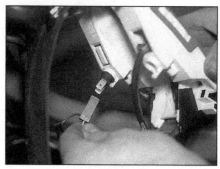

30.11b . . . and unplug the wiring harness from it at the multiplug connector(s)

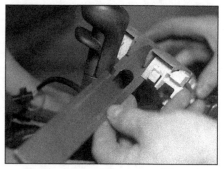

30.11c Slide out the cover strip and remove the indicator panel from the selector lever

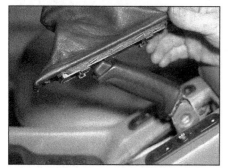

30.13 Unclip and remove the handbrake lever gaiter

30.14a Removing a centre console rear retaining screw

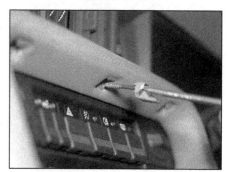

30.14b Removing a centre console upper retaining screw

30.14c Removing a centre console screw via the gear/selector lever aperture . . .

30.14d . . . and via the ashtray aperture

30.15a Lift the centre console away from the floorpan slightly . . .

11 On models with automatic transmission, unclip the selector lever indicator panel from the console and unplug the wiring harness from it at the multiplug connector. Slide out the cover strip and remove the indicator panel from the selector lever **(see illustrations)**.

12 On models with manual transmission, unscrew the gear lever knob, then unclip the gear lever gaiter from the centre console and lift it up over the end of the gear lever.

13 Unclip and remove the handbrake lever gaiter **(see illustration)**.

14 Remove the securing screws for the console moulding: two beneath the oddments storage box, two at the front edge of the gear/selector lever aperture, one behind the ashtray, and three behind plastic covers on the underside of the upper edge of the console padding **(see illustrations)**.

15 Lift the centre console away from the floorpan slightly, then disconnect the wiring harness from the console at the multiway connectors, labelling each one to aid refitting **(see illustrations)**.

16 Remove the centre console from the vehicle.

Refitting

17 Refitting is a reversal of the removal procedure.

30.15b . . . then disconnect the wiring harness from the console at the multiway connectors

Chapter 12
Body electrical system

Contents

Anti-theft alarm system - component removal and refitting 31
Battery - charging 4
Battery - removal and refitting 3
Bulbs - renewal 16
Central locking system - component removal and refitting 25
Check control system - general 29
Cigarette lighter - removal and refitting .10
Clock - removal and refitting 9
Courtesy light switch - removal and refitting 8
Cruise control components 27
Electrical system - general information and precautions 1
Electrical fault finding - general information 2
Exterior lamp units - removal and refitting 18
Facia switches - removal and refitting 7
Fuses and relays - general 5
Headlamp and associated components - removal and refitting 17

Headlamp - beam alignment 19
Heated seats - general 28
Heater control switch - removal and refitting 11
Horn - removal and refitting 15
ICE components - removal and refitting .30
Ignition switch - removal and refitting 12
Instrument panel - removal and refitting .13
Radio equipment - suppression of interference 32
Speedometer cable - renewal 14
Steering column combination switches - removal and refitting 6
Tailgate wiper motor - removal and refitting 23
Tailgate washer pump - removal and refitting 24
Trip computer - general 26
Windscreen wiper motor and linkage - removal and refitting 21
Windscreen washer pump - removal and refitting 22
Wiper blades and arms - removal and refitting 20

Degrees of difficulty

Easy, suitable for novice with little experience	Fairly easy, suitable for beginner with some experience	Fairly difficult, suitable for competent DIY mechanic	Difficult, suitable for experienced DIY mechanic	Very difficult, suitable for expert DIY or professional

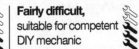

Specifications

System type . . . . 12 volt, negative earth

Fuses (typical)

No	Rating (Amps)		Circuits protected
1	10		LH parking lamp, LH tail lamp
2	10		RH parking lamp, RH tail lamp
3	10		LH main beam
4	10		RH main beam
5	10		LH dipped beam
6	10		RH dipped beam
7	-		Not used
8	15		Stop-lamps, turn signal lamps, ABS
9	30		Reverse lamps, windscreen wipers, horn
10	10		Rear foglamp
11	-		Not used
12	30		Heater motor
13	20		Cigarette lighter, heated front seats, glovebox light
14	20		Constant current for caravan or trailer, level control system
15	15		Hazard warning flashers, clock, luggage compartment lamp, courtesy light, radio
16	20		Fuel injection system
17	20		Fog lamps
18	20		Heated rear window
19	30		Front electric windows
20	30		Rear electric windows
21	10		Instrument panel, number plate light, engine compartment light
22	30		Air conditioning system additional cooling fan
23	30		Central door locking system, heated rear seats
24	20		Long range headlamps
25	30		Electrically operated sunroof, front electric windows
26	10		Headlamp washer system
27	10		Automatic transmission

Bulbs (typical)

Function	Watts
Headlamp main/dip	60/55
Driving lights	55
Parking light	5
Direction indicator lamp (front and rear)	21
Stop-lamp	21
Rear foglamp	21
Tail lamp	10
Number plate light	5 or 10
Reversing lamp	21

Wiper blades

Carlton Saloon and Estate - front	Champion VX48 or X48
Carlton Estate - rear	Champion X36
Senator	Champion VX45 or X45

1 Electrical system - general information and precautions

General information

1 The electrical system is of 12 volt, negative earth type. Electrical power is produced by an alternator, belt-driven from the crankshaft pulley. A lead-acid battery provides a reserve of power for starting the engine and for periods when the electrical load exceeds the alternator's output.

2 The reader whose competence or interest extends beyond the items covered in this Chapter may wish to study the Automobile Electrical Manual; available from the publishers of this book.

Precautions

 Warning: It is necessary to take extra care when working on the electrical system to avoid damage to semiconductor devices (diodes and transistors) and to avoid the risk of personal injury. In addition to the precautions given in "Safety first!" at the beginning of this manual, observe the following when working on the system.

3 Always remove rings, watches, etc before working on the electrical system. Even with the battery disconnected, capacitive discharge could occur if a component live terminal is earthed through a metal object. This could cause a shock, or a nasty burn.

4 Do not reverse the battery connections. Components such as the alternator or any other having semiconductor circuitry could be irreparably damaged.

5 Never disconnect the battery terminals, or alternator wiring connections, when the engine is running.

6 The battery leads and alternator connections must always be disconnected before carrying out any electric-arc welding on the car, or the alternator will be ruined.

7 Never use a high-voltage resistance tester for automotive circuit or continuity testing.

2 Electrical fault finding - general information

Note: Refer to the precautions given in `Safety first!' and in Section 1 of this Chapter before starting work. The following tests relate to testing of the main electrical circuits, and should not be used to test delicate electronic circuits (such as anti-lock braking systems), particularly where an electronic control unit (ECU) is used.

General

1 A typical electrical circuit consists of an electrical component, any switches, relays, motors, fuses, fusible links or circuit breakers related to that component, and the wiring and connectors which link the component to both the battery and the chassis. To help pinpoint a problem in a circuit, wiring diagrams are included at the end of this manual.

2 Before attempting to diagnose an electrical fault, first study the appropriate wiring diagram, to obtain a more complete understanding of the components included in the particular circuit concerned. The possible sources of a fault can be narrowed down by noting whether other components related to the circuit are operating properly. If several components or circuits fail at one time, the problem is likely to be related to a shared fuse or earth connection.

3 Electrical problems usually stem from simple causes, such as loose or corroded connections, a faulty earth connection, a blown fuse, a melted fusible link, or a faulty relay (refer to Section 5 for details of testing relays). Visually inspect the condition of all fuses, wires and connections in a problem circuit before testing the components. Use the wiring diagrams to determine which terminal connections will need to be checked, in order to pinpoint the trouble-spot.

4 The basic tools required for electrical fault-finding include a circuit tester or voltmeter (a 12-volt bulb with a set of test leads can also be used for certain tests); a self-powered test light (sometimes known as a continuity tester); an ohmmeter (to measure resistance); a battery and set of test leads; and a jumper wire, preferably with a circuit breaker or fuse incorporated, which can be used to bypass suspect wires or electrical components. Before attempting to locate a problem with test instruments, use the wiring diagram to determine where to make the connections.

5 To find the source of an intermittent wiring fault (usually due to a poor or dirty connection, or damaged wiring insulation), an integrity test can be performed on the wiring, which involves moving the wiring by hand, to see if the fault occurs as the wiring is moved. It should be possible to narrow down the source of the fault to a particular section of wiring. This method of testing can be used in conjunction with any of the tests described in the following sub-Sections.

6 Apart from problems due to poor connections, two basic types of fault can occur in an electrical circuit - open-circuit, or short-circuit.

7 Open-circuit faults are caused by a break somewhere in the circuit, which prevents current from flowing. An open-circuit fault will prevent a component from working, but will not cause the relevant circuit fuse to blow.

8 Short-circuit faults are caused by a `short' somewhere in the circuit, which allows the current flowing in the circuit to `escape' along an alternative route, usually to earth. Short-circuit faults are normally caused by a breakdown in wiring insulation, which allows a feed wire to touch either another wire, or an earthed component such as the bodyshell. A short-circuit fault will normally cause the relevant circuit fuse to blow.

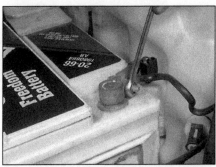

3.2a Loosen the clamp nut and bolt on the negative (-) terminal clamp . . .

3.2b . . . then remove the clamp and move it to one side

3.4a Unbolt the battery clamp . . .

 Warning: A short circuit that occurs in the wiring between a circuits battery supply and its fuse will not cause the fuse in that particular circuit to blow. **This part of the circuit is unprotected - bear this in mind when fault-finding on the vehicles electrical system.**

Finding an open-circuit

9 To check for an open-circuit, connect one lead of a circuit tester or voltmeter to either the negative battery terminal or a known good earth.

10 Connect the other lead to a connector in the circuit being tested, preferably nearest to the battery or fuse.

11 Switch on the circuit, bearing in mind that some circuits are live only when the ignition switch is moved to a particular position.

12 If voltage is present (indicated either by the tester bulb lighting or a voltmeter reading, as applicable), this means that the section of the circuit between the relevant connector and the battery is problem-free.

13 Continue to check the remainder of the circuit in the same fashion.

14 When a point is reached at which no voltage is present, the problem must lie between that point and the previous test point with voltage. Most problems can be traced to a broken, corroded or loose connection.

Finding a short-circuit

15 To check for a short-circuit, first disconnect the load(s) from the circuit (loads are the components which draw current from a circuit, such as bulbs, motors, heating elements, etc).

16 Remove the relevant fuse from the circuit, and connect a circuit tester or voltmeter to the fuse connections.

17 Switch on the circuit, bearing in mind that some circuits are live only when the ignition switch is moved to a particular position.

18 If voltage is present (indicated either by the tester bulb lighting or a voltmeter reading, as applicable), this means that there is a short-circuit.

19 If no voltage is present, but the fuse still blows with the load(s) connected, this indicates an internal fault in the load(s).

Finding an earth fault

20 The battery negative terminal is connected to 'earth' - the metal of the engine/transmission and the car body - and most systems are wired so that they only receive a positive feed, the current returning via the metal of the car body. This means that the component mounting and the body form part of that circuit. Loose or corroded mountings can therefore cause a range of electrical faults, ranging from total failure of a circuit, to a puzzling partial fault. In particular, lights may shine dimly (especially when another circuit sharing the same earth point is in operation), motors (eg wiper motors or the radiator cooling fan motor) may run slowly, and the operation of one circuit may have an apparently-unrelated effect on another. Note that on many vehicles, earth straps are used between certain components, such as the engine/transmission and the body, usually where there is no metal-to-metal contact between components, due to flexible rubber mountings, etc.

21 To check whether a component is properly earthed, disconnect the battery, and connect one lead of an ohmmeter to a known good earth point. Connect the other lead to the wire or earth connection being tested. The resistance reading should be zero; if not, check the connection as follows.

22 If an earth connection is thought to be faulty, dismantle the connection, and clean back to bare metal both the bodyshell and the wire terminal or the component earth connection mating surface. Be careful to remove all traces of dirt and corrosion, then use a knife to trim away any paint, so that a clean metal-to-metal joint is made. On reassembly, tighten the joint fasteners securely; if a wire terminal is being refitted, use serrated washers between the terminal and the bodyshell, to ensure a clean and secure connection. When the connection is remade, prevent the onset of corrosion in the future by applying a coat of petroleum jelly or silicone-based grease, or by spraying on (at regular intervals) a proprietary ignition sealer, or a water-dispersant lubricant.

3.4b . . .and remove the battery

3 Battery - removal and refitting

Removal

1 The battery is located in the front left-hand side of the engine compartment.

2 Loosen the clamp nut and bolt on the negative (-) terminal clamp, remove the clamp then move it and the cable to one side **(see illustrations)**.

3 Lift the plastic cover and disconnect the positive (+) terminal clamp in a similar manner.

4 Unscrew the clamp bolt at the base of the battery and remove the battery **(see illustrations)**.

Refitting

5 Refitting is a reversal of removal, connecting the negative (-) terminal clamp last. Apply a little petroleum jelly to the terminal posts and clamps before tightening them.

4 Battery - charging

1 In normal use the battery should be kept charged by the alternator. Except in extremely adverse conditions a regular need to charge the battery from an external source suggests that the battery or alternator is faulty, or that a short-circuit is draining the battery.

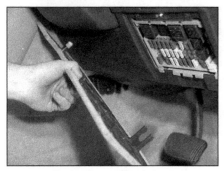

5.1a Facia mounted fuse/relay box

5.1b Relays located in the engine compartment

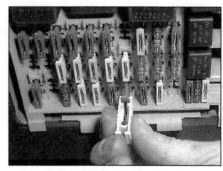

5.3 Using the removal tool to extract a fuse

2 Charging from an external source may be useful to temporarily revive a flagging battery. A battery which is not in use should be given a refresher charge every six to eight weeks.

3 The state of charge of the battery fitted as original equipment is shown by a "magic eye" indicator on the top face of the battery. If the indicator is green the battery is charged. It if turns darker and eventually to black then the battery needs charging. If the indicator is clear or yellow this indicates that the electrolyte level is too low to allow further use and the battery should be renewed.

4 Disconnect both leads or better still remove the battery before charging it.

5 As a general guide the charging rate (in amps) should not exceed one tenth of the battery capacity (in amp-hours). Make sure that dual voltage equipment is set to 12 volts.

6 Connect the charger to the battery, observing the correct polarity (+ to +, and - to -), then switch on the mains. Switch off the mains before disconnecting the charger. Ensure adequate ventilation during charging. If using the "magic eye" indicator to determine the state of charge, shake the battery occasionally to encourage the indicator to move.

7 Rapid or boost charging should be avoided as there is a risk of explosion, due to the rapid build-up of gas inside the battery.

5 Fuses and relays - general

1 All the car's electrical circuits are protected by fuses; most of the fuses are found in a fuse/relay box located under a cover to the right of and below the steering column. Unclip the cover and pull out the fusebox. Relays are located in, and behind, the fusebox. On some models an additional relay box is located in the left-hand rear corner of the engine compartment **(see illustrations)**.

2 The fuse applications are given in the Specifications and this information is also to be found on the rear of the fuse cover.

3 A fuse remover and spare fuses are to be found in the bottom right corner of the fusebox **(see illustration)**.

4 When renewing a fuse, switch off the circuit(s) concerned first. If the new fuse blows immediately when switching on, find and rectify the cause. The most usual cause of a blown fuse is a short-circuit to earth somewhere along the wire feeding the component concerned. The wire may be disconnected, trapped or frayed. Pay special attention to wire that runs through grommets, under carpets etc.

5 Where a blown fuse serves more than one component, the defective circuit can be traced by switching on each component in turn until the replacement fuse blows.

6 Never attempt to bypass a fuse with silver foil or wire, nor fit a fuse of a higher rating than specified. Serious damage, or even fire, may result.

6 Steering column combination switches - removal and refitting

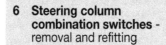

Removal

1 Unscrew the steering wheel height adjustment knob.

2 Disconnect the battery negative lead.

3 Remove the screws and withdraw the steering column shroud sections.

4 For better access remove the steering wheel as described in Chapter 10.

5 Unclip the switch and disconnect the wiring plug **(see illustration)**.

6.5 Disconnecting the combination switch wiring

Refitting

6 Refitting is a reversal of removal.

7 Facia switches - removal and refitting

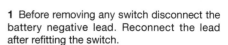

1 Before removing any switch disconnect the battery negative lead. Reconnect the lead after refitting the switch.

Lighting switch

2 Turn the knob to the Low beam position and pull it out.

3 Using a small screwdriver in the bottom hole, depress the catch and remove the knob as shown **(see illustration)**

4 Press together the retaining tabs and pull out the switch **(see illustrations)**.

5 Refitting is a reversal of removal.

7.3 Removing the knob from the headlamp/interior lamp switch

7.4a Press together the tabs . . .

7.4b . . . and pull out the switch

7.7 Use a strip of tape (arrowed) to protect the facia trim when removing a switch unit

7.8 Fitting a centre facia switch

7.10 Fitting the headlamp range adjuster switch

7.12 Glovebox illumination switch

9 Clock - removal and refitting

Removal

1 Disconnect the battery negative lead.
2 Carefully pull the clock from the facia. Disconnect the supply and illumination leads from the clock and remove it (see illustration).

Refitting

3 Refitting is a reversal of removal.

Centre facia switches

6 Protect the panel immediately above the switch with a strip of adhesive tape.
7 Using a screwdriver under the rocker switch and another on top of the switch, lever out the switch from the socket board as shown. (see illustration).
8 Refit by pressing the switch into position (see illustration).

Headlamp range adjuster switch

9 Using a screwdriver under the switch, lever out the switch.
10 Refit by pressing the switch into position (see illustration).

Glovebox switch

11 Remove the glovebox, referring to Chapter 11.

12 Slide the switch from the side of the glovebox (see illustration).
13 Refit in reverse order.

8 Courtesy light switch - removal and refitting

Removal

1 Open the door and unscrew the cross-head screw (see illustration).
2 Remove the switch from the door pillar and pull the wire out sufficiently to prevent it from springing back into the pillar.
3 Disconnect the wire and remove the switch.

Refitting

4 Refitting is a reversal of removal.

10 Cigarette lighter - removal and refitting

Removal

1 Disconnect the battery earth lead.
2 Pull the heater element from the lighter socket.
3 Carefully prise the lighter socket out of the illuminating ring. Unplug the socket and remove it (see illustration).

Refitting

4 Refitting is a reversal of removal. When inserting the socket into the illuminating ring, make sure that the ring lugs pass over the smooth part of the socket. Twist the socket clockwise to engage the lugs.

8.1 Courtesy light switch screw (arrowed)

9.2 Disconnecting the clock wiring

10.3 Rear view of cigarette lighter (facia panel removed)

11.2 Heater control switch removal

13.2 Removing the cigarette lighter cover

13.8a Removing a plastic cap from the centre screws

11 Heater control switch - removal and refitting

Removal

1 Remove the heater control panel as described in Chapter 3.
2 Unclip the switch from the control panel **(see illustration)**.

Refitting

3 Refitting is a reversal of removal.

12 Ignition switch - removal and refitting

Removal

1 Disconnect the battery negative lead.
2 Unscrew the steering wheel height adjustment knob.
3 Remove the screws and withdraw the steering column shroud sections.
4 Pull off the multi-plug.
5 With the ignition key inserted and at position II, depress the small detent spring and pull out the lock cylinder.
6 Unscrew the two grub screws and remove the ignition switch.

Refitting

7 Refitting is a reversal of removal.

13 Instrument panel - removal and refitting

Removal

1 Disconnect the battery negative lead.
2 Prise off the cigarette lighter cover, and remove the two screws revealed **(see illustration)**.
3 Pull out the bottom of the heater control panel and unhook it at the top.
4 Remove the heater or air conditioning control panel.
5 Remove the lighting switch (refer to Section 7).
6 Remove the headlamp range adjuster switch (refer to Section 7).
7 Remove the steering column combination switches (refer to Section 6).

13.8b Removing the surround panel

8 Remove the screws and withdraw the surround panel from the facia **(see illustrations)**. Note that the centre screws are covered with plastic caps. Disconnect the wiring plug for the headlamp height adjuster.
9 Unclip the bezel from the surround **(see illustration)**.
10 Unscrew the instrument panel retaining screws **(see illustration)**.
11 Where applicable, release the speedometer cable from its retaining clips in the engine compartment.
12 Pull out the instrument panel, then depress the spring plate and disconnect the speedometer cable (where applicable)**(see illustration)**.
13 Note the location of the wiring plugs and disconnect them **(see illustrations)**.
14 Remove the instrument panel.
15 If required, access to the tachometer, temperature gauge, fuel gauge, voltage

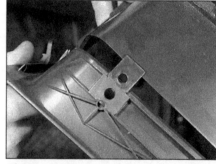

13.9 Unclipping the instrument panel bezel

13.10 Unscrewing the instrument panel retaining screws - Carlton model shown

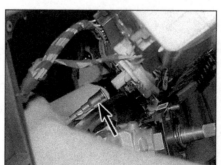

13.12 Disconnecting the speedometer cable (arrowed)

13.13a Disconnecting the left-hand wiring plugs . . .

13.13b . . . and right-hand wiring plug from the instrument panel

stabiliser, printed circuit board, and speedometer may be gained by removing the casing held by five screws (analogue display).

Refitting

16 Refitting is a reversal of removal.

14 Speedometer cable - renewal

1 Remove the instrument panel as described in Section 13 .
2 Working in the engine compartment draw the cable through the bulkhead and recover the grommet.
3 Jack up the front of the car and support on axle stands (see "*Jacking and Vehicle Support*").
4 Unscrew the knurled nut and disconnect the cable from the gearbox **(see illustration)**. Remove the cable.
5 Refitting is a reversal of removal, but make sure that the cable is not kinked or bent.

15 Horn - removal and refitting

Removal

1 The horn is located behind the radiator grille. First remove the grille (see Chapter 11).
2 Disconnect the battery negative lead.
3 Disconnect the two horn wires, then unbolt the horn from the bracket **(see illustration)**.

16.4 Removing the headlamp bulb wiring

14.4 Disconnecting the speedometer cable from the gearbox

4 If the horn does not operate, use a voltmeter to check that 12 volts is available at one of the wires with the ignition on and the horn push depressed.

Refitting

5 Refitting is a reversal of removal.

16 Bulbs - renewal

1 When renewing a bulb always switch off the respective circuit, and when changing halogen bulbs do not touch the glass part of the bulb. If the glass is inadvertently touched, clean it with white spirit.

16.2 Cover on rear of headlamp

16.5 Bulb retaining spring clip (arrowed)

15.3 Horn mounting and wiring

Headlamp and parking lamp

2 Release the spring clip then swivel out the cover and remove it from the rear of the headlamp **(see illustration)**.
3 Pull out the parking lamp bulbholder and extract the bulb without turning it **(see illustration)**.
4 Pull the wiring plug from the headlight bulb terminals **(see illustration)**.
5 Squeeze together the ends of the spring clip and swivel it outwards **(see illustration)**.
6 Remove the old bulb **(see illustration)**.
7 Fit the new bulb using a reversal of the removal procedure, but make sure the bulb lug(s) engage with the recess(es) provided.

Front direction indicator bulb

Carlton

8 Twist and remove the bulbholder from the rear of the lamp.

16.3 Removing the parking lamp bulbholder

16.6 Removing the headlamp bulb

16.9 Front direction indicator lamp bulb removal (lamp removed for clarity)

16.12a Swivel the lens unit away from the bodywork . . .

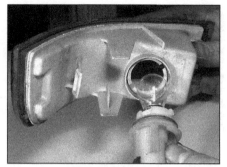

16.12b . . . then twist the bulb holder out of the lens unit

16.15 Front fog lamp wiring and bulb retaining spring clip (arrowed)

16.18 Slacken and remove the foglamp lens unit retaining screw

16.19 Removing the fog lamp bulb

9 Depress and twist the bulb to remove it **(see illustration)**.
10 Fit the new bulb and reconnect the bulbholder.

Senator

11 Apply pressure to the outside edge of the lamp lens and carefully lever against the inner edge with a plastic instrument.
12 Swivel the lens unit away from the bodywork, then twist the bulbholder out of the lens unit (bayonet fit) **(see illustrations)**.
13 Remove the bulb from the holder and fit a new item. Twist the bulb holder into position and refit the lens unit.

Front foglamps

Carlton

14 Reach under the bumper/front valance and remove the cover from the rear of the

lamp by turning it anti-clockwise.
15 Release the spring clip, remove the bulb, and disconnect the wiring **(see illustration)**.
16 Fit the new bulb in reverse order, making sure that the lugs engage the recesses.

Senator

17 Remove the adjacent direction indicator lens unit as described in the previous sub-Section.
18 Slacken and remove the foglamp lens unit retaining screw and lift out the lens unit **(see illustration)**. Prise the protective cap from the rear surface.
19 Squeeze together the tangs of the retaining clip, then twist and lift out the bulbholder **(see illustration)**.
20 Pull the bulb from the bulbholder and unplug the cabling at the connector.
21 Fit the new bulb and reconnect the cable, then refit the bulbholder and retaining clip.

Front driving lamps

22 On Carlton models, remove the radiator grille (refer to Chapter 11).
23 Release the spring clip (where applicable) and remove the cover **(see illustration)**.
24 Pull the wire from the bulb terminal.
25 Release the spring clip and withdraw the bulb.
26 Fit the new bulb in reverse order, ensuring that the locating tab on the bulb flange engages with the recess in the bulbholder.

Rear lamp cluster

Carlton Saloon and Senator

Note: *On Senator models, the rear fog and reversing lamps are housed in a separate cluster, mounted on the bootlid - refer to the relevant sub-Section.*
27 Where applicable, unclip the lamp cover.
Note: *If the bulb to be renewed is on the left hand side of the vehicle, it will be necessary to first remove the spare wheel from its housing.*
28 Press the two lugs apart and withdraw the bulbholder **(see illustration)**.
29 Depress and twist the relevant bulb to remove it **(see illustration)**.
30 The bulbholder may be removed if required by disconnecting the wiring plug.
31 Fit the new bulb in reverse order.

Carlton Estate

32 Turn the catch and open the trim cover.
33 Release the lug and withdraw the bulbholder **(see illustration)**.

16.23 Front driving lamp cover removal

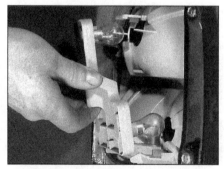

16.28 Removal of the rear lamp cluster bulbholder - Senator model shown

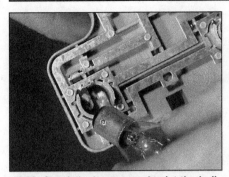
16.29 Carefully depress and twist the bulb to remove it

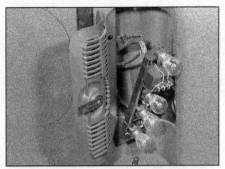
16.33 Rear lamp cluster bulbholder removal (Estate)

16.39 Removing the number plate lamp surround (Saloon)

16.40a Remove the number plate lamp . . .

16.40b . . . and withdraw the lens

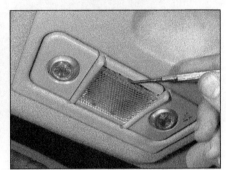
16.45a Removing the front interior lamp lens . . .

34 Depress and twist the relevant bulb to remove it.
35 Fit the new bulb in reverse order.

Senator (bootlid mounted lamp cluster)

36 Rotate the plastic fixings through one quarter turn and swivel open the protective cover.
37 Twist the relevant bulbholder out of the lens unit, then remove the bulb and unplug the cabling at the connector.
38 Fit the new bulb to the holder and reconnect the cabling connector. Refit the bulbholder to the lens unit and fold back the protective cover. Rotate the fixings through one quarter turn to secure the cover in position.

Number plate lamp

Carlton Saloon and Senator

39 Open the boot lid and prise off the lamp surround with a screwdriver (see illustration).
40 Remove the lamp then depress the lugs and withdraw the lens (see illustrations).
41 Depress and twist the bulb to remove it.

Carlton Estate

42 Open the tailgate. Remove the screws and withdraw the lens.
43 Release the festoon type bulb from the terminals.
44 Fit the new bulb in reverse order.

Interior lamps, luggage compartment lamp, engine compartment lamp, and glovebox lamp

45 Using a small screwdriver prise out the lamp and lens (see illustrations).
46 Prise the festoon type bulb from the terminals.
47 Fit the new bulb in reverse order.

Reading lamp

48 Using a small screwdriver prise the complete lamp from the headlining.
49 Pull out the bulbholder and extract the wedge type bulb.
50 Fit the new bulb in reverse order.

Side direction indicator repeater lamp

51 Twist and remove the lens.
52 Extract the wedge type bulb.

Instrument panel warning and illumination lights

53 Remove the instrument panel (Section 13).
54 Twist and remove the bulbholder.
55 Extract the wedge type bulb.

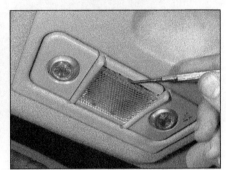
16.45b . . . to gain access to the bulb

Heater control illumination lamp

56 Remove the heater control panel as described in Chapter 3.
57 Pull the bulb from the bulbholder.

Ashtray illumination light

58 Remove the facia front panel with reference to Chapter 11.
59 Pull out the bulbholder and extract the bulb .

Passenger sunvisor vanity mirror lamp

60 Lower the sunvisor then, using a small flat-bladed screwdriver, carefully prise off the lamp cover. Remove the bulb(s).
61 Refitting is a reverse of the removal procedure.

17.3 Disconnecting the headlamp wiring plug

17.4 Disconnecting the headlamp range control wiring

17.6a Headlamp mounting bolts (arrowed) - Carlton model shown

17 Headlamp and associated components - removal and refitting

Headlamp unit - removal and refitting

Carlton

1 Remove the front direction indicator lamp (Section 18).

2 Remove the radiator grille (Chapter 11).

3 Disconnect the headlamp wiring plug **(see illustration)**.

4 On models with a headlamp range control, disconnect the wiring plug **(see illustration)**.

5 On models with a headlamp wash/wipe system the front bumper must be moved to one side. To do this, unscrew the bolt located beneath the wheel arch, unclip the wheel arch

protector, and release the bumper sideways. The wiper arm may also be removed at this stage and the washer tube disconnected.

6 Unscrew the three mounting bolts and withdraw the headlamp from the location slot **(see illustrations)**.

7 Where applicable remove the headlamp wiper motor (two screws) and the headlamp range control motor.

8 The lens and gasket may be renewed by prising off the spring clips.

9 Refitting is a reversal of removal but adjust the headlamp alignment as described in Section 19.

Senator

10 With reference to Chapter 11, remove the radiator grille and front bumper.

11 On models with a headlamp wash/wipe system, disconnect the washer tube from the jet housing.

12 Remove the two screws from the upper edge of the headlamp unit, then carefully ease the lower press stud fixings out of the clips in the rear mounting bracket **(see illustrations)**.

13 Unplug all wiring connectors from the rear of the headlamp unit, labelling them to aid refitting later.

14 If the headlamp unit is to be renewed, prise off the trim strips and transfer them to the new unit. Where applicable, remove the screws and detach the headlamp wiper motor from the headlamp unit.

15 Where applicable, refer to the relevant sub-Sections and remove the range control servo motor from the headlamp unit.

16 The lens and gasket may be renewed by prising off the spring clips.

17 Refitting is a reversal of removal; on completion, check and if necessary adjust the headlamp alignment as described in Section 19.

Headlamp wash/wipe components - removal and refitting

Wiper arm

18 Lift the spindle cover, then slacken and remove the wiper arm retaining nut **(see illustration)**. Release the arm from the spindle splines, and remove it from the vehicle.

19 Refitting is a reverse of the removal procedure, ensuring that the wiper blade is correctly positioned on the spindle splines, and its retaining nut is securely tightened.

Washer jet

20 Remove the wiper arm as described above.

21 Pull the washer jet off the wiper motor spindle, and disconnect it from the washer tubing **(see illustration)**. Tie a piece of string to the tubing, to prevent it disappearing behind the bumper.

22 Refitting is a reverse of the removal procedure.

Washer pump

23 The pump is identical to the windscreen washer pump, and can be removed and refitted using the information in Section 22.

17.6b Headlamp bottom location slot

17.12a Headlamp press stud lower fixings (arrowed)

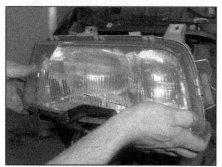

17.12b Removing the headlamp unit - Senator model shown

17.18 Removing the headlamp wiper arm

17.21 Disconnecting the headlamp washer tubing

18.5 Removing the front direction indicator unit - Senator model shown

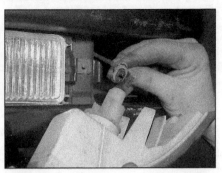

18.6 Unplug the wiring at the connector

Solenoid valve

24 Unbolt the windscreen washer reservoir from the wheel arch, emptying the contents into a suitable container.
25 Disconnect the solenoid wiring connector, then remove the solenoid from the reservoir.
26 Label the hoses, to ensure that they are correctly reconnected on refitting, then disconnect them and remove the solenoid from the vehicle.
27 Refitting is a reversal of the removal procedure, ensuring that the washer hoses are reconnected correctly. On completion, refill the reservoir with fluid.

Wiper motor assembly

28 Refer to the information given in the headlamp removal section.

Headlamp range adjustment servo - removal and refitting

Carlton

29 Remove the headlamp unit as described at the beginning of this Section.
30 Remove the cover from the rear of the headlamp unit, then release the servo pushrod from the rear of the reflector.
31 Rotate the servo housing clockwise, releasing it from its bayonet mounting and withdraw from the headlamp unit.
32 Refitting is a reversal of removal.

Senator

33 On the upper surface of the headlamp unit, fully slacken the vertical adjustment screw until the threaded section of the servo

18.13a Rear lamp cluster mounting bolts (arrowed)

connecting rod is disconnected from the lamp reflector.
34 Rotate the servo housing anticlockwise, releasing it from its bayonet mounting and extract it from the headlamp unit.
35 Refitting is a reversal of removal.

18 Exterior lamp units - removal and refitting

Headlamp units

1 Refer to Section 17.

Front direction indicator lamp - removal and refitting

Carlton

2 Remove the bulb as described in Section 27.
3 Pull back and release the spring clip, then withdraw the lamp forwards.
4 Refitting is a reversal of removal but make sure that the lamp locates correctly on the lugs.

Senator

5 Apply pressure to the outside edge of the lamp lens and carefully lever against the inner edge with a plastic instrument **(see illustration)**.
6 Swivel the lens unit away from the bodywork, then unplug the wiring at the connector **(see illustration)**.
7 Refitting is a reversal of removal; ensure

18.13b Removing the rear lamp cluster - Senator model shown

that the lugs at either end of the lamp locate in the recesses provided.

Rear lamp clusters - removal and refitting

Carlton

8 On Saloon models, open up the boot lid, then release the relevant luggage compartment trim panel to gain access to the lamp unit. Depress the two bulbholder retaining lugs, and remove the holder from the lamp unit. Undo the four retaining bolts, and remove the lamp unit from the vehicle.
9 On Estate models, from within the luggage compartment, turn the catch and open up the relevant lamp cover. Depress the retaining lugs and remove the bulbholder assembly. Undo the three retaining bolts, and remove the lamp unit from the vehicle.
10 Refitting is a reverse of the removal procedure.

Senator - wing mounted lamp cluster

11 Loosen the trim material and fold it back.
Note: *If working on the left hand side of the vehicle, it will be necessary to remove the spare wheel from its housing.*
12 Press the two lugs apart and withdraw the bulbholder.
13 Remove the mounting bolts and lift the lamp cluster away from the wing **(see illustrations)**.
14 Refitting is a reverse of the removal procedure.

Senator - bootlid mounted lamp clusters

Note: *Both the lamp clusters are integral with the bootlid trim panel and can only be renewed as a complete assembly.*
15 Extract the stud fixings and loosen the trim material from the underside of the bootlid.
16 Working inside the bootlid void, slacken and remove the screws and nuts securing the trim panel to the bootlid.
17 Disconnect the lamp cluster cabling at the multiplugs.
18 Remove the screws that secure the lamp clusters to the bootlid.
19 Slacken and withdraw the screws and lift off the number plate. Prise off the plastic cap

18.20 Removing the bootlid trim panel and lamp clusters - Senator model shown

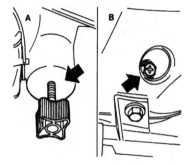

19.2a Headlamp beam adjustment knobs - models without electric range control

A Vertical adjustment
B Horizontal adjustment

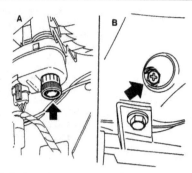

19.2b Headlamp beam adjustment knobs - models with electric range control

A Vertical adjustment
B Horizontal adjustment

and remove the trim panel mounting screw beneath.

20 Lift off the trim panel together with the lamp clusters, guiding the bootlid lock button through the aperture in the trim panel **(see illustration)**.

21 Refitting is a reverse of the removal procedure.

Front foglamps - removal and refitting

Carlton

22 Apply the handbrake, then jack up the front of the car and support on axle stands (see "*Jacking and Vehicle Support*").

23 Disconnect the wiring connector from the relevant foglamp, then slacken and remove its retaining bolts, and withdraw the lamp from the rear of the bumper.

24 Refitting is a reverse of the removal procedure.

Senator

25 Remove the adjacent direction indicator lens unit as described in Section 18.

26 Slacken and remove the foglamp lens unit retaining screw and lift out the lens unit. Prise the protective cap from the rear surface.

27 Squeeze together the tangs of the retaining clip, then twist and lift out the bulbholder.

28 Refitting is a reverse of the removal procedure.

Indicator side repeater lamps - removal and refitting

29 Where necessary, undo the mudflap retaining screws, then slacken and remove the retaining bolts from the front relevant wheel arch liner. Unclip the rear of the liner until access can be gained to the side repeater lamp wiring connector.

30 Disconnect the wiring connector, then release its retaining tabs and withdraw the lamp from the wing.

31 Refitting is a reversal of the removal procedure, ensuring that the wheel arch liner is correctly refitted and its retaining bolts are securely tightened.

19 Headlamp - beam alignment

1 Correct alignment of the headlamp beams is most important, not only to ensure good vision for the driver but also to protect other drivers from being dazzled. Accurate alignment should be carried out by a GM dealer using optical setting equipment.

2 In an emergency, adjustments may be made by turning the adjustment knobs shown **(see illustrations)**; accurate adjustment should be carried out at the first opportunity.

20 Wiper blades and arms - removal and refitting

Removal

1 To remove a blade, see '*Weekly Checks*'.

2 The wiper motor should be in its parked position before removing a wiper arm. Mark the position of the blade on the screen with adhesive tape as a guide for refitting.

3 Lift up the cover (where applicable) and unscrew the nut from the spindle **(see illustration)**. Pull the arm from the spindle.

Refitting

4 Refitting is a reversal of removal.

20.3 Removing a windscreen wiper arm

21 Windscreen wiper motor and linkage - removal and refitting

Removal

1 Remove the windscreen wiper arms as described in Section 20 .

2 Disconnect the battery negative lead.

3 Unscrew the plastic nuts securing the spindles to the windscreen valance.

4 Pull off the rubber moulding and remove the plastic water deflector.

5 Disconnect the wiring multi-plug from the motor **(see illustration)**.

6 Unbolt the motor and withdraw it together with the linkage.

Refitting

7 Refitting is a reversal of removal.

22 Windscreen washer pump - removal and refitting

Removal

1 Remove the battery as described Section 4.

2 Unbolt the windscreen washer reservoir from the wheel arch and empty its contents into a suitable container.

21.5 Windscreen wiper motor and wiring multi-plug

23.5 Tailgate wiper motor and bracket

3 Disconnect the wiring plug(s) then twist the pump slightly to remove it. Disconnect the washer hose.

Refitting

4 Refitting is a reversal of removal. Top-up the reservoir with a washer fluid solution.

23 Tailgate wiper motor - removal and refitting

Removal

1 Remove the wiper arm (see Section 20).
2 Remove the tailgate trim and, if fitted, the loudspeakers as described in Chapter 11.
3 Disconnect the battery negative lead.
4 Disconnect the wiring multi-plug from the motor. Also unscrew the earth lead screw.
5 Unbolt and remove the motor and bracket (see illustration).
6 Unbolt the motor from the bracket.

Refitting

7 Refitting is a reversal of removal.

24 Tailgate washer pump - removal and refitting

The tailgate washer pump is located in the same reservoir as the windscreen washer pump and its removal and refitting procedures are therefore as described in Section 22.

25 Central locking system - component removal and refitting

General information

1 All models are fitted with a central door locking system to allow simultaneous locking of all doors and the fuel filler cap.
2 Each lock is provided with an electrically operated servo, and an electronic control unit generates the electrical impulses needed to operate the servos.
3 The servos should operate when the locking knob or key is half way through its

travel. Adjustment is made by loosening the appropriate servo screws, repositioning the servo and tightening the screws.
4 The electronic control unit is located behind the main facia panel.

Central locking system components - removal and refitting

5 Disconnect the battery negative terminal.

Door lock servo motor - pre-1988 models

6 Remove the door trim inner panel, as described in Chapter 11.
7 Peel back the plastic water shield from the door frame, to gain access to the servo unit.
8 Slacken and remove the servo motor retaining screws, then detach it from its control rod. Disconnect the wiring connector, and remove the servo motor from the door.
9 On refitting, reconnect the wiring connector to the servo, then connect the servo to the control rod. Refit the servo unit retaining screws, tightening them finger-tight only at this stage. Adjust the servo motor as follows.
10 Using a suitable marker pen, make a mark "A" on the door locking knob control rod. Push the control rod down into the locked position, and mark the position of the mark on the control rod on the door frame "B". Pull the control rod up into the unlocked position, and again mark the position of the mark on the control rod on the door frame "C". Make a third alignment mark "D" on the door frame, exactly halfway between marks "B" and "C". Slowly move the control rod from the locked to unlocked position, while listening to servo motor switch. The switch in the servo should operate, indicated by an audible click, when the control rod is exactly halfway between the locked and unlocked position - ie when mark "A" aligns with mark "D". Adjust the position of the servo motor until this is so, then securely tighten its retaining screws.
11 Once the servo motor is correctly adjusted, refit the plastic water shield to the door frame, and install the door trim panel as described in Chapter 11.

Door lock servo motor - 1988-on models

12 On 1988-on models, remove the lock assembly as described in Chapter 11. Undo the two servo motor retaining screws, then detach the motor and remove it from the bracket.
13 On refitting, reconnect the servo motor actuating lever to its control rod, then refit its retaining screws, tightening them finger-tight only. Prior to refitting the lock assembly, adjust the servo motor position as described in the relevant following paragraph.
14 *Driver's door :* press the actuating lever firmly into the servo motor and, while holding it securely in the locked position, adjust the position of the servo motor until the lock lever abuts its stop. Hold the servo in this position, and tighten its retaining screws securely.

15 *Front passenger door:* press the actuating lever firmly into the servo motor and, while holding it securely in the locked position, adjust the position of the servo motor until there is a clearance of 2 mm (0.08 in) between the lock lever and its stop. Hold the servo motor in this position, and tighten its retaining screws securely.
16 *Rear passenger doors:* press the actuating lever firmly into the servo motor and, while holding it securely in the locked position, adjust the position of the servo motor until there is a clearance of 2 mm (0.08 in) between the lock lever and its stop. Hold the servo motor in this position, and tighten its retaining screws securely.
17 Once the servo motor is correctly adjusted, refit the lock assembly to the door as described in Chapter 11.

Boot lid/tailgate servo motor

18 Open up the boot lid or tailgate, then slacken and remove the two servo motor retaining screws. Detach the servo from its operating rod, then disconnect its wiring connector and remove the servo motor.
19 On refitting, connect the wiring connector, then engage the servo actuating lever with its operating rod. Refit the servo motor retaining screws, and tighten them by hand only at this stage. Adjust the position of the servo motor as follows.
20 Insert the key into the lock, and set the lock in the horizontal position. Slowly turn the key up and down while listening to the servo motor. The switch in the servo should operate, indicated by an audible click, when the key is at the same position on either side of the horizontal. Adjust the position of the servo motor until this is the case, then securely tighten its retaining screws.

Fuel filler cap servo motor

21 From within the luggage compartment, carefully peel back the right-hand trim panel until access to the servo motor can be gained.
22 Disconnect the wiring connector from the rear of the motor, then undo the two retaining screws and remove the motor from the vehicle.
23 Refitting is a reverse of the removal procedure.

Operating switch assembly

24 The operating switch assembly takes the form of two microswitches clipped onto the rear of the lock cylinder. There are two switches, one connected to the central locking system, and the other connected to the electric window system.
25 To remove a switch, first remove the door trim panel as described in Chapter 11.
26 Peel back the plastic water shield sufficiently to gain access to the exterior door handle.
27 Trace the wiring back from the microswitch assembly, and disconnect it at its wiring connectors. Unclip the switch assembly from the handle, and remove it from the door.

28 Refitting is a reversal of the removal procedure.

Electronic control unit

29 The central locking electronic control unit is located behind the driver's footwell right-hand side trim panel.
30 To remove the unit, peel back the rubber moulding and remove the trim panel from the right-hand side of the driver's footwell.
31 Disconnect the wiring connector, then undo the two retaining bolts and remove the control unit from the vehicle.
32 Refitting is a reversal of the removal procedure.

26 Trip computer - component removal and refitting

General information

1 A trip computer is optional equipment on some models. The computer collects fuel consumption and distance data and integrates them with respect to time. In this way it can provide estimates of fuel consumption (both instantaneous and average), average speed and range on fuel remaining. Normal time clock and stopwatch functions are available, and an external temperature sensor is also provided.
2 For detailed operating instructions, refer to the owner's handbook supplied with the vehicle.
3 Testing of the trip computer and its associated components is deemed to be beyond the scope of the average DIY mechanic.

Trip computer components - removal and refitting

4 Before attempting to remove any of the trip computer components, first disconnect the battery negative cable and position it away from the terminal.

Trip computer

Carlton
5 Remove the instrument panel as described in Chapter 12.
6 Push the trip computer out from the facia, and disconnect its wiring connector.

Senator
7 Remove the two screws and lift off the face level air vent assembly, together with the trip computer bezel and module. The screws are located above the trip computer display and between the two face level air vents.
8 Unplug the multiway connector from the rear of the trip computer module.
9 Press in the four plastic lugs and release the trip computer module from the air vent assembly.
All models
10 If a new trip computer is being installed, remove the program memory from the back of the original unit, and install it in the new computer. If the computer display bulb has failed, take the computer to a Vauxhall dealer to have the bulb renewed; a special tool is required to remove the bulb.
11 Refitting is a reverse of the removal procedure, noting that no pressure should be exerted upon the front of the computer display panel, or damage may result.

Trip computer switch

12 Remove the middle cover from the console, and disconnect the trip computer switch wiring connector. If access to the switch connector cannot be gained via the cover aperture, remove the centre console retaining screws, and lift the console slightly until the connector can be reached. Refer to Chapter 11 for further information.
13 Once the switch wiring connector has been disconnected, depress the switch retaining tangs, and remove the switch from the cover.
14 Refitting is a reversal of the removal procedure.

Outside air temperature sensor

15 The outside air temperature sensor is fitted to the underside of the front bumper. To remove the sensor, unclip it from the bumper and unplug the wiring connector.
16 Refit using a reverse of the removal procedure.

27 Cruise control components - removal and refitting

1 Before attempting to remove any of the cruise control components, first disconnect the battery negative cable and position it away from the terminal.

Regulating unit

2 The regulating unit is mounted onto the engine compartment bulkhead on Carlton models and onto the side of the left hand suspension turret on Senator models. To remove the unit, first disconnect its wiring connector **(see illustration)**.
3 Undo the three retaining screws, and release the regulating unit from the bulkhead **(see illustration)**.
4 Release the small spring clip, and detach the accelerator cable ball end from the throttle linkage. Carefully prise off the spring clip, and detach the cruise control cable from the throttle linkage.
5 Screw the adjusting screw fully into the guide piece, then unclip the guide piece from the regulating unit **(see illustration)**.
6 Slide the guide piece away from the regulating unit, and detach the cruise control cable from the regulating unit belt. Remove the regulating unit from the vehicle.
7 On refitting, attach the nipple of the cruise control cable to the regulating unit adjusting belt, then feed the adjusting belt into the guide piece, ensuring that the belt clip is correctly located in the guide piece elongated slot. Clip the guide piece into position in the regulating unit.
8 Refit the cruise control cable to the throttle linkage, and secure it in position with the spring clip. Reconnect the accelerator cable, and secure it in position with its spring clip.
9 Refit the regulating unit retaining screws, and tighten them securely. Reconnect the wiring connector.
10 Adjust the accelerator cable as described in Chapter 4, then adjust the cruise control cable as described in the next sub-Section.

Cruise control cable

11 Carry out the operations described in the previous sub-Section.

27.2 Disconnect the wiring plug from the cruise control regulator unit

27.3 Undo the three retaining screws and lift off the regulator unit

27.5 Unclip the guide piece from the regulator unit

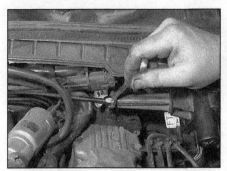

27.16 Adjusting the cruise control cable

30.1a Removing the Allen screws covering the rod removal holes

30.1b Removing the radio/cassette unit

12 Release the outer cable retaining clip from the throttle housing, and remove the cable from the engine compartment.

13 If a new cable is being fitted, unscrew the guide piece from the adjusting nut of the original cable, and screw it fully onto the adjusting nut of the new cable.

14 On refitting, clip the outer cable into position on the throttle housing, then reconnect the cable to the regulating unit as described in the previous sub-Section.

15 Adjust the accelerator cable as described in Chapter 4, then adjust the cruise control cable as follows.

16 Screw the adjusting nut out of the guide piece, until all slack is removed from the cable and the throttle linkage just starts to move **(see illustration)**. From this point, screw the adjusting nut two complete turns back into the guide piece, so that a small amount of free play exists in the cable.

Control unit

17 The control unit is located behind the glovebox, at the left-hand end of the facia.

18 To gain access to the unit, open up the glovebox, then slacken and remove the five glovebox retaining bolts. Remove the glovebox from the facia, disconnecting the wiring connectors from the illumination lamp and switch as they become accessible. Note that, on models with air conditioning, it will also be necessary to detach the cool-air hose from the rear of the glovebox.

19 Disconnect the wiring connector from the control unit, then undo its retaining screw and remove the unit through the glovebox aperture.

20 Refitting is a reversal of the removal procedure.

Operating switches

21 The cruise control operating switches are situated on the end of the left-hand steering column combination switch assembly stalk. Refer to Section 6 for details of removal and refitting.

28 Heated seats - general

1 Heated front and rear seats are optional equipment on some models. Heating elements are fitted inside the seats and controlled thermostatically.

2 In the event of malfunction, first check the wiring runs and connectors. If a heating element is proved faulty, a GM dealer should be consulted.

29 Check control system - general

1 Fitted to some higher specification models, the check control system monitors important fluid levels, brake pad wear and bulb failure. A bank of warning lights on the instrument panel conveys the information to the driver.

2 All the warning lights should come on for a few seconds when the ignition is first switched on; they should then all go out, except for the stop-lamp warning light which will go out once the brake pedal is operated. If any warning light stays on, or comes on during operation, the components or system indicated should be checked.

3 The main bulb failure indicator light monitors dipped headlights and tail lights. In brackets this light monitors the stop-lamp bulbs.

4 The check control display unit may be removed from the rear of the instrument panel by extracting three screws.

5 The bulb sensor is located behind the fusebox. If a tow bar is fitted, an additional bulb sensor is located behind the left-hand rear trim panel.

6 Sensors for the coolant and brake fluid levels are located in the relevant reservoir filler caps. A separate sensor is fitted to the washer fluid reservoir. The sensor for the engine oil level is located on the side of the sump.

30 ICE components - removal and refitting

Radio/cassette player - removal and refitting

1 The radio is manufactured to the latest DIN standard and is removed by inserting two special rods into the holes on each side of the unit. The rods are pressed in until they snap into place, then used to pull the radio out of its aperture. The rods can be obtained from a car entertainment specialist. Note that the rod holes may be covered with side covers or Allen screws **(see illustrations)**.

2 On some models the radio is automatically disconnected from the battery, aerial and loudspeakers by means of a multiple socket, however on other models separate connections are provided.

3 Where applicable the cassette storage box may be removed using the rods described in paragraph 1.

4 To remove the front loudspeakers remove the trim from the A-pillar then prise out the speakers and disconnect the wiring. Access to the rear speakers is gained from the luggage compartment on Saloon models. Removal of the door and tailgate mounted speakers is described in Chapter 11.

5 Refitting is a reversal of removal.

CD player and graphic equaliser - removal and refitting

6 Both the CD player and graphic equaliser (where fitted) can be removed using the information given in the previous sub-Section. Prior to removal, make a note of the correct fitted positions of all the wiring connectors, to help ensure that they are correctly reconnected on refitting. At the time of writing, no information was available on the boot-mounted CD autochanger fitted to later high-specification models.

Loudspeakers - removal and refitting

Front door speakers

7 Refer to the information in Chapter 11.

Facia panel speakers

8 Carefully prise the trim panel away from the relevant A-pillar, noting that the trim panels are retained by three retaining clips .

9 Prise the speaker out of the facia panel, disconnecting its wiring connectors as they become accessible.

10 Refitting is a reversal of the removal procedure, ensuring that the trim panel is clipped securely in position.

Rear speakers - Carlton Saloon and Senator models

11 Unclip the speaker cover from the rear parcel shelf.

12 Undo the four speaker retaining screws, then lift the speaker out and disconnect its wiring connectors.

13 Refitting is a reversal of the removal procedure.

Rear speakers - Carlton Estate models

14 Refer to the information in Chapter 11.

Windscreen aerial amplifier - removal and refitting

15 On models with an aerial which is built into the windscreen, an amplifier is incorporated in the aerial lead, to help boost the signal. The amplifier can be removed as follows.

16 Remove the right-hand front speaker from the facia panel as described above.

17 Remove the radio/cassette or CD player as described earlier in the this Section.

18 Trace the radio/CD player wiring back to the amplifier wiring connector, which is approximately 60 mm (2.5 in) from the main connector. Disconnect the amplifier supply wire.

19 Tie a piece of string to the radio end of the aerial lead, and disconnect the upper end of the lead from the windscreen.

20 Undo the retaining bolt, then withdraw the amplifier through the speaker aperture. Once the end of the aerial lead emerges, untie the string and leave it in position behind the facia; the string can then be used on refitting, to draw the aerial lead and amplifier wiring connector through into position in the radio aperture.

21 Refitting is a reverse of the removal.

31 Anti-theft alarm system - component removal and refitting

General information

1 From 1990 onwards, an anti-theft alarm system was fitted to all high-specification Saloon models as standard equipment, and was offered as an optional extra on most other models.

2 Great care should be taken when disturbing any of the components in the anti-theft alarm system. Incorrect refitting may lead erratic alarm operation, which compromises the vehicles security and may cause unwanted engine immobilisation. Erroneous alarm triggering may also result, causing unnecessary noise pollution.

Anti-theft alarm system components - removal and refitting

3 Before attempting to remove any components, first disconnect the battery negative cable and position it away from the terminal.

Electronic control unit

4 The electronic control unit is located behind glovebox aperture in the facia; refer to Chapter 11 and remove the glovebox from the facia.

5 Disconnect the ducting from the air vent assembly.

6 Unplug the cabling from the electronic control unit at the multiway connector.

7 Remove the retaining screws and lift the electronic control unit away from the bodywork.

8 Refitting is a reversal of the removal procedure.

Ultrasonic sensors

9 The ultrasonic sensors are mounted on the B-pillars in the cabin headlining. Unscrew the fixings at the top of the B-pillar trim panel and prise it away from the pillar slightly.

10 Unclip the sensor bezel, then lift out the sensor and unplug the wiring harness from it at the multiway connector.

11 Refitting is a reversal of the removal procedure.

Bonnet switch

12 Press in the switch housing spring clip and withdraw the switch from the wing. Unplug the wiring at the multiway connector.

13 Refitting is a reversal of the removal procedure.

32 Radio equipment - suppression of interference

1 Adequate radio interference suppression equipment is fitted during manufacture. If vehicle-generated interference is a problem, make sure first that the radio is properly trimmed (see manufacturer's instructions) and that the aerial is well earthed.

2 Radio equipment which is fitted instead of the original items may be more sensitive to interference. If not already present, the use of an in-line choke in the radio power supply, as close as possible to the receiver, is often of benefit.

3 If interference from the windscreen wiper motor is a problem, an in-line choke can be fitted to its supply leads. Make sure that the choke is of adequate current carrying capacity.

4 The ignition system is already suppressed and no further attempt should be made in that direction.

5 Consult a GM dealer or car entertainment specialist for further advice if necessary.

Key to wiring diagrams for Carlton models up to 1993

No	Description	Track
E1	LH parking light	306
E2	LH tail light	307, 505
E3	Number plate light	313
E4	RH parking light	309
E5	RH tail light	310, 507
E6	Engine compartment light	318
E7	LH high beam	337
E8	RH high beam	338
E9	LH low beam	339, 509
E10	RH low beam	340, 511
E11	Instrument lights	316
E12	Selector lever light	314
E13	Boot light	385
E15	Glovebox light	466
E16	Cigarette lighter light	463
E17	LH reversing light	436
E18	RH reversing light	437
E19	Heated rear window	458
E20	LH foglight	347
E21	RH foglight	348
E22	LH spot light	344
E23	RH spot light	345
E24	LH rear foglight	353
E25	LH heated front seat	536
E30	RH heated front seat	540
E32	Clock light	397
E33	Ashtray light	464
E37	Make-up mirror lamp	399
E38	Computer light	471
E39	RH rear foglight	354
E41	Courtesy light (with delay)	387..390
E47	LH heated rear seat	544
E48	RH heated rear seat	550
F1 to		
F26	Fuses in fusebox	various
F25	Voltage stabiliser	269
F30	Fuse (radiator fan)	231
F31	Fuse (EZV carburettor)	236
F32	Fuse (mixture preheater)	262
F33	Fuse (mixture preheater)	118
G1	Battery	101
G2	Alternator	108, 109
G3	Battery (Diesel)	183
G6	Alternator (Diesel)	184..186
H2	Horn	431, 434
H3	Turn signal warning light	378, 379
H4	Oil pressure warning light	281
H5	Handbrake/brake fluid warning light	283
H6	Hazard warning system warning light	373
H7	No-charge warning light	285
H8	Main beam warning light	336
H9	LH stop-light	362, 513
H10	RH stop-light	363, 515
H11	LH front turn signal light	374
H12	LH rear turn signal light	375
H13	RH front turn signal light	382
H14	RH rear turn signal light	383
H15	Low fuel warning light	275
H16	Preheater warning light	193
H17	Trailer turn signal warning light	370
H18	Dual horns	432
H19	Headlights on warning buzzer	394, 395
H21	Clutch/parking brake warning light	287
H23	Radio with electric aerial	762..763
H25	Mirror heater warning light	684, 694
H26	ABS warning light	574
H27	Safety check warning buzzer	756..758
H28	Seat belt warning light	758
H29	4-speed automatic warning light	443
H30	Engine warning light	148
H33	LH repeater turn signal light	377
H34	RH repeater turn signal light	380

No	Description	Track
H41	Warning light (only with LCD)	317
H44	EZV warning light	253
K1	Heated rear window relay	456..458
K2	Flasher unit	370, 371
K4	Spotlight relay	343, 344
K5	Foglight relay	348, 349
K6	Air conditioning relay	701, 702
K7	Air conditioning fan relay	702, 703
K8	Windscreen wiper intermittent relay	405..408
K9	Headlamp washer relay	412, 413
K10	Trailer flasher unit	370, 371
K14	Cruise control	747..753
K15	Fuel injection timing control	204..220
K19	Level control relay	449, 450
K21	Level control sensor	447..449
K23	Cruise control relay	743, 744
K24	Radiator fan relay	231, 232
K25	Preheater relay	193..196
K30	Rear wiper intermittent relay	426..428
K35	Heated exterior mirror delay relay	697..699
K37	Central locking relay	606..611
K45	Mixture preheater relay	117, 118, 261, 262
K47	Over-voltage protection relay	570, 571
K48	ABS pump relay	576..579
K49	ABS solenoid valve relay	585..588
K50	ABS timing control	577..590
K51	Auxiliary radiator fan relay	732, 733
K53	Timing control (EV 61)	124..131
K54	Carburettor control unit (EZV)	238..258
K55	Carburettor relay (EZV)	236, 237
K56	Automatic kick-down control unit	440..444
K59	Day running light relay	319..325
K60	Compressor relay	706..707
K61	Control unit (Motronic)	138..173
K62	Control unit (dim-dip lights)	328..332
K63	Dual horn relay	432, 433
K65	LH seat heating relay	544..546
K66	RH seat heating relay	550..552
K67	Radiator fan relay	735, 736
K68	Fuel injection relay	175..179, 224, 228
K72	Engine revolution relay	113..115
K73	Ignition module (EZ 61)	121, 122
L3	Ignition coil (inductive sensor)	134, 135, 256, 257
L4	Ignition coil (inductive sensor, EZ 61)	122, 123
M1	Starter motor	105, 106
M2	Windscreen wiper motor	403..406
M3	Heater fan motor	293..296
M4	Radiator fan motor	231
M5	Washer pump	402
M6	LH headlight wiper motor	415..417
M7	RH headlight wiper motor	419..421
M8	Rear window wiper motor	424..426
M9	Rear window washer pump	429
M10	Air conditioning fan motor	710..713
M11	Auxiliary radiator fan motor	733
M12	Starter motor (Diesel)	190, 191
M13	Sunroof motor	488..491
M14	LH front door window motor	668..670
M15	RH front door window motor	673..675
M18	Front door locking motor	606..609
M19	LH rear door locking motor	617..619
M20	RH rear door locking motor	621..623
M21	Fuel pump	175, 224
M22	Level control compressor	450
M26	Electric aerial motor	761, 762
M30	LH exterior mirror adjustment and heating	679..682, 688..691
M31	RH exterior mirror adjustment and heating	694..697
M32	Front door locking motor	612..615
M33	Idle control unit	157, 158
M34	ABS return pump	574
M35	Auxiliary radiator fan relay	738

Key to wiring diagrams for Carlton models up to 1993 (continued)

No	Description	Track
M37	Bootlid/tailgate locking motor	625..628
M39	LH headlight levelling motor	558..560
M40	RH headlight levelling motor	562..564
M41	Fuel filler cap locking motor	630, 631
M42	Air conditioning actuator	717..721
M47	LH front electric window motor	635..639
M48	RH front electric window motor	653..657
M49	LH rear electric window motor	641..645
M50	RH rear electric window motor	659..663
P1	Fuel gauge	273
P2	Temperature gauge	271
P3	Clock	396
P4	Fuel sensor	273
P5	Temperature sensor	271
P7	Tachometer	276
P10	Oil pressure sensor	787
P11	Airflow meter	156..160
P12	Temperature probe (coolant)	146, 216
P13	Outside air temperature sensor	476, 477
P15	Fuel flowmeter	469, 470
P17	LH front wheel sensor (ABS)	582, 583
P18	RH front wheel sensor (ABS)	584, 585
P19	LH rear wheel sensor (ABS)	586, 587
P20	RH rear wheel sensor (ABS)	588, 589
P21	Instrument optical frequency sensor	278, 279
P24	Oil temperature sensor	128, 129
P25	Bulb test sensor	505..517
P27	LH front brake lining sensor	523
P28	RH front brake lining sensor	523
P29	Inlet manifold temperature sensor	243, 244
P30	Coolant temperature sensor	246, 247
P31	Main throttle potentiometer	245, 247
P32	Heated Lambda sensor	170, 171
P35	Crankshaft inductive sensor	125..127, 165..167, 255..257
P39	Trailer bulb test sensor	518, 520
R2	Carburettor preheater	111, 260
R3	Cigarette lighter	461
R5	Glow plugs	197
R7	Mixture preheater	118..120, 262
R13	LH heated washer jet	409
R14	RH heated washer jet	410
R15	Resistor	130, 131, 147
S1	Starter motor switch	105, 106, 190, 191
S2	Light switch assembly	
S2.1	Light switch	305..308, 506, 507
S2.2	Courtesy light switch	389
S2.3	Instrument lights dimmer	315, 776
S3	Heater fan switch	291..297
S4	Heated rear window switch	454..457
S5	Turn signal switch assembly	
S5.2	Headlight dip switch	338, 339, 511
S5.3	Turn signal switch	381..383
S5.4	Parking light switch	301..303
S5.5	Horn switch	433
S7	Reversing light switch	436
S8	Stop-light switch	362, 513
S9	Windscreen wiper switch assembly	
S9.2	Windscreen wiper switch (intermittent)	402..406
S9.3	Rear window wiper switch (intermittent)	427, 428
S10	Automatic transmission switch	
S10.1	Automatic transmission switch	106
S10.2	Reversing light switch	437
S10.4	Speed telltale switch	793..799
S11	Brake fluid level switch	283
S12	Clutch control switch	286
S13	Handbrake warning light switch	287
S14	Oil pressure switch	281
S15	Boot light switch	385
S17	LH courtesy light switch	390
S18	Glovebox light switch	466
S21	Foglight switch	349..351
S22	Rear foglight switch	354, 356

No	Description	Track
S24	Air conditioning fan switch	707..714
S27	Pressure switch	727
S28	Compressor cut-off switch	727
S29	Radiator fan switch	232, 732
S30	LH front heated door switch	536..538
S31	LH rear door courtesy light switch	391
S32	RH rear door courtesy light switch	392
S35	Sunroof micro switch	488
S36	Sunroof micro switch	490
S37	Electric window switch assembly	636..662
S37.1	LH front electric window switch	636..638
S37.2	RH front electric window switch	654..656
S37.3	LH rear electric window switch	662..644
S37.4	RH rear electric window switch	660..662
S37.5	Safety switch	640
S37.6	Anti-jamming switch	658
S37.7	Electronic control	645..648
S39	LH rear door window motor switch	602..604
S40	RH rear door window motor switch	664..666
S41	RH anti-theft lock switch	602..604
S42	LH central locking switch	605
S43	Cruise control switch	747..750
S44	Throttle valve switch	142, 143, 204, 205
S45	Cruise control clutch switch	741, 742
S47	Doors open/headlamps on warning switch	393, 394
S52	Hazard light switch	371..376
S53	LH front electric window switch	668..671
S55	RH front seat heating switch	540..542
S57	Sunroof switch	487..491
S63	Board computer switch assembly	474..478
S63.1	Function reset switch	475
S63.2	Clock hour adjustment switch	476
S63.3	Function selection switch	477
S63.5	Clock minute adjustment switch	478
S68	Exterior mirror switch	
S68.1	Exterior mirror adjustment switch	678..681, 686..690
S68.2	Exterior mirror heater switch	683, 684, 692, 693
S73	Temperature switch	117
S76	Compressor pressure switch	731
S78	RH front window motor switch	673..676
S81	Brake fluid low level switch	525
S82	Washer fluid low level switch	524
S87	4-speed automatic switch	441
S89	Seat belt switch	756
S93	Coolant low level switch	526
S95	Engine oil low level switch	527
S96	LH rear seat heating switch	546..548
S97	RH rear seat heating switch	552..554
S98	Headlight levelling switch	557..559
S99	RH front window switch (2V)	650
S100	LH front window switch (2V)	651
S101	Compressor switch	727..729
S102	Circulation switch	723..725
S109	Motronic compressor pressure switch	730
S111	Fuel cut-off vacuum switch	115
U2	Board computer	470..481
U4	ABS system	574..588
U5	Check control display assembly	521..530
U5.1	Tail light and low beam warning light	522
U5.2	Brake light warning light	523
U5.3	Low oil level warning light	525
U5.5	Low front brake lining warning light	526
U5.6	Low washer fluid warning light	528
U5.7	Low coolant level warning light	529
U6	LCD instrument assembly	771..798
U6.1	Charging indicator light	781
U6.2	Voltmeter	782..784
U6.3	Fuel indicator	782
U6.4	Oil pressure warning light	785
U6.5	Oil pressure gauge	787
U6.6	Coolant temperature indicator	790
U6.8	Speedometer	772

Key to wiring diagrams for Carlton models up to 1993 (continued)

No	Description	Track	No	Description	Track
U6.14	Tachometer	786	Y5	Diesel solenoid valve	199
U6.22	Display lights	775, 776	Y6	Auxiliary air slide valve	221, 222
U6.26	Automatic transmission lever display	793..798	Y7	Fuel injection solenoid valve	160..167, 207..214
U7	Air conditioning adjustment unit	716..721	Y8	Cruise control actuator	747..753
U7.1	Temperature selector lever potentiometer	716	Y9	Level control solenoid	451
U7.2	Demister lever limit switch	718, 719	Y19	LH front ABS solenoid	581
U7.3	Electronic control	716..721	Y20	RH front ABS solenoid	583
V1	Brake fluid test bulb diode	284, 779	Y21	Rear axle ABS solenoid	582
V3	ABS solenoid valve diode	587	Y26	Throttle valve positioner	236..242
V8	Compressor diode	728	Y27	Pre-throttle valve	250, 251
X1	Trailer socket	various	Y33	Distributor	125, 136, 258
X5 to			Y34	Tank ventilation valve	177
X15E	Connectors	various	Y35	Circulation valve	723
Y1	Air conditioning compressor	727	Y39	Fuel cut-off solenoid valve	114
Y4	Headlight washer solenoid valve	413	Y40	4-speed automatic transmission	442, 444

Not all items are fitted to all models

Colour code

BL	Blue
BR	Brown
GE	Yellow
GN	Green
GR	Grey
HBL.	Light blue
LI	Lilac
RT	Red
SW	Black
VI	Violet
WS	White

Abbreviations

ABS	Anti-lock brake system		M 1.5	Motronic M 1.5
AC	Air conditioning		M 2.5	Motronic M 2.5
AT	Automatic transmission		MOT	Motronic in general
ATC	Automatic temperature control		MT	Manual transmission
AZV	Trailer hitch		N	Norway
BR	On-board computer		NS	Foglights
CC	Check control		NSL	Rear foglights
D	Diesel		OEL	Oil level control (oil pressure)
DS	Theft protection		OPT	Optional equipment
DWA	Anti-theft warning system		P/N	Park/Neutral (automatic transmission)
DZM	Tachometer		PBSL	Park and brake shift block
EFC	Electric folding roof, convertible		POT	Potentiometer
EKS	Pinch guard (electric windows)		RC	Electric ride control
EMP	Radio		RHD	Right-hand drive
EUR	Euronorm engine		S	Sweden
EZ +	EI Plus with self-diagnosis		SD	Sliding roof
EZV	Ecotronic		SH	Seat heating
FH	Window winders		SRA	Headlight cleaning system
GB	Great Britain		TANK	Fuel gauge
HS	Rear screen		TD	Turbodiesel
HW	Rear screen wiper		TEMP	Temperature gauge
HZG	Heating		TFL	Daytime driving light
HRL	Luggage compartment light		TKS	Door contact switch
INS	Instrument		TSZI	Transistor ignition (inductive)
IRL	Interior light		VGS	Carburettor
KAT	Catalytic converter		WEG	Odometer frequency sensor
KBS	Wiring harness		WHR	Car level control
KV	Contact distributor		WS	Warning buzzer
L3.1	Jetronic L3.1		ZV	Central door locking
LCD	LCD instrument		ZYL	Cylinder
LHD	Left-hand drive		4WD	Four wheel drive
LWR	Headlight range control			

Wiring identification

eg GE WS 1.5

GE	Basic colour
WS	Identification colour
1.5	Section (mm²)

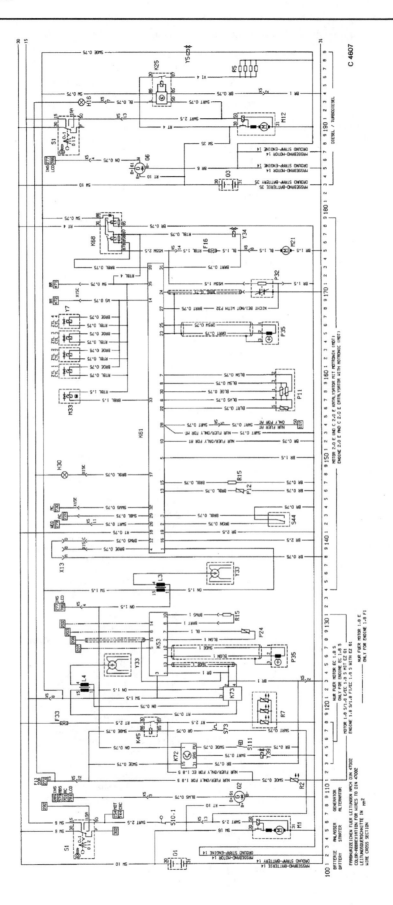

Wiring diagram for Carlton models up to 1993

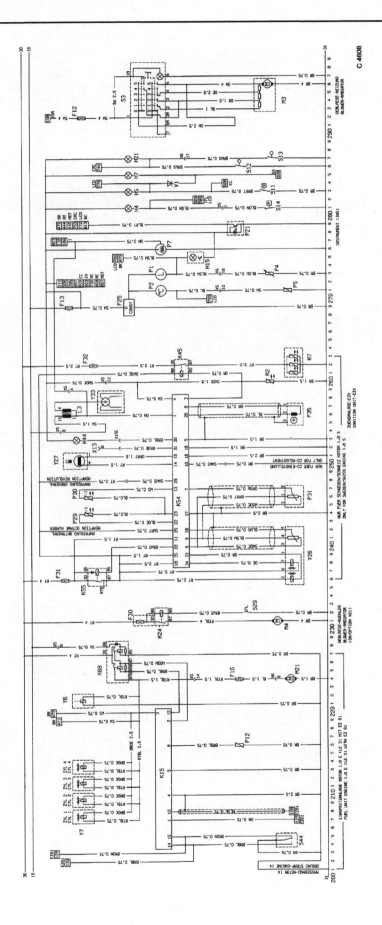

Wiring diagram for Carlton models up to 1993 (continued)

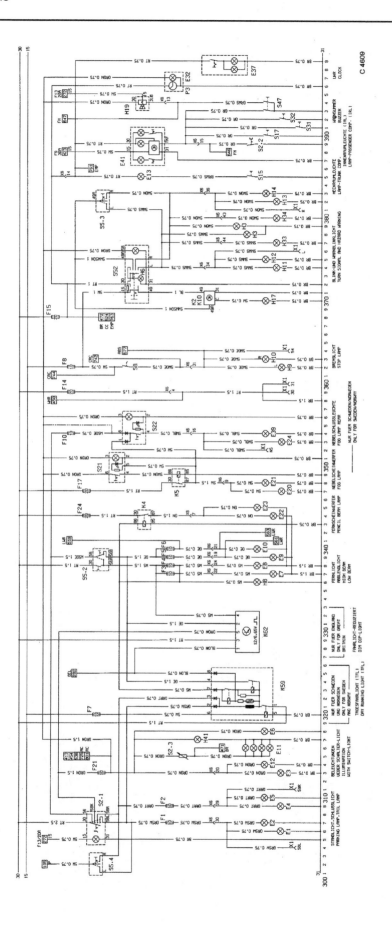

Wiring diagram for Carlton models up to 1993 (continued)

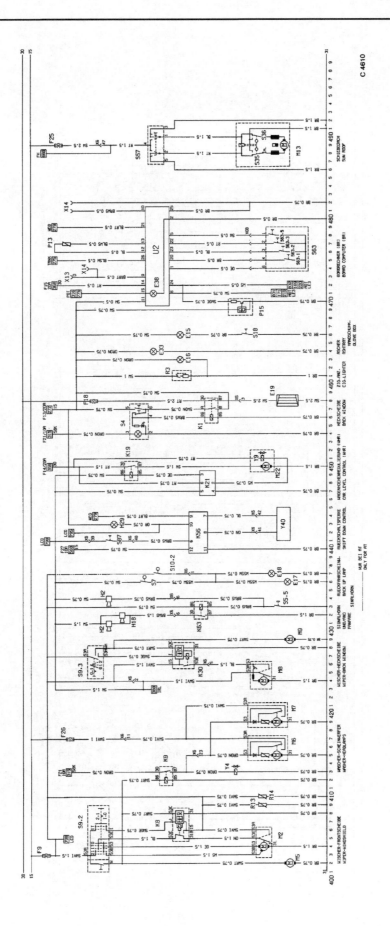

Wiring diagram for Carlton models up to 1993 (continued)

C 4610

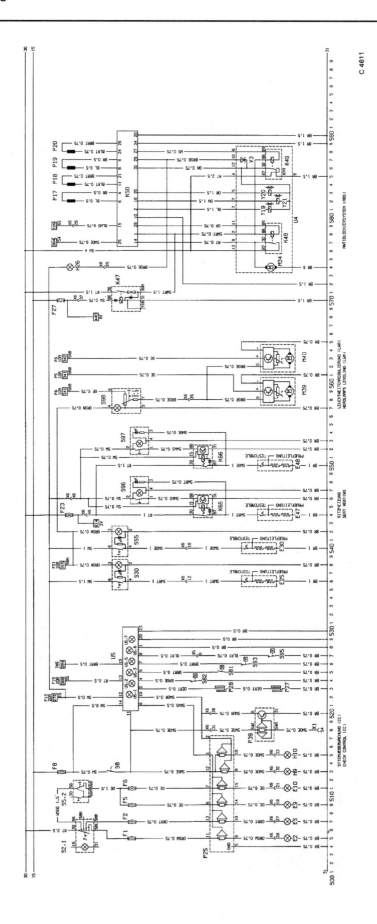

C 4611

Wiring diagram for Carlton models up to 1993 (continued)

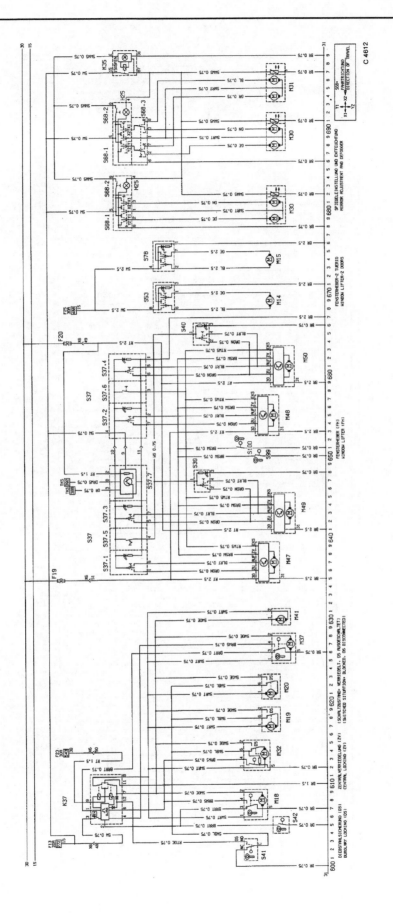

Wiring diagram for Carlton models up to 1993 (continued)

C 4612

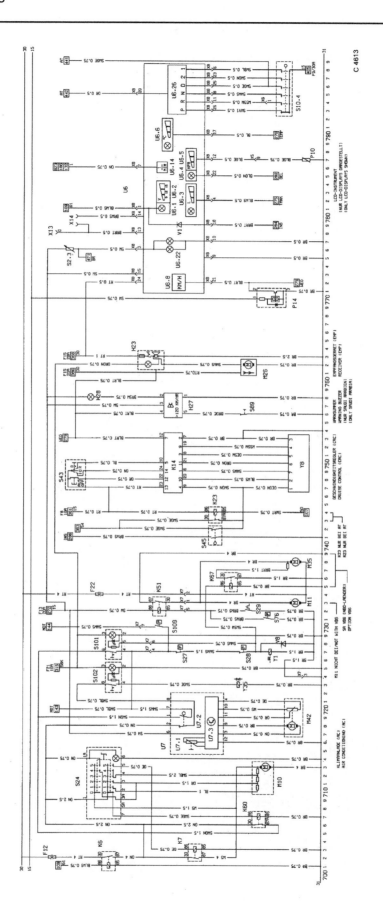

Wiring diagram for Carlton models up to 1993 (continued)

Key to wiring diagrams for Carlton models from 1993

No	Description	Track
E1	Sidelight, left	302
E2	Tail light, left	303, 502, 533
E3	Number plate light	311, 316, 318
E4	Sidelight, right	309
E5	Tail light, right	308, 504, 535
E6	Engine compartment light	320
E7	Main beam, left	337
E8	Main beam, right	339
E9	Dipped beam, left	338, 506, 537
E10	Dipped beam, right	340, 508, 539
E11	Instrument lighting	877
E12	Selector lever lighting (auto. trans.)	233, 447
E13	Luggage compartment light	383
E15	Glovebox light	469
E16	Cigarette lighter illumination	467
E17	Reversing light, left	436
E18	Reversing light, right	437
E19	Heated rear window	663, 833
E20	Foglight, left	347
E21	Foglight, right	348
E22	Headlight main beam, left	344
E23	Headlight main beam, right	342
E24	Foglight, rear, left	352
E25	Heating mat – front seat, left	551
E30	Heating mat – front seat, right	555
E32	Light – clock	399
E33	Light – ashtray	468
E37	Light – make-up mirror, left	385,
E38	Light – on-board computer	474
E39	Foglight, rear, right	354
E40	Light – make-up mirror, right	387
E41	Interior light, delayed switch-off	389..391
E47	Heating mat – rear seat, left	559
E48	Heating mat – rear seat, right	565
E61	Number plate light, left (Japan)	313
E62	Number plate light, right (Japan)	314
F1-F28	Fuses (in fusebox)	various
F31	Fuse – radiator cooling fan	126
F34	Fuse – radiator cooling fan	757
F35	Voltage stabilizer	880
F37	Fuse – water pump	779
F38	Fuse – anti-theft warning unit	635
F42	Fuse – radiator cooling fan (maxi)	749, 768
F47	Fuse – air conditioning (maxi)	702
G1	Battery	101
G2	Alternator	114..116
H1	Radio	820..836
H3	Warning light – direction indicator light	874, 875
H4	Warning light – oil pressure	892
H5	Warning light – brake fluid	894
H6	Warning light – hazard warning system	373
H7	Charging indicator light	896
H8	Warning light – main beam	893
H9	Stop-light, left	362, 510, 541
H10	Stop-light, right	364, 512, 543
H11	Direction indicator light, front, left	374
H12	Direction indicator light, rear, left	375
H13	Direction indicator light, front, right	380
H14	Direction indicator light, rear, right	381
H15	Warning light – fuel	887
H16	Warning light – glow time (diesel)	868
H17	Warning light – trailer direction indicators	871
H18	Trumpet horn	431
H19	Buzzer – headlights-on warning (in fusebox)	396, 397
H21	Warning light – clutch & handbrake	897
H25	Warning light – mirror heating	207, 654
H26	Warning light – ABS	866
H27	Warning buzzer – safety checking	815..817
H28	Warning light – seat belt warning	867
H30	Warning light – engine	870
H33	Direction indicator repeater light, left	377
H34	Direction indicator repeater light, right	378

No	Description	Track
H37	Loudspeaker – front left	821, 824
H38	Loudspeaker – front right	825, 828
H39	Loudspeaker – rear left	821, 822
H40	Loudspeaker – rear right	824, 825
H41	Warning light – lights	861
H42	Warning light – automatic transmission	869
H46	Warning light – catalytic conv. temperature	872
H47	Siren – anti-theft warning unit	635
H48	Trumpet horn	432
H52	Loudspeaker – door, front left	822, 823
H53	Loudspeaker – door, front right	826, 827
K3	Relay – starter, anti-theft warning unit	111, 112
K4	Relay – headlights, main beam	343, 344
K5	Relay – foglights	347, 348
K6	Relay – air conditioning	701, 702
K7	Relay – blower, air conditioning	702, 703
K8	Relay – windscreen intermittent wipe	405..408
K9	Relay – headlight washer unit	412, 413
K10	Flasher unit	370, 371
K14	Cruise control	806..812
K19	Relay – car level control	453, 454, 460, 461
K21	Sensor – car level control	451..453, 458..460
K23	Relay – cruise control	802, 803
K24	Relay – blower, radiator	126, 127
K30	Relay – tailgate intermittent wipe	426..428
K35	Relay – time delay, heated rear window & mirrors	657..660
K37	Control unit – central locking	602..610
K41	Control unit – power steering	485..488
K47	Relay – over-voltage protection (ABS)	581, 582
K50	Timing control – ABS	586..599
K51	Relay – radiator cooling fan	748, 749, 759, 760
K52	Relay – radiator cooling fan	763..765
K56	Control unit – kickdown control	440..445
K59	Relay – day running lights	321..327
K61	Control unit – Motronic	133..162, 261..295
K63	Relay – trumpet horn (in fusebox)	432, 433
K64	Relay – blower, air conditioning stage 1	715, 716
K65	Relay – heating mat, rear left	559..561
K66	Relay – heating mat, rear right	565..567
K67	Relay – radiator cooling fan	752, 753, 767, 768
K68	Relay – fuel injection unit	163..167, 296..299
K81	Relay – water pump	779..782
K85	Control unit – automatic transmission	235..259
K86	Control unit – check control	526..547
K87	Relay – radiator cooling fan	756, 757
K88	Control unit – catalytic conv. temperature	223..225
K90	Relay – compressor (auto. trans.)	741, 742
K93	Relay – compressor (C30SE)	742, 743
K94	Control unit – anti-theft warning unit	630..644
K101	Relay – exterior mirror, parking position	217..220
K102	Control unit – handbrake shift lock	229..231
L1	Ignition coil	133, 268
M1	Starter	105, 106
M2	Motor – windscreen wiper	403..406
M3	Motor – heater blower	787..790
M4	Motor – radiator cooling fan	126, 780
M5	Windscreen washer pump	402
M6	Motor – headlight wiper, left	415..417
M7	Motor – headlight wiper, right	418..420
M8	Motor – tailgate wiper	424..426
M9	Tailgate washer pump	429
M10	Motor – blower, air conditioning	709..712
M11	Motor – radiator cooling fan	749, 752, 757
M13	Motor – sunroof	795..798
M18	Motor – central locking, driver's door	603..606
M19	Motor – central locking, rear left door	618..620
M20	Motor – central locking, rear right door	622..624
M21	Fuel pump	171
M22	Compressor – car level control	454, 461
M26	Motor – electric aerial	836..838
M30	Exterior mirror – driver's side	649..652

Key to wiring diagrams for Carlton models from 1993 (continued)

No	Description	Track
M31	Exterior mirror – passenger's side	655..658
M32	Motor – central locking, passenger's door	611..614
M33	Actuator – idle speed	151, 152, 278, 279
M35	Motor – radiator cooling fan	765
M37	Motor – central locking, bootlid/tailgate	615..618
M39	Motor – headlight levelling, left	572..575
M40	Motor – headlight levelling, right	576..579
M41	Motor – fuel filler flap, central locking	622, 624
M42	Actuator – air conditioning	720..724
M47	Motor – electric window, driver's door	667..671
M48	Motor – electric window, passenger's door	685..689
M49	Motor – electric window, rear left	673..677
M50	Motor – electric window, rear right	691..695
M57	Water pump	422, 782
M62	Exterior mirror – driver's side	203..209
M63	Exterior mirror – passenger's side	212..218
P1	Fuel gauge	885
P2	Water temperature gauge	883
P3	Clock	398
P4	Sensor – fuel	852, 885
P5	Sensor – coolant temperature	859, 883
P7	Tachometer	888
P10	Sensor – oil pressure	852
P11	Airflow meter	145..149
P12	Coolant temperature sensor	136, 267
P13	Sensor – outside air temperature	478
P14	Sensor – distance (WEG)	841, 842
P17	Sensor – ABS, front left	592
P18	Sensor – ABS, front right	594
P19	Sensor – ABS, rear left	596
P20	Sensor – ABS, rear right	598
P21	Sensor – distance (WEG)	890, 891
P25	Sensor – bulb test	501..514
P27	Sensor – brake lining, front left	519, 530
P28	Sensor – brake lining, front right	519, 530
P32	Sensor – (heated), oxygen in exhaust gas	161, 162, 294, 295
P34	Potentiometer – throttle valve	141..143, 268..270
P35	Impulse sensor – crankshaft	156..158, 289..291
P39	Sensor – bulb test, trailer	515, 517, 546..548
P46	Sensor – knock control	281, 282
P47	Sensor – cylinder identification	285..287
P50	Temperature sensor – catalytic converter	224, 225
P51	Sensor – speed	242, 243
P52	Airflow meter	271..274
P53	Sensor – anti-theft unit, driver's side	636..644
P54	Sensor – anti-theft unit, passenger's side	636..644
P56	Sensor – knock control	283, 284
P57	Aerial	836
P58	Pane breakage sensor, rear left – anti-theft unit (KW)	644
P59	Pane breakage sensor, rear right – anti-theft unit (KW)	645
R3	Cigarette lighter	466
R13	Washer nozzle – heated, left	409
R14	Washer nozzle – heated, right	410
R19	Pre-resistor – radiator cooling fan	752
S1	Starter switch assembly	103..106
S1.2	Switch – key contact (Japan)	833
S2	Light switch assembly	
S2.1	Light switch	305..308
S2.2	Interior light switch	391
S2.3	Instrument light dimmer	846, 876
S3	Heater fan switch	785..791
S4	Switch – heated rear window & mirrors	663..665
S5	Direction indicator switch assembly	
S5.2	Switch – dipped beam	338, 339
S5.3	Switch – direction indicators	379..381
S5.4	Switch – sidelights	301..303
S5.5	Switch – horn	433
S7	Switch – reversing lights	486
S8	Switch – stop-lights	362
S9	Wiper switch assembly	
S9.2	Windscreen intermittent wipe switch	402..406

No	Description	Track
S9.3	Tailgate intermittent wipe switch	427, 428
S10	Switch assembly – auto. transmission (AW71L)	
S10.1	Switch – park/neutral	106
S10.4	Switch – selector lever position	441..445
S11	Control switch – brake fluid	894
S12	Control switch – clutch	899
S13	Switch – handbrake	897
S14	Switch – oil pressure	854, 892
S15	Switch – boot light	383
S17	Contact switch – passenger's door	392
S18	Switch – glovebox light	469
S21	Switch – foglight	348..350
S22	Switch – foglight, rear	353, 356
S24	Switch – blower, air conditioning	706..713
S27	Switch – compressor, low pressure	736, 775
S28	Switch – compressor, high pressure	736, 775
S29	Switch – coolant temperature	127, 746, 779
S30	Switch – heating mat, front seat, left	551..553
S31	Contact switch – rear left door	393
S32	Contact switch – rear right door	394
S35	Micro-switch – sunroof	795
S36	Micro-switch – sunroof	797
S37	Switch assembly – electric windows	
S37.1	Switch – electric window, driver's door	668..670
S37.2	Switch – electric window, passenger's door	686..688
S37.3	Switch – electric window, rear left	674..676
S37.4	Switch – electric window, rear right	692..694
S37.5	Safety switch	672
S37.6	Switch – anti-jam off (elec. window pinch guard off)	690
S37.7	Control – automatic, electric window	677..680
S39	Switch – electric window, rear left door	678..680
S40	Switch – electric window, rear right door	696..698
S41	Switch – anti-theft locking, driver's door	600..602
S42	Switch – central locking, passenger's door	609
S43	Switch – cruise control	806..809
S45	Switch – clutch, cruise control	800, 801
S47	Contact switch – driver's door 2-pin	395, 396
S51	Switch – temperature, coolant (compressor)	773
S52	Switch – hazard warning	371..376
S55	Switch – heating mat, front seat, right	555..557
S57	Switch – sunroof	793..799
S63	Switch assembly – on-board computer	
S63.1	Switch – function reset	477
S63.2	Switch – hour adjustment, clock	478
S63.3	Switch – function select	479
S63.5	Switch – minute adjustment, clock	480
S68	Switch assembly – exterior mirror	
S68.1	Switch – exterior mirror adjustment	201..205, 647..652
S68.3	Switch – exterior mirror, left/right	201..206, 647..652
S68.4	Switch – exterior mirror, parking position	207, 208
S76	Switch – compressor, high pressure (blower)	748, 778
S82	Control switch – washer fluid, min. capacity	521, 526
S87	Switch – 4-speed automatic	445
S89	Switch – seat belt	815
S93	Control switch – coolant, min. capacity	522, 527
S95	Control switch – engine oil, min. capacity	523, 528
S96	Switch – heating mat, rear seat, left	561..563
S97	Switch – heating mat, rear seat, right	567..569
S98	Switch – headlight levelling	571..573
S99	Switch – electric window, driver's door	672
S100	Switch – electric window, passenger's door	684
S101	Switch – compressor	734, 736
S102	Switch – circulation	728..730
S104	Switch – kickdown	240
S105	Switch – Winter mode (auto. transmission)	234..236
S106	Switch – Economy/Sport mode (auto. trans.)	238
S109	Switch – compressor (Motronic)	741
S116	Switch – stop-light (AR25 auto. trans.)	365, 366
S118	Switch – automatic transmission	237..240
S120	Switch – bonnet	631
S128	Switch – coolant temperature	744, 745
U2	On-board computer	471..482

Key to wiring diagrams for Carlton models from 1993 (continued)

No	Description	Track
U4	Hydraulic unit assembly – ABS	584..597
U4.1	Relay – ABS pump	585..588
U4.2	Relay – solenoid valves, ABS	594..597
U4.3	Pump – ABS hydraulic unit	584
U4.4	Diode – ABS hydraulic unit	596
U4.5	Solenoid valve – ABS, front left	590
U4.6	Solenoid valve – ABS, front right	592
U4.7	Solenoid valve – ABS, rear left	591
U5	Display assembly – check control system	
U5.1	Warning light – washer fluid, min. capacity	526
U5.2	Warning light – engine oil, min. capacity	527
U5.3	Warning light – coolant, min. capacity	528
U5.4	Warning light – tail light & dipped beam	529
U5.5	Warning light – stop-light failure	530
U5.6	Warning light – brake lining, front	531
U6	LCD instrument assembly	
U6.1	Charging indicator light	852
U6.2	Voltmeter	853
U6.3	Fuel gauge	852
U6.4	Warning light – oil pressure	854
U6.5	Oil pressure gauge	856
U6.6	Water temperature gauge	859
U6.8	Speedometer	843
U6.14	Tachometer	857
U6.22	Warning lights	846..848
U6.26	Selector lever indicator, auto. transmission	861..864
U6.30	Warning light – washer fluid, min. capacity	517
U6.31	Warning light – engine oil, min. capacity	518
U6.32	Warning light – coolant, min. capacity	519
U6.33	Warning light – tail light & dipped beam	521
U6.34	Warning light – stop-light failure	522
U6.35	Warning light – brake lining, front	523
U7	Air conditioning unit assembly	
U7.1	Potentiometer – temperature selector	719
U7.2	Limit switch – defroster lever	721
U7.3	Control unit – electronic	718..724
U10	Transmission assembly – 4-speed automatic	
U10.1	Pressure switch – 4-speed automatic	443
U10.2	Solenoid valve – 4-speed automatic	445
U13	Main automatic transmission housing	
U13.1	Solenoid valve – 2/3 shift	245
U13.3	Solenoid valve – 1/2/3/4 shift	246
U13.3	Solenoid valve – brake band	247
U14	Intermediate automatic transmission housing	
U14.1	Solenoid valve – converter clutch	250
U14.2	Temperature sensor – transmission fluid	251
U14.3	Solenoid valve – hydraulic pressure regulator	252
U17	Amplifier – aerial, roof (caravan)	830
U18	Amplifier – aerial, rear window	832..834
U19	Amplifier – windscreen aerial	828
V1	Diode – brake fluid level tester	850, 895
V8	Diode – compressor	735, 777
X	Connectors and multi-plugs	
X1	Trailer socket – 7-pin	304, 306, 357..360, 376, 379, 517, 548
X4	Instrument panel & air conditioning 3-pin (D)	775..778
X5	Instrument panel & engine 7-pin/ 14-pin (D)	106..116, 523, 528, 782, 854..859, 883, 892
X6	Instrument panel & body 51-pin	171, 231..238, 231..238, 302, 309, 315, 337..362, 374..396, 415, 417, 424, 426, 432, 437, 443..445, 502..517, 533..561, 572, 581..586, 663, 667, 696, 796, 837, 852, 885, 897
X6A	Instrument panel & body 6-pin	476..480, 640
X6C	Instrument panel & door 4-pin	486, 632, 658
X6D	Body & door 6-pin (ZV)	615..618, 678, 679
X7	Instrument panel & air conditioning 7-pin	702, 735..760
X8	Instrument panel & LCD instrument 26-pin	842..864
X9	Instrument panel & LCD instrument 26-pin (CC)	517..523

No	Description	Track
X10	Code countries 6-pin	312, 313, 351, 354
X11	Instrument panel & temperature sensor 2-pin	224, 225
X12	Code anti-theft warning unit 4-pin	634
X13	Diagnostic link 10-pin	145, 146, 252, 264, 265, 368, 371, 481, 482, 632, 633, 849, 850
X15	Octane plug 3-pin	138, 139
X16	Instrument panel & Motronic 26-pin	145..149, 169, 235..265, 272..275, 471, 472, 860, 882
X17	Instrument panel & instrument 14-pin	874..897
X18	Instrument panel & instrument 16-pin	861,866..872
X20	Door & driver's door 24-pin	201..214, 600..606, 650..657, 667..671, 822, 823
X21	Door & passenger's door 24-pin	211..218, 609..614, 655..658, 685..689, 826, 827
X22	Door & rear door, left 11-pin	618..620, 673..680
X23	Door & rear door, right 11-pin	622..624, 691..698
X24	Body & tailgate 5-pin (KW)	615..618
X25	Body & bootlid 6-pin	314, 615..618
X26	Body & tailgate 3-pin (KW)	317, 425, 426
X27	Body & car level control 3-pin	450..454
X28	Body & car level control 6-pin	458..461
X29	Car level control & height sensor 5-pin	450..460
X30	Motronic & switch – auto. transmission 8-pin	237..242
X31	Instrument panel & switch – automatic transmission (AW71L) 5-pin	106, 441, 445
X32	Air conditioning & engine 1-pin	778
X33	Engine & blower 3-pin	779..782
X34	Motronic & fuel injection sol. valves 3-pin	285..289
X35	Motronic & fuel inj. valves (C26NE) 15-pin	860, 882
X36	Motronic & engine (C24NE) 1-pin	858, 884
X37	Body & water pump 3-pin	421, 422
X40	Body & console 8-pin	231..238, 436, 443..447
X41	Body & loudspeaker, rear 4-pin (KW)	821..825
X42	Instrument panel & cruise control (AR25 automatic transmission) 4-pin	802, 803
X43	Instrument panel & body 6-pin	644, 821..826
X44	Body & loudspeaker, rear 6-pin (limousine)	821..826, 837
X45	Door & console 5-pin	558,562
X46	Door & console 8-pin	668..679
X47	Door & console 7-pin	685..694
X48	Instrument panel & switch – auto trans. 5-pin	443
X49	Body & trailer socket 9-pin	304, 306, 357..360, 376, 379, 517, 548
X50	Motronic & automatic transmission 10-pin	242..253
X51	Instrument panel 16-pin	533..547
X52	Instrument panel 26-pin	526..537, 546
X53	Instrument panel & compressor 5-pin	774..778
X54	Instrument panel & instrument 8-pin (CC)	526..532
X55	Instrument panel & door 4-pin	822..827
X66	Driver's door & switch – ext. mirror 9-pin	201..208, 647..654
X67	Instrument panel & Jetronic 5-pin	
X68	Instrument panel & door 9-pin	631, 633, 636..644
X69	Instrument panel & radio 16-pin	820..836
X70	Door & sensor – anti-theft unit 4-pin	636..639
X71	Door & sensor – anti-theft unit 4-pin	641..644
X72	Motronic & automatic transmission 2-pin	245, 246
X73	Instrument panel & kickdown sw. 4-pin (LHD)	240
X75	Instrument panel & warning buzzer 2-pin	816, 817
X76	Instrument panel & Motronic 2-pin	135, 136, 268, 270
X77	Air conditioning & blower, radiator 3-pin	751, 752
X78	Body & tailgate 2-pin (KW)	663
X79	Engine & alternator 2-pin (D)	115, 116
X80	Engine & Motronic 2-pin	239, 240
X81	Body & tailgate 2-pin (KW)	383
X83	Instrument panel & cruise control 1-pin	813
X84-87	Body & sensor – ABS 2-pin	592..599
X89	Tailgate & number plate light 1-pin	317
Y1	Clutch – compressor, air conditioning	736, 775
Y4	Solenoid valve – headlight washer	413
Y7	Fuel injection valves	153..160, 281..292
Y8	Actuator – cruise control	806..812

Key to wiring diagrams for Carlton models from 1993 (continued)

No	Description	Track	No	Description	Track
Y9	Solenoid valve – car level control	455, 462	Y34	Solenoid valve – fuel tank ventilation	165, 298
Y14	Valve – coolant (Japan)	718	Y35	Valve – circulation	728
Y25	Solenoid valve – power steering	485	Y46	Solenoid valve – inlet manifold	277
Y33	Ignition distributor	132, 260	Y47	Lifting magnet – handbrake shift lock	231

Not all items are fitted to all models

Colour code

BL	Blue
BR	Brown
GE	Yellow
GN	Green
GR	Grey
HBL	Light blue
LI	Lilac
RT	Red
SW	Black
VI	Violet
WS	White

Abbreviations

ABS	Anti-lock brake system		M 2.7	Motronic M 2.7
AC	Air conditioning		M 2.8	Motronic M 2.8
AT	Automatic transmission		MID	Multi-info-display
ATC	Automatic temperature control		MOT	Motronic in general
AZV	Trailer hitch		MT	Manual transmission
BR	On-board computer		MUL	Multec in general
CC	Check control		NS	Front foglights
CRC	Cruise control		NSL	Rear foglights
D	Diesel		OEL	Oil/fluid level control (oil/fluid level)
DID	Dual-info-display		OPT	Optional equipment
DIS	Direct ignition system		PBSL	Park/brake lockout
DS	Theft protection		P/N	Park/Neutral (AT)
DWA	Anti-theft warning system		POT	Potentiometer
DZM	Tachometer		RC	Electronic ride control
EFC	Electric folding roof, convertible		RFS	Reversing lights
EKS	Pinch guard (electric windows)		RHD	Right-hand drive
EMP	Radio (receiver)		SD	Sliding roof
EZ +	El Plus with self-diagnosis		SH	Seat heating
FH	Window winders		SRA	Headlight washer system
HRL	Luggage/load compartment light		TANK	Fuel tank sensor
HS	Rear screen		TC	Traction control
HW	Rear screen wiper		TD	Turbodiesel
HZG	Heating		TEMP	Temperature gauge
INS	Instrument		TFL	Daytime driving light
IRL	Interior light		TKS	Door contact switch
KAT	Catalytic converter		TSZI	Transistor ignition (inductive)
KBS	Wiring harness		VGS	Carburettor
KV	Contact distribution		WEG	Odometer frequency sensor
L3.1	Jetronic L3.1		WHR	Car level control
LCD	LCD instrument		WS	Warning buzzer
LHD	Left-hand drive		ZV	Central door locking
LWR	Headlight range control		ZYL	Cylinder
M 1.5	Motronic M 1.5		4WD	Four wheel drive
M 1.5.2	Motronic M 1.5.2			

Wiring identification

eg GE WS 1.5

GE	Basic colour
WS	Identification colour
1.5	Section (mm²)

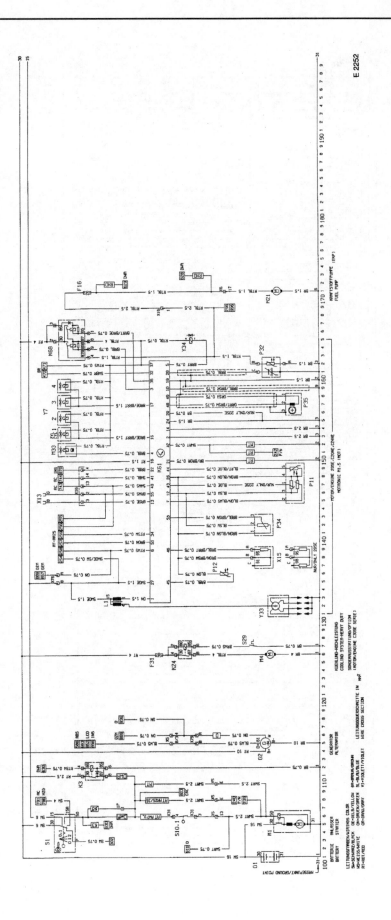

Wiring diagram for Carlton models from 1993

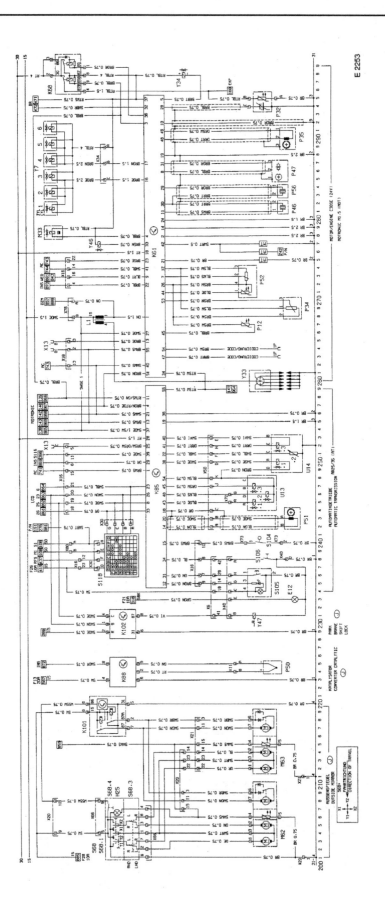

E 2253

Wiring diagram for Carlton models from 1993 (continued)

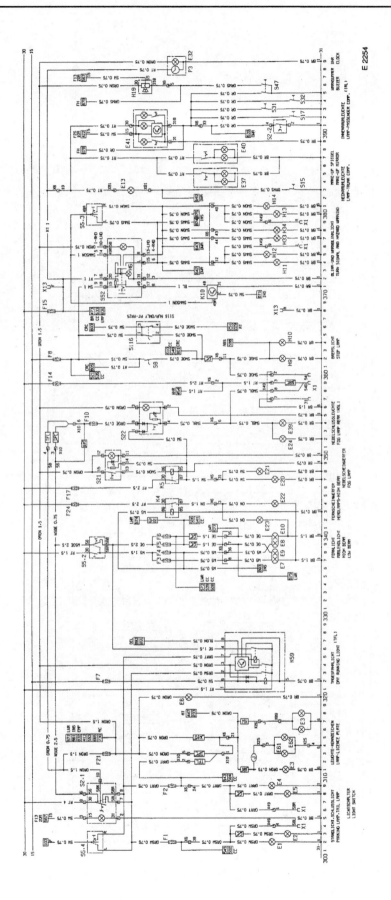

Wiring diagram for Carlton models from 1993 (continued)

E 2254

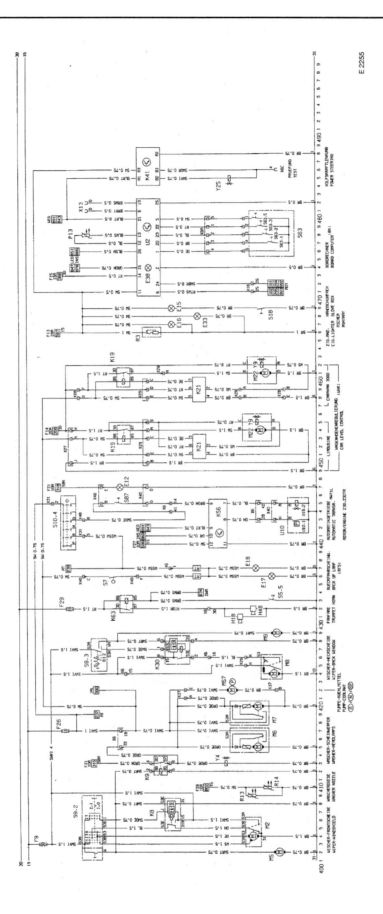

Wiring diagram for Carlton models from 1993 (continued)

E 2255

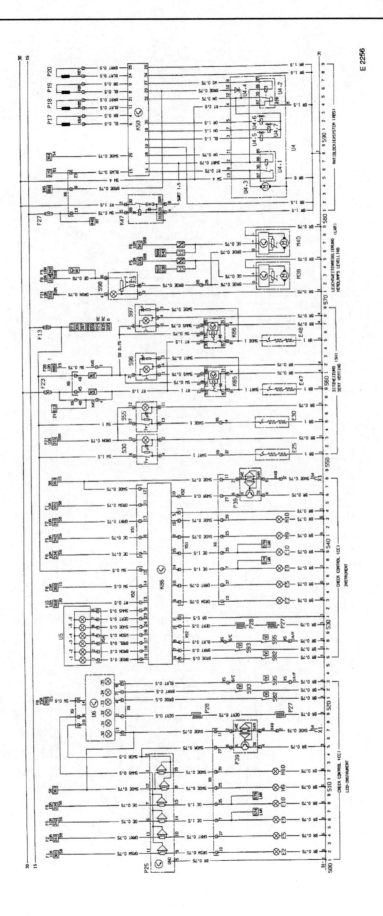

E 2256

Wiring diagram for Carlton models from 1993 (continued)

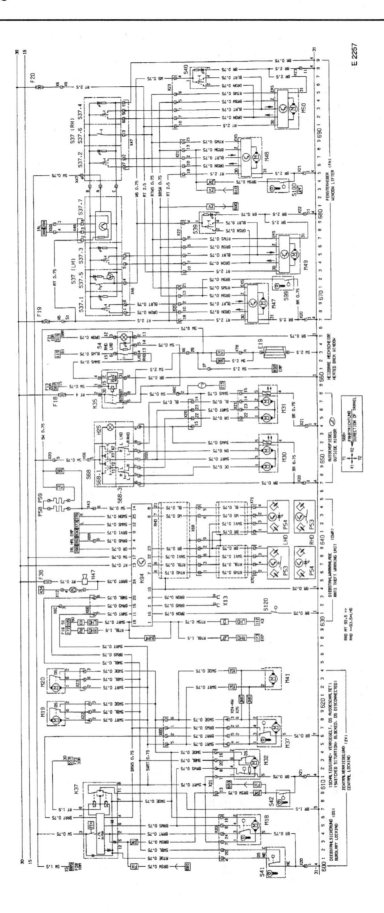

Wiring diagram for Carlton models from 1993 (continued)

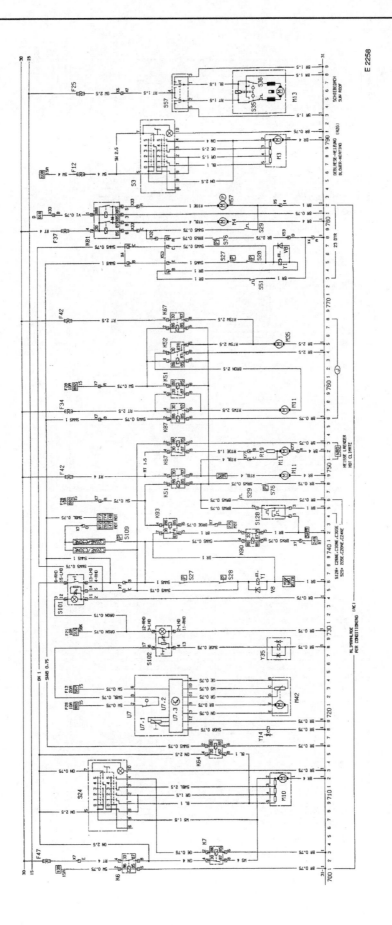

Wiring diagram for Carlton models from 1993 (continued)

E 2258

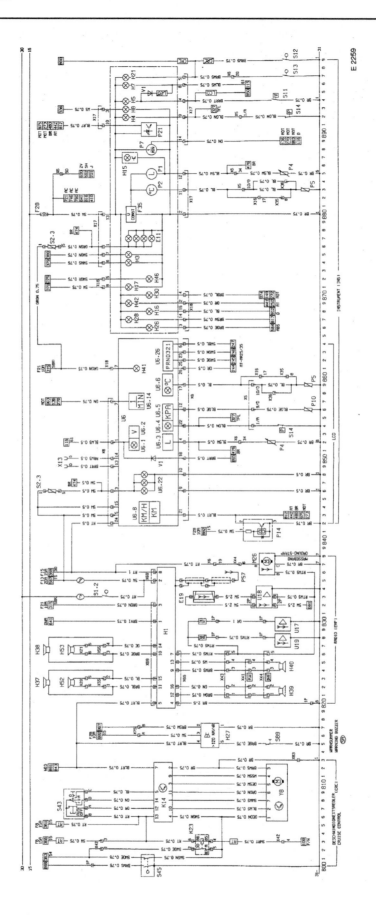

Wiring diagram for Carlton models from 1993 (continued)

E 2259

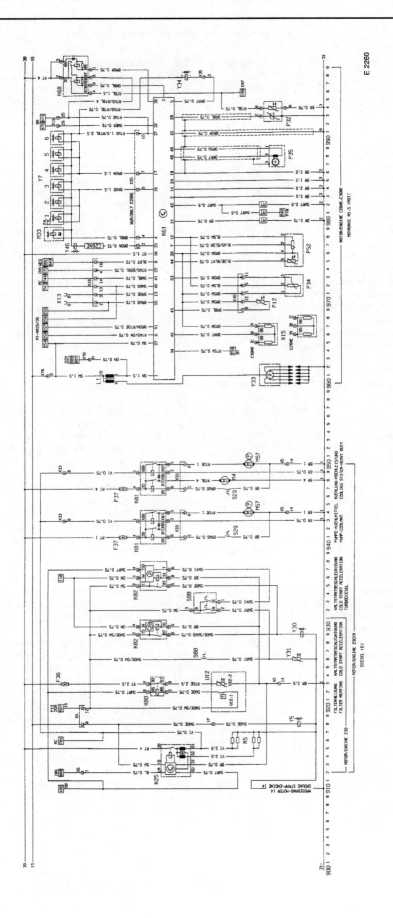

Wiring diagram for Carlton models from 1993 (continued)

E 2260

Key to wiring diagram for Senator models up to 1993

No	Description	Location	No	Description	Location
U4.3	ABS hydraulic pump	560	P28	Brake lining (front right) sensor	424
U4	ABS hydraulic pump assembly	560 to 573	H43	Brake lining (front) indicator	423 to 425
U4.4	ABS hydraulic pump diode	572	U5.5	Brake lining indicator - front	522
H26	ABS indicator	560	P27	Brake lining sensor - front left	519
U4.1	ABS pump relay	561 to 564	P28	Brake lining sensor - front right	519
P17	ABS sensor - front left	562, 563	P25	Bulb test sensor	500 to 513
P18	ABS sensor - front right	564, 565	M22	Car level control compressor	466
P19	ABS sensor - rear left	566, 567	K19	Car level control relay	465, 466
P20	ABS sensor - rear right	568, 569	K21	Car level control sensor	463 to 465
U4.5	ABS solenoid - front left	566	Y9	Car level control solenoid valve	467
U4.6	ABS solenoid - front right	568	K37	Central locking control unit	606 to 611
U4.7	ABS solenoid - rear axle	567	M37	Central locking motor - boot compartment	616 to 619
U4.2	ABS solenoid valves relay	570 to 573	M18	Central locking motor - driver's door	606 to 609
K50	ABS timing control	562 to 575	M41	Central locking motor - fuel filler flap	623, 625
M10	Air conditioning blower motor	709 to 712	M32	Central locking motor - passenger door	612 to 615
K7	Air conditioning blower relay	702, 703	M19	Central locking motor - rear left door	619 to 621
U7.6	Air conditioning blower switch	706 to 713	M20	Central locking motor - rear right door	623 to 625
Y1	Air conditioning compressor clutch	721	S42	Central locking switch - passenger door	605
K60	Air conditioning compressor relay	705, 706	H7	Charging indicator light	421
K6	Air conditioning relay	701, 702	U6.1	Charging indicator light	782
U7	Air conditioning unit assembly adjustment	706 to 723	U5	Check control display assembly	517 to 526
X7	Air conditioning wiring harness connector	714, 721, 722, 725 to 728	R3	Cigarette lighter	427
			E16	Cigarette lighter lamp	428
M51	Air flap actuator - driver's side	737 to 741	U7.5	Circulation switch	716 to 718
M52	Air flap actuator - passenger side	742 to 746	Y35	Circulation valve	718
P11	Air flow meter	152 to 156, 230 to 234, 282 to 286	P3	Clock	363
			S63.2	Clock - hours adjustment switch	476
S74	Air temperature switch	209	E32	Clock lamp	362
E55	Air vent lamp - centre	433	S12	Clutch control switch	416
E57	Air vent lamp - left	432	Y30	Cold start acceleration solenoid valve	266
E58	Air vent lamp - right	433	V8	Compressor diode	722
G2	Alternator	111	U7.4	Compressor switch	721 to 723
G6	Alternator (Diesel)	251	S109	Compressor switch (Motronic) >1200KPA	723
S37.6	Anti-jam 'off' switch (EKS)	659	U2	Computer	470 to 481
S41	Anti-theft locking switch - driver's door	602 to 604	E38	Computer lamp	471
H29	Automatic 4-speed indicator	553	S63	Computer switch assembly	
S87	Automatic 4-speed switch	551	S93	Cooling agent control switch	522
M26	Automatic aerial motor	768, 769	U5.7	Cooling fluid minimum capacity indicator	525
H23	Automatic aerial receiver	769, 770	S29	Cooling temperature blower switch	726
U10	Auto gearbox 4-speed assembly	551 to 553	S51	Cooling temperature compressor switch	721
U10.1	Auto gearbox 4-speed pressure switch	551	P2	Cooling temperature indicator	404
U10.1	Auto gearbox 4-speed solenoid valve	553	U6.6	Cooling temperature indicator	791
Y36	Auto gearbox solenoid valve (1)	181	P12	Cooling temperature sensor	148, 241, 242, 275
Y37	Auto gearbox solenoid valve (2)	182			
Y38	Auto gearbox solenoid valve (clutch)	183	P5	Cooling temperature sensor	404
S10.1	Auto gearbox starter switch	107	S29	Cooling temperature switch	194
S10	Auto gearbox switch assembly		P35	Crankshaft impulse sensor	136 to 138
S37.7	Automatic window control	646 to 649	P35	Crankshaft inductive sensor	289 to 291
H33	Auxiliary indicator lamp - left	373	K14	Cruise control	756 to 762
H34	Auxiliary indicator lamp - right	376	Y8	Cruise control actuator	756 to 762
G1	Battery	101	S45	Cruise control clutch switch	751, 752
G3	Battery (Diesel)	249	K23	Cruise control relay	753, 754
U7.7	Blower lamp switch	714	S43	Cruise control switch	756 to 759
X6	Body wiring harness connector	Various	U7.2	Defroster limit switch	717 to 720
X6A	Body wiring harness connector 5 pin	474 to 478	K62	Dim-dip light control unit	328 to 332
X6D	Body wiring harness connector 6 pin	616 to 619	S2.3	Dimmer instrument lights	315
X6D	Body/door wiring harness connector 6 pin	647, 648	U6.22	Display lights	777, 778
E13	Boot compartment lamp	397	P14	Distance sensor	411, 412
S15	Boot compartment lamp switch	397	S47	Door contact switch & lamps 'on' warning	387, 388
S11	Brake fluid control switch	419	S17	Door contact switch - front right (TKS)	384
S81	Brake fluid control switch	521	S31	Door contact switch - rear left	385
H5	Brake fluid indicator	419	S32	Door contact switch - rear right	386
V1	Brake fluid test bulb diode	420, 784	E52	Door lamp - rear left	391
P27	Brake lining (front left) sensor	424	E53	Door lamp - rear right	392

Key to wiring diagram for Senator models up to 1993 (continued)

No	Description	Location	No	Description	Location
S38.1	Door mirror adjustment switch	671 to 674, 679 to 683	E25	Heating pad - front seat left	529
			E30	Heating pad - front seat right	535
S68.3	Door mirror left/right switch	680 to 684	E47	Heating pad - rear seat left	538
S68	Door mirror switch assembly		E48	Heating pad - rear seat right	543
E50	Driver's door lamp	389	K65	Heating pad relay - rear seat left	538 to 540
X20	Driver's door wiring harness connector	432	K66	Heating pad relay - rear seat right	543 to 545
S106	Economy/power switch	185	S30	Heating pad switch - front seat left	529 to 531
K40	Electronic idling regulator	242 to 247	S46	Heating pad switch - front seats	533 to 535
E6	Engine compartment lamp	318	S96	Heating pad switch - rear seat left	540 to 542
H30	Engine instrument indicator	158, 274	S97	Heating pad switch - rear seat right	545 to 547
S95	Engine oil minimum capacity control switch	523	S76	High pressure compressor switch (blower)	725
X5	Engine wiring harness connector	Various	S28	High pressure compressor switch >2800KPA	721
K70	ETM control unit	171 to 188	H18	Horn	455
H42	ETM programme power indicator	185	H18A	Horn	456
K2	Flasher unit	365 to 367	K63	Horn relay	456, 457
E20	Fog lamp - left	346	S5.5	Horn switch	457
E24	Fog lamp - rear left	352	Y31	Idling control actuator	267
E39	Fog lamp - rear right	353	M33	Idling power unit	148, 149, 243 to 245
E21	Fog lamp - right	347			
K5	Fog lamp relay	347, 348	L2	Ignition coil Hall sensor system	203, 204
S21	Fog lamp switch	348 to 350	L3	Ignition coil HEI inductive sensor system	270, 271
S22	Fog lamp switch - rear	352 to 355	K52	Ignition coil module	202, 203
H15	Fuel indicator	408	L3	Ignition coil sensor system	122, 123
P1	Fuel indicator	406	Y33	Ignition distributor - MHDI	124, 272
U6.3	Fuel indicator	782	Y22	Ignition distributor EAI	209
K68	Fuel injection relay unit	126 to 130	S63.5	Illumination switch	478
Y7	Fuel injectors	135 to 146, 227 to 238, 285 to 292	H11	Indicator lamp - front left	370
			H13	Indicator lamp - front right	378
K68	Fuel injection unit relay	296 to 299	H12	Indicator lamp - rear left	371
K15	Fuel injection unit timing control	220 to 239	H14	Indicator lamp - rear right	379
X15A	Fuel injection wiring connector 10 pin	Various	H3	Indicator lamp indicator	374, 375
X15B	Fuel injection wiring connector 8 pin	176, 179, 185, 187, 188	S5.3	Indicator switch	377 to 379
			S5	Indicator switch assembly	
M21	Fuel pump	126, 216, 297	P41	Inside air temperature sensor - driver's side	735
K31	Fuel pump relay	216 to 218	P42	Inside air temperature sensor - passngr side	736
P4	Fuel sensor	406	M53	Inside temperature blower sensor	749
Y5	Fuel solenoid valve	264	X17	Instrument connector 14 pin	Various
S63.1	Function reset switch	475	X18	Instrument connector 16 pin	Various
S63.3	Function select switch	477	E11	Instrument lights	316
F1 to	Fuse (in fuse box)	Various	S2.3	Instrument lights dimmer	778
E49	Fuse box lamp	380	S104	Kickdown switch	179
E15	Glove box lamp	430	P32	Lambda sensor	132, 133, 293, 294
S18	Glove box lamp switch	430			
R5	Glow plugs	263	E22	Lamp pencil beam - left	344
Y11	Hall sensor	205 to 207	E23	Lamp pencil beam - right	345
S52	Hazard warning switch	367 to 372	H41	LCD indicator light	317
H6	Hazard warning system indicator	369	U6	LCD instrument assembly	774 to 798
H19	Headlamp 'on' warning buzzer	388, 389	X8	LCD instrument connector 26 pin	
S98	Headlamp levelling switch	491 to 493	S2.1	Light switch	305 to 308, 502, 503
M39	Headlamp levelling unit motor - left	492 to 495			
M40	Headlamp levelling unit motor - right	496 to 499	S2	Light switch assembly	
Y4	Headlamp washer solenoid valve	447	S5.2	Low beam	507
K9	Headlamp washer unit relay	446, 447	E9	Low beam - left	339, 505
M6	Headlamp wiper motor - left	449 to 451	E10	Low beam - right	340, 507
M7	Headlamp wiper motor - right	453 to 455	S5.2	Low beam switch	338, 339
M30	Heated door mirror adjustment - left	672 to 675, 681 to 684	S27	Low pressure compressor switch >215KPA	721
			E7	Main beam - left	337
M31	Heated door mirror adjustment - right	687 to 690	E8	Main beam - right	338
K35	Heated door mirror time delay relay	690 to 692	H8	Main beam indicator	336
H25	Heated mirror indicator	676, 685	K4	Main beam lamp relay	343, 344
E19	Heated rear window	694	K61	Motronic control unit	131 to 164, 269 to 295
S4	Heated rear window switch	695 to 697			
M3	Heater blower motor	116 to 119	X15C	Motronic wiring harness connector 5 pin	793, 795 to 798
S3	Heater blower switch	115 to 120	E3	Number plate lamp	313

Key to wiring diagram for Senator models up to 1993 (continued)

No	Description	Location	No	Description	Location
X26	Octane number connector	150, 277	M12	Starter (Diesel)	256, 257
U5.3	Oil minimum capacity indicator	521	S1	Starter switch	106, 107,
U6.5	Oil pressure gauge	787			256, 257
H4	Oil pressure indicator	414	H9	Stop lamp - left	359, 509
U6.4	Oil pressure indicator	785	H10	Stop lamp - right	360, 511
P10	Oil pressure sensor	787	S8	Stop lamp switch	360, 509
S14	Oil pressure switch	414	U5.2	Stop light indicator	519
S75	Oil temperature switch	207	S57	Sun roof - open/close/tilt/close	484 to 488
P13	Outside air temperature sensor	477	S35	Sun roof micro switch	485
P40	Outside air temperature sensor	734	S36	Sun roof micro switch	487
K47	Over voltage protection relay	557, 558	M13	Sun roof motor	485 to 488
H21	Parking brake & clutch indicator	417	P7	Tachometer	409
S13	Parking brake switch	417	U6.14	Tachometer	788
E1	Parking lamp - left	306	Y34	Tank ventilation valve	131, 298
E4	Parking lamp - right	309	U8	Temperature control - driver's side	
S5.4	Parking lamp switch	301 to 303	U8.1	Temperature control - driver's side	743 to 746
E27	Passenger compartment lamp - rear left	392, 393	U9	Temperature control - passenger side	734 to 747
E28	Passenger compartment lamp - rear right	394, 395	U9.1	Temperature control potentiometer	740 to 742
E41	Passenger compartment lamp delay	382 to 384	S88	Temperature cooling switch	266, 267
S2.2	Passenger compartment lamp switch	381	X13	Test connector	Various
E51	Passenger door lamp	390	S107	Throttle valve ETM switch	223 to 228
X21	Passenger door wiring harness connector	433	S44	Throttle valve switch	158, 159,
K41	Power steering control unit	596 to 598			219, 221, 271, 272
Y25	Power steering solenoid valve	596	S107	Throttle valve switch (ETM)	161 to 167
H16	Preheating time indicator	259	K46	Timing control EAI	204 to 212
K25	Preheating time relay	259 to 262	P39	Trailer bulb test sensor	514 to 516
X14	Programme pins	474, 480,	K10	Trailer flasher unit	365 to 367
		481, 791, 792	H17	Trailer indicator lamp indicator	366
M11	Radiator auxiliary blower motor	727	X1	Trailer socket	Various
M35	Radiator auxiliary blower motor	732	S66	Vacuum ISC switch	208
K51	Radiator auxiliary blower relay	726, 727	F35	Voltage stabiliser	402
F31	Radiator blower fuse	193	U6.2	Voltmeter	783 to 785
M4	Radiator blower motor	193	S82	Washer fluid control switch	520
K24	Radiator blower relay	193, 194	U5.6	Washer fluid minimum capacity indicator	524
K67	Radiator blower relay	729, 730	R13	Washer nozzle (heated) - left	443
R17	Rear cigarette lighter	548	R14	Washer nozzle (heated) - right	444
E54	Rear cigarette lighter lamp	549	M14	Window lifter motor - front left	627, 629
E59	Rear heater air vent lamp	550	M47	Window lifter motor - front left	636 to 640
E2	Rear lamp - left	307, 501	M15	Window lifter motor - front right	631,633
E5	Rear lamp - right	310, 503	M48	Window lifter motor - front right	654 to 658
U5.1	Rear light & low beam indicator	518	M49	Window lifter motor - rear left	642 to 646
E17	Reversing lamp - left	459	M50	Window lifter motor - rear right	660 to 664
E18	Reversing lamp - right	460	S99	Window lifter switch - driver's door ZV	651
S7	Reversing lamp switch	459	S53	Window lifter switch - front left	627 to 630
S10.2	Reversing lamp switch	460	S78	Window lifter switch - front right	631 to 634
M43	Ride control actuator - front left	579 to 581	S37.1	Window lifter switch - left	637 to 639
M44	Ride control actuator - front right	583 to 585	S100	Window lifter switch - passenger door ZV	652
M45	Ride control actuator - rear left	587 to 589	S37.3	Window lifter switch - rear left	643 to 645
M46	Ride control actuator - rear right	591 to 593	S39	Window lifter switch - rear left door	647 to 649
S110	Ride control switch	578 to 583	S37.4	Window lifter switch - rear right	661 to 663
K71	Ride control unit	579 to 594	S40	Window lifter switch - rear right door	665 to 667
K59	Running light relay	319 to 325	S37.2	Window lifter switch - right	655 to 657
H27	Safety checking warning buzzer	764 to 765	S37	Window lifter switch assembly	637 to 663
S37.5	Safety switch	641	M5	Windscreen washer pump	436
S89	Seat belt switch	764	K8	Windscreen wiper interval relay	439 to 442
H28	Seat belt warning indicator	766	M2	Windscreen wiper motor	437 to 440
E12	Selector lever lamp	314	S9.2	Windshield wiper interval switch	436 to 440
K56	Shift down control unit	551 to 555	S9	Wiper unit switch assembly	
U6.26	Speed indicator	793 to 798	X6B	Wiring body harness connector 8 pin	587 to 593
S10.4	Speed indicator switch	793 to 798	X6C	Wiring harness connector - door 2 pin	690, 691
P43	Speedometer	413	X20	Wiring harness connector - driver's door	Various
U6.8	Speedometer	775	X21	Wiring harness connector - passenger door	Various
S105	Start up assistance switch	187 to 189	X22	Wiring connector - rear left door	Various
M1	Starter	106, 107	X22A	Wiring connector - rear left door 2 pin	391, 642, 649

Key to wiring diagram for Senator models up to 1993 (continued)

No	Description	Location	No	Description	Location
X23	Wiring connector - rear right door	Various	X15A	Wiring harness connector F1 10 pin	Various
X23A	Wiring connector - rear right door 2 pin	392, 660, 667	X15D	Wiring harness connector F1 3 pin	Various
X25	Wiring connector boot lid 4 pin	616 to 619	X15B	Wiring harness connector F1 8 pin	281, 143

For colour code, abbreviations key and wiring identification, see page 12•30

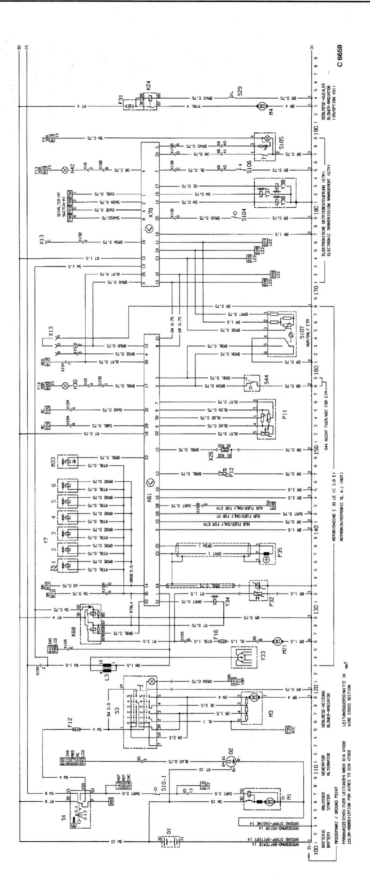

Wiring diagram for Senator models up to 1993

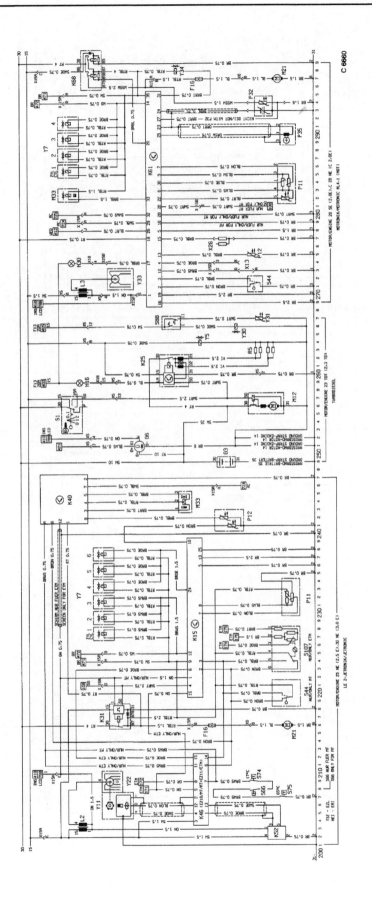

Wiring diagram for Senator models up to 1993 (continued)

C 6660

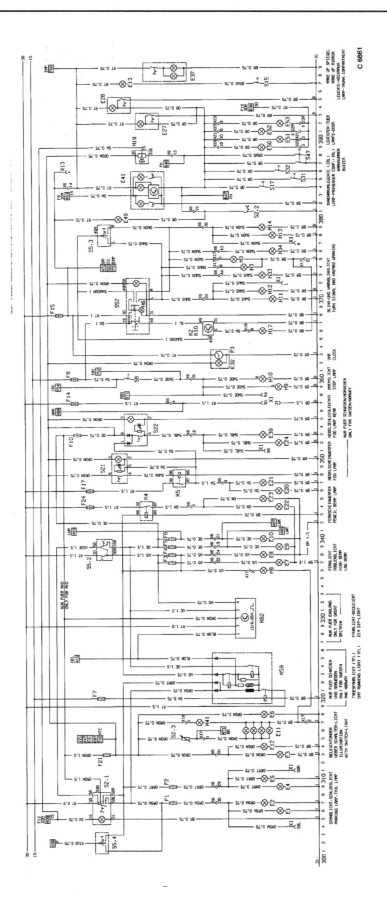

Wiring diagram for Senator models up to 1993 (continued)

C 6661

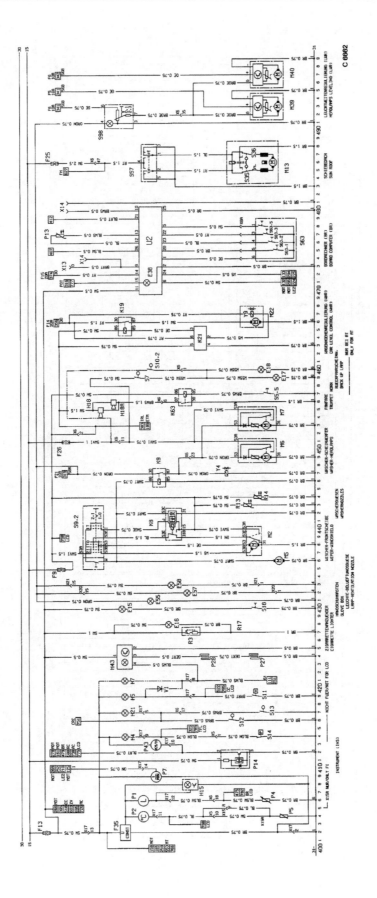

Wiring diagram for Senator models up to 1993 (continued)

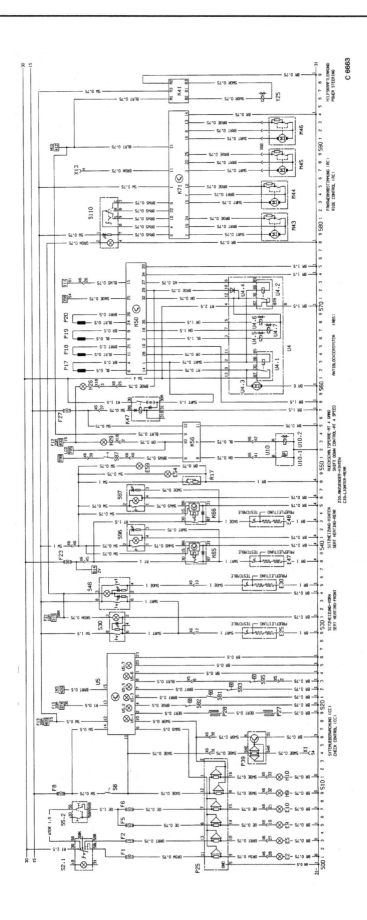

Wiring diagram for Senator models up to 1993 (continued)

C 6663

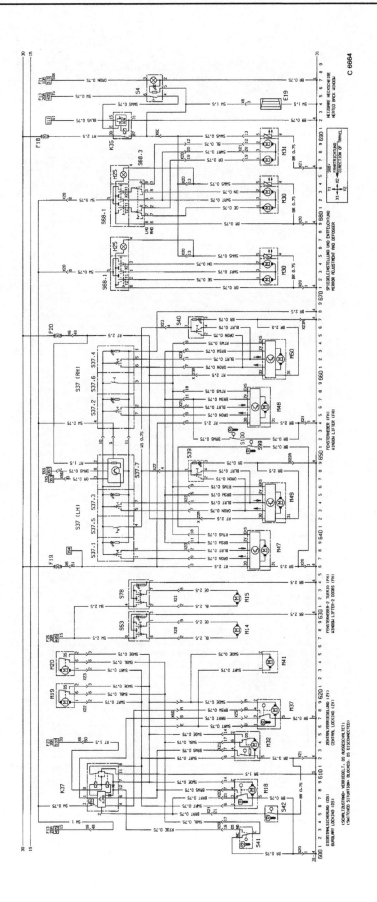

Wiring diagram for Senator models up to 1993 (continued)

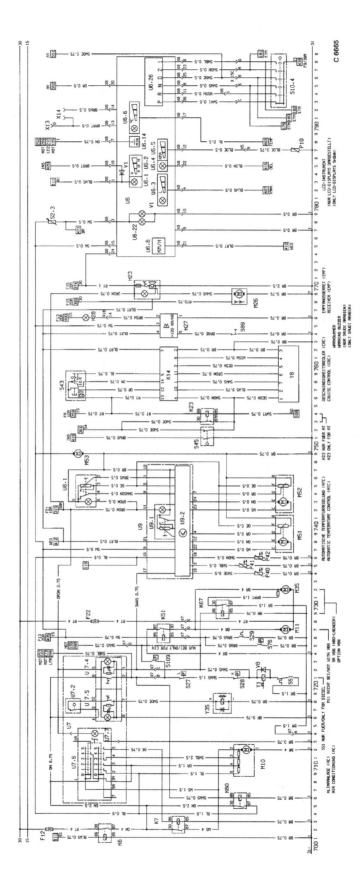

Wiring diagram for Senator models up to 1993 (continued)

Key to wiring diagram for Senator models from 1993

No	Description	Location	No	Description	Location
X84 to X87	ABS 2 pin revolution body & sensor	227 to 234	X60	Body & door 6 pin	395
U4.3	ABS hydraulic pump	219	X6D	Body & door 6 pin (ZV)	615 to 618,
U4.4	ABS hydraulic pump diode	231			679
U4.1	ABS pump relay	220, 223	X44	Body & rear loudspeaker 6 pin	818 to 825,
U4.2	ABS relay solenoid valves	229 to 232			833
U4.5	ABS solenoid valve - front left	225	X49	Body & socket - trailer 9 pin	370, 373
U4.6	ABS solenoid valve - front right	227	S120	Bonnet switch	632
U4.7	ABS solenoid valve - rear axle	226	S15	Boot light switch	377
P17	ABS wheel sensor - front left	227	S11	Brake fluid control switch	891
P18	ABS wheel sensor - front right	229	V1	Brake fluid level test diode	892
P19	ABS wheel sensor - rear left	231	H5	Brake fluid warning indicator	891
P20A	BS wheel sensor - right right	233	X29	Car level control & height sensor 5 pin	462 to 466
H26	ABS warning indicator	863	M22	Car level control compressor	466
S109	Acceleration revolution switch (C30SE)	736	K19	Car level control relay (mini)	465, 466
P57	Aerial	832	K21	Car level control sensor	463 to 465
X77	Air conditioning & radiator blower 3 pin	746, 748	Y9	Car level control solenoid valve	467
U7	Air conditioning adjustment unit assembly		K88	Catalytic converter temperature control unit	123 to 125
M10	Air conditioning blower motor	709 to 712	P50	Catalytic converter temperature sensor	124, 125
K7	Air conditioning blower relay	702, 703	H46	Catalytic converter temperature	
K64	Air conditioning blower relay (stage 1)	705, 706		warning indicator (JAPAN)	869
S24	Air conditioning blower switch	707 to 714	K37	Central locking control unit	602 to 610
Y1	Air conditioning clutch compressor	737	M37	Central locking motor - boot lid	615 to 618
F47	Air conditioning fuse (MAXI)	702	M18	Central locking motor - driver's door	603 to 606
K6	Air conditioning relay	701, 702	M41	Central locking motor - fuel filler flap	622, 624
M51	Air flap actuator - driver's side	769 to 773	M32	Central locking motor - passenger door	611 to 614
M52	Air flap actuator - passenger side	774 to 778	M19	Central locking motor - rear left door	618 to 620
P52	Air flow meter	171 to 174,	M20	Central locking motor - rear right door	622 to 624
		269 to 272	S42	Central locking switch - passenger door	609
G2	Alternator	111, 112	U6.1	Charging indicator light	847
S37.6	Anti-jam off switch (EKS)	690	H7	Charging indicator light	893
S41	Anti-theft locking switch - driver's door	600 to 602	U5	Check control display assembly	
X12	Anti-theft warning unit code 4 pin	634	R3	Cigarette lighter	428
K94	Anti-theft warning unit control unit	630 to 644	R17	Cigarette lighter - rear	570
F38	Anti-theft warning unit fuse	636	Y35	Circulation solenoid valve	718
P53	Anti-theft warning unit sensor - driver's side	637 to 644	U7.5	Circulation switch	716 to 718
P54	Anti-theft warning unit sensor - passngr side	637 to 644	S63.2	Clock - hours adjustment switch	476
H47	Anti-theft warning unit signal horn	636	S63.4	Clock - minutes adjustment switch	478
K3	Anti-theft warning unit starter relay	109, 110	H21	Clutch & parking brake warning indicator	894
U13.2	Auto gearbox 1/2 - 3/4 shift solenoid valve	146	V8	Compressor diode	739
U13.1	Auto gearbox 2/3 shift solenoid valve	145	K93	Compressor relay (C30SE)	734, 735
U14	Auto gearbox assembly intermedia housing		U7.4	Compressor switch	721, 722
U13	Auto gearbox assembly main housing		U2	Computer	470 to 480
U14.2	Auto gearbox ATF temperature sensor	151	E38	Computer lamp	473
X40	Auto gearbox body & console 8 pin	131 to 138	S63	Computer switch assembly	
U13.3	Auto gearbox brake brand solenoid valve	147	K86	Control unit - check control	526 to 547
K90	Auto gearbox compressor relay	728, 729	S93	Coolant control switch	522, 527
K85	Auto gearbox control unit	135 to 159	Y14	Coolant solenoid valve (JAPAN)	782
K23	Auto gearbox cruise control relay	202, 203	U6.6	Coolant temperature indicator	854
U14.3	Auto gearbox hydraulic pressure		P2	Coolant temperature indicator	880
	regulator solenoid valve	152	P12	Coolant temperature sensor	167, 264
X42	Auto gearbox instrument panel		P5	Coolant temperature sensor	854, 880
	& cruise control 4 pin	202, 203	S29	Coolant temperature switch	119
X30	Auto gearbox Motronic & switch 8 pin	137 to 142	S128	Coolant temperature switch	729, 730
E12	Auto gearbox selector level lamp	133	X10	Countries code 6 pin	312, 313,
S118	Auto gearbox switch	137 to 140			346, 348
U14.1	Auto gearbox torque converter solenoid	150	P35	Crankshaft impulse sensor	189 to 191,
H42	Auto gearbox warning indicator	866			281 to 283
H33	Auxiliary indicator lamp - left	371	K14	Cruise control	206 to 212
H34	Auxiliary indicator lamp - right	372	Y8	Cruise control actuator	206 to 212
G1	Battery	101	S45	Cruise control clutch switch	201
X26	Body & boot lid 3 pin	348, 459	S43	Cruise control switch	206 to 209
X25	Body & boot lid 4 pin	615 to 618	P47	Cylinder identification sensor	185 to 187
X27	Body & car level control 3 pin	462, 465,	K59	Day running light relay	321 to 327
		466	U7.2	Defroster lever limit switch	717, 718

Key to wiring diagram for Senator models from 1993 (continued)

No	Description	Location	No	Description	Location
X13	Diagnostic link 10 pin	152, 164, 165, 264, 265, 362, 365, 409, 479, 480, 633, 634, 844, 845	M39	Headlamp levelling motor - left	492 to 494
			M40	Headlamp levelling motor - right	496 to 498
			S98	Headlamp levelling switch	491 to 493
P14	Distance sensor (WEG)	898, 899	E22	Headlamp main beam - left	338
X45	Door & console 5 pin	559, 563	E23	Headlamp main beam - right	336
X47	Door & console 7 pin	685 to 694	K4	Headlamp main beam relay	337, 338
X46	Door & console 8 pin	668 to 679	Y4	Headlamp washer solenoid valve	444
X20	Door & driver's door 24 pin	318, 574 to 587, 600 to 606, 647 to 657, 667 to 671, 818, 819	K9	Headlamp washer unit relay	443, 444
			M6	Headlamp wiper motor - left	446 to 448
			M7	Headlamp wiper motor - right	450 to 452
X21	Door & passenger door 24 pin	319, 393, 584 to 591, 609 to 614, 654 to 658, 685 to 689, 823, 824	H19	Headlamps 'on' warning buzzer	390
			E19	Heated rear window	663
			E19	Heated rear window aerial	829
			M3	Heater blower motor	790 to 793
X22	Door & rear left door 11 pin	394, 618 to 620, 673 to 680	S3	Heater blower switch	788 to 795
			E25	Heating pad - driver's seat	551
X23	Door & rear right door 11 pin	395, 622 to 624, 691 to 698	E30	Heating pad - passenger seat	557
			E47	Heating pad - rear seat left	560
X70	Door & sensor -anti-theft warning unit 4 pin	637 to 640	E48	Heating pad - rear seat right	565
X71	Door & sensor- anti-theft warning unit 4 pin	641 to 644	K65	Heating pad relay - rear left seat	560 to 562
S31	Door contact switch - rear left	387	K66	Heating pad relay - rear right seat	565 to 567
S32	Door contact switch - rear right	388	S76	High pressure compressor (blower) switch	732
M62	Door mirror - driver's side	576 to 583	S28	High-pressure compressor switch	737
M30	Door mirror - driver's side	649 to 652	H18	Horn	454
M63	Door mirror - passenger side	585 to 592	H48	Horn	455
M31	Door mirror - passenger side	655 to 658	K63	Horn relay	455, 456
S68.1	Door mirror adjustment switch	574 to 578, 647 to 652	S5.5	Horn switch	456
			U4	Hydraulic pump assembly -ABS	
S68	Door mirror adjustment switch assembly		M33	Idle speed actuator	178, 179, 272, 273
S68.3	Door mirror left/right switch	574 to 579, 647 to 652	L1	Ignition coil	168, 255
			Y33	Ignition distributor	160, 255
X66	Door mirror- driver's door 9 pin	647 to 654	H11	Indicator lamp - front left	368
X66	Driver's door & switch - outside mirror 9 pin	574 to 581	H13	Indicator lamp - front right	374
S47	Driver's door contact switch 2 pin	389, 390	H12	Indicator lamp - rear left	369
S106	Economy/Power switch programme	138	H14	Indicator lamp - rear right	375
M26	Electric aerial motor	832, 833	S5.3	Indicator switch	373 to 375
U9.2	Electronic control	766 to 779	S5	Indicator switch assembly	
X80	Engine & Motronic 2P	139, 140	H3	Indicator warning lamp indicator	871, 872
E6	Engine compartment lamp	317	M53	Inside temperature blower sensor	784
S95	Engine oil minimum capacity control switch	523, 528	P41	Inside temperature sensor - driver's side	767
H30	Engine warning indicator	867	P42	Inside temperature sensor - passenger side	768
K10	Flasher unit	363 to 365	U6	Instrument assembly LCD	
E20	Fog lamp - left	341	E11	Instrument lamps	874
E24	Fog lamp - rear left	346	S2.3	Instrument lights dimmer	841, 873
E39	Fog lamp - rear right	348	X7	Instrument panel & air conditioning 7 pin	702, 727 to 739
E21	Fog lamp - right	342			
K5	Fog lamp relay	341, 342	X82	Instrument panel & blower switch 2 pin	713, 714, 794, 795
U6.3	Fuel indicator	847			
P1	Fuel indicator	882	X6	Instrument panel & body 51 pin	131 to 138, 216 to 221, 297, 302 to 332, 338 to 353, 368 to 390, 446 to 460, 486, 492, 502 to 517, 663, 667, 696, 833, 847, 882, 894
K68	Fuel injection unit relay	196 to 199, 290 to 294			
Y7	Fuel injectors	181 to 192, 274 to 285			
M21	Fuel pump	297	X6A	Instrument panel & body 6 pin	474 to 478, 641
P4	Fuel sensor	847, 882			
H15	Fuel warning indicator	884	X43	Instrument panel & body 6 pin	818 to 825
S63.1	Function reset switch	475	X6	Instrument panel & body/door 51 pin	419, 425, 534 to 562
S63.3	Function select switch	477			
F1 to	Fuse (in fuse box)	Various	X51	Instrument panel & check control 16 pin	533 to 547
S18	Glove box lamp switch	430	X52	Instrument panel & check control 26 pin	526 to 536, 546
S13	Handbrake switch	894			
S52	Hazard warning switch	365 to 370	X83	Instrument panel & cruise control 1 pin	213
H6	Hazard warning system indicator	367			

Key to wiring diagram for Senator models from 1993 (continued)

No	Description	Location
X6C	Instrument panel & door 4 pin	319, 633, 658
X55	Instrument panel & door 4 pin	818 to 824
X68	Instrument panel & door 9 pin	631 to 633, 636 to 644
X5	Instrument panel & engine 7 pin	106, 107, 112, 523, 528, 849, 851, 889
X17	Instrument panel & instrument 14 pin	871 to 894
X18	Instrument panel & instrument 16 pin	856, 863 to 867, 868, 869
X54	Instrument panel & instrument 8 pin (CC)	526 to 532
X73	Instrument panel & kickdown switch 4 pin (LHD)	140
X8	Instrument panel & LCD instrument 26 pin	837 to 859
X9	Instrument panel & LCD instrument 26 pin (CC)	517 to 523
X76	Instrument panel & Motronic 2 pin	168, 170, 255, 257
X16	Instrument panel & Motronic 26 pin	135 to 165, 172 to 195, 264 to 295, 854, 880
X69	Instrument panel & radio 16 pin	816 to 832
X68	Instrument panel & ride control - rear 6 pin	409 to 415
X75	Instrument panel & safety checking 2 pin	812, 813
X11	Instrument panel & temperature sensor 2P	124, 125
Y46	Intake manifold solenoid valve	177
Y46	Intake manifold solenoid valve (C26NE)	271
S104	Kickdown switch	140
P46	Knocking control sensor	181, 182
P56	Knocking control sensor	183, 184
P32	Lambda/exhaust sensor	194, 195, 287, 288
E13	Lamp - boot	377
E55	Lamp - centre air vent	320
E16	Lamp - cigarette lighter	428
E50	Lamp - driver's door	392
E51	Lamp - driver's door	392
E49	Lamp - fuse box	382
E15	Lamp - glove box	430
E57	Lamp - left air vent	318
E41	Lamp - passenger compartment - disconnect delay	383 to 386
E27	Lamp - passenger compartment - rear left	393, 394
E28	Lamp - passenger compartment - rear right	396, 397
E52	Lamp - rear left door	394
E53	Lamp - rear right door	395
E58	Lamp - right air vent	319
E37	Lamp - vanity mirror - left	378, 379
E40	Lamp - vanity mirror - right	381, 382
U6.22	Light display	841 to 843
S2.1	Light switch	305 to 308
S2	Light switch assembly	
H37	Loudspeaker - front left	817, 820
H52	Loudspeaker - front left door	818, 819
H38	Loudspeaker - front right	822, 825
H53	Loudspeaker - front right door	823, 824
H39	Loudspeaker - rear left	818, 819
H40	Loudspeaker - rear right	823, 824
E9	Low beam - left	506, 542
E10	Low beam - right	508, 544
S27	Low-pressure compressor switch	737
E7	Main beam - left	331
E8	Main beam - right	332

No	Description	Location
H8	Main beam warning indicator	890
X40	Manual gearbox body & console 8 pin	459
H25	Mirror heater warning	654
X50	Motronic & automatic gearbox 10 pin	142 to 153
X72	Motronic & automatic gearbox 2 pin	145, 146
X35	Motronic & fuel injection valves 15 pin (C26NE)	263 to 292, 854, 880
X34	Motronic & fuel injection valves 3 pin	185 to 189
K61	Motronic control unit	161 to 195, 255 to 289
E3	Number plate lamp	314
X15	Octane number 3 pin	260, 261
U6.5	Oil pressure gauge	851
P10	Oil pressure sensor	851
S1.4	Oil pressure switch	849, 889
U6.4	Oil pressure warning indicator	849
H4	Oil pressure warning indicator	889
P13	Outside air temperature sensor	477
P40	Outside temperature sensor	766
K47	Over voltage protection relay (ABS)	216, 217
K102	Park brake control unit, Shift lock	129 to 131
Y47	Park brake shift lock solenoid	131
E1	Parking lamp - left	302
E4	Parking lamp - right	309
S5.4	Parking lamp switch	301 to 303
S68.4	Parking position switch	580
S2.2	Passenger compartment lamp switch	385
S17	Passenger door contact switch	386
K41	Power steering control unit	418 to 420
Y25	Power steering solenoid valve	418
F31	Radiator blower fuse	118, 751
F42	Radiator blower fuse (MAXI)	744, 762
M35	Radiator blower motor	759
M11	Radiator blower motor	742, 746, 751
R19	Radiator blower pre-resistor	746
K87	Radiator blower relay	750, 751
K52	Radiator blower relay	757 to 759
K51	Radiator blower relay	741, 742, 753, 754
K67	Radiator blower relay	745, 746, 761, 762
M4	Radiator motor blower	118
H1	Radio	816 to 832
E54	Rear cigarette lighter lamp	571
E59	Rear heater air vent lamp	572
S4	Rear window & outside mirror switch	663 to 665
K35	Rear window & outside mirror time delay relay	657 to 660
U18	Rear window aerial amplifier	827 to 830
K101	Relay - outside mirror, parking position	590 to 593
E17	Reversing lamp - left	459
E18	Reversing lamp - right	460
S7	Reversing lamp switch	459
S110	Ride control switch	400 to 405
K71	Ride control unit	401 to 416
H27	Safety checking warning buzzer	811 to 813
S37.5	Safety switch	672
S89	Seat belt switch	811
H28	Seat belt warning indicator	864
U6.26	Selector level display	856 to 859
P25	Sensor - bulb test	501 to 514
P27	Sensor - front left brake lining	519 to 530

Key to wiring diagram for Senator models from 1993 (continued)

No	Description	Location	No	Description	Location
P28	Sensor - front right brake lining	519, 530	H17	Trailer indicator lamp warning indicator	868
P39	Sensor - trailer bulb test	546 to 548, 515, 517	X1	Trailer socket 7 pin	304, 306, 351, 353, 370, 373, 517, 548
M43	Shock absorber actuator - front left	401 to 403	F35	Voltage stabiliser	878
M44	Shock absorber actuator - front right	405 to 407	U6.2	Voltmeter	848
M45	Shock absorber actuator - rear left	409 to 411	U6. 35	Warning - brake lining, front	524
M46	Shock absorber actuator - rear right	413 to 415	U5.6	Warning - brake lining, front	532
P51	Speed sensor	142, 143	U6. 32	Warning - coolant minimum capacity	519
P43	Speedometer	887	U5.3	Warning - coolant minimum capacity	529
U6.8	Speedometer	838	H25	Warning - heated outside mirror	580
S105	Start-up assistance switch	134 to 136	U6.31	Warning - oil minimum capacity	518
M1	Starter	105, 106	U5.2	Warning - oil minimum capacity	528
S1.2	Starter key contact switch	829	U6. 34	Warning - stop light failure	522
S1	Starter switch	103 to 106	U5.5	Warning - stop light failure	531
H9	Stop lamp - left	510, 534	U6.33	Warning - tail light & low beam	521
H10	Stop lamp - right	512, 536	U5.4	Warning - tail light & low beam	530
S35	Sun roof micro switch	485	U5.1	Warning - washer fluid minimum capacity	527
S36	Sun roof micro switch	487	U6.30	Warning -washer fluid minimum capacity	517
M13	Sun roof motor	485 to 488	H41	Warning light indicator	856
S57	Sun roof switch	484 to 488	S82	Washer fluid control switch	521, 526
S21	Switch - fog lamp	342 to 344	R13	Washer nozzle - heated - left	440
S22	Switch - fog lamp rear	347 to 350	R14	Washer nozzle - heated - right	441
S30	Switch - heating pad - driver's side	551 to 553	S37.7	Window lifter control	677 to 680
S46	Switch - heating pad - front seats	555 to 557	M47	Window lifter motor - driver's door	667 to 671
S96	Switch - heating pad - rear left seat	562 to 564	M48	Window lifter motor - passenger door	685 to 689
S97	Switch - heating pad - rear right seat	567 to 569	M49	Window lifter motor - rear left	673 to 677
S5.2	Switch - low beam	332, 333	M50	Window lifter motor - rear right	691 to 695
S8	Switch - stop lamp	356	S99	Window lifter switch - driver's door	672
S116	Switch - stop lamp	359, 360	S37.1	Window lifter switch - driver's door	668 to 670
U6.14	Tachometer	852	S100	Window lifter switch - passenger door	684
P7	Tachometer	885	S37.2	Window lifter switch - passenger door	686 to 688
E2	Tail lamp - left	502, 538	S37.3	Window lifter switch - rear left	674 to 676
E5	Tail lamp - right	504, 540	S37.4	Window lifter switch - rear right	692 to 694
Y34	Tank ventilation solenoid valve	198, 292	S37	Window lifter switch assembly	
U8	Temperature control - driver's side		S39	Window lifter switch, door - rear left	678 to 680
U9	Temperature control - passenger side		S40	Window lifter switch, door - rear right	696 to 698
U9.1	Temperature control potentiometer	768 to 771	M5	Windscreen washer pump	433
U8.1	Temperature control potentiometer	772 to 775	K8	Windscreen wiper interval relay (in fuse box)	436 to 439
P34	Throttle valve potentiometer	168 to 170, 265 to 267	S9.2	Windscreen wiper interval switch	433 to 437
K50	Timing control (ABS)	221 to 235	M2	Windscreen wiper motor	434 to 437
X49	Trailer body & socket 9 pin	304, 306, 351 to 353, 517, 548	S9	Wiper unit switch assembly	

For colour code, abbreviations key and wiring identification, see page 12•30

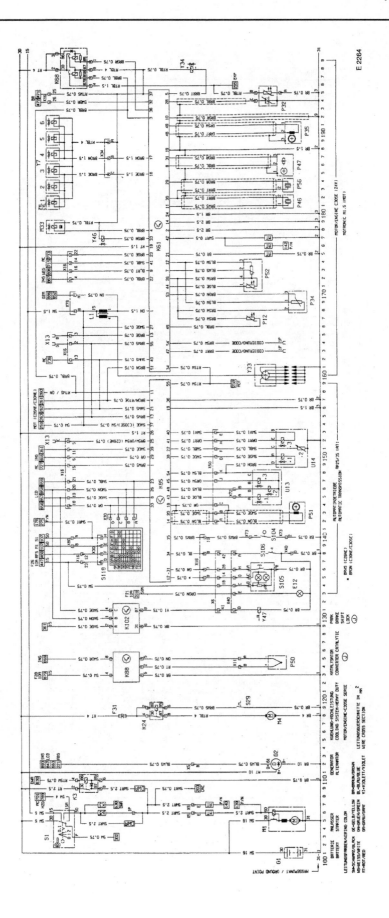

Wiring diagram for Senator models from 1993

E 2264

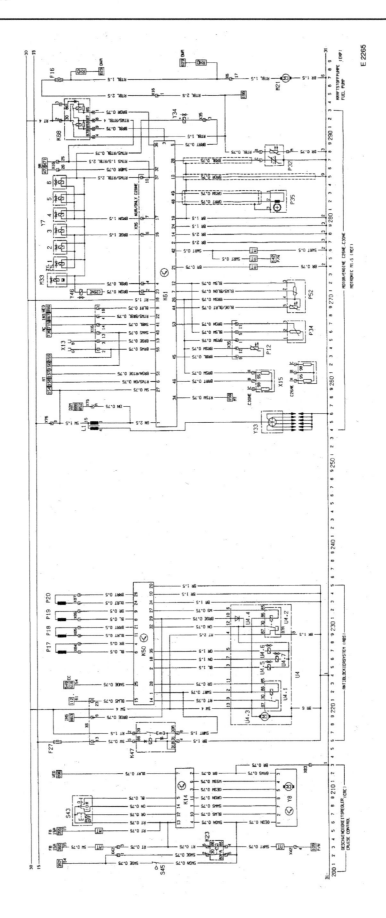

Wiring diagram for Senator models from 1993 (continued)

E 2265

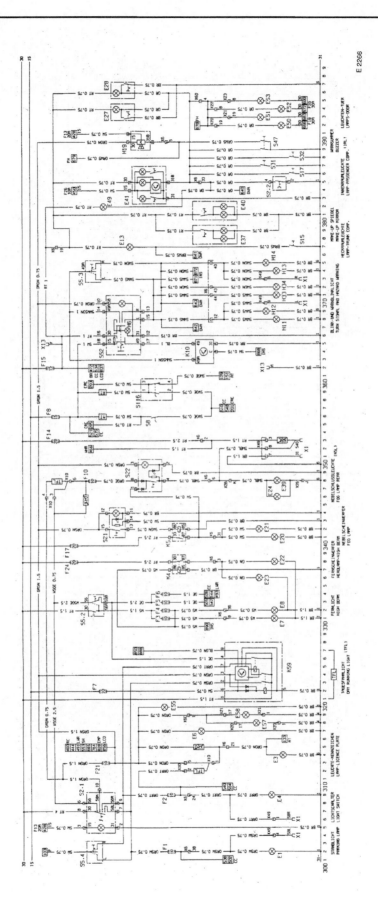

Wiring diagram for Senator models from 1993 (continued)

E 2266

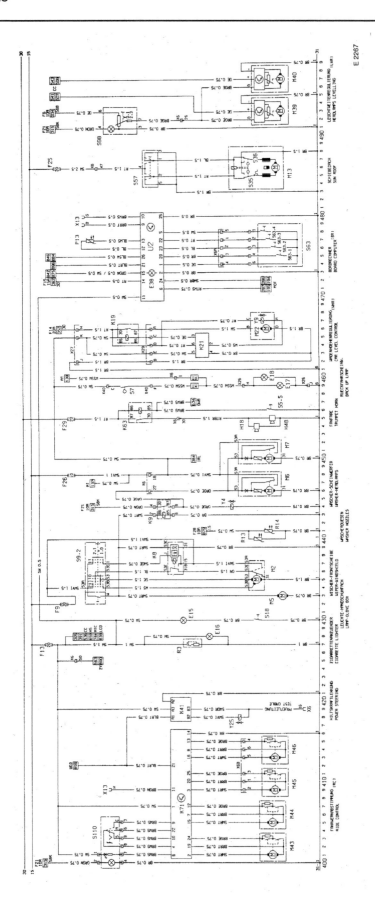

Wiring diagram for Senator models from 1993 (continued)

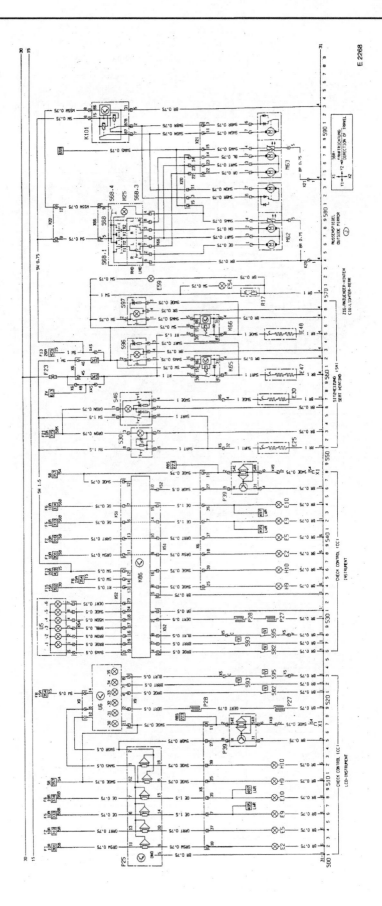

Wiring diagram for Senator models from 1993 (continued)

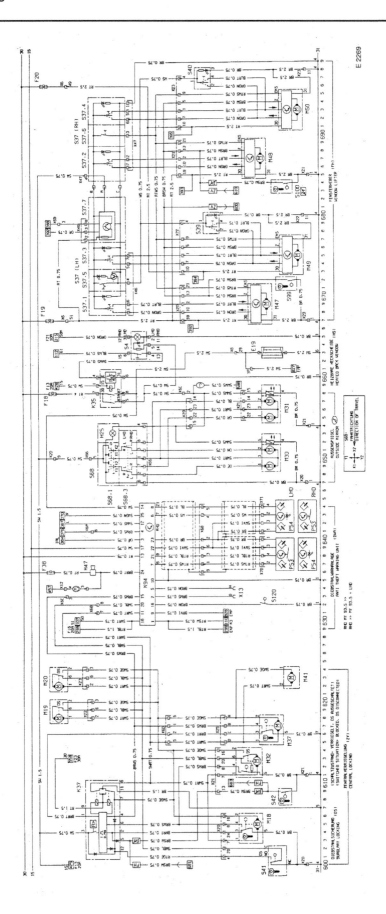

Wiring diagram for Senator models from 1993 (continued)

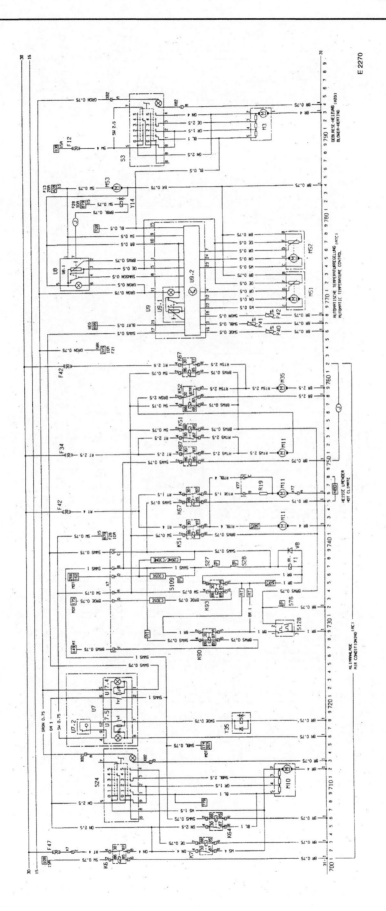

Wiring diagram for Senator models from 1993 (continued)

E 2270

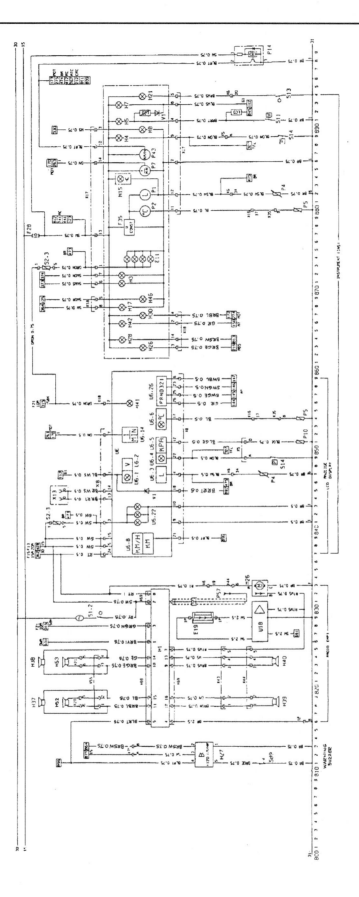

Wiring diagram for Senator models from 1993 (continued)

Dimensions and Weights .... **REF•1**
Conversion Factors .... **REF•2**
Buying Spare Parts ....**REF•3**
Vehicle Identification .... **REF•3**
General Repair Procedures .... **REF•4**
Jacking and Vehicle Support .... **REF•5**

Radio/cassette unit Anti-theft System .... **REF•5**
Tools and Working Facilities .... **REF•6**
MOT Test Checks ....**REF•8**
Fault Finding .... **REF•12**
Glossary of Technical Terms .... **REF•19**
Index .... **REF•23**

Dimensions and Weights

Note: *All figures are approximate, and may vary according to model. Refer to manufacturer's data for exact figures.*

Dimensions

Carlton

Overall length:
  Saloon models ....4738 mm
  3000 GSi ....4742 mm
  Estate models ....4768 mm
Overall width:
  Excluding 3000 GSi ....1760 mm
  3000 GSi ....1772 mm
Overall height (unladen):
  Saloon models ....1448 mm
  3000 GSi ....1425 mm
  Estate models (excluding 3.0 24V) ....1483 mm
  3.0 24V Estate models ....1530 mm

Senator

Overall length ....4845 mm
Overall width ....1763 mm
Overall height (unladen) ....1452 mm

Weights

Carlton

Kerb weight*:
  1.8 saloon with manual transmission ....1265 kg
  3.0 24V GSi with auto transmission and air conditioning ...1515 kg
Maximum gross vehicle weight*:
  1.8 saloon with manual transmission ....1955 kg
  3.0 24V GSi with auto transmission and air conditioning ...2015 kg
Maximum roof rack load ....100 kg

Senator

Kerb weight*:
  2.5i with manual transmission ....1445 kg
  3.0i 24V CD with auto transmission and air conditioning ...1574 kg
Maximum gross vehicle weight*:
  2.5i with manual transmission ....2005 kg
  3.0i 24V CD with auto transmission and air conditioning ...2065 kg
Maximum roof rack load ....100 kg

Depending on model and specification.

Conversion Factors

Length (distance)
Inches (in)	25.4	= Millimetres (mm)	x 0.0394	= Inches (in)
Feet (ft)	0.305	= Metres (m)	x 3.281	= Feet (ft)
Miles	1.609	= Kilometres (km)	x 0.621	= Miles

Volume (capacity)
Cubic inches (cu in; in³)	x 16.387	= Cubic centimetres (cc; cm³)	x 0.061	= Cubic inches (cu in; in³)
Imperial pints (Imp pt)	x 0.568	= Litres (l)	x 1.76	= Imperial pints (Imp pt)
Imperial quarts (Imp qt)	x 1.137	= Litres (l)	x 0.88	= Imperial quarts (Imp qt)
Imperial quarts (Imp qt)	x 1.201	= US quarts (US qt)	x 0.833	= Imperial quarts (Imp qt)
US quarts (US qt)	x 0.946	= Litres (l)	x 1.057	= US quarts (US qt)
Imperial gallons (Imp gal)	x 4.546	= Litres (l)	x 0.22	= Imperial gallons (Imp gal)
Imperial gallons (Imp gal)	x 1.201	= US gallons (US gal)	x 0.833	= Imperial gallons (Imp gal)
US gallons (US gal)	x 3.785	= Litres (l)	x 0.264	= US gallons (US gal)

Mass (weight)
Ounces (oz)	x 28.35	= Grams (g)	x 0.035	= Ounces (oz)
Pounds (lb)	x 0.454	= Kilograms (kg)	x 2.205	= Pounds (lb)

Force
Ounces-force (ozf; oz)	x 0.278	= Newtons (N)	x 3.6	= Ounces-force (ozf; oz)
Pounds-force (lbf; lb)	x 4.448	= Newtons (N)	x 0.225	= Pounds-force (lbf; lb)
Newtons (N)	x 0.1	= Kilograms-force (kgf; kg)	x 9.81	= Newtons (N)

Pressure
Pounds-force per square inch (psi; lbf/in²; lb/in²)	x 0.070	= Kilograms-force per square centimetre (kgf/cm²; kg/cm²)	x 14.223	= Pounds-force per square inch (psi; lbf/in²; lb/in²)
Pounds-force per square inch (psi; lbf/in²; lb/in²)	x 0.068	= Atmospheres (atm)	x 14.696	= Pounds-force per square inch (psi; lbf/in²; lb/in²)
Pounds-force per square inch (psi; lbf/in²; lb/in²)	x 0.069	= Bars	x 14.5	= Pounds-force per square inch (psi; lbf/in²; lb/in²)
Pounds-force per square inch (psi; lbf/in²; lb/in²)	x 6.895	= Kilopascals (kPa)	x 0.145	= Pounds-force per square inch (psi; lbf/in²; lb/in²)
Kilopascals (kPa)	x 0.01	= Kilograms-force per square centimetre (kgf/cm²; kg/cm²)	x 98.1	= Kilopascals (kPa)
Millibar (mbar)	x 100	= Pascals (Pa)	x 0.01	= Millibar (mbar)
Millibar (mbar)	x 0.0145	= Pounds-force per square inch (psi; lbf/in²; lb/in²)	x 68.947	= Millibar (mbar)
Millibar (mbar)	x 0.75	= Millimetres of mercury (mmHg)	x 1.333	= Millibar (mbar)
Millibar (mbar)	x 0.401	= Inches of water (inH₂O)	x 2.491	= Millibar (mbar)
Millimetres of mercury (mmHg)	x 0.535	= Inches of water (inH₂O)	x 1.868	= Millimetres of mercury (mmHg)
Inches of water (inH₂O)	x 0.036	= Pounds-force per square inch (psi; lbf/in²; lb/in²)	x 27.68	= Inches of water (inH₂O)

Torque (moment of force)
Pounds-force inches (lbf in; lb in)	x 1.152	= Kilograms-force centimetre (kgf cm; kg cm)	x 0.868	= Pounds-force inches (lbf in; lb in)
Pounds-force inches (lbf in; lb in)	x 0.113	= Newton metres (Nm)	x 8.85	= Pounds-force inches (lbf in; lb in)
Pounds-force inches (lbf in; lb in)	x 0.083	= Pounds-force feet (lbf ft; lb ft)	x 12	= Pounds-force inches (lbf in; lb in)
Pounds-force feet (lbf ft; lb ft)	x 0.138	= Kilograms-force metres (kgf m; kg m)	x 7.233	= Pounds-force feet (lbf ft; lb ft)
Pounds-force feet (lbf ft; lb ft)	x 1.356	= Newton metres (Nm)	x 0.738	= Pounds-force feet (lbf ft; lb ft)
Newton metres (Nm)	x 0.102	= Kilograms-force metres (kgf m; kg m)	x 9.804	= Newton metres (Nm)

Power
Horsepower (hp)	x 745.7	= Watts (W)	x 0.0013	= Horsepower (hp)

Velocity (speed)
Miles per hour (miles/hr; mph)	x 1.609	= Kilometres per hour (km/hr; kph)	x 0.621	= Miles per hour (miles/hr; mph)

Fuel consumption*
Miles per gallon (mpg)	x 0.354	= Kilometres per litre (km/l)	x 2.825	= Miles per gallon (mpg)

* It is common practice to convert from miles per gallon (mpg) to litres/100 kilometres (l/100km), where mpg x l/100 km = 282

Temperature
Degrees Fahrenheit = (°C x 1.8) + 32   Degrees Celsius (Degrees Centigrade; °C) = (°F - 32) x 0.56

Spare parts are available from many sources, including maker's appointed garages, accessory shops, and motor factors. To be sure of obtaining the correct parts, it will sometimes be necessary to quote the vehicle identification number. If possible, it can also be useful to take the old parts along for positive identification. Items such as starter motors and alternators may be available under a service exchange scheme - any parts returned should be clean.

Our advice regarding spare parts is as follows.

Officially appointed garages

This is the best source of parts which are peculiar to your car, and which are not otherwise generally available (eg, badges, interior trim, certain body panels, etc). It is also the only place at which you should buy parts if the vehicle is still under warranty.

Accessory shops

These are very good places to buy materials and components needed for the maintenance of your car (oil, air and fuel filters, light bulbs, drivebelts, greases, brake pads, touch-up paint, etc). Components of this nature sold by a reputable shop are usually of the same standard as those used by the car manufacturer.

Besides components, these shops also sell tools and general accessories, usually have convenient opening hours, charge lower prices, and can often be found close to home. Some accessory shops have parts counters where components needed for almost any repair job can be purchased or ordered.

Motor factors

Good factors will stock all the more important components which wear out comparatively quickly, and can sometimes supply individual components needed for the overhaul of a larger assembly (eg, brake seals and hydraulic parts, bearing shells, pistons, valves). They may also handle work such as cylinder block reboring, crankshaft regrinding, etc.

Tyre and exhaust specialists

These outlets may be independent, or members of a local or national chain. They frequently offer competitive prices when compared with a main dealer or local garage, but it will pay to obtain several quotes before making a decision. When researching prices, also ask what "extras" may be added - for instance fitting a new valve and balancing the wheel are both commonly charged on top of the price of a new tyre.

Other sources

Beware of parts or materials obtained from market stalls, car boot sales or similar outlets. Such items are not invariably sub-standard, but there is little chance of compensation if they do prove unsatisfactory. in the case of safety-critical components such as brake pads, there is the risk not only of financial loss, but also of an accident causing injury or death.

Second-hand components or assemblies obtained from a car breaker can be a good buy in some circumstances, but this sort of purchase is best made by the experienced DIY mechanic.

Vehicle Identification

Modifications are a continuing and unpublicised process in vehicle manufacture, quite apart from major model changes. Spare parts manuals and lists are compiled upon a numerical basis, the individual vehicle identification numbers being essential to correct identification of the component concerned.

When ordering spare parts, always give as much information as possible. Quote the car model, year of manufacture and registration, chassis and engine numbers as appropriate.

The *Vehicle Identification Number (VIN)* plate is riveted to the body panel above the radiator. The vehicle identification number is also stamped into the floorpan, beneath the carpet between the driver's door and seat **(see illustrations)**.

The *engine number* is stamped on the left hand face of the cylinder block.

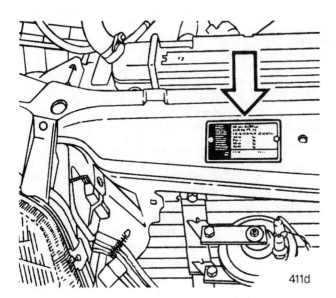

The VIN plate is riveted to the body panel above the radiator

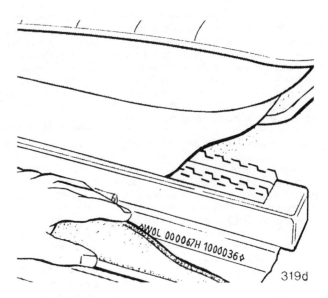

The vehicle identification number is also stamped into the floorpan, beneath the carpet between the driver's door and seat

Whenever servicing, repair or overhaul work is carried out on the car or its components, it is necessary to observe the following procedures and instructions. This will assist in carrying out the operation efficiently and to a professional standard of workmanship.

Joint mating faces and gaskets

When separating components at their mating faces, never insert screwdrivers or similar implements into the joint between the faces in order to prise them apart. This can cause severe damage which results in oil leaks, coolant leaks, etc upon reassembly. Separation is usually achieved by tapping along the joint with a soft-faced hammer in order to break the seal. However, note that this method may not be suitable where dowels are used for component location.

Where a gasket is used between the mating faces of two components, ensure that it is renewed on reassembly, and fit it dry unless otherwise stated in the repair procedure. Make sure that the mating faces are clean and dry, with all traces of old gasket removed. When cleaning a joint face, use a tool which is not likely to score or damage the face, and remove any burrs or nicks with an oilstone or fine file.

Make sure that tapped holes are cleaned with a pipe cleaner, and keep them free of jointing compound, if this is being used, unless specifically instructed otherwise.

Ensure that all orifices, channels or pipes are clear, and blow through them, preferably using compressed air.

Oil seals

Oil seals can be removed by levering them out with a wide flat-bladed screwdriver or similar tool. Alternatively, a number of self-tapping screws may be screwed into the seal, and these used as a purchase for pliers or similar in order to pull the seal free.

Whenever an oil seal is removed from its working location, either individually or as part of an assembly, it should be renewed.

The very fine sealing lip of the seal is easily damaged, and will not seal if the surface it contacts is not completely clean and free from scratches, nicks or grooves. If the original sealing surface of the component cannot be restored, and the manufacturer has not made provision for slight relocation of the seal relative to the sealing surface, the component should be renewed.

Protect the lips of the seal from any surface which may damage them in the course of fitting. Use tape or a conical sleeve where possible. Lubricate the seal lips with oil before fitting and, on dual-lipped seals, fill the space between the lips with grease.

Unless otherwise stated, oil seals must be fitted with their sealing lips toward the lubricant to be sealed.

Use a tubular drift or block of wood of the appropriate size to install the seal and, if the seal housing is shouldered, drive the seal down to the shoulder. If the seal housing is unshouldered, the seal should be fitted with its face flush with the housing top face (unless otherwise instructed).

Screw threads and fastenings

Seized nuts, bolts and screws are quite a common occurrence where corrosion has set in, and the use of penetrating oil or releasing fluid will often overcome this problem if the offending item is soaked for a while before attempting to release it. The use of an impact driver may also provide a means of releasing such stubborn fastening devices, when used in conjunction with the appropriate screwdriver bit or socket. If none of these methods works, it may be necessary to resort to the careful application of heat, or the use of a hacksaw or nut splitter device.

Studs are usually removed by locking two nuts together on the threaded part, and then using a spanner on the lower nut to unscrew the stud. Studs or bolts which have broken off below the surface of the component in which they are mounted can sometimes be removed using a stud extractor. Always ensure that a blind tapped hole is completely free from oil, grease, water or other fluid before installing the bolt or stud. Failure to do this could cause the housing to crack due to the hydraulic action of the bolt or stud as it is screwed in.

When tightening a castellated nut to accept a split pin, tighten the nut to the specified torque, where applicable, and then tighten further to the next split pin hole. Never slacken the nut to align the split pin hole, unless stated in the repair procedure.

When checking or retightening a nut or bolt to a specified torque setting, slacken the nut or bolt by a quarter of a turn, and then retighten to the specified setting. However, this should not be attempted where angular tightening has been used.

For some screw fastenings, notably cylinder head bolts or nuts, torque wrench settings are no longer specified for the latter stages of tightening, "angle-tightening" being called up instead. Typically, a fairly low torque wrench setting will be applied to the bolts/nuts in the correct sequence, followed by one or more stages of tightening through specified angles.

Locknuts, locktabs and washers

Any fastening which will rotate against a component or housing during tightening should always have a washer between it and the relevant component or housing.

Spring or split washers should always be renewed when they are used to lock a critical component such as a big-end bearing retaining bolt or nut. Locktabs which are folded over to retain a nut or bolt should always be renewed.

Self-locking nuts can be re-used in non-critical areas, providing resistance can be felt when the locking portion passes over the bolt or stud thread. However, it should be noted that self-locking stiffnuts tend to lose their effectiveness after long periods of use, and should be renewed as a matter of course.

Split pins must always be replaced with new ones of the correct size for the hole.

When thread-locking compound is found on the threads of a fastener which is to be re-used, it should be cleaned off with a wire brush and solvent, and fresh compound applied on reassembly.

Special tools

Some repair procedures in this manual entail the use of special tools such as a press, two or three-legged pullers, spring compressors, etc. Wherever possible, suitable readily-available alternatives to the manufacturer's special tools are described, and are shown in use. In some instances, where no alternative is possible, it has been necessary to resort to the use of a manufacturer's tool, and this has been done for reasons of safety as well as the efficient completion of the repair operation. Unless you are highly-skilled and have a thorough understanding of the procedures described, never attempt to bypass the use of any special tool when the procedure described specifies its use. Not only is there a very great risk of personal injury, but expensive damage could be caused to the components involved.

Environmental considerations

When disposing of used engine oil, brake fluid, antifreeze, etc, give due consideration to any detrimental environmental effects. Do not, for instance, pour any of the above liquids down drains into the general sewage system, or onto the ground to soak away. Many local council refuse tips provide a facility for waste oil disposal, as do some garages. If none of these facilities are available, consult your local Environmental Health Department, or the National Rivers Authority, for further advice.

With the universal tightening-up of legislation regarding the emission of environmentally-harmful substances from motor vehicles, most current vehicles have tamperproof devices fitted to the main adjustment points of the fuel system. These devices are primarily designed to prevent unqualified persons from adjusting the fuel/air mixture, with the chance of a consequent increase in toxic emissions. If such devices are encountered during servicing or overhaul, they should, wherever possible, be renewed or refitted in accordance with the vehicle manufacturer's requirements or current legislation.

OIL BANK LINE
0800 66 33 66

Note: It is antisocial and illegal to dump oil down the drain. To find the location of your local oil recycling bank, call this number free.

Jacking and Vehicle Support

The jack supplied with the vehicle tool kit should only be used for changing the roadwheels - see *"Wheel changing"* at the front of this manual. When carrying out any other kind of work, raise the vehicle using a hydraulic (or "trolley") jack, and always supplement the jack with axle stands positioned under the vehicle jacking points.

When using a hydraulic jack or axle stands, always position the jack head or axle stand head

under, or adjacent to one of the relevant wheel changing jacking points **(see illustrations)**.

The jack supplied with the vehicle locates in the jacking points on the underside of the sills. Ensure that the jack head is correctly engaged before attempting to raise the vehicle.

Never work under, around, or near a raised vehicle, unless it is adequately supported in at least two places.

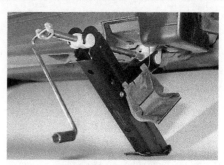

Vehicle jack in use

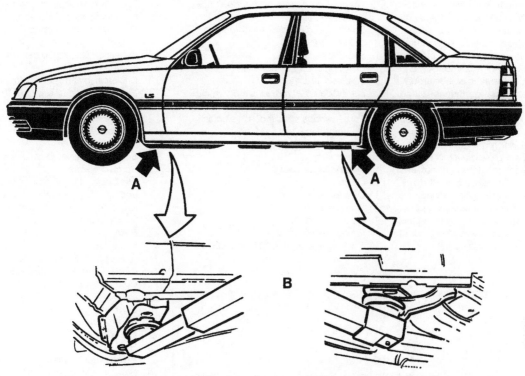

Jacking points for (A) vehicle jack and (B) trolley jack or vehicle hoist

Radio/cassette unit Anti-theft System - Precaution

The radio/cassette/CD player/autochanger unit fitted to later models as standard equipment by Vauxhall is equipped with a built-in security code, to deter thieves. If the power source to the unit is cut, the anti-theft system will activate. Even if the power source is immediately reconnected, the unit will not

function until the correct security code has been entered. Therefore if you do not know the correct security code for the unit, **do not** disconnect the battery negative lead, or remove the radio/cassette unit from the vehicle.

The procedure for reprogramming a unit that has been disconnected from its power supply varies from model to model - consult the handbook supplied with the unit for specific details or refer to your GM dealer.

Introduction

A selection of good tools is a fundamental requirement for anyone contemplating the maintenance and repair of a motor vehicle. For the owner who does not possess any, their purchase will prove a considerable expense, offsetting some of the savings made by doing-it-yourself. However, provided that the tools purchased meet the relevant national safety standards and are of good quality, they will last for many years and prove an extremely worthwhile investment.

To help the average owner to decide which tools are needed to carry out the various tasks detailed in this manual, we have compiled three lists of tools under the following headings: *Maintenance and minor repair, Repair and overhaul*, and *Special*. Newcomers to practical mechanics should start off with the *Maintenance and minor repair* tool kit, and confine themselves to the simpler jobs around the vehicle. Then, as confidence and experience grow, more difficult tasks can be undertaken, with extra tools being purchased as, and when, they are needed. In this way, a *Maintenance and minor repair* tool kit can be built up into a *Repair and overhaul* tool kit over a considerable period of time, without any major cash outlays. The experienced do-it-yourselfer will have a tool kit good enough for most repair and overhaul procedures, and will add tools from the *Special* category when it is felt that the expense is justified by the amount of use to which these tools will be put.

Maintenance and minor repair tool kit

The tools given in this list should be considered as a minimum requirement if routine maintenance, servicing and minor repair operations are to be undertaken. We recommend the purchase of combination spanners (ring one end, open-ended the other); although more expensive than open-ended ones, they do give the advantages of both types of spanner.

☐ *Combination spanners:*
  Metric - 8 to 19 mm inclusive
☐ *Adjustable spanner - 35 mm jaw (approx.)*
☐ *Spark plug spanner (with rubber insert) - petrol models*
☐ *Spark plug gap adjustment tool - petrol models*
☐ *Set of feeler gauges*
☐ *Brake bleed nipple spanner*
☐ *Screwdrivers:*
  Flat blade - 100 mm long x 6 mm dia
  Cross blade - 100 mm long x 6 mm dia
  Torx - various sizes (not all vehicles)
☐ *Combination pliers*
☐ *Hacksaw (junior)*
☐ *Tyre pump*
☐ *Tyre pressure gauge*
☐ *Oil can*
☐ *Oil filter removal tool*
☐ *Fine emery cloth*
☐ *Wire brush (small)*
☐ *Funnel (medium size)*
☐ *Sump drain plug key (not all vehicles)*

Repair and overhaul tool kit

These tools are virtually essential for anyone undertaking any major repairs to a motor vehicle, and are additional to those given in the *Maintenance and minor repair* list. Included in this list is a comprehensive set of sockets. Although these are expensive, they will be found invaluable as they are so versatile - particularly if various drives are included in the set. We recommend the half-inch square-drive type, as this can be used with most proprietary torque wrenches.

The tools in this list will sometimes need to be supplemented by tools from the *Special* list:

☐ *Sockets (or box spanners) to cover range in previous list (including Torx sockets)*
☐ *Reversible ratchet drive (for use with sockets)*
☐ *Extension piece, 250 mm (for use with sockets)*
☐ *Universal joint (for use with sockets)*
☐ *Flexible handle or sliding T "breaker bar" (for use with sockets)*
☐ *Torque wrench (for use with sockets)*
☐ *Self-locking grips*
☐ *Ball pein hammer*
☐ *Soft-faced mallet (plastic or rubber)*
☐ *Screwdrivers:*
  Flat blade - long & sturdy, short (chubby), and narrow (electrician's) types
  Cross blade - long & sturdy, and short (chubby) types
☐ *Pliers:*
  Long-nosed
  Side cutters (electrician's)
  Circlip (internal and external)
☐ *Cold chisel - 25 mm*
☐ *Scriber*
☐ *Scraper*
☐ *Centre-punch*
☐ *Pin punch*
☐ *Hacksaw*
☐ *Brake hose clamp*
☐ *Brake/clutch bleeding kit*
☐ *Selection of twist drills*
☐ *Steel rule/straight-edge*
☐ *Allen keys (inc. splined/Torx type)*
☐ *Selection of files*
☐ *Wire brush*
☐ *Axle stands*
☐ *Jack (strong trolley or hydraulic type)*
☐ *Light with extension lead*
☐ *Universal electrical multi-meter*

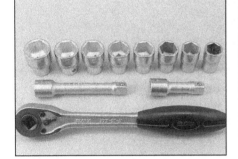
Sockets and reversible ratchet drive

Brake bleeding kit

Torx key, socket and bit

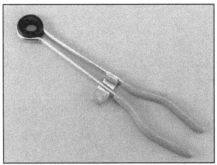
Hose clamp

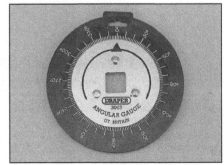
Angular-tightening gauge

Special tools

The tools in this list are those which are not used regularly, are expensive to buy, or which need to be used in accordance with their manufacturers' instructions. Unless relatively difficult mechanical jobs are undertaken frequently, it will not be economic to buy many of these tools. Where this is the case, you could consider clubbing together with friends (or joining a motorists' club) to make a joint purchase, or borrowing the tools against a deposit from a local garage or tool hire specialist. It is worth noting that many of the larger DIY superstores now carry a large range of special tools for hire at modest rates.

The following list contains only those tools and instruments freely available to the public, and not those special tools produced by the vehicle manufacturer specifically for its dealer network. You will find occasional references to these manufacturers' special tools in the text of this manual. Generally, an alternative method of doing the job without the vehicle manufacturers' special tool is given. However, sometimes there is no alternative to using them. Where this is the case and the relevant tool cannot be bought or borrowed, you will have to entrust the work to a dealer.

- [ ] Angular-tightening gauge
- [ ] Valve spring compressor
- [ ] Valve grinding tool
- [ ] Piston ring compressor
- [ ] Piston ring removal/installation tool
- [ ] Cylinder bore hone
- [ ] Balljoint separator
- [ ] Coil spring compressors (where applicable)
- [ ] Two/three-legged hub and bearing puller
- [ ] Impact screwdriver
- [ ] Micrometer and/or vernier calipers
- [ ] Dial gauge
- [ ] Stroboscopic timing light
- [ ] Dwell angle meter/tachometer
- [ ] Fault code reader
- [ ] Cylinder compression gauge
- [ ] Hand-operated vacuum pump and gauge
- [ ] Clutch plate alignment set
- [ ] Brake shoe steady spring cup removal tool
- [ ] Bush and bearing removal/installation set
- [ ] Stud extractors
- [ ] Tap and die set
- [ ] Lifting tackle
- [ ] Trolley jack

Buying tools

Reputable motor accessory shops and superstores often offer excellent quality tools at discount prices, so it pays to shop around.

Remember, you don't have to buy the most expensive items on the shelf, but it is always advisable to steer clear of the very cheap tools. Beware of 'bargains' offered on market stalls or at car boot sales. There are plenty of good tools around at reasonable prices, but always aim to purchase items which meet the relevant national safety standards. If in doubt, ask the proprietor or manager of the shop for advice before making a purchase.

Care and maintenance of tools

Having purchased a reasonable tool kit, it is necessary to keep the tools in a clean and serviceable condition. After use, always wipe off any dirt, grease and metal particles using a clean, dry cloth, before putting the tools away. Never leave them lying around after they have been used. A simple tool rack on the garage or workshop wall for items such as screwdrivers and pliers is a good idea. Store all normal spanners and sockets in a metal box. Any measuring instruments, gauges, meters, etc, must be carefully stored where they cannot be damaged or become rusty.

Take a little care when tools are used. Hammer heads inevitably become marked, and screwdrivers lose the keen edge on their blades from time to time. A little timely attention with emery cloth or a file will soon restore items like this to a good finish.

Working facilities

Not to be forgotten when discussing tools is the workshop itself. If anything more than routine maintenance is to be carried out, a suitable working area becomes essential.

It is appreciated that many an owner-mechanic is forced by circumstances to remove an engine or similar item without the benefit of a garage or workshop. Having done this, any repairs should always be done under the cover of a roof.

Wherever possible, any dismantling should be done on a clean, flat workbench or table at a suitable working height.

Any workbench needs a vice; one with a jaw opening of 100 mm is suitable for most jobs. As mentioned previously, some clean dry storage space is also required for tools, as well as for any lubricants, cleaning fluids, touch-up paints etc, which become necessary.

Another item which may be required, and which has a much more general usage, is an electric drill with a chuck capacity of at least 8 mm. This, together with a good range of twist drills, is virtually essential for fitting accessories.

Last, but not least, always keep a supply of old newspapers and clean, lint-free rags available, and try to keep any working area as clean as possible.

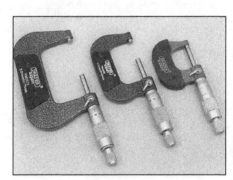

Micrometers

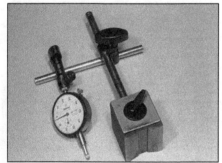

Dial test indicator ("dial gauge")

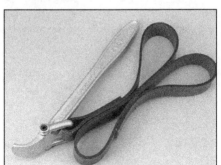

Strap wrench

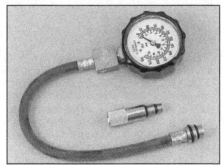

Compression tester

Fault code reader

This is a guide to getting your vehicle through the MOT test. Obviously it will not be possible to examine the vehicle to the same standard as the professional MOT tester. However, working through the following checks will enable you to identify any problem areas before submitting the vehicle for the test.

Where a testable component is in borderline condition, the tester has discretion in deciding whether to pass or fail it. The basis of such discretion is whether the tester would be happy for a close relative or friend to use the vehicle with the component in that condition. If the vehicle presented is clean and evidently well cared for, the tester may be more inclined to pass a borderline component than if the vehicle is scruffy and apparently neglected.

It has only been possible to summarise the test requirements here, based on the regulations in force at the time of printing. Test standards are becoming increasingly stringent, although there are some exemptions for older vehicles. For full details obtain a copy of the Haynes publication Pass the MOT! (available from stockists of Haynes manuals).

An assistant will be needed to help carry out some of these checks.

The checks have been sub-divided into four categories, as follows:

1 Checks carried out **FROM THE DRIVER'S SEAT**

2 Checks carried out **WITH THE VEHICLE ON THE GROUND**

3 Checks carried out **WITH THE VEHICLE RAISED AND THE WHEELS FREE TO TURN**

4 Checks carried out on **YOUR VEHICLE'S EXHAUST EMISSION SYSTEM**

1 Checks carried out **FROM THE DRIVER'S SEAT**

Handbrake

☐ Test the operation of the handbrake. Excessive travel (too many clicks) indicates incorrect brake or cable adjustment.

☐ Check that the handbrake cannot be released by tapping the lever sideways. Check the security of the lever mountings.

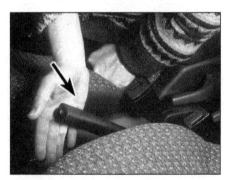

Footbrake

☐ Depress the brake pedal and check that it does not creep down to the floor, indicating a master cylinder fault. Release the pedal, wait a few seconds, then depress it again. If the pedal travels nearly to the floor before firm resistance is felt, brake adjustment or repair is necessary. If the pedal feels spongy, there is air in the hydraulic system which must be removed by bleeding.

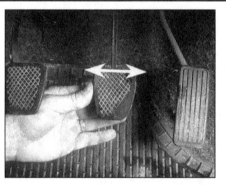

☐ Check that the brake pedal is secure and in good condition. Check also for signs of fluid leaks on the pedal, floor or carpets, which would indicate failed seals in the brake master cylinder.

☐ Check the servo unit (when applicable) by operating the brake pedal several times, then keeping the pedal depressed and starting the engine. As the engine starts, the pedal will move down slightly. If not, the vacuum hose or the servo itself may be faulty.

Steering wheel and column

☐ Examine the steering wheel for fractures or looseness of the hub, spokes or rim.

☐ Move the steering wheel from side to side and then up and down. Check that the steering wheel is not loose on the column, indicating wear or a loose retaining nut. Continue moving the steering wheel as before, but also turn it slightly from left to right.

☐ Check that the steering wheel is not loose on the column, and that there is no abnormal

movement of the steering wheel, indicating wear in the column support bearings or couplings.

Windscreen and mirrors

☐ The windscreen must be free of cracks or other significant damage within the driver's field of view. (Small stone chips are acceptable.) Rear view mirrors must be secure, intact, and capable of being adjusted.

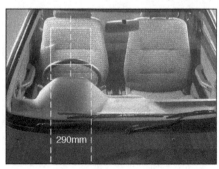

290mm

Seat belts and seats

Note: *The following checks are applicable to all seat belts, front and rear.*

☐ Examine the webbing of all the belts (including rear belts if fitted) for cuts, serious fraying or deterioration. Fasten and unfasten each belt to check the buckles. If applicable, check the retracting mechanism. Check the security of all seat belt mountings accessible from inside the vehicle.
☐ The front seats themselves must be securely attached and the backrests must lock in the upright position.

Doors

☐ Both front doors must be able to be opened and closed from outside and inside, and must latch securely when closed.

2 Checks carried out WITH THE VEHICLE ON THE GROUND

Vehicle identification

☐ Number plates must be in good condition, secure and legible, with letters and numbers correctly spaced – spacing at (A) should be twice that at (B).

☐ The VIN plate and/or homologation plate must be legible.

Electrical equipment

☐ Switch on the ignition and check the operation of the horn.
☐ Check the windscreen washers and wipers, examining the wiper blades; renew damaged or perished blades. Also check the operation of the stop-lights.

☐ Check the operation of the sidelights and number plate lights. The lenses and reflectors must be secure, clean and undamaged.
☐ Check the operation and alignment of the headlights. The headlight reflectors must not be tarnished and the lenses must be undamaged.
☐ Switch on the ignition and check the operation of the direction indicators (including the instrument panel tell-tale) and the hazard warning lights. Operation of the sidelights and stop-lights must not affect the indicators - if it does, the cause is usually a bad earth at the rear light cluster.
☐ Check the operation of the rear foglight(s), including the warning light on the instrument panel or in the switch.

Footbrake

☐ Examine the master cylinder, brake pipes and servo unit for leaks, loose mountings, corrosion or other damage.

☐ The fluid reservoir must be secure and the fluid level must be between the upper (**A**) and lower (**B**) markings.

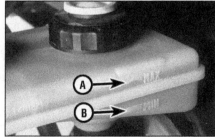

☐ Inspect both front brake flexible hoses for cracks or deterioration of the rubber. Turn the steering from lock to lock, and ensure that the hoses do not contact the wheel, tyre, or any part of the steering or suspension mechanism. With the brake pedal firmly depressed, check the hoses for bulges or leaks under pressure.

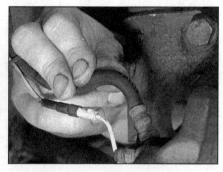

Steering and suspension

☐ Have your assistant turn the steering wheel from side to side slightly, up to the point where the steering gear just begins to transmit this movement to the roadwheels. Check for excessive free play between the steering wheel and the steering gear, indicating wear or insecurity of the steering column joints, the column-to-steering gear coupling, or the steering gear itself.
☐ Have your assistant turn the steering wheel more vigorously in each direction, so that the roadwheels just begin to turn. As this is done, examine all the steering joints, linkages, fittings and attachments. Renew any component that shows signs of wear or damage. On vehicles with power steering, check the security and condition of the steering pump, drivebelt and hoses.
☐ Check that the vehicle is standing level, and at approximately the correct ride height.

Shock absorbers

☐ Depress each corner of the vehicle in turn, then release it. The vehicle should rise and then settle in its normal position. If the vehicle continues to rise and fall, the shock absorber is defective. A shock absorber which has seized will also cause the vehicle to fail.

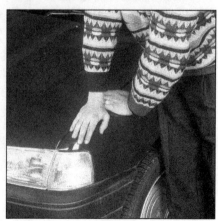

Exhaust system

☐ Start the engine. With your assistant holding a rag over the tailpipe, check the entire system for leaks. Repair or renew leaking sections.

3 Checks carried out
WITH THE VEHICLE RAISED AND THE WHEELS FREE TO TURN

Jack up the front and rear of the vehicle, and securely support it on axle stands. Position the stands clear of the suspension assemblies. Ensure that the wheels are clear of the ground and that the steering can be turned from lock to lock.

Steering mechanism

☐ Have your assistant turn the steering from lock to lock. Check that the steering turns smoothly, and that no part of the steering mechanism, including a wheel or tyre, fouls any brake hose or pipe or any part of the body structure.
☐ Examine the steering rack rubber gaiters for damage or insecurity of the retaining clips. If power steering is fitted, check for signs of damage or leakage of the fluid hoses, pipes or connections. Also check for excessive stiffness or binding of the steering, a missing split pin or locking device, or severe corrosion of the body structure within 30 cm of any steering component attachment point.

Front and rear suspension and wheel bearings

☐ Starting at the front right-hand side, grasp the roadwheel at the 3 o'clock and 9 o'clock positions and shake it vigorously. Check for free play or insecurity at the wheel bearings, suspension balljoints, or suspension mountings, pivots and attachments.
☐ Now grasp the wheel at the 12 o'clock and 6 o'clock positions and repeat the previous inspection. Spin the wheel, and check for roughness or tightness of the front wheel bearing.

☐ If excess free play is suspected at a component pivot point, this can be confirmed by using a large screwdriver or similar tool and levering between the mounting and the component attachment. This will confirm whether the wear is in the pivot bush, its retaining bolt, or in the mounting itself (the bolt holes can often become elongated).

☐ Carry out all the above checks at the other front wheel, and then at both rear wheels.

Springs and shock absorbers

☐ Examine the suspension struts (when applicable) for serious fluid leakage, corrosion, or damage to the casing. Also check the security of the mounting points.
☐ If coil springs are fitted, check that the spring ends locate in their seats, and that the spring is not corroded, cracked or broken.
☐ If leaf springs are fitted, check that all leaves are intact, that the axle is securely attached to each spring, and that there is no deterioration of the spring eye mountings, bushes, and shackles.

☐ The same general checks apply to vehicles fitted with other suspension types, such as torsion bars, hydraulic displacer units, etc. Ensure that all mountings and attachments are secure, that there are no signs of excessive wear, corrosion or damage, and (on hydraulic types) that there are no fluid leaks or damaged pipes.
☐ Inspect the shock absorbers for signs of serious fluid leakage. Check for wear of the mounting bushes or attachments, or damage to the body of the unit.

Driveshafts (fwd vehicles only)

☐ Rotate each front wheel in turn and inspect the constant velocity joint gaiters for splits or damage. Also check that each driveshaft is straight and undamaged.

Braking system

☐ If possible without dismantling, check brake pad wear and disc condition. Ensure that the friction lining material has not worn excessively, (A) and that the discs are not fractured, pitted, scored or badly worn (B).

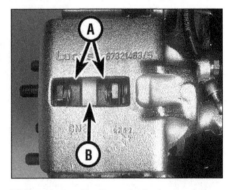

☐ Examine all the rigid brake pipes underneath the vehicle, and the flexible hose(s) at the rear. Look for corrosion, chafing or insecurity of the pipes, and for signs of bulging under pressure, chafing, splits or deterioration of the flexible hoses.
☐ Look for signs of fluid leaks at the brake calipers or on the brake backplates. Repair or renew leaking components.
☐ Slowly spin each wheel, while your assistant depresses and releases the footbrake. Ensure that each brake is operating and does not bind when the pedal is released.

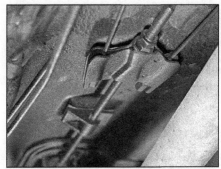

☐ Examine the handbrake mechanism, checking for frayed or broken cables, excessive corrosion, or wear or insecurity of the linkage. Check that the mechanism works on each relevant wheel, and releases fully, without binding.

☐ It is not possible to test brake efficiency without special equipment, but a road test can be carried out later to check that the vehicle pulls up in a straight line.

Fuel and exhaust systems

☐ Inspect the fuel tank (including the filler cap), fuel pipes, hoses and unions. All components must be secure and free from leaks.

☐ Examine the exhaust system over its entire length, checking for any damaged, broken or missing mountings, security of the retaining clamps and rust or corrosion.

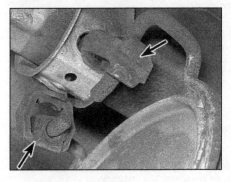

Wheels and tyres

☐ Examine the sidewalls and tread area of each tyre in turn. Check for cuts, tears, lumps, bulges, separation of the tread, and exposure of the ply or cord due to wear or damage. Check that the tyre bead is correctly seated on the wheel rim, that the valve is sound and

properly seated, and that the wheel is not distorted or damaged.

☐ Check that the tyres are of the correct size for the vehicle, that they are of the same size and type on each axle, and that the pressures are correct.

☐ Check the tyre tread depth. The legal minimum at the time of writing is 1.6 mm over at least three-quarters of the tread width. Abnormal tread wear may indicate incorrect front wheel alignment.

Body corrosion

☐ Check the condition of the entire vehicle structure for signs of corrosion in load-bearing areas. (These include chassis box sections, side sills, cross-members, pillars, and all suspension, steering, braking system and seat belt mountings and anchorages.) Any corrosion which has seriously reduced the thickness of a load-bearing area is likely to cause the vehicle to fail. In this case professional repairs are likely to be needed.

☐ Damage or corrosion which causes sharp or otherwise dangerous edges to be exposed will also cause the vehicle to fail.

4 Checks carried out on YOUR VEHICLE'S EXHAUST EMISSION SYSTEM

Petrol models

☐ Have the engine at normal operating temperature, and make sure that it is in good tune (ignition system in good order, air filter element clean, etc).

☐ Before any measurements are carried out, raise the engine speed to around 2500 rpm, and hold it at this speed for 20 seconds. Allow the engine speed to return to idle, and watch for smoke emissions from the exhaust tailpipe. If the idle speed is obviously much too high, or if dense blue or clearly-visible black smoke comes from the tailpipe for more than 5 seconds, the vehicle will fail. As a rule of thumb, blue smoke signifies oil being burnt (engine wear) while black smoke signifies unburnt fuel (dirty air cleaner element, or other carburettor or fuel system fault).

☐ An exhaust gas analyser capable of measuring carbon monoxide (CO) and hydrocarbons (HC) is now needed. If such an instrument cannot be hired or borrowed, a local garage may agree to perform the check for a small fee.

CO emissions (mixture)

☐ At the time of writing, the maximum CO level at idle is 3.5% for vehicles first used after August 1986 and 4.5% for older vehicles. From January 1996 a much tighter limit (around 0.5%) applies to catalyst-equipped vehicles first used from August 1992. If the CO level cannot be reduced far enough to pass the test (and the fuel and ignition systems are otherwise in good condition) then the carburettor is badly worn, or there is some problem in the fuel injection system or catalytic converter (as applicable).

HC emissions

☐ With the CO emissions within limits, HC emissions must be no more than 1200 ppm (parts per million). If the vehicle fails this test at idle, it can be re-tested at around 2000 rpm; if the HC level is then 1200 ppm or less, this counts as a pass.

☐ Excessive HC emissions can be caused by oil being burnt, but they are more likely to be due to unburnt fuel.

Diesel models

☐ The only emission test applicable to Diesel engines is the measuring of exhaust smoke density. The test involves accelerating the engine several times to its maximum unloaded speed.

Note: *It is of the utmost importance that the engine timing belt is in good condition before the test is carried out.*

☐ Excessive smoke can be caused by a dirty air cleaner element. Otherwise, professional advice may be needed to find the cause.

Engine 1

- ☐ Engine fails to rotate when attempting to start
- ☐ Engine rotates, but will not start
- ☐ Engine difficult to start when cold
- ☐ Engine difficult to start when hot
- ☐ Starter motor noisy or rough in engagement
- ☐ Starter motor turns engine slowly
- ☐ Engine starts, but stops immediately
- ☐ Engine idles erratically
- ☐ Engine misfires at idle speed
- ☐ Engine misfires throughout the driving speed range
- ☐ Engine stalls
- ☐ Engine lacks power
- ☐ Engine backfires
- ☐ Oil pressure warning light illuminated with engine running
- ☐ Engine runs-on after switching off
- ☐ Engine noises

Cooling system 2

- ☐ Overheating
- ☐ Overcooling
- ☐ External coolant leakage
- ☐ Internal coolant leakage
- ☐ Corrosion

Fuel and exhaust systems 3

- ☐ Excessive fuel consumption
- ☐ Fuel leakage and/or fuel odour
- ☐ Excessive noise or fumes from exhaust system

Clutch 4

- ☐ Pedal travels to floor - no pressure or very little resistance
- ☐ Clutch fails to disengage (unable to select gears)
- ☐ Clutch slips (engine speed increases, with no increase in vehicle speed)
- ☐ Judder as clutch is engaged
- ☐ Noise when depressing or releasing clutch pedal

Manual transmission 5

- ☐ Noisy in neutral with engine running
- ☐ Noisy in one particular gear
- ☐ Difficulty engaging gears
- ☐ Jumps out of gear
- ☐ Vibration
- ☐ Lubricant leaks

Automatic transmission 6

- ☐ Fluid leakage
- ☐ Transmission fluid brown, or has burned smell
- ☐ General gear selection problems
- ☐ Transmission will not downshift (kickdown) with accelerator fully depressed
- ☐ Engine will not start in any gear, or starts in gears other than Park or Neutral
- ☐ Transmission slips, shifts roughly, is noisy, or has no drive in forward or reverse gears

Differential and propshaft 7

- ☐ Vibration when accelerating and decelerating
- ☐ Low-pitched whining, increasing with road speed

Braking system 8

- ☐ Vehicle pulls to one side under braking
- ☐ Noise (grinding or high-pitched squeal) when brakes applied
- ☐ Excessive brake pedal travel
- ☐ Brake pedal feels spongy when depressed
- ☐ Excessive brake pedal effort required to stop vehicle
- ☐ Judder felt through brake pedal or steering wheel when braking
- ☐ Brakes binding
- ☐ Rear wheels locking under normal braking

Suspension and steering systems 9

- ☐ Vehicle pulls to one side
- ☐ Wheel wobble and vibration
- ☐ Excessive pitching and/or rolling around corners, or during braking
- ☐ Wandering or general instability
- ☐ Excessively-stiff steering
- ☐ Excessive play in steering
- ☐ Lack of power assistance
- ☐ Tyre wear excessive

Electrical system 10

- ☐ Battery will only hold a charge for a few days
- ☐ Ignition/no-charge warning light remains illuminated with engine running
- ☐ Ignition/no-charge warning light fails to come on
- ☐ Lights inoperative
- ☐ Instrument readings inaccurate or erratic
- ☐ Horn inoperative, or unsatisfactory in operation
- ☐ Wipers inoperative, or unsatisfactory in operation
- ☐ Washers inoperative, or unsatisfactory in operation
- ☐ Electric windows inoperative, or unsatisfactory in operation
- ☐ Central locking system inoperative, or unsatisfactory in operation

Introduction

The vehicle owner who does his or her own maintenance according to the recommended service schedules should not have to use this section of the manual very often. Modern component reliability is such that, provided those items subject to wear or deterioration are inspected or renewed at the specified intervals, sudden failure is comparatively rare. Faults do not usually just happen as a result of sudden failure, but develop over a period of time. Major mechanical failures in particular are usually preceded by characteristic symptoms over hundreds or even thousands of miles. Those components which do occasionally fail without warning are often small and easily carried in the vehicle.

With any fault-finding, the first step is to decide where to begin investigations. Sometimes this is obvious, but on other occasions, a little detective work will be necessary. The owner who makes half a dozen haphazard adjustments or replacements may be successful in curing a fault (or its symptoms), but will be none the wiser if the fault recurs, and ultimately may have spent more time and money than was necessary. A calm and logical approach will be found to be more satisfactory in the long run. Always take into account any warning signs or abnormalities that may have been noticed in the period preceding the fault - power loss, high or low gauge readings, unusual smells, etc - and remember that failure of components such as fuses or spark plugs may only be pointers to some underlying fault.

The pages which follow provide an easy-reference guide to the more common problems which may occur during the operation of the vehicle. These problems and their possible causes are grouped under headings denoting various components or systems, such as Engine, Cooling system, etc. The Chapter and/or Section which deals with the problem is also shown in brackets. Whatever the fault, certain basic principles apply. These are as follows:

Verify the fault. This is simply a matter of being sure that you know what the symptoms are before starting work. This is particularly important if you are investigating a fault for someone else, who may not have described it very accurately.

Don't overlook the obvious. For example, if the vehicle won't start, is there fuel in the tank? (Don't take anyone else's word on this particular point, and don't trust the fuel gauge either!) If an electrical fault is indicated, look for loose or broken wires before using the test gear.

Cure the disease, not the symptom. Substituting a flat battery with a fully-charged one will get you off the hard shoulder, but if the underlying cause is not attended to, the new battery will go the same way. Similarly, changing oil-fouled spark plugs for a new set will get you moving again, but remember that the reason for the fouling (if it wasn't simply an incorrect grade of plug) will have to be established and corrected.

Don't take anything for granted. Particularly, don't forget that a "new" component may itself be defective (especially if it's been rattling around in the boot for months), and don't leave components out of a fault diagnosis sequence just because they are new or recently-fitted. When you do finally diagnose a difficult fault, you'll probably realise that all the evidence was there from the start.

1 Engine

Engine fails to rotate when attempting to start

☐ Battery terminal connections loose or corroded (*"Weekly Checks"*).
☐ Battery discharged or faulty (Chapter 5).
☐ Loose or disconnected wiring in the starting circuit (Chapter 5).
☐ Defective starter solenoid or switch (Chapter 5).
☐ Defective starter motor (Chapter 5).
☐ Starter pinion or flywheel ring gear teeth loose or broken (Chapters 2 or 5).
☐ Engine earth strap broken or disconnected (Chapter 5).

Engine rotates, but will not start

☐ Fuel tank empty.
☐ Battery discharged (engine rotates slowly) (Chapter 5).
☐ Battery terminal connections loose or corroded (*"Weekly Checks"*).
☐ Air filter element dirty or clogged (Chapter 1).
☐ Low cylinder compressions (Chapter 2A).
☐ Major mechanical failure (eg broken timing belt) (Chapter 2).
☐ Ignition components damp or damaged (Chapter 5).
☐ Fuel injection system fault - fuel injection models (Chapter 4).
☐ Stop solenoid faulty - carburettor models (Chapter 4).
☐ Worn, faulty or incorrectly-gapped spark plugs
☐ Choke mechanism worn, faulty or incorrectly adjusted - carburettor models (Chapter 4)
☐ Broken, loose or disconnected wiring in ignition circuit (Chapter 5)

Engine difficult to start when cold

☐ Battery discharged (Chapter 5).
☐ Battery terminal connections loose or corroded (*"Weekly Checks"*).
☐ Air filter element dirty or clogged (Chapter 1).
☐ Worn, faulty or incorrectly-gapped spark plugs
☐ Choke mechanism worn, faulty or incorrectly adjusted - carburettor models (Chapter 4)
☐ Low cylinder compressions (Chapter 2).
☐ Fuel injection system fault - fuel injection models (Chapter 4)
☐ Ignition system fault (Chapter 5)

Engine difficult to start when hot

☐ Battery discharged (Chapter 5).
☐ Battery terminal connections loose or corroded (*"Weekly Checks"*).
☐ Air filter element dirty or clogged (Chapter 1).
☐ Choke mechanism worn, faulty or incorrectly adjusted - carburettor models (Chapter 4)
☐ Fuel injection system fault - fuel injection models (Chapter 4)

Starter motor noisy or rough in engagement

☐ Starter pinion or flywheel ring gear teeth loose or broken (Chapter 2 or 5).
☐ Starter motor mounting bolts loose or missing (Chapter 5).
☐ Starter motor internal components worn or damaged (Chapter 5).

Starter motor turns engine slowly

☐ Battery discharged (Chapter 5).
☐ Battery terminal connections loose or corroded (*"Weekly Checks"*).
☐ Earth strap broken or disconnected (Chapter 5).
☐ Starter motor wiring loose (Chapter 5).
☐ Starter motor internal fault (Chapter 5).

Engine starts, but stops immediately

☐ Loose ignition system wiring (Chapter 5)
☐ Dirt in fuel system (Chapter 4).
☐ Fuel injector fault (Chapter 4).
☐ Fuel pump or pressure regulator fault (Chapter 4)
☐ Incorrectly adjusted idle speed (Chapter 1).
☐ Choke mechanism worn, faulty or incorrectly adjusted - carburettor models (Chapter 4)
☐ Vacuum leak at carburettor/throttle body, inlet manifold or hoses (Chapters 2 and 4)
☐ Blocked carburettor jets or internal passages - carburettor models (Chapter 4)

Engine idles erratically

☐ Incorrectly-adjusted idle speed (Chapter 1).
☐ Air filter element clogged (Chapter 1).
☐ Air in fuel system (Chapter 4).
☐ Incorrect tappet adjustment (Chapter 2).
☐ Worn, faulty or incorrectly-gapped spark plugs
☐ Vacuum leak at carburettor/throttle body, inlet manifold or hoses (Chapters 2 and 4)
☐ Blocked carburettor jets or internal passages - carburettor models (Chapter 4)
☐ Uneven or low cylinder compressions (Chapter 2).
☐ Timing belt incorrectly fitted or tensioned (Chapter 2).
☐ Camshaft lobes worn (Chapter 2).
☐ Faulty fuel injector(s) (Chapter 4).

Engine misfires at idle speed

☐ Distributor cap cracked or tracking internally (Chapter 5).
☐ Faulty fuel injector(s) (Chapter 4).
☐ Incorrect tappet adjustment (Chapter 2).
☐ Uneven or low cylinder compressions (Chapter 2).
☐ Disconnected, leaking, or perished crankcase ventilation hoses (Chapter 4).
☐ Vacuum leak at the carburettor, throttle body, inlet manifold or associated hoses (Chapter 4).

1 Engine (continued)

Engine misfires throughout the driving speed range

- ☐ Fuel filter choked (Chapter 1).
- ☐ Fuel pump faulty, or delivery pressure low (Chapter 4).
- ☐ Fuel tank vent blocked, or fuel pipes restricted (Chapter 4).
- ☐ Uneven or low cylinder compressions (Chapter 2).
- ☐ Worn, faulty or incorrectly-gapped spark plugs (Chapter 1).
- ☐ Faulty spark plug HT leads (Chapter 1).

Engine stalls

- ☐ Incorrectly adjusted idle speed (Chapter 1).
- ☐ Fuel filter choked (Chapter 1).
- ☐ Blocked injector/fuel injection system fault (Chapter 4).
- ☐ Fuel pump faulty, or delivery pressure low (Chapter 4).
- ☐ Vacuum leak at the throttle body, inlet manifold or associated hoses (Chapter 4).
- ☐ Fuel tank vent blocked, or fuel pipes restricted (Chapter 4).

Engine lacks power

- ☐ Fuel filter choked (Chapter 1).
- ☐ Timing belt incorrectly fitted or tensioned (Chapter 2).
- ☐ Fuel pump faulty, or delivery pressure low (Chapter 4).
- ☐ Worn, faulty or incorrectly-gapped spark plugs (Chapter 1).
- ☐ Vacuum leak at the carburettor, throttle body, inlet manifold or associated hoses (Chapter 4).
- ☐ Uneven or low cylinder compressions (Chapter 2).
- ☐ Brakes binding (Chapters 1 and 9).
- ☐ Clutch slipping (Chapter 6).
- ☐ Blocked injector/fuel injection system fault (Chapter 4).

Engine backfires

- ☐ Timing belt incorrectly fitted (Chapter 2A).
- ☐ Faulty injector/fuel injection system fault (Chapter 4).

Oil pressure warning light illuminated with engine running

- ☐ Low oil level, or incorrect oil grade ("Weekly Checks").
- ☐ Faulty oil pressure sensor (Chapter 5).
- ☐ Worn engine bearings and/or oil pump (Chapter 2).
- ☐ Excessively high engine operating temperature (Chapter 3).
- ☐ Oil pressure relief valve defective (Chapter 2).
- ☐ Oil pick-up strainer clogged (Chapter 2).

Note: *Low oil pressure in a high-mileage engine at tickover is not necessarily a cause for concern. Sudden pressure loss at speed is far more significant. In any event, check the gauge or warning light sender before condemning the engine.*

Engine runs-on after switching off

- ☐ Excessive carbon build-up in engine (Chapter 2).
- ☐ Excessively high engine operating temperature (Chapter 3).

Engine noises

Pre-ignition (pinking) or knocking during acceleration or under load

- ☐ Incorrect fuel/air mixture setting (Chapter 4).
- ☐ Ignition timing over-advanced (Chapter 5B).
- ☐ Faulty fuel injector(s) (Chapter 4).
- ☐ Excessive carbon build-up in engine (Chapter 2).

Whistling or wheezing noises

- ☐ Leaking exhaust manifold gasket (Chapter 4).
- ☐ Leaking vacuum hose (Chapter 4 or 9).
- ☐ Blowing cylinder head gasket (Chapter 2).

Tapping or rattling noises

- ☐ Worn valve gear or camshaft (Chapter 2).
- ☐ Ancillary component fault (coolant pump, alternator, etc) (Chapters 3, 5, etc).

Knocking or thumping noises

- ☐ Worn big-end bearings (regular heavy knocking, perhaps less under load) (Chapter 2).
- ☐ Worn main bearings (rumbling and knocking, perhaps worsening under load) (Chapter 2).
- ☐ Piston slap (most noticeable when cold) (Chapter 2).
- ☐ Ancillary component fault (coolant pump, alternator, etc) (Chapters 3, 5, etc).

2 Cooling system

Overheating

- ☐ Insufficient coolant in system ("Weekly Checks").
- ☐ Thermostat faulty (Chapter 3).
- ☐ Radiator core blocked, or grille restricted (Chapter 3).
- ☐ Electric cooling fan or thermostatic switch faulty (Chapter 3).
- ☐ Inaccurate temperature gauge sender unit (Chapter 3).
- ☐ Airlock in cooling system (Chapter 3).
- ☐ Expansion tank pressure cap faulty (Chapter 3).

Overcooling

- ☐ Thermostat faulty (Chapter 3).
- ☐ Inaccurate temperature gauge sender unit (Chapter 3).

External coolant leakage

- ☐ Deteriorated or damaged hoses or hose clips (Chapter 1).
- ☐ Radiator core or heater matrix leaking (Chapter 3).
- ☐ Pressure cap faulty (Chapter 3).
- ☐ Coolant pump internal seal leaking (Chapter 3).
- ☐ Coolant pump-to-block seal leaking (Chapter 3).
- ☐ Boiling due to overheating (Chapter 3).
- ☐ Core plug leaking (Chapter 2).

Internal coolant leakage

- ☐ Leaking cylinder head gasket (Chapter 2).
- ☐ Cracked cylinder head or cylinder block (Chapter 2).

Corrosion

- ☐ Infrequent draining and flushing (Chapter 1).
- ☐ Incorrect coolant mixture or inappropriate coolant type (Chapter 1).

3 Fuel and exhaust systems

Excessive fuel consumption
☐ Air filter element dirty or clogged (Chapter 1).
☐ Fuel injection system fault (Chapter 4).
☐ Ignition timing incorrect/ignition system fault (Chapters 1 and 5).
☐ Tyres under-inflated (*"Weekly Checks"*).

Fuel leakage and/or fuel odour
☐ Damaged or corroded fuel tank, pipes or connections (Chapter 4).

Excessive noise or fumes from exhaust system
☐ Leaking exhaust system or manifold joints (Chapters 1 and 4).
☐ Leaking, corroded or damaged silencers or pipe (Chapters 1 and 4).
☐ Broken mountings causing body or suspension contact (Chapter 1).

4 Clutch

Pedal travels to floor - no pressure or very little resistance
☐ Broken clutch cable - cable-operated clutch (Chapter 6).
☐ Incorrect clutch cable adjustment/automatic adjuster faulty - cable-operated clutch (Chapter 6).
☐ Hydraulic fluid level low/air in the hydraulic system - hydraulically-operated clutch
☐ Broken clutch release bearing or fork (Chapter 6).
☐ Broken diaphragm spring in clutch pressure plate (Chapter 6).

Clutch fails to disengage (unable to select gears)
☐ Incorrect clutch cable adjustment/automatic adjuster faulty - cable-operated clutch (Chapter 6).
☐ Incorrect clutch cable adjustment/automatic adjuster faulty - cable-operated clutch (Chapter 6).
☐ Hydraulic fluid level too high - hydraulically-operated clutch
☐ Clutch disc sticking on gearbox input shaft splines (Chapter 6).
☐ Clutch disc sticking to flywheel or pressure plate (Chapter 6).
☐ Faulty pressure plate assembly (Chapter 6).
☐ Clutch release mechanism worn or badly assembled (Chapter 6).

Clutch slips (engine speed increases, with no increase in vehicle speed)
☐ Incorrect clutch cable adjustment/automatic adjuster faulty - cable-operated clutch (Chapter 6).
☐ Hydraulic fluid level too high - hydraulically-operated clutch
☐ Clutch disc linings excessively worn (Chapter 6).
☐ Clutch disc linings contaminated with oil or grease (Chapter 6).
☐ Faulty pressure plate or weak diaphragm spring (Chapter 6).

Judder as clutch is engaged
☐ Clutch disc linings contaminated with oil or grease (Chapter 6).
☐ Clutch disc linings excessively worn (Chapter 6).
☐ Clutch cable sticking or frayed - cable-operated clutch (Chapter 6).
☐ Faulty or distorted pressure plate or diaphragm spring (Chapter 6).
☐ Worn or loose engine or gearbox mountings (Chapter 2A or 2B).
☐ Clutch disc hub or gearbox input shaft splines worn (Chapter 6).

Noise when depressing or releasing clutch pedal
☐ Worn clutch release bearing (Chapter 6).
☐ Worn or dry clutch pedal bushes (Chapter 6).
☐ Faulty pressure plate assembly (Chapter 6).
☐ Pressure plate diaphragm spring broken (Chapter 6).
☐ Broken clutch disc cushioning springs (Chapter 6).

5 Manual transmission

Noisy in neutral with engine running
☐ Input shaft bearings worn (noise apparent with clutch pedal released, but not when depressed) (Chapter 7).*
☐ Clutch release bearing worn (noise apparent with clutch pedal depressed, possibly less when released) (Chapter 6).

Noisy in one particular gear
☐ Worn, damaged or chipped gear teeth (Chapter 7).*

Difficulty engaging gears
☐ Clutch fault (Chapter 6).
☐ Worn or damaged gearchange linkage/cable (Chapter 7).
☐ Incorrectly-adjusted gearchange linkage/cable (Chapter 7).
☐ Worn synchroniser units (Chapter 7).*

Jumps out of gear
☐ Worn or damaged gearchange linkage/cable (Chapter 7).
☐ Incorrectly-adjusted gearchange linkage/cable (Chapter 7).
☐ Worn synchroniser units (Chapter 7).*
☐ Worn selector forks (Chapter 7).*

Vibration
☐ Lack of oil (Chapter 1).
☐ Worn bearings (Chapter 7).*

Lubricant leaks
☐ Leaking differential output oil seal (Chapter 7).
☐ Leaking housing joint (Chapter 7).*
☐ Leaking input shaft oil seal (Chapter 7).*
*Although the corrective action necessary to remedy the symptoms described is beyond the scope of the home mechanic, the above information should be helpful in isolating the cause of the condition, so that the owner can communicate clearly with a professional mechanic.

6 Automatic transmission

Note: *Due to the complexity of the automatic transmission, it is difficult for the home mechanic to properly diagnose and service this unit. For problems other than the following, the vehicle should be taken to a dealer service department or automatic transmission specialist. Do not be too hasty in removing the transmission if a fault is suspected, as most of the testing is carried out with the unit still fitted.*

Fluid leakage

☐ Automatic transmission fluid is usually dark in colour. Fluid leaks should not be confused with engine oil, which can easily be blown onto the transmission by airflow.
☐ To determine the source of a leak, first remove all built-up dirt and grime from the transmission housing and surrounding areas using a degreasing agent, or by steam-cleaning. Drive the vehicle at low speed, so airflow will not blow the leak far from its source. Raise and support the vehicle, and determine where the leak is coming from. The following are common areas of leakage:

a) *Oil pan (Chapter 1 and 7).*
b) *Dipstick tube (Chapter 1 and 7).*
c) *Transmission-to-fluid cooler pipes/unions (Chapter 7).*

Transmission fluid brown, or has burned smell

☐ Transmission fluid level low, or fluid in need of renewal (Chapter 1).

General gear selection problems

☐ Chapter 7B deals with checking and adjusting the selector cable on automatic transmissions. The following are common problems which may be caused by a poorly-adjusted cable:

a) *Engine starting in gears other than Park or Neutral.*
b) *Indicator panel indicating a gear other than the one actually being used.*
c) *Vehicle moves when in Park or Neutral.*
d) *Poor gear shift quality or erratic gear changes.*

☐ Refer to Chapter 7B for the selector cable adjustment procedure.

Transmission will not downshift (kickdown) with accelerator pedal fully depressed

☐ Low transmission fluid level (Chapter 1).
☐ Incorrect selector cable adjustment (Chapter 7).

Engine will not start in any gear, or starts in gears other than Park or Neutral

☐ Incorrect starter/inhibitor switch adjustment (Chapter 7).
☐ Incorrect selector cable adjustment (Chapter 7).

Transmission slips, shifts roughly, is noisy, or has no drive in forward or reverse gears

☐ There are many probable causes for the above problems, but the home mechanic should be concerned with only one possibility - fluid level. Before taking the vehicle to a dealer or transmission specialist, check the fluid level and condition of the fluid as described in Chapter 1. Correct the fluid level as necessary, or change the fluid and filter if needed. If the problem persists, professional help will be necessary.

7 Differential and propshaft

Vibration when accelerating or decelerating

☐ Worn universal joint (Chapter 8).
☐ Bent or distorted propeller shaft (Chapter 8).

Low-pitched whining, increasing with road speed

☐ Worn differential (Chapter 8)

8 Braking system

Note: *Before assuming that a brake problem exists, make sure that the tyres are in good condition and correctly inflated, that the front wheel alignment is correct, and that the vehicle is not loaded with weight in an unequal manner. Apart from checking the condition of all pipe and hose connections, any faults occurring on the anti-lock braking system should be referred to a GM dealer for diagnosis.*

Vehicle pulls to one side under braking

☐ Worn, defective, damaged or contaminated brake pads/shoes on one side (Chapters 1 and 9).
☐ Seized or partially-seized front brake caliper/wheel cylinder piston (Chapters 1 and 9).
☐ A mixture of brake pad/shoe lining materials fitted between sides (Chapters 1 and 9).
☐ Brake caliper or backplate mounting bolts loose (Chapter 9).
☐ Worn or damaged steering or suspension components (Chapters 1 and 10).

Noise (grinding or high-pitched squeal) when brakes applied

☐ Brake pad or shoe friction lining material worn down to metal backing (Chapters 1 and 9).
☐ Excessive corrosion of brake disc or drum. (May be apparent after the vehicle has been standing for some time (Chapters 1 and 9).
☐ Foreign object (stone chipping, etc) trapped between brake disc and shield (Chapters 1 and 9).

Excessive brake pedal travel

☐ Inoperative rear brake self-adjust mechanism - drum brakes (Chapters 1 and 9).
☐ Faulty master cylinder (Chapter 9).
☐ Air in hydraulic system (Chapters 1 and 9).
☐ Faulty vacuum servo unit (Chapter 9).

Brake pedal feels spongy when depressed

☐ Air in hydraulic system (Chapters 1 and 9).
☐ Deteriorated flexible rubber brake hoses (Chapters 1 and 9).
☐ Master cylinder mounting nuts loose (Chapter 9).
☐ Faulty master cylinder (Chapter 9).

8 Braking system (continued)

Excessive brake pedal effort required to stop vehicle

- [ ] Faulty vacuum servo unit (Chapter 9).
- [ ] Disconnected, damaged or insecure brake servo vacuum hose (Chapter 9).
- [ ] Primary or secondary hydraulic circuit failure (Chapter 9).
- [ ] Seized brake caliper or wheel cylinder piston(s) (Chapter 9).
- [ ] Brake pads or brake shoes incorrectly fitted (Chapters 1 and 9).
- [ ] Incorrect grade of brake pads or brake shoes fitted (Chapters 1 and 9).
- [ ] Brake pads or brake shoe linings contaminated (Chapters 1 and 9).

Judder felt through brake pedal or steering wheel when braking

- [ ] Excessive run-out or distortion of discs/drums (Chapters 1 and 9).
- [ ] Brake pad or brake shoe linings worn (Chapters 1 and 9).
- [ ] Brake caliper or brake backplate mounting bolts loose (Chapter 9).
- [ ] Wear in suspension or steering components or mountings (Chapters 1 and 10).

Brakes binding

- [ ] Seized brake caliper or wheel cylinder piston(s) (Chapter 9).
- [ ] Incorrectly-adjusted handbrake mechanism (Chapter 9).
- [ ] Faulty master cylinder (Chapter 9).

Rear wheels locking under normal braking

- [ ] Rear brake shoe linings contaminated (Chapters 1 and 9).
- [ ] Faulty brake pressure regulator (Chapter 9).

9 Suspension and steering

Note: *Before diagnosing suspension or steering faults, be sure that the trouble is not due to incorrect tyre pressures, mixtures of tyre types, or binding brakes.*

Vehicle pulls to one side

- [ ] Defective tyre (*"Weekly Checks"*).
- [ ] Excessive wear in suspension or steering components (Chapters 1 and 10).
- [ ] Incorrect front wheel alignment (Chapter 10).
- [ ] Accident damage to steering or suspension components (Chapter 1).

Wheel wobble and vibration

- [ ] Front roadwheels out of balance (vibration felt mainly through the steering wheel) (Chapters 1 and 10).
- [ ] Rear roadwheels out of balance (vibration felt throughout the vehicle) (Chapters 1 and 10).
- [ ] Roadwheels damaged or distorted (Chapters 1 and 10).
- [ ] Faulty or damaged tyre (*"Weekly Checks"*).
- [ ] Worn steering or suspension joints, bushes or components (Chapters 1 and 10).
- [ ] Wheel bolts loose (Chapters 1 and 10).

Excessive pitching and/or rolling around corners, or during braking

- [ ] Defective shock absorbers (Chapters 1 and 10).
- [ ] Broken or weak spring and/or suspension component (Chapters 1 and 10).
- [ ] Worn or damaged anti-roll bar or mountings (Chapter 10).

Wandering or general instability

- [ ] Incorrect front wheel alignment (Chapter 10).
- [ ] Worn steering or suspension joints, bushes or components (Chapters 1 and 10).
- [ ] Roadwheels out of balance (Chapters 1 and 10).
- [ ] Faulty or damaged tyre (*"Weekly Checks"*).
- [ ] Wheel bolts loose (Chapters 1 and 10).
- [ ] Defective shock absorbers (Chapters 1 and 10).

Excessively-stiff steering

- [ ] Lack of steering gear lubricant (Chapter 10).
- [ ] Seized track rod end balljoint or suspension balljoint (Chapters 1 and 10).
- [ ] Broken or incorrectly-adjusted drivebelt - power steering (Chapter 1).
- [ ] Incorrect front wheel alignment (Chapter 10).
- [ ] Steering rack or column bent or damaged (Chapter 10).

Excessive play in steering

- [ ] Worn steering column intermediate shaft universal joint (Chapter 10).
- [ ] Worn steering track rod end balljoints (Chapters 1 and 10).
- [ ] Worn rack-and-pinion steering gear (Chapter 10).
- [ ] Worn steering or suspension joints, bushes or components (Chapters 1 and 10).

Lack of power assistance

- [ ] Broken or incorrectly-adjusted auxiliary drivebelt (Chapter 1).
- [ ] Incorrect power steering fluid level (*"Weekly Checks"*).
- [ ] Restriction in power steering fluid hoses (Chapter 1).
- [ ] Faulty power steering pump (Chapter 10).
- [ ] Faulty rack-and-pinion steering gear (Chapter 10).

Tyre wear excessive

Tyres worn on inside or outside edges

- [ ] Tyres under-inflated (wear on both edges) (*"Weekly Checks"*).
- [ ] Incorrect camber or castor angles (wear on one edge only) (Chapter 10).
- [ ] Worn steering or suspension joints, bushes or components (Chapters 1 and 10).
- [ ] Excessively-hard cornering.
- [ ] Accident damage.

Tyre treads exhibit feathered edges

- [ ] Incorrect toe setting (Chapter 10).

Tyres worn in centre of tread

- [ ] Tyres over-inflated (*"Weekly Checks"*).

Tyres worn on inside and outside edges

- [ ] Tyres under-inflated (*"Weekly Checks"*).

Tyres worn unevenly

- [ ] Tyres/wheels out of balance (Chapter 1).
- [ ] Excessive wheel or tyre run-out (Chapter 1).
- [ ] Worn shock absorbers (Chapters 1 and 10).
- [ ] Faulty tyre (*"Weekly Checks"*).

10 Electrical system

Note: *For problems associated with the starting system, refer to the faults listed under "Engine" earlier in this Section.*

Battery will only hold a charge for a few days

- ☐ Battery defective internally (Chapter 5).
- ☐ Battery terminal connections loose or corroded (*"Weekly Checks"*).
- ☐ Auxiliary drivebelt worn or incorrectly adjusted (Chapter 1).
- ☐ Alternator not charging at correct output (Chapter 5).
- ☐ Alternator or voltage regulator faulty (Chapter 5).
- ☐ Short-circuit causing continual battery drain (Chapters 5 and 12).

Ignition/no-charge warning light remains illuminated with engine running

- ☐ Auxiliary drivebelt broken, worn, or incorrectly adjusted (Chapter 1).
- ☐ Alternator brushes worn, sticking, or dirty (Chapter 5).
- ☐ Alternator brush springs weak or broken (Chapter 5).
- ☐ Internal fault in alternator or voltage regulator (Chapter 5).
- ☐ Broken, disconnected, or loose wiring in charging circuit (Chapter 5).

Ignition/no-charge warning light fails to come on

- ☐ Warning light bulb blown (Chapter 12).
- ☐ Disconnected or loose wiring in warning light circuit (Chapter 12).
- ☐ Alternator faulty (Chapter 5).

Lights inoperative

- ☐ Bulb blown (Chapter 12).
- ☐ Corrosion of bulb or bulbholder contacts (Chapter 12).
- ☐ Blown fuse (Chapter 12).
- ☐ Faulty relay (Chapter 12).
- ☐ Broken, loose, or disconnected wiring (Chapter 12).
- ☐ Faulty switch (Chapter 12).

Instrument readings inaccurate or erratic

Instrument readings increase with engine speed

- ☐ Faulty voltage regulator (Chapter 12).

Fuel or temperature gauges give no reading

- ☐ Faulty gauge sender unit (Chapters 3 and 4).
- ☐ Wiring open-circuit (Chapter 12).
- ☐ Faulty gauge (Chapter 12).

Fuel or temperature gauges only give maximum reading

- ☐ Faulty gauge sender unit (Chapters 3 and 4).
- ☐ Wiring short-circuit (Chapter 12).
- ☐ Faulty gauge (Chapter 12).

Horn inoperative, or unsatisfactory in operation

Horn operates all the time

- ☐ Horn push either earthed or stuck down (Chapter 12).
- ☐ Horn cable-to-horn push earthed (Chapter 12).

Horn fails to operate

- ☐ Blown fuse (Chapter 12).
- ☐ Cable or cable connections loose or disconnected (Chapter 12).
- ☐ Faulty horn (Chapter 12).

Horn emits intermittent or unsatisfactory sound

- ☐ Cable connections loose (Chapter 12).
- ☐ Horn mountings loose (Chapter 12).
- ☐ Faulty horn (Chapter 12).

Wipers inoperative, or unsatisfactory in operation

Wipers fail to operate, or operate very slowly

- ☐ Wiper blades stuck to screen, or linkage seized or binding (Chapters 1 and 12).
- ☐ Blown fuse (Chapter 12).
- ☐ Cable or cable connections loose or disconnected (Chapter 12).

- ☐ Faulty relay (Chapter 12).
- ☐ Faulty wiper motor (Chapter 12).

Wiper blades sweep over the wrong area of glass

- ☐ Wiper arms incorrectly positioned on spindles (Chapter 1).
- ☐ Excessive wear of wiper linkage (Chapter 12).
- ☐ Wiper motor or linkage mountings loose or insecure (Chapter 12).

Wiper blades fail to clean the glass effectively

- ☐ Wiper blade rubbers worn or perished (*"Weekly Checks"*).
- ☐ Wiper arm tension springs broken, or arm pivots seized (Chapter 12).
- ☐ Insufficient windscreen washer additive to adequately remove road film (*"Weekly Checks"*).

Washers inoperative, or unsatisfactory in operation

One or more washer jets inoperative

- ☐ Blocked washer jet (Chapter 1).
- ☐ Disconnected, kinked or restricted fluid hose (Chapter 12).
- ☐ Insufficient fluid in washer reservoir (*"Weekly Checks"*).

Washer pump fails to operate

- ☐ Broken or disconnected wiring or connections (Chapter 12).
- ☐ Blown fuse (Chapter 12).
- ☐ Faulty washer switch (Chapter 12).
- ☐ Faulty washer pump (Chapter 12).

Washer pump runs for some time before fluid is emitted

- ☐ Faulty one-way valve in fluid supply hose (Chapter 12).

Electric windows inoperative, or unsatisfactory in operation

Window glass will only move in one direction

- ☐ Faulty switch (Chapter 12).

Window glass slow to move

- ☐ Regulator seized or damaged, or in need of lubrication (Chapter 11).
- ☐ Door internal components or trim fouling regulator (Chapter 11).
- ☐ Faulty motor (Chapter 11).

Window glass fails to move

- ☐ Blown fuse (Chapter 12).
- ☐ Faulty relay (Chapter 12).
- ☐ Broken or disconnected wiring or connections (Chapter 12).
- ☐ Faulty motor (Chapter 11).

Central locking system inoperative, or unsatisfactory in operation

Complete system failure

- ☐ Blown fuse (Chapter 12).
- ☐ Faulty relay (Chapter 12).
- ☐ Broken or disconnected wiring or connections (Chapter 12).
- ☐ Faulty vacuum pump (Chapter 11).

Latch locks but will not unlock, or unlocks but will not lock

- ☐ Faulty master switch (Chapter 12).
- ☐ Broken or disconnected latch operating rods or levers (Chapter 11).
- ☐ Faulty relay (Chapter 12).
- ☐ Faulty vacuum pump (Chapter 11).

One solenoid/motor fails to operate

- ☐ Broken or disconnected wiring or connections (Chapter 12).
- ☐ Faulty operating assembly (Chapter 11).
- ☐ Broken, binding or disconnected latch operating rods or levers (Chapter 11).
- ☐ Fault in door latch (Chapter 11).

A

ABS (Anti-lock brake system) A system, usually electronically controlled, that senses incipient wheel lockup during braking and relieves hydraulic pressure at wheels that are about to skid.

Air bag An inflatable bag hidden in the steering wheel (driver's side) or the dash or glovebox (passenger side). In a head-on collision, the bags inflate, preventing the driver and front passenger from being thrown forward into the steering wheel or windscreen.

Air cleaner A metal or plastic housing, containing a filter element, which removes dust and dirt from the air being drawn into the engine.

Air filter element The actual filter in an air cleaner system, usually manufactured from pleated paper and requiring renewal at regular intervals.

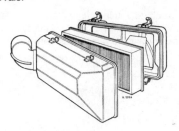

Air filter

Allen key A hexagonal wrench which fits into a recessed hexagonal hole.

Alligator clip A long-nosed spring-loaded metal clip with meshing teeth. Used to make temporary electrical connections.

Alternator A component in the electrical system which converts mechanical energy from a drivebelt into electrical energy to charge the battery and to operate the starting system, ignition system and electrical accessories.

Ampere (amp) A unit of measurement for the flow of electric current. One amp is the amount of current produced by one volt acting through a resistance of one ohm.

Anaerobic sealer A substance used to prevent bolts and screws from loosening. Anaerobic means that it does not require oxygen for activation. The Loctite brand is widely used.

Antifreeze A substance (usually ethylene glycol) mixed with water, and added to a vehicle's cooling system, to prevent freezing of the coolant in winter. Antifreeze also contains chemicals to inhibit corrosion and the formation of rust and other deposits that would tend to clog the radiator and coolant passages and reduce cooling efficiency.

Anti-seize compound A coating that reduces the risk of seizing on fasteners that are subjected to high temperatures, such as exhaust manifold bolts and nuts.

Asbestos A natural fibrous mineral with great heat resistance, commonly used in the composition of brake friction materials. Asbestos is a health hazard and the dust created by brake systems should never be inhaled or ingested.

Axle A shaft on which a wheel revolves, or which revolves with a wheel. Also, a solid beam that connects the two wheels at one end of the vehicle. An axle which also transmits power to the wheels is known as a live axle.

Axleshaft A single rotating shaft, on either side of the differential, which delivers power from the final drive assembly to the drive wheels. Also called a driveshaft or a halfshaft.

B

Ball bearing An anti-friction bearing consisting of a hardened inner and outer race with hardened steel balls between two races.

Bearing The curved surface on a shaft or in a bore, or the part assembled into either, that permits relative motion between them with minimum wear and friction.

Bearing

Big-end bearing The bearing in the end of the connecting rod that's attached to the crankshaft.

Bleed nipple A valve on a brake wheel cylinder, caliper or other hydraulic component that is opened to purge the hydraulic system of air. Also called a bleed screw.

Brake bleeding Procedure for removing air from lines of a hydraulic brake system.

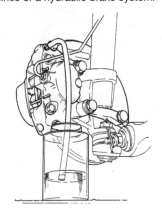

Brake bleeding

Brake disc The component of a disc brake that rotates with the wheels.

Brake drum The component of a drum brake that rotates with the wheels.

Brake linings The friction material which contacts the brake disc or drum to retard the vehicle's speed. The linings are bonded or riveted to the brake pads or shoes.

Brake pads The replaceable friction pads that pinch the brake disc when the brakes are applied. Brake pads consist of a friction material bonded or riveted to a rigid backing plate.

Brake shoe The crescent-shaped carrier to which the brake linings are mounted and which forces the lining against the rotating drum during braking.

Braking systems For more information on braking systems, consult the *Haynes Automotive Brake Manual*.

Breaker bar A long socket wrench handle providing greater leverage.

Bulkhead The insulated partition between the engine and the passenger compartment.

C

Caliper The non-rotating part of a disc-brake assembly that straddles the disc and carries the brake pads. The caliper also contains the hydraulic components that cause the pads to pinch the disc when the brakes are applied. A caliper is also a measuring tool that can be set to measure inside or outside dimensions of an object.

Camshaft A rotating shaft on which a series of cam lobes operate the valve mechanisms. The camshaft may be driven by gears, by sprockets and chain or by sprockets and a belt.

Canister A container in an evaporative emission control system; contains activated charcoal granules to trap vapours from the fuel system.

Canister

Carburettor A device which mixes fuel with air in the proper proportions to provide a desired power output from a spark ignition internal combustion engine.

Castellated Resembling the parapets along the top of a castle wall. For example, a castellated balljoint stud nut.

Castor In wheel alignment, the backward or forward tilt of the steering axis. Castor is positive when the steering axis is inclined rearward at the top.

Catalytic converter A silencer-like device in the exhaust system which converts certain pollutants in the exhaust gases into less harmful substances.

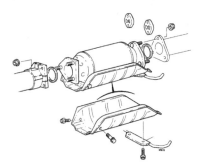

Catalytic converter

Circlip A ring-shaped clip used to prevent endwise movement of cylindrical parts and shafts. An internal circlip is installed in a groove in a housing; an external circlip fits into a groove on the outside of a cylindrical piece such as a shaft.

Clearance The amount of space between two parts. For example, between a piston and a cylinder, between a bearing and a journal, etc.

Coil spring A spiral of elastic steel found in various sizes throughout a vehicle, for example as a springing medium in the suspension and in the valve train.

Compression Reduction in volume, and increase in pressure and temperature, of a gas, caused by squeezing it into a smaller space.

Compression ratio The relationship between cylinder volume when the piston is at top dead centre and cylinder volume when the piston is at bottom dead centre.

Constant velocity (CV) joint A type of universal joint that cancels out vibrations caused by driving power being transmitted through an angle.

Core plug A disc or cup-shaped metal device inserted in a hole in a casting through which core was removed when the casting was formed. Also known as a freeze plug or expansion plug.

Crankcase The lower part of the engine block in which the crankshaft rotates.

Crankshaft The main rotating member, or shaft, running the length of the crankcase, with offset "throws" to which the connecting rods are attached.

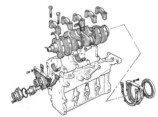

Crankshaft assembly

Crocodile clip See Alligator clip

D

Diagnostic code Code numbers obtained by accessing the diagnostic mode of an engine management computer. This code can be used to determine the area in the system where a malfunction may be located.

Disc brake A brake design incorporating a rotating disc onto which brake pads are squeezed. The resulting friction converts the energy of a moving vehicle into heat.

Double-overhead cam (DOHC) An engine that uses two overhead camshafts, usually one for the intake valves and one for the exhaust valves.

Drivebelt(s) The belt(s) used to drive accessories such as the alternator, water pump, power steering pump, air conditioning compressor, etc. off the crankshaft pulley.

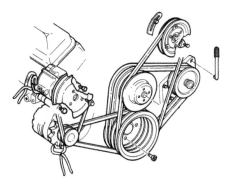

Accessory drivebelts

Driveshaft Any shaft used to transmit motion. Commonly used when referring to the axleshafts on a front wheel drive vehicle.

Drum brake A type of brake using a drum-shaped metal cylinder attached to the inner surface of the wheel. When the brake pedal is pressed, curved brake shoes with friction linings press against the inside of the drum to slow or stop the vehicle.

E

EGR valve A valve used to introduce exhaust gases into the intake air stream.

Electronic control unit (ECU) A computer which controls (for instance) ignition and fuel injection systems, or an anti-lock braking system. For more information refer to the *Haynes Automotive Electrical and Electronic Systems Manual.*

Electronic Fuel Injection (EFI) A computer controlled fuel system that distributes fuel through an injector located in each intake port of the engine.

Emergency brake A braking system, independent of the main hydraulic system, that can be used to slow or stop the vehicle if the primary brakes fail, or to hold the vehicle stationary even though the brake pedal isn't depressed. It usually consists of a hand lever that actuates either front or rear brakes mechanically through a series of cables and linkages. Also known as a handbrake or parking brake.

Endfloat The amount of lengthwise movement between two parts. As applied to a crankshaft, the distance that the crankshaft can move forward and back in the cylinder block.

Engine management system (EMS) A computer controlled system which manages the fuel injection and the ignition systems in an integrated fashion.

Exhaust manifold A part with several passages through which exhaust gases leave the engine combustion chambers and enter the exhaust pipe.

F

Fan clutch A viscous (fluid) drive coupling device which permits variable engine fan speeds in relation to engine speeds.

Feeler blade A thin strip or blade of hardened steel, ground to an exact thickness, used to check or measure clearances between parts.

Feeler blade

Firing order The order in which the engine cylinders fire, or deliver their power strokes, beginning with the number one cylinder.

Flywheel A heavy spinning wheel in which energy is absorbed and stored by means of momentum. On cars, the flywheel is attached to the crankshaft to smooth out firing impulses.

Free play The amount of travel before any action takes place. The "looseness" in a linkage, or an assembly of parts, between the initial application of force and actual movement. For example, the distance the brake pedal moves before the pistons in the master cylinder are actuated.

Fuse An electrical device which protects a circuit against accidental overload. The typical fuse contains a soft piece of metal which is calibrated to melt at a predetermined current flow (expressed as amps) and break the circuit.

Fusible link A circuit protection device consisting of a conductor surrounded by heat-resistant insulation. The conductor is smaller than the wire it protects, so it acts as the weakest link in the circuit. Unlike a blown fuse, a failed fusible link must frequently be cut from the wire for replacement.

G

Gap The distance the spark must travel in jumping from the centre electrode to the side electrode in a spark plug. Also refers to the spacing between the points in a contact breaker assembly in a conventional points-type ignition, or to the distance between the reluctor or rotor and the pickup coil in an electronic ignition.

Adjusting spark plug gap

Gasket Any thin, soft material - usually cork, cardboard, asbestos or soft metal - installed between two metal surfaces to ensure a good seal. For instance, the cylinder head gasket seals the joint between the block and the cylinder head.

Gasket

Gauge An instrument panel display used to monitor engine conditions. A gauge with a movable pointer on a dial or a fixed scale is an analogue gauge. A gauge with a numerical readout is called a digital gauge.

H

Halfshaft A rotating shaft that transmits power from the final drive unit to a drive wheel, usually when referring to a live rear axle.

Harmonic balancer A device designed to reduce torsion or twisting vibration in the crankshaft. May be incorporated in the crankshaft pulley. Also known as a vibration damper.

Hone An abrasive tool for correcting small irregularities or differences in diameter in an engine cylinder, brake cylinder, etc.

Hydraulic tappet A tappet that utilises hydraulic pressure from the engine's lubrication system to maintain zero clearance (constant contact with both camshaft and valve stem). Automatically adjusts to variation in valve stem length. Hydraulic tappets also reduce valve noise.

I

Ignition timing The moment at which the spark plug fires, usually expressed in the number of crankshaft degrees before the piston reaches the top of its stroke.

Inlet manifold A tube or housing with passages through which flows the air-fuel mixture (carburettor vehicles and vehicles with throttle body injection) or air only (port fuel-injected vehicles) to the port openings in the cylinder head.

J

Jump start Starting the engine of a vehicle with a discharged or weak battery by attaching jump leads from the weak battery to a charged or helper battery.

L

Load Sensing Proportioning Valve (LSPV) A brake hydraulic system control valve that works like a proportioning valve, but also takes into consideration the amount of weight carried by the rear axle.

Locknut A nut used to lock an adjustment nut, or other threaded component, in place. For example, a locknut is employed to keep the adjusting nut on the rocker arm in position.

Lockwasher A form of washer designed to prevent an attaching nut from working loose.

M

MacPherson strut A type of front suspension system devised by Earle MacPherson at Ford of England. In its original form, a simple lateral link with the anti-roll bar creates the lower control arm. A long strut - an integral coil spring and shock absorber - is mounted between the body and the steering knuckle. Many modern so-called MacPherson strut systems use a conventional lower A-arm and don't rely on the anti-roll bar for location.

Multimeter An electrical test instrument with the capability to measure voltage, current and resistance.

N

NOx Oxides of Nitrogen. A common toxic pollutant emitted by petrol and diesel engines at higher temperatures.

O

Ohm The unit of electrical resistance. One volt applied to a resistance of one ohm will produce a current of one amp.

Ohmmeter An instrument for measuring electrical resistance.

O-ring A type of sealing ring made of a special rubber-like material; in use, the O-ring is compressed into a groove to provide the sealing action.

Overhead cam (ohc) engine An engine with the camshaft(s) located on top of the cylinder head(s).

Overhead valve (ohv) engine An engine with the valves located in the cylinder head, but with the camshaft located in the engine block.

Oxygen sensor A device installed in the engine exhaust manifold, which senses the oxygen content in the exhaust and converts this information into an electric current. Also called a Lambda sensor.

P

Phillips screw A type of screw head having a cross instead of a slot for a corresponding type of screwdriver.

Plastigage A thin strip of plastic thread, available in different sizes, used for measuring clearances. For example, a strip of Plastigage is laid across a bearing journal. The parts are assembled and dismantled; the width of the crushed strip indicates the clearance between journal and bearing.

Plastigage

Propeller shaft The long hollow tube with universal joints at both ends that carries power from the transmission to the differential on front-engined rear wheel drive vehicles.

Proportioning valve A hydraulic control valve which limits the amount of pressure to the rear brakes during panic stops to prevent wheel lock-up.

R

Rack-and-pinion steering A steering system with a pinion gear on the end of the steering shaft that mates with a rack (think of a geared wheel opened up and laid flat). When the steering wheel is turned, the pinion turns, moving the rack to the left or right. This movement is transmitted through the track rods to the steering arms at the wheels.

Radiator A liquid-to-air heat transfer device designed to reduce the temperature of the coolant in an internal combustion engine cooling system.

Refrigerant Any substance used as a heat transfer agent in an air-conditioning system. R-12 has been the principle refrigerant for many years; recently, however, manufacturers have begun using R-134a, a non-CFC substance that is considered less harmful to the ozone in the upper atmosphere.

Rocker arm A lever arm that rocks on a shaft or pivots on a stud. In an overhead valve engine, the rocker arm converts the upward movement of the pushrod into a downward movement to open a valve.

Rotor In a distributor, the rotating device inside the cap that connects the centre electrode and the outer terminals as it turns, distributing the high voltage from the coil secondary winding to the proper spark plug. Also, that part of an alternator which rotates inside the stator. Also, the rotating assembly of a turbocharger, including the compressor wheel, shaft and turbine wheel.

Runout The amount of wobble (in-and-out movement) of a gear or wheel as it's rotated. The amount a shaft rotates "out-of-true." The out-of-round condition of a rotating part.

S

Sealant A liquid or paste used to prevent leakage at a joint. Sometimes used in conjunction with a gasket.

Sealed beam lamp An older headlight design which integrates the reflector, lens and filaments into a hermetically-sealed one-piece unit. When a filament burns out or the lens cracks, the entire unit is simply replaced.

Serpentine drivebelt A single, long, wide accessory drivebelt that's used on some newer vehicles to drive all the accessories, instead of a series of smaller, shorter belts. Serpentine drivebelts are usually tensioned by an automatic tensioner.

Serpentine drivebelt

Shim Thin spacer, commonly used to adjust the clearance or relative positions between two parts. For example, shims inserted into or under bucket tappets control valve clearances. Clearance is adjusted by changing the thickness of the shim.

Slide hammer A special puller that screws into or hooks onto a component such as a shaft or bearing; a heavy sliding handle on the shaft bottoms against the end of the shaft to knock the component free.

Sprocket A tooth or projection on the periphery of a wheel, shaped to engage with a chain or drivebelt. Commonly used to refer to the sprocket wheel itself.

Starter inhibitor switch On vehicles with an automatic transmission, a switch that prevents starting if the vehicle is not in Neutral or Park.

Strut See MacPherson strut.

T

Tappet A cylindrical component which transmits motion from the cam to the valve stem, either directly or via a pushrod and rocker arm. Also called a cam follower.

Thermostat A heat-controlled valve that regulates the flow of coolant between the cylinder block and the radiator, so maintaining optimum engine operating temperature. A thermostat is also used in some air cleaners in which the temperature is regulated.

Thrust bearing The bearing in the clutch assembly that is moved in to the release levers by clutch pedal action to disengage the clutch. Also referred to as a release bearing.

Timing belt A toothed belt which drives the camshaft. Serious engine damage may result if it breaks in service.

Timing chain A chain which drives the camshaft.

Toe-in The amount the front wheels are closer together at the front than at the rear. On rear wheel drive vehicles, a slight amount of toe-in is usually specified to keep the front wheels running parallel on the road by offsetting other forces that tend to spread the wheels apart.

Toe-out The amount the front wheels are closer together at the rear than at the front. On front wheel drive vehicles, a slight amount of toe-out is usually specified.

Tools For full information on choosing and using tools, refer to the *Haynes Automotive Tools Manual*.

Tracer A stripe of a second colour applied to a wire insulator to distinguish that wire from another one with the same colour insulator.

Tune-up A process of accurate and careful adjustments and parts replacement to obtain the best possible engine performance.

Turbocharger A centrifugal device, driven by exhaust gases, that pressurises the intake air. Normally used to increase the power output from a given engine displacement, but can also be used primarily to reduce exhaust emissions (as on VW's "Umwelt" Diesel engine).

U

Universal joint or U-joint A double-pivoted connection for transmitting power from a driving to a driven shaft through an angle. A U-joint consists of two Y-shaped yokes and a cross-shaped member called the spider.

V

Valve A device through which the flow of liquid, gas, vacuum, or loose material in bulk may be started, stopped, or regulated by a movable part that opens, shuts, or partially obstructs one or more ports or passageways. A valve is also the movable part of such a device.

Valve clearance The clearance between the valve tip (the end of the valve stem) and the rocker arm or tappet. The valve clearance is measured when the valve is closed.

Vernier caliper A precision measuring instrument that measures inside and outside dimensions. Not quite as accurate as a micrometer, but more convenient.

Viscosity The thickness of a liquid or its resistance to flow.

Volt A unit for expressing electrical "pressure" in a circuit. One volt that will produce a current of one ampere through a resistance of one ohm.

W

Welding Various processes used to join metal items by heating the areas to be joined to a molten state and fusing them together. For more information refer to the *Haynes Automotive Welding Manual*.

Wiring diagram A drawing portraying the components and wires in a vehicle's electrical system, using standardised symbols. For more information refer to the *Haynes Automotive Electrical and Electronic Systems Manual*.

Note: *References throughout this index are in the form - "Chapter number" • "page number"*

A

ABS brakes - 9•13
Accelerator cable - 1•10, 4A•3,4B•3
Accelerator pedal - 4A•3
Air cleaner - 4A•2, 4B•2
Air conditioning system - 1•15, 3•8
Air filter element - 1•3, 1•10
Alternator - 5A•3
Anti-roll bars - 10•5, 10•8
Anti-theft alarm system - 12•16
Antifreeze - 0•9, 0•11, 0•16, 1•2
ATF - 0•16, 1•2, 1•11, 1•15
Automatic transmission - 7B•1 et seq
    ECU and switches - 7B•6
    fault finding - REF•12, REF•16
    fluid - 0•16, 1•2, 1•11, 1•15
    inhibitor switch - 7B•5
    kickdown cable - 7B•3
    removal and refitting - 7B•2
    selector lever - 7B•4
Auxiliary drivebelt - 1•9

B

Battery:
    booster - 0•7
    checks - 0•15
    connections - 0•6
    removal and refitting - 5A•3, 12•3
    testing and charging - 5A•2
Bearings - 2A•13
Bleeding the brakes - 9•11
Bleeding the clutch - 6•3
Body electrical
    system - 12•1 et seq
Bodywork and fittings- 11•1 et seq
Bodywork damage - 11•2
Bodywork maintenance - 11•1
Bonnet - 11•3
Boot lid - 11•4
Brake fluid - 0•9, 0•12, 0•16, 1•16
Braking system - 9•1 et seq
    ABS - 9•13
    bleeding the brakes - 9•11
    brake pad check - 1•12
    brake pads front - 9•2
    brake pads rear - 9•6
    brake caliper front - 9•6
    brake caliper rear - 9•8
    brake disc - 9•8
    brake pedal - 9•13
    faultfinding - REF•12, REF•16
    handbrake shoes - 9•9
    handbrake cable - 9•9
    handbrake lever - 9•10
    hydraulic lines and hoses - 1•12, 9•12
    master cylinder - 9•10
    rear brake proportioning valve - 9•10
    vacuum servo unit - 1•12, 9•12

Bulbs
    driving lamps - 12•8
    foglamps - 12•8
    general - 0•15
    headlamp - 12•7
    indicator - 12•7
    interior - 12•9
    number plate - 12•9
    parking lamp - 12•7
    ratings - 12•2
    rear lamps - 12•8
Bumpers - 11•11

C

Cables
    accelerator - 1•10, 4A•3, 4B•3
    clutch - 6•2
    handbrake - 9•9
    kickdown - 7B•3
    speedometer - 12•7
Camshaft - 2A•14, 2B•9, 2C•9
Carburettor - 4A•3
Carpets - 11•2
Catalytic converter - 4B•16
Central locking system - 12•13
Charging system testing - 5A•3
Cigarette lighter - 12•5
CIH 2.5, 2.6 and 3.0 litre engines -
    2B•1 et seq
Clock - 12•5
Clutch - 6•1 et seq
    bleeding the clutch - 6•3
    cable - 6•2
    fault finding - REF•12, REF•15
    hydraulic pipes/hoses - 6•3
    master cylinder - 6•2
    pedal - 1•14, 6•2
    release bearing - 6•5
    removal, inspection and refitting - 6•4
    slave cylinder - 6•3
Coil - 1•10, 5B•4
Compression test - 2A•3
Console - 11•13
Contents - 0•2
Conversion factors - REF•2
Coolant - 0•9, 0•11, 0•16, 1•2
Cooling, heating and air conditioning
    systems - 3•1 et seq
    air conditioning system - 1•15, 3•8
    coolant pump - 3•4
    draining/refilling - 3•2
    drivebelts - 3•6
    expansion tank - 3•6
    fan - 3•3, 3•4
    fault finding - REF•12, REF•14
    heater control panel - 3•7
    heater control switch - 12•6
    heater fan motor - 3•7
    heater matrix - 3•7
    leaks - 0•9, 1•9
    radiator - 3•2
    temperature gauge sender unit - 3•6
    thermostat - 3•3

Crankshaft - 2A•13
Cruise control - 12•14
Cylinder block - 2A•15
Cylinder bores - 2A•13
Cylinder head - 2A•14, 2A•15, 2B•7,
    2B•9, 2C•6, 2C•11

D

Dents - 11•2
Differential and propshaft fault finding -
    REF•12, REF•16
Dimensions and weights - REF•1
Distributor - 5B•2
Distributor cap - 1•10
DOHC 3 0 litre engine - 2C•1 et seq
Door - 11•9
Door handle - 11•8
Door lock - 11•8
Door trim - 11•6
Driveshaft removal and refitting - 8•4

E

Earth fault - 12•3
Electric windows - 11•9
Electrical system fault finding - 12•2,
    REF•12, REF•18
Engine:
    bearings - 2A•13
    camshaft - 2A•14, 2B•9, 2C•9
    compression test - 2A•3
    crankshaft - 2A•13
    cylinder block - 2A•15
    cylinder bores - 2A•13
    cylinder head - 2A•11, 2A•15, 2B•7, 2B•9,
        2C•6, 2C-11
    dismantling - 2A•5, 2B•5, 2C•5
    fault finding - REF•12, REF•13
    hydraulic valve lifters - 2B•8
    mountings - 2A•11, 2B•7, 2C•6
    oil - 0•11, 0•16, 1•2, 1•8
    oil filter - 0•9, 1•2, 1•8
    oil pressure relief valve - 2B•9, 2C•10
    oil pump - 2C•10
    piston rings - 2A•14, 2B•9, 2C•11
    pistons - 2A•14, 2B•9, 2C•11
    reassembly - 2A•17, 2B•10, 2C•11
    refitting - 2A•21, 2B•12, 2C•13
    removal - 2A•4, 2B•5, 2C•4
    sump - 0•9, 2A•10, 2B•6, 2C•6
    timing belt - 1•16, 2A•3, 2A•12, 2A•14
    timing chain - 2B•9, 2C•11
    valves - 2A•1, 2A•15, 2B•3, 2C•2
Environmental considerations - REF•4
Exhaust manifold - 4A•7, 4B•11, 4B•14
Exhaust system removal and
    refitting - 4A•7,4B•15
Expansion tank - 3•6

F

Facia - 11•12
Fault finding - REF•12 et seq
  automatic transmission - REF•12, REF•16
  braking system - REF•12, REF•16
  clutch - REF•12, REF•15
  cooling system - REF•12, REF•14
  differential and
    propshaft - REF•12, REF•16
  electrical system - 12•2, REF•12, REF•18
  engine REF•12, REF•13
  fuel and exhaust system - REF•12, REF•15
  manual transmission - REF•12, REF•15
  suspension and steering - REF•12, REF•17
Final drive, driveshafts and propeller
  shaft - 8•1 et seq
  driveshaft removal and refitting - 8•4
  driveshaft rubber bellows - 8•4
  final drive unit oil check - 1•12, 8•3
  final drive unit removal and refitting - 8•2
  final drive unit oil seals - 8•3
  final drive unit damping bracket - 8•3
  final drive unit rear cover gasket - 8•3
  propeller shaft - 8•4
Fuel and exhaust systems:
  accelerator cable - 1•10, 4A•3, 4B•3
  accelerator pedal - 4A•3
  air cleaner - 4A•2, 4B•3
  carburettor system - 4A•1 et seq
  catalytic converter - 4B•16
  depressurisation - 4B•4
  exhaust system removal and
    refitting - 4A•7, 4B•16
  fault finding - REF•12, REF•15
  fuel gauge sender unit - 4A•2, 4B•5
  fuel injection system - 4B•1 et seq
  fuel injectors - 4B•6
  fuel pump - 4A•2, 4B•5
  fuel tank - 4A•2, 4B•5
  idle speed mixture
    adjustment - 4A•3, 4B•5
  manifolds - 4A•7, 4B•11, 4B•14
  preheater element - 4A•6
  thermotime valve - 4A•6
Fuses - 0•15, 12•1, 12•4

G

Gearbox - see Manual transmission
Gearbox oil - 0•9, 0•16, 1•2, 1•15
Gearchange lever - 7A•3
Gearchange linkage - 7A•5
Glass - 11•9, 11•10, 11•11
Glossary of technical terms - REF•19

H

Handbrake cable - 9•9
Handbrake lever - 9•10
Handbrake shoes - 9•9
Headlamp beam alignment - 1•13, 12•12
Headlamp unit - 12•10
Headrests - 11•11

Heated seats -12•15
Heater:
  control panel - 3•7
  control switch - 12•6
  fan motor - 3•7
  matrix - 3•7
Horn - 12•7
HT leads - 1•10
Hydraulic lines and hoses
  brakes - 1•2, 9•12
Hydraulic system bleeding clutch - 6•3
Hydraulic system bleeding brakes - 9•11
Hydraulic valve lifters - 2B•8
Idle speed/mixture
  adjustment - 4A•3, 4B•5

I

Ignition system - 5B•1 et seq
  coil - 1•10, 5B•4
  switch - 12•6
  system testing - 5B•2
  timing - 5B•3
Inlet manifold - 4A•7, 4B•11
Interior lamps - 12•9
Instrument panel - 12•6
Introduction to your Carlton/Senator - 0•4

J

Jacking and vehicle support - REF•5
Jump starting - 0•7

K

Kickdown cable - 7B•3

L

Lamps
  cluster rear - 12•11
  foglamp - 12•12
  indicator - 12•11, 12•12
Leaks - 0•9, 1•9
Loudspeakers - 11•8, 12•15

M

Maintenance schedule - 1•4
Manifolds - 4A•7, 4B•11, 4B•14
Manual transmission - 7A•1 et seq
  draining and refilling - 7A•1
  fault finding - REF•12, REF•15
  gearchange lever - 7A•3
  gearchange linkage - 7A•5
  oil - 0•9, 0•16, 1•2, 1•15
  oil seals - 7A•5
  removal and refitting - 7A•2
  reversing light switch - 7A•5
Master cylinder brake - 9•10
Master cylinder clutch - 6•2
Mirrors - 11•10
MOT test checks - REF•8

N

Number plate lamp - 12•9

O

OHC 1.8 and 2.0 litre engines - 2A•1 et seq
Oil engine - 0•11, 0•16, 1•2, 1•8
Oil gearbox - 0•9, 0•16, 1•2, 1•15
Oil filter - 0•9, 1•2, 1•8
Oil level sensor - 5A•4
Oil pressure relief valve - 2B•9, 2C•10
Oil pressure warning light sensor - 5A•4
Oil pump - 2C•10
Oil seals:
  final drive unit - 8•3
  general - REF•4
  manual transmission - 7A•5

P

Parts - REF•3
Pedals:
  accelerator - 4A•3
  brake - 9•13
  clutch - 1•14, 6•2
Piston rings - 2A•14, 2B•9, 2C•11
Pistons - 2A•14, 2B•9, 2C•11
Plastic components - 11•3
Power steering fluid - 0•9, 0•12, 0•16
Power steering pump - 10•12
Propeller shaft - 8•4
Punctures - 0•8

R

Radiator - 3•2
Radiator fan - 3•3, 3•4
Radiator grille - 11•6
Radio cassette anti-theft system - REF•5
Radio/cassette player - 12•15
Rear axle - 10•8
Relays - 12•4
Respraying - 11•2
Reversing light switch - 7A•5
Rotor arm - 1•10
Routine maintenance and servicing -
  1-1 et seq
Rust - 11•2

S

Safety first - 0•5
Screen washer fluid - 0•13
Seat belts - 11•11
Seats - 11•12
Shock absorber - 10•7
Short circuit - 12•3
Slave cylinder clutch - 6•3
Spare parts - REF•3
Spark plugs - 1•3, 1•13
Speakers - 11•8, 12•15
Specifications - see Chapter starts
Speedometer cable - 12•7

Starter motor - 5A•4
***Starting and charging systems -
5A•1 et seq***
Starting problems - 0•6
Starting system testing - 5A•3
Steering
  and suspension check - 1•12
  column - 10•10
  fault finding - REF•12, REF•17
  gear - 10•11
  hub and bearings - 10•5, 10•9
  idler - 10•12
  knuckle - 10•5
  power steering fluid - 0•9, 0•12, 0•16
  power steering pump - 10•12
  tierods - 10•12
  wheel alignment - 10•2, 10•13
  wheel - 10•10
Sump - 0•9, 2A•10, 2B•6, 2C•6
Sunroof - 11•12
Suspension and steering - 10•1 et seq
  anti-roll bars - 10•5, 10•8
  crossmember - 10•6, 10•9
  fault finding - REF•12, REF•17
  front lower arm - 10•4
  front lower balljoint - 10•4
  front strut - 10•3
  rear axle - 10•8
  semi-trailing arm - 10•7
  shock absorber - 10•7

Switches:
  centre facia - 12•5
  courtesy light - 12•5
  glovebox - 12•5
  headlamp range - 12•5
  heater control - 12•6
  ignition - 12•6
  lighting - 12•4
  steering column - 12•4

T

Tailgate - 11•5
Temperature gauge sender unit - 3•6
Thermostat - 3•3
Throttle cable - 1•10, 4A•3, 4B•3
Throttle pedal - 4A•3
Timing - 5B•3
Timing belt - 1•16, 2A•3, 2A•12, 2A•14
Timing chain - 2B•9, 2C•11
Tools - REF•4, REF•6
Towing - 0•9
Trip computer - 12•14
Tyre pressures - 0•16
Tyres - 0•14, 10•2

U

Underbody - 1•13
Underbody views - 1•6, 1•7
Underbonnet views - 0•10, 1•5
Unleaded petrol - 4A•3, 4B•3
Upholstery - 11•2

V

Vacuum servo unit - 1•12, 9•12
Valves - 2A•1, 2A•15, 2B•3, 2C•2
Vehicle identification - REF•3

W

Washer pumps - 12•12, 12•13
Washer jet - 12•10
Weekly checks - 0•10
Wheel alignment - 10•2, 10•13
Wheel changing - 0•8
Windows - 11•9, 11•10, 11•11
Windscreen - 11•9
Wiper arm - 12•10
Wiper blades - 0•13, 12•2
Wiper motors - 12•12, 12•13
Wiring diagrams - 12•17 et seq

Preserving Our Motoring Heritage

< The Model J Duesenberg Derham Tourster. Only eight of these magnificent cars were ever built – this is the only example to be found outside the United States of America

Almost every car you've ever loved, loathed or desired is gathered under one roof at the Haynes Motor Museum. Over 300 immaculately presented cars and motorbikes represent every aspect of our motoring heritage, from elegant reminders of bygone days, such as the superb Model J Duesenberg to curiosities like the bug-eyed BMW Isetta. There are also many old friends and flames. Perhaps you remember the 1959 Ford Popular that you did your courting in? The magnificent 'Red Collection' is a spectacle of classic sports cars including AC, Alfa Romeo, Austin Healey, Ferrari, Lamborghini, Maserati, MG, Riley, Porsche and Triumph.

A Perfect Day Out

Each and every vehicle at the Haynes Motor Museum has played its part in the history and culture of Motoring. Today, they make a wonderful spectacle and a great day out for all the family. Bring the kids, bring Mum and Dad, but above all bring your camera to capture those golden memories for ever. You will also find an impressive array of motoring memorabilia, a comfortable 70 seat video cinema and one of the most extensive transport book shops in Britain. The Pit Stop Cafe serves everything from a cup of tea to wholesome, home-made meals or, if you prefer, you can enjoy the large picnic area nestled in the beautiful rural surroundings of Somerset.

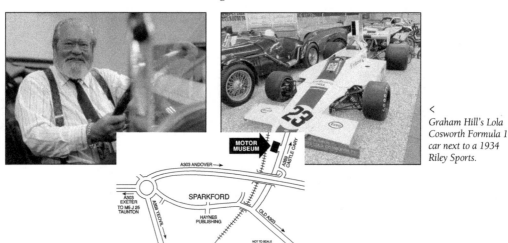

> John Haynes O.B.E., Founder and Chairman of the museum at the wheel of a Haynes Light 12.

< Graham Hill's Lola Cosworth Formula 1 car next to a 1934 Riley Sports.

The Museum is situated on the A359 Yeovil to Frome road at Sparkford, just off the A303 in Somerset. It is about 40 miles south of Bristol, and 25 minutes drive from the M5 intersection at Taunton.
Open 9.30am - 5.30pm (10.00am - 4.00pm Winter) 7 days a week, *except Christmas Day, Boxing Day and New Years Day*
Special rates available for schools, coach parties and outings Charitable Trust No. 292048